D0481974

The Fourth Crusade

THE MIDDLE AGES SERIES

Ruth Mazo Karras, General Editor

Edward Peters, Founding Editor

A complete list of books in the series
is available from the publisher.

The Fourth Crusade

The Conquest of Constantinople

SECOND EDITION

Donald E. Queller and
Thomas F. Madden

With an essay on primary sources by
ALFRED J. ANDREA

PENN

University of Pennsylvania Press

Philadelphia

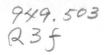

Published by
University of Pennsylvania Press
Philadelphia, Pennsylvania 19104–6097

Library of Congress Cataloging-in-Publication Data
Queller, Donald E.
  The Fourth Crusade : the conquest of Constantinople / Donald E.
Queller and Thomas F. Madden ; with an essay on primary sources
by Alfred J. Andrea. — 2nd [rev.] ed.
    p.   cm.
  Includes bibliographical references (p.   ) and index.
  ISBN 0-8122-3387-5 (alk. paper)
    1. Crusades—Fourth, 1202–1204.   2. Istanbul (Turkey)—History—
Siege, 1203–1204.   3. Civilization, Medieval—13th century.
4. Military history, Medieval.   I. Madden, Thomas F.   II. Title.
D164.Q38   1997
949.5′03—dc21   96-39139
                                                              CIP

Dedicated in love and respect to our parents:
†Dolph and †Lee Queller
Thomas and Joyce Madden

Contents

Preface to the Second Edition

Because of the rich diversity of subjects that the Fourth Crusade touches, it will always remain a topic of interest to scholars from many disciplines. We should rejoice, not decry, that this fascinating event continues to attract investigators who offer new insights on a host of important topics. Since 1977, when the first edition of this volume appeared, historians have continued to add substantially to our understanding of the crusade. The large number of new studies on Innocent III, Venice, Byzantium, and the crusading movement prompted us to blend this wealth of material with new ideas of our own to produce this revised edition.

Aside from correcting errors (some minor, others embarrassing), we have, in this edition, also updated the bibliography and endnotes. More profound, however, is the revision and expansion of many portions of the book. In some cases large sections have been completely rewritten, in others we have added new text resulting from our own or others' research. This is most evident in our treatment of activities in the papal court as well as our attempt to better place the crusade into the larger context of Venetian history. We have also looked much more closely at the situation in Byzantium. The Byzantines' unique culture shaped their view of the Fourth Crusade and informed their reactions to it. We have, therefore, devoted more attention to them and examined more carefully events in Constantinople's court and streets.

Reviewers of the first edition were quite generous, but some did criticize the book's narrow chronological scope and its alleged pro-Venetian bias. We have attempted to meet these criticisms insofar as we can without sacrificing our fundamental convictions, which are founded upon very intensive, very nearly exhaustive research. We believe that there have been quite a lot of generalizations and judgments, indeed, in some cases, too many. We do not believe in minute, picky antiquarianism, but we do believe in meticulous and intensive microhistory, so long as it has broader implications. We think that our narrative bears upon perhaps the broadest and most important of themes, the nature and condition of humankind. Other scholars have dealt adequately with the background of the Fourth Crusade; we have tried, as far as possible, to march along with the crusaders, to become observers in their councils, to view events as they saw them. And they saw themselves almost overwhelmed by immediate and recurring crises and were preoccupied with dealing with them. Therefore, while we have expanded the scope somewhat, we have consciously and deliberately written a highly focused book.

As for a Venetian bias, it was not the intent of the first edition, nor is it here, to depict the Venetians as Galahads. We, who are both Christians, see them, as we see all people, created in the image of God, but marred by sin. Put that in secular terms of moral ambiguity, if you choose, as we have done in the text, where one is less free to be personal than in a preface. Whether we speak in religious or secular terms, the Venetians shared with other crusaders ideals and baser motives. We have tried in the second edition to emphasize that the Venetians were not saintly, and we have added material on their relations with the Greeks in the twelfth century.

Although the Fourth Crusade had a clear beginning with Pope Innocent III's summons in 1198, it is not so easy to say when it ended. The first edition concluded with the capture of Constantinople and devoted a few pages in an epilogue to the sack of the city and subsequent events. We have expanded the discussion of the fall of the city and devoted a new chapter to the sack of Constantinople and the subsequent imperial election. With the coronation of Baldwin of Flanders, it seems to us, the crusade had come to an end and the Latin Empire was born. The overriding concern of the Latins was no longer making their way to the Holy Land, but consolidating and defending their newly won base in the Levant.

Professor Madden came to this subject by reading the first edition of this book as an undergraduate at the University of New Mexico. Fascinated by the event, he went to the University of Illinois to pursue his doctorate under Professor Queller. After co-authoring two articles together, we decided to collaborate on a revised edition of *The Fourth Crusade*. Professor Madden wrote the original revision, which Professor Queller then edited. On a few matters we disagreed, but that is the nature of collegial scholarship. We think the book is much better for those debates. On the basics, however, we have always seen eye-to-eye.

We would like to warmly thank Alfred J. Andrea of the University of Vermont. His many studies on the minor sources of the Fourth Crusade have added greatly to our understanding of the event and its chroniclers. As of this writing, his translation and commentary on Gunther of Pairis's *Hystoria Constantinopolitana* is in press (University of Pennsylvania Press, 1997). Professor Andrea, however, was kind enough to provide us with the entire text in electronic form. Even more kindly, he agreed to write an essay on the primary sources for the Fourth Crusade that appears at the end of this volume, and he went over the entire finished manuscript and offered many excellent suggestions and criticisms. We thank also Dr. Janet Rabinowitch, who assisted us with her expertise in the Russian language. We must also remember and thank the participants in the medieval seminars, both formal and informal, at the University of Illinois, especially Mark Angelos, Gerald Day, James Everett, Louis Haas, Irene Katele, Ellen Kittell, Laurence Marvin, Michael Pedrotty, Cristina Perisinotto, Pongracz Sennyey, Francis Swietek, and Patricia Wenzel. If we go back to Professor Queller's seminars at the University of Southern California, Susan Stratton clearly deserves thanks. All have listened, commented, and criticized bits and pieces of this and many other of our studies. Many of them have also published studies on the Fourth Crusade or peripheral topics.

Our financial benefactors for the revision of this work are few, since few were needed. Some of the archival material from Venice was collected by Professor Madden while working on a separate study on Enrico Dandolo and his family that was funded by the Gladys Krieble Delmas Foundation. The Mellon Faculty Development Fund at Saint Louis University also provided Professor Madden funds to facilitate in the final writing and editing process. We warmly thank them both.

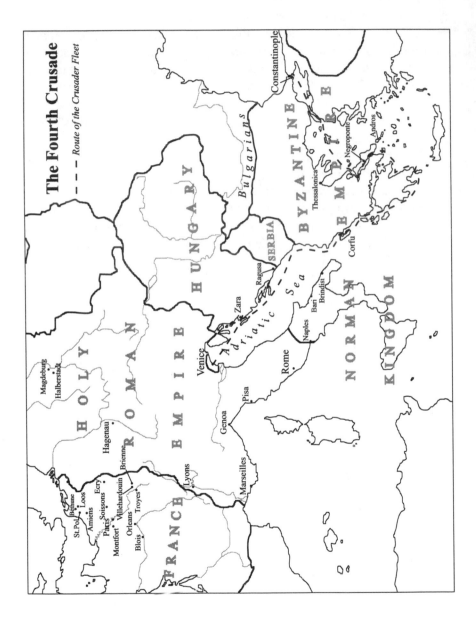

The Fourth Crusade

- - - - *Route of the Crusader Fleet*

I

The Preaching and Taking
of the Cross

In his letter announcing to the patriarch of Jerusalem the death of his predecessor and his own elevation to the papacy on 8 January 1198, Innocent III
proclaimed his intention to work for the cause of the Holy Land and the
deliverance of Jerusalem.[1] Infidel possession of the Holy City offended the
hearts and minds of medieval Christians in a way scarcely comprehensible
even to the most religious among us.[2] The young pope, acutely conscious
of his responsibility as the head of Christendom, intended to reassume papal
leadership of the holy war.[3] On 15 August he proclaimed a new crusade, sum-
moning the *militia Christi* for March of 1199. All towns, as well as counts and
barons, should provide crusaders for two years at their own expense according to their resources. Kings were not mentioned, for he meant this crusade to
be wholly under papal control.[4] Prelates of the church should also contribute
either men or money according to their means. Both those who would undertake the pilgrimage and those who would provide the means were offered the
crusading indulgence for the remission of sins. Crusaders would also receive
the usual protection of their goods and a moratorium on the interest of their
debts. The pope named Cardinal-priest Soffredo and Cardinal-deacon Peter
Capuano as his legates to direct the enterprise.[5]

Political conditions in Latin Europe, however, were not auspicious for a
crusade. England and France were at war, as they had been on and off since
Richard Lion-Heart's return from captivity in 1194. The powerful and wealthy
Count Baldwin of Flanders was also at loggerheads with his French suzerain.
Germany was rent by two rival claimants to the imperial crown, Philip of
Swabia, allied with France, and Otto of Brunswick, allied with England. Sicily
was unsettled under the boy-king Frederick and his regent mother, Constance,
struggling to maintain Hohenstaufen rule. Genoa and Pisa, two of the great
maritime powers, were also at war. Innocent III pursued a policy aimed at
solving or stabilizing the conflicts of the secular powers. The Fourth Crusade

was both the end toward which this policy was directed and a means intended to achieve it by enlisting the contentious powers in the war against the infidel.[6]

To the bitter disappointment of the pope the appointed time passed with no response to his summons or to his repeated demands for men and money. In late December and early January Innocent took the step of levying a general papal tax upon the clergy. The pope and cardinals taxed themselves a tenth of their incomes for the following year; other clergy were to pay a fortieth of their revenues, with the exception of certain privileged monastic orders, the Cistercians, Carthusians, Premonstratensians, and Grandmontines, who had to pay only a fiftieth. Although we have no records that enable us to determine how much money was collected, various sources indicate considerable clerical opposition.[7] Other measures to gain financial support for the Holy Land were also taken. A chest was placed in each church for weekly offerings, in return for which donors would receive a remission of sins and a weekly public mass said for them. Bishops converted penances into cash for the Holy Land.[8]

Results were disappointing until religious fervor was fanned by the preaching of the charismatic Fulk of Neuilly. Before he acquired his fame Fulk had been rector or curate of the country church of Neuilly near Paris. Discouraged by his lack of success he had turned for improvement to the university. Fortified with new learning and confidence, his sermons gained popularity. It seemed to many that the Holy Spirit spoke through him.[9] Jacques of Vitry wrote: "Come and hear the priest Fulk, because he is another Paul."[10] Intent upon reforming the moral abuses of his day, he harangued huge crowds in the open air, focusing his denunciations upon the sins of usury and lechery.[11] Clerical concubinage was a favorite target. Not only did Fulk condemn priests and their concubines generically, but he pointed them out in the crowd.[12] He had considerable success in redeeming prostitutes, either settling them under vows of celibacy in the convent of Saint Anthony near Paris or finding them dowries and husbands.[13] When Fulk denounced sin he filled the streets with innumerable penitents. His followers believed that he worked miracles, giving sight to the blind, hearing to the deaf, mobility to the lame. As he journeyed, the sick were carried from long distances to lie along his route, so that they might touch his clothes as he passed.[14] Great as his eloquence and the force of his personality were, however, his success was also due to the foibles of his hearers. Readily moved to a high pitch of emotion, they all too often proved to be the shallow soil, on which the seed sprouted quickly, but as quickly withered, for it had no root.[15]

Just how Fulk became a preacher of the crusade remains obscure. Some believed that the Blessed Virgin appeared to him, commanding this mission.[16] We know that in September 1198 Fulk sought the aid of the white monks in preaching the crusade, but was refused.[17] Less than two months later, however, Innocent III authorized him to enlist both black and white monks in his campaign.[18] He traveled abroad, beyond his parish and the environs of Paris, subject only to the jurisdiction of the legate Peter. Fulk's crusade preaching recalls the fervor of Peter the Hermit and the First Crusade.[19] He touched the hearts of the common people. Although he also enlisted nobles, Fulk bestowed the crusader's cross upon many thousands of the poor.[20]

Cardinal-legate Peter Capuano, meanwhile, had proceeded to France where at Dijon he had promulgated the papal bull offering the full remission of the temporal penalties for sins to those who would take the cross or bear its financial burden. He succeeded in negotiating a truce between Philip Augustus and Richard, probably because Philip found himself in difficult straits and therefore ready to listen to the legate's proposals.[21] Peter, however, soon clashed with Philip over the king's displacement of the queen, Ingeborg of Denmark, in favor of Agnes of Meran. After the legate had placed France under the interdict, he was withdrawn by the pope.[22]

The enlistment of a real crusading army of knights finally began at a tournament held by Count Thibaut of Champagne at his castle at Ecry-sur-Aisne in the Ardennes region of northern France on 28 November 1199.[23] This was fifteen months after Innocent had proclaimed the crusade, a year after he had authorized Fulk to enlist monks to preach it, and six months after the pope's original scheduled date of departure for the crusading army. From Champagne itself and from nearby lands a numerous and illustrious assemblage of knights had gathered to test their military prowess, to win honor before the ladies, and to enjoy the banqueting, the minstrelsy, and other social amenities of their class. Suddenly, when they were all armed and ready for the sport, the knights, led by Count Thibaut himself and by his cousin, Count Louis of Blois, put aside their weapons and, swept by a common enthusiasm, committed themselves instead to the crusade.[24] Older historians painted a colorful picture of Fulk of Neuilly denouncing the frivolity in which they were engaged and turning their souls toward Christ. It is regrettable to have to give up such a romantic scene, but there is no evidence that he was present.[25] We do not know, in fact, what sparked their ardor: perhaps some preacher did take advantage of the gathering to issue his plea; or perhaps the fervor sprang spontaneously from Thibaut and Louis, for such waves of enthusiasm were not uncommon in the Middle Ages. In any case, the knights, uttering solemn oaths, converted the momentary passion into vows of a lasting and enforceable obligation.[26] As an outward sign of their commitment they received crosses of cloth to be worn proudly on their shoulders. They also gained the spiritual and temporal privileges of crusaders, the most important of which was the indulgence—the remission of the temporal penalties for sins. Those who died on crusade were believed to enter straightway into the kingdom of heaven, rising from the dust of battle to the company of the saints. In popular estimation, the fallen heroes of the crusades were regarded as Christian martyrs.[27]

By this time the Latin church possessed a well-developed doctrine of the crusade.[28] The concept of Christian war appears alien to the thought and personality of Jesus, and, in fact, it was not looked upon favorably by the Greek church.[29] Throughout its history, however, the Christian church has survived and flourished by adaptation to its cultural milieu. As the Germanic tribes began to sweep over the Roman Empire, Saint Augustine had discussed the just war.[30] At the time of the disintegration of the Carolingian Empire and the invasions by Vikings, Magyars, and Muslims, the Christians of western Europe, who were not far removed from their warlike barbaric ancestors, quite understandably had asserted the virtue of holy war in defense of the interests of the church.[31]

Another important component of the crusading idea was the pilgrimage, the journey of the penitent to sacred shrines to gain religious benefit. Originally pilgrims went unarmed, and as late as 1065 a devout band of pilgrims had refused to defend their lives with arms.[32] To Gregory VII's zeal for a holy war belongs the credit for sanctifying the armed pilgrimage by transforming the meaning of *militia Christi* from monastic asceticism to military combat, from a figurative to a quite literal interpretation.[33] The concept of a holy pilgrimage remained vital; medieval writers do not refer to the armed pilgrimage as a "crusade," but as an *expeditio, iter in terram sanctam*, or *peregrinatio*, the technical term for pilgrimage.[34] When the First Crusade had set out for Jerusalem the concept was not fully formed, but it had developed during the course of the movement. In the late twelfth century the canonists had elaborated a quite specific doctrine of the crusade, which was summoned and authorized by the pope for a definite period against a specific enemy.[35]

Not all the knights who assumed the cross at Ecry, to be sure, were moved solely by religious considerations. The feudal noble's position in society, his code of honor, and his chivalric self-esteem urged him to the crusade. No measure of success in the lists could win for a knight such admiration from the ladies as he gained by taking the cross.[36] To men reared for warfare, moreover, the sheer joy of battle was a strong motive often neglected by bookish scholars. The winning of lands and, for the greater men, an enhanced role in power politics joined in the complex of motives that led men to devote themselves to a dangerous campaign in a distant land.

The two young counts, Thibaut and Louis, were among the most powerful and distinguished French nobles. Grandsons of Louis VII and Eleanor of Aquitaine, they were double cousins, for the two daughters of the royal marriage had married two noble brothers.[37] Thibaut and Louis, of course, were also nephews of Philip II Augustus and of Richard Lion-Heart and John. They were both young men in their twenties.[38] Thibaut's mother was Marie of Champagne, famed patroness of the gentled chivalry of the twelfth century, and from her circle he imbibed the code of the Arthurian romances, in which the armed pilgrimage played a prominent part. Thibaut's brother, Count Henry II, had earlier taken the cross, received the government of the Kingdom of Jerusalem in 1192, and died in the Levant in 1197.[39] Louis, too, was a model of crusading chivalry, who had previously accompanied his father on the Third Crusade and would later prove his mettle by a valorous, if foolhardy, death in 1205.[40] The example of the two young barons, therefore, encouraged many to follow them in taking the crusaders' vow.[41] The tournament at Ecry provided the first tangible nucleus for a crusading army.

Soon after Ecry, other nobles of northern France were also inspired to join the holy war. On Ash Wednesday, 23 February 1200, at the city of Bruges where several drops of the blood of Christ were treasured, Count Baldwin of Flanders took the cross.[42] Baldwin was known as a pious and just man, charitable to the poor, and generous to the clergy.[43] His beloved wife Marie, sister of Thibaut of Champagne, was also moved by the Lenten spirit of sacrifice and assumed the crusader's burden along with her husband.[44] Afterwards, Baldwin's two brothers, Henry and Eustace, his nephew Thierry, and other Flemish nobles took their vows.[45] The count of Flanders was perhaps the most powerful of all the vassals of the French king. At twenty-eight years of age, ruler of his country since 1194, he had achieved a reputation for political sagacity, which was respected throughout Europe.[46] He had proven his military ability by defeating Philip Augustus and had shown great diplomatic skill by entering into an alliance with England, thereby forcing Philip to accept the provisions of the Treaty of Péronne.[47]

In Perche, Count Geoffrey and his brother, Stephen, who were also cousins of Thibaut and Louis, enlisted in the growing ranks of the crusade.[48] The interrelationships among the great nobles of France help to account for the wave of those taking up the cross, as the crusade took on something of the character of a family affair. But other great nobles, unrelated to the above, also enlisted. In Picardy, the powerful Count Hugh of Saint Pol, a veteran crusader, committed himself to the new enterprise, and naturally many lesser nobles followed suit.[49] At Ecry, Renaud of Montmirail, cousin to the counts of Champagne and Blois, Simon de Montfort, future leader of the Albigensian Crusade, Geoffrey of Villehardouin, marshal of Champagne and chronicler of the Fourth Crusade, and many other knights had taken up the cross.[50] In Flanders, there were John of Nesle, the châtelain of Bruges, Conon of Béthune, and Baldwin of Beauvoir.[51] Perche supplied Rotrou of Montfort, Yves of La Jaille, and many others.[52] And from Picardy came Nicholas of Mailly, Walter of Nesle, and his son, Peter.[53]

It has been estimated that the initial wave of enlistments, which began with Ecry, netted about a hundred companies of eighty to a hundred men each. These were not, of course, all knights: many were commoners. The usual proportions for armies of that time were one heavily armored knight to two lightly armed squires or sergeants on horseback to four foot soldiers or sergeants on foot.[54]

In consequence of this popular response to the crusading call, the leading nobles held a *"parlament"* in early 1200 at Soissons.[55] Honored as guests of the city's bishop, Nivelon, one of the earliest ecclesiastics to enlist in the crusade, they met in order to settle upon a time of departure and a route.[56] Because a sufficient number had not yet enlisted, however, they disbanded without achieving anything.[57] Later in the year every count and baron who had been crossed met at Compiègne, on the border of Vermandois and the Ile-de-France, to deal with the organization and strategy of the coming expedition.[58] However, they found themselves in disagreement on many points, and few conclusive decisions were made. Since earlier pilgrimages, most recently that of Frederick Barbarossa, however, had demonstrated the innumerable difficulties of the journey by land, its slowness, physical fatigue, and spiritual ennui, it was decided to go by sea. Many crusaders in the past had come to the same conclusion. Venice, Genoa, and Pisa regularly sent two fleets a year to the Levant carrying crusaders and supplies for the settlers.[59] None of the feudal nobles possessed a fleet, of course, and only the count of Flanders could readily obtain one. Thus, they determined to seek transportation from one of the great Mediterranean maritime cities. The meeting ended with an agreement to appoint the best envoys they could find, give them full diplomatic powers to act in the names of their lords, and send them to secure transportation for the crusading army.[60]

The counts of Flanders, Champagne, and Blois appointed six plenipotentiaries for this purpose, among whom were Conon of Béthune and Geoffrey of Villehardouin.[61] Conon was a member of an illustrious family of Artois, a famed troubadour, and a veteran of the Third Crusade.[62] Geoffrey, the marshal of Champagne, a mature man of about fifty, was well known for his wisdom in council.[63] His chronicle of the Fourth Crusade reveals to us a mind well-organized and clear, though not profound.[64] Among the leaders of the crusade, he falls into a rank just below the great counts of Flanders, Blois, and Champagne, a position of leadership higher than his relatively modest estate would in itself suggest.[65] The count of Champagne trusted none of his men more than the marshal, and, on this and other occasions when diplomatic skill was required, the crusaders invariably turned to Villehardouin for his counsel.[66]

Great trust was placed in these six envoys. Their principals, the counts of Flanders, Champagne, and Blois, had left all the details to be worked out by them; the envoys' agreements would be as binding as their own. As was not uncommon in medieval diplomacy, the principals did not even specify the parties with whom their representatives should negotiate, but agreed to be bound by whatever conventions they might make "in all the ports of the sea, in whatever place they might go."[67] Since no French port was capable of providing the number of ships they believed they would need, the envoys were left with a choice among the three great Italian maritime cities, Genoa, Pisa, and Venice, whose flourishing commerce contributed so much to the revival of western Europe.[68] Robert of Clari contends that the envoys first sought aid from Genoa and Pisa before turning to Venice,[69] but the Picard knight is notoriously misinformed about the preliminaries of the crusade, confusing, in this case, actual visits to Pisa and Genoa by four of the envoys on the return trip.[70] These two western ports, weakened by their long struggles for maritime supremacy against each other, were in no condition at this time to undertake new ventures.[71] Genoa may also have been opposed by the French knights, for there had been numerous complaints concerning Genoese fulfillment of their contract to transport the army of Philip Augustus on the Third Crusade.[72] The envoys decided, therefore, in favor of the great port at the head of the Adriatic, the only one where they could find available the maritime resources required to meet their needs.[73]

There has been considerable debate over the attitude of Pope Innocent III toward the choice of Venice. One group of historians has argued that the pontiff not only favored the choice, but ordered it, trusting the Venetians more than the Genoese or Pisans.[74] The *Gesta Innocentii*, a Roman apologia for Innocent III, which is by no means a pro-Venetian source, tells of a papal legation sent to the two warring western ports in an effort to make peace between them in the interest of the crusade: the Genoese and Pisans, however, would not accept "the word of peace, because they were not sons of peace."[75] This, of course, left no alternative to Venice. A few of the pro-Venetian authorities, misinterpreting a passage in the *Devastatio Constantinopolitana*, hold that Innocent ordered the crusaders to take passage from Venice. He did do this, but it was two years later in 1202, long after a contract with Venice had been made and while crusaders were hesitating in Lombardy.[76] Innocent had urged the Venetians, in fact, to take the cross, both through a legate and in a letter of December 1198.[77] The letter is important for it demonstrates Innocent's willingness to compromise on certain issues in order to assure the future success of the crusade. Undoubtedly conceding to Venetian demands, the pope granted them permission to carry on trade with Egypt in nonstrategic goods. Until the crusaders had committed themselves to the Venetians, however, there is no solid evidence that Innocent III favored Venice rather than other Italian seaports.[78] That he ordered or demanded its selection is, indeed, a myth.

A larger group of historians has taken exactly the opposite approach.[79] They find a history of papal complaints against the Venetians throughout the crusades because of their refusal to give up their trade with the enemy. Venice showed greater interest in commercial privileges, they assert, than in the holy war. The pope, therefore, according to this line of reasoning, was displeased with the choice of Venice, foreseeing a conflict between the mercantile spirit of the Republic of Saint Mark and the aims of the crusade. However, when the historian goes below the surface of this seemingly logical argument, the error of their interpretation becomes apparent. Although Venice had maintained profitable relations with the infidel for some time, commerce with the Muslim East was neither limited nor peculiar to Venice.[80] A generation earlier, Benjamin of Tudela had declared that people from all parts of Christendom frequented Alexandria for trade. His extensive list includes Tuscany, Lombardy, Apulia, Amalfi, Sicily, Genoa, and Pisa, but not (incorrectly, of course) Venice.[81] It is evident that other Italian sea powers were just as interested as the Venetians in taking advantage of lucrative trade with the infidel. While the church might well distrust the profit motive, Venetian merchants were not unique in pursuing it.[82] Innocent III neither encouraged nor discouraged the choice of Venice, which was the only port able to serve the crusaders' purposes.

The pope's preferences, in fact, had little or no bearing on the course of the crusade. Innocent's vision of papal leadership was already anachronistic in an increasingly secular society. The crusading leaders faced a practical problem of transportation, and they dealt with it in their own way, seeking counsel from neither the pope nor his legate. Venice seemed more likely to be able to supply what they needed, and so the envoys decided to go there.[83]

The Ill-fated Treaty of Venice, 1201

In the dead of winter of 1200–1201 the crusaders' envoys struggled through the Mont Cenis Pass into the north Italian marquisate of Montferrat. Passing through Piacenza on the Po, they traversed the length of the Lombard Plain, and arrived at Venice during the first week of Lent.[1] They came to the great port at the head of the Adriatic, seeking ships to bear their armies to the Levant for the reconquest of Jerusalem. They were welcomed warmly and honorably, as befitted ambassadors of great feudal lords, by the venerable doge Enrico Dandolo, garbed in almost imperial splendor and preceded by a sword, a chair of state draped in cloth of gold, and a parasol.[2]

Dandolo was a very old man in 1201—contemporary and near contemporary sources make this abundantly clear.[3] Marino Sanudo, the great sixteenth-century chronicler of Venetian affairs, declared that the doge was eighty-five at the time of his election in 1192.[4] Modern historians have accepted that Dandolo was old, but generally doubted Sanudo's claim, tempering it by differing degrees.[5] There is no compelling reason to do so. Sanudo's statement is in agreement with contemporary sources—modern skepticism less so. Furthermore, Dandolo came from a family of men (and presumably women) who lived into their eighties or nineties with some regularity.[6] If Sanudo is right, Enrico Dandolo was ninety-four when he greeted the crusader envoys: extremely old but hardly outside human experience.

Beyond advanced age, Doge Dandolo had yet another handicap: he was blind. Villehardouin, who was closely associated with him for four years, says that he did not see at all, and this is supported by other sources.[7] Dandolo told Villehardouin that he had lost his sight as a result of a blow on the head, which must have occurred sometime between 1176 and 1192.[8] After the conquest of Constantinople in 1204, a rumor began circulating in the defeated city that Dandolo had been blinded by Manuel Comnenus during an embassy to the emperor in 1172.[9] According to the story, Dandolo swore to avenge himself on Byzantium, thus explaining the outcome of the Fourth Crusade. The rumor, like much of the city's urban folklore, is completely false: Dan-

dolo could still see as late as 1176.[10] Unfortunately, the story has been seized
on by otherwise excellent historians attempting to cast Dandolo in the darkest terms and thus explain the tragedy of 1204 as a personal vendetta.[11] There
is no doubt that in 1201 Enrico Dandolo was both blind and old: the Byzantines had as little to do with the former as they did the latter.

Old and handicapped he was, yet Enrico Dandolo still possessed remarkable energy. He had lost nothing of his mental acuity, but had indeed
continued to sharpen it upon the whetstone of experience. The sources that
reflect a direct acquaintance with the man reveal him as benevolent, eloquent,
and universally respected.[12] Of course he possessed vast experience in affairs
of commerce and of state. Novices were not elected to head the Republic of
Saint Mark. He possessed a great and penetrating sense of politics. He was
also an ingenious and skilled diplomat and an equally skilled strategist and
tactician.[13] He was one of those men whose qualities make others turn naturally to them for leadership, as the young crusading barons would learn to
do. Many historians picture him as extraordinarily ruthless and unscrupulous
when the glory, wealth, and power of the republic were at stake.[14] He was
certainly an ardent Venetian patriot: he was certainly also not a saint, but a
man of the world. As a Venetian and a bourgeois his values were not identical
with those of northern European chivalry, nor should that be expected. No
absolute scale, however, places chivalric virtues on a higher plane than those
of the bourgeoisie.[15] Dandolo was ambitious for his own glory and for the
prosperity and power of the republic; he was not, however, the unscrupulous
manipulator that some historians have depicted.

The envoys delivered to the doge their letters of credence to which were
appended clauses giving them full powers to commit their principals. When
Dandolo had seen them, he appointed an audience for the envoys four days
hence with the Small Council, an executive body consisting of the doge himself and a fluctuating group of ducal judges.[16] Some historians have blamed
Venice for delays in the negotiations process, comparing the alacrity with
which the envoys responded to Venetian proposals. But the envoys were but
six men with blank parchments, Dandolo and his council had a state to run.
The Small Council was kept extremely busy by a constant stream of litiga-
tion and petitions, many of which could not be postponed. That the envoys
received an audience in only four days suggests that Dandolo did all that he
could to expedite the process.[17] At the agreed time Villehardouin and his
companions were led to the ducal palace. There they presented their request:
"Lord, we have come to you on behalf of the great barons of France, who have
taken the sign of the cross to avenge the shame done to Jesus Christ and to
conquer Jerusalem, if God permits. And because they know that no one has

as great power as you and your people, they beg you for the love of God to have pity on the land beyond the sea and on the shame done to Jesus Christ, and to consider how they can obtain vessels and a fleet."[18] Villehardouin does not record giving any estimation of the number of crusaders for whom transportation would be needed, but it is not believable that the envoys had failed to receive such an estimate from the magnates at Compiègne or that they neglected to communicate it to the doge. They could not, after all, have opened negotiations by requesting a fleet of unspecified size. The treaty subsequently concluded states that the envoys requested transportation for 4,500 horses, 4,500 knights, 9000 squires, and 20,000 foot soldiers.[19] Responsibility for the estimate of the number of crusaders is no mere detail of the dickering with the Venetians, for the overestimation was crucial to the outcome of the Fourth Crusade. The doge replied that he would respond in eight days, for this was a very serious matter that required much thought.[20]

When the French knights rejoined the doge and his council on the determined day, the Venetians were ready with an offer. On condition of approval by the Great Council and the popular assembly, the doge proposed to provide horse transports (*usserii*) and transports (*naves*) for the specified numbers of men and horses. The Venetians would also provision the army for a year.[21] The doge asked in payment four marks for each knight and each horse and two marks for each squire and foot soldier, or a total of ninety-four thousand marks. In addition to the transportation that the French had requested, Dandolo offered to supply fifty war galleys at the expense of Venice on condition that the Venetians should receive a half-share in any conquests made by the combined forces.[22] The envoys replied that they would consult together and respond on the following day. By and large they found the offer acceptable, but, if the requested price given above is correct, they must have determined to seek a reduction in the rate for knights from four marks to two, or a new basis of four marks per horse and two marks per man. Thus, on the following day, the French and the Venetians agreed upon terms at a cost of eighty-five thousand marks of Cologne to be paid in four installments by April 1202, when the crusaders should come to Venice. The fleet would be ready to sail on the feast of Saints Peter and Paul, 29 June.[23]

Some scholars have charged that the Venetians imposed extortionate terms upon the guileless warriors from the north, but it was overestimation of the numbers of the crusaders, not the price demanded by the doge, that proved disastrous.[24] Villehardouin was no innocent babe, but a man of experience whose judgment was greatly trusted. Among the entire host of crusaders and Venetians only Dandolo was more highly regarded in council than he.[25] We can also compare the treaty of 1201 with other contracts for transportation of crusaders to determine whether its terms were reasonable. In the earliest such contract that we possess, Genoa agreed in 1184 to carry a small band of thirteen knights, twenty-six horses, and twenty-six squires with provisions for eight months at a cost of eight and one-half marks per unit of one knight, two horses, and two squires.[26] The treaty of 1201 would have charged fourteen marks for a knight, two horses, and two squires, but for a year. The price of the contract of 1184 for a comparable time would presumably have been twelve and three-fourths marks. In 1190 Philip Augustus contracted with Genoa for an army of 650 knights, 1,300 horses, and 1,300 squires at a rate of nine marks per unit of one knight, two horses, and two squires for eight months, or, presumably, thirteen and a half marks for a year. Moreover, under the contract of 1190, wine was to be provided for only four months. The Genoese were also to receive concessions in the conquered cities.[27] Genoese performance of the earlier contract, furthermore, was a source of French complaints, while our sources on the Fourth Crusade have only praise for the fleet prepared by Venice.[28] The treaty of the crusaders with the Venetians was slightly more costly than the contracts of 1184 and 1190, but the Venetians were also throwing in fifty war galleys at no additional cost.[29]

Beyond just the cost, Werner Maleczek has argued that the clause giving one-half of the booty to Venice and the other to the Franks was itself extraordinary, and would never have been accepted by Innocent III. He points out that if the crusade was successful in Egypt or Palestine only one-half of the conquered lands would return to the lordship of the king of Jerusalem, the other half going to the Republic of Saint Mark. This one clause was Venice's greatest deception, since it assured that, of the Fourth Crusade's victories, only one-half would be gains for Christendom, the rest acquisitions for Venice. This was a direct distortion of the crusading ideal, which the Venetians with colonies in the Latin East well knew. Indeed, Maleczek argues, the division clause in the Treaty of Venice should be seen in light of other treaty arrangements made between Venice and the Latin Kingdom in the East.[30] The argument is compelling, but not convincing. While the treaty makes clear that anything the Franks and Venetians acquired was to be split evenly between the two, it says nothing about conquests of land.[31] The word *aliquid* (anything) was understood to mean spoils of war, not foreign lands; nor was it ever taken to mean that by the crusaders. None of the crusade's territorial conquests was split evenly between Venetians and Franks. To be sure, Dandolo probably hoped that victories in Egypt and the Levant would translate into improved positions and larger quarters in eastern cities, as it had on previous occasions when Venice fought in defense of the Holy Land. But these had always been matters for later treaties, dictated by events of the time. If the

Treaty of Venice was taken by any party to mean that Venice should receive one-half of all land conquests then the Treaty of Partition, which laid out the division of the Byzantine Empire, would have been superfluous. As it turned out, Venice ended up with three-eighths rather than one-half of the Empire, although she received her full one-half of booty.

As the doge had told the envoys, he now had to seek the assent of the Great Council (an oversight body of forty) and the people. In former days a doge could have acted on the basis of the consent of the popular assembly alone, but little by little the ducal power, like that of the people, was eroding before the rise of the Venetian oligarchy. Now, apart from his powers as commander in chief, the doge could do little without the his council's approval.[32] Enrico Dandolo, of course, was no common doge. His age, his great ability, and his reputation earned him an extraordinary influence upon his countrymen.[33] When the treaty was presented to the Great Council it was applauded and approved. Then Dandolo summoned increasingly larger groups, first one hundred, then two hundred, finally a thousand, according to Villehardouin, which approved in their turn. It is not precisely clear what Villehardouin was witnessing, since there is no record of any other progressive assemblies being summoned in Venice before. It was probably not a strictly constitutional mechanism, but rather a means by which Dandolo could convince leading Venetians of the merits of the treaty, and then broaden popular approval with their help.[34]

At last, for the final acceptance of the treaty on the part of the Venetians, Dandolo assembled the *arengo* or popular assembly, consisting of ten thousand persons, according to Villehardouin. The doge's strategy of assembling leading citizens to approve the treaty beforehand had the added benefit of informing the general populace about the proposal before they were all assembled. According to Villehardouin, Dandolo asked the people to hear a mass of the Holy Spirit in San Marco church and pray for guidance on this important matter.[35] This assumes that the people already knew what they were praying about. After mass, Dandolo invited the crusaders to address the assembled. Villehardouin tells how the crowd stared curiously at the French envoys, who were the center of attention, since few Venetians until this moment had seen these strangers whose request promised to transform their lives for good or ill. Villehardouin himself spoke for the envoys, telling his hearers how the most powerful lords in France had sent him and his colleagues to Venice, knowing that no other city had such great power on the sea.[36] Moved by the solemn setting and his zeal for the cross, the marshal of Champagne implored his hearers to have mercy on the Holy City and to avenge the shame done to Jesus Christ by the desecration of the Holy Places. Finishing his plea,

Villehardouin, joined by the other envoys, fell to his knees, weeping copiously, and swearing that they would not arise until their request was granted. Such a display was not regarded as unseemly in the Middle Ages, for men showed their emotions more openly then than we do today. Dandolo and his Venetians, equally moved by the plight of the Holy Land, also wept and stretched their arms on high, crying, "We grant it! We grant it!" And then there went up such a shout, says Villehardouin, that the earth itself seemed to tremble. Finally the doge spoke once more from the lectern, telling his people how highly honored they were that the greatest men in the world had chosen them as their companions in this exalted enterprise.[37] The envoys had fulfilled their mission, and more than fulfilled it, in that the Venetians had agreed not only to provide transportation, but to join the expedition as allies. Only details and formalities remained.

On the following day, according to Geoffrey, the treaty was officially redacted.[38] Two copies of it, both in the name of the doge, survive. We do not possess the complementary copies in the names of the crusaders, but the envoys bore with them blank parchments previously sealed by their principals that were undoubtedly used for this purpose. Villehardouin and his colleagues met with the doge and his councils in the ducal palace for the concluding ceremonies. When the doge delivered the treaty to the envoys he fell to his knees in tears swearing to maintain the covenants in good faith. The French, who had used some of their blank sealed parchments to inscribe oaths on behalf of the counts of Flanders, Champagne, and Blois, also were in tears as they swore their adherence.[39]

The treaty did not name a specific destination, although the envoys and Venetians made a secret agreement that the crusade should land in Egypt (*Babilloine*), because they believed that the Holy Land could be recovered more easily from the Muslims in this way than by direct assault.[40] Villehardouin fails to tell us who made this decision on the destination, but it is not credible that the envoys themselves would have had such freedom that they could direct the entire enterprise wherever they willed. According to Gunther of Pairis, the leading barons unanimously decided to attack Alexandria, both because it was an attractive and strategic target and because they did not wish to break the five-year truce signed by the kingdom of Jerusalem in 1198.[41] The strategy of taking Jerusalem by attacking Egypt was not new. There were hints of it during the First Crusade. King William I of Sicily sent sixty vessels on a very successful raiding mission to Egypt in 1154.[42] King Amalric of Jerusalem (1163–1174) took Alexandria in 1167 and laid siege to Cairo the following year.[43] In 1174 Amalric planned an assault against Alexandria in conjunction with an enormous fleet sent by William II of Sicily and the help of some

Shiite rebels. The plan unraveled, however, when Amalric died, the rebels were executed, and the Normans were routed.[44] Renaud of Chatillon, lord of Transjordan, had incensed Saladin in 1183 by his foray into the Red Sea area. The idea of an attack by Western crusaders upon this center of Muslim power had gained even greater support after Richard Lion-Heart had considered it, and it was to prevail in the crusades of the coming century.[45] Gradually, the single-minded zeal of the earlier crusaders was giving way to the development of a strategy. It has been argued that the failure of the Westerners to seize and hold the great interior cities, such as Damascus and Aleppo, possession of which would have posed a threat to Baghdad itself and to the valley of the Tigris-Euphrates, was responsible for the ultimate defeat of the crusaders. The failure to gain a foothold in Egypt, however, was more important. The crusaders themselves were aware of the precarious nature of their possessions along the Syrian coast, vulnerable to a pincer movement from Egypt in the south and from upper Mesopotamia in the north. The Egyptian littoral, on the other hand, was critical to communications among the Muslims. Not for nothing was Alexandria called the market of the two worlds. If the crusaders could cut the lines between North Africa and the eastern Muslim world, the whole of Islam would be in jeopardy, and Jerusalem would fall like ripe fruit into their hands. As it turned out, of course, neither the Fourth Crusade nor subsequent attempts upon the delta succeeded, and ultimately a Muslim offensive launched from Egypt drove the Latins from the Levant.[46] To the Franks and Venetians in 1201, however, there seemed every promise of success. They knew that Egypt was in the midst of hard times. For five years the Nile had failed to deliver its fruitful flood, and the land was in a weakened state, overwhelmed by famine and poverty.[47] As for the cities, Alexandria was in steady decline and Cairo's fortifications, begun by Saladin, remained unfinished in 1201.[48] Enrico Dandolo knew Alexandria's problems firsthand. He had traveled to the city immediately after the failed Frankish-Norman attack in 1174 and had a good chance to inspect its weaknesses.[49]

Prospects for the crusade in the Holy Land itself, moreover, did not present an encouraging aspect. The Christians of the Levant had entered into a five-year truce with the Muslims in 1198, and were not disposed to violate it.[50] When Renaud of Dampierre, one of the French crusaders who was to sail directly from Apulia to the Holy Land in 1202, arrived there, he pleaded with King Aimery to break the truce, which the king would not do.[51] Such incidents as this confirmed in the minds of the crusaders their distrust for their coreligionists of Syria. Decades of dwelling in the East as conquerors had softened their natures and dulled their ardor for war. The religious zeal that had driven their ancestors had given way to the enjoyment of the good life.

Their great concern in these matters was that what they possessed should not be put in jeopardy. They were even suspected of having set a trap with the Muslims for earlier crusaders out of a fear that the newcomers would dispossess them, a charge that is probably extreme and ill-founded, but that reflects the attitude of some of the new crusaders. Certainly no one counted upon the Christians of the Levant for much help.[52] To the leading men, therefore, the plan to attack the Nile Delta made a great deal of sense. If they succeeded in seizing one of the great port cities, the sultan would be compelled to yield Jerusalem to protect his more vital interests.

Strategic considerations were supported by a shift in religious attitude. In the course of a century of crusading the Holy Land had ceased to be the specific and unique objective of some of those who bore the cross. The concept of the crusade had become less specifically associated with the places consecrated by the life of Christ. A Christian who made war at the behest of the Church against the enemies of Christendom in Spain or elsewhere was conceived to be fighting for the heavenly Jerusalem and entitled to the privileges of a crusader. For those who saw the crusade in these broader terms, therefore, it was no less sacred a task to attack Egypt than Palestine.[53]

This liberal view, however, had failed to capture the minds of many crusaders, particularly those in the ranks. Simple men were still drawn to the actual places where the Lord had lived and died and they felt bound, as we shall see, to a literal accomplishment of their vows. For this reason, although the negotiators agreed upon Egypt, the treaty was deliberately vague concerning the destination. The envoys did not wish to arouse dissension among the mass of crusaders when the terms of the treaty became known to them. In general, the great barons, more inclined to strategic considerations, favored Egypt, while many of the lesser men simply assumed that their single and immediate goal was Jerusalem. Probably not even the barons were all of one mind. A crusading army was a rather disorderly mass. Each man, certainly each of the more powerful men, remained free to follow the dictates of his own will or his own conscience. In order to attract as many of the crusaders as possible to Venice, therefore, deliberate obscurity concerning the destination was sound policy. Announcement that they planned to sail for Egypt could only cause discord and defection. Once all were gathered in Venice, however, a certain commitment to the common enterprise would already have been made and the influence of the leaders would be stronger.[54]

Before leaving Venice the envoys borrowed two thousand marks to pay the Venetians to begin construction of the fleet.[55] They may have used blanks presealed by the three counts for this also.[56] It is true that the terms of the treaty do not seem to require any payment before August, but Villehardouin tells of borrowing the money.[57] This earnest money permitted the building of the fleet to begin.

The preparation of ships to transport an army of 33,500 men, plus the fifty galleys that Venice was to provide at her own cost, was a massive undertaking, even for the great Adriatic maritime republic. We know that the fleet before Constantinople numbered approximately two hundred ships.[58] Villehardouin tells us, however, and there is every reason to believe him, that the Venetians had prepared ships for at least three times as many crusaders as appeared in Venice.[59] We must conclude, therefore, that the Venetians had prepared, in addition to the 50 galleys, some 450 transports. Robert of Clari reports that the doge suspended Venetian commerce for eighteen months, ordering the vessels back home in order to concentrate upon preparing this massive fleet.[60] Although these were, for the most part, private merchant vessels, it was within the doge's power to contract their services for the state. Beyond existing vessels, however, the state had to pay for the construction of a great many new ships. In later centuries the doge could have ordered vessels from the famous Venetian Arsenal, but in 1201 shipbuilding was still largely a private enterprise practiced in small shipyards throughout the lagoon.[61] Payment for the labor involved in the fleet construction may have stimulated the issuance of two new coins, the quarter-penny or *quartarolo*, and the *grosso*, the first pure silver coin minted in western Europe since antiquity.[62] Beyond the vessels, Venice also had to secure the tons of provisions necessary for the enterprise: an undertaking made doubly difficult by poor harvests, which had afflicted the Mediterranean for the past few years.[63] Finally, and most difficult for the small republic, was the manpower requirement. Crews for the 450 transport vessels and 50 war galleys would require around fourteen thousand men, a figure equal to one-half of Venice's able-bodied male population.[64] To raise so large a force, the Venetian state could not rely solely on voluntary assumptions of the cross. Instead, a lottery was instituted at the parish level, which was set to tap half of all Venetian men of military age.[65] Enrico Dandolo did not stretch the truth when he told the envoys that their request was a weighty matter. The preparation of the crusading fleet consumed Venice's attention, resources, and commerce for over one year. It was the largest endeavor in Venetian history, the largest state project in western Europe since the time of the Romans. These facts have been too little noted by critics of the Venetian role in the Fourth Crusade. The city made a tremendous effort and committed itself deeply to the enterprise. Failure would be a disaster for the merchants of the Rialto and the city whose well-being depended upon them.

No one could then anticipate it, but the treaty of transportation of 1201 set the crusade on a course that was to lead to Constantinople. It was not that the Venetians took advantage of the knights from beyond the Alps, but that the envoys of the crusaders committed themselves to conventions impossible to fulfill. Contracting for ships and supplies for an army of 33,500 men was extravagantly optimistic, to say the least. Presumably the envoys were not completely uninstructed by their principals, so the full blame does not rest upon them, but must be shouldered in large measure by the young counts of Flanders, Champagne, and Blois. Even a king or emperor could raise such a force only with the greatest difficulty.[66] Events were to prove that the leaders of the crusade could not. As a result of their failure, necessity and circumstance would draw the Fourth Crusade step by step to the shores of the Bosporus.

The marshal of Champagne, Geoffrey of Villehardouin, has often been indicted as an official historian of the crusade, cleverly appearing to tell the whole story, but actually concealing devious plots to divert the army to Constantinople. Revelation of the whole truth, according to this view, would have been most embarrassing to the small circle of leaders to which he belonged.[67] Where Villehardouin's account can be checked against official documents, however, he proves to be relatively accurate and quite specific, if somewhat superficial. His description of the negotiations at Venice in early 1201 can be verified in considerable detail by the treaty itself and other official documents. In spite of a few minor deviations, which do not appear to reflect any desire to mislead, he analyzes the conventions carefully and accurately. His chronology is also detailed and relatively precise, although his date for the conclusion of the treaty is difficult to reconcile with the date the official document bears. Again, however, there seems to be no deep significance in the discrepancy. The tone and style of certain passages, moreover, particularly those recounting the speeches of the envoys, suggest that he was working with documents or notes in hand. It has been suggested that when he wrote his account some years later he possessed copies of numerous official documents and possibly a journal that he had kept day by day.[68] Certainly the style of his chronicle is very different from the impressionistic one of Robert of Clari. The evidence brought against his honesty is not convincing. He does not probe underlying causes and motives, it is true, for his approach, while detailed, is not profound. It is the style of a soldier, not that of a trained historian. If, as the fate of the crusade unfolds, he appears to be pleading for the defense, it is not because he is concealing some secret plot, but because he himself played such a prominent role in making the treaty from which all subsequent difficulties followed.[69]

Finally the envoys joined the Venetians in dispatching messengers to Rome to obtain papal confirmation of the treaty. This would lend added sanction to their covenants. Such confirmation was granted between 5 May and 8 May. Opinions differ, however, concerning Innocent's reaction to the news brought by the envoys from Venice.[70] Villehardouin reports simply that the pope confirmed the treaty "very willingly."[71] Innocent's clerical biographer, however, describes the attitude of the pope in quite different terms. Fore-seeing the future, Innocent cautiously replied that he would confirm those conventions, provided the crusaders should not harm Christians, unless they wrongfully impeded the passage of the crusade or another just or necessary cause should occur. The consent of the papal legate would be required be-fore any attack on Christians could be undertaken. The author of the *Gesta Innocentii* continues that the Venetians would not accept the confirmation with these provisions, from which he concludes that they planned an attack upon Christian territory from the beginning.[72] Which of the two, the mar-shal of Champagne or the Roman cleric, tells the truth? Supporters of the *Gesta* (those who blame Venetian greed for the outcome of the crusade) point to the long-standing Venetian trade with the infidel and the reluctance of the merchants of the lagoons to give up their profits in spite of repeated papal prohibitions. Innocent, according to this view, saw the Venetians as danger-ous and untrustworthy allies, and granted even qualified approval to the pact only very reluctantly. Those who support Villehardouin reply that the papacy had not shown itself fearful of the Venetians, that Innocent had sought their participation in the crusade, that he had given them the right to deal with Egypt in non-military goods, and that his letter to them of 8 May 1201 spoke in warm terms of their commitment to the crusade. These historians concede that the *Gesta* is a generally reliable source often based directly upon papal letters. It was not written until 1208, however, seven years after the events in question, and it is an apologia for Innocent III, who may have inspired its composition himself. Writing long after the conquest of Constantinople and after Innocent had finally recognized the failure of the Fourth Crusade, and unwilling to burden the pope with any share of responsibility for the out-come, the author, according to this view, knowingly or unknowingly trans-ferred to May 1201 the prohibition against attacking Christians first actually delivered in November 1202. In doing so he not only sought to avoid embar-rassment for the pope, but attributed to him remarkable foresight.[73]

It is possible, however, to believe that the pope confirmed the treaty very willingly, yet also imposed conditions. A letter of the pope to Dandolo of 25 February 1204, recounts "how we gave warning to your envoys, who came to the Apostolic See seeking that the pacts undertaken between you should be confirmed, and through them to you and to the Venetians, lest you should harm the lands of that king [of Hungary] in any way." This can scarcely refer to any other agreements than those of 1201. The prohibition seems to have been verbal and it is not identical with the prohibition in the *Gesta*, since it deals specifically with the Hungarian kingdom. The papal letter, however, continues, that "through our letters" the Venetians had been strictly admonished not to invade or harm the lands of Christians with the exceptions and conditions given in the *Gesta*.[74] It is possible, of course, that the pope here refers to a document considerably later than the verbal prohibition, but it is probably not so. Very likely, given the record of earlier crusaders in becoming involved in peripheral campaigns and interventions, Innocent did deliver a specific oral warning to the envoys in an effort to protect the king of Hungary, and then shortly in the written confirmation of the treaty broadened the prohibition to include attacks upon any Christian lands. Since the *Gesta* is, in general, a reliable source, it seems preferable to adopt this interpretation, which is in no way contradictory to Villehardouin.

Innocent's prescience and his distrust of the Venetians, however, need not be accepted. For one thing, the author of the *Gesta* is not here writing from documents, but speculating concerning his hero's frame of mind. For another, no specific foresight and suspicion need be predicated, for the crusades had already given ample evidence of the likelihood that conflicts among Christians would arise. The papal prohibition was simply the product of experience and common sense.[75]

Papal confirmation could not make a bad treaty a good one. No doubt the pope rejoiced at the huge army that was intended to assemble at Venice in the spring of 1202, but Innocent had no power to transform unrealistic plans into realities. The fateful treaty of 1201 was to lead to one crisis after another for the crusaders who did assemble in Venice, and they had to meet these crises one by one, as best they could, papal prohibitions notwithstanding.

3

The Election of Boniface
of Montferrat

After Villehardouin and his five colleagues had arranged for transportation of the crusade, they set out for home to report the success of their mission. When they reached Piacenza the party divided: Geoffrey the marshal and Alard Maquereau continued toward France, while the other four journeyed to Genoa and Pisa to discover what those cities would do to aid Jerusalem. Since the envoys had already entered into a binding contract with the Venetians for ships to convey an enormous army, they could not have been seeking in Genoa and Pisa additional transportation or more favorable terms. Villehardouin, moreover, the chief negotiator, was not among them. Perhaps they considered it worth the detour to see if they might gain Genoese or Pisan participation in the crusade, or it might have been merely a courteous gesture in the hope of averting any adverse reaction to the alliance by Venice's rivals. In any case, the Genoese and Pisans replied that they could do nothing.[1]

While their two colleagues were occupied with this fruitless journey, Geoffrey and his companion retraced their way home via the western Alps. Between Piacenza and the Mont Cenis pass they would have had to pass through the marquisate of Montferrat, and it is highly probable that there they visited with Marquis Boniface.[2] The crusader envoys were seeking men and money in support of their enterprise. Boniface was a famous knight, and, moreover, a relative by marriage of Count Thibaut of Champagne. The court of Montferrat, in addition, was a center for chivalric entertainment. Noble visitors gathered there to hear the songs of some of the most famous troubadours in Europe. Considering Villehardouin's status, connections, and interests, it is unlikely that he would pass by the court of Marquis Boniface without stopping. In all probability he told the marquis of the mission to Venice, and Boniface may have shown himself inclined to join the French crusaders. Perhaps Geoffrey and Boniface established then the friendly relationship that was to become so strong and enduring. All of this, of course, is merely reasonable speculation. Still, a month or so later, when the crusaders were seeking a leader, Villehardouin was entirely confident that the lord of Montferrat would accept a summons to that post. It seems plausible to conclude, therefore, that there was a meeting at the time of Geoffrey's return from Venice.[3]

Resuming their homeward journey, Villehardouin and Maquereau traversed the Mont Cenis Pass. On their way they encountered Walter of Brienne, accompanied by a considerable number of crusaders from Champagne and elsewhere. The count of Brienne had been enlisted by Pope Innocent as an instrument in the faltering papal struggle against the Hohenstaufen party for control of Italy and Sicily. Walter had married the eldest daughter of Tancred, last of the Norman kings of Naples and Sicily, and the foe of the imperial Hohenstaufen. The pope promised support for Walter's efforts to conquer, in the name of his wife, the county of Lecce and the principality of Taranto in Apulia, the heel of the Italian boot.[4] Innocent regarded his war against the Germans in Italy as a crusade and once even threatened to divert the entire Fourth Crusade to Sicily, though he likely did not mean it.[5] In exchange for news of Walter's affairs, Villehardouin recounted the accomplishments of the crusader envoys at Venice. He reports that the count of Brienne and his companions rejoiced at the news and congratulated the negotiators. Walter declared that he and his men were already en route, and that when the main body of crusaders would come they would find him and his followers quite ready.[6] It appears that the count and his men regarded the campaign in Apulia as a side journey on their expedition to the Holy Land, which offers a key to understanding the later excursions to Zara and Constantinople. Villehardouin tells of the encounter with joy, but it was fraught with evil portents. Although Innocent did not, like some pontiffs, cynically sacrifice the cause of the Holy Land to other interests, he was here making use of crusaders pledged to the pilgrimage overseas for papal warfare in Italy.[7] This hardly comported with his pleas to other rulers to cease their wars in the interest of the crusade. No doubt he hoped and Walter confidently expected that their battle would be swiftly won and that these crusaders would indeed be ready within a year to fulfill their vows, but, if so, they were tragically wrong. Furthermore, Villehardouin does not record, nor is it logical to expect, that the count promised to lead his men back up the peninsula to the rendezvous at Venice. If he were able to join the crusading army at all, he would naturally embark his troops directly from an Apulian port. Thus already lost to the future assemblage at Venice were a number of men described as "a great part of the crusaders from Champagne."[8] As it turned out, the pope was able to lend Walter of Brienne only a little support. Even so, within a few months he had marched to victory near Capua and gained a great part of Apulia. Later he put his German foe to flight upon the historic field at Cannae. Many enthusiastic Italians flocked to follow his banners, including the young Francis of Assisi, who fell out, however, upon the way, converted to a new and greater cause.[9] Provençal and Italian troubadours, who hated the Germans, sang the praises of the count of Brienne.[10] In the end, however, Walter was surprised in his camp and slain by the enemy in June of 1205, long after the departure of the crusade from Venice.[11] A considerable number of good fighting men were thus lost to the crusade. The chances of fulfilling the newly made compact with the Venetians were, thereby, also diminished.[12]

Without further incident Geoffrey and Alard hastened by way of Burgundy to Troyes to report their success to Count Thibaut. They found the young count very ill, but he received the news of the progress of his project with such joy that he rose from his bed and mounted his horse, which he had not ridden since his illness. The exercise exacerbated the ailment, which, in any case, may have been fatal, and he took once more to his bed, never to rise again. Anticipating death, the count made what preparations he could. Deprived of the opportunity of fulfilling personally his pilgrimage to the Holy Land, he appointed a knight, Renaud of Dampierre, to go in his place, and provided him with sufficient money. Then he made his testament. Of the money that he had gathered for the crusade, he distributed some among his Champenois followers for their expenses on the journey.[13] He made each of them swear to follow the army assembling at Venice. Many of these, Villehardouin complains, later violated that oath. The remainder of this money was reserved for the crusading army as a whole. Having made what preparations were possible for the repose of his soul and for the holy cause to which he had dedicated himself, on 24 May the young count of Champagne died. He left his widow Blanche and a small daughter, and only a few days later, perhaps 30 May, Blanche gave birth to a son, Count Thibaut IV of Champagne. Thibaut III's body was laid to rest with great pomp beside that of his father in the Church of Saint Stephen, which the latter had built at Troyes.[14] Over the new tomb they raised an inscription:

> Intent upon making amends for the injuries of the Cross and the land
>   of the Crucified
> He paved a way with expenses, an army, a fleet.
> Seeking the terrestrial city, he finds the one celestial;
> While he is obtaining his goal far away, he finds it at home.[15]

Scholars have differed on Thibaut's precise role in the Fourth Crusade. Was he the leader of the entire crusading army or only one of several great crusading barons? Robert of Clari declares that the count was elected to lead the enterprise shortly before his death, which Robert incorrectly places before the Treaty of Venice.[16] Ernoul and Bernard le Trésorier's *Chronique* (Ernoul-Bernard) reports that the election took place after the treaty at an assembly of the crusaders at Corbie.[17] Robert, however, cannot be trusted until his own arrival in Venice in the summer of 1202 and Ernoul-Bernard cannot be counted upon for details of events in far away France. Both are obviously confused on the various assemblies of the barons.

Most modern historians have followed these unreliable sources or one another.[18] Other scholars, including Queller in the first edition of this book, deny Thibaut real and formal leadership, but allow that he had informal preeminence.[19] Benjamin Hendrickx states in passing that when the barons recruited Boniface of Montferrat, they asked him to replace the count of Champagne and, at the same time (i.e., as a distinct and separate matter), take command of the entire army.[20] Ellen E. Kittell agrees, further arguing that Thibaut was neither formally nor informally the head of the entire host.[21]

It is clear that Thibaut was not sole commander prior to the spring of 1201. Despite Villehardouin's prominence in negotiating the Treaty of Venice, the six envoys were formally of equal status, two representing each of the three French magnates. The Treaty of Venice lists the counts of Flanders, Champagne, and Blois in that order, as does a letter of Innocent III.[22] Medieval scribes customarily listed names in order of rank. Indeed, if there were any informal preeminence it would belong to the count of Flanders. Kittell argues that the successive offers to the duke of Burgundy and the count of Bar-le-Duc to replace the dead count were from the latter's Champenois followers. She finds Villehardouin's silence concerning his lord's position in the host to be the most telling bit of evidence. Had Thibaut been supreme leader, she contends, Villehardouin would have mentioned it.[23] The question, while intriguing, is largely academic. The command of the crusading army, even when it was given to Boniface of Montferrat, did not amount to what we would regard as command. It was merely a title. No more than Agamemnon could command Achilles before the walls of Troy could Boniface command Baldwin of Flanders before the walls of Constantinople.

Although Villehardouin does not mention an assembly at Corbie, it does seem reasonable to believe that the leading men gathered to hear the report of the envoys to Venice and to ratify the treaty. The Venetians had included in the document requirements that the three principals must ratify it and that the other crusaders should swear their own adherence to its terms.[24]

After Thibaut's burial his followers sought a successor. Matthew of Montmorency, Simon de Montfort, Geoffrey of Joinville (the seneschal of

Champagne), and Villehardouin were sent to offer the command of the Champenois to Duke Eudes of Burgundy, a cousin of Thibaut. They requested him to take the cross and come to the succor of the Holy Land. If he consented he would receive the allegiance of the crusaders from Champagne and the money that Thibaut had left for the crusade. When the duke of Burgundy refused, Joinville then was sent to make the same offer to Count Thibaut of Bar-le-Duc, also a cousin of the deceased count of Champagne. He in turn declined.[25] So in late June another assembly was held at Soissons to determine what should be done. All the chief men of the French crusaders were present, Baldwin of Flanders, Louis of Blois, Geoffrey of Perche, Hugh of Saint Pol, and many others. Villehardouin proposed that the command of Thibaut's men and leadership of the whole army should be offered to Boniface, marquis of Montferrat, one of the most highly regarded men alive. He assured the assembled barons that the marquis would accept.[26] Villehardouin's confidence has been interpreted as a sign of prior collusion between the Italian marquis and the marshal of Champagne to place Boniface at the head of the crusade, but there is no evidence of this.[27] The two had probably conferred at the time of the marshal's return from Venice, but it is not at all credible that Geoffrey and Boniface could have foreseen the tangled skein of events, the death of the count of Champagne and the refusals of the duke of Burgundy and the count of Bar-le-Duc, which led to the choice at Soissons. There was much debate among the crusaders, now troubled by their failure to obtain a replacement for the count of Champagne, but they finally agreed upon the Italian marquis.[28]

One may well ask why the command was not offered to the powerful and popular Baldwin of Flanders. No one would seem to possess a better claim to leadership than he. He was wealthy and, among the crusaders, the only one with his own fleet. There are two reasons why Baldwin may have been overlooked. The offers to the duke of Burgundy, the count of Bar-le-Duc, and the marquis of Montferrat, none of whom had at that time joined the crusade, suggest that the barons were seeking to use the position to add to their ranks. The enlistment of a prominent baron with his followers would entail a sizable increase in the numbers of the crusaders. Perhaps they already had a premonition of difficulty in fulfilling the treaty with the Venetians. Baldwin, moreover, was no favorite of the king of France, whom he had humiliated.[29] Apart from personal feelings, the king would have had a natural reluctance to enhance so greatly the prestige of one of his most powerful vassals. If it is true, as it appears to be, that Philip Augustus intervened on behalf of Boniface, his opposition to the count of Flanders provides a motive.

The marquis of Montferrat, to be sure, had imposing qualifications on his own account to attract the attention of the leaderless crusaders. He belonged to the great international aristocracy. The house of Montferrat was related to both the German Hohenstaufen and the French Capetians and it had played a celebrated role in the earlier crusades.[30] In his early fifties Boniface was a mature leader with long experience of command. He had governed Montferrat since 1183 and had been marquis since 1192, when his brother Conrad died in the East.[31] His aptitude in diplomacy is proved by his ability to retain the trust of the pope in spite of his loyalty to the Hohenstaufen.[32] He was widely regarded as an ideal Christian knight. His impetuous valor finally brought about his death in 1207 when he rushed into battle armed only with a sword.[33] He was one of the best fighting men and commanders of his day. According to his faithful troubadour, Raimbaut de Vaqueiras, Boniface was also renowned for compassion toward the weak and distressed and respect toward ladies. As young men Boniface and Raimbaut had shared romantic expeditions in the service of ladies, emulating the heroes of romance. The court of Montferrat was a center of chivalry. In his *Epic Letter*, Raimbaut celebrates the courtly life, the fine raiment and armor, the jousts and song, the hospitality of Montferrat.[34]

The marquis of Montferrat was without question a brilliant choice. Recognized as the greatest of the Italian nobles, he possessed formidable power and large numbers of fighting men. His marquisate lay in the Piedmont, straddling the banks of the Tanaro River between Turin on the west and Tortona on the east. As a Lombard prince, Boniface would be relatively acceptable to the various national components of the crusading army, the Italians, the Germans, and the many French.[35]

The *Gesta* of Innocent III informs us, in fact, that the selection of Boniface was made upon the advice of Philip Augustus, the king of France.[36] Contrary to the opinion of those who believe that many crusaders enlisted to escape the wrath of Philip, it was quite natural that the French barons should consult with their king on so important a matter.[37] That the Venetians recognized the king's influence among the crusaders is proved by their demand that his oath be sought in support of the treaty for transportation.[38] Boniface's later visit to the court of France immediately before his acceptance of the command also lends support to the belief that Philip Augustus influenced the selection.

Philip of Swabia, Hohenstaufen claimant to the German kingship and the Holy Roman Empire, also was favorably inclined, since the house of Montferrat had a heritage of allegiance to the Ghibelline cause. During Frederick Barbarossa's wars against the Lombard League, Boniface and his brothers joined in defending the marquisate against the attacks of the anti-imperial

communes of the Piedmont and Lombardy.[39] In these wars the young nobleman grew up, disciplined by experience in battle to the duties of his position
in life. At the *Reichstag* at Mainz in February of 1194 the Piedmontese marquis ranked among the great princes of the empire, the duke of Austria, the
duke of Swabia, and others.[40] He joined Henry VI's campaign of the same
year against the Normans of Naples and Sicily, received the title of imperial
legate, and, along with the podesta of Genoa, was placed in command of the
fleet. He was nearly killed at Messina for the Ghibelline cause, but survived to
enjoy Henry's coronation at Palermo on Christmas of 1194.[41] After the pre-
mature death of Henry VI, Boniface continued to enjoy the friendship and
favor of the new Hohenstaufen leader, Henry's brother, Philip of Swabia.

Boniface was a choice agreeable also to Pope Innocent. In 1199 the pontiff
had chosen the marquis of Montferrat as a colleague of the highly regarded
Conrad, cardinal-archbishop of Mainz, in a vain effort to settle the struggle
over the German throne between the Hohenstaufen Philip of Swabia and the
Welf Otto of Brunswick, or at least to try to obtain a truce of five years.[42] In
light of the well-known Hohenstaufen loyalties of the marquis of Montferrat,
his employment by the pope in this prominent role is surprising. Innocent
must have had great confidence in Boniface, a relative, vassal, and friend of
the feared German dynasty, to entrust him with this task.[43]

Few families could rival the reputation of the house of Montferrat in the
Levant. Boniface's father, William the Old, had fought with distinction on the
Second Crusade. When the barons of the kingdom of Jerusalem decided to
seek a successor from Europe for the leper Baldwin IV, who had no hope of an
heir of his body, the renown of the marquis William and his flourishing family
attracted their attention. Boniface's eldest brother, William Longsword, was
therefore called to Palestine in 1176 to marry Baldwin's sister Sibyl and to provide for the succession to the crown. William's energy, intelligence, and valor
soon gained a predominant influence over the sick king, arousing the envy of
some of the magnates. A bare three months after his marriage William died
mysteriously. The posthumous son of this brief marriage was the future king,
Baldwin V.[44] William the Old himself returned to the Holy Land, falling captive in 1187 to Saladin at the fateful Battle of Hattin, which sealed the fate of
Jerusalem.[45] In the midst of the shock of this disaster, William's second son,
Conrad, arrived at Tyre. He, too, was a knight of renown, highly praised for
valor and wisdom. When the people of Tyre heard that the son of the marquis
of Montferrat was at hand they went forth in joyous procession to welcome
him and rendered the city into his hands. His defense of Tyre, both before
and after the fall of Jerusalem earned him the highest glory. He flung into the
city's ditch the standards that Saladin had sent to be flown from Tyre's walls

after its surrender, which had already been arranged.[46] When Saladin, confident that he held a trump card in the person of Conrad's captive father, tried to bargain with the son, Conrad refused to surrender the smallest stone in order to gain the liberation of William the Old.[47] Conrad married Isabel, the other sister of Baldwin IV, and succeeded in gaining election as king. That he was already married to the Byzantine princess Theodora Angelina he conveniently ignored. Very soon after his election, however, Conrad was murdered in the streets of Tyre by the minions of the Old Man of the Mountain, the chief of the feared sect of the Assassins.[48]

The house of Montferrat also had played an exalted role in Byzantium. In 1179 the emperor Manuel Comnenus proposed the marriage of his daughter Maria to one of the sons of the illustrious William the Old. The emperor's aim was to win over to his Italian policy a powerful family that had been loyal to his enemies, the Hohenstaufen. At this time the house of Montferrat had been left by Barbarossa's capitulation in the Treaty of Venice of 1177 to face alone the fury of the nearby towns. The inducement offered by Manuel was high indeed—his own daughter, second in succession to the throne.[49] The lord of Montferrat leaped at the opportunity, giving up for a time his support of the German emperor who had abandoned him. Since William Longsword was dead in Palestine, Conrad and Boniface were already married, and Frederick had donned clerical vestments, the honor fell to the youngest son, Renier.[50] This seventeen-year-old youth married the princess Maria, a strong-minded woman of thirty. Renier received the title of "Caesar" and the high honors of a member of the imperial family. Although two Latin sources declare that Renier became king of Thessalonica, the youth in fact received little if any real authority. No doubt, however, the Latin sources do reflect a fact in distorted form. Manuel very likely granted him Thessalonica as a *pronoia*, an estate for life normally given as payment for high military command.[51] The princess Maria could not forget that she had been deprived of the right of succession to the throne by the birth of her much younger half-brother Alexius. By her maturity and her determined and energetic character she gained domination over her younger spouse, who became caught up in affairs too great for his limited experience. When Emperor Manuel died and the throne passed to the youngster Alexius II in September 1180, Maria saw her chance. Manuel's young, beautiful, frivolous, and spoiled widow abandoned herself and the empire into the hands of Alexius the *protosebastos*, a high official and a member of the imperial family. This scandalous liaison upset the entire court. The lover of the empress-dowager arrogantly assumed an almost imperial role. He also foolishly alienated his subjects, particularly the more ambitious courtiers, by his reliance upon the Latins, whose wealth and influence aroused bitter resentment. This pro-Latin policy had been Manuel's as well, but a policy disliked under a strong emperor became intolerable in the hands of the despicable paramour. Maria, Renier, and many nobles of the court plotted to overthrow the *protosebastos*, secretly harboring the aim of usurping her brother's throne for herself. Renier of Montferrat seems to have been a passive follower of his ambitious wife. The conspiracy was prematurely exposed, and some of the conspirators were arrested. Maria and Renier with about a hundred and fifty followers, mostly Latin, perhaps Renier's own Piedmontese, took refuge in Hagia Sophia. Reduced to these desperate straits, young Renier proved his mettle as a fighter. He led his little band out of the sanctuary to repulse the imperial army, at least for the time, before returning to the churchly fortress. To put an end to the spectacle, which Byzantines later referred to as the "Holy War" since it took place in their great church, the *protosebastos* offered the conspirators an amnesty. They willingly accepted. A few years later, however, Maria, Renier, and Alexius II alike fell victims to the usurper Andronicus I. Renier and Maria had a more solid claim to the Byzantine throne than did the new emperor, so it is not surprising that Andronicus poisoned Renier.[52] The call of the East proved fatal to all four of the brave sons of William of Montferrat who answered it. One learned scholar believed that Boniface was present in Constantinople with Renier while these events unfolded, but this is unsupported by evidence.[53] At any rate, Boniface no doubt harbored resentment at least against Byzantium, and a desire for revenge for the murder of his youngest brother. He may also have dreamed of reclaiming what he conceived to be Renier's rights to Thessalonica, if not to the Byzantine throne itself. This is not to say that revenge and ambition were necessarily in the forefront of Boniface's mind when he took the cross. The tragic career of Renier, however, must have constituted a portion of the memories that influenced the mind of Boniface of Montferrat.

If Renier's poor luck in Constantinople affected Boniface, so too did the very favorable treatment of his other brother, Conrad of Montferrat. Before his brilliant and ill-fated career in the kingdom of Jerusalem, Conrad had played a prominent role in Constantinople, even becoming something of a local hero there. It was probably late in the year of 1186 when the emperor Isaac II Angelus, seeking an able Latin commander for the imperial troops, turned once more to the house of Montferrat. He first offered the hand of his sister Theodora to Boniface, and discovering that he had a wife, willingly accepted Conrad, then a widower, as a substitute. Conrad was already known for his military exploits and had previously paid an extended visit to Constantinople. Almost immediately after his marriage, Conrad proved himself the main support of the emperor against the revolt of Alexius Branas.

Conrad's brilliant defense of Constantinople earned him the gratitude of the Angeli and the respect of the people. Nicetas Choniates, no friend of Italians, wrote that Conrad "so excelled in bravery and sagacity that he was far-famed, not only among the Romans but also celebrated among his countrymen."[54] Not long after his victory over the rebel, however, Conrad began to find his position at court uncomfortable, since many of the nobles were relatives or friends of Branas. He could not have remained unaware, moreover, of the popular hatred of Westerners, even though it was not directed against him personally. He also failed to receive from the emperor rewards commensurate with his success. He had gained from Isaac the title of "Caesar," formerly held by his brother, but he was not permitted to don the blue buskins that signified the office. This title, formerly so important, was in the twelfth century only an empty honor given to the emperor's son-in-law. Nevertheless, Conrad's currency with the military and general popularity in the city might have foreshadowed even greater things in Byzantium, perhaps even elevation to the imperial throne. But Conrad had another appointment to keep. Before the Byzantine marriage offer he had taken the crusader's cross. While he was willing to stop in the great city and secure his position, he was determined to fulfill his vow and journey to the Holy Land. Hated by some Greek courtiers, cheated of the full recognition he deserved, and apparently not enamored of Theodora, when Conrad heard that Saladin threatened to sweep the Christians of Palestine into the sea, he answered the call of duty and adventure. Without a by-your-leave to either emperor or wife he left Constantinople on 14 July 1187.[55] In the Holy Land, as mentioned previously, he won renown at Tyre but soon was assassinated. Boniface of Montferrat's three brothers who had gained glory and met their deaths in the East marked him as the likely leader of the crusading host.

Emissaries were sent from the crusaders at Soissons to offer command of the army to the marquis of Montferrat. They found him at Castagnola delle Lanze, a castle in the territory of Asti. They asked him to come to Soissons on a certain day to consult with the leaders about accepting the command, and he agreed with thanks.[56]

Journeying to Soissons where the nobles awaited him in the late summer of 1201, Boniface stopped in Paris to consult with Philip Augustus.[57] Apart from his relationship with the French king and the latter's role in promoting the offer that Boniface had just received, there were other reasons for speaking with Philip before proceeding. Prior to accepting command of an army dominated by French nobles it was certainly appropriate for a Lombard prince to confer with the king of France, not only as a mark of courtesy, but because the king would be able to tell him much about the men he was asked to lead.

There were also matters not directly related to the crusade, but to the general political background in which it was set. Philip received Boniface warmly. The marquis did not let pass the opportunity to intercede with the French monarch on behalf of the Hohenstaufen faction in the struggle for the German throne. The king convinced Boniface that he remained attached to the cause of Philip of Swabia and had no understanding with his rival Otto of Brunswick. It was probably at this time, in fact, that Philip Augustus entrusted Boniface with a message for the pope in which he complained strongly of Innocent's support of Otto. If the pope feared Hohenstaufen policy, the king of France wrote, he himself would serve as a guarantor for Philip of Swabia.[58]

Boniface then proceeded to Soissons to meet the French crusaders. Accompanying him, as the crusaders had no doubt hoped, were various Lombard nobles who had elected to share the work of God. Also included in the group were two abbots of the white-garbed Cistercian order, one of whom was Peter of Locedio, who was to play a prominent role in the crusade. The proceedings took place in an orchard adjoining the Benedictine abbey of Notre Dame. Here the crusading barons offered the Lombard marquis the command of the whole army, as well as the money left by Thibaut and the latter's men. Kneeling in tears before him, they begged him to accept. Falling in turn at their feet, Boniface declared that he would do as they wished.[59] On his knees before the nobles he committed himself to them and their cause. Yet it was not for the crusading ideal alone that he assumed the cross. Most crusaders were driven by a complex of religious and secular motives, and ambition ran deep in the souls of the Montferrats. No doubt he envisioned for himself a powerful position in Palestine, and the thought of the honors his brothers had enjoyed in Constantinople must also have entered his mind[60]

The assembled knights and clergy at Soissons moved to the abbey church to solemnize the work of giving the host a commander. It is surely not coincidental that the abbey church of Notre Dame at Soissons contained the tomb of Saint Drausius, seventh-century bishop of Soissons, who was venerated, among other things, as the protector of those who were preparing to fight the infidel.[61] Then the bishop of Soissons, Nivelon, together with the popular crusade preacher Fulk of Neuilly and the two Cistercian abbots, fastened the cross on the shoulder of the marquis. After the ceremony they consulted over their plans and agreed to meet in Venice. The day after taking the cross the marquis departed to settle his affairs.[62]

On his homeward journey the marquis visited the great abbey of Cîteaux in the Burgundian wilderness, motherhouse of the white monks whose annual general chapter met on 13 September, the eve of the Exaltation of the Holy Cross.[63] For the occasion were assembled at Cîteaux not only abbots of the order, but many nobles, for the focus of attention of the general chapter of 1201 was the forthcoming crusade. Since their foundation at the time of the First Crusade, the white monks, who came largely from aristocratic and military backgrounds, had been deeply involved in the crusading movement. Their own Saint Bernard of Clairvaux had been closely associated with the Knights Templar and was the heart and soul of the Second Crusade. His preaching had called it into being and its failure was his greatest disappointment. Cistercians had thrown themselves into the Third Crusade as well. Discouraged, perhaps, at the outcome of their earlier efforts, they had not been active in Innocent III's endeavors to promote the Fourth Crusade, but once the tournament at Ecry had given distinguished leaders for a holy war, the white monks rallied enthusiastically to the new effort. They not only provided preachers to exhort the faithful to take the cross, but some of them joined the crusaders to care for their spiritual needs. The wealthy Cistercian order also lent its financial support to the enterprise.[64]

Perhaps Fulk, the miracle-working preacher of the crusade, accompanied Boniface on his journey to Burgundy, for he too was present at the general chapter, and in fact the main attraction. Before the assembled monks and nobles the fiery evangelist preached the cross, as he had done so successfully over the past three years. During this period Fulk is said to have crossed some 200,000 soldiers of Christ.[65] All too many of them, however, were the untrained and the unarmed, the poor and the sick. He gained much praise for awaking this mass enthusiasm, but it is doubtful that many of these enlistments were taken seriously by the secular leaders responsible for planning the crusade in practical terms. Many enthusiasts would have been worse than useless for reasons of sex, age, debility, or poverty. Others had come forward under the influence of the immediate fervor aroused by the spellbinding Fulk, but they were seeds that had no root and withered away. Not even the overly sanguine counts of Flanders, Champagne, and Blois had dared to think in numbers of anything like this magnitude. Perhaps it was hoped that many who did not participate as crusaders would redeem their vows with money for the undertaking. Had they done so, the crusade might have taken a different course.

Greater men were not immune to Fulk's eloquence. At the general chapter of September 1201 his emotional summons to succor the land sanctified by the feet of Christ resulted in the enlistment of many additional knights from Burgundy, Champagne, and elsewhere, who had perhaps come to Cîteaux for this purpose.[66] Each of the greater men who took vows naturally attracted the enlistment of lesser folk. The monks at Cîteaux, of course, were not allowed to take the cross without the approval of their superiors, but Fulk had brought a letter from Innocent III designating certain white abbots to assist him in the spiritual care of the crusaders.[67] Boniface made a special plea in addition for the company of Abbot Peter of Locedio, whose counsel he required, and permission was granted.[68]

Upon leaving Cîteaux the new leader of the crusade did not return directly to Montferrat, but instead paid a visit to his lord and cousin, Philip of Swabia. At the court of the German king at Hagenau he passed the Christmas holidays, attending an assembly of the king's vassals of the left bank of the Rhine.[69] Boniface and Philip were on familiar terms. The marquis had served the Hohenstaufen well, and after Philip's election as king of Germany, Boniface had visited him as a papal envoy in an attempt to settle the struggle over the German throne. Very recently, Boniface had represented the Hohenstaufen cause at Paris, and wished to report to Philip of Swabia his success there. As chief of the crusade, moreover, the marquis had reason to visit Germany to discover what aid the German barons might lend to the venture. There had been relatively few enlistments from Germany because of the Hohenstaufen-Welf struggle, which divided Germany into armed camps. Most of the German nobles had their attention focused upon this conflict: one reason why Pope Innocent had been anxious to seek a truce, if a true peace was not possible. Not much was to be hoped from Germany, perhaps, but it was incumbent upon the new leader, who was himself a vassal of the empire, to make a try.

At Hagenau, Boniface encountered an unexpected guest, the refugee Byzantine prince Alexius, son of the deposed emperor Isaac II Angelus.[70] Alexius, consistently referred to as a youth in the sources, was a late adolescent; he was not porphyrogenitus, so his birth must be dated prior to Isaac's ascent to the throne in 1185, perhaps in 1183.[71] He was the brother of Irene, Philip's Greek wife. Their father Isaac had been dethroned in 1195 by the treachery of his older brother, also named Alexius, whom Isaac had completely trusted and highly honored. Early in Isaac's reign the emperor had sought and gained through Saladin his brother's release from prison. Returned to Constantinople, the elder Alexius had been given high office and is said to have received the imperial palace of Boukoleon and the revenues of the adjacent port, which provided an enormous income. Those hostile to Isaac, however, sought to turn the older brother against him, and in time they worked upon his ambitions and a palace coup was plotted. Reports of the conspiracy frequently reached the emperor, but he trusted his brother too blindly to investigate. The conspirators found their opportunity when Isaac and his brother were encamped in southern Thrace in early April 1195. The emperor had decided to go hunting, accompanied by only a small retinue. The conspirators seized the opportune moment. Alexius, the treacherous brother, had excused himself from the hunt, saying that he did not feel well. As soon as Isaac was a short distance from the camp the conspirators led his brother to the imperial tent and hailed him emperor. Attracted by the uproar, the whole camp ran to the scene, and finding the soldiers ready to accept the result, all others had perforce to accept it. Isaac, still within earshot, heard the tumult, and attendants quickly brought him the news. His first reaction was to attack the camp, calling upon Christ and an icon of the Virgin for heavenly aid. His companions, however, seeing how things stood, refused to follow him in a hopeless cause, so he was forced to flee. Across the Maritza River and down the main road to the west the frightened emperor fled, closely pursued by his brother's men. Shortly he was taken, led to a nearby monastery, and was there blinded, the usual fate of deposed rulers, since blindness was conceived as a disqualification for rule. Later he was imprisoned in Constantinople.[72]

The new emperor Alexius III was surprisingly careless in keeping his blinded brother and young nephew under surveillance. His own treacherous ascent to the throne should have put him fully on his guard against treachery, for one who rises to power by an act of violence sets a dangerous precedent against himself. As Nicetas puts it in his ornate style, however, Alexius III forgot that "vengeance does not sleep forever, but takes delight in the chronic changes and eagerly pursues those who perform lawless acts, pouncing swiftly and noiselessly."[73] The blinded Isaac enjoyed considerable freedom. Anybody could visit him without fear in his relatively comfortable confinement, and there flocked all those with grievances against the government. Among the callers were disgruntled Latin inhabitants of the capital and visiting merchants from the West, jealous of their economic privileges, who proposed schemes to overthrow the usurper. Not surprisingly, Isaac welcomed these overtures. He even wrote to his daughter Irene in Germany urging her to rally her husband, Philip of Swabia, to avenge her wronged father. Irene's replies also had no trouble reaching Isaac.

The emperor allowed great freedom to young Alexius as well, who was not blinded, but youthful and ambitious, although not very clever. Father and son willingly promised not to plot against the throne, a declaration upon which the elder Alexius foolishly placed his trust. Bare promises, insufficiently sanctioned by an appropriate balance of benefits, are frequently broken. In fact, Isaac and his son conspired that young Alexius should escape to the West and, with the aid of Irene and her German husband, should attempt to overthrow the treacherous emperor. When Alexius III was engaged in repressing the rebellion of Michael Camytzes in the late summer and early fall of 1201, young Alexius accompanied him to Damokraneia in Thrace. The young prince had come to an agreement with two prominent Pisan merchants of Constantinople to assist his escape by sea. Their great ship set sail at the appropriate time for Athyra on the Sea of Marmara, where it anchored, ostensibly to load sand for ballast. Young Alexius, at the first opportunity, fled his uncle's camp and hurried to Athyra, where a skiff awaited to row him to the merchant ship. The emperor soon learned of his nephew's escape, of course, and ordered that all outgoing ships should be searched for the fugitive. When the emperor's agents searched the Pisan vessel, however, the young prince had cut off his long hair, put on Western clothing, and was mingling with the Pisans aboard, so they did not discover him.[74] The merchantman then conveyed the prince to the Adriatic port of Ancona, where he sent word of his escape to Irene in Germany. Irene sought her husband's aid for her brother, who, as Nicetas tells us, "was homeless and without a country and wandered about like the planets, taking with him no more than his body."[75] Irene dispatched a considerable bodyguard to escort her brother to Germany.[76]

Thus Alexius journeyed from Ancona to Germany, arriving in late September or October of 1201, and met Boniface at Hagenau. The young prince and the Italian veteran had a great deal in common. Boniface's brother Conrad had saved Alexius's father's reign with his military skill. Alexius's aunt was Boniface's former sister-in-law (although this may have been a topic best avoided). Indeed, it would not be odd if Boniface and the prince had met before in better times. They also shared resentment against more-or-less recent developments in Constantinople. Alexius had seen his father deposed and blinded, himself deprived of the succession and forced to become a refugee without possessions or power, dependent upon others. Boniface recalled the fate of his brothers in Constantinople: Renier murdered and Conrad cheated of his rewards. The possibility of leading the crusading army to Jerusalem by way of Constantinople, where young Alexius could be installed as emperor by the crusaders, must have arisen. Alexius professed and probably believed that he would be welcomed as the rightful heir to the throne by the inhabitants of the imperial city.[77] That he was rejected when it came to the test does not alter the significance of the belief that he held and communicated to his new friends in the West. Alexius, however, would not have requested an armed conquest of Constantinople, but rather a show of force to encourage his supporters in a palace coup. The difference between the two is vast, but frequently forgotten today.

Philip also had his reasons to join in the discussions. Frederick Barbarossa's relations with Byzantium had been so bad during his journey across Byzantine territory on the Third Crusade that he had considered attacking the city. Ironically, the Byzantine emperor at that time had been Isaac II, the father of the young Alexius who now sought the aid of Frederick's son.[78] Henry VI, Philip's brother, had also threatened the conquest of Constantinople by a crusading army.[79] But proposals and threats are not attacks: the size and strength of Constantinople continued to daunt Westerners.

Even a casual observer knew Constantinople as the largest, wealthiest, and best defended city in the Western world. There were no casual observers at Hagenau. In nine centuries New Rome had never fallen to a foreign aggressor, shrugging off besieging armies many times larger and better supplied than the Fourth Crusade could ever hope to be.[80] The First Crusade's attacks against the city had been pitiful failures. Since then, the city's mammoth fortifications had been further strengthened.[81] Although it was common in the West to bluster about attacking Constantinople, this should hardly surprise given the wealth of the city, its general contempt for Westerners, its recalcitrance in crusading and ecclesiastical matters, and the celebration of martial prowess in chivalric culture. Indeed, it would be amazing if kings and nobles did not boast of plans to conquer the great city.[82] But none made any serious attempt. Neither Philip of Swabia nor Boniface of Montferrat would be lured into such a plot. They would, however, be intrigued by a plan to provide a show of force in support of an armed coup. Although Constantinople had never fallen to a foreign aggressor, it had often surrendered to a rival emperor, usually after a brief assault. This was the case in the imperial accessions of 610, 743, 963, 1057, 1078, and 1081. Had it not been for the brilliance of Conrad of Montferrat, it would also have been the case in 1187. In such instances, it was not necessary to have sufficient troops to conquer the city, only enough to lend support to dissident factions in their attempts to topple the current emperor. Typically, then, a palace coup either deposed the current emperor, or someone hoping to gain favor with the new emperor orchestrated the opening of one of the gates.[83] The fact that young Alexius was requesting help from purely Latin troops need not have been a serious handicap either: Alexius I Comnenus had succeeded in his armed coup of 1081 with a predominantly foreign army and even allowed the troops to sack Constantinople for three days.[84] The young Alexius believed that, for him, the gates would be opened immediately. But, failing that, Boniface and Philip knew that the presence of the Fourth Crusade army might well topple Alexius III's administration.

But talk is cheap, and that is all that was offered at Hagenau. Despite Irene's fervent pleas on behalf of her brother, neither Philip nor Boniface were in a position to help the young man. Philip's struggle with Otto, the pope's protégé, was not going well. Philip had been excommunicated in March, and the anathema had deprived him of crucial supporters. The duke of Austria, the bishop of Basel, the abbot of Pairis, and others had taken the cross perhaps in part to escape the censure of the pope while providing justification for declining to perform their duty toward the king.[85] Even those who took the cross but did not actually join the army in 1202 withheld their active military support from Philip. In Italy, meanwhile, the Ghibellines were at odds among themselves, while the Germans of the Regno were taking a beating at the hands of Walter of Brienne.[86] Philip had too many problems of his own to concern himself in any direct way with the claims of his brother-in-law.[87]

Historians who attribute the Latin conquest of Constantinople to a plot laid primarily by Philip of Swabia see in the election of Boniface of Montferrat to head the crusade precisely the instrument required by the Hohenstaufen to achieve his ends.[88] The author of the *Gesta Innocentii*, desiring not only to clear his hero of any responsibility for the sack of Constantinople, but also to cast blame upon the hated house of Hohenstaufen, states that Boniface "was said" to have treated with Philip concerning the installation of Alexius in Constantinople by means of the crusading army.[89] Such a discussion surely took place. Historians, however, sometimes leap too readily from discussions to deeds, from idle talk to careful plans, to successful execution. Bookish themselves, they tend to overestimate the powers of leaders of men to grasp the various threads of an already evolving pattern of events and to weave them into a desired design. Philip, it is agreed, was powerless; so, these historians contend, he worked his way by wile through Boniface.[90] But neither Philip nor Boniface had any way of foreseeing the fortuitous concatenation of circumstances that ultimately led the crusade to Constantinople. Boniface did not have a crusading army at his disposal just because he had been elected commander. A crusading army was not like a modern army, disciplined, and ruled by a fixed and well-organized chain of command. Nor, in fact, is even a modern army so rational an instrument of the commander's will as would appear from the tables of organization. A crusading army was an inchoate mass of men moved unpredictably by enthusiasms, fears, ambitions, superstitions, and lusts.[91] Boniface could not reasonably anticipate any effective authority over such barons as Baldwin of Flanders or Simon de Montfort. They in turn had not much more real control over their followers.[92] The commander of such an army was rather like a man shooting a rapids in a canoe. He cannot control the stream, and he has only a very limited control over the course of the canoe. But by energetic and constant care, he can keep it headed in the right direction, even turn it briefly against the current, avoid the rocks, and come safely through. Boniface would have been not only arrogant, but foolish, if he believed at Christmas of 1201 that he had power to manage the crusade according to his will.[93]

Having found commiseration, but no promise of aid at Philip's court, young Alexius now journeyed to Rome to seek the pope's assistance. This visit took place shortly after the meeting at Hagenau, perhaps in late February 1202, not immediately upon the arrival of Alexius in the West.[94] Innocent himself later described it in a letter to Alexius III of 16 November 1202. His word *olim* (formerly), which, it has been argued, must refer to a time at some distance in the past,[95] could certainly refer as well to early 1202 as to late 1201. Alexius complained to the pontiff of the wrongs he had suffered at the hands of his uncle. The pope should condemn his former captor and help him to regain his rightful place. The citizens of Constantinople, he asserted, desired him as emperor. Innocent was underwhelmed and sent the young man back to Germany.[96] The pope would not risk the crusade, to which he was so deeply committed, upon this young man. Not born to the purple, Alexius had a weak claim to the Byzantine throne. True, Alexius III had come to power by a criminal act, but that was hardly new in Byzantium. Alexius III was as favorable to Rome as Isaac II had been, in fact more favorable, since the new emperor had hinted at recognizing papal authority and, in any event, did not actively impede crusades. Besides, why should the pope do anything to aid the relatives of the Hohenstaufen?[97]

Not long after the departure of Alexius, Boniface of Montferrat also journeyed to Rome, probably about the middle of March.[98] He wished to consult with the head of the Church concerning the great enterprise over which he had recently assumed command. The visit had been planned before Boniface had gone to Germany and had met young Alexius, for he had agreed during his visit to Paris to become the emissary of Philip Augustus to the pope.[99] The original purpose of the journey to Rome was not, therefore, to win the pope for a Constantinopolitan adventure. Still, as long as he was there, there was no harm in sounding out the pope on the possibility of stopping off at Constantinople on the way east. Already acquainted with this proposal from the mouth of the Byzantine prince, Innocent was not happy to hear it from the leader of the new crusade. He had not been impressed by young Alexius, his claims, or his promises: a judgment that proved in the end to be extremely sound. Innocent commanded Boniface to banish the scheme from his mind, warning that the crusade must not attack Christians, but should proceed as quickly as possible to the Holy Land. Wishing to retain the favor of the Holy See, Boniface renounced the idea, at least for the moment. He then moved the discussion on to various details concerning the crusade that required attention.[100] One of these was probably the continuing enmity between Genoa and Pisa, for in late April we find him at Lerici, a coastal town about midway between the feuding cities, no doubt on his return journey, attempting to mediate a peace between them. If it is true that Boniface acted as a collaborator with Innocent, an assumption difficult to avoid, it indicates that his hints concerning the route of Constantinople did not drive a wedge between the pope and the marquis. From Lerici, Boniface returned to Montferrat, where he had little time to make his own personal preparations for departure.[101]

4

The Poverty of the
Army at Venice

The failing spirits of the crusaders, depressed by the death of the count of Champagne and the difficulty of finding a new leader, revived when Boniface accepted the command at Soissons. Once again the preparations for the crusade were moving forward. The gathering at Cîteaux shortly afterwards provided a grand opportunity to whip up enthusiasm and to gain recruits, a chance that Fulk the preacher did not fail to seize. Abbot Martin of Pairis and other ecclesiastics also sounded again and again the call to arms against the infidel.[1] In the aftermath of the journey of Boniface to the assembly at Hagenau, German troops under Bishop Conrad of Halberstadt, Count Berthold of Katzenellenbogen, and other nobles took the cross.[2] Raimbaut de Vaqueiras and his fellow troubadours did their part too in propagandizing the venture in song.[3]

In the spring of 1202 the marquis of Montferrat and all those who were destined to serve under his command, from the highest baron to the lowest sergeant, had much to do. In the great castles of the barons and in the solitary towers of lesser nobles complex preparations were underway.[4] Lands were sold or pledged to raise money for the journey, horses and arms were made ready. In anticipation of a long absence, affairs at home had to be put in order. Facing the likelihood of death, for they well knew that many of them would never return, they also had to look to their spiritual state. Some just grievances against them might yet be satisfied to the easing of their souls. With an eye to sins that could no longer be remedied, nobles of wealth about to depart on an undertaking of great danger made gifts to monasteries and provided for prayers and masses to insure their well-being in this life or in the life to come. The preparations of crusaders of lower rank, who had less of this world's goods and power, were on a smaller scale. But they too had money and equipment to provide, families to leave, and death to fear.[5]

Their spirits were cast down again by the loss of another of the leaders.

About the middle of April, Count Geoffrey of Perche took ill and died. By his testament he provided that his brother Stephen should receive the money he had gathered for the crusade in order to lead his men and fulfill his vow. There was great grief for his loss within his own lands and among the ranks of the crusaders.[6]

Between Easter (14 April) and Pentecost (2 June) of 1202 the most timely pilgrims said good-bye to homes and families, and many were the tears and laments, as both Villehardouin and Robert of Clari inform us.[7] Some consideration of the emotions of the crusaders and their loved ones is not amiss if we are to understand these men so that we can comprehend the crusade, as much as possible, from their point of view. The poets, always sensitive to the interplay of emotion between the lover and his beloved, describe the lady trembling at the thought of the danger facing her lover and fearing that she will die of grief or go insane. Months earlier, when he had taken the cross, it seemed a romantic adventure, undertaken in part, perhaps, to display his chivalry before her. Now harsh reality was at hand: the vow had been taken, and the lover must depart, perhaps never to return.[8] The poets also show the crusader himself torn between love and duty. Duty prevails, but though his body goes to Palestine, his heart will never leave his kind and beautiful lady.[9]

The troubadour Raimbaut, friend and comrade in arms of the marquis of Montferrat, describes his own emotions and reveals some of the motivations that led these men to abandon their loved ones. The insufferable thought of leaving his sweetheart, Beatrice, warred against the pride he felt in the honor that had been paid his friend and patron. He had not been enthusiastic about the crusade, and he had agreed to go only out of loyalty to Boniface. Romantic devotee of knighthood that he was, Raimbaut pictured to himself the banners of the knights of Champagne, he imagined the count of Flanders crying "Flanders!" and the marquis shouting "Montferrat and the lion!" as they charged. He also thought of the joy of serving God and the reward of Paradise should he die in His service. Yet over against the imagined joys of battle appeared the beauty of Beatrice, and he did not know whether he should go or stay. He, in fact, delayed until the spring of 1203 before joining the expedition.[10] Another poet presents a parting crusader who had a different concern:

> I have ta'en the cross, the stern crusader's token:
> To purge my sins to Palestine I fare:
> A lady's heart at parting nigh is broken:
> If e'er again I breathe my native air,
> God grant I find her honor never faltered,
> Then my dearest wish is mine:

But if her life is altered,
God grant to me a grave in Palestine.[11]

Conon of Béthune consoles himself with the thought that ladies unfaithful to their crusading lovers can sin only with cowards, because all the good men are overseas.[12]

Although many delayed, a multitude of soldiers of the cross parted from their loved ones and set out toward the south.[13] At last the *militia Christi* were on the march. Some were small bands, like that of Villehardouin; some were great, like Baldwin's. The French crusaders followed the customary route via the Mont Cenis Pass and Lombardy.[14] As they marched they sang crusading songs, whiling away the tiresome hours and reinforcing the bonds that linked them together and bound them to a common cause. On their journey they visited centers of piety, such as Clairvaux and Cîteaux, to venerate the precious relics and to renew their faith that their fearful venture was indeed the will of God.[15] Many of those coming from France, including Count Baldwin, must have stopped at Montferrat to pay their respects to their leader, for his lands were on their route of march, and they would not have passed up the opportunity to enjoy his hospitality and to rehearse their plans.[16]

Most departures were tardy. It had been agreed in the treaty that the journeys should be made during the month of April in order to be prepared for embarkation on 29 June,[17] but, as Villehardouin informs us, many crusaders did not get underway until toward Pentecost, which was 2 June.[18] Many, in fact, did not leave so soon. Synchronizing the movements of any army is enormously difficult; for a crusading army it was impossible. Some started earlier, some later. Some enjoyed a more leisurely journey than others. While the most prompt departed early enough to arrive in Venice before the scheduled date for sailing, they would have to wait for the latecomers. In this respect, as well as for lack of numbers, the crusaders were to fail the Venetians and to get into a predicament from which they were never fully able to extricate themselves.

About 1 June the first crusaders began to arrive at the rendezvous in the city on the lagoons.[19] From Flanders, Picardy, the Ile-de-France, Blois, Chartres, Champagne, Burgundy, the lands bordering the Rhine, and the subalpine provinces of Italy they came, their varied languages mingling in the confusion of tongues common in this city of international commerce. If they kept to the old tradition, the crusaders from various lands wore crosses of different colors, such as red for the French and green for the Flemings. There were few or no English. The preaching campaign of Abbot Eustace of Saint Germer de Flay in England had produced disappointing results. While King John enacted the fortieth tax on ecclesiastical and secular lands for the support of the crusade, the funds trickled in very slowly. Still, John had sufficient funds to give his nephew Louis of Blois one thousand marks for his pilgrimage. Beyond that King John could not help.[20] He was deeply engaged in a struggle for his throne with his nephew Arthur, who had the support of Philip Augustus. The English king, therefore, had not only declined to take the cross himself, but had placed obstacles in the way of English enlistments.[21] Some of the Germans arrived early, and so did Baldwin of Flanders, Hugh of Saint Pol, and Geoffrey of Villehardouin.[22] They pitched their tents on the island of Saint Nicholas (the Lido), the long narrow sandbar fronting the Adriatic behind which lie the lagoons of Venice. Robert of Clari states that the crusaders decided to encamp on the Lido after discovering that they could not find quarters on Rialto, the main island.[23] The anonymous author of the *Devastatio Constantinopolitana*, on the other hand, complains that the Venetians deliberately isolated the crusaders there.[24] Each states the same basic truth, although from different points of view. It simply was not feasible to host a large alien army in the city proper. After all, they were expecting an army of 33,500 men to descend upon a city with a population of around 100,000.[25] Housing could have been found only by expelling the rightful owners, a means used freely enough in conquered places, but not even to be considered in an allied city, which was to supply the essential fleet. No city, moreover, certainly not proud Venice, would tolerate even a friendly army within its confines over a long period of time, and it now appeared that the assembling of the crusaders was to be a drawn out process. The burgesses, and their wives and daughters, could sleep more soundly if the lagoon separated them from the host. Some of the crusaders, no doubt, shared the piety and chastity of Count Baldwin. Others possessed the desires for drink and sex common among most soldiers throughout history, and the common soldierly lack of inhibitions in seeking them. Far better that a wall of water should separate these foreigners from the homes of their allies.

Among the early arrivals was probably also the chronicler Robert of Clari, although he does not tell us exactly when he came to Venice. Robert's lord, Peter of Amiens, was related to Hugh of Saint Pol, in whose company they likely traveled, and we know that the count of Saint Pol was among the early comers.[26] Whatever its failings for the earlier period, from the time of Robert's arrival in Venice his chronicle becomes an invaluable source of information, especially about the experiences and feelings of the men in the ranks. This is a rare advantage, since most of our sources were either written by men of higher estate or composed according to their testimony. Robert continues to display some weaknesses, however. He had no head for numbers or dates, so he should never be relied upon for amounts of money, numbers of men, or chronology without the greatest caution.[27] He was a poor knight from near Amiens, an adventurer, like so many members of his class. Though a simple man, he was not completely uncultured. He knew the chivalric romances and through them legends about Alexander the Great, the fall of Troy, and the Trojan origin the Franks had attributed to themselves. He possessed the gift of a fresh eye, and so he gives us clear and colorful details of battles and buildings and all sorts of things.[28]

The Venetians were prepared for their allies. Doge Enrico Dandolo had prohibited all commercial voyages, had set the whole of Venice to work on building the fleet, and so everything was in readiness.[29] The Venetians had fulfilled their contract to the letter.[30] Even the anti-Venetian *Gesta Innocentii* concedes that they had ready a fleet, the like of which had not been known for a long time.[31] We may estimate it at about five hundred vessels, not counting petty auxiliary craft.[32] It was an amazing feat, a project that must have consumed Venetian resources and attention nonstop from March 1201 to June 1202. It is unfortunate for the historian that the Venetian record is so silent when it comes to their contribution to the crusade. In a city where notaries did a thriving business it is striking that no extant documents describe any of Venice's preparatory activities. We have no ducal decrees, contracts for shipbuilding or the purchase of provisions, petitions for exemption from service, or much else that one would expect from the building and outfitting of a great armada. While it is true that the documentary record is very sparse from this early period in Venetian history, there remain a great many notarial documents made in Venice during the fleet's construction. Venetian monasteries continued to make and break land tenure agreements, private land disputes continued to be put before the ducal court, people married, borrowed money, and made wills—all without a mention of the effort that must have shaped Venetian life for over a year.[33] While the lacuna is frustrating, it does not completely hide the effects of the fleet's construction on Venice. In a quantitative analysis of surviving archival material in Venice dating from 1193 to 1205, Thomas Madden found a sharp decline in ecclesiastical and secular business in the lagoon at the time of the crusade's preparation.[34] While Venetians continued with their everyday affairs, much of their economic vitality was siphoned off by their construction of the crusader fleet and the acquisition of supplies. The armada rode at anchor off the Lido; sails, ropes, supplies, and all the many things needed for the voyage were aboard; an appropriate number of passengers had been assigned to each ship. Only one thing was lacking: passengers.[35]

Already in June it was clear that the crusade was in trouble. Crusaders were not arriving soon enough or in sufficient numbers.[36] Not to speak of the 200,000 who reportedly received the cross from Fulk, nothing approximating the 33,500 anticipated by the Treaty of Venice were to keep the rendezvous at the city on the lagoons. Some never set out. Others coming from France gathered at Marseilles or Genoa, and either crossed through many perils (as Robert of Auxerre puts it) directly to Palestine or were detained by adverse circumstances.[37] Many sought transportation from Apulian ports.[38] Some joined Walter of Brienne in his campaign against the Germans.[39] In this over-estimation of the number of the crusaders, not in Venetian or Hohenstaufen treachery, nor in territorial ambitions more worldly than those of Baldwin of Edessa or Bohemond of Antioch a century before, lies the reason for the failure of the Fourth Crusade.

Not even Count Baldwin's full strength assembled in Venice. A sizable force of Flemings, perhaps half of Baldwin's entire following, took ship in Flanders under the command of John of Nesle, sworn to join Baldwin in Venice or wherever else he should command.[40] All summer they struggled with contrary winds before passing through the Straits of Gibraltar.[41] Ernoul-Bernard reports that they sacked an unnamed Muslim port on the Mediterranean with great profit.[42] They arrived at Marseilles in the fall and decided to remain there for the winter.[43]

Some scholars believe that those who failed to join the host in Venice resented the leadership of Boniface of Montferrat. The crusade was primarily a French undertaking, they contend, and he was a Lombard prince of whom they had perhaps never heard. The Champenois, in spite of their vows to the dying Thibaut to meet the army in Venice, smoldered at Boniface's receiving both the money that Thibaut had gathered as well as direct command over his followers. Some also were apprehensive over Boniface's visit to Philip of Swabia, who was under the ban of excommunication. Villehardouin, a leader of the Champenois, mentions nothing unfavorable to Boniface, of course, but according to this theory, the chronicler deliberately obscured the real cause for the failure of the crusade, since he himself was responsible for nominating the marquis.[44] Some crusaders may have avoided Venice through distaste for the Italian marquis, but this is sheer speculation and not even especially plausible. It anachronistically introduces modern nationalism into the minds of medieval men, and fails to take sufficient account of the brotherhood of chivalry and the renown of the marquis of Montferrat in that international community of arms. It is doubtful, moreover, that many crusaders knew anything about his journey to Hagenau. Robert of Clari, who is our key to what was in the minds of the mass of the crusaders, does not mention it until Boniface himself speaks openly to the host at Zara of his meeting with young Alexius.[45] The argument that resentment or fear of the leadership of Boniface kept many crusaders from the rendezvous is not convincing.

If a plot to install young Alexius on the Byzantine throne had existed, of course, rumors of this might have deterred from assembling at Venice those who held a strict view of their crusading vows. It has been shown, however, that although the marquis, the German king, and the young prince undoubtedly discussed the use of the crusading army to return Alexius to Constantinople, no realistic plans could have been made. Boniface's trip to Rome was not primarily to attempt to enlist the pope's support for such a scheme, for the journey had been planned before the encounter at Hagenau. If a plot had existed, moreover, surely such prominent foes of any attack upon Christians as Simon de Montfort, Enguerrand of Boves, and the abbot of Vaux-de-Cernay would have learned of it and abandoned the army at this time, as in fact they did later.

There is no need for historians to resort to such spurious arguments, for an abundance of good reasons for the paucity of crusaders at Venice can be found. First, the cohesion of the crusading host must not be exaggerated. Every prominent crusader had his own goals and his own plans, and felt bound to the army only insofar as it served his purposes. The same was true to a lesser extent even of the common people.[46] Villehardouin, of course, shows an intense loyalty to the host, but his was a special case, since his own honor and reputation rested upon its success. The Treaty of Venice had not been made in the name of the army, but of the counts of Flanders, Champagne, and Blois.[47] The army, indeed, could not make a treaty, for it had no corporate character, no standing as an entity in law. The greater men had probably ratified the treaty by oaths at Corbie, but we have no way of knowing who was present on that occasion. The mass of crusaders certainly was not.[48] The cost of transportation was another factor. It was not expected to be paid from a common treasury, but, in general, each crusader was to pay his own way.[49] As they finally set themselves in motion, many probably decided to sail from Marseilles, Genoa, or Apulia simply because they thought they could find more favorable terms for passage than had been agreed upon with the Republic of Saint Mark. These considerations, as well as the long overland journey to Venice, likely prompted the force under John of Nesle to sail from Flanders. Another very important reason why many crusaders failed to keep the rendezvous at Venice may have been the codicil to the treaty providing that Egypt should be the place of debarkation.[50] Although it was to be kept secret, knowledge of the agreement had probably come into the hands of the more prominent men, at any rate. Everyone involved in the assemblies at Soissons, Compiègne, and Corbie would have sought information on the details of the conventions with the Venetians. The six envoys and their three principals, at least, were initially privy to the plan, not counting the doge and his small council, and it is likely that rumors of the destination were abroad. Those who believed that the only legitimate goal for a man under the crusader's vow was Palestine would be the first to seek alternate means of reaching the Holy Land if they learned of the Egyptian codicil.

The lack of cohesion of a crusading army and the possible aversion to the Egyptian route were compounded by the problem of numbers. Knowledgeable leaders very likely had qualms about their ability to muster so large an army as anticipated by the treaty, fearing precisely what occurred in fact: the inability of the crusaders to meet their obligations to Venice. Their fears, valid enough in themselves, were self-fulfilling. Some changed plans to save themselves from the disarray of a reduced and indebted host. Some held back, waiting to see how many others appeared, and, as the result was not encouraging, they headed for Apulian ports.[51] One of those who hesitated was the count of Blois, one of the original leaders and one of the principals of the Treaty of Venice. If even Count Louis wavered, we may imagine the hesitancy of others not so deeply obligated as he. Hugh of Saint Pol and Geoffrey of Villehardouin were sent out from Venice to meet the count of Blois, and to plead with him and others to keep the rendezvous. They found him at Pavia. Here, before the road to the south branched off at Piacenza, he vacillated. Geoffrey and Hugh prevailed upon his sense of honor, and Count Louis agreed to join his friends at Venice, but we may imagine with what trepidation. The great joy with which he and his large force were received there accentuates how crucial the arrival of additional pilgrims was. After the count and his men united with the other crusaders on the Lido, Villehardouin tells us how great and fine an army was assembled there, but he admits that it was only one-third as great as anticipated.[52]

Although Count Louis had been persuaded to keep his faith, many other crusaders did turn south from Piacenza to seek passage in Apulian ports. By this means several hundred knights found their way to Palestine, not at all the puissant force that was expected.[53] This was naturally a great disappointment to the more warlike of the embattled Christians of the Holy Land. Seeing that so little aid was at hand, King Aimery II refused to break the truce with the Muslims, despite the pleas of Renaud of Dampierre, one of the newcomers.[54] Since Renaud was the knight who had been entrusted with the duty of fulfilling the crusading vow of the dying count of Champagne, perhaps this obligation to his dead lord weighed on his mind and influenced him toward a narrow interpretation of his duty. Not content to wait for the expiration of the truce, Renaud and others departed for Antioch. Against advice he tried to force his passage and was ambushed by the Muslims. The entire band of eighty knights was wiped out, with only one escaping. Renaud himself was taken prisoner and remained in captivity for thirty years.[55]

Villehardouin passes harsh judgment on those who sailed from other ports than Venice. Here we see the bitter disappointment of our author, writing after the events and possessing a full grasp of the consequences of the lack of men.[56] Lack of men and money kept the crusaders from meeting their obligations to the Venetians, and so they were drawn to Constantinople by the promises of young Alexius. When Alexius could not fulfill those promises, they lacked the resources to go on to the Holy Land, and so they conquered the city. Even after the conquest, they could not muster a sufficient force to hold their new possessions and to mount the long-anticipated assault upon the Holy Land, and so, after marching through Christian blood to the Bosporus, they were unable to free the land of Christ. Villehardouin's bitterness is understandable, but, at least partially, misdirected. The failure of the crusade did result from insufficiency of men and money, as Villehardouin protests, but those who sailed from Marseilles, Genoa, or Apulia were not guilty of betraying the holy war. They reacted according to their best conscience and judgment to a tragic train of events already set in motion and irreversible. Those whom Villehardouin condemns as defectors were not the villains of this piece; that role belongs to the unrealistic treaty itself. No wonder Villehardouin does not stress it, for he himself stands out among those responsible for the ruinous blunder.[57] We know that some three hundred knights came directly to the Holy Land.[58] If those taking the direct course were in the common proportions of one knight to two squires to four sergeants, their total number would be twenty-one hundred men.[59] Villehardouin tells us that only one-third of the 33,500 expected at Venice actually assembled there, and this figure seems the most reliable.[60] If we add, then, the number who went directly to Palestine to those gathered in Venice, we arrive at no more than about fourteen thousand men—still far short of those for whom passage had been prepared.

If those who failed to keep the rendezvous at Venice followed their consciences, they disobeyed, nonetheless, the will of the pope. Innocent saw clearly enough in the fragmentation of the army the ruination of his plans. He therefore ordered those hesitating in Lombardy to take ship from Venice. Many did not obey.[61]

The papal legate, Cardinal Peter Capuano, did not arrive at the port of embarkation until 22 July, nearly a month after the scheduled date of departure.[62] Upon his arrival, according to the *Devastatio*, he took the wise measure of sending home the poor, the sick, and the women.[63] Peter Capuano's position was a tricky one. Papal legates had played almost no role in recent crusades.[64] While Peter and Soffredo had been busy enough preparing for the Fourth Crusade, their efforts had never intersected with those of the crusaders themselves. When Peter arrived in Venice, he was a stranger to the French and Venetians. Villehardouin mentions Peter Capuano only once (and then not by name) between his preaching in France before the tourney at Ecry and the Battle of Adrianople in 1205.[65] There is no hint that the French planned to consult him on matters of destination or strategy, although they were surely willing to accept him as a papal legate. But the Venetians begrudged him even that recognition. It may be that Peter's quick dismissal of the vows of the unfit caused Enrico Dandolo and others to worry that he might later release the entire army from their obligations to Venice, thus freeing them to seek transport from other ports. Such an action would ruin Venice and further cripple the crusade. From the Frankish point of view Peter Capuano added little, from the Venetian point of view he threatened a great deal. He was, therefore, informed by the Venetians that while he was welcome to accompany the crusade as a preacher, he would not be accepted as a papal legate.[66]

At this late date there also arrived a detachment of Germans led, according to Gunther of Pairis, by his abbot Martin of the Cistercian monastery of that name near Colmar in Alsace.[67] Gunther's chronicle was both a eulogy of Martin and a *translatio* for the numerous relics which the abbot brought back to Pairis.[68] Gunther describes Martin as pleasant looking, affable, eloquent, humble among his monks, and wise in counsel. He had assumed the responsibility for preaching the crusade in the lands along the upper Rhine.[69] We have Gunther's account, possibly as recalled years later by the abbot, of Martin's crusading sermon delivered in Basel before the end of September 1201. A great crowd of clergy and laity jammed the cathedral to hear him. He began by echoing the words of Saint Bernard of Clairvaux: "Heed my word to you, my lords and brothers; heed my word to you! Indeed, not my word, but Christ's. Christ himself is the author of this sermon; I am his fragile instrument. Today Christ addresses you in his words through my mouth. It is he who grieves before you over his wounds."[70] So, in the fashion of the typical crusading sermon, he deplored the plight of the Holy Land and urged the necessity of assisting its defenders. Speaking of the desecration of the sanctified places, the abbot wept, and the cathedral was filled with the groans, sobs, and sighs of his hearers. He recalled the triumphs of the crusaders of a century before. He enumerated the spiritual advantages of taking the cross and did not leave out the material rewards.[71] After preaching at Basel, he had gone about the whole region, giving the cross to many. Finally, having committed himself and his followers to the protection of the Virgin, he set out for

Venice by way of the upper Rhine, Innsbruck, and the Brenner Pass. Many remarked, according to Gunther, the unarmed monk riding at the head of a military array of almost 1,200 men.[72] Toward the end of the journey, Abbot Martin spent eight weeks, late May to late July, visiting with the bishop of Verona.[73] By the beginning of June, therefore, it must have been clear that the fleet would not sail on schedule on 29 June.

On 13 August, shortly after the arrival of Abbot Martin and his followers, a leading German prelate, Conrad of Krosigk, bishop of Halberstadt, joined the host on the Lido.[74] Bishop Conrad was one of the most devoted supporters of Philip of Swabia. Pressed by the pope and his legate in Germany to support Philip's rival Otto, Conrad did nothing, thus incurring the ban of excommunication. He therefore sought refuge and perhaps absolution in the crusader's cross, which he assumed on Palm Sunday of 1202.[75] Within a few weeks he journeyed by way of Bohemia and Austria to the patriarchate of Aquileia and Venice.[76] The bishop was to be the informant for the narrative of the crusade by the anonymous chronicler of Halberstadt.[77] Accompanying Conrad was Count Berthold of Katzenellenbogen, Henry of Ulmen, and many other German lords.[78]

Boniface of Montferrat, the leader of the crusade, did not depart from home until early August. At Pavia on the ninth he formally transferred to his son the reins of government of the marquisate. He then left for Venice to assume command, arriving there on 15 August.[79] Had the host assembled in anything like the order planned Boniface would surely have made his appearance at a much earlier date.[80]

While the crusaders were too slowly trickling into Venice, they were further disheartened by the sad news of the death in May of Fulk of Neuilly, the popular preacher of the crusade.[81] Many of those who were present, and thousands who were not, had taken the cross at his exhortation. Fulk's death on the eve of the crusade was an evil omen. Not even the large sum of money that he had gathered from his overwrought hearers was to aid the expedition directly. Some had been given to individual poor crusaders to enable them to fulfill their vows. The greater part, however, was destined by the Cistercians, to whom it was entrusted, for the direct aid of the Holy Land, where it was warmly welcomed. An earthquake in Palestine had destroyed fortifications; much of the money raised by Fulk was used to repair the walls of Acre, Tyre, and Beirut. Ugly suspicions arose that Fulk had diverted funds to his own use. Although these were untrue, one of his associates, Peter of Rossi, was guilty of peculation. Even Innocent III felt compelled to deny publicly that the pope himself had profited at the expense of the Holy Land.[82]

When it seemed that as many had arrived as would in fact appear the doge went to talk with the barons on the Lido. He demanded that they now pay what was owed. The Venetians were prepared to embark. They had performed what was required of them; a fleet to transport 33,500 men stood ready. Villehardouin and other crusading sources agree that the Venetians had indeed fulfilled their promises admirably. So the barons asked that the host, the great and the small, should pay. Some of the poorer crusaders declared that they could not, but the barons collected as much as they could. The sum was augmented by the money that Thibaut of Champagne had reserved for the army after distributing part of his treasure among his own followers.[83] Still they could not gather half enough to pay what they owed to the Venetians. Dandolo remonstrated that the crusaders must pay the covenanted price. Venice had undergone enormous expense and disruption of her usual commerce. Shipbuilders had been paid. Owners whose merchant vessels had been requisitioned had been recompensed. Provisions had been bought. For a year and a half Venetian traders had lost their normal gain while preparing this great armada. No one ought to expect the Venetians out of Christian charity and crusading zeal to have renounced payment for the fleet and to have sailed off on a wave of piety and good fellowship. The greatest commercial city in Latin Christendom faced a financial disaster. The evil consequences of the foolish treaty now stood starkly revealed. The crusaders could not pay; the Venetians could not renounce payment.

Later, after the crusaders had sacked Constantinople and failed to reach the Holy Land, there circulated in Palestine rumors that the Venetians had been bribed with gifts and commercial concessions to form a treaty with the sultan of Egypt to divert the crusade from his lands. This rumor found its way into the continuation of William of Tyre's history. Some scholars have accepted it as a fact, and there was even an abortive attempt to identify the treaty and date it 13 May 1202, just about the time when the first crusaders were arriving in Venice. This latter effort, at least, must be definitively discarded, and, in fact, the whole story should be regarded as nothing more than an interesting example of the suspicions and accusations that would naturally arise among the Christians of Palestine cheated of the aid upon which they had counted.[84] When affairs go badly men all too often seek a villain upon whom to dump responsibility. This not only helps them to avoid self-accusation and achieve self-righteousness, but also enables them to escape responsibility for serious thought about the issues. The wealthy and arrogant Venetians, who gained greatly from the conquest of Constantinople, were plausible candidates for the villain's role.

Unable to pay their debt, the leading men among the crusaders conferred in desperation. The situation was clear. The Venetians had fulfilled their contract, but the crusaders could not, because they were far short of the required number of men. Some pleaded: "For the love of God, let's each give in addition as much as we can. It is better to spend all our wealth here than to default on our agreement and lose all we have spent. If this expedition does not take place, the opportunity for aiding the Holy Land will be lost."[85] But not everyone agreed. The majority argued that they had already individually paid what each man owed for passage. It was not their fault if others had failed to appear. If the Venetians would transport them, they were ready. If not, they would seek ships elsewhere. There was no sense in throwing good money after bad. Villehardouin says that these crusaders wanted to break up the army, but this is the harshness of a partisan.[86] Far from villainous, they simply took a more personal view of the crusade than Villehardouin and his party. They had a specific vow to fulfill, individual obligations under the contract with Venice, and rights of their own. Villehardouin's party held a more practical and collective point of view. They were the establishment, the responsible men, adaptable as to means of achieving a more generally defined end—aid to the Holy Land. These were the same leaders who had seen the practical advantages of the landing in Egypt. This party urged that it was better that they should be impoverished than that the army should disperse. So the counts of Flanders, Blois, and Saint Pol, the marquis of Montferrat, and others of their persuasion gave all they had and could borrow to make up the deficit. They not only gave their money, but their gold and silver vessels were borne to the ducal palace in payment. And yet they still lacked 34,000 marks of the 85,000 originally owed.[87]

Was there no other source of funds? Innocent III had imposed upon all clerics the general income tax of 1199 and had established other means for gathering money for the Holy Land. Political unrest, resistance of the clergy, and the weakness of canonical sanctions, however, had hampered collections. Records which would provide us with any approximation of the sums collected are not extant. Various letters from the pope prodding the clergy to pay their quotas prove, however, that collection was neither easy nor efficient.[88] In any case, from the beginning of the crusades the pilgrims had been expected to provide their own financial support. The Second and Third Crusades, it is true, had been largely financed by the kings, but there is no indication that the expenses of the crusading armies were regarded as a responsibility of the church.[89] In the papal mandate of 1199 there is a minor provision for the support of knights and other soldiers who did not have sufficient money of their own, but this was to come only from the alms given by the faithful into the chests placed in the churches, not from the income tax or other sources of subsidy for the Holy Land.[90] That money was to be sent to the Levant for the use of the Christians there.[91] The disposal after his death of the money garnered by Fulk of Neuilly also suggests this, for it was sent to the Holy Land and used to repair fortifications.[92] This explains why collections continued long after the Fourth Crusade had ended, because the subsidy for the Holy Land was still needed there.[93] If the crusaders at Venice had any expectation of receiving aid from the papacy, it is unlikely that the chroniclers would have failed to mention it. The crusaders knew full well that their financial predicament was their own responsibility.[94]

Matters were growing desperate for the crusaders on the Lido. The original plan had been that they should encamp there only until 29 June, the intended date of embarkation. Those who arrived on time, expecting the prompt assembling of the host, at first found no great fault with their accommodations. As summer wore on, however, life on the Lido became more trying. Although today it is a charming and famous beach resort, in the summer of 1202 the Lido was merely a sandy island baked by the subalpine sun. The Italian summer has always been hard on armies from northern Europe. Fortunately epidemic disease does not appear to have struck the crusaders, although among an army of eleven to twelve thousand encamped in a foreign land, eating unaccustomed food, drinking strange water, and suffering from poor sanitation, a few naturally died over the course of the summer and early fall.[95] When the crusaders failed to pay, according to Robert of Clari, Dandolo threatened to cut off their supplies of food and water, although he did not carry out his angry ultimatum.[96] Food did become a serious problem however, for bad harvests in recent years, not only in Italy and the West, but overseas, had made food scarce and dear.[97] And so, as the army languished, their money dwindled. The greater men were grieved and angered at all they had spent without getting any nearer to their goal.[98] Some of the poorer crusaders had nothing left. Those who could borrowed from Venetian merchants, and, as the days and weeks passed, the load of debt became more and more worrisome.[99] As it became apparent that the expected number of pilgrims would never arrive, their insolvency seemed irreparable. While the summer dragged on the host was threatened with dissolution. Although it is often claimed that the crusaders were virtual prisoners on the Lido, utterly reliant on Venice for sustenance, the numerous defectors from the host attest to the easy travel on and off the island. Others, in technical violation of the Treaty of Venice, sailed to the Italian mainland to purchase food in other markets.[100] With each departure the confidence of those remaining was further shaken, sowing the seeds of future defections. Nothing is worse for the morale of an army than prolonged inactivity. Men grow frustrated and irritable. They do not know what is going on, and wild rumors circulate. A crusading army did not even have sufficient discipline to impose the contrived work that is supposed to give to simple minds the illusion of meaningful activity. So they daily diminished in numbers and spirit. And they grumbled, mostly against the Venetians. They complained that the cost of the fleet was excessive, that they were overcharged for their supplies, that they were exploited. It seemed to the men in the ranks that their hosts had been paid plenty.[101] They had no accurate information, only impressions. They had paid—most of them. They had seen the gold and silver vessels of the barons carried off to the ducal palace. They knew that Fulk of Neuilly had left money for the crusade, and they believed that this large sum had gone to fill Venetian pockets. Surely the avaricious Venetians had gained outrageously. Were the crusaders their allies or not?

Looking at their situation in another way, time was becoming a crucial factor. The winter season, when medieval men did not sail the seas, even the relatively mild Mediterranean, loomed before them. Much of their lease of the Venetian fleet had already passed, leaving them less time to perform their vows. To many on the lonely island, the Holy Land now seemed an impossibly distant place.

5

The Conquest of Zara

The crusading chiefs informed the doge of Venice that they were utterly unable to pay any more, since they were impoverished by their efforts and had scarcely enough money to live on.[1] Despite the complaints of the ill-informed, the Venetians were not responsible for this plight. Neither Villehardouin nor even Robert of Clari, who came from a lower rank, blames them. The merchant republic, in fact, suffered along with the crusaders in their crisis, having expended vast sums and sacrificed customary profits that could not now be recovered. Worse yet, Venice had on its hands a destitute, disgruntled, and ill-disciplined foreign army. The Venetians too stood under the threat of impending debacle.

Although it makes little sense, it has become almost a cliché among some historians to describe the desperate situation in the summer of 1202 as the outcome of careful planning by Doge Enrico Dandolo. Dandolo, it is said, knew that the crusaders would never number 33,500 nor would they ever come up with the agreed payment. Thus the doge was able to entrap the enterprise in parchment and seals by forcing its leaders to promise what he knew they could not deliver. With the crusade in his power, Dandolo could divert it against his enemies, namely Zara and Constantinople.[2] The problem with this oft-stated scenario is that there is no evidence for it, abundant evidence against it, and it relies on a prescience that no human, Dandolo included, possesses.[3] Had the doge and his council believed only eleven or twelve thousand troops would appear at Venice they would have contracted to provide transportation for no more. There are easier ways to affect the direction of a crusade (namely joining it) than committing your state to providing three times more ships and food than can be paid for by the contracting customer. This is forgotten by historians who sit at their desks and without a care write a fleet of five hundred vessels into being.[4] What if the crusaders refused to pay at all? What if they chose to find transportation elsewhere (as many did), thus leaving Venice holding the bag of an enormous fleet, crushing debt, and no army? These were real risks to which no doge would willingly expose the republic. Venice was sorely injured by the crusaders' miscalculation, and so too must have been the reputation of Enrico Dandolo himself. It was he who had endorsed the plan before the ducal council, Great Council, and popular assembly back in 1201. While the Venetians blamed the Franks for their mutual predicament, their faith in their doge, who had led them into this mess, must also have been shaken.

Enrico Dandolo desperately needed a solution that would send the crusade on its way without Venice renouncing payment. He realized that the crusaders truly could pay no more. The Venetians could keep the sums already paid, but their right to them would not be universally recognized, and if the crusade failed, Venice would receive much criticism throughout Christendom.[5] More importantly, if Venice simply kept the 50,000 marks paid, accepted her losses, and disbanded the fleet, what would be the reaction of the restive army of crusaders? So large a military force had never been allowed into the lagoon before. While the Lido is separate from Venice itself, the distance is not great. Dandolo and his advisers had to consider the possibility that Venice itself could be in danger. If, then, they could not forgive the debt, nor end their contractual association, perhaps they could find some other means by which the crusaders could fulfill their obligations to the Venetians. Dandolo searched his old head, crammed with the experience of a long life of statecraft, for a solution. Although not prescient, he was wise. Dandolo called to the attention of his counselors the Venetian desire to reconquer the port of Zara on the eastern coast of the Adriatic. All efforts to subjugate Zara had failed, and there seemed no hope of achieving this goal without outside assistance. Now fate had provided a means. If the crusaders would help the Venetians to conquer Zara, they in turn could postpone payment of the 34,000 marks still owed until such time as God permitted them to gain conquests to divide as provided by the treaty. Out of their share the crusaders could then pay.[6] The crusade would be preserved. The fortune that Venice had invested in the fleet would not be wasted. There would even be a positive gain. The interest of Christendom in the holy war and the self-interest of Venice in reconquering Christian Zara coincided.

Zara was no small issue to the Venetians. After the Istrian towns it was the first of those ports along the eastern shore of the Adriatic upon which Venice had depended for the refurbishing and resupplying of ships setting out for the Levant.[7] Perhaps even more important was its use as a port through which the high quality oak of Dalmatian forests could be transported to the shipyards of Venice. Oak was not available to the Venetians in quantity from their own Italian hinterland. Dalmatian oak was therefore crucial for the fleet, and hence for the maritime mastery of Venice, its trade, its wealth and power.

Although other ports, such as Ragusa, could serve, they were more distant than Zara, and the supply was more vulnerable.[8]

In the last century and a half Zara had changed hands repeatedly. Every time Zara revolted against Venice the hand of the king of Hungary was seen in the background. After every loss until the last, Venice had won back the vital but recalcitrant port. Finally in late 1180 or 1181 Zara again revolted and threw off Venetian control. Venice was too hampered by the foul state of its affairs in Constantinople to take vigorous action at once. Her privileges in the Eastern Empire had been revoked and her wealth expropriated in 1171. Attempts to negotiate compensation for these losses dragged on year after year. Once agreement for compensation was reached with Isaac II Angelus in 1185, Venice took the opportunity to concentrate once more upon the troubled Adriatic. Zara stood alone on the Dalmatian coast in its defiance of Venice. Doge Orio Mastropiero asked for and received loans from Venice's leading nobles to prosecute a war against Zara. Seeing danger impending, Zara put herself under the protection of Bela III of Hungary, who constructed a strong fortress there. The Venetian attack was short-lived. Almost immediately after the siege began in summer 1187, Pope Gregory VIII ordered a cessation of all hostilities in preparation for the Third Crusade. Venice complied, signing a two year truce. Zara then signed a rather loose treaty of "peace and friendship" in 1188 with Pisa, one of the great maritime powers and a major commercial rival of Venice in the East.[9] Pisa, however, had its own peace treaty with Venice, which would not expire until 1193. In the meantime, the truce between Venice and Zara ended and, therefore, in 1190, Venetians attacked Zarans again with little effect.[10] Enrico Dandolo turned his attention to Zara almost immediately after his election to the ducal throne. In 1192, a fleet was sent to attack, if not Zara itself, then Zaran interests. The island of Pago fell to Venice, but Zara remained defiant.[11] Other matters then diverted Venice's attention. With the expiration of the truce with Pisa in 1193, Dandolo may have worried that an additional assault on Zara would prompt open war with Pisa.[12] Nevertheless, rancor between Zarans and Venetians remained high.[13]

It would be instructive to know in more detail what the ducal council thought of Dandolo's proposal. Zara was long a thorn in Venice's side that was directly responsible for disrupting the Adriatic, Venice's own sea. When the Fourth Crusade sailed it would take much of Venice's manpower, leaving Venetian controlled areas on their honor to remain loyal while the Venetians crusaded. It was universally accepted in medieval Europe that a ruler had a right to stabilize his domains, quashing rebels and exacting oaths of loyalty, before leading his armies on a crusade. This was done either during the prepa-

ratory activities, as occurred in all of the major crusades, or on the journey to
the East. Richard I fought often in his French domains after taking the cross,
and later led his crusaders against Christians in Sicily, taking Messina, on his
way to the Holy Land. More recently, as we have seen, Innocent III toyed
with the idea of using the Fourth Crusade itself to attack Sicily to help stabilize papal power in Italy.[14] King Emeric of Hungary, who had taken the cross
in 1200, did little else but wage war to stabilize his kingdom. Venice had the
same right to insure the stability of her territory before departing with most
of her military force. Indeed, when the Fourth Crusade did sail it stopped at
a large number of Dalmatian ports to receive oaths of loyalty to Venice. Zara
was different only in that it was in open rebellion.[15] It is difficult to believe,
therefore, that Dandolo did not envision a stop at Zara from the beginning.
A full-scale siege was probably out of the question (although Richard, Innocent, and Emeric had few qualms about such actions to further their own
goals), but Zara might very well surrender to the Venetians and swear future
loyalty to the republic when it saw the massive crusader fleet. Dandolo's proposal, therefore, was not revolutionary: a stop at Zara was within Venice's
rights. To defer the debt, however, the crusaders would have to agree to besiege the city if it refused to surrender.

The Venetians quickly grasped the advantages of Dandolo's proposal, so
he presented it to the crusading leaders. He pointed to the onset of winter,
which was not favorable for long voyages or extensive naval operations. He
stressed the blamelessness of the Venetians, who would have transported the
army overseas long ago, had it not been for the failure of the crusaders to live
up to the contract. Then he proposed that the barons make the best of a bad
situation by helping the Venetians to recover Zara. In return the payment
of the debt would be deferred. The Dalmatian city was a fine one, supplied
with all good things, so that they could comfortably winter there and toward
Easter set sail for Egypt.[16]

Dandolo is often criticized for taking advantage of the crusaders' position by forcing them to advance Venetian interests with arms. If Dandolo
was willing to defer the debt, why not just defer it? Why compel the crusaders into the moral dilemma of attacking Christians? The question is fair
enough if looked at from the standpoint of an autocratic state. A pious and
wealthy monarch might well have put off the debt without imposing conditions. But Dandolo was no monarch and Venice no autocracy. The doge
had no authority to forgive or postpone a debt without support of the ducal
council and Great Council. Given the large number of purveyors in Venice
who wanted their promised payments, a deferment would have probably also
required broad popular approval. Something had to be offered to those Vene-

tians injured by the crusaders' inability to pay. By choosing a landing at Zara, Dandolo was able to gain the necessary support.

The barons discussed Dandolo's proposal among themselves. It did not take long to conclude that their options were extremely limited. They could assist the Venetians at Zara, as the doge proposed, or they could return home in shame, having set out bravely to succor the Holy Land, but having gone no farther than Venice. A few, no doubt, could have proceeded to Palestine as individuals or in small groups to fulfill their vows, but the army as a whole was by this time impoverished and would have dissolved. By accepting Dandolo's proposal the crusade could at last get underway. The troops would soon have action and a needed change of scene. Soldiers become restive when nothing seems to be happening. The burdensome debt could be deferred until a more propitious time. And in the spring they could at last be off to fight the infidel. So the leaders agreed to aid the Venetians in restoring Zara to Venetian control.[17]

Robert of Clari, it is true, tells of two meetings of the doge and the crusaders. In the first of these Dandolo offered to defer the debt until the Venetians could be paid out of the first conquests, and only later, and to the leaders alone, did he raise the subject of Zara.[18] Those historians who seek to make Dandolo the villain of the piece find here a devious and successful conspiracy with the chiefs.[19] No doubt Robert of Clari tells the story as he learned it. As a simple knight in the ranks he was not involved in the councils of the mighty. He reports only what was known to the common soldiers, that the debt was to be deferred and that they were to sail overseas. Only later did the host learn of the agreement to attack Zara. It is not at all likely, however, that he has events in their true sequence. The astute doge would scarcely have sacrificed publicly and without advantage so strong a bargaining point as the debt before raising the issue of Zara, nor would the ducal council have allowed him to float so large a loan without some recompense. Villehardouin tells us of Dandolo's discussions with the Venetians, and then simply adds that the proposals were made to the crusaders.[20] Privy to the most secret councils, the marshal no doubt also reports the incident accurately from his vantage point. The proposals were made to the leaders of the army. To these experienced and responsible men Dandolo's scheme made sense, but, as once before in the case of Egypt, they concealed from the rank and file the details of their plans. They saw no necessity for confiding in the common people. The stop at Zara was a minor detail, of which the host, as Robert declares, knew nothing in advance. When the deferral of the debt and their imminent departure were announced to them, the multitude naturally rejoiced, falling at the feet of the doge. That night they burned great fires on the Lido, and they attached torches to the ends of their lances and paraded about with them. It seemed as if the whole camp was aflame with joy.[21]

On a Sunday that was a great holiday, probably the Nativity of the Virgin, 8 September, San Marco was filled with Venetians and crusaders.[22] Before the mass began in this solemn and awe-inspiring setting, the doge in full ceremonial garb mounted the pulpit to address his people: "Sirs, you are joined with the most valiant men in the world in the greatest enterprise that anyone has ever undertaken. I am old and weak and in need of rest, and my health is failing. But I see that no one knows how to govern and direct you as I do, who am your lord. If you agree that I should take the sign of the cross to protect and lead you, and that my son should remain and guard the country, I will go to live or die with you and the pilgrims."[23] Dandolo and his Venetian audience saw in this emotional spectacle more than we do today. They heard in Dandolo's plea an echo of that delivered at the same podium by their national hero, Doge Domenico Michiel, when he donned the cross in 1121. Then, it was a young Enrico Dandolo who watched as Michiel filled the church with his crusading zeal, causing thousands of Venetians to follow his example and join the Venetian crusade.[24] Among them were Dandolo's grandfather, father, and uncle. The success of the Venetian crusade against an Egyptian fleet made Michiel a revered figure. Dandolo had already imitated the crusading doge by suspending all overseas trade in preparation for the enterprise. Now he completed the process by taking the cross, delivering a moving speech, and leaving his son in charge of Venetian affairs during his absence: all just as Michiel had done.[25] Although our French sources knew nothing of this subtext, the assembled Venetians surely recognized it at once. Venice was again to wage a holy war, and her doge, they felt certain, would once again lead them to victory.

As in 1121, San Marco rang with the cries of Venetians assenting to Dandolo's request and clamoring to take up the burden themselves. Dandolo then descended from the pulpit and knelt in tears before the high altar. Others too wept at the thought of this ancient, blind warrior enlisting in the cause of the Holy Land. He received his cross, not in the customary fashion, upon the shoulder, but upon the cloth crown of the Venetian doge, where it would be more prominent.[26] Many of those who had avoided the crusade by luck in the lottery now begged to be crossed as well.[27] The French crusaders rejoiced at Dandolo's enlistment, not only because of the numbers he drew in his train, but because of their confidence in his wisdom and prowess.[28] Time and again they were to turn to him for leadership, and in the heat of battle no man would show greater courage than his.

Modern, and therefore more cynical, observers might be tempted to dismiss the emotional crossing of the doge as a charade, staged by Dandolo to convince the French to accept him as one of the crusading leaders and the Venetians to allow him to leave his son as vice-doge. Thus by shedding a few tears Dandolo gained control of the Fourth Crusade and established a possible dynasty at home.[29] While it is surely true that Dandolo and the Venetians hoped to gain wealth, power, and glory on the crusade, this made them no different than anyone who took the pilgrim's vow. The sincere piety expressed in San Marco that day, however, cannot be dismissed as elaborate deception. Medieval men felt strongly about their faith and the sacrifice of the crusade. Venetians were just as pious as their allies: Venice itself was filled with churches and Venetians were regular crusaders.[30] Although sophisticated scholars may find religious enthusiasm distasteful, it was a regular facet of medieval life that cannot be ignored. Dandolo's crossing had slight effect on Venetian politics as well. It was hardly unusual for a doge to leave his son to oversee the state while he was away; Dandolo needed no popular approval.[31] With this, however, Giorgio Cracco disagrees. Cracco argues that the entire scene in San Marco was an invention of Villehardouin. Dandolo, Cracco believes, lacked the constitutional authority either to take command of the Venetian crusaders or to leave his son as vice-doge. Indeed, Cracco contends that Dandolo was *incapable* of such a performance, since he was blind, old, and feeble. Rather, Dandolo was co-opted by the Venetian crusaders who led him to Constantinople, not the other way around.[32] The problem with this novel interpretation is that it lacks supporting evidence and is contradicted by what evidence we have. There is no law nor any clause in Dandolo's oath of office that prohibited him from taking the cross and commanding the Venetian troops.[33] Even if such a law existed, it would have been overridden by the popular acclamation of approval, the theoretical source of all power in Venice. Dandolo was old and blind, but certainly not weak. Cracco's interpretation of Dandolo forces him to discard virtually every description of the doge from friend and enemy alike.[34]

The crossing of the doge was a splendid event, but Gunther of Pairis tells of widespread disaffection in the army, which indicates that rumors of the agreement to coerce Zara into submission to Venice may have leaked beyond the circle of leaders.[35] For crusaders to become involved in an attack upon a Christian city seemed to many detestable. To fall upon Christians with burning, raping, and slaughter was sinful for those marked with the cross of Christ, however commendable these activities might be when inflicted upon unbelievers. The problem was compounded in that the king of Hungary, Emeric, was also signed with the cross and enjoyed the same papal protection as themselves. Surely they risked the pope's anathema and the loss of their own crusading privileges if they attacked Hungarian possessions. Behind the proposal of the doge some crusaders saw the greed of the Venetians, the same rapacity that some of them believed they had already experienced at the hands of their hosts. Many poor crusaders, having consumed what little money they had brought with them and having nothing left for the direct journey to Palestine, abandoned the cause, sorrowfully retracing their steps toward home. The great adventure was over for them. The spiritual and worldly bene-fits were lost. Some of the richer men, too, not suffering from penury, but unwilling to soil their consciences, also turned back. Not only was the army deprived of these defectors, but on their homeward journey they encountered Germans and others who were either on their way to join the host in Venice or hesitating in Lombardy to see how matters developed. Hearing the news of the expedition to Zara, these remained in a waiting position, sought Apu-lian ports, or joined the homeward trek.[36]

Other crusaders took a different view of the Venetian proposal. To return home with the crusading vow unfulfilled would be a greater public disgrace and a greater sin than taking part in the attack upon Christian Zara.[37] Men often find themselves in situations where no ethically commendable choices are open to them. They must, as Dandolo said, "make the best of it."[38] Each crusader had to weigh his own values, and those who accepted the logic of the leaders placed very great weight upon the preservation of the army and effective aid to the Holy Land. If the pope himself could not embrace their de-cision to accept the sin of attacking Christians, he did subsequently recognize that they were driven by a necessity that mitigated their guilt.[39] His earlier prohibition against attacking Christians, moreover, contained an exception for the case of necessity.[40] The conflict within the crusaders' camp concerning the attack on Zara also reveals the contrast between two types of men. Those who turned away were inwardly responsible to their consciences. Those who chose the lesser evil, the Zaran expedition, were outwardly responsible for practical results. The best of the former are saints, but they are not the leaders of armies, states, or even the church. Villehardouin, spokesman for the prac-tical men, stresses that even those who proceeded to the Holy Land apart from the army, as well as those who returned home, accomplished nothing.[41] His party was concerned with attainable ends and the means by which these might be reached in a world that does not run according to the dictates of conscience.

Even the clergy were not of one mind. Abbot Martin of Pairis, shocked at the prospect that the crusading army would attack Christians, not knowing where to turn or what he should do, sought out the papal legate. Torn by con-science, he begged for absolution from his crusading vow, so that he might return to the accustomed quiet of his monastery. But one cannot lightly leave the cloister to ride at the head of an army, then simply return when threatened by the evil that engulfs the world in which armies ride. Peter Capuano, the legate, absolutely refused the abbot's request In no case should Martin or the other monks abandon the army, but remain with it and try to prevent, as much as possible, the shedding of Christian blood. Martin, denied his wish for moral security in the womb of his monastery, submitted, as he must, with sighs and a grieving heart.[42]

Other churchmen were less opposed to the expedition to Zara than Martin of Pairis. Bishop Conrad of Halberstadt discussed the question with the papal legate, but made no pleas to be freed from his vow. Rather, Conrad's uncertainty arose only from the fact that he had not taken part in the negotiations between the Venetian and French leaders, and was therefore unsure whether the decision to sail to Zara had received the assent of the pope. Peter Capuano replied cautiously, saying that while Innocent could not condone an attack on Christians, the pope was willing to overlook it if the alternative was the disintegration of the crusade The legate ordered Bishop Conrad to act according to his conscience, but under no circumstances was he to abandon the host.[43]

The papal legate was thus among those who accepted the lesser evil, as he judged it, for the sake of the greater good. At all costs Capuano wished to prevent the disintegration of the army for which he was responsible to the pope, so he used all his powers to overcome the scruples of those more squeamish than him.[44] Perhaps his moral judgment was distorted by his legatine office, for men tend to overvalue those activities for which they bear direct responsibility. Cardinal Peter has been accused of betraying Innocent's trust, but, although the pope could not condone the attack upon Zara, there is no evidence that he repudiated his legate. In fact Capuano's decision was consistent with Innocent's own policy of preserving his crusade by adapting to situations that he could not change. Capuano acted within the terms of the papal prohibition, which forbade crusaders to attack Christians except in case of necessity and after consultation with the legate. Whether or not Peter's judgment was correct could be argued endlessly. The doctrine of necessity is fraught with moral peril—as is life itself. The legate's decision, although it may not have been right, was reasonable, defensible, and within the limits of his authority. In a way, the cardinal's moral character appears more admirable than that of the pontiff, for he grasped the thistle resolutely.

While not a perfect solution, the decision to land at Zara at last gave the participants a certainty that the crusade would indeed sail. It also gave another interested party, young Alexius Angelus, that same certainty. The imperial refugee had for some time been hovering nearby in Verona, watching with interest the plight of the foundering crusade. At some point, probably in September, Alexius sent envoys to Boniface of Montferrat and the French barons in Venice.[45] They recounted in detail Alexius III's treachery toward his brother Isaac and the escape of the young prince.[46] The messengers assured the barons that the magnates of the Byzantine Empire and the more powerful elements in Constantinople longed to receive the prince as emperor.[47] At no great cost or effort the crusaders could restore a rightful ruler against a wicked tyrant and, in return, would be rewarded with aid for their own enterprise in Palestine. This was all new to Villehardouin and the rest of the small group of French barons who met with the envoys.[48] Villehardouin was told that it was only happenstance that the young Alexius was in Verona, resting while on his way to the court of Philip of Swabia. Yet that trip had taken place a year earlier: since then Alexius had already spoken to Boniface and then the pope about the possibility of using the crusade on his behalf. Boniface alone knew that Alexius's presence in Verona was purposeful and that Innocent had forbade the crusade to take up the young man's cause. He said nothing. Indeed, according to Villehardouin, Boniface along with the other barons "marveled greatly" at Alexius's story.[49] It is clear that the marquis wanted the French to view Alexius's proposal as a providential boon, not an old scheme twice forbidden by the pope. Despite the subterfuge and misrepresentation, the plan did commend itself to the leading barons. To carry out their crusading purpose the barons saw by now that they must have additional support. Though they were an impressive army in spite of the failure of many to keep the rendezvous, they found themselves in extreme financial straits. They were not yet willing to commit themselves fully to the plan, but they were willing to send envoys with Alexius to the court of Philip of Swabia "whither he [Alexius] is going." It is important to point out that, according to Villehardouin, the number of men involved in this discussion was very small.[50] Enrico Dandolo and the Venetians were not included, nor were the majority of the French, who wanted nothing to do with the plan when they first heard it in Zara that winter. Although the plan to use the crusade to install the young Alexius had progressed somewhat from the musing discussions at Hagenau the previous Christmas, it had moved only from talk to negotiations.

Meanwhile, Cardinal Peter Capuano had left Venice, returning to Rome with a bundle of bad news for Innocent III. Probably uppermost in Capuano's mind was the refusal of the Venetians to receive him in his legatine role. He also had to inform Innocent of the disappointing number of crusaders who had arrived in Venice, and of the decision to stop off at Zara on the way down the Adriatic, which Capuano had already tacitly endorsed. Finally, the cardinal was instructed by the barons to sound out the pope on what they believed was a new proposal from the young Alexius.[51] Capuano was not destined to rejoin the army until after the conquest of Constantinople. Rejected as legate by the Venetians, neither he nor the pope could accept with dignity his proposed role as a mere preacher. Furthermore, Innocent had no intention of sanctifying with the presence of a legate, who represented the very person of the pope himself, the attack on a city belonging to the king of Hungary. Capuano was not in disgrace or relieved of his legatine office.[52] Innocent simply adopted that most difficult and sometimes most effective policy of watchful waiting.

On the eve of the crusaders' departure the marquis of Montferrat also journeyed to consult the pope. With him came his friend Abbot Peter of Locedio, a man who had enjoyed Innocent's confidence for many years. Boniface was not to rejoin the army until after the conquest of Zara. If this attack upon the lands of a crusader could not be avoided, Innocent wished, at any rate, to disassociate the official leader of the crusade from it.[53] Boniface was just as happy to avoid the incident himself. As a partisan of Genoa, he had no desire to assist Venice in her local wars.

Innocent did not like what he heard from his legate and the leader of his crusade. Both men brought him news of their support for different diversions of the enterprise. Capuano told him of the unfortunate necessity of the attack on Zara, which the legate hoped to discourage but was forced to accept. Boniface brought the now tiresome story of the dispossessed Alexius and his promises of aid for the Holy Land. The latter was easily dispensed with: Innocent hated the idea when he first heard it, and time had done nothing to change his mind. As for Zara, Innocent could not support Capuano's position. The pope wrote a strong letter threatening religious sanctions against any crusader who should attack Christians and entrusted it to the abbot of Locedio.[54] The letter did not reach the army, however, until it stood before Zara. It has been charged that Innocent's prohibition was merely for the record, that he knew that it would not arrive in time to have any effect. It is true that politically Innocent had little to lose and something to gain by an attack on Zara. The city was a hotbed of the Bogomil heresy, a dualism akin to Albigensianism. Repeated attempts to cajole King Emeric of Hungary into rooting out the Bogomils had elicited little response.[55] The king of Hungary was skating on thin ice with Innocent III. Emeric had taken the crusader's vow two years earlier, but he continued to put off his departure with excuse after excuse.[56] Only a few weeks after the departure from Rome of the abbot of Locedio and Boniface of Montferrat, Innocent received another embassy from Emeric asking the pope to relieve him of his vow so that he could crush the "multitudes" of Bogomils in his kingdom (the existence of which he had previously denied). In a letter dated 9 November 1202, only two days before the attack on Zara, Innocent scolded Emeric for his incessant delays and for his continuous attacks on Christians since his donning of the cross.[57] Beyond his anger toward the king of Hungary and discontent concerning the heretical Dalmatia, Innocent had other reasons to favor the attack on Zara. He was pursuing negotiations with Johannitsa, the Bulgarian "emperor," in an attempt to bring the Bulgarian church into the Catholic fold. An attack on the Bulgarians' mortal enemy, Hungary, could only advance that cause.[58] None of this, however, is sufficient to prove that Innocent approved of the attack on Zara but cynically sent a letter forbidding it, which he knew would never make it in time. The effective relief of the Holy Land was far more important to the pope than any political objectives. He had refused to divert the Fourth Crusade for his own purposes in Italy; he would not do so now in Hungary. Besides, if Innocent truly believed that his letter would not arrive at Zara in time to stop the attack then he made a serious miscalculation. The letter did arrive before the assault; the majority of crusaders simply chose to ignore it. The crusade had a momentum of its own.

Only a few weeks later the problem of the troublesome Byzantine prince Alexius again found its way into the papal court. An embassy arrived from his uncle, Alexius III, seeking to dissuade the pontiff from lending any support or encouragement to the refugee. The emperor was uncomfortably aware of the army poised on the Lido and knew also that his nephew was attempting to enlist its aid through Philip of Swabia. It was only prudent, then, to warn Innocent of the danger to his crusade and thus avert the messiness of another angry crusade army on the Bosporus. The imperial envoys appealed both to Innocent's religious ideals and his political sense. They argued that he should prevent any attack upon Christians by an army dedicated to war against the infidel. They also presented the constitutional arguments against the claims of young Alexius: he had not been elected by the nobles; and he had no hereditary claim, since he was born before his father's coronation.[59] They appealed to the pope's own political interests, since the connection between the young prince and the anti-papal Hohenstaufen was obvious to all. Innocent was even reminded that Philip of Swabia, the brother-in-law of Alexius and his sponsor in the West, was under the ban of excommunication as a cleric who had put aside his robe for the sword of knighthood. The envoys of the emperor did not, however, touch upon the two subjects closest to Innocent's heart: aid to the crusade and the reunion of the Greek and Latin churches. Still, they were preaching to the choir. Innocent, as we have seen, had repeatedly forbidden the crusade to take up the young Alexius's cause.

He had no intention of allowing this opportunity for victory in Jerusalem to become bogged down in Byzantine politics. On 16 November, Innocent replied to the emperor with a letter that contained both a friendly response and a thinly veiled threat. While he assured the emperor that after consultation with the cardinals he had come to a decision that would please him, Innocent took care to point out that the young Alexius offered aid to the Holy Land and reunion of the churches. Innocent surely had in mind the letters he had previously exchanged with Patriarch John X Camaterus, which, while cordial, made clear that Byzantium would never accept Rome as "head and mother" of the church.[60] Innocent also suggested in his letter to Alexius how serious a matter the triumph of Philip of Swabia in Germany would be for the Byzantine Empire, since the Hohenstaufen would be free to lend effective support to his brother-in-law.[61] Innocent and Alexius had mutual interests in defeating Philip of Swabia's initiatives and in ensuring that the crusade avoid Constantinople. Both men erred, however, in believing that the pope was still at the helm of his crusade. When Innocent bade farewell to his Byzantine guests, he hoped never again to hear of young Alexius Angelus. In Constantinople, Alexius III turned his attention to other more pressing matters. According to Nicetas these included "building lavish bathhouses, leveling hills to plant vineyards, and filling in ravines."[62]

The crusaders meanwhile were pressing forward the final preparations for their belated departure. The transports and horse transports were turned over to the various leaders. Food and other supplies were loaded on board. Petraries and mangonels, three hundred of them, were loaded on the vessels.[63] The crusaders got themselves and their gear ready for embarkation. Baldwin of Flanders, who had contributed generously of his wealth to the sums paid Venice, at the last moment borrowed from four Venetian merchants a sum of over 118 marks sterling.[64] The odd figure suggests that it was for some specific purchase.

The Venetians too were busy preparing for departure. It is unfortunate that the documentary record in Venice is so poor in this early period, for it prevents us from getting a clear view of the activities and attitudes of one-half of the crusaders. A small piece of evidence, however, has recently come to light. A will, made by a Venetian crusader just before the fleet departed, gives a rare glimpse into the human side of one of the thousands of Venetians who took the cross in 1202.[65] The will was made in October 1202 (Venetians did not at this time specify dates beyond the month) by Walframe of Gemona, a very un-Venetian name. In fact, he calls himself an "inhabitant" of Venice, meaning that he was not native to the lagoon, dwelling in the parish of San Stae. Walframe was probably a young man since his father Enrico was still alive and, although he was married, he mentions no children. In the opening remarks, Walframe resolutely states that he is "prepared to go in the service of the Lord and his Holy Sepulcher." In his will, he returns to his wife, Palmera, her dowry of seventy lire and leaves her three houses and four slaves that he and his father had given to her as a morning gift after their wedding. He further left Palmera three hundred lire to be piously distributed for his soul if he was killed on crusade. Given the lateness of the will, it is clear that it was made immediately before the fleet sailed. It is interesting that the will was drawn up by a priest at San Marco, rather than by a private notary or a priest in Walframe's own parish. It may be that the clergy of San Marco provided notarial services for Venetians preparing to board the crusade vessels near the church. It is not difficult to imagine hundreds of men gathering their goods, bidding farewell to their loved ones, and putting their final affairs in order in the great open space of the still unpaved Piazza San Marco.[66] What became of Walframe, whether he ever returned to Palmera in San Stae or died along the way, we shall probably never know. But it remains that with the exception of Enrico Dandolo, Walframe of Gemona is the only Venetian crusader whose name we know with certainty.[67]

There is a slight disagreement in the sources on the date of departure. Villehardouin says that they sailed in the octave of Saint Remi, 2–8 October, while the authors of the *Gesta episcoporum Halberstadensium* and the *Devastatio* say 1 October.[68] Since Baldwin's loan from Venetian merchants and Walframe of Gemona's will bear October as their date, we probably ought to conclude that both men did not conduct their important business on the very day of departure. It has been suggested that the fleet sailed in two sections, which is possible.[69]

The sources are also in disagreement concerning the size of the fleet, ranging from about 200 vessels to 480, and modern scholars follow one or another without consensus.[70] The eyewitnesses, however, are in approximate agreement. The author of the *Devastatio* counted 40 transports, 100 horse transports, and 62 galleys, for a total of two hundred two ships. Hugh of Saint Pol described the fleet before Constantinople in 1203 as numbering 200 vessels, and he had specifically accounted for the loss of 4 transports and 2 horse transports, so this is good confirmation of the *Devastatio*. Moreover, from the walls of Constantinople, Nicetas counted in the fleet of the enemy more than 70 transports, a 110 horse transports, and 60 galleys, for a total of two hundred forty or slightly more, which remains in the same range. Hugh of Saint Pol specifically excludes small auxiliary craft, as we assume the others do also.[71] We may safely accept a figure, then, of slightly over two hundred major vessels, approximately half of which were horse transports, and very roughly one quarter transports and the other quarter galleys.

The galley was the fighting ship of the Middle Ages, long, narrow, low, light, and swift. It was some one hundred to one hundred and thirty feet long and only fifteen to seventeen feet wide. Its long narrow *corsia*, or deck, stood no more than five or six feet above the keel. In action it was propelled by rowers, although it used an auxiliary sail for cruising. A typical galley of the period had 120 rowers seated two to a bench with thirty benches on each side, although there were larger and smaller galleys.[72] In battle or other urgent need the rowers could propel a galley with great speed. They were protected from sun and rain by a large awning, which was removed for combat. Two great lateral oars near the stern served as a double rudder. There was a single mast about a third of the length from the bow surmounted by a cage for lookouts or for marines. When the galley was under canvas a triangular lateen sail was spread on a yard, which was often longer than the vessel. There was a boarding platform with a beak for grappling on the prow, which might be furnished with a catapult, mangonel, or other artillery piece. In older times ramming had been more important, and in some cases the platform had not replaced the pointed underwater ram. Sometimes, too, a heavy metal spike was suspended from the yard to be dropped on opposing galleys to bilge them. In addition to the rowers there were forty or fifty officers and marines to each galley, and the rowers, as well, were armed.[73]

The transports were converted roundships, which were normally used for carrying bulky goods. They were large, high, and broad in the beam, as much as two hundred feet long and thirty or forty feet wide. They were sailing ships, normally two-masters, although some bore three. Their raised castles fore and aft gave them a crescent shape. Here siege weapons were mounted. In battle they were primarily useful for assailing walled ports, although they could also be used in the open sea to protect the galleys as a sort of floating fortress. They bore a relatively small force of marines. A few of them were of enormous size, able to carry a thousand or more passengers.[74] These giants were exceptional: in the fleet sailing from Venice there were the *Paradise*, assigned to the bishop of Soissons; the *Pilgrim*, assigned to the bishop of Troyes; the *Violet*, assigned to Stephen of Perche; and the *Eagle*, nicknamed "*The Entire World*," which bore Venetians. In April 1204, Robert of Clari counted only four or five ships great enough to assault the wooden towers that the defenders of Constantinople had built atop the stone ones.[75] These were the few giant transports.

A generation earlier the Byzantines had introduced the horse transport to the Latins. Loading and unloading horses was a ticklish business. When one tried to walk a horse up or down the narrow inclined plank used to embark men the animal became very nervous and tended to shy. There was no efficient means of putting them aboard by sling. Once on board there was a difficulty in placing them in the hold. To meet these problems the Byzantines devised the technique of cutting a door in the side of the vessel not much above the water, which opened to form a ramp. Not having to face a steep incline, the horses remained somewhat more calm, and they walked directly to the proper level. The horse transports were also fitted to handle these extremely valuable beasts so as to bring them to their destination in reasonably good shape. They were transported in individual box stalls, each horse suspended by leather straps so that its feet barely touched the deck. They were thus protected against the pitching and rolling of the ship, and their immobility also helped preserve the stability of the vessel. They suffered greatly from chafing and other discomforts and from the enforced immobility, but this method of transport was the best available. The Byzantine type of horse transport was simply a roundship with a door in the side. The Westerners also employed a horse transport, which was long and low, more like a galley, although much larger. Actually it was a cross between a transport and a galley, having two masts, but also 150 rowers.[76] According to Villehardouin, the horse transports had to be towed by galleys in the strong current of the Bosporus, suggesting that these were the large sailing vessels rather than the oared variety.[77]

The enormous fleet that the Venetians had built was uniquely designed for an attack on Egypt. Fifty or more galleys would be required to defeat the Ayyubid navy, which would attempt to destroy the crusader fleet. The horse transports, designed to operate in shallow water and back up to sandy beaches, were perfectly suited for the Egyptian shore. Indeed, Egypt was the only maritime power in the Mediterranean that necessitated such an imposing battle fleet. It was certainly not designed for an attack on Constantinople. The squadron of galleys had no opposing navy in the Bosporus. Its duties were limited to towing transports and breaking chains. Constantinople also lacked broad sandy beaches on which the amphibious horse transports could launch their armored knights. The Venetians knew Constantinople and Egypt well: they designed their fleet to oppose the latter.[78]

The departure of the fleet was a magnificent spectacle. The impressionable Robert of Clari calls it the finest sight since the creation of the world. The blind doge, garbed in his colorful robes of state and wearing the cloth crown with the prominent crusader's cross, boarded his galley, painted vermilion like that of an emperor. A canopy of vermilion samite sheltered him on board. Above him fluttered the banner of Saint Mark. Four silver trumpets used on solemn occasions blared before him and drums rattled to attract attention to the show.[79] The various colored banners were raised and the sides of the ships and the castles were girded with the shields of the crusaders, each painted brilliantly to distinguish its owner. These belts of steel around the ships provided at once a measure of defense and ornament. When the pilgrims were all aboard, the clergy mounted the castles or poops of the ships to chant the *Veni creator spiritus*. As Dandolo's vermilion galley began to move followed by the rest of the fleet a hundred trumpets of silver and brass signaled the departure and countless drums and tabors beat excitedly. Never was there such rejoicing among great and small, clergy and laymen, who all, according to Robert of Clari, wept with joy. Soon they passed the familiar Lido on the right and moved out of the lagoon into the Adriatic. Then the sails of the galleys were raised. With the whole fleet of over two hundred vessels dancing under sail, with the banners and ensigns snapping in the breeze, the sea, Robert says, seemed to be swarming with life.[80]

The departure was not without its foreboding aspect, however. The huge transport *Violet*, which had been assigned to Stephen of Perche, sank. Stephen himself remained ill at Venice, either not having embarked with the others or perhaps having been injured in the sinking of the *Violet*. He was lost to the army until after the conquest of Constantinople. In March of 1203, after his recovery, he proceeded to Apulia, and thence sailed with many others directly for Palestine.[81] After the fall of the Byzantine capital he rejoined the host to serve in defense of the conquest and to claim a part in the division of fiefs.[82] Another of the barons, Matthew of Montmorency, also remained behind, sick and incapable of travel, but he shortly resumed his place in the army before Zara.[83] The marquis of Montferrat, too, was absent. Under the transparent excuse that his affairs detained him, the titular head of the crusade avoided the whole problem of Zara. Had he joined the crusaders he would have been under pressure to inform them of the pope's prohibition of the attack and perhaps even to forbid it himself. Boniface also had no interest in helping the Venetians secure their hold on the Adriatic for any reason. Best to stay away until the matter resolved itself.

Zara was not the fleet's first stop, only the most important. As was Venice's right, the armada stopped at a number of ports along the Dalmatian coast to insure their loyalty and support. Since these cities owed military service to Venice, the doge could fill out his complement of rowers and marines and put aboard additional supplies.[84] Part of the fleet under command of the doge sailed directly across the Gulf of Venice at the head of the Adriatic to Pirano in western Istria, arriving on 9 October.[85] Trieste, the greatest of the Istrian ports, and Muggia, a smaller town about five miles down the coast, fearing the power the doge had assembled, hurriedly dispatched large embassies of prominent citizens to do him honor. Overlooking their wrongdoings, which both towns were forced to acknowledge in new treaties, Dandolo received them into his grace, sending the emissaries back to their cities to prepare his reception. Shortly thereafter the doge sailed up the coast to the port huddled beneath the rocky, wooded hills overlooking the Gulf of Trieste. Here the citizens of Trieste received him with all the honors due a determined man whose will was backed by a large fleet. The priests turned out in their finest vestments, innumerable candles were burned, and all the bells of the city rang noisily. In a solemn pact Trieste pledged its loyalty to Venice.[86] The ceremony was then repeated at Muggia. The pacts are almost identical.[87]

The other portion of the fleet, if we believe Robert of Clari, who does not mention the events described above, sailed directly for Pola near the southern tip of the Istrian peninsula. Here they landed, refreshed themselves, bought provisions, and stayed a little while.[88] Pola too owed Venice rowers and marines, and these were no doubt claimed.[89] The vessels then set sail for Zara, making as spectacular a display as when they departed Venice, as Robert tells it, so that the people of Pola were amazed at the show of power and splendor.[90] We hear nothing more of them until their arrival before Zara on 10 November.

Venice has been charged by Paul Riant and other historians with deliberately delaying the fleet between the sailing from Venice and the arrival at Zara, so that winter would be facing them and it would no longer be possible to sail overseas.[91] They overlook the announcement prior to the departure from Venice of the plan to winter at Zara.[92] Early October was much too late for voyages from western European ports to Alexandria. The scholarly critics of Venice, moreover, are unaware of what was going on at Pirano, Trieste, Muggia, Pola, and perhaps other cities not recorded in the documents. Rowers and marines, as well as provisions, were being put on board. This was the service owed by the subject cities to the Republic of Saint Mark. In some cases these services took some persuading: according to the *Devastatio*, Trieste and Muggia had to be forced into submission.[93] This took considerable time, for the obligation became effective only when the Venetian fleet set forth from the lagoons. The enlistment of men and gathering of provisions could not be accomplished overnight. Furthermore, the trip from Venice to Zara was not to be sailed quickly. It was (and is) fraught with rocks and shoals ready to destroy the ship of an unwary captain.[94] All of these factors account for the relative slowness of this part of the voyage.[95]

The first division of ships lowered their anchors within sight of Zara on 10 November. On the next morning, the feast of Saint Martin, which was bright and clear, the remainder of the fleet joined them. Zara is sheltered from the waves, like so much of the eastern coast of the Adriatic, by a range of mostly submerged mountains protruding from the sea. The ancient Roman city, the richest in Dalmatia, is situated on a near-island linked to the continent by a tongue of land.[96] The crusaders took note of Zara's high walls and formidable towers, and they said to one another: "How could such a city be taken by force except with the help of God?"[97] As Dandolo had warned, the fleet received here a far different reception than in the Istrian ports. When the inhabitants of Zara saw ranged before their city the greatest naval force they had ever beheld they were filled with fear—but prepared to resist. They raised their great chain across the mouth of the harbor, closed the gates of the city, and made ready for the impending assault.

The Venetian galleys ran upon the chain and broke it, opening the way for Venetian ships to swarm into the harbor. Knights and sergeants came ashore. The doors in the sides of the horse transports opened and the horses were led blindfolded to land. Siege machinery was removed from the large transport vessels. Tents and pavilions were unloaded and pitched. The Zarans did not oppose the landing, so the army encamped.[98]

Although the Fourth Crusade did not reach its projected size, it remained a massive force by Western standards. Dandolo, who had been to Zara before and may have participated in previous sieges of it, knew well that the city could never hold out. Close as they were to Venice and encamped on the Adriatic shore, which Venice controlled, the besieging army could rely on virtually limitless provisions. Since departure for Egypt was out of the question until the following March, the crusaders also had plenty of time to reduce the city. The fact that the fall of Zara was now a certainty also did not escape the Zarans themselves. Without their Pisan or Hungarian allies to relieve them, they had no choice but to offer terms. Two days after the fleet arrived, on 12 November, a deputation of Zarans came to the crimson pavilion of the doge. They offered the surrender of the city and its goods to his discretion with the sole condition that the lives of its inhabitants should be spared.[99] This was a rich moment for Enrico Dandolo. He had expended much energy both before and during his dogeship in dealing with rebellious Zara.[100] Now, at last, it was at his mercy. The surrender was, for all practical purposes, total. There were a few members of the Zaran ruling class that Dandolo hoped to do away with, but the slaughter of the inhabitants had never been part of the plan, nor was it in Venice's commercial interests to do so. Still, the doge replied that he would have to confer with his French allies before accepting the surrender.[101] What did Dandolo feel he had to discuss? Surely, the barons would not oppose sparing Christian lives. It is not clear that the doge was required to confer with the French at all: the siege of Zara was a Venetian initiative in which the French had been persuaded to participate in order to defer their debt. They had no interest or right either to accept or reject the terms by which Venice would reclaim its recalcitrant port. There may have been an element of piling on in Dandolo's decision to leave the envoys waiting in his tent, wringing their hands over their own lives and those of their fellow citizens, while he conferred with the French. Whatever the case, the decision was a bad one. Had the doge immediately accepted the surrender much of the trouble that followed would have been avoided.

The progress of the Zaran dignitaries to the doge's pavilion did not go unnoticed among the crusading host. It was clear to all that a surrender was in progress. For most of the crusaders this was the best news possible. They could winter in Zara and leave for the Holy Land in March, all without shedding Christian blood. For others, however, the news rankled. Simon de Montfort, one of the first French barons to take the cross back at Ecry, had been unhappy about the direction of the crusade for some time. Despite his great prominence among the French lords, he had not been involved in the decision to acquire transport from Venice, nor did his suggestions for French leaders of the crusade meet with success. It has been suggested that Simon saw his own power dwindling in favor of Italians, namely Boniface of Montferrat and Enrico Dandolo.[102] The count of Montfort also felt that the attack on Zara was a perversion of the crusade, and he was determined to stop it. He was not alone: many of his friends, relatives, and vassals were also angered by the slighting of their lord and the perceived misdirection of the crusade. Among them was Enguerrand of Boves, who, like many of Simon's friends, would later play an important role in the Albigensian Crusade, which Simon led.[103] A number of white monks, led by Abbot Guy of Vaux-de-Cernay, also backed Simon's position. The abbey of Vaux-de-Cernay was a frequent beneficiary of the largesse of the counts of Montfort and seems to have played an important role in the education of young members of Simon's family.[104] This party, for both pious and political reasons, was determined that Zara would not fall to the crusaders.

It is almost certain that the letter Innocent III had entrusted to the abbot of Locedio forbidding the attack on Zara had arrived, and that the abbot of Vaux-de-Cernay had it in his possession.[105] This seemed to be the trump card for which Simon de Montfort and his party had been waiting. It was clear to them that when faced with the pope's commands the crusaders would turn from their sin, which the papal legate had wrongfully condoned. The Venetians, too, would have to accept the papal ban and take their proper role as transporters, not leaders. For this party, the surrender of the Zarans was unjust and tragic. Nothing in the pope's letter forbade the crusaders from wintering at Zara, provided they did not attack the city. The pope could not prohibit the Venetians from accepting a surrender if it was freely given. The dissidents moved quickly to inform the Zarans of the pope's friendship and that of many of the crusaders. While the Zaran delegates anxiously awaited the return of Enrico Dandolo, Simon de Montfort paid them a visit. He probably told them of the papal letter forbidding the assault and certainly made it clear that the French, who bore the crosses of pilgrims, would never attack the Christian city of Zara. The large force was hollow, he assured them; half of it there only for show. If the Zarans could defend themselves against the Venetians they would be safe enough. Leaving nothing to chance, Robert of Boves, the brother of Enguerrand, rode to the walls of the city and announced to the defenders just what Simon was telling to their representatives. The latter thanked the count of Montfort for his honesty and support, and returned to Zara.[106]

The meeting between Dandolo and the crusading leaders took very little time. It is interesting that no one seems to have missed Simon de Montfort, further suggesting the erosion of his power in the host. The barons immediately voted to accept the surrender of Zara and then accompanied the doge back to his pavilion to conclude the agreement. There they found no Zaran delegates, but rather Simon de Montfort and his supporters.[107] The doge and the Frankish leaders were astonished and angered. Before very much could be said, Guy of Vaux-de-Cernay stepped forward, probably with the papal letter in hand, and exclaimed, "I forbid you, on behalf of the Pope of Rome, to attack this city, for those within are Christians and you are crusaders!"[108] To ignore this prohibition, he continued, would mean excommunication. A violent scene erupted. According to the abbot's nephew, the Venetians tried to kill Guy but were stopped by Simon de Montfort.[109] Enrico Dandolo was angriest of all. Rather than accusing the dissidents, he turned to the crusading leaders saying, "Lords, I had this city at my mercy, and your people have deprived me of it; you have promised to assist me to conquer it, and I summon you to do so."[110]

The crusading leaders, Villehardouin among them, were now thrust onto the horns of a terrible dilemma. On the one hand they had Guy of Vaux-de-Cernay's condemnation of an attack on Zara, backed up by the threat of papal excommunication. Pilgrims enlisted in the crusade to win the heavenly Jerusalem by means of the crusading indulgence.[111] If they went against the pope's will, not only did many believe that they would lose the indulgence and other crusader privileges, but they would be cut off utterly from the sacraments of the church, the instruments of grace. These concerns had to be

weighed against their solemn commitments to the Venetians to attack Zara if
it failed to surrender. Many of the French nobles might not have agreed to the
Zaran expedition in the first place had it not been for the papal legate's tacit
approval. Since then they had given their word to fight for Venice, a promise
their feudal morality would not easily allow them to break. They were particularly shamed by the actions of Simon de Montfort, who had willfully scuttled
the peaceful surrender of the city and thrown them into this crisis. It was their
anger at him and his supporters that finally tipped the scales in Venice's favor.
The barons had been aware for some time of Simon's grumbling, and they
were fed up. In their private deliberations they remarked on the outrageous
nature of the dissidents' actions, and exclaimed that "there has not been a day
that passed that they have not tried to break up this host."[112] To refuse to attack the city would not only cause shame to fall on their heads and probably
spell the dissolution of the army, but it would also reward Simon de Montfort for his interference. The barons decided that, excommunication or no,
they would fulfill their obligation to attack the city.[113]

The dissidents' desire to preserve Zara was not only thwarted, but their
clumsy attempts to bring it about forced the assault that they hoped to avoid.
If they believed that the crusaders would turn from their present leadership to
the blameless figure of Simon de Montfort, they were disappointed. Among
the magnates only Simon de Montfort himself and Enguerrand of Boves declared that they would not go against the command of the pope. They withdrew from the camp and set up their tents at a distance, disassociating themselves from the sinful act.[114]

Peaceful surrender was still not impossible, but it would be much harder
to negotiate. The Venetian assurances to the Zarans that the crusaders would
indeed attack their city were scoffed at. Simon de Montfort had done his work
well, the citizens of Zara were convinced that the French would not attack
their walls, no matter what their eyes told them. Preparations for the siege by
anyone other than the Venetians were passed off as mere bluff. The king of
Hungary had surrounded their city with formidable walls and towers and had
placed there a garrison of troops.[115] In order to work upon the consciences
and weaken the morale of the attackers, the Zarans suspended crucifixes from
their walls.[116] Their confidence in their military and moral defense, as well as
the assurances of Simon de Montfort, however, was misplaced. The Venetians
and the majority of the crusaders did not hesitate to attack the city.

The Venetian fleet assaulted the walls from the harbor to the west from
the Val di Maestro to the Porta Terraferma. The vessels were equipped with
projectile weapons that battered the fortifications and with ladders prepared

for scaling the battlements of the defenders. To the east, from the Porta Terraferma back around to the Val di Maestro, the crusaders dug siege trenches
around the walls. With mangonels, petraries, and other engines of war they
hammered the city's defenses from the landward side for about five days.[117]
Martin, the abbot of Pairis, who had been denied release from his crusading
vow when the attack on Zara was first proposed, informed his monk Gunther
that the crusaders went about their work sadly and with heavy hearts, but all
the more vigorously in order to get the hateful business finished as quickly
as possible.[118] Whatever their feelings, they did a thorough job. The city was
surrounded without communication by land or sea and without hope of succor or supplies. The defenders cast javelins and stones from the walls at their
tormentors, but without inflicting many casualties. They soon saw that they
could not resist the superior force that faced them. The allies ignored their demand that their quarrel with the Venetians be submitted to the pope. Finally
the crusaders began to undermine the walls of the city. Unable to beat off
the sappers, the terrified Zarans saw that they were lost, that the walls would
soon fall open. They were constrained to offer once more to surrender the city
to the mercy of the attackers on the sole condition that their lives should be
spared. This was accepted. On 24 November, the feast of Saint Chrysogonus,
whose body rested within the walls of Zara helpless to protect them, the city
was occupied and put to sack.[119] A poverty-stricken soldiery was unleashed
upon the defenseless town. They snatched everything of value they could find;
they destroyed buildings; they even plundered and profaned churches. The
city was divided: the Venetians quartered in the harbor area and the Franks
further inland.[120]

Evidence concerning Zaran casualties is conflicting. Gunther reports that
there was little bloodshed or destruction, but he has an ulterior motive for
giving this impression, since Abbot Martin lent his presence to an attack
that he thought sinful, but was powerless to halt.[121] Pope Innocent, casti-
gating the crusaders after the fact, declares that the conquest of Zara was not
achieved without considerable effusion of blood.[122] And Thomas, archdeacon
of Spalato, reports that mortality in the city was so great that there were not
enough healthy men to bury the dead, so corpses lay exposed in homes and
churches.[123] Thomas wrote after 1268, however, and was a mere infant in 1202.
He misdates the attack on the city by an entire year. Moreover, his unburied
corpses have more the odor of literary convention than of decaying flesh.

At any rate, the terms of surrender were not honored by the conquerors.
Dandolo ordered various citizens especially hateful to the Venetians decapitated and others exiled. Many sought refuge in Belgrade or Arbe or in the

monastery of Saints Cosmas and Damian of the Mountain. The more adventurous men of Zara took to the hills as partisans, and an expedition from Venice under Dandolo's son eventually was necessary to suppress them.[124]

Much later, possibly in 1205, the doge wrote to Innocent attempting to justify the conquest of Zara.[125] He mentioned that it had been necessary because of the approach of bad weather to winter there. Since the Zarans were rebels of long standing against Venice, having betrayed their oaths, he deemed it just to wreak vengeance upon them as enemies. He admitted that he was told that Zara was under papal protection, but he did not believe it. He told the pope the he felt certain that neither Innocent nor his predecessors would receive under the papal mantle those who did not take the cross as genuine pilgrims, but rather as a cover for the seizure and detention of the goods of others. Dandolo had respected King Emeric's vow since 1200, but the crusading ploy had worn thin.[126] We may dismiss much of Dandolo's argument as special pleading, of course, yet the conquest of Zara was not the simple, one-sided moral abomination that many historians have represented.[127] If we resist the temptation to oversimplify moral issues, a case can be made for the Venetians, as well as for their allies. Zara was a former Venetian dependency, which had revolted. Zaran pirates preyed on Venetian shipping within the Adriatic, control of which was absolutely vital to Venetian prosperity. The Zarans had even allied with Pisa to challenge Saint Mark's dominion in that sea. Like many crusaders before them, Venetians claimed the right to stabilize their domain before departing to fight for the Church. Venice, moreover, had made a massive financial commitment to the crusade, which was in danger of collapse. Abandonment of the enterprise would mean a real financial disaster. The attack upon Zara preserved the crusade and protected the investment of the Venetians. If we do not find them guiltless, as we should not, we should at least comprehend sympathetically the Venetians' legitimate concerns.

6

The Treaty of Zara

The interest of the Venetians and the intention of Dandolo, of course, was not merely to take Zara, but to secure it under their own hegemony. The fleet and the army needed to remain there for a time, therefore, on guard against any effort by the king of Hungary to retake the city. In any case travel in the Mediterranean Sea customarily came to an almost complete halt in the winter from November until March. Venetian commerce with the Levant was organized around two great voyages each year. The spring fleet was scheduled to leave Venice about Easter, although it often was delayed until perhaps mid-May. The summer fleet was expected to depart on the feast of John the Baptist (24 June), but sometimes was held up until as late as August or even September.[1] In conformity with this pattern of sailing and in view of the need to protect the newly won city, Dandolo informed the barons that they must winter at Zara.[2] A more suitable place would be hard to find. Around the city were numerous olive groves, ample vineyards, and rich grainfields. Game and fish were found in abundance. The winter climate was more mild than that of Venice, not to mention the crusaders' northern homelands. The Mediterranean sun almost always warmed the winter days. Only rarely was Zara afflicted with icy winds and snow. As early as January the flowering of the almond trees would foretell the advent of spring.[3]

Pleasant as Zara was, it was now many months since the crusaders had left their homes, and Jerusalem remained distant. Even among those who accepted the necessity of the attack on Zara, frustration and discontent against their leaders and the Venetians were great. Although Villehardouin tells us that the houses in the conquered city were allotted equitably, from the *Devastatio* we hear the common complaint that the rich and powerful seized all the best places, leaving nothing for the poor.[4] The crusaders could undoubtedly observe Venetians stacking goods on the shore for shipment to Venice and concluded that their allies had gotten the better of them.[5] The Venetians were getting rich. What had they, the poor crusaders, gained? Had the Venetians not already received more than was just? The mass of crusaders probably believed that the large sums left by Fulk of Neuilly had gone into Venetian purses. Many felt used by their allies.

On the third day after the conquest, about the hour of vespers, a bloody fight erupted in the city between the disgruntled crusaders and the Venetians. From both sides men ran to arms to join the widespread conflict in the streets. The chief men donned their armor and rushed into the midst of the melee to separate the combatants. No sooner did they quench the flames in one quarter, however, than fighting broke out anew in another. Everywhere the Venetians had the worst of it, not being able to resist the resentful fury of the French. According to the *Devastatio*, about a hundred Venetians and French were killed and many more wounded. Most were common folk, but a prominent Flemish knight named Giles of Landas was slain, struck in the eye by a Venetian shaft. The night had nearly ended before the barons were able to calm the excited troops. The doge and the leaders of the crusade spent the rest of the week soothing bitter feelings and restoring peace.[6] Even so, the fray added to the animosities between opposing factions and increased disaffection among the conquerors.

When the king of Hungary heard that the crusaders had joined in the sack of Zara he was very angry, sending messengers to reproach them for this unjustifiable deed. He had taken the cross, as they had, to deliver the Holy Land, only to be attacked by brothers-in-arms. They should give up Zara at once. If they wanted anything from him, he was prepared to give it freely, and he would then go overseas with them. The last was a lie: Emeric was at that moment attempting to be relieved of his vow; he had no intention of leaving Hungary. Indeed, Emeric never did crusade. He had taken the cross to garner support from Innocent III in his war with his brother Andrew. Now that the war was over, Emeric found the burden useful in trying to hold attackers at bay. Although his reasoning was self-serving, Enrico Dandolo was right about King Emeric: he only used the cross as a shield.[7] The barons replied to the king that they would not yield the city, for they had sworn to help the Venetians. Emeric then sent to the pope, pleading for protection against these pilgrims who were pillaging his lands.[8] Innocent's reaction to the fall of Zara and the plea of the Hungarian king is contained in a letter undated, but written at the end of 1202 or the very beginning of 1203. He denounced the crusaders for their conquest and plundering of Zara and for the great effusion of blood that they had caused. They had refused the Zarans' appeal for papal judgment of their dispute with the Venetians. They had assaulted walls from which the inhabitants had suspended the sign of the cross. They had attacked the lands of a crusader. They had ignored the strict prohibition of the pope, which was backed by the sanctions of excommunication and withdrawal of crusading indulgences. He enjoined them most strictly not to harm the city further, but to restore it to representatives of the aggrieved king.[9]

It has often been assumed that Innocent launched a formal bull of excommunication, but he did not. None was needed. In his previous letter, the pope had made it clear that to attack Zara was to incur the ban: therefore excommunication of the host was automatic.[10] Innocent probably delayed issuing the formal bull of excommunication, hoping that the crusaders would show contrition for their sins. But there is no doubt that the pope considered his crusaders to be excommunicated, as did members of the crusading clergy.[11] Among the laity there was general agreement that they were now under the ban, but some rationalized the predicament, arguing for one reason or another that the excommunication did not take place. Villehardouin omitted any mention of it at all, although he did report the pope's anger at the attack.[12] In a letter to the pope dated April 1203, the crusading leaders mentioned "the apostolic excommunication which we incurred before Zara, or we fear we incurred," which sums up their view nicely.[13] Some of the modern confusion arises because of the testimony of Peter of Vaux-de-Cernay, who provides us with the story from the dissident party's point of view. Peter assures his reader in the strongest terms that he had seen the bull of excommunication with his own eyes.[14] Scholars have suggested different reasons for this statement. Andrea believes that Peter made an honest mistake, interpreting a later papal letter as a formal excommunication.[15] Monique Zerner-Chardavoine and Hélène Piéchon-Palloc argue that Peter reported the non-existent bull to remove any lingering doubt over the penalties of the sin that Simon de Montfort piously avoided.[16] This may have been a technique that Guy of Vaux de Cernay and others in his party used when trying to recruit crusaders to their side. Whatever the case, the papal bull is a mirage. From Innocent's point of view it was unnecessary and imprudent. Let the offenders be in doubt. In the event, the crusaders begged forgiveness so quickly that the pope scarcely had time to issue a decree.

Formal bull or no, many at Zara were deeply concerned about the state of their souls. As a counterweight to the condemnations of the dissident party, the majority of the crusading bishops agreed to absolve the army from their sin and lift the ban of excommunication.[17] This probably had a soothing effect on the rank and file, but it was plainly uncanonical. The episcopal absolution was merely a stopgap to comfort the consciences and alleviate the fury of the soldiers. The crusading leaders also sent a delegation to the pope, consisting of two bishops and two knights, to explain their situation to the Holy See and obtain proper forgiveness. According to Villehardouin, these were the eloquent and pious Bishop Nivelon of Soissons; John Faicete of Noyon, the bishop-elect of Acre; John of Friaise who had helped to negotiate the Treaty of Venice; and Robert of Boves.[18] The first three were committed to their mission, but the fourth was not. Robert of Boves was a stupid choice for such a task. It is scarcely likely that the leaders were ignorant of his opposition to the attack upon Zara and his role under the walls in subverting the proposed surrender. Robert seized the opportunity of the mission to Rome to defect, not returning to the army, but going directly to Acre.[19] Only Gunther of Pairis names Abbot Martin as a member of the mission, and he seems confused on the subject, for he names only the clerics.[20] It is clear, however, that Martin did go to Rome at this time. Riant and others have suggested that he represented only the German contingent, whereas Villehardouin names those representing the whole army or, perhaps, since all four were from the French-Flemish group, only that segment of it.[21] More recently, Andrea has argued that Martin simply tagged along to request a dispensation from his vow. He had already expressed serious misgivings about Zara, and was now clearly troubled by his presence there.[22] There were no Venetian representatives, for they would not confess the sinfulness of the attack.[23]

About mid-December the leader of the crusade, Boniface of Montferrat, with Matthew of Montmorency and others, rejoined the army.[24] He found a very unstable situation. Simon de Montfort, Enguerrand of Boves, the abbot of Vaux-de-Cernay, and a number of lesser men who had objected to the attack upon a Christian city were disaffected. The men in the ranks mistrusted their leaders and envied and hated the Venetians. The Venetians, in turn, were angered by the heavy losses they had suffered in the recent outburst of violence and by the repeated failure of the crusaders to honor their obligations. The latter continued to owe a very large sum, thirty-four thousand marks, to their allies: the agreement to conquer Zara had merely postponed the day of reckoning. The army remained extremely short of money, since the unexpected delays had consumed so much of their resources. The crusade was not to set sail from Zara until about Easter, moreover, and by that time the year for which the Venetians owed support would be half gone.

Boniface's arrival in Zara was quickly followed by the arrival on 1 January 1203 of German envoys from the court of Philip of Swabia bearing news of the young Byzantine prince Alexius.[25] Their arrival was not unexpected by Villehardouin and the other leading barons, since it was they who had sent their own envoys to Philip's court to profess their interest in supporting the imperial hopeful. For the vast majority of crusaders, however, the story of Alexius's sorry plight and his request for assistance came as a complete surprise. The Venetians, too, had probably heard nothing of this before;

we cannot even be certain that Enrico Dandolo was informed of the French negotiations with the young prince.[26]

The German envoys met with the Frankish barons and the doge in the palace where Dandolo was staying.[27] Villehardouin does not say who or how many attended this audience, but it was probably very small. The envoys presented their credentials as legates for both Philip of Swabia and the young Alexius. They then affirmed Philip's desire to send his brother-in-law to the host, and stressed the responsibility of all crusaders to the downtrodden. "Because you march for God, and for right, and for justice," the Germans proclaimed, "you must return the inheritance to those who have been despoiled of it, if you are able."[28] This was a clever argument, for indeed crusading was seen as an act of love and charity, restoring Christ's patrimony, which had been unjustly stolen from him.[29] In this case the crusaders could perform this good work on behalf of the Byzantine prince and materially help their crusade in the bargain. The envoys then turned to the reward for this service. First, young Alexius would place the Greek church in obedience to Rome. He would supply the crusading army and provide them in addition with two hundred thousand marks. He himself would raise an army of ten thousand to join in the crusade for one year, and throughout his life he promised to maintain five hundred knights in the Holy Land. The envoys possessed full powers to conclude a treaty on those terms.[30] Nicetas implies that the inexperienced young prince did not comprehend the enormity of the commitment he was making.[31] This may well be true. In any case, desperate men are disposed to promise anything, leaving the fulfillment to be worried about at a later time. Not only did Alexius overestimate his potential military and financial resources and his influence over the Byzantine church, but the envoys assured the crusaders that the magnates of the empire and the greater part of the population of the capital desired the overthrow of the usurper who occupied the throne.[32]

On the following day the leaders met again in the palace where the doge was lodged to discuss the German proposal. This meeting was larger. Gathered were the bishops and abbots accompanying the army, the barons from France and Flanders and their most important vassals, the German princes, Boniface and the other Lombard lords, and the Venetian doge with his council. The assembly was polarized. The marquis, and the counts of Flanders, Blois, and Saint Pol had already more or less committed themselves to the project the previous summer, providing that Philip of Swabia would guarantee the word of his young brother-in-law, as he now did through his emissaries.[33] Naturally the most faithful followers of these great barons, such as the officials of their courts and the former envoys to Venice, were of their party. The Germans had been ordered by the emissaries of Philip of Swabia to support his initiative, although we do not know how vigorously they did so.[34] Some of them had joined the crusade to escape excommunication for their support of the Hohenstaufen, and they perhaps still feared the papal ban.[35]

Enrico Dandolo and the Venetians also came down on the side of the German proposal, but certainly not without grave thought. It is very common for modern historians to see Dandolo as the foremost proponent of the plan to sail to Constantinople.[36] Still seething at the Byzantine seizure of Venetian merchants and goods in the Eastern Empire three decades earlier, Dandolo, it is argued, jumped at the chance to turn the crusade into his own mission of vengeance.[37] Subsequent arguments between Venice and Byzantium further convinced Dandolo that the only remedy for the republic's threatened position in Constantinople was conquest. Dandolo, it is depressingly common to read, simply hated Byzantines.[38] Such statements are incorrect, derived from uninformed sources, and promulgated by modern scholars with insufficient understanding of Venetian history. While it is true that Dandolo, like all Venetians, was enraged by the Byzantine seizure of 1171, it is also true that he and his father, Vitale, devoted much of their careers to rebuilding the relationship between Venice and Constantinople.[39] Their efforts, and those of other Venetians, bore fruit. By 1180 Manuel Comnenus began releasing Venetian prisoners and their goods. After the anti-Latin riots of 1182, Andronicus I released all of the remaining Venetians, restored the Venetian Quarter in Constantinople, and agreed to repay them for the losses they sustained in 1171.[40] Venetians, who had suffered little or no harm from the 1182 pogrom, flocked back to Constantinople. Enrico Dandolo himself served as a ducal legate to the restored Venetian community in the city.[41] By 1189 the young Alexius's father, Isaac II, had extended Venetian privileges thoughout the empire.[42] The overthrow of Isaac in 1195 was initially bad news for Venice. Alexius III took advantage of the war between Venice and Pisa by playing the former against the latter. He also suspended reparation payments and taxed Venetian shipping in violation of their treaty rights.[43] Doge Dandolo responded by diligently negotiating a new chrysobull with Alexius III in 1198, which affirmed and extended Venetian trading rights in the empire.[44] Although Alexius openly ignored the treaty's provisions, he did resume reparation payments. By 1203, Venice had been reimbursed for about 85 percent of her losses in 1171.[45] Although Venice's position in Constantinople was not ideal, it was very profitable. Dandolo, therefore, had a difficult decision to make. He alone among the crusading leaders had a great deal to lose by steering the crusade to Constantinople. For the possibility of installing a friendlier emperor, Dandolo would have to jeopardize Venice's profitable position in the empire. The risk/return ratio was far more favorable to Venice if the crusade sailed to Egypt as planned. Venetians did only a tiny fraction of overseas business in Egypt, and there they saw an excellent chance of conquering port cities for themselves.[46] In the end, though, Dandolo accepted the arguments of the French leaders that the detour to Constantinople would preserve the crusade. Dandolo knew firsthand the fickle nature of Byzantine politics and therefore considered the prospects of sparking a palace coup in favor of the young Alexius favorable. What neither Dandolo nor any other rational leader considered at the time was the possibility of conquering Constantinople outright.[47] The Fourth Crusade was big, but it was not that big. Those who believe otherwise are guilty of the common historical fallacy of reading an event from back to front.[48]

The opposing faction was led by Simon de Montfort, who, as later in the Albigensian Crusade, saw himself as the staunch defender of papal policy.[49] Some of the knights from Champagne, jealous of the leadership of Montferrat and the money he had received from Count Thibaut's legacy, stood against the German proposals.[50] The churchmen divided along similar lines. Abbot Simon of Loos, a follower of the count of Flanders, was prominent in the party favoring young Alexius.[51] Abbot Peter of Locedio surely followed his lord and friend Boniface, although he was also attached to Innocent and trusted by him.[52] Abbot Guy of Vaux-de-Cernay, follower of the count of Montfort, was chief of the clerical foes of the undertaking. As in his courageous opposition to the attack upon Zara, he conceived himself as representing the papal will.[53] The abbot of Cercanceaux was also of this faction.[54] The five bishops in the army similarly stood on different sides of the issue. Nivelon of Soissons, who had helped to negotiate the treaty of 1198 between Philip Augustus and Philip of Swabia, showed himself later to be favorable to the policy of the Hohenstaufen. He was not, however, in Zara for the debate, since he had gone to Rome in the delegation to the pope.[55] John Faicete, bishop-elect of Acre and chancellor of Flanders, was also in Rome, but later followed Baldwin in endorsing the plan. Conrad Krosigk of Halberstadt, like Abbot Martin, had shown at Venice a fear of ecclesiastical censure for failure to proceed directly against the infidel. Nevertheless, his loyalty to Philip of Swabia remained very strong, and that coupled with the dire necessity of the host led the bishop of Halberstadt to support the German proposal.[56] Bishop Garnier of Troyes may not have been active in the debate, for he was so old that Innocent had sought to relieve him of his crusading vow three years earlier.[57] The only prelate who could be counted upon to oppose the German blandishments was Peter, bishop-elect of Bethlehem.[58]

The greater men thus were deeply divided over the German proposal, and its merits and demerits were argued abroad in the camp. The abbot of Vaux-de-Cernay and those of his party urged that the crusaders should proceed directly to Jerusalem to accomplish whatever they could. In no way would his partisans consent to the German plan.[59] They called to the minds of the crusaders the vows that they had sworn so long ago, which remained unfulfilled. Men could not with impunity forswear those promises made in the sight of God. Their arms had been blessed to fight the infidel, not to shed Christian blood.[60] They may have pointed out that Constantinople had a legitimate emperor, Alexius III, who was on good terms with the Holy See, and there was no acceptable motive for attacking him.[61] To turn from the holy war to seek booty in a Christian city could bring only disgrace. If they did it, they would have to face the wrath of the pope, who possessed the keys of heaven. Moreover, how could they put their trust in the deposed and blinded Isaac and his son? The father had allied with Saladin, greatest of the Muslim foes of the crusade, against Frederick Barbarossa.[62] The son was a refugee without power, money, or subjects, who could only be a hindrance to them. Their strength, moreover, was not sufficient for the task proposed by the German envoys. Constantinople was unbelievably large and massively fortified. It had stood impregnable for nine centuries, it could surely withstand their small force.

Abbot Simon of Loos and those on his side begged that the army accept the proposed treaty in order to survive. The essential thing was to prevent the dissolution of the crusading army.[63] Before his departure from Venice for Rome, the papal legate himself had recognized the overwhelming importance of this objective, to which he had been willing to sacrifice his qualms concerning the attack upon Zara. This faction argued that the crusaders must bow before the ineluctable facts. Their contract with the Venetians for provisions had only about six months to run, and they had not even paid what they already owed. They could not help the Holy Land without money and supplies. Those of their number who had gone directly to Palestine from other ports had accomplished nothing there. Only via Egypt or Constantinople could they aid the Christians of the Levant and fulfill their vows. Alexius provided an excuse to go to the Byzantine capital and an expectation of easy success.[64] Constantinople seemed to them as acceptable a step as Cairo on the way to Jerusalem. The Byzantines had been indifferent to the cause of Christ from the beginning of the crusades and had increasingly become an obstacle to the crusaders from the West. The empire was very rich, however, and if the Greeks under young Alexius would renounce their schism and throw their resources into the common cause, victory over the infidel would be facilitated. Such an outcome would not only save the present expedition, but would establish secure lines of communication and supply for the future. In the circumstances in which they found themselves the offer of young Alexius and Philip of Swabia appeared nothing less than providential. The restoration would not be an end of the crusade, but a means to attain Jerusalem, their ultimate goal.

To some of the pilgrims who interpreted their vows more liberally than others the appeal of Alexius appeared to coincide with their Christian duty. They believed that the young prince was the legitimate heir to the Byzantine throne. Their chivalric code committed them to the defense of the weak and the oppressed, and they were moved by his dolorous account of his treacherously blinded father.[65] They were told, moreover, that Alexius had the support of a large and powerful party in Constantinople, so the crusaders would come to his aid, not as conquerors, but as welcome restorers and liberators.[66] To romantic minds, like the troubadours Conon of Béthune and Raimbaut of Vaqueiras, aiding Alexius could appear a point of honor. Boniface also was no stranger to chivalric adventure. Even most of the bishops accepted the restoration of the Greek youth as legitimate and just.[67]

Whether or not an open appeal was made to the attractiveness of Constantinople as a center for sacred relics we do not know. Since at least the days of the Venerable Bede in the eighth century, however, Constantinople had been known in the West as a holy city, sanctified by its relics, a great center of pilgrimage.[68] The renown of the relics resting in the Byzantine capital had been exalted by the popular legend of *The Voyage of Charlemagne to Jerusalem.* In the twelfth century the imperial capital was one of the holy places listed on the pilgrimage route. The crusaders regarded themselves as pilgrims, of course, and many probably considered the religious benefits to be gained by visiting and venerating so many holy objects.[69]

Certainly the proponents of the German proposal urged the virtue of reuniting the Greek church to Rome. Bishops and nobles joined in their enthusiasm for the return of the schismatics to the true fold and the genuine pastor. It was argued that the pope himself regarded Alexius III as a schismatic and a heretic. Surely he would not punish the crusaders for opposing such a foe.[70]

Still there was no consensus in the host. Therefore, the greatest of the barons, Boniface of Montferrat, Baldwin of Flanders, Louis of Blois, and Hugh of Saint Pol, with a few of their followers who favored the expedition to Constantinople, met once more with the German envoys in the doge's palace and accepted the offer. They would be shamed, they said, if they refused it.[71] Boniface and Hugh would both later claim that they had been moved by the shortage of provisions in the army of which they were leaders.[72] Boniface also professed that he was following the advice of Peter Capuano, the papal legate.[73] The agreement of the Venetians was essential of course, for the army could go nowhere without the fleet. Dandolo had probably already made it known that he was willing to support the Hohenstaufen proposal. The conventions were therefore drawn up, sanctioned by oaths, and sealed. The German envoys, as they had said, possessed full powers to seal the treaty in the name of young Alexius. On the side of the crusaders, not many could be found to support the oaths of the four barons, only eight others, according to Villehardouin, so great was the opposition and apprehension in the army. Among the eight, predictably, was the marshal of Champagne.[74] Throughout his chronicle runs the theme of the necessity of keeping the army intact and the bad faith of those "who wished to destroy it."[75] Whatever the decision of the chosen leader of the army, Villehardouin would follow him, laying aside every consideration, even the fear of excommunication, in the interest of the unity and preservation of the crusade. The treaty to restore the refugee Greek prince was thus concluded, at least with a small group of leaders, and the German envoys, accompanied by two crusaders, returned to their king. Young Alexius was to join the host at Zara before 20 April 1203.[76]

The decision of the Venetians and a few of the chief crusaders to accept the German offer by no means put an end to the debate. There was great dissatisfaction in the camp, especially among the poorer and simpler men, who naturally suffered more from the delays and the financial difficulties of the army than did the rich. They might have borne their privations more readily if they could see that they suffered them in pursuit of their vows, but these seemed as far from fulfillment as ever. Some of the pilgrims, moreover, who had not been able to meet the cost of the journey had been subsidized with funds collected by the church. These had obligated themselves not to return home without letters from the king of Jerusalem, the patriarch, the master of the Hospital or the Temple, or the papal legate attesting that they had performed their pilgrimage to the Holy Land. Otherwise they had to repay the money.[77] This weighed on their minds. The poor crusaders mistrusted the Venetians and their own leaders, all of whom, they were coming to believe, were more interested in material gains than in religious ideals. But discontent was rampant also among the barons themselves. Like the poor, the dissident nobles had not joined the expedition to fight against Christians, but for Christ. They too feared the censure of the church. Some suspected that they had already incurred automatic excommunication for the conquest of Zara, and they were not sanguine about the absolutions they had received from the crusading bishops. Others believed that the proposed intervention in Byzantine affairs was foolish and rash. Alexius would not be accepted with rejoicing, as he claimed, and Constantinople would have to be purchased with the blood of crusaders, if, indeed, they could win so strong and great a city at all. They swore that they would not go to Greece.[78]

Things were not made better by the return to Zara of the crusader envoys to the pope. The had arrived in Rome in the early weeks of 1203 and were admitted to an audience.[79] They begged papal absolution for their sin, which they had committed with grief and was compelled by necessity. According to Villehardouin, they pleaded that the barons had acted "as men who could not do better, given the defection of those who sailed from other ports. If they had not done it, they would not have been able to hold the army together."[80] They were prepared to make amends.[81] If the pope, their good father, would now instruct them, they were ready to do his will.[82]

Innocent was angry. In a letter he wrote a year later to the bishop of Soissons, the pope recalled how severely Bishop Nivelon and his fellow envoys were received by the pope, and how saddened he was by the sins of his sons.[83] Innocent had explicitly forbidden the crusaders to attack Zara, and he learned from the envoys that his instructions were made known to the leaders before the siege began. The Zarans had offered to put the dispute before the pope, and even that was refused. Innocent found it unbelievable that the crusaders could assail walls draped with the images of the cross that they had sworn to protect. The pope accepted the difficult circumstances that led the army to its actions, but that did not excuse the sin. Now, however, the crusader envoys assured him that the host was contrite. Innocent had no desire to destroy the crusade by refusing to forgive them if they were truly sorry for their sins and willing to do penance, and as a priest he had no right to refuse absolution to the penitent. But what of the Venetians? Why were no Venetians sent to ask forgiveness for their greater role in the attack? The envoys responded that the citizens of the lagoon considered the attack to be a justified action to crush rebels in their domain. They would not beg absolution for something they considered blameless. Robert of Boves would not have failed to point out that it was the doge who had demanded that the crusaders attack the city even after the papal prohibition was read by Guy of Vaux-de-Cernay. Without recognizing their sin, showing contrition, or expressing their willingness to make amends, the Venetians were not eligible for papal absolution. Without absolution, the Venetians remained excommunicated.[84]

When three of the envoys returned to Zara, they brought with them two letters and oral instructions given to the bishop of Soissons.[85] They found that events had moved quickly since their departure. The German envoys had come and gone, and the host was horribly divided over the plan to install the young Alexius in Constantinople. The news that the envoys bore could only make things worse. The first papal letter was very harsh, omitting even the customary salutation. Innocent condemned the crusaders for the harm they had done to their vows and the cause of the Holy Land. He was willing to accept that part of the blame lay in the difficulties with which the crusade wrestled, but he stressed that these problems were self-inflicted. He decreed that the absolutions given by the crusade bishops were void, but that he would offer papal absolution if the crusaders showed proper repentance. The leaders were to ask pardon of the king of Hungary and return to him the spoils of Zara. This, in fact, was never done, nor could it be without the cooperation of the Venetians, but at least the pope had required it. Next, the clergy was ordered to inform the rank and file that they were forbidden by the Holy See from attacking any Christians, unless a just cause forced them to do so and then only with the approval of the pope. Finally, the crusade leaders were to send to Rome sealed statements swearing that they would henceforth obey all papal orders. Once this was done, Innocent authorized the papal legate or his nuncio to absolve the penitent by apostolic authority.[86]

While the first letter was for public consumption, Innocent's second letter was likely aimed at the lay and clerical leaders.[87] Innocent was faced with a grave problem by the Venetians' refusal to accept the sinfulness of the capture of Zara. They remained excommunicates, and Christians were forbidden from having any dealings with those under the ban.[88] How could the crusade continue if the owners of the fleet were now untouchable? How could one-half of the crusaders have no commerce with the other half? Innocent still held open the possibility for the Venetians to show remorse and, therefore, enjoy the same absolution given to their allies. But if they remained obdurate, the pope gave the penitent crusaders permission to continue to work with the excommunicated Venetians since their fleet was essential to the success of the crusade. Just as canon law allowed family members to remain with an excommunicated paterfamilias, so too, Innocent argued, should the crusaders remain with the doge of Venice, who was the paterfamilias of the fleet. It was a stretch, and Innocent knew it. He, therefore, gave the crusade leaders permission to "dissemble" in their discussions with the Venetians: in effect, telling the Venetians whatever it took to make them deliver the army to their destination. After they arrived, Innocent continued, "you may seize the opportunity to repress their evil."[89] The language is deliberately vague, but it seems to suggest that if the crusaders from the lagoon had not repented of their sin by the time they reached the Levant, the other crusaders were justified in destroying them.[90]

In the same letter, Innocent addressed matters in the Byzantine Empire. He had already heard from Alexius III's envoys of the proposals that the emperor's nephew was making to the crusaders. The pope had proscribed this

scheme once to the young Alexius and twice to Boniface of Montferrat. Innocent's oral instructions entrusted to the bishop of Soissons probably reiter-
ated this prohibition.[91] Nevertheless, Innocent was very aware of the financial
difficulties that might force the leaders to undertake the Constantinopolitan detour. He did not want to hear the same excuse of necessity when the
host again disobeyed him. He, therefore, did his best to ease the constraints.
Stressing his support for Alexius III, Innocent stated that he would write to
"his beloved son in Christ" the emperor instructing him to make provisions
ready for the crusaders as he had previously promised to do. If the emperor
was recalcitrant, however, Innocent left the door open for them to take what
they required by force.[92] "Necessity," wrote Innocent perceptively, "especially
when an important cause is at stake, excuses many things." He did not mean
to grant a right of robbery, but only to tolerate it, "for one cannot escape
grave necessity without great cost."[93] The argument from necessity is dubious and fraught with danger for any meaningful moral code. We must bear
in mind, of course, the enormous value that Innocent placed upon the success of the crusade. He was compelled to choose the lesser evil, as he saw it.
He was no saintly fanatic, but a practical man who knew how to survive and
thrive amidst life's moral ambiguities. The irony and his tragedy is that all his
compromising did not achieve his aim. His moral predicament calls for understanding and compassion—as do the quandaries of Dandolo, Montferrat,
Villehardouin, and the other protagonists who were faced with hard choices.

While the offer of papal absolution was good news for the crusade
leaders, everything else that came from Rome was bad. The leading barons had already committed themselves and the crusade to helping the young
Alexius. It was too late to change their minds without receiving much blame.
There was already a good amount of dissent about the plan among the crusading ranks; if word of the papal prohibition leaked out among the soldiers,
the deal would be ruined. This was Innocent's intention and it is why he
ordered the clergy to preach to the entire host his condemnation of turning swords against Christians. The pope's alternative, to take provisions from
Greek lands, was no help. The crusade had food, at least as long as the contract
lasted with the Venetians. What they needed was money to pay off their debts
and perhaps renew the lease on the fleet for an additional year. The Byzantine prince offered them that; the pope did not. The barons also did not favor
the pope's suggestion that they sail immediately to Egypt or Syria and then
"repress the evil" of the Venetians. An element of greed must also have been
present. The Byzantine prince offered enormous wealth for a simple task: an
offer some naturally found hard to refuse.

The papal correspondence was suppressed.[94] The leaders said nothing more of the advice concerning dealings with the excommunicated Venetians and the pope's prohibition against sailing to Constantinople. None of it reached the rank and file. Robert of Clari was told that the pope had willingly absolved all of the crusaders, French and Venetian alike.[95] Even Villehardouin excised the troublesome status of Venetian souls from his history.[96] The crusade bishops also agreed to refrain from preaching the pope's message as they had been ordered to do.[97] Instead, they and the lower clergy informed the rank and file that the pope actually favored the plan since it would bring the Greek church back into communion with Rome.[98] This was the first time that the bishops chose to ignore or misrepresent Innocent's position in order to further the goals of the crusading leaders. It would not be the last.

Keeping the pope's commands secret only kept the crusaders from instantly refusing to go to Constantinople. It did not convince them to agree to the detour. Despite the efforts of the clergy in commending the plan, there remained a great many who wanted nothing to do with it. Under pressure the leaders granted permission for about a thousand to leave the host and find their own way to fulfill their crusading vows. Orders were then given that no more should leave the camp, but orders could not check the flight of dissident nobles and undisciplined masses. More than another thousand deserted.[99] Many embarked upon merchant vessels, two of which were lost at sea. One of the ships that sank, undoubtedly overloaded with pilgrims, took all five hundred aboard to watery deaths.[100] Other crusaders departed by land through Slavonia, where the inhabitants attacked and murdered many of them, and the survivors had to return to the army at Zara.[101]

One of the leading dissidents, Renaud of Montmirail, with the support of Louis of Blois, his kinsman, was made head of an embassy to the Christians of the Holy Land. Why a member of this faction was entrusted with such a charge is a puzzle. Perhaps the leaders hoped that Renaud would become convinced himself, and then convince his friends, that at that time nothing really could be accomplished in Palestine by the crusading army. They also may have wished to give evidence to the dissidents that the ultimate goal of the expedition, the Holy Land, remained unchanged. At any rate, although Renaud and the knights who accompanied him swore on relics that they would return within fifteen days after delivering their messages, they did not, and nothing more was heard from them until after the conquest of Constantinople.[102]

The famous and powerful Simon de Montfort had also had enough. In his view, the crusade was out of control—or at least out of his control—bending to the will of men with few Christian scruples. He decided to find his own way to the Holy Land and fulfill his vow.[103] Simon, according to Peter of Vaux-de-Cernay, whose uncle, the abbot, was very close to the count, was a man of orthodox faith, a virtuous way of life, and great bravery.[104] What we know of his life and deeds confirms this judgment, but we may also conclude that he was a narrow-minded zealot. It is not absolutely clear when Simon and his followers left the host, but it was probably sometime in the late winter after the conclusion of the treaty with young Alexius.[105] He had made a treaty with the king of Hungary, presumably for safe conduct. Simon's brother Guy and the abbots of Vaux-de-Cernay and Cercanceaux were among the important men who followed him. Enguerrand of Boves, who had opposed the attack on Zara, also defected a little later.[106] According to Peter, Simon de Montfort and his party made their way with great suffering by land up the rugged coast of the Adriatic to regain Italy. In Apulia, Simon hired ships to take his men to Palestine.[107] This was a most grievous loss to the army.

Another serious setback was the failure of the fleet that had sailed from Flanders under John of Nesle to join the army at Venice. The count of Flanders and his allies counted heavily upon it, for it contained a great number of sergeants. The Flemish fleet had arrived safely at Marseilles to pass the winter. Messengers seeking instructions from the count came from there to Zara not long after the debate over the Alexian proposals. Baldwin commanded the fleet to set sail at the end of March to rendezvous with the main body off the town of Modon at the southwestern corner of Morea just before the routes for Egypt and Constantinople diverged. It may be assumed, however, that the messengers carried back to the Flemish fleet news of the decision to go to Constantinople, and that the heated debate of Zara was reenacted at Marseilles. This time, though, those who were determined to go directly to Palestine prevailed, and when warm weather arrived the Flemings sailed for Syrian waters. Villehardouin, always conscious of the diminishing size of the main host, bitterly laments this loss.[108] The total number who abandoned the army at Venice or Zara, or who sailed with the Flemish fleet, he declares, was greater than those who followed the leaders to Constantinople. No good could come of their desertion. The unhealthy climate of Syria proved fatal to some, he says. Others returned home. None accomplished anything.[109]

Not all of those who defected from the army were single-minded zealots for the Holy Land like Simon de Montfort. Some of them, too, like some of those who favored the route of Constantinople, can be charged with confusing lucrative private undertakings with the crusading venture. Walter of Brienne's campaign in south Italy to claim the inheritance of his wife was of this sort.[110] A bizarre private enterprise was pursued by a knight in the Flemish fleet. A daughter of the last Greek emperor of Cyprus of the Comnenian line had been carried off to the West by Richard Lion-Heart. This Flemish knight, a relative of Count Baldwin, encountered her in Marseilles and promptly married her to gain a claim upon the fertile island. Although he was among those who failed to obey Baldwin's order to rendezvous with the main army, Ernoul-Bernard tells us that the knight had every confidence that he would have the support of the count and the Flemings in his endeavor. This reveals a lot about the lack of discipline and fixed purpose in a crusading army. Not only was the commander's order ignored, but it was assumed that he would not mind, and would even assist the private venture. Our ambitious—and naive—knight hurried to Jerusalem to demand Cyprus of King Aimery. "Who is this beggar?" asked the king. "Let him clear out of here fast, if he values his life." And so he did, joining other crusaders in the war between Christian Antioch and Christian Armenia.[111]

Ernoul-Bernard, our source from the Christian community of the Levant, confirms that those who proceeded to Palestine failed to achieve anything, because of the truce between the two religions in the Holy Land.[112] Apart from a few unproductive skirmishes against Muslims, they became entangled in the internecine wars that the Christian states of the East waged against one another. Although their accomplishments were meager or even negative, however, we should not accept Villehardouin's attribution of bad faith to those who disagreed with his party. Most of them were motivated by a strong desire to fulfill their vows, which they interpreted simply and rigorously. When many of those who had gone to Palestine returned home in September of 1204, some of the dissenters most bitterly attacked by the marshal, Simon and Guy de Montfort, John of Nesle, and Robert of Boves, remained in the Holy Land still determined to do their duty for Christ.[113]

While dissenters abandoned the crusade and others wrestled with the moral questions surrounding the trip to Constantinople, the papal legate, Peter Capuano, waited at Benevento. He had left Rome along with the crusade envoys but did not join them on their trip to Zara. Along with Robert of Boves and Martin of Pairis, who were both determined to find their own way to Palestine, Peter Capuano waited in the Italian city for word on the crusaders' reaction to Innocent's letters and instructions.[114] From there he could proceed to an Apulian port to join the army on its journey or sail on his own for the Levant. The pope sent him twelve hundred pounds for his expenses in either event.[115] Only if the army were prepared to obey like the true army of Christ did the pope and the legate intend that the latter should dignify it with his presence. By February or March 1203, word had reached Capuano of the defections in the army, the plan to sail to Constantinople, and the Venetians' continued unwillingness to admit their sin or accept him as spiritual leader of the crusade. He wrote to Innocent requesting further instructions. The pope replied that if these rumors were true, Capuano should go straight to the kingdom of Jerusalem. As for the French leaders, if they had sworn to no longer serve the greed of Venice and to be henceforth obedient to the papacy, the cardinal should absolve them. If they balked at signing oaths of obedience that would bind their heirs, Capuano should do as God inspired him.[116] In fact, the French had not completed all of the requirements for absolution that Innocent had originally demanded: while they had shown contrition and sworn with parchment and seals to obey future orders from the Holy See, they had not asked pardon from Emeric of Hungary nor did they return any of the spoils from Zara.[117] The commitment to follow the directives of the pope did not ring true either, since they were apparently planning to assist the young Alexius. The legate, nonetheless, took what he could get and ordered his envoys to grant full papal absolution to the French. By April, however, word reached Capuano that the rumors were true: the Byzantine pretender was on his way to Zara. The crusade, from his point of view, had run amok. He would not condone its actions by his presence. In late April he sent a formal bull of excommunication of the Venetians to Boniface of Montferrat, and then, along with Martin of Pairis, boarded a vessel bound for Acre.[118] Neither was to rejoin the crusade for one year.

When the bull of excommunication arrived, Boniface gave it the same treatment that the leadership had given to the previous papal missives. He suppressed it. Thanks to the efforts of the bishops who remained, it was generally believed in the rank and file that the pope had absolved all of the crusaders, both French and Venetian.[119] While Innocent had given permission to the pilgrims to travel with the excommunicated Venetians, this would have been cold comfort for many soldiers who would question the legitimacy of a crusade in which one-half of its members were also the enemies of Christ. The bull could only have a divisive effect on the already fragmenting enterprise. Many of the Venetians, too, would have balked at continuing without absolution. Men like Walliame of Gemona had sworn to fight "in the service of the Lord and the Holy Sepulcher."[120] These Venetians fought to save their souls, not lose them. Mindful of these concerns, Boniface entrusted the bull to one of the abbots in favor of the German plan, while awaiting further orders from Innocent.[121] Boniface felt his action was sufficiently justified: the pope had already advised him to "dissemble" whenever necessary in his dealings with the Venetians.[122]

On 7 April, the Monday after Easter, the winter having drawn to an end and the season for sailing at hand, the crusaders evacuated Zara and encamped near the harbor, while the Venetians leveled the city to its foundations. No more, they vowed, should pirates from Zara oppress Venetian shipping in the Adriatic. They destroyed not only fortifications, but palaces and other build-

ings, leaving only churches and bell towers above the rubble, calling no one
to worship, presiding over a dead city.[123] Not long afterwards Dandolo's son
sent a force from Venice to build a castle on the island called Malconsiglio to
stand as a permanent outpost against Zaran piracy.[124]

Young Alexius was expected to join the crusaders at Zara by 20 April.[125]
The leaders, having made their decision, were eager to get the army underway.
Soldiers become restive unless they are making recognizable progress toward
a goal, and the bitter dispute over the crusade's course had left many of them
in a mood to desert. So, when the date of Alexius's expected arrival came
without the appearance of the prince, the fleet was ordered to sail for Corfu,
leaving Dandolo and Montferrat behind at Zara to await him.[126] The chronicler of Halberstadt tells of the fleet's stop at Ragusa where Bishop Conrad
met a hermit who prophesied the capture of Constantinople and its subjec-
tion to the crusaders.[127] About 1 May they reached the Greek island where
they were to await the others. They pitched their tents and pavilions in front
of the city and led the horses out of their transports to graze on fresh grass
and to exercise. There they remained for three weeks awaiting their leaders
and the Greek pretender.[128]

At Zara, meanwhile, the marquis and the doge expected day by day the
coming of Alexius. On 25 April he arrived and was received with great joy and
what solemnity the small number of those remaining there could muster.[129]
They promptly set sail before a favorable wind to rejoin the host. At various Greek ports along the way, such as Durazzo, the western terminus of the
ancient road from the Adriatic to the Bosporus, they stopped to claim the
citizens' allegiance to the pretender.[130] Late in May they cast anchor before
Corfu. When the chief men in the camp heard that their claimant was at hand
they hurried to the shore to greet and honor him. The common soldiers too,
of course, flocked to see the young prince who had been the cause of so much
debate among the leaders. Alexius took great pleasure, not only in the honors that were paid him, but in the power of the host that he beheld. His tent
was raised in the place of honor and security in the middle of the camp, right
beside it, the tent of the marquis of Montferrat, into whose care the German
king had commended the youth.[131]

The crusaders were initially well-received on the island. Nevertheless,
there arose an incident that foreshadowed the acrimony to come, not only at
Corfu, but at Constantinople. As the anonymous chronicler of Halberstadt
reports it, the archbishop of Corfu had invited some of the Latin clergy to
lunch, presumably including Bishop Conrad. As might have been expected
where churchmen from the East and West were gathered, the subject of papal
supremacy came under discussion. The Greek prelate commented wryly that

the only justification for Roman primacy that he could see was that Roman soldiers had crucified Christ.[132] This small incident gives a hint of the Greek attitude toward Rome. The Byzantine church would never accept the submission to the pope that Alexius, who lacked authority and responsibility to match his ambition, had so glibly promised. The pretender's appearance at Corfu, in fact, aroused violent resistance. The natives shelled the Venetian armada with their petraries, so that the ships had to withdraw from the harbor in haste with large stones splashing in the water about them. In revenge, the Latins laid waste to at least part of the island.[133] If the crusaders could sense in this conflict only the isolated perversity of Corfu, the historian, who has the advantage of hindsight, can easily discern the real depth of the bitterness between East and West and the hostility that any Latin-supported pretender would enkindle among some Byzantines.[134]

Although a few of the chief men of the crusade had sealed convenants embodying the plan to place young Alexius on the Byzantine throne, this project still had very little support among the other leaders and the lesser knights and ordinary crusaders. The issue was by no means settled. The pretender sought to appeal to the compassion of these rough warriors, who were accustomed, as we have seen, to be easily moved to weeping and other signs of emotion, by appearing before them as a supplicant begging their aid on his knees.[135]

Alexius's performance had the opposite of its desired effect. For many in the ranks, the plan was still a lark, a loose proposal favored by the highest barons but not endorsed by the crusade. When they saw the Byzantine prince himself begging for their aid, they were determined to put a stop to the plan. They shouted their disapproval, which prompted shouts from those who favored the plan. But the dissenters were in the majority. Rather then engender support for the Constantinopolitan plan, Alexius's speech allowed the opposition to rise up and speak with one angry voice. According to Robert of Clari they cried, "Bah! what have we to do in Constantinople? We have our pilgrimage to make, and also our plan of going to Babylon or Alexandria. Moreover, our navy is to follow us for only a year, and half the year is already past."[136] The proposed enterprise was fraught with peril. It was not their fault if a few barons had placed their seals on a ill-conceived treaty. The majority had made it clear when the German envoys arrived in January that they would not join this effort. If the barons who had sworn to assist the pretender felt that they must go to Constantinople, then Godspeed. The majority would remain at Corfu and send word to Walter of Brienne in Apulia that he should send ships to bring them to Brindisi to join him.[137] After seven months the crusade was still little nearer than Walter's forces to the goal of Jerusalem. To proceed to Apulia would not represent much of a reversal. Even Villehardouin, who had every reason to minimize this opposition and fix the blame upon a few malcontents, admits that more than half of the crusaders refused to follow the official leadership—one more sign of the chronicler's essential veracity.[138] Now the leaders were faced not merely with defections that weakened their army, but with its utter collapse.

The leaders, and above all Boniface of Montferrat, used every imaginable argument to win supporters to the cause of Alexius. They tried in vain to persuade the army that it was profitless and dangerous to go to Jerusalem. They were short of money and supplies. The chief men could not pay their knights and sergeants or afford the construction of additional machines of war.[139] The clergy, seduced perhaps by the hope of rich Byzantine sees, tried to convince the crusaders of the justice of the undertaking. They declared that the enthronement of young Alexius, who had been wronged by his uncle, was a righteous cause, as was the unification of the churches under Rome.[140] Constantinople, moreover, the home of sacred relics since the days of Constantine's mother, Saint Helena, was a worthy goal of pilgrimage. Religious benefits could be gained without sacrificing those already possessed as crusaders.

To no avail. The dissident majority withdrew from the camp before the city and pitched their tents in a valley at a distance, firmly intending to send word to Walter of Brienne that they were prepared to serve him. The situation was desperate, the leaders' plans lay in ruins, the crusade had essentially dissolved. Boniface urged those who favored the Constantinopolitan plan to go to the camp of the dissidents and to beg them humbly, for God's sake, to have pity on the army and not to dishonor themselves by being responsible for the failure of the crusade. So the leaders of the expedition, along with Alexius and all the bishops and abbots, went together to the valley where the dissidents were encamped.[141] When they arrived, they dismounted, and the dissidents, who were also mounted, possibly even fearing attack, also descended from their horses to greet their comrades. The leaders then fell to their knees protesting with many tears that they would not rise until those who had withdrawn would promise not to abandon the army. According to Villehardouin, the dissidents had great pity on the suppliants, as well they might, seeing their own lords and their relatives and friends there weeping at their feet. So they agreed to talk it over among themselves, and they withdrew to a distance. After some discussion, they told the marquis and others of his party that they would agree, after all, to go to Constantinople, on condition that they should remain there no more than a month unless they consented to an extension of time. One of the concerns that the majority had expressed was the ticking away of their lease on the Venetian vessels. The proposed trip

to Constantinople would likely consume the remainder of that lease. Therefore, the dissidents demanded that the leaders swear on the Gospels that at
any time after the expiration of the Treaty of Venice on Saint Michael's day,
29 September, they would provide ships for transportation to the Holy Land
within fifteen days after they were requested. The leaders joyously accepted
these terms, but pointed out that they should (as was becoming customary)
keep secret the one-month limit on their stay at Constantinople. If it became
known to the Byzantines it would only encourage opposition to the young
Alexius. Those who wished to push on to Jerusalem, however, were adamant,
and so the terms of the agreement were made public.[142]

The army was saved from its latest crisis and its gravest so far. They
would go to Constantinople to gain the throne for Alexius and to obtain the
money, troops, and supplies he promised for the recovery of the Holy Land.
The young prince was required to swear upon relics that he would keep his
convenants.[143]

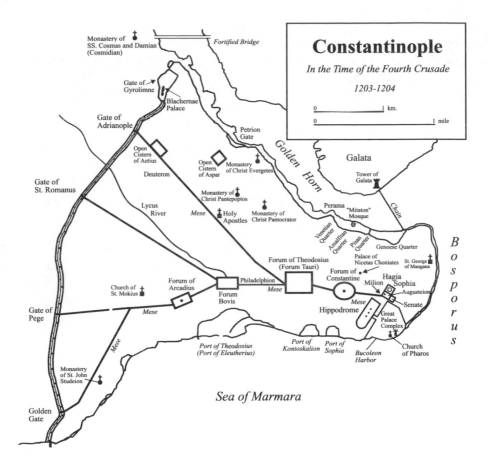

Constantinople

In the Time of the Fourth Crusade

1203-1204

0   1 km.

0   1 mile

Monastery of
SS. Cosmas and Damian
(Cosmidian)

Fortified Bridge

Gate of
Gyrolimne

Blachernae
Palace

Petrion
Gate

Golden Horn

Galata

Gate of
Adrianople

Open
Cistern
of Aetius

Open
Cistern
of Aspar

Monastery
of Christ Evergetes

Tower of
Galata

Deuteron

Perama

Mitaton"
Mosque

Chalti

Gate of
St. Romanus

Monastery of
Christ Pantepoptos

Venetian
Quarter

Lycus
River

Mese

Holy
Apostles

Monastery of
Christ Pantocrator

Amalfitan
Quarter

Pisan
Quarter

Genoese Quarter

Forum of Theodosius
(Forum Tauri)

Palace of
Nicetas Choniates

St. George
of Mangana

Church of
St. Mokius

Forum of
Arcadius

Philadelphion

Forum
Bovis

Mese

Forum of
Constantine

Milion

Hagia
Sophia

Augusteion

Senate

Gate of
Pege

Mese

Mese

Hippodrome

Great
Palace
Complex

*B
o
s
p
o
r
u
s*

Mese

Monastery
of St. John
Studeion

*Port of Theodosius
(Port of Eleutherius)*

*Port of
Kontoskalion*

*Port of
Sophia*

*Bucoleon
Harbor*

Church
of Pharos

Golden
Gate

Sea of Marmara

7

The Taking of the
Tower of Galata

That necessity that is said to know no law had once more prevailed, and on 24 May, the eve of Pentecost, the fleet bearing the crusading host turned its prows toward the Christian capital on the shores of the Bosporus.[1] It was a beautiful day with bright sunshine and a gentle, favoring wind. The pilgrims committed themselves to the protection of Saint Nicholas of Bari, the protector of those who voyage by sea, and the Venetians set their sails to catch the breeze.[2] The usually reserved marshal of Champagne tells enthusiastically of the beauty of the spectacle. The water was crowded with galleys, transports, horse transports, and merchant ships that had joined to take advantage of the escort; their sails filled the sea from the shore to the edge of the horizon. The hearts of men rejoiced at the sight. The mind of Villehardouin, however, never dwelt for long upon pure spectacle, but always returned promptly to practical matters. This thing of splendor, the host of dancing sails moved gently by wind and wave, seemed to him, as it was, an instrument fit for conquering lands.[3]

While imposing and awe-inspiring, the crusader fleet was still bound for Christian, not infidel lands. Back in Rome, Innocent had already learned from his legate, Cardinal Capuano, that the crusaders were headed for Constantinople. On 21 April the pope had written to Capuano expressing his anger that the crusaders had agreed to help the young Alexius despite his warnings.[4] Although Innocent still had some hope that the barons would honor their sealed oaths to obey papal directives, it was becoming painfully clear that the pope had little control over his crusade.[5] The leaders, while apparently determined to push on to the Holy Land, were just as determined to have the help promised by young Alexius to reach that goal. That Innocent ordered his legate to sail to Syria without an army reveals much about the pope's thinking in the first days after he learned of the impending detour to Byzantium. Capuano was a legate to the Fourth Crusade, not the Latin Kingdom. His departure for the Levant was not an abandonment of the enterprise, but rather a temporary removal of papal sanction while the crusade again acted outside its spiritual mission. If the pope could not stop the crusade from sinning again, at least he could put his legate in a position to forgive the transgression when the host finally arrived in the Holy Land. In the meantime, Innocent would remain silent—allowing to happen what he could not prevent.[6]

Sometime in May or June 1203, probably earlier rather than later, Innocent changed his mind and wrote directly to the crusade leaders to forbid the trip to Byzantium. As with the letter after the fall of Zara, Innocent omitted the customary salutation. He told them that he was deeply grieved for himself, for the crusaders, and for all Christendom. In their repeated disobedience, the crusaders were harming all three and aiding the infidels whom they had sworn to fight. The barons had repented of their sins and solemnly bound themselves and their successors to obey the Holy See. Innocent warned them not to return to their previous sins like dogs returning to their own vomit. The pope knew the rationalizations that the crusading clergy was using to promote the Constantinopolitan venture, and he addressed them directly: "Let no one among you rashly convince himself that he may seize or plunder Greek lands on the pretext that they show little obedience to the Apostolic See, or because the emperor of Constantinople deposed his brother, blinded him, and usurped the empire." While unjust, these were not the crimes that the crusaders had sworn to avenge. Rather, their duty was to punish the greater injuries to the crucified Christ. Innocent wanted to hear no more of these frivolous side issues or fake necessities. If it was wealth they wanted, let them take it from the infidel, not their Greek brethren. Innocent was also displeased by Boniface's decision to suppress the excommunication of the Venetians. He ordered the leaders to publish the bull lest they share in the ban.[7]

Great scholarly controversy has swirled around the dating of this letter that so clearly forbids the voyage to Constantinople. Since it was made at the summer residence it could not have been sent before 7 May and could even have gone out as late as July. August Potthast tentatively dated it to 20 June, which has become the standard date; Jules Tessier put it in the second week of May, which has gained more recent acceptance.[8] Whether May or June, the letter was still late. Innocent knew of the decision to assist Alexius in April, but he waited for at least two weeks to send the letter forbidding the action. Why? Some see sinister motives in the delay, arguing that Innocent, in fact, favored the journey to Constantinople, longing for reunification of the Church, but unable to openly support it. According to this theory, he waited until he was certain that his prohibition could not reach the host in time and then sent the missive only "for the record."[9] Others believe that while Innocent sincerely opposed the plan to enthrone Alexius, he was nonetheless willing to turn a blind eye if it would materially help the crusade on the way to Jerusalem.[10] The tardy prohibition, therefore, expressed the pope's true position, but did so in a way that it would have no effect. Still others argue that the lateness of the letter was due to other factors, such as uncertainty in the curia concerning the acceptance of the Alexian plan or hope that the French would change their minds.[11]

None of these arguments sufficiently explain the delay. Innocent had enough experience with the crusade leaders to know that they were keeping his directives from the rank and file. His prohibition of the attack on Zara had done little, and his later condemnations, orders, and excommunications had been suppressed. This letter forbidding the detour to Constantinople would surely also make it no farther than the eyes of the barons and bishops, after which it would be filed with the other papal missives kept secret from the host. That, in fact, is what happened when the letter eventually arrived. If Innocent wished to condemn the voyage to Constantinople only "for the record," he would have done better to have dashed off his letter in April. The crusade leaders could just as easily suppress this letter in spring as they could in summer. As it stands, sending the letter in May or June actually marred the record, creating the present controversy about Innocent's motives. A better explanation of the delay is that Innocent experienced the same moral uncertainty and conflict that plagued the crusaders on Corfu. In April he was willing to avert his eyes from the venture, ordering his legate to await the host in the Holy Land where they would again take up Christ's cause. Weeks later he thought better of this strategy of silence. It was his responsibility as pope to condemn this prostitution of the crusade, to make clear to the leaders that he did not support this plan, and to inform them of the peril to their souls. He surely suspected that the letter, whenever it arrived, would have little effect on men who had repeatedly ignored his commands. The lateness of the letter tells us nothing about any secret papal agenda for Constantinople, since its earlier dispatch would have had the same result. Instead, the delay points to the complexity of the moral issues that the Vicar of Christ as well as the commanders in the field found difficult to resolve.

The fleet sailed for Byzantium, and none could have wished for a more fortunate journey. The canvas bulged before a favoring breeze bearing the Western warriors south along the Greek coast. As they rounded Cape Malea they met two ships filled with pilgrims returning from Syria, among whom were some of those who had sailed from Marseilles rather than join the main body of the army at Venice.[12] Like others who had proceeded directly to the Holy Land, they had encountered a serious plague at Acre. They had soon despaired of the arrival of their comrades from Venice and had decided to return home. According to Villehardouin, who was prejudiced against them, they were so ashamed that they did not want to make themselves known to those whom they had betrayed. Count Baldwin, however, sent the small boat from his ship to inquire who they were, and they replied. One sergeant jumped over the side of his ship into the small boat. He shouted back to his companions on board: "You men can do what you like with anything I've left behind. I'm going with these people, for it certainly seems to me they'll win some land for themselves." The crusaders naturally rejoiced over this prodigal son, returned to his duty.[13]

After passing Malea medieval ships hugged the Greek coast, sailing north before turning northeast past the islands of Idhra and Ayios Eoryiose and entering the Gulf of Euboea.[14] The crusade fleet continued to Negroponte on the island of Euboea, where the young prince received the submission of the inhabitants. The barons then held a council and decided to send Alexius with a large part of the fleet under the marquis of Montferrat and the count of Flanders southward again to the island of Andros to gain its adherence to their cause. When they landed there the knights armed themselves and ravaged the land until its people surrendered to the pretender. They provided him with money and goods, and the ships filled their water barrels from the island's abundant springs. Then they sailed off once more to rejoin the remainder of the fleet. On this voyage they suffered the loss of Guy the castellan of Coucy, who was buried at sea.[15]

The portion of the fleet that had remained at Negroponte sailed northwest along the Gulf of Euboea, then turning to the northeast to pass through the straits of Trikeri and out into the Aegean.[16] Passing the island of Lemnos, they entered the Dardanelles, which, along with the Sea of Marmara and the Bosporus, the crusaders called the Straits of Saint George from the monastery of Saint George of Mangana. They found the straits undefended, and the armada sailed up as far as the ancient town of Abydos, a beautiful and well-situated city on the Asiatic side. The crusaders left their ships in the harbor and went ashore, where the people of the city surrendered at once, earning the contempt of Villehardouin for lacking the courage to defend themselves. The inhabitants achieved their purpose, however, for the crusaders placed a guard over the city to prevent looting. The peasants were not so fortunate. Supplies in the fleet were running dangerously low, so the pilgrims spent their time while awaiting the detachment from Negroponte in seizing the harvest of winter wheat, which now stood ripe in the fields.[17] About mid-June at Abydos the two sections of the fleet reunited.[18]

Emperor Alexius III meanwhile did little to prepare for the Latin fleet descending on the capital. By treachery to his brother he had gained rule over a social and political system in decay.[19] Although the overall Byzantine economy was expanding, the process of feudalization and political disintegration was in full swing.[20] Virtually independent political entities had sprung up on both sides of the straits and in the islands. The senate, clergy, and artisans of Constantinople had even refused to contribute to a special fund for defense against the German Henry VI.[21]

Nicetas can find little good to say of Alexius III: he was gracious, approachable, and opposed to cruel punishments and tortures, but he was cowardly and incompetent.[22] Alexius had come to the throne amidst hopes for a warlike and strong rule, but at the test he proved far from valorous. His very coronation was shadowed with evil portents. The horse on which he was to ride to Hagia Sophia reared, casting the imperial crown into the street and almost unseating him.[23] As ruler he surrounded himself with flatterers and calumniators. He had no aptitude for administration, and, according to Nicetas, knew as little of the affairs of the empire, as if he inhabited far-distant Thule.[24] When faced by foreign ambassadors threatening war he relied upon a dazzling show of court ceremonial to overawe them.[25] So had his predecessors, of course, but they had other more substantial resources in reserve. Such successes as he did enjoy were due to a certain subtlety that his enemies called duplicity. He was devoted to astrology like his contemporaries and undertook nothing without consulting the practitioners of this arcane art. It is alleged that he lived in terror of fate's retribution for his sin against his brother.[26] His idleness was made worse by a painful disease, which may have been gout.[27] His wife, Euphrosyne, is said to have deceived him brazenly, making the emperor a laughingstock in the eyes of his subjects.[28]

When Alexius III heard of the reception of his nephew as emperor within the empire he made what preparations he could, but it was much too late. Shaking himself out of his customary lethargy the emperor ordered the imperial fleet prepared for action.[29] What a fantasy! Manuel Comnenus in the mid-twelfth century had been able to put into the water against the Normans a fleet of five hundred galleys and more than a thousand transports.[30] Even in 1171, when Byzantine sea power was again declining before the rise of the Italian maritime states, Manuel was able to assemble one hundred fifty galleys against the Venetians.[31] After the death of Manuel in 1180, however, his successors allowed the fleet to decay. They abandoned the financial burden of it to rely upon hiring pirate vessels, which were then numerous in the eastern Mediterranean.[32] Mercenaries, however, are often unavailable when they are most needed. In 1196 only thirty vessels could be mustered for a campaign against pirates.[33] There were, indeed, a myriad of exalted naval functionaries drawing large stipends for doing nothing. These officers vaunted their proud titles and posed as admirals and captains—but there was no fleet.[34] The keeper of the imperial forests, as if these were sacred groves or the Garden of Eden planted by God himself, would not allow wood to be cut for ships.[35] An even more blatant culprit was the brother-in-law of the empress Euphrosyne, the Lord Admiral Michael Stryphnos, who had chief responsibility for naval affairs. This venal beneficiary of Byzantine nepotism possessed, according to Nicetas, a remarkable gift for turning anchors into gold and ropes into silver. He sold off from the arsenals entire ships, pocketing the proceeds. He had been prosecuted for corruption, but had survived to pull down from power his accuser. The incapable emperor did nothing to restrain these fools and criminals. So, in the spring of 1203, the successor of the Caesars could put into the water only twenty decaying and worm-eaten ships incapable of putting out into the open sea to face the Venetian fleet of some two hundred vessels.[36]

The army was not in quite such a disastrous condition, but neither was it in good order. By the end of the eleventh century, the Byzantine army had been largely replaced with mercenaries or defeated foreigners who owed the emperor military service. The trend was reversed by John II Comnenus and his son Manuel Comnenus, who attempted to rebuild a national army. They instituted the *pronoia*, a grant of land that would provide revenue to pay soldiers.[37] Although the system probably did swell the ranks of the army, it also diluted its quality. Military men, and particularly officers of which Byzantium had an abundance, became more concerned with extracting wealth from their territory than in defending the empire. According to Nicetas, the new practice drove out men who hoped to win honor and glory in war, and drew in the weak, unqualified, and greedy.[38] These men had a natural inclination to put local concerns over imperial orders, thus giving rise to the numerous military revolts that erupted with regularity in twelfth-century Byzantium. Nevertheless, while the Byzantine army was not of the highest caliber, it remained quite large. Alexius III had approximately fifty thousand regular troops under his command in Constantinople alone.[39]

Beyond regular forces, Constantinople was also defended by a variety of foreigners. The Pisans had a large quarter along the Golden Horn very close to the Venetian Quarter. The hostilities between Venice and Pisa in the Adriatic and Aegean were actually reflections of the deeper rivalry between the two commercial powers in Constantinople. Although Alexius III had made concessions to Venice in the chrysobull of 1198, he continued to favor the Pisans. The Pisans, therefore, had a great deal to lose if the Fourth Crusade was successful in installing the young Alexius, who favored Venice. To avoid that prospect, the Pisans stood ready to assist in the defense of the city. Pisan armed forces probably stood at about two thousand men.[40]

Constantinople was also known for its foreign mercenaries. Benjamin of Tudela, who was in Constantinople in 1198, spoke harshly of the citizens of the great city who preferred to hire men from all nations to fight for them, rather than disrupt their luxurious life-styles.[41] Constantinople regularly hired contingents of Slavs, Turks, Hungarians, and Franks (or West Europeans). Altogether, these constituted a sizable defending force. Nevertheless, the importance of these foreigners was still overshadowed by the emperor's famed Varangian Guard.

Originally Scandinavians who came to Constantinople in the ninth century, the Varangian Guard later expanded to include Anglo-Saxon warriors after William's Norman invasion in 1066. By 1203 the Guard was composed of approximately equal portions of both. Varangians typically wielded deadly single-edged axes that they carried on their shoulders. They were also known to use swords. Varangians were fierce fighters, easily the best mercenaries under imperial command. The corps was an extremely elite group, crowned with victories and indispensable in ceremonies. Each member of the Guard took a solemn vow to protect and obey the emperor. That vow ruled them for centuries: it should not be underestimated.[42] A century earlier, Anna Comnena noted that the Varangians "regarded their loyalty to the emperors and the protection of the imperial persons as a pledge and ancestral tradition, handed down from father to son, which they keep inviolate and will certainly not listen to even the slightest word about treachery."[43] One of Alexius III's first actions after seizing the throne in 1195 was to write to three kings of Scandinavia asking for additional men for the Varangian Guard. Guard levels in Constantinople were usually around five thousand men; expecting trouble, Alexius III had requested twelve hundred more. He probably received some, although perhaps not the number he requested.[44] Alexius made good use of the Guard. In 1200 the Varangians put down a popular rebellion led by John Lagos.[45] Shortly afterward, John "the Fat" Comnenus took one of the crowns suspended over the main altar in Hagia Sophia, proclaimed himself emperor, and occupied the Great Palace with a small force. Alexius, who was away at the time, ordered the Varangians to deal with the rebel. They marched on the palace, defeated John's troops, and decapitated the usurper.[46]

With the protection of the massive walls of Theodosius and the presence of defenders who outnumbered the attackers by three to one, Alexius III felt reasonably secure. In the days before the crusaders arrived he inspected the city's garrisons and ordered the houses razed that were built outside the walls to avoid their use as cover for the attackers.[47] From hindsight, Alexius III's meager preparations for defense against the crusaders seem the product of stupidity, lethargy, or both. Certainly that is the way Nicetas Choniates saw things as he looked back on the events that befell his beloved city. But in May

1203, from the vantage point of the imperial palace, things looked very differently. While Alexius III would have preferred to have a fleet, even this was a minor matter. Only a mighty armada could have stopped the large crusader convoy from making its way up the Bosporus. The emperor's strength was in his seemingly impregnable city and its vast military garrison. In the long history of foreign armies that attacked Constantinople before and after 1203, the army of the Fourth Crusade remains pitifully small. The danger to Alexius III was not that the crusaders could take the massive city by storm, something no one considered a serious possibility, but rather that their presence might undermine his administration. What the emperor had to guard against was not the knights of France or Venetian marines, but the assassin in his chambers or the traitor at the city gate.

Once the crusaders had reunited at Abydos they embarked once more for Constantinople. The many sails appeared like flowers blossoming on the narrow straits. Against the stiff current that flows down the Dardanelles the fleet made its way into the tranquil Sea of Marmara. On the eve of Saint John the Baptist, 23 June, they cast anchor before the abbey of Saint Stephen about seven miles southwest of Constantinople. Here they were in full view of their destination.[48] Although Saint Stephen's does not offer the most picturesque of the many panoramas of Constantinople, the crusaders were nonetheless astounded by the grandeur of the scene before their eyes. They had never imagined there could be such a beautiful city in all the world. They had never beheld so many and such magnificent palaces, and the many domes of Orthodox churches were also a strange and marvelous sight.[49] Since they were not mere sightseers, but men with a mission, they were awed by the high walls and loftier towers encircling the city. Constantinople was simply outside the ken of the northerners. The ten largest cities in western Europe would have fit comfortably in the walls of this teeming megalopolis. Here these hardy knights of the medieval world came face-to-face with the still beating heart of antiquity. No man, says Villehardouin, was so brave and daring that he did not shudder at the sight.[50] Robert of Clari was just as stunned by the city. After describing its enormous size and some of its palaces and marvels, Robert finally gave up, saying, "if anyone should recount to you the hundredth part of the richness and the beauty and the nobility that was found . . . in the city, it would seem like a lie and you would not believe it."[51] The population of the city at this time is still in dispute. Scholarly estimates range from two hundred thousand inhabitants to one million. Precision is impossible, but it probably stood at around five hundred thousand souls within the walls in 1203, with perhaps eight hundred thousand if we include the greater metropolitan area.[52] In any event, it was big; so big that Villehardouin was surely not the only one who had the sinking feeling that the host had bitten off far more than it could chew.

After landing, the leaders held a conference to determine what they should do next. There were many opinions, but the doge advised that they must not go overland, for they were again short of food, and it would be impossible to keep the men from scattering in search of provisions. He pointed out the Isles of the Monks (now called Princes' Islands) to the southeast of the city where they should put ashore to lay in stores. These would be much less well defended than either shore of the Bosporus, and so could more easily be seized and used as a base of operations to attack Constantinople from the sea. A regular siege of the land walls, the tactic to which the Western knights were accustomed and which they would have preferred, was impossible, since they did not have sufficient numbers for such a great and well-fortified city. The barons agreed with the plan of the doge and returned to their ships.[53]

On the day of Saint John the Baptist, 24 June, they boarded their vessels, which were now arrayed so finely that the fleet seemed to the crusaders the most beautiful thing in the world. The pennons and banners of all the lords with their lively and variegated colors were unfurled. The shields, each furbished with the arms of its owner, were ranged around the bulwarks like a wall of steel. Each man had looked to his arms to see that all was in readiness.[54] These preparations were not so much for actual battle, although the crusaders were ready if it should be joined, but rather to impress the people of Constantinople. Like all armed coups in Byzantine history, it was important that the Fourth Crusade make clear the mischief that it could cause for the surrounding areas and the disruption it could inflict on daily business in the great city. These factors would be the sources of dissatisfaction that could topple the sitting emperor.

The ships did not sail to the Isles of the Monks as agreed, perhaps because of a strong southerly wind.[55] Instead, they formed a long line, running right under the towering walls of the capital. The galleys led, canvas furled and propelled by rowers, as in combat, followed by the larger transports under sail. Some of the bowmen shot at Greek ships from a distance as they sailed by, but their shots fell short into the water. The sea wall of the city stood right at the water's edge, so crowds of Greeks mounted the walls. Because of the high hills in Constantinople many other citizens could see the impressive fleet from rooftops or even on grassy knolls in the old acropolis (modern Seraglio Point). In a city saturated with spectacle, where the unusual was commonplace, the colorful crusader fleet remained a sight to behold. The crusaders in the ships were likewise struck with awe as they sailed under the domineering sea walls.[56]

Entering the Bosporus they beheld the beautiful scenery along its banks.

On the Asiatic side, opposite Constantinople, picturesque cliffs and gentle slopes alternated. They viewed luxuriant gardens, handsome houses, and magnificent palaces, some of them imperial summer residences, where the emperor was accustomed to withdraw from the noisome city to enjoy the fresh air and the beauties of nature.[57] The fleet made port at Chalcedon across the straits from the imperial city. There some of the crusaders took up quarters in a splendid palace belonging to the emperor, some appropriated houses in the town, and others pitched their pavilions. At the first opportunity they led the horses from their transports to graze and regain the use of their legs. Only the Venetian sailors were left aboard the ships. Foragers were put to work. The country was not only beautiful, but fertile, and the harvest of winter wheat had been gathered and stood in stacks in the fields.[58] From their encampment Constantinople stood in full view at the distance of only a mile. From this vantage they could see the city in its most splendid aspect. Dominating the landscape was Justinian's enormous church, Hagia Sophia, and surrounding it were the numerous buildings of the imperial palace complex, patriarchal palace, and senate. Beyond, the city stretched on as far as the eye could see, bustling with activity. During the day the crusaders could see the colossal equestrian statue of Justinian riding at the top of its monumental column, with the hand of the emperor stretched out toward the crusaders almost as a warning. At night they marveled at the lights of the city, including the dome of Hagia Sophia used as a marker by passing ships, and the lighthouse situated near the port of Sophia.

The rapid current that emanates from the Black Sea and courses through the straits makes it easier to cross from the Asiatic side to Constantinople from above the city, and so the Latins decided to move their quarters another mile or so to the north to the town of Scutari. On the third day, 26 June, the Venetians sailed the ships up the straits, while the crusaders marched by land along the shore. At Scutari the leaders occupied another of Alexius III's summer palaces.[59] Upon learning of the crusaders' movement the emperor arrayed his army on the European side of the straits opposite them to resist an attempted landing.[60]

At Scutari the crusaders waited for the expected palace coup, or at least for word from supporters of young Alexius within the city of their desire to overthrow their tyrant. They were disappointed. In a letter to the West written that summer, Hugh of Saint Pol remarked on how disturbed they were by the silence from the megalopolis. No friend, no relative, no partisan of the young Alexius came to the crusaders to inform them of conditions in the city.[61] They had made this side journey because they believed they would be greeted as liberators and would work hand-in-hand with the people of

Constantinople in removing their usurping emperor.[62] The attack that young Alexius had assured them would be unnecessary now seemed increasingly likely. Looking across at the enormous city defended by its massive garrison and monumental walls, the crusaders felt the grip of fear close around their spirits. They remained at Scutari, waiting for young Alexius's supporters, for nine long days.[63]

Grasping at straws, the leaders began to consider the possibility that no one in the city knew of the presence of the rightful emperor in the crusader camp or that those who did know were fearful about speaking out. In fact, the situation in Constantinople was far more complex. While the young Alexius did have some supporters among the aristocracy, they were a tiny minority. Among the populace, some were concerned about rumors spread by Alexius III that the pretender had promised to lay the Greek church prostrate before the throne of Saint Peter in Rome.[64] Others were prejudiced against the young Alexius because he was making his bid with paid Latin troops, although that was hardly without precedence in recent Byzantine history.[65] Most of Constantinople's citizens, however, did not give the matter too much thought. Whether Isaac II's brother or his son ruled the empire was a matter of minor interest to people who had seen far more drastic changes in leadership in their lives. While Alexius III was in power, and they were not inconvenienced, the people were content to embrace the status quo and, in the bargain, hand the pompous Latins a defeat. If conditions changed, they could change their minds just as quickly. But until then, the people of New Rome were willing to heed the advice Isaac II gave in 1187 when Constantinople was attacked by another imperial hopeful: "remain at home, offering assistance to neither side until the issue is resolved by battle and then submit with the others to the victor."[66]

During this period, on 1 July, occurred the first skirmish between Greeks and Latins. The crusaders had assigned a detachment of some eighty knights to prevent a surprise attack upon the camp and to protect the foragers. While engaged in reconnaissance this party came upon some pavilions pitched at the foot of a hill several miles east of Scutari.[67] This proved to be the encampment of a force of some five hundred Greek cavalry under Lord Admiral Michael Stryphnos. The Latin reconnaissance party drew up in four companies to attack, and the Greeks also drew up in battle formation in front of their tents to await the enemy. Though faced by far superior numbers, the reconnaissance party couched their pennoned lances and rode upon the foe as strongly as they could. At the shock of the first encounter the Greeks broke ranks and fled, led by their commanders, who, according to Nicetas, turned their backs and ran before these "soul-snatching angels" like frightened deer.[68] The crusaders pursued the enemy for several miles before turning back to loot the camp. They gained chargers and other horses and mules, the tents, and other booty. The horses were especially prized, for there were far more men in the host trained for cavalry warfare than there were mounts. When the reconnaissance party returned to the crusaders' camp they were welcomed warmly by their comrades, with whom they shared the booty.[69]

On the following day there appeared at Scutari an embassy from the emperor Alexius III, headed by a native of Lombardy, Nicolò Rosso. He found the barons and the doge conferring at the emperor's summer palace and delivered his letters of credence to the marquis, who gave him permission to speak. Rosso inquired on behalf of the emperor why the crusaders had entered his lands, for he was a Christian, as they were, and he knew that they were bound to deliver the Holy Land, the Holy Cross, and the Holy Sepulcher. If they were poor and needed supplies, he would gladly give them provisions and money, provided that they withdraw from his land. If they would not do this, the emperor would do them harm, albeit reluctantly. He warned the crusaders that he had sufficient power to crush them even if they were twenty times stronger than they were. Conon of Béthune replied for the crusaders. Conon was an older man, like Villehardouin, a member of an illustrious family of Artois, and a relative of Baldwin of Flanders.[70] He was an eloquent and fervent speaker, and shared with the marshal of Champagne the heaviest diplomatic burdens of the crusade. When negotiation was required, Villehardouin usually spoke for the crusaders. When Conon spoke it was in defiance.[71] He said: "We have not entered his dominions, since he has wrongfully taken possession of this land, in defiance of God, and of right and justice. It belongs to his nephew, seated here on a throne amongst us, who is his brother the emperor Isaac's son. However, if your lord will consent to place himself at the mercy of his nephew, and give him back his crown and his empire, we will beg the prince to allow him enough money to live in a wealthy style. But unless you return to give us such a message, pray do not venture to come here again."[72] Rosso replied, of course, that the emperor would do nothing of the sort, and then departed.[73]

Alexius III, like Innocent III, had operated under the assumption that the crusaders needed only food and basic supplies to make their way to Jerusalem. But the web of contracts and oaths under which the Western knights labored made their situation more complicated. The emperor's professed amazement that these soldiers of Christ should come to his domains was, of course, pure subterfuge. He knew full well that they were escorting his well-traveled nephew. But the emperor had also received assurances from the pope that the Latins were forbidden to take up the pretender's cause. By presenting the face of Christian brotherhood and an open hand filled with provisions, the emperor, like the pope, believed the crusaders would abandon the young prince. He learned differently. The crusaders learned something too from the imperial embassy. Until now they could only guess at why the people of Constantinople had not overthrown Alexius III when the fleet sailed into the Bosporus. The possibility that the city was ignorant of the presence of its true lord among the crusaders was ratified by the emperor's envoy. The impression that Rosso gave to the Westerners was that even the usurping emperor himself did not know why the crusade had traveled to Byzantium. Surely, then, the crusaders reasoned, the common people were also in the dark.

To dispel that darkness, the day after Rosso's visit the doge proposed that they take their ward on a galley under the walls of Constantinople, show him to the people, and call upon them to receive their true emperor. This would not only reveal the presence of Prince Alexius to the people, but also provide the cue for the young man's faction to begin the expected palace coup. So the doge ordered ten galleys prepared. Dandolo, Boniface, and young Alexius boarded one, probably the sumptuous vessel of the doge. All the knights who wished to accompany them climbed aboard the other galleys. Under a flag of truce the galleys rowed back and forth under the sea walls, perhaps as close as ten feet at times, displaying the prince to the Greeks and calling for his recognition. They cried out the crimes of Alexius III and stressed that they had not come to do harm to the people, but rather to defend them and assist them in overthrowing their tyrant. They urged the Greeks to take action, but if they refused the crusaders promised to do as much damage to the city as they were able.[74] Their words were well chosen, perhaps by Dandolo, who had sufficient experience with Byzantine politics to understand the mechanics of armed coups. It was essential to make the citizens understand both the goodwill of the army if their claimant was accepted as well as their intention to become a destructive force if he was not.

For once the sagacious Enrico Dandolo had given bad advice. Rather than a popular uprising, the exhibition of the young pretender sparked popular revelry. The sea walls, now lined with people to see the strange sight, exploded with laughter, hoots, whistles, and derisive insults. Despite the flag of truce, each time the galleys approached too close to the walls they were showered with missiles. The crusaders' hopes were dashed by this display. Dandolo and the leaders had seriously miscalculated the response of Constantinople to the young Alexius. That Dandolo proposed the exhibition of Alexius in the first place provides solid proof that the doge, like the other crusaders, believed the young man's assurances of popular support.[75] Putting young Alexius between Dandolo and Montferrat on a conspicuously Venetian vessel was also a mistake. While Boniface's family was well known and generally liked in Constantinople, the same could not be said for Dandolo or the Venetians.[76] Furthermore, since all the ships in the Fourth Crusade were Venetian, this undoubtedly led the average Byzantine to view young Alexius as the Venetian candidate, brought to the city to unseat Alexius III, who favored the Pisans. Surely among the loudest criers on the walls were Pisans, who lived very close to the Bosporus.

The shouting of abuse from the walls was so loud that the crusaders complained that they were unable to make the Greeks understand their reasons for coming to Constantinople. So they returned to Scutari.[77] There was no choice now but to recognize that the prince's party in Constantinople was a figment of the young man's imagination. The assurances of Alexius, his sister, and his German brother-in-law had probably not been consciously false. Philip of Swabia did not know the temper of the Greeks directly, but only through his wife and her brother. Irene, of course, had been long absent from Constantinople, relying for news solely on the optimistic letters of her father and his intimates. We have all seen older and wiser men than young Alexius deceive themselves concerning the measure of their own support. His did not exist. In fact, the overwhelming mood of the Greeks was resentment against a Venetian or papal pawn. The crusaders had hoped that they could use Alexius as the instrument of a bloodless coup d'état. Now they saw clearly that they must risk all in battle.

On the next day, after hearing mass, the leaders of the crusaders held a council of war on horseback in an open field.[78] They had observed that the walls of Constantinople facing the Sea of Marmara and the Bosporus rose almost immediately out of the water, leaving practically no space for attackers to gain a foothold. The tiny shore that existed there was dominated by the towers that projected from the walls, leaving assailants exposed to a rain of javelins, arrows, and stones from above. Any assault upon these walls would also be endangered by the strong current sweeping the ships southward. On the north shore of the Golden Horn, however, where the suburbs of Pera and Galata flourished, there was a larger beach defended only by the strong tower of Galata. The barons agreed that their first objective must be to gain a foothold on this north shore and control of the Golden Horn. From there they could launch an attack upon the city itself.[79]

After much discussion of details they agreed upon an order of battle for an attack the next day. The army of about ten thousand men, not counting the Venetians, was arranged in seven battalions. Baldwin of Flanders received the advance guard since he had under his command the most skilled and numerous archers.[80] A feudal army, while it relied upon the charge of heavily armed knights for the blow-giving victory, customarily tried to shelter that mounted mass behind a screen of infantry until the critical moment. Archers and crossbowmen were especially favored, so that they could soften up the enemy with a shower of arrows and bolts before the chivalric charge. Many of Baldwin's archers were undoubtedly well equipped with iron caps and leather or quilted linen protection for the body, if not chain mail. Less favored infantrymen wore their ordinary clothing, having only a spear or a bow to distinguish them from peaceful pilgrims.[81] Baldwin's brother Henry commanded the second battalion. Hugh of Saint Pol, had the third. The numerous vassals and followers of Louis of Blois formed the fourth battalion. Like Baldwin's, this was an especially strong force. The valiant Matthew of Montmorency had charge of the Champenois and the fifth battalion. Geoffrey the Marshal, of course, was one of the outstanding nobles in this group, perhaps the second in command or a sort of chief of staff.[82] Much has been seen of Villehardouin already as diplomat and counselor, but he was also a noteworthy knight. In him are reflected the dominant values of his age and class. Individual honor, in the sense of renown, was foremost in his mind. "He does ill," he wrote, "who through fear of death does anything that will cause him to be reproached forever."[83] Yet his courage was not of the foolhardy sort, but rather consisted in a firm resolution in the face of peril. It was tempered too by his consciousness of the common good and the practical problems. We find his mind always occupied with plans of operations, alignments of forces, and the availability of supplies.[84] The sixth battalion was composed of Burgundians, while the seventh embraced Lombards, Tuscans, Provençals, and Germans under the command of Boniface. The marquis's battalion was the rearguard. The Venetians, of course, were to be responsible for the fleet, which was so vital to success and the survival of all.[85]

Now it was cried through the host that everyone should arm himself. For the moment, all disaffection with the course of the crusade seemed to disappear. The hour of decision had passed, and the hour of battle was upon them. Now they must either fight or die.[86] If they were successful, their obligation to young Alexius would be fulfilled, and they need only collect their reward and continue toward Jerusalem. Yet the result of battle was uncertain and, indeed, not very promising, and the heart of many brave men trembled at the thought of forcing a landing. The priests among them reminded the crusaders of the imminence of death and exhorted them to cast themselves upon the mercy of God. Through confession and absolution the warriors prepared to face the Eternal Judge. Men also made wills, not only to provide for the disposal of their temporal goods, but to take advantage of a possible last chance to provide for pious works worthy to be weighed in their favor before the throne of judgment. Masses were heard, and collectively and individually the crusaders placed themselves under the protection of the saints, especially those warrior-saints who were known to join miraculously in battle in favor of their devotees. Armed as fully as could be in body and spirit, the crusaders entered the vessels.[87]

Just after sunrise on the fine morning of 5 July the early stillness was broken by the blare of trumpets and the rolling of drums and tabors. When those in Constantinople heard the racket the walls filled with armed men, while householders gaped from their rooftops. The Venetian galleys were moving forward in order of battle, and each towed behind it one of the more unwieldy sailing ships in order to cross over more securely.[88] Presumably this was to take advantage of the greater maneuverability of the oared galleys against the strong current. To Robert of Clari, it seemed that land and sea trembled, and that the sea was covered with ships.[89] The attack was not against the city itself, however, but against the suburb of Galata across the Golden Horn. This was a novel strategy. Constantinople's attackers had always arrayed themselves against the land walls, while the Golden Horn remained a safe harbor for Byzantine vessels. No fleet had ever been successful in defeating the defenses of the Golden Horn; even centuries later in 1453 Sultan Mehmed II would be forced to transport his vessels overland above Pera to bring them into the harbor. Alexius III was determined to keep the Fourth Crusade from being the first to crack that defense. Near the northern shore of the entrance to the harbor, less than a mile from Scutari, the emperor disposed his forces to meet the attack. The crusaders sent barks packed with crossbowmen and archers ahead of the galleys to attempt to clear the shore for landing. As missiles cast by mangonels and petraries on the walls of Constantinople splashed in the water about them the vessels made their way across the treacherous Bosporus without mishap. As they drew near the shore each ship strained to be first to land. When they ran aground the ports in the sides of the horse transports were quickly lowered to form ramps, down which the fully armored knights rode into the water up to their waists, lances in hand. The archers followed the knights, and then the other foot soldiers. As these lesser men clambered to shore they drew up in front of the various battalions of knights in the accustomed formation.[90]

The Byzantines made only a feeble pretense of contesting the landing. Some volleys of arrows were fired from a distance at the knights with their long lances poised for the thunderous mounted charge. When Count Baldwin set in motion his vanguard under the banners bearing the Lion of Flanders, and the other battalions began to move forward after the Flemings, the Greeks quickly turned tail and showed their heels in such precipitous flight that not even the arrows of the crusaders could catch them. The knights chased their fleeing quarry all along the north shore of the harbor as far as the fortified bridge beyond the northwest extremity of Constantinople. Over this bridge the frightened Greeks escaped to the other shore. The warlike Westerners seized the tents and pavilions of the emperor with much booty. Without the loss of a man they had gained the whole north shore of the Golden Horn except for the suburb of Galata and its critical tower.[91]

The crusaders camped on the slope of the hill behind the tower in Estanor, the Jewish quarter.[92] Along with the surrounding shops and homes of Genoese and other foreigners it formed a wealthy suburb of Constantinople.[93] The Venetians urged that they should make an assault upon the tower on the following day, for it was essential to get the fleet out of the unsheltered straits and into the safety of the Golden Horn. The barons realized that any risk to the ships placed them all in mortal danger, so the council of war agreed with the Venetian proposal.[94] The tower was the key to the harbor, for to it was fastened one end of the great chain that barred the mouth. It was a strong fortification, well defended by mercenary troops, the English and Danes of the elite Varangian Guard, Pisans, perhaps Genoese, and others.[95] That night the crusaders kept a good watch, and on the morrow they set up their siege equipment, while the ships bearing petraries moved within range. The engineers prepared to mine the strong walls. Meanwhile the guard within the tower had been reinforced from Constantinople by small boats crossing the harbor. The defenders of the tower made several sorties, inflicting some damage upon the crusaders with their arrows. In response to the last of these, however, the crusaders successfully counterattacked, dividing the enemy force and demolishing it. Many fell bloodily under the lances and swords of the Latins. Others fled in terror into the water of the harbor, where they attempted to haul themselves hand over hand along the great chain to recover the boat that had brought reinforcements across. Many of them drowned miserably in their flight, but some regained the vessels and safety. Others still ran back toward the protecting tower. The crusaders pressed after them so hard that it was impossible to close the gate, so the pursuers crowded in. In hand-to-hand conflict the crusaders prevailed, the tower fell, and its defenders were taken prisoners.[96] Among the attackers, Peter of Bracieux, a tall knight who seems always to have sought the midst of the fray, distinguished himself in the assault. Robert of Clari also boasts of the valor of his brother, the cleric Aleaumes.[97] James of Avesnes, as well, who was perilously wounded in the face with a lance and nearly killed, survived to win an abundant share of the victor's glory.[98]

Now the attackers set about the destruction of the chain that extended, supported by wooden floats, from the tower to what we now call Seraglio Point, barring the mouth of the Golden Horn. Ernoul-Bernard says that it was as thick as a man's arm.[99] The greatest ship in the armada, the *Eagle*, gaining a full head of sail before the wind and the current, ran with its reinforced and iron-cased prow upon the chain, and broke it.[100] Pulling hard on their oars, the rowers drove the galleys into the Golden Horn in the wake of the *Eagle*, and the other transports and horse transports followed. The overwhelming force of the Venetian fleet fell upon the few and dilapidated Byzantine galleys, barges, and light craft drawn up behind the chain. Some were captured. Others were deliberately run aground by their crews beneath the walls, abandoned, and later sunk.[101] The vast Venetian fleet now covered the Golden Horn, safely protected from the elements. The crusaders and Venetians were elated with their brilliant victory. A part of the broken chain was sent as a token to the Christian port of Acre in the Holy Land.[102] For Constantinople, this was a momentous event. Bereft of sea power, the city's secure harbor was now infested by an enemy. Although the walls along the Golden Horn were extremely high and strong, they remained the city's weakest fortifications. More important to the citizens of Constantinople, however, was the enormous amount of damage the crusaders could do to the surrounding areas and even the city itself. The vibrant commerce that took place along the quays and in the warehouses of the Golden Horn, thus giving the harbor its name, was also halted. From the Greek perspective, the crusaders were no longer an oddity or a spectacle, but a real threat.

8

The First Conquest of Constantinople

A council of war held by the magnates and the leading Venetians determined to follow up their advantage with an attack before Alexius III should have time to improve his defensive position. The northern knights and the Venetians, however, disagreed upon tactics. The Venetians favored a water-borne assault across the harbor against the enemy's weaker fortifications. On the side of the Golden Horn the city was protected by a single wall about thirty feet high, flanked, of course, with many projecting towers. The Venetian sons of the sea proposed to attack the heights of these fortifications from bridges mounted upon their ships. The knights on the other hand, naturally preferred fighting on land. The shifting foothold of a flying bridge perched precariously on a ship had no attraction for feudal warriors unfamiliar with the sea. They preferred to attack the land walls, despite the greater strength of these defenses. The disagreement was settled by a compromise: the crusaders would attack the land walls near the Blachernae Palace at the northern apex of the triangle of Constantinople; the Venetians in their ships would assault the nearby harbor walls.[1]

The compromise made the tasks of both Franks and Venetians more difficult. While the northern corner of the city allowed all of the crusaders to fight in their favored element, it also meant that all would have to attack some of the city's strongest fortifications. Armies that attacked Constantinople by land before and after the Fourth Crusade concentrated on the weakest part of the Theodosian walls, called the *Mesoteichion* or middle wall. This portion of the land wall stretched from the Rhegium Gate (modern Mevlevihane Kapı) to the Pempton or Saint Cyriac Gate, also known as the Fifth Military Gate.[2] There the Lycus River entered the city, making a deep moat impossible. The dip in the river valley also put the defenders on the walls at a lower level than the attackers outside.[3] But the *Mesoteichion* was far beyond the northern knights' reach. Marching so far south would allow Alexius III to sally

forth with his superior numbers from northern gates, thus splitting the crusaders in two and cutting the Franks off from their retreat across the bridge.
The Venetians too had to concentrate their attacks along the northern harbor
walls to avoid becoming separated from their allies. The Venetians, therefore,
were forced to attack near the Gate of Petria, which was the only section of
the Golden Horn fortifications protected by a double wall.[4] This combined
operation was not a siege, nor even a full scale attack, but rather a small, concentrated assault on one corner of Constantinople.

With their plans laid, the Latins spent the next four days after the taking
of the tower in preparing for battle, readying supplies, and resting the troops.[5]
On the morning of 10 July the battalions of the crusaders in full battle array
set out in line of march along the north shore of the Golden Horn. They intended to pass over the stone bridge across the Barbysis River where it enters
into the harbor. By this bridge the great city was joined to its suburbs on
the north shore, and by means of it Alexius III and his fleeing troops had
regained the safety of the walls on the day before the tower fell. It was two
or three miles from the crusaders' camp at Galata. When they arrived at the
bridge they discovered that the Greeks had prudently demolished it. The next
crossing was several miles farther upstream, and its use would necessitate the
separation of the army from the fleet, which had followed the troops along
the shore. The crusaders therefore set men to work the rest of the day and
through the night to repair the broken bridge. The next day it was ready for
crossing. The Byzantines ought to have defended the bridge vigorously. It was
long and narrow, so narrow that three horses could scarcely cross it abreast,
and long enough so that its capture against a determined defense would have
been very costly. After their reverses, however, the Greeks had no heart for
battle, and they offered little or no opposition to the crossing. The crusaders
thus passed over in good order and set up camp facing the wall in front of a
hill within the city that had the imperial palace of Blachernae at the base of its
northern slope. The fleet anchored nearby.[6] Here the army and the fleet could
attack almost side by side.

The camp was on a hill crowned by a monastery, which the crusaders
called Bohemond's castle after the bellicose Norman, who had occupied it at
the time of the First Crusade. It was actually the monastery of Saints Cosmas and Damian, or the Cosmidion. Between the two hills and before the
wall was a small valley. Nicetas tells us that the camp was so close to the walls
that the besiegers before the Gate of Gyrolimne could almost converse with
the defenders.[7] Conversation was not the order of the day, however; instead
they fired their arrows at the windows of the palace. The walls of the city, of
course, also overlooked the crusaders' camp, and the defenders returned the

fire.[8] From their camp and especially from the hill behind them the attackers had a view of the awesome city. First, they beheld the formidable walls of Constantinople. These huge fortifications, built by Theodosius II, consisted of a triple wall studded with mammoth towers, allowing defenders to fall back to a higher and stronger wall if one or even two should be breached. No assailant had ever made it that far, however, because of the very wide and deep moat that ran outside the land fortifications. As the crusaders looked south this imposing wall stretched for miles out of sight until it met the Sea of Marmara. But the moat and triple wall were of less interest to the northerners than the larger and newer single wall of Blachernae, which they prepared to attack. While this wall lacked a moat, it was about fifteen feet thick, forty-five to fifty-five feet high, internally reinforced by a buttressing system, and built with larger stone blocks than those used even in the Theodosian giants to the south. Much of this wall had been built by Manuel Comnenus to extend the city's defenses around the Blachernae suburb.[9] Isaac Angelus had further reinforced the defenses of Blachernae with an additional great square tower.[10] Behind the Comnenian wall stretched the old Blachernae wall, which provided an excellent second line of defense.[11] Blachernae was an affluent area, not least because of the vast and splendid imperial palace that dominated the district. Emperors had increasingly favored this residence over the older Great Palace in the southeastern corner of the city.[12] Beyond the palace extended a vista of churches and public buildings, columns, and towers. Far off the great domes of Hagia Sophia hung in the sky.

Because of their decisions, if the crusaders were successful in breaching Constantinople's defenses, they would have found themselves in possession of the Blachernae district, not Constantinople. Blachernae had been incorporated into Constantinople's defenses as an afterthought. Its fortifications were a patchwork quilt of various projects.[13] Although it was now within the city's defenses, its leftover fortifications inside the outer walls made it an excellent stronghold. Much of Blachernae Palace's attraction for recent emperors was its strategic position: flanked by walls and towers, and removed from the tumultuous city center. If the Blachernae suburb were taken, the crusaders could seize the imperial palace, crown Alexius, and use the Blachernae Palace and towers to defend themselves against the Greeks. Rather than camping in the open, the Westerners would hold high ground surrounded by massive fortifications.[14] Dandolo and Montferrat may have felt that such a scenario would spark the coup they anticipated in the Great Palace. In any event, sitting tight in Blachernae was infinitely preferable to advancing into the city where the crusaders could be picked off by soldiers or citizens in the narrow streets of the megalopolis.[15]

Since the besiegers were under fire from the defenders on the walls and sallies against the camp were feared, they set to work fortifying their position. They provided it with earthworks and a palisade constructed of good heavy planks and crossbeams. Then they set up their petraries and mangonels and other siege machinery to pound the walls and the palace, which was seriously damaged.[16]

The Venetians also made ready for the assault. Dandolo ordered the construction of flying bridges on the transports. These bridges of planks with rope railings were suspended from the masts and supported by lashed yards. They hung high above the water before the vessels. The bridge could be maneuvered onto the tops of the walls, making the vessels fast and forming a passage by which as many as three soldiers abreast could advance from the ship to the ramparts.[17] The ships were covered with hides to protect them from the fearful Greek fire, the Byzantine equivalent of the flame thrower.[18] The bridges also were padded with hides and canvas to protect the attackers. Siege weapons were readied on the prow of each vessel to batter the walls and threaten the defenders. From cages aloft crossbowmen also could soften the defense for the swordsmen on the bridges.[19]

Alexius III ordered his archers and artillery to pelt the crusaders' camp, while also sending out sorties from the gates as many as six or seven times a day.[20] In these skirmishes the Western knights had a chance to measure lances with their foes. Nicetas claims that the Byzantines fought well in these engagements.[21] Even at night there was no respite, for the whole camp had to be called to arms whenever one of these sorties occurred. Day and night one of the seven divisions stood guard before the Gyrolimne Gate to protect the siege machinery and repulse sallies. The Latins had little rest, but they did repel the thrusts vigorously.[22] On one occasion Matthew of Wallincourt had his horse killed under him as he bravely pursued his foes upon the very drawbridge before the gate.[23] Peter of Bracieux, whose quarters were pitched right before the gate from which most of the sorties issued, again distinguished himself in combat.[24]

The sallies and the fire from the walls took their toll upon the Latins. Villehardouin tells us that it was impossible to venture in search of supplies more than four bowshots from the fortified camp. Since foraging parties could not function, provisions became painfully short, although there was a sufficient store of flour and salt meat. Fresh meat was completely lacking except for the flesh of horses killed in the skirmishing. Because of their lack of provisions the leaders knew that they could not sustain the assault beyond two or three weeks. They knew that their situation was desperate. As the marshal lamented, "never . . . have so many been besieged by so few."[25]

So on 16 July the leaders decided to assault the city on the morrow. At the break of day the doge prepared his vessels to draw close to the walls on the other side of the harbor and the crusaders arrayed their divisions in the field facing the Blachernae Palace.[26] From the landward side the crossbowmen opened fire upon the wall. The crusaders also drew up a ram in an effort to smash a hole in the fortifications.[27] Three battalions of knights and infantry-men under the marquis of Montferrat stationed themselves before the camp to protect it. The four battalions assigned to the assault under Baldwin of Flanders, his brother Henry, Louis of Blois, and Hugh of Saint Pol hurled themselves at the wall with scaling ladders.[28] In spite of fierce resistance they planted two of these ladders against a barbican close to the sea. From this description it must have been some part of the citadel of Blachernae formed by the Heraclian and Leonine fortifications at the very northern extremity of the land walls.[29] Many attackers were cast down as they strove to mount the walls, their bodies broken as they tumbled from the heights. Two knights and two sergeants, whose names have not been given to us, scaled the ladders and with their swords forced their way, in spite of the blows rained upon them, onto the parapet. They held their foothold tenaciously, while a handful of others succeeded in following them, for a total of about fifteen men. Here they found themselves faced by the select foreign mercenaries of the Varangian Guard and by some Pisans. They fought bloodily, the swords of the crusaders against the dread axes of the Varangians. The efficient savagery of the Varangians drove the Latins off the wall, and two Latins were captured. These were led before the triumphant Alexius III, who was pleased by the ease of his victory. Despite the valor and bravery with which the Franks attacked the Queen of Cities, it remained that they were far too few to do the job. The land attack was an utter failure. Many of the attackers had been wounded or received broken limbs in falls from the scaling ladders. They retreated behind their protecting palisades, greatly upset by their defeat.[30]

The Venetians had more success in attacking the harbor walls. Dandolo had drawn up his ships in battle formation along the shore, a line extending the length of three crossbow shots.[31] From his vermilion galley with the banner of Saint Mark waving proudly from the bow, the venerable and blind doge ordered the attack. To the Greeks within the city, according to the orator Nicholas Mesarites, the water appeared covered with trees bearing baneful and deadly fruit.[32] Upon this forest of masts the defenders showered a torrent of stones from the artillery mounted on the towers, but no ships were lost. The mangonels from the fleet returned the Greek bombardment, and, as the ships drew within range for crossbowmen and archers, bolts and arrows filled the air. The flying bridges from some vessels came so close to the walls that the attackers, suspended precariously in the air above sea and shore, exchanged pike thrusts and sword blows with the defenders. The din was so tremendous, says Villehardouin, that it seemed as if both land and sea were crumbling into pieces.[33]

At first the galleys remained behind the larger vessels. Blind old Dandolo stood in the prow of his galley grasping the staff of the Venetian banner, which, as it is shown on coins and seals, he had received from the hands of the evangelist Mark. He shouted angrily at his men to put him on shore, threatening them with dire punishments if they failed to do so. The oarsmen drove the galleys forward in short and choppy rhythm in a series of leaps, the vermilion galley in the van. Dandolo's was the first vessel to run aground on the narrow strip between the walls and the water, and the men leaped ashore, bearing the ensign of the winged lion before the doge. When those in the other galleys saw their banner on the shore they strained to emulate their venerable leader. The crews of the galleys piled ashore. Under fire upon the narrow strip of beach they raised scaling ladders against the wall and mounted to attack. After a time, amidst the confusion of the fray, they saw the winged lion flying from one of the towers. More than forty men told Villehardouin that they saw it, though none could report who had borne it there.[34] However it got there, the banner stirred the patriotic Venetians to redouble their efforts. The Venetians on the shore also breached the wall perhaps with a battering ram near the imperial landing dock and gained a foothold within the city.[35]

Some of the roundships meanwhile had maneuvered their flying bridges onto the tops of towers. The attackers on the bridges, once these were made fast, had the advantage of height, and the Venetians fought fiercely to claw their way onto the ramparts. Here the defenders were primarily regular Byzantine forces, who lacked the martial skill of the imperial guard. When a large number of Venetians had gained a footing the defenders simply fled, allowing the Venetians to open gates for their companions on the shore. These rushed in, and soon the attackers were in possession of twenty-five or thirty towers fronting the quarter called the Petrion.[36] Since the wall facing the Golden Horn had one hundred and ten towers the Venetians held something like one-fourth of the entire harbor wall.[37] They tried to penetrate into the city, and did gain some booty from the nearby quarter, but met ferocious resistance, probably from the Varangian Guard. Many Venetians were wounded, and they fell back to the wall. The defenders of the city rallied to attempt to retake the captured towers, but were beaten off. Dandolo sent word of his success to his allies, reporting that a large section of wall was held fast, news that caused great rejoicing. The doge even sent horses captured in the city as a symbol of his victory and because of the known shortage of mounts among the Franks. But the Venetians did not dare again advance beyond their section of wall into the city itself.[38]

In order to protect their position the doge's men set fire to the houses near the wall. The same wind that drove the Venetians' vessels onto the shores of Constantinople also fanned their fire into a massive and uncontrollable blaze. From near the Petrion Gate the fire consumed homes and shops along the lower ground along the wall, but was unable to climb the steep hill toward the Monastery of the Virgin Pammacaristos (modern Fethiye Camii). It then raged farther into Constantinople by way of the milder grade in the Petra valley, devastating a wide expanse of the city, and stopping only at the open cistern of Aetius in the Deuteron region. Altogether this tragic fire reduced 125 acres (50.5 hectares) to smoldering rubble, leaving as many as twenty-thousand Byzantines bereft of homes and possessions.[39]

While the hellish fire raged, Dandolo received word from his allies that they were in trouble and needed help.[40] Emperor Alexius had issued from the walls on the landward side of Constantinople at the head of a large force. Everyone in the city had seen the smoke, flame, and embers, and many knew that the harbor wall had been breached by the Venetians. While the citizens of Constantinople were willing to support Alexius III against a rival supported by the Franks and Venetians, they were not willing to see their homes and businesses sacrificed in the process. Amidst the confusion could be heard shouts denouncing Alexius III's negligence and inactivity and vilifying his character. Finally a group of influential men came to the emperor threatening to hand over the city to his nephew unless he would deliver them from the "dogs" who were attacking it.[41]

Alexius had no way of expelling the Venetians from the wall on the Golden Horn while the fire still raged. He therefore decided to draw them away from their positions by attacking their Frankish allies outside the land walls. From three gates, one of which was the Gate of Saint Romanus about a mile to the south of the crusaders' camp, Alexius led the best troops he could muster in an effort to catch the crusaders in the right flank. The emperor commanded an enormous force, probably more than thirty thousand troops, and he arrayed his might in full view of the battered Western knights.[42] The sight was so overwhelming, in fact, that the magnates sent a plea for reinforcements to the doge, who ordered his Venetians to abandon their hard-won towers and go to live or die in an effort to rescue their allies.[43] Meanwhile Alexius marshaled his troops and advanced slowly and in good order. Villehardouin records that the entire plain was covered with the enemy.[44]

One battalion of the crusaders had remained outside the palisade as usual to guard the siege equipment. Now the other six moved out and drew up in front of their fortification facing the enemy to the south, so that they could not be attacked on the flank.[45] Baldwin of Flanders asked for the vanguard, and again it was given to him. Hugh of Saint Pol commanded the second battalion and Henry, Baldwin's brother, the third. The other four under the general command of the marquis of Montferrat were assigned to guard the camp and the machines. They were not to move from their defensive stance unless the battalions of Baldwin, Hugh, and Henry should be threatened with imminent destruction. So they stood quite still in front of the palisade. Each battalion was arranged with archers and crossbowmen in front, then the mounted knights, and behind them three or four companies of squires and sergeants. There was also a company of knights on foot, for a number of them had lost their horses.[46] Robert of Clari tells us that the seven battalions included only seven hundred knights. Hugh of Saint Pol's letter to the duke of Louvain counts five hundred knights and two thousand mounted sergeants.[47] Opposite the emperor's common infantry, which had formed along the wall, and to protect their left, which was now the flank toward the city, the crusaders armed every man possible: horseboys, cooks, and all. These flunkies draped themselves for minimal protection in quilts and saddle cloths. In lieu of helmets they donned pots from the kitchens. They armed themselves with whatever everyday implements lay at hand with which injury could be inflicted, such as pestles and skewers. The Picard knight Robert reports that these lackeys appeared so hideous that the emperor's infantry trembled at the sight of them.[48] Indeed, they must have looked like something out of the fantastic visions of Pieter Brueghel, though we may wonder whether they incited fear or amazement.

For some time the armies stood facing each other.[49] Despite his enormously superior numbers, Alexius III had no desire to risk battle against the French on an open plain. His aim was merely to frighten them into calling the Venetians from their positions on Constantinople's walls, something they did with alacrity. Robert of Clari gives a colorful account of the skirmishing that followed. The Picard knight did not really understand all the ramifications of what was going on, but he reports what he saw before his eyes and what he garnered from his companions in the ranks. His account also offers valuable insight into the minds and mores of the crusaders. He tells how two of the worthiest and wisest were appointed in each of the crusaders' attack divisions to pass on the commands. If they shouted "Spur!" all should spur. If they commanded "Trot!" all should do that. The count of Flanders, who had the honor of leading the attack, rode forward with his battalion. The battalions of Henry of Hainaut and Hugh of Saint Pol fell in behind him. Robert marvels at the glorious sight of the knights with their colorful shields and their horses all caparisoned with cloth of silk and coats of arms. They moved forward at first in a tight, disciplined formation, a feat that feudal armies were often unable to achieve, since glory-hungry knights often dug their spurs into the flanks of their horses prematurely to gallop out ahead of their comrades and get themselves killed. At the tails of the tight ranks of horses advanced the companies of infantry. The Byzantine emperor rode to meet them with nine battalions, each of which, according to Robert, was much larger than the battalions of the crusaders. When Baldwin's contingent had ridden two bowshots from the camp, his advisers warned him not to go farther, for the crusaders in reserve before the palisades would not be able to come to his aid in case of need. They counseled that he return to the camp and await the attack of the emperor there. This seemed good advice to the count, so he turned his battalion around, and his brother Henry did the same. But the count of Saint Pol and Peter of Amiens and others in their battalion did not want to turn back and came to a confused halt in the middle of the field. Their pride would not allow them to retreat. In their eyes the count of Flanders, who had requested the vanguard, had acted shamefully. They shouted to their men: "Now that he draws back, he leaves you the van, so let us take it, in God's name!" When the count of Flanders saw that Hugh's battalion had not followed him, he sent word beseeching them to do so, but Peter of Amiens replied that they would not. A second time Baldwin pleaded with them to follow his example, but again the counts of Saint Pol and Amiens refused. Then Peter and Eustace of Canteleux, the two assigned to issue the commands in that battalion, ordered the company to resume the advance at a trot. The crusaders guarding the palisade saw all this, and they cried out: "Look, see! The count of Saint Pol and my lord Peter of Amiens mean to attack the emperor! Lord God," they cried, "Lord God guard them this day and all their company. Look! They have taken the van that belonged to the count of Flanders. Lord God, bring them to safety." Robert, who was probably himself in the ranks following Peter of Amiens, cannot resist remarking that the ladies and maidens of the palace were watching from the windows and others from the walls. He imagines them saying to one another, for it is his own image of himself and his companions that we read here, that the crusaders looked like angels, they were so beautifully and finely armed, and their horses were so magnificently accoutered.[50]

The knights in Baldwin's battalion were not now enjoying the glow of vanity felt by Robert and his fellows who had refused to turn back. They charged Baldwin with shame at failing to advance and threatened to withdraw their allegiance from him if he did not at once resume the attack. Baldwin was no coward, and as soon as he heard these words he spurred his charger forward, and his knights spurred after him. They pulled abreast of the count of

Saint Pol's battalion with Henry's battalion riding after them. Now the opposing forces came so near that the archers and crossbowmen exchanged fire.
The crusaders were coming up a small rise of ground that lay between them
and the enemy. When the emperor saw them appear over the crest of the rise
he ordered a halt. The imperial forces that had been sent to try to surround
the camp of the crusaders rejoined him there. The Latins also came to a halt
at the top of the ridge. Via messengers the leaders of the three crusader battalions took counsel. They were far from their camp and their companions, and
if they advanced beyond the rise they would be out of sight of their friends,
who would not be able to aid them. Moreover, between them and the emperor's forces there was the Lycus River, and crossing it would be dangerous.[51]

While the crusaders were considering what to do, the emperor also had a
decision to make. According to our Latin sources, he was overcome with fear
of the courage, size, and strength of the Latins, and it is true that the Greeks
had an acute awareness of the "irresistible first shock" of the feudal charge of
Western knights. Anna Comnena had written long ago that a Frank on horseback "would make a hole through the walls of Babylon."[52] So Alexius declined battle and turned his forces back into the city.[53] Raimbaut de Vaqueiras
boasts, "We were hawks and they were herons, and we chased them as the
wolf chases the sheep,"[54] but actually the crusaders did not cross the stream
to pursue their foe, fearing a trap. Robert reports that Alexius was blamed by
the ladies who were watching and by one and all for his failure to join battle
with his greater forces against the puny numbers of the attackers.[55] This again
reflects the Picard knight's simplistic understanding of events. Alexius III retreated into the city because the objective of his sortie had been achieved: the
Venetians had abandoned the harbor walls to assist their allies. Had it been
the emperor's intention to fight the Western knights he would not have arrayed his forces below the Lycus River nor would he have waited while the
crusaders arranged themselves into battalions and planned out their strategy.
Byzantine emperors defending the city against imperial rivals were not in the
habit of forfeiting their tremendously fortified position in Constantinople for
the honor of meeting their rivals in pitched battles on open plains.[56]

In spite of some temporary successes, the attack upon the city was a failure. Villehardouin reveals the sense of peril among the crusaders. At day's
end, as they removed their armor, they were weary and overwrought. They
ate and drank sparingly, because they were short of supplies.[57]

The retreat of the imperial forces created within Constantinople a great
clamor against Alexius III.[58] The scope of the devastation left by the Venetians' fire enraged those who had lost their homes and possessions, and
profoundly disturbed everyone else.[59] Never before had an armed rebellion

caused such damage to the great city. Many began to favor accepting the claims of the young Alexius rather than remaining loyal to Alexius III and suffering further destruction. When the emperor had sallied forth from the city with so many troops, a great many Greeks believed that he would make the Latins pay for their injury to Constantinople. Alexius III's tactical maneuver to make the crusaders believe that he would attack them on an open plain also fooled many Byzantines, who were embittered and ashamed when they saw the pride of Byzantium retreat into the city amid scornful cries from the Latins. And so the emperor had managed to alienate both the aristocracy, who wanted no more damage done to their city in defense of Alexius's administration, and the common people, who despised their emperor's cowardice and were humiliated by the Latins' insults. When he returned to his palace, Alexius feared that his time on the throne was limited.[60] As one who had himself led a coup, he knew what they smelled like. While he tried to patch things up by proclaiming his firm intention to destroy the insolent Latins on the morrow, it was clear that he might never get that chance.[61] Angry troops on the walls could now more easily be bribed by Latins or Greeks into ending this argument between Alexius and his nephew by simply opening a gate and allowing the crusaders to enter. The Varangian Guard could not be everywhere. Alexius III must have shuddered to think what would happen to him if he was captured by his nephew and brother. Blinding would be only the beginning. When Isaac II had led his palace coup against Andronicus I, he had horribly tortured the old emperor, giving him over to the people, who ended his life, as Donald Nicol says, "with a frenzied and horrible bestiality unparalleled even by Byzantine standards."[62] How much worse Alexius III would fare after all the injuries and betrayals he had heaped on Isaac! Far better to put as much distance between himself and Constantinople as possible.

Near midnight Alexius secretly fled the city, professing to follow the example of David, who had found safety in flight from Saul. He also imitated Moses fleeing Egypt, for he took with him a thousand pounds of gold and as many precious stones and shining pearls as he could. His favorite daughter, Irene, some other relatives, and his choice concubines accompanied him. He left behind the empress Euphrosyne and another daughter, Eudocia.[63] Alexius had had troubles with Euphrosyne before, but they seem to have patched things up by this time. Several years earlier, when Alexius was on campaign, the empress's brother and son-in-law had accused her to the emperor's face of dishonoring his bed like a whore, and they expressed fear lest she help her lover to usurp the throne. As a consequence, the alleged lover was assassinated, and Euphrosyne had been compelled to plead with friends of the emperor to save her, not only from public dishonor, but from death. After a brief exile in a convent, she was restored to her position.[64] The anonymous chronicler of Gaeta, on what grounds we do not know, states that she had a hand in the flight of young Alexius in 1201.[65] A third daughter, Anna, the wife of Theodore Lascaris, also remained behind with her brave husband.[66] The fleeing emperor and his entourage hurried to a prepared refuge at the town of Develtos a hundred miles to the north near the Black Sea.[67]

Although Alexius had fled Constantinople, he was by no means relinquishing the crown. Careful to bring the imperial regalia with him, Alexius III would continue to rule in various provinces, always claiming to be the true emperor of Byzantium, until 1211. The large sums he took with him were not for strictly personal use, but rather to raise additional troops to defend his rule.[68] The family members he left behind were not unknowing victims of his cowardice, but rather proxies who were to administer Constantinople and direct its defense during his absence. This was not the first time the empress Euphrosyne had exercised power to maintain order. Theodore Lascaris, Alexius III's heir to the throne and later the first emperor of Nicaea, was to act in the emperor's stead, and in so doing make crystal clear to the aristocracy that Alexius, his family, and his faction were still in power.[69]

But not all of the aristocracy saw things as did Alexius III. Some worried that once the enemy outside the walls learned that the emperor had fled they would resume the attack. The emperor's retreat the day before and the discovery of his flight the next morning led many to believe that he had forfeited his position. His actions seemed foolish at best and treasonous at worst. Why should the capital accept an emperor who feared capture so much that he left their defense to his heir? If he was unwilling to endure the crusaders' attacks, why then should the people of Constantinople? The claims of authority by Theodore Lascaris fell on deaf ears. He and the other partisans of Alexius III were arrested and imprisoned.[70] The Byzantines needed a new emperor at once. Normally, when an emperor fled before an armed coup, the city accepted the rival claimant as the new emperor.[71] In this case, however, there was the added difficulty of the Latin crusaders' firm hold on the young Alexius and the anger many citizens felt toward the Westerners for the damage done to the city. To offer the crown to young Alexius would be to give the haughty Latins too much. Instead, an inspired alternative was proposed. Since the crusaders professed to be fighting for the rightful emperor and against the usurper Alexius III, why not restore blind Isaac II?[72] This would present the Latins with a *fait accompli*. These soldiers of Christ would no longer have reason to attack Constantinople in the name of young Alexius Angelus since his father would again be on the throne of the Caesars.

The fighting could stop with both sides saving face: the crusaders ousting the tyrant, the Byzantines resisting Latin demands.

While an excellent plan, there was one obstacle: the Varangian Guard. There was a real question among the Byzantine magnates whether the Guard would accept Isaac II as emperor. To survive in Byzantium's turbulent political environment, the Varangians, whose loyalty was only to the emperor, were forced to interpret their vow very strictly. They could accept that their vow to Alexius III was no longer binding, since they had long held that flight from the city meant the relinquishing of imperial power. When Andronicus I fled Constantinople in 1185, the Guard had no difficulty in taking a new vow to Isaac II.[73] When Isaac was overthrown by Alexius III in 1195 the Varangians again accepted that the mantle of authority had shifted, since Isaac's blindness was thought to disqualify him for the imperial throne. Now, in 1203, however, the Guard would have to hail Isaac II again as emperor, despite the fact that he was blind, meaning that blindness did not disqualify him. This would logically lead to the conclusion that the Guard had failed to honor its vow to protect and defend the emperor through Isaac's years in prison. And so the time-honored vow of the Varangians was again tested by the twists and turns of Byzantine politics. Constantine Philoxenites, the Eunuch of the Imperial Treasury, called the "ax-bearers" together to gain their acceptance of Isaac's resurrection. Without that acceptance it could not be done. The Varangians agreed to the proposal, but in so doing pushed their vow into a new shade of gray.[74] This was the first time that the Guard was consulted before the crowning of a new emperor. It would not be the last. In the maelstrom of events that would thunder across Byzantium over the next nine months, the Varangian Guard would be swept from the role of loyal bodyguards into that of kingmakers, like the Praetorian Guard before and the Janissaries after them.

With Alexius III gone, Theodore Lascaris imprisoned, and the Varangian Guard sanguine, the way was cleared for Isaac II's reinstatement. The blind man was clothed once more in the purple robes of state, borne to the Blachernae Palace, placed on the throne, and honored as emperor.[75]

In the middle of the night Isaac sent news of his revived state to his son in the camp of the crusaders. The marquis, the protector of the young prince, was promptly notified, and he at once summoned a meeting of the leaders in the tent of Alexius. Here the young man informed his friends of the flight of the tyrant and the enthronement of Isaac. The news was totally unexpected, and Villehardouin tells us that their joy was full. They praised God for delivering them from the hardship and danger of the previous day.[76] Their chivalric zeal to aid the oppressed against the powerful, which was not feigned but real, had finally borne fruit. Of course they had thought of the young prince who was among them, not his father, as the victim of oppression. But they knew the tale of the treachery of the vile uncle, and it was apparent that the blinded father had suffered the wrongs of the tyrant to an even greater degree than his son. Jubilation did not entirely prevail over caution, however, and when dawn broke the host was ordered to don their armor and to have their weapons at hand, lest they fall into a trap. The Latins placed little trust in the Greeks, although the news now was repeatedly verified by those coming from the city. A delegation of Byzantine magnates soon appeared to ask for the prince. They were sent to find him at the tent of the marquis. There his Greek "friends," who had been so strangely silent since his appearance before the city, made a great fuss over him. They thanked the crusaders profusely for the services they had rendered him and invited them into the city and into the palace as the most welcome guests.[77]

The leaders of the host slowly realized that the situation was more complex than it had at first appeared. Assuming that Isaac had indeed been restored, their position was not so favorable as it had seemed in the middle of the night. True they were delivered from immediate danger and were now welcomed into the imperial city, but they began to see that they had staked their lives and the future of the crusade on young Alexius, not upon his father, whom they had never met and who was not their creature. They probably recalled too that this Isaac was the very man who had entered into alliance with Saladin at the time of the Third Crusade to betray and destroy Frederick Barbarossa.[78] So they drew back in hesitation from the proffered triumphal entry with the young prince. They would keep him in the camp as a hostage until the intentions of Isaac were clear. A delegation would be sent to the emperor to demand his confirmation of the promises of his son contained in the Treaty of Zara. Villehardouin, Matthew of Montmorency, and two Venetians were entrusted with the mission. They rode to the Gate of Gyrolimne, where they dismounted and proceeded on foot between two lines of the awesome ax-bearing Varangians to the palace of Blachernae.[79]

The palace itself was situated in a low place at the foot of the hill of Blachernae, but it was so tall that it overlooked, as we have seen, the walls and the country beyond. Its exterior was of incomparable beauty. The interior, too, defied description, being covered with mosaics of gold and many colors and floored with costly and colorful marbles. Led into the audience chamber, the envoys saw Isaac sitting on his throne, probably the golden and bejeweled one described by Benjamin of Tudela with a golden crown sparkling with diamonds suspended above it by a golden chain.[80] Isaac was red-haired and florid,[81] dressed in the costliest robes imaginable. Beside him was his very beautiful wife, Margaret, the sister of the king of Hungary. They were surrounded by such a huge array of lords and ladies, says Villehardouin, that there was hardly room to turn around. The ladies especially were richly attired in precious cloths and adorned with gems.[82] The Byzantine court, as was its custom, put on a brilliant display of wealth in an effort to overawe the visitors. Even the marshal of Champagne, who knew well enough how to discriminate between the show of power and its reality, was impressed—although not enough to distract him from hard negotiating. The envoys were received with every honor, but soon they expressed their desire to speak privately with the emperor, and the four of them retired to a smaller room with Isaac, the empress, the chancellor, and an interpreter. As spokesman for the Latins, Villehardouin stated that they could not allow Alexius to enter the city until his father had confirmed the Treaty of Zara. The marshal stated its terms: submission of the Greek church to the pope; two hundred thousand marks for the host and provisions for a year; ten thousand men for one year to join the crusaders; and five hundred knights to be maintained continually in the Holy Land. Isaac immediately recognized that the young prince had committed himself to promises that he could not fulfill. The father knew his subjects and the resources of the state much better than did his son. He protested that the financial conditions were impossible and that he could not impose papal authority upon the Greeks. After much lively discussion gaining nothing from the Byzantine point of view, in despair and knowing full well that he could not keep his promises, Isaac yielded to their demands and ratified the conventions of young Alexius. He took an oath and had the imperial golden seal affixed to the ratification, which the envoys triumphantly bore back to their camp.[83]

Later in the same day the gates of the city were flung open to them, and the crusading chieftains proudly conducted young Alexius into the presence of his father. Isaac embraced the son who had restored his fortunes and seated him by his side on a golden throne.[84] The Byzantine nobles and ministers prostrated themselves before the prince who had so recently been treated with derision. Alexius and his Latin friends were outwardly received with feasting, rejoicing, and every mark of honor.[85]

The scheme hatched at Zara to extricate the crusaders from their financial difficulties and to gain Byzantine support for the Holy Land seemed, after all their hardships and dangers, to have succeeded. They would now have abundant resources of men and money for their sacred cause. Hugh of Saint Pol wrote to friends in the West of the joy and anticipation among the crusaders for the upcoming crusade in Egypt. He related with pride how the emperor had sent envoys to the sultan to defy him and warn him of the impending Christian force that would soon remove the infidels from the lands of Christ.[86]

There were, however, foreboding clouds on the crusading horizon, dimly perceived, if seen at all, by the cross-bearers. Isaac II Angelus, known to them as the betrayer of Barbarossa, held the imperial power. Alexius, their trump card, had now been played. Restored to the side of his father he would come under Greek influence. The power of the crusaders over him would inevitably decline. Even if Isaac and Alexius proved true to their word, the protestations of Isaac had forewarned the Latin leaders that fulfilling the promises would be anything but simple.

9

The Uneasy Alliance of
Latins and Greeks

The successful armed rebellion of young Alexius Angelus against his uncle ranks among the most bloodless coups in Byzantine history. Apart from those killed in the fighting on the walls, no one that we know of lost his life as a result of the change in leadership. It was usual after an armed rebellion to see a good deal of violence and theft in Constantinople. In 1081 Alexius Comnenus had allowed his foreign mercenaries to plunder the capital for three days. As his daughter, Anna Comnena tells us, the army "spared neither houses, churches, nor even the innermost sanctuaries."[1] After his armed rebellion in 1182, Andronicus Comnenus ordered his mercenaries to inform citizens of Constantinople that they were free to plunder the Latin quarters. Thousands, including women, children, and the aged, were massacred.[2] Nothing like this occurred in 1203. Young Alexius Angelus's foreign mercenary army (for that is how the Byzantines saw the crusaders) acted with extraordinary restraint. They entered the city peacefully and without incident, marveling at the wonders of the megalopolis that they had just tried to storm.

Still, there was a risk, and Isaac II moved quickly to remove it. The manners of Latins and Greeks were mutually abrasive, and they regarded each other as—at best—religious schismatics. For the moment tempers were cool. The Westerners saw themselves as deliverers of the Greeks from a tyrant's hands, and the Greeks were willing enough to confirm this view. But how long could this last? Many Byzantines resented the Latins' presence in the city, and others, particularly those who had lost so much in the fire, despised them. Isaac probably also realized the advantages in disassociating himself as much as possible in the eyes of his subjects from the army of Latins to which he owed his imperial crown and robes. He and his son therefore prevailed upon the crusaders to withdraw outside the walls and across the Golden Horn to the quarter of Pera. The crusading leaders agreed, because they too saw the risks, according to some Western sources, and did not wish to offend.[3] Robert of Clari, who probably reflects the opinion of the rank and file, says, however, that the Latins withdrew to the opposite shore because of mistrust of the Greeks, who were traitors. Robert also tells us that Peter of Bracieux remained with his men in the palace of Blachernae to safeguard the interests of the pilgrims.[4] Despite their change in quarters, both Villehardouin and Clari report that the crusaders had complete freedom to enter the city whenever they chose.[5]

By raising Isaac from captivity to his old throne, the Greek magnates and ministers had for the moment outmaneuvered the Latins and young Alexius.[6] The prince had planned to gain the crown for himself, believing his father disqualified by blindness.[7] It was the young man's claim that the crusaders had supported. It did not take the leading crusaders, who were not fools, long to grasp the political significance of the Greek maneuver. It was probably, therefore, as a price for the crusaders' withdrawal from the city that Isaac and his Greek advisers reluctantly agreed to the coronation of his son as co-emperor.[8] And so the crusaders drew back across the harbor to the neighborhood of Galata and Estanor. Here the emperor saw that they were plentifully supplied with food. On the north shore of the Golden Horn they would await Isaac's fulfillment of his promises and the resumption of their pilgrimage.[9]

The solemn coronation of young Alexius was set for 1 August, the day of Saint Peter in Chains.[10] The ceremonies were celebrated with all the pomp and circumstance that the Byzantines always employed to buttress political authority. Richly garbed, the young prince was led in procession to Hagia Sophia with crowds along the way admiring the pageantry and shouting their ritual acclamations. Beneath the awe-inspiring golden dome, surrounded by the rich glow of the mosaics, before the glorious high altar, with every solemn sanction that the most ceremonious of churches could offer, Alexius received an imperial diadem as symbol of the sacred office.[11] The protégé of the marquis of Montferrat was now emperor. From this time on the crusading magnates tended to ignore Isaac, speaking of only one emperor, Alexius IV.[12]

Not long after the taking of the city, the barons were granted audience to receive the appreciation of Isaac and his son.[13] Shortly they also began to receive more tangible signs of gratitude. They probably received rich gifts, which Byzantine emperors were accustomed to bestow on allies. Boniface of Montferrat, who had rescued young Alexius from obscurity, championing his cause before the pope and crusaders, was particularly honored. The great friendship that had long existed between the Montferrat clan and the Angeli was remembered, and Boniface may at this time have been given the island of Crete.[14] As for the rest of the crusaders, Alexius paid to them a sizable portion of the money that he had promised, though not all of it. According to Villehardouin, Alexius made an initial payment on his debt sufficient to allow all of the crusaders to settle accounts with the Venetians.[15] At long last the Treaty of Venice had been fulfilled. Robert of Clari provides additional detail. He records that the new emperor immediately paid one hundred thousand marks, or half of the promised reward. Half of this sum went to the Venetians, who, according to the Treaty of Venice, received half of the enterprise's income. The other half went to the Franks. Of the latter sum, the French paid thirty-six thousand marks to the Venetians for the fleet and provisions. The remaining twenty thousand marks (Clari's arithmetic leaves something to be desired) was paid to "those who had loaned their money to pay for the passage."[16] The meaning and amount of the last sum is not clear. It probably refers to money loaned by wealthier knights to poorer crusaders. In that case the Venetians and wealthier knights were flush, while the poorer soldiers remained poor.[17]

Naturally the crusaders spent much of their time visiting the great city across the bustling harbor. From its hills they overlooked the awe-inspiring vista of palaces, churches, and endless houses of the greatest city in Christendom: a city, as Villehardouin describes it, "richer than any other since the beginning of time."[18] The Latins marveled at the Greeks, dressed like princes in garments of silk with gold embroidery.[19] People from many lands, of many races, customs, and religions swarmed about the wharves, the streets, and the forums. Not all of the city was wealthy, of course, although tourists tend to frequent the nicer places, which please the eye and do not offend the nose. Yet some of the visitors must have wandered away from the Mese and the forums to the crowded squalor of the slums, where the imperial splendor was contradicted by unspeakable misery.[20] Most of the pilgrims, however, stuck to the centers of imperial and ecclesiastical magnificence.

They marveled at the mighty church of Hagia Sophia; built by Justinian, it was Western civilization's greatest architectural achievement until the construction of Saint Peter's in Rome in the sixteenth century. Now given the opportunity to visit the interior, the crusaders were overwhelmed by Hagia Sophia's treasures of gold and silver, of marble and porphyry and granite. The visitors gazed in wonder upon the mosaics of its walls and vaults. They were awed by the "gold-embedded saints and emperors" towering above them in the enormous dome.[21] Outside, between Hagia Sophia and the complex of buildings making up the Great Palace, extended the porticoed plaza called the Augusteion. Here was the massive column of Justinian that bore at its top a thrice life-size bronze equestrian statue of the emperor. Dressed in the raiment of Achilles, Justinian held in one hand the orb of empire, while the other was stretched out to the East in a warding gesture against the Persians.[22] To the east of the Augusteion stood the Senate House, where that ancient body still met.[23] To the west was the beautifully decorated Milion, the milestone from which all distances were reckoned in the Roman East.[24] And to the south stretched the sprawling complex of the Great Palace.[25] Westerners often called it Bucoleon for the sculpted lion and bull locked in mortal combat that decorated its landing on the Sea of Marmara at the foot of a beautiful flight of marble steps.[26] The greater men were admitted to the sixth-century Triclinos of gold, which had served as the throne room and center of the palace since the tenth century. Here was the famous tree of gold with mechanical singing golden birds, so often reported by visitors.[27] North of the palace was the lavish Hippodrome where the chariots of the empire still raced to crowds that could number one hundred thousand.[28] Yet chariot racing was but one of the spectacles in the Hippodrome. Exotic wild animal shows, acrobats, and musicians often performed for the people's amusement.[29] The central spina, around which the chariots raced, was decorated with hundreds of bronze statues, most dating back to antiquity.[30] Among them was the Serpent Column of Delphi, a bronze pillar in the form of three entwined serpents. Originally a votive offering to Apollo crafted by the Greek poleis after their defeat of the Persians in 479 B.C., it was transported from Delphi to the Hippodrome by Constantine.[31] Thrusting upward from the spina were two obelisks. One was Egyptian, taken from Thebes by Constantine, transported to New Rome by Julian, and erected in the Hippodrome by Theodosius the Great.[32] The other was made of brick and covered with bronze plate so that it gleamed strikingly in the sun.[33]

As the rank and file of pilgrims wandered the streets and the forums they came upon many towering columns commemorating the deeds of past emperors. In the circular Forum of Constantine stood the enormous column of the founder. Made from nine massive porphyry drums stretching to a height of fifty meters, the column originally bore a colossal bronze statue of Constantine as Apollo. The statue was lost in a storm in 1105, but some years later Manuel Comnenus replaced it with a golden cross.[34] Further along the covered Mese street was the expansive Forum Tauri, also called the Forum of Theodosius. There the crusader/tourists could climb the winding staircase inside the tower of Theodosius for a view of the city—that is, if they could get past the hermits who often camped on the column's summit. The column was modeled on Trajan's Column in Rome, and like its twin on the Tiber its exterior was covered in the spiraling sculpted triumphs of the emperor.[35] An almost identical column stood a little farther down Mese in the Forum of Arcadius.[36] In 1203, both columns were thought to depict future rather than past events in their reliefs.[37]

The pilgrims crowded the churches, not just as sightseers, but to venerate the treasures of holy relics. Villehardouin reports that these were beyond all description, for there were as many in Constantinople as in all the rest of the world.[38] The cult of the cross, the emblem of the crusade, had played a large role in attracting many of the crusaders to the holy war, so they hastened to view and venerate the holy wood, to gain its salutary power, and to fulfill in some measure the objective of their pilgrimage. With only slightly reduced zeal they accumulated additional spiritual benefits by making the rounds of the many other precious relics contained in the city. Those who felt guilt over their attack on Zara and the pilgrimage not yet completed found considerable comfort in visiting and venerating the relics of Constantinople.[39]

No Westerner who visited Constantinople before has given us such a detailed description of the city as the impressionable Robert of Clari.[40] An innocent sightseer, the typical tourist, open-eyed and widemouthed, Robert was entranced by the marvels of the imperial city. As in his accounts of battles, the simple knight, in contrast to the more aloof marshal of Champagne, displays his flair for the specific and the concrete. Hagia Sophia, the Great Palace, the Hippodrome, the Golden Gate, and other monuments are pictured for us in his words. He rhapsodizes the riches of Hagia Sophia: the magnificent columns of jasper and porphyry, the great altar of alloyed noble metals and crushed precious stones, the silver canopy over the altar supported by silver columns, the shining silver lamps. Within the confines of the Great Palace he visited the Church of the Blessed Virgin of the Lighthouse to venerate the True Cross and other relics of the Passion, including the crown of thorns, which had points, he said, as sharp as daggers, although one suspects that he was not allowed to touch them. At the Church of the Holy Apostles he viewed with reverence the column against which Jesus was scourged. At the abbey of Christ Pantocrator (All-Powerful) he beheld the marble slab upon which the body of the Lord was laid with the visible spots of the very tears of the Holy Mother.[41] Sometimes Robert gives us a garbled account of the wonders that he saw. He tells us, for example, of the *sydoine*, which miraculously opened every Friday to reveal the features of Christ. Here he seems to confuse the grave cloth, or *sindon*, with the *sudarium*, or handkerchief, of Saint Veronica, which captured the image of the Lord.[42]

Robert apparently did much of his touring of the city with the help of native guides and interpreters. They told him how the Golden Gate at the far south corner of the land walls was opened only for the triumphal entry of a victorious emperor, and they described the pageantry of such occasions in some detail. Other tales they related to our gullible tourist were colored by unbridled imagination, superstition, and local pride. Robert reports the miraculous cures obtained by rubbing against the columns of Hagia Sophia.

Indeed the interior of the church apparently functioned like a great clinic, for various columns had their special ailments. Just as Robert often described events he did not witness by reporting dialogues he did not hear, so too he described the urban legends surrounding Constantinople's marvels by reporting inscriptions he did not read. The equestrian statue of Justinian (which Robert believed was Heraclius) had an inscription on it, Robert claims, which read that "he swore that the Saracens should never have truce from him."[43] The statue, of course, had no such inscription, nor could Robert have seen it on its lofty perch if it did. But the words did capture the essential meaning of the monument, which was built to extol the victories of Justinian and to ward off foes from the East.[44] On the mantled statue above the gate that Robert calls the Gate of the Golden Mantle, perhaps, though not clearly, the Gyrolimne, Robert reads the words, "Anyone who lives in Constantinople a year can have a mantle of gold, just as I have."[45] His guides told him too of the Cassandra-like prophetic reliefs on the columns of Theodosius and Arcadius, which could not be understood until after the event. The credulous knight viewed with amazement the Hippodrome and described its wonders in some detail. He was told that the many statues of men and beasts ranged along the spina used to move by enchantment, taking part in the games, although they did so no longer.[46]

Robert of Clari was also quite taken by a story he was told by one of the barons, probably Peter of Bracieux, about a black man in Constantinople. He was a Nubian, or perhaps Ethiopian, king or prince who was visiting Constantinople during a pilgrimage. That he was there at all says much about the continued ties between Constantinople and the Monophysite Orthodox Christians of Africa.[47] The French barons who saw the prince were startled not only by his black skin, but also by his forehead, which was branded with the sign of the cross. He told the Franks through an interpreter that in his land all children were so branded after baptism. To see the Holy Sites, he had left his home with sixty men. By the time he reached Jerusalem only ten had survived; when he reached Constantinople only two remained alive. He had come to the city before the crusaders had arrived and had been put up in royal surroundings by Alexius III in a sumptuous monastery. He told them of his intention to continue on to Rome and then to Santiago de Compostela. Finally, if he lived that long, he hoped to return to Jerusalem and stay there the remainder of his days.[48] Robert of Clari was very impressed by the story of this remarkable man.

Although Villehardouin tells of the friendly relations of the crusaders and their hosts,[49] the long-developing animosity between Greeks and Latins soon prevailed. Much of the rancor of the Greeks toward the crusaders fell upon the immature head of Alexius IV. In their eyes the young emperor de-graded by his unseemly behavior the imperial dignity so jealously preserved by his predecessors. He wasted whole days with his Latin friends in drink-ing and dicing. Nicetas complains that he allowed his drinking companions to don the golden and bejeweled diadem. Abandoning Byzantine decorum, he gave himself over to the rude manners of the Westerners, imitating their vulgarity.[50] In his foolishness, as Nicetas sees it, he even tried to fill up the bottomless gulf of their desire for money.[51] The imperial treasures, in fact, did not go far toward meeting his need to pay his benefactors. More was gained by expropriating the wealth of Euphrosyne and others associated with Alexius III, such as the Lord Admiral Michael Stryphnos, who thus lost the gains of his corruption in office. One by one other wealthy families were plun-dered of their treasures to meet the demands of the Latins, who were eager to get on their way. Yet, although Alexius seemed from the Greek viewpoint to pour a sea of gold upon them, they were never satisfied, for they never did receive all that had been promised.[52]

When secular resources failed, imperial officials turned to the treasures of the church. Precious ecclesiastical plate was confiscated. Holy icons of gold and silver were struck with axes from the walls to the ground to be melted down for bullion. This was the source of some of the money that the cru-saders spent like any other in the shops and brothels of Constantinople. Of course this was sacrilege in the eyes of pious Greeks—and even of those not so pious. Stripping churches and destroying icons not only deprived Con-stantinople of those items that protected her, but also invited God's wrath to thunder down on his people. Nicetas believed that all of the misfortunes that later befell the Queen of Cities stemmed from this reckless sacrilege.[53] The effect was all the worse because Alexius III, unlike his brother, had been care-ful to placate the church lest it support the dethroned Isaac and his son.[54]

Even more sensitive than the plundering of ecclesiastical wealth was the question of the submission of the Greek church to Rome as required by the Treaty of Zara. Alexius IV and Patriarch John X Camaterus communicated their submission to the pope, but they made no effort to impose Roman doc-trine and usages upon the people.[55] This must have been a particularly bitter pill for Camaterus to swallow. In one terse letter he contradicted or nulli-fied all of his objections to Roman primacy that he had sent to Innocent in 1199 and 1200.[56] While Innocent recognized here a great opportunity to re-unify the churches, he had sufficient experience with the Greeks generally and the patriarch in particular to be less sanguine than the crusaders. He urged them to require Camaterus to acknowledge publicly his submission to Rome and to seek the pallium from the pope as first steps toward real reunion.[57]

These demands were impossible, and therefore never fulfilled. Many Byzantines already branded young Alexius a traitor who had sold his country and his faith to the Latins for his own advantage.[58] He was caught along with his father on the horns of a terrible dilemma: the longer the crusaders remained in Constantinople the more his administration was viewed with suspicion and anger; but he could not raise the money that would send them on their way without exacerbating the hatred of his subjects, which was already bubbling to the surface.[59]

The crusading leaders were also in a difficult fix. According to the oaths they had sworn on the Gospels to the crusading host, they were bound to lead the army away from Constantinople one month after its arrival, unless they received the consent of the host to remain longer. It had been more than a month since the crusade cast anchor off Scutari on 26 June, but the leadership likely argued that the one month clock should start ticking only after the crusaders actually entered the city on 18 July. Whatever the reckoning, it was clear that they would have to be on their way soon. The rank and file were acutely aware that their transportation treaty with Venice would expire on 29 September and they had no intention of having spent all of their money for a trip to Constantinople. Something had to be done.

Alexius came to the camp of the crusaders to discuss both his and their difficulties and to propose a means of solving them. The doge and the magnates gathered in the quarters of the count of Flanders to confer with the emperor. Alexius explained to them how the Greeks resented him because he had gained the throne through Latin aid. Many of his subjects hated him so much that if the crusaders abandoned him now they would surely kill him. He was well aware of the oath that the barons had sworn at Corfu and the upcoming expiration of the Treaty of Venice, and he wanted to help. But there was simply no way he could pay the rest of the money so quickly and have any hope of retaining his throne. His uncle, Alexius III, still controlled much of the empire. If the crusaders left Constantinople it would be only a matter of time before the tyrant marched on the capital and deposed his brother and nephew. Alexius IV needed time: time to consolidate his hold on the empire and time to collect the remaining sum he owed to the Westerners. To give him that time, Alexius proposed that the crusading host should remain in his service until the beginning of the next sailing season in March 1204. At his own expense he would renew the lease on the Venetian fleet for an additional year, thus to 29 September 1204. He would also supply the material needs of the crusaders until spring, when they would be free to pursue their pilgrimage. By then he would be in firm control of the whole empire, from which would come the wealth to enable him to fulfill his obligations. In March, the crusaders with the promised Greek aid could sail to Palestine, having the whole summer campaigning season before them.

The leaders discussed the issue in private. They realized that the young emperor described accurately the situation in the city, and that his proposal made sense, not only from his point of view, but from theirs. Yet because of their vow to the army, they had no authority to accept Alexius's proposition without the approval of the host. On the next day, therefore, the leaders summoned all the other powerful men and most of the knights to an assembly, where they informed them of the emperor's request. Heated discussion ensued, as might have been anticipated. Those who felt strongly compelled to accomplish promptly their long deferred vows were understandably outraged. Time and again the leaders had put them off. At Corfu they had been won over only at the sight of their companions and chief on their knees and in tears, promising that as soon as Alexius was restored the pilgrimage would be resumed. Now they said to their leaders, "Give us the ships as you swore to do, for we wish to go off to Syria."[60] The leaders were swayed by more complex considerations. They argued that if they sailed promptly to Palestine winter would soon be upon them and they would accomplish nothing. Moreover, they had need of provisions and the aid promised by Alexius. The Venetians also were reluctant to leave their colony in Constantinople to face alone the fury of the Greeks should Alexius fall. Finally, the imposition upon Constantinople of an emperor friendly to the West and submissive to Rome was too great an accomplishment to risk. At last they had overcome one of the major obstacles to the entire crusading movement and had provided for the crusade a firm base—at least it would be a firm base if they could make Alexius IV secure on the throne. This should not be lightly tossed away just to fulfill their vows six months earlier. Most of the dissidents were won over, however reluctantly, and they agreed to remain at Constantinople until March 1204. Alexius then contracted with Doge Dandolo for an additional year of the Venetian fleet's service.[61]

Aside from a few areas that had already professed allegiance to him, Alexius IV ruled only Constantinople and its neighboring lands. Much of the empire was in tacit rebellion, ignoring the changes in the capital. More of it was under the control of Alexius III, who lacked the capital, but ruled an empire.[62] Upon the advice of his counselors, both Greek and Latin, Alexius decided to undertake an expedition to pursue his uncle and to assert his authority over the provinces.[63] With promises of liberal pay he persuaded many of the crusaders to accompany him. It is said that the marquis of Montferrat and his followers received sixteen hundred pounds of gold for their part in the expedition.[64] Of all the magnates Boniface was most closely tied to the inter-

ests of the young emperor, really part of his administration, so it was natural
that he should accompany his protégé and enjoy his role of kingmaker and
mentor. Hugh of Saint Pol, Henry of Flanders, and many others joined the
march toward Thrace in mid-August. The doge, Baldwin of Flanders, Louis
of Blois, and the majority of the Latins remained in the camp to protect it and
to watch over the city.[65] About this time the crusaders lost to death through
illness the deeply respected Matthew of Montmorency.[66]

Alexius III had set up his temporary capital at nearby Adrianople in
Thrace.[67] In their assault upon his forces the crusaders and the young emperor
captured at least twenty towns and forty castles, but Alexius III escaped them.
Many of the inhabitants, though, came to offer their submission to young
Alexius, and the wealth of the conquered cities was peeled off to serve the
needs of the emperor and the crusaders. Johannitsa, tsar of the Bulgars, however, did not submit.[68] He was to become an important player in the drama
of the crusaders in Byzantium after the fall of the city in 1204.

During the absence of the expeditionary force two related disasters
rocked the capital and undermined the fragile foundations of cooperation between Greeks and Latins.[69] Around or probably on 18 August the smoldering
resentment of the Greek mob flared up in a vicious attack upon the Latin inhabitants of the city.[70] Jealous of the wealth of the aliens, embittered at the
prospect of religious union, humiliated by their own weakness, in rage they
fell upon the foreigners. From Seraglio Point the quarters of the Italians extended to the west along the south shore of the harbor, the choicest spots in
the great city for seafaring trade, first the Genoese, then the Pisans, next the
Amalfitans, and finally the Venetians.[71] The xenophobic wrath of the rabble
made no distinction between friend and foe. They attacked the Amalfitans,
who, Nicetas says "had been nurtured in Roman customs," as well as the
Pisans, who had only one month earlier fought valiantly to defend the city
against the crusaders. Many of the Pisans had been brought up in Constantinople and regarded it as home.[72] The mob descended on the Venetian Quarter as well, but here they were closer to the mark, since Venice had played so
prominent a role in the Fourth Crusade. The outnumbered victims saw their
churches, homes, hospitals, warehouses, and shops reduced to ashes.[73] Fearful
for their lives, a large number took to their ships and boats and sought refuge
with the Latin army on the other side of the harbor. This was a tragedy for
Constantinople, as well as the Italians. Through irrational violence the city
lost some of those who had been among its best defenders. In one day the
Byzantine mob had done the previously impossible: reconciling Pisans with
Venetians.[74]

Tempers flared in the crusader camp when they saw the wanton destruction and heard the tales of the refugees. It was because of the army's presence that these good people had lost their homes—a fact the refugees surely emphasized. Given the course of subsequent events it seems likely that the dispossessed Pisans and Venetians asked for help from the Latin army to avenge themselves on their assailants. The crusading leaders could not comply. They had been contracted to protect Alexius's reign and, therefore, keep peace in Constantinople.[75]

On 19 August, probably one day after the anti-Latin riot, a group of armed Flemings, Pisans, and Venetians crossed the Golden Horn on fishing boats and descended on a seaside mosque that stood outside the city walls just across the harbor.[76] It is not clear whether this expedition was sanctioned by the leadership as a "shot across the bow," or whether it was undertaken only on the authority of those who participated. The fact that Venetian vessels were not used suggests the latter. The mosque was in a very unlucky location. Called the Mitaton mosque, the structure was built by Isaac II as a gesture to Saladin sometime before 1195.[77] Constantinople had a number of mosques, but the others were safely tucked away in the Moslem Quarter further up the Golden Horn. Only the Mitaton mosque stood defenseless on the shore. For crusaders who longed to prove their mettle against infidels, the Islamic place of worship was an inviting target.[78]

The Latins landed and attacked the mosque, but the worshipers fought back vigorously. They called to their Byzantine neighbors for help, who came immediately, driving the raiders back to their boats, but not before they were able to set fire to the mosque.[79] That was not the only fire the expedition set. Some of the Latins, almost certainly the Pisans and Venetians, left the storming of the mosque to the crusaders and returned to their ruined quarters through the open gates. There they set fire to the homes and shops of their Greek neighbors who had so recently done the same to them. Running from building to building these arsonists planted their deadly seeds of destruction in, as Nicetas says, a "goodly number" of places.[80]

By the time the Westerners had made it back to the opposite shore, one of the world's most destructive fires had been born. Whipped into a roaring inferno by strong winds, the flames, Nicetas reported, "rose unbelievably high above the ground." "While in the past many conflagrations had taken place in the City . . . ," he continued, "the fires ignited at this time proved all the others to be but sparks." Shifting erratically, the strong winds blew the enormous fire in a zigzag path. Buildings that seemed to have been spared were again turned upon and destroyed. Columns, statues, great structures "went up in smoke like so much brushwood." "Nothing," Nicetas lamented, "could stand before those flames."[81] Across the Golden Horn the crusaders looked on the inferno with dumbfounded horror. Villehardouin recorded that the barons "were extremely grieved and filled with pity, seeing the great churches and the rich palaces melting and collapsing, the great streets filled with merchandise burning in the flames, but they could do nothing."[82]

The fire raged southward during much of the first day, destroying enormous numbers of buildings, including the palace of Nicetas Choniates situated just northeast of the Forum of Constantine.[83] This region was one of Constantinople's most densely populated. The flames darted down the northern covered street that ended at the Milion. There the fire came within a hair's breadth of consuming Hagia Sophia. The fire burned part of the great church's atrium, but the structure itself was spared. The Forum of Constantine was not so lucky. Its covered walkways were leveled. Mese had become a river of fire. A little farther west the ancient and splendid church of Saint Anastasia was destroyed. To the east the Hippodrome narrowly escaped destruction. On the next day the wind shifted to blow the fire westward. The blaze ran along the southern portion of the city destroying homes, churches, and warehouses on the Sea of Marmara. Finally it halted at the Port of Theodosius.[84]

By the third day the fire had largely subsided. The winds probably abated and the citizens, using the plethora of cisterns in the city, got to work extinguishing the last of the flames. Localized fires continued to erupt here and there for another week.[85] This fire, the second that the Latins had inflicted on the great city, was a devastating blow. In two days approximately 450 acres (182 hectares) of Constantinople's most opulent and most congested areas had been reduced to ashes and rubble. The material cost was enormous, but so too were the human costs. Death tolls were probably not high: it is estimated that about 150 lost their lives as a result of the blaze. But homeless figures were colossal. At least 100,000 souls saw their dwellings destroyed.[86] Some, like Nicetas Choniates, had alternate accommodations.[87] Others simply left the city for greener pastures. But most returned to the devastation, building squatters camps and tent villages in the pathetic ruins of their neighborhoods.[88]

It is not unusual for the victims of a cataclysm like the second fire in Constantinople to look for a scapegoat. For Romans in A.D. 64 it was the Christians; for Londoners in 1666 it was the Dutch and Catholics. For Byzantines in 1203 it was the Latins. In this case, though, some of the accused were guilty: Latins had indeed set Constantinople ablaze. Aware of what was in store for them, the remaining Westerners living in the city packed their bags, gathered their families, and fled to the welcoming arms of the crusaders in Galata. Villehardouin counted fifteen thousand refugees, "and it was to be a great boon to the crusaders that they crossed over."[89]

Not surprisingly the fire poisoned relations between the Byzantines and the crusaders. Most Greeks now truly detested the Latins and began looking for someone who could wreak vengeance on them for their crime. Most Latins were torn between their horror at the fire's devastation, their sorrow for having inflicted it, and their growing belief that the Greeks had it coming.[90] Villehardouin noted that "neither side knew on whom to cast the blame for the fire; and this rankled in men's hearts on both sides."[91]

The Byzantines did not blame only the Latins: they also reproached Alexius IV, who had brought the crusaders to Constantinople and fattened them with wealth and honors. To retain his throne, Alexius would have to address the anger of his subjects. But to do so would mean turning his back on his friends, who would naturally then turn their backs on him. His situation was desperate.

"And So Began the War . . ."

The expeditionary force led by Alexius and Boniface turned back to Constantinople after about three months in the field.[1] At an even earlier date Henry of Flanders, disappointed with his pay, had led his men back to the crusaders' camp.[2] Before long the others were to follow. During their absence animosity between the Greeks and Latins had exploded in the wake of the great fire. Constantinople was, for the first time since the massacres of 1182, virtually free of Latin residents.[3] Only small numbers still ventured into the city. Isaac II had also failed to make any additional payments to the Latins. No doubt he could not pay them. Financially it had become more and more difficult; politically it had become impossible. Crusade leaders who remained in the camp, therefore, sent a message to their comrades in the field that they should return no later than 1 November.[4] The barons who had accompanied Alexius agreed to comply, and Alexius himself decided to return with them, perhaps fearing that his Greek soldiers might take his life if he no longer had the immediate protection of the marquis of Montferrat.[5]

The expeditionary force did not quite make it back to Constantinople by the prescribed date, but on 11 November they returned to be greeted by a magnificent reception.[6] Byzantine society was ruled by ritual, and the necessary ceremonies were not forgotten when the young emperor returned to his capital. Although he had not been successful in capturing his imperial rival, Alexius IV had brought additional territory under his control. This was not enough to warrant the opening of the Golden Gate for a triumphal procession, but it was sufficient to bring out a body of dignitaries, who met the emperor outside the walls, extolled his achievements with ritual acclamations, and escorted him to Blachernae Palace.[7] Isaac II was not as happy to see his son return. He noted with bitterness how Alexius's name preceded his in the acclamations. He resented his own increasingly powerless role and began openly criticizing Alexius for his inexperience and revolting familiarity with the vulgar Westerners.[8] For their part the crusaders also joyously rode forth from their camp to greet their comrades in arms. Boniface and his companions joined the pilgrims in the encampment on the northern side of the harbor.[9]

From the day of his return the crusaders noticed a marked change in the attitude of the young emperor toward them. Villehardouin says that Alexius was filled with pride and adopted a haughty manner toward those who were his benefactors.[10] Viewing from afar, and one hopes with greater understanding, we can imagine the struggle going on in the youth's mind. He had learned to depend upon Boniface and to defer to the older man. To this protector and the other Latins he owed his rise to the throne, and he feared the outcome should he be left to face his subjects without their support. On the other hand, his situation had changed with the great fire and the anti-Latin wrath of his subjects. Moreover, no man, least of all a young man, likes to see himself as the puppet of others. Surrounded now by the ego-inflating pomp of the Byzantine court, Alexius could not help feeling that his Latin friends failed to appreciate adequately the change in his position. He was no longer the erratically wandering refugee of Zara and Corfu, but the solemnly enthroned emperor of Rome. It was easy and natural to flatter himself that he could now make it on his own—a fatal conceit.[11]

Alexius's problem, of course, was not just personal and psychological, but political. Although he had brought Thrace under submission, the majority of the provinces still did not recognize his authority. For the first time Constantinople was largely isolated from her empire.[12] The emperor was equally estranged from the people of the capital, who were demoralized by financial exactions, humiliated by the Latins' control over the emperor, and enraged by the horrible fires that had devastated their homes. Anti-Latin emotions in the city reached a fevered pitch, not only among the commoners but also the nobility. Isaac II seems to have become the focal point for a palace faction favoring a complete break with the crusaders.[13] Yet Isaac's increasing marginalization in state affairs hamstrung the proponents of this course of action. It was Alexius who, for the moment, controlled the loyalist army, the Varangian Guard, and the crusader forces. The young emperor was not ready to spurn his Latin friends, indeed he feared doing so. Still, he knew that paying them their due would be extremely difficult.

Beginning with Nicetas and continuing with all subsequent historians, Alexius IV has been seen as a naive fool, a reckless youth drowning in the course of events that he evoked, but could not control. In many ways this assessment is true, but it is not the whole truth. Unlike most of the other members of the imperial government, Alexius had experienced the dynamics at work in the crusading host. He had been at Corfu when the army scorned his appeal for aid. He had seen how delicately the leaders had jury-rigged the enterprise to take advantage of the opportunity to further the crusade and reunite the churches. He alone among the Byzantine aristocracy knew the greatest weakness of the Latin army: the fervent desire of the majority to be on their way to Syria. This imperative had been postponed momentarily by Alexius's extension of the Treaty of Venice, but the emperor knew that when March arrived the crusade army would brook no more delays. They had been assured that no matter the situation in Constantinople, they would be aboard Venetian vessels, fully supplied, and headed for infidel lands. To disappoint them again would spell the complete dissolution of the crusade. March 1204 hung over everyone's heads. Alexius IV had until then to finish paying the crusaders; the crusading leaders had until then to depart.[14] The young emperor knew well that if he was unable to pay the Latins by March they would have to leave Byzantium anyway. They would have no choice. His strategy, it seems, was to stall his old friends, making only token payments and avoiding them as much as possible—much the way any overextended borrower deals with debt collectors. In this way he could retain the use of the Latin army while at the same time attempting to rebuild his image as a loyal Roman among the people of New Rome. Alexius was not alone in this view of events—a faction of moderates in the court supported him.[15] These probably included the grand logothete, Nicetas Choniates.[16]

In reality, Alexius was stalling not only the crusaders, who wanted their promised reward, but also the Byzantines, who wanted revenge. It was an intensely tricky balancing act that would have taxed even the ablest statesman. Alexius did not have those credentials. The trifling payments the emperor made to the crusaders angered both the anti-Latin elements, who believed the crusaders had already received too much, as well as the crusaders, who wanted their accounts settled, not pocket change.[17] In an undelivered oration eulogizing Alexius IV, the orator Nicephorus Chrysoberges expressed the prevalent anti-Latin sentiment: "Let them not blow their cheeks out against us like Olympic victors!" Yet he also accepted the usefulness of some of the Latins, suggesting that they become part of Alexius's administration.[18] Forced to lean one way or the other, Alexius began to inch his way toward the anti-Latin faction.[19] He probably hoped to appease them with high words and small measures until March when the whole problem, he believed, would evaporate. Therefore, token payments stopped and even Boniface found it difficult to get access to the emperor.[20]

It may have been at this time that Alexius Ducas was promoted to *protovestiarius*, or chamberlain. Called Mourtzouphlus for his bushy eyebrows, Alexius Ducas knew a great deal about palace politics and intrigue.[21] In 1195 he was probably one of the conspirators behind the overthrow of Isaac II.[22] He later also turned against Alexius III, supporting the coup of John "the Fat" Comnenus in 1201. John's reign lasted no more than a day before the Varangians crushed the rebellion.[23] Alexius III imprisoned Mourtzouphlus, where he probably remained until Isaac was restored by the crusaders.[24] Brand identifies Mourtzouphlus as the leader of the anti-Latin faction in Alexius IV's court, a very reasonable conclusion.[25] Mourtzouphlus probably had some family ties, however tenuous, to the dynasty of the Comneni and thus could flatter himself with an imperial heritage.[26] Haughty and arrogant, he proudly wore the green shoes to which his new office entitled him.[27] He had a deep voice and harsh speech.[28] Mourtzouphlus was ambitious and energetic, and, as we shall see, not lacking in personal courage.[29] He is understandably portrayed as a villain in the Latin sources, and Nicetas also hated him, for Mourtzouphlus later removed the historian from office to make room for one of his partisans.[30] Nicetas describes him as a hollow man, who confused cunning for wisdom.[31] Few men since Pilate have received such uniformly bad press; Mourtzouphlus made the mistake of wronging the single historian of the period on the Greek side. And yet, had matters ended up differently in April 1204, he might well have been hailed as one of Byzantium's greatest heroes.

Alexius's incremental moves toward the anti-Latin sentiments of the palace and populace had the added effect of undercutting what little support his blind father enjoyed. For all practical purposes, Alexius IV was now the sole emperor. Isaac had already sensed the sea change when his name was demoted to second place after Alexius's triumphant return to Constantinople. According to the *Chronicle of Novgorod*, Alexius taunted his father that his blindness made him unfit for rule. He, Alexius, alone was emperor![32] The young man probably did not actually utter these words to his father, but like the speeches in Thucydides, they represent what might have been said to reveal the reality underlying what actually happened. In the oration of Chrysoberges, composed in late November, Alexius is treated as if he were sole emperor.[33] Isaac was edged out. He was not alone: Nicetas would later lose his high office at the hands of Mourtzouphlus, and other members of the conciliatory faction were also deprived of influence.[34]

Isaac, shunted aside from the center of power, though retaining the imperial title, could do no more than mutter through his teeth about the vices, recklessness, and frivolity of his son.[35] Involved in Isaac's decline, as cause or result or, more likely, a combination of the two, was his increasing mental incapacity.[36] He had never been a strong emperor, but was given to inconsistency, impetuosity, weakness, and mystical superstition.[37] He had suffered much in his life, which likely contributed to the breaking of his health. By

1203, he apparently alternated between states of confusion and lucidity. Such intermittent rationality in the mentally ill is not uncommon. By January 1204 he had sunk into powerlessness and utter incompetence. He occupied himself in babbling with favorite astrologers and prophets, who promised the miraculous restoration of his sight, the shedding of his aching limbs like the skin of a snake, and his transformation into a godlike world emperor. His foolish superstition led him to bring to the palace from the Hippodrome the statue of the Calydonian boar, in the expectation that it would destroy his enemies, as the original boar had rent in pieces the enemies it had been sent to attack. Nicetas damns the monks who fed the broken man's fantasies for the sake of the choice fish and rich wines they enjoyed at his table.[38]

While intrigue and madness walked the corridors of Blachernae, the crusaders in Galata watched events with anxious expectation. Immediately upon their return from the expedition into Thrace the crusaders had requested the payments that were due them. Alexius pled his poverty, pointing out that the foray had been less profitable than anticipated, and gained a delay. At first he continued to make feeble installments, but once more was forced by penury and politics to request a postponement.[39] The marquis of Montferrat, who had a considerable claim upon the young man's gratitude, frequently reproached Alexius for not repaying them for the great service they had done him.[40] The emperor continued to stall with paltry payments.[41] Alexius now understood too well that he had made extravagant promises that he could never keep. He learned, as Steven Runciman wisely says, that an emperor cannot be as irresponsible as a pretender.[42] Soon Alexius, supported by his new advisers, terminated even the token payments.[43] Torn between his affection for his Latin friends and his desire to hold on to his throne, Alexius IV did his best to seem independent and defiant toward the crusaders, while ensuring that no actual break developed between himself and the Latin army.[44] Although the money dried up, food continued to be supplied to the crusading host.

Extreme anxiety prevailed in the crusaders' camp. They had come to Constantinople and had won the throne for Alexius at great risk in the expectation of proceeding to Palestine with the support of the Byzantine Empire. Now they were not even paid the hard cash owed them under the Treaty of Zara. What could they expect of the additional sums promised to keep them at Constantinople through the winter and the military support that Alexius was to send to the aid of the Holy Land? The ordinary men saw their hopes betrayed again and again. The dissatisfaction and grumbling that is to be expected of an army in camp grew to an intensity that could not be ignored.

Then things got worse. On 1 December, armed Latins, probably crusaders but perhaps former Latin residents, became engaged in an altercation with a number of Greeks in the city.[45] Our only source for the event, the *Devastatio Constantinopolitana*, says nothing about the cause of the disturbance, but the author does put some of the blame on Latins who "so rashly took up arms against the Greeks."[46] The fighting spread into various areas playing out in violent skirmishes, some of which resulted in Greek and others in Latin retreat. But as word spread of the fighting more Byzantines joined in, prompting the Latin combatants to appeal to the crusading host to assist them.[47] A war was brewing and the crusading chiefs wanted nothing to do with it. While they had little love for the mobs of the city, the ruler of Constantinople remained their sworn friend. Despite his coolness, which perhaps in part the leaders understood, Alexius had broken neither of the contracts he had made with the Westerners.[48] The leaders could not condone an invasion of the city to aid Latins who should never have drawn their swords in the first place. Some of the Latin fighters escaped, but others were captured. The Greek mob took these captives, added to them Latin women, children, and elderly (who must have been resident aliens who felt secure in the city), murdered them, and burned the corpses. Mistaking restraint for cowardice, the belligerent Greeks then boarded small craft and rowed across to destroy Latin vessels docked in the harbor. The Venetians quickly manned their galleys and routed the Byzantine assailants, chasing them back to the walls of the city where many Greeks were killed. They also captured some Byzantine boats laden with merchandise and food.[49]

Alexius's policy of appeasing the anti-Latin majority without renouncing his continued commitments to the crusaders was crumbling into dust. He had long been trapped in a difficult political dilemma. Naively hoping that everyone would just get along, the young emperor was able neither to extinguish nor to satisfy the rage now boiling over among the populace. He could straddle the fence no longer. The Byzantines were bent on revenge against the Latins, the angry crusaders were stuck at Constantinople until the sailing season in March, and Alexius was caught in the middle. The crusading leaders were in a similar fix. Faced with a grumbling army, a hostile population, and an aloof emperor, the chiefs could no longer let matters remain as they were. Blood had been shed, and more would follow if relations between Constantinople and the crusade could not be repaired.

The leading knights and Doge Dandolo convened a parliament, probably one or two days after the riot and massacre.[50] Given their circumstances it is not surprising that the general sentiment at the meeting was hostile to Alexius IV. After all they had done for him, the emperor had cravenly abandoned his friends in favor of the duplicitous Greeks. It was only his cowardice, some undoubtedly believed, that kept Alexius from informing the crusaders of his change of heart. The leaders were particularly concerned because of the onset of winter, which meant that they no longer had any choice but to remain at Constantinople until March. On the other hand, Alexius continued to supply the crusaders with provisions; they had no wish to unnecessarily anger him. The emperor had not, after all, refused to pay his debt. Since his assumption of the throne, Alexius had paid about half of the sum and, in principle at least, had placed the Greek church in obedience to Rome. So, they wondered, what was the emperor's game? Was he simply stalling the Latins until March when the crusading host would demand departure, or did he truly intend to fulfill his sworn obligations to his friends? If the former, they were justified in issuing a formal defiance. If the latter, they wanted to hear it from Alexius's lips.

The crusading leaders decided to appoint an embassy of six men, three French and three Venetians, to go to the Byzantine court and question Alexius on his intentions. The French envoys were Villehardouin, Conon of Béthune, and Miles the Brabantine; the names of the Venetians are not known. The six envoys, girded with their swords, rode around the north side of the harbor and crossed the bridge near the Blachernae Palace. Villehardouin tells us that they rode in fear that the treacherous Greeks would not respect the sanctity that was supposed to surround them as envoys. At the palace gate they dismounted, for it was reserved to the emperor alone to enter the palace grounds on horseback. They were promptly admitted to the audience chamber where they saw Isaac and Alexius seated on thrones side by side with the empress Margaret, Isaac's wife, and many courtiers in attendance. Since hard language was the order of the day, Conon, rather than the marshal, once more assumed the role of spokesman. He appears to have addressed Alexius alone, although we know that Isaac was present. Once more he reminded the young man of the services performed in his behalf, of his covenants, and his failure to honor them. As the envoys had been instructed, Conon demanded that Alexius fulfill his promises. If he did not, Conon threatened, the crusaders would no longer hold him for their lord and friend, but would take by force what was owed them. They would not commence hostilities without this warning, for it was not their custom to act treacherously. (The implication of moral superiority to the Greeks, of course, was clear.) Alexius now must choose.[51]

Although Conon's tone was harsh, his ultimatum was weak. The crusaders were not demanding the immediate payment of the outstanding debt—something they had no right to demand—but rather a solemn assurance that the debt would indeed be paid. The covenants that Conon called on Alexius to honor clearly stated that the emperor had until March 1204 to settle his debt.[52] It was only November; he had plenty of time. To calm the crusaders' ire, Alexius needed only to assure them that they would be paid—something he had been doing right along.[53] But the threatening demeanor and frank speech of the envoys put Alexius in a difficult bind. His court was now stocked with members of the anti-Latin faction who favored a complete break from the Westerners. To cave in to Conon's ultimatum would be more than unseemly, it would spell the end of his reign. On the other hand, a bellicose dismissal of the crusader envoys would mean the loss of the Latin army and the acquisition of a troublesome enemy.

Alexius never had a chance to reply.[54] No sooner had Conon's ultimatum ceased echoing from the palace walls than the Byzantine court exploded in outrage. Never, they proclaimed, had any envoy had the audacity to defy a Roman emperor in is own court, as Conon had done. This is what came of befriending barbarians! Amid the swelling anger and violent shouts of the Byzantine aristocracy, Villehardouin looked to his former friend, Alexius IV. The emperor remained still, frozen between his people and his friends, between ambition and security. He returned the marshal's gaze with "evil looks." That was enough. The crusader envoys turned on their heals, strode out of the palace, and mounted their horses. They all breathed a sigh of relief when the palace gates swung shut, for they had feared they would be taken prisoner or killed. Spurring their horses, they returned to their camp.[55]

The envoys gave a full relation of their embassy to the crusading leaders.[56] It confirmed their worst fears. Villehardouin provides no details concerning any subsequent deliberations, but it is clear that the chiefs considered the angry response of the Byzantine court to be the equivalent of Alexius IV's refusal to meet his obligations. He was the emperor, after all. Had he wished, he could have quieted his nobles with a word and assured his old friends of his continued commitment to them and their holy enterprise. His failure to do so and his evil countenance spoke volumes. The Greek and Latin alliance was now ended.[57]

"And so began the war," says Villehardouin.[58] But war is a slippery term with shifting meanings. What was the nature of this new war? According to Robert of Clari, whose account is marred by jumbled chronology and outright invention, the object of this war was the conquest of Constantinople. Like some modern historians, Robert projects the final result onto the previous events. Faced with the fact that no attack occurred on Constantinople until many months later, Robert explains that the crusaders were forced to delay the conquest until after winter had passed since it was too cold for the Venetians to rig their ships with ladders.[59] This seems very unlikely, since it was not too cold for the Venetians vessels and sailors to see frequent activity throughout the winter as they sailed up and down the Bosporus and Golden Horn.[60] According to Baldwin of Flanders, the Venetian vessels were not outfitted for an attack against Constantinople until February 1204, when, as we shall see, the nature of the "war" had changed drastically.[61] Since it was still cold in February when the vessels were finally prepared, Robert of Clari's explanation is further discredited.[62]

The nature of this new war is explained by the events and words that led up to it. Its object was not the conquest of Constantinople, but rather the acquisition of the money and supplies that the crusaders believed Alexius legally and morally owed them. The words of the Latins' ultimatum were exact, and Conon did not soften them for the imperial ear. If Alexius refused to acknowledge his outstanding debt to the crusaders, then the Latins would take the money from him in any way that they could. In describing the war, Villehardouin states simply "what could be seized was seized."[63] Robert of Clari echoes this in one of his accounts of the ultimatum: "if he [Alexius IV] did not pay them, they would seize enough of his possessions to pay themselves."[64] And so they did. The rich villas and churches that surrounded Constantinople in every direction were the easiest and, therefore, the first targets of the crusaders. They stripped these estates of all wealth and then burned the empty buildings to the ground. They also took what food and supplies they needed from the local population.[65] Local militia and some imperial troops moved to protect Byzantine property, sometimes with success but usually without.[66] Looting by the Latins did not trouble their consciences for they were simply recovering their due from the lands of the faithless emperor.[67] The war, viewed from the Latin perspective as the act of "paying ourselves," also solved many problems for the crusade leaders. Although they would have preferred payment in full, the raids of December and January provided an effective alternative. Money was once again flowing into crusaders' pockets, the rank and file were no longer restless, and they could reasonably expect to be on their way to the East in March.[68]

Ironically, the formal break with the crusaders also solved a number of problems for Alexius—at least at first. The enmity of the Westerners earned him the support of the anti-Latin elite and probably gave him some measure of popularity among the general public. The crusader's looting of the rich structures of Byzantium to "pay themselves" made Alexius's looting of similar structures no longer necessary. In a perverse sense, the emperor was still making installment payments on his debt.[69] From his point of view, the crusaders' defiance did not change all that many things. Like the crusaders, Alexius knew that the larger problem would evaporate in March when the common soldier's vow would irresistibly pull him to the land of Christ. The emperor also knew that the grievance between him and the crusaders still remained financial. If a coup reared its head in Constantinople, Alexius believed that he could call on the crusaders to defend him by simply agreeing to fulfill his previous covenants.[70] He had, after all, never formally repudiated them.

Although Alexius often dispatched troops to defend areas under crusaders' attacks, he avoided as much as possible associating himself with these forays. This decision was probably based on both personal and strategic reasoning. Strategically, the emperor wanted to avoid a battle with the crusaders. In so doing he preserved his ability to plausibly deny responsibility for open hostilities should he need to patch matters up with the crusaders at a later date. Leading Byzantine troops and the mighty Varangian Guard against the Latins would remove that option. Personally, Alexius simply did not want to engage directly his former allies. The young man felt great affection for the crusaders, who had rescued him from obscurity, brought him home, and fought for his cause. He had been through enormous hardships with them—hardships that strengthened the bond of friendship between Alexius and the Latin leaders. Although political necessities now forced the emperor to keep the crusaders at arm's length, he remained fond of them.[71] Alexius's subjects saw this too. According to Nicetas, Alexius was under increasing pressure to personally lead imperial troops against the Latins, "unless indeed he was siding with the Romans with his lips only and had inclined his heart to the Latins." Alexius responded with bold promises of impending attacks, but they came to nothing. Nicetas remarked that the young man "could not bring himself to take up arms against the Latins, thinking it to be unnatural and inexpedient."[72]

As December wore on and the crusaders' raids continued, the citizens of Constantinople again began to turn against Alexius IV. It was humiliating to them that the arrogant Latins now gorged themselves on the fat of the Byzantine land, while the successor of the Caesars cowered in his palace. Given all the harm that they had done to the God-guarded Queen of Cities, the Latins deserved to be crushed by the anointed emperor. Anti-Latin aristocrats were also increasingly exasperated with the young man who had brought enemies to the capital but lacked the grit to fight them.[73] Others, like Nicetas Choniates, began to suspect that the break between Alexius and the Latins was largely a farce, designed to allow the latter to take forcibly the wealth that the former could not legally extract.[74]

Sometime around 20 December the Byzantines decided to attack the Latin fleet with fire ships.[75] They loaded a number of vessels with dry wood, old barrels, shavings, tow, pitch, pieces of fat, and other combustibles. One night about midnight, when a strong wind blew directly toward the enemy fleet across the harbor, they set torch to the fire ships and launched them under full sail toward the Venetian vessels. The wind blew the flaming ships rapidly across the Golden Horn. The fleet was saved by the naval skill of the Venetians, who leaped aboard their ships and expertly maneuvered them out of the path of fiery destruction.[76] One week later the crusaders boarded their vessels and raided the Byzantine harbor, capturing many ships.[77]

On 1 January, within two weeks of their first failed attempt to burn the Venetian fleet, the Greeks tried again. They loaded some fifteen to seventeen old vessels with combustibles, awaited once more the cover of a dark night with a strong south wind, and set the blazing flotilla on a course for the enemy ships. This time they improved the tactic by chaining the prows of the fire ships together, so that they came on in a fiery line. The trumpets in the crusaders' camp sounded the alarm. The men sprang to arms and tumbled out into the plain in the best order they could manage to face a possible attack by land from the direction of the bridge. The danger was of a different kind, of course, and in confusion and consternation they beheld the flaming line bearing down upon their fleet. It seemed, says Villehardouin, as if the whole world were on fire. The marshal, who specifies that he was an eyewitness, praises the heroism and skill of the Venetians. They quickly boarded their galleys and other vessels. Some struggled to maneuver their ships out of danger. Others in small boats and barges courageously laid hold of the fire ships with grappling irons to divert them from their destructive course. Large numbers of Greeks had flocked to the shore of the harbor to view the fiery spectacle and to rejoice at the discomfiture of the enemy. They raised such a tumult that it seemed as if earth and sea would be swallowed up. When the Greeks saw the Venetians grappling with the fire ships, some of them jumped into whatever boats they could find and drew near enough to shoot at them, wounding many. The seafarers from the lagoons did not panic, however, but, enduring toil and danger through the night, succeeded in drawing the whole fiery mass out of the harbor and into the strong current of the straits. There the burning ships were set free to drift spectacularly, but harmlessly, past the city and into the open sea. The Westerners lost only one ship, a Pisan merchantman that caught fire and sank.[78]

Although the Latins won at least their share of skirmishes, there remained great hardship in the camp. They were not a large enough force actually to besiege the great city, yet they were still a large number of men to be fed, more than twenty thousand, plus the refugees from the city. Since the emperor had cut off their supplies they had lived largely by foraging, but the same area had by now been covered many times, and less and less food was available within the range of their operations. Foraging was hampered, moreover, by the sallies of the Greeks. Robert of Clari tells of the dearth and high cost of food in the camp: a *setier* of wine cost twelve or even fifteen sous, a hen twenty sous, an egg two pence.[79] Alberic of Trois-Fontaines reports that twopenny bread three days old sold for twenty-six pence, which, if true, reflects an extremely punishing inflation of prices.[80] Robert says that they had plenty of biscuits, however, which were undoubtedly not very pleasant, but adequate to stave off starvation.[81] At any rate, a merchant vessel arrived from Brindisi loaded with food, so there was plenty for everyone for a time.[82]

As Alexius IV's popularity plunged to its nadir in Constantinople, a more aggressive and able leader emerged. On 7 January, one week after the last fire ship attack, the protovestiarius, Alexius Ducas Mourtzouphlus, led a contingent of Byzantine troops against the crusaders.[83] Nicetas Choniates, who greatly disliked the protovestiarius, reports that Mourtzouphlus made the sortie to curry public favor for a possible bid for the throne. Nevertheless, Nicetas gives the bushy-browed man his due, remarking on his skill and valor.[84] The encounter occurred at a place known as the Pierced Stone and a nearby arch, both of which were situated outside the city walls somewhere between the Cosmidion and Blachernae.[85] The attack may have been on Mourtzouphlus's own initiative, since Alexius refused to allow any troops to go to his aid when the project went awry.[86] Facing Mourtzouphlus was his old nemesis in court: Boniface of Montferrat. Although the protovestiarius had bested the marquis in the political arena, Boniface and his troops had little trouble defeating Mourtzouphlus on the field of battle.[87] During the melee, Mourtzouphlus's horse stumbled and he was almost captured by the Latin troops. He was saved only by a band of young archers who fired arrows at the crusaders from the city walls.[88] According to the *Devastatio*, the Greeks lost many men while among the Latins only two knights and a squire fell.[89]

Although Mourtzouphlus's sortie was a military failure, it was a political success. He had proven his willingness to lead the city's considerable forces against the Latin marauders and he had displayed the martial valor traditionally associated with a Roman emperor. But most of all, he had demonstrated that Alexius IV was unwilling to send troops against the Latins even when his own protovestiarius was in danger of being captured or killed. For the masses the conclusion was inescapable: Alexius IV still favored the Latins despite his now tiresome patriotic rhetoric. During the next two weeks anger toward the emperor grew to such a level that people openly criticized him and cursed his name.[90] A popular rebellion was brewing that threatened to rival any that Constantinople had seen. Yet unlike other rebellions in Byzantine history, this one lacked a leader around whom opposition could crystallize. Instead it erupted in isolated outbursts and local disturbances, many with damaging effects.

It was probably at this time that a drunken mob destroyed one of Constantinople's greatest treasures, the lifelike bronze statue of Athena attributed to Phidias. Nicetas, disgusted with this senseless vandalism, described in detail every aspect of the ancient artwork that future generations would never behold.[91] In one hand Athena had previously grasped the shaft of a long spear, but it seems that the weapon had long ago been lost. The empty hand, therefore, appeared to the mob to be beckoning someone, and they assumed it was the Latins.[92] The fact that the statue was facing south, actually with its back toward the Latins, was of no consequence to the vandals who shattered the priceless treasure of antiquity.[93] So a great work, perhaps a product of the finest sculptor of classical Greece, was lost to the passions of a superstitious and besotted rabble.

The bronze Athena was not the only antiquity that the angry mobs defiled. They also looked warily on the relief-covered columns of Theodosius and Arcadius. The past victories of Roman armies pictured there became for the Greeks the future conquest of their beloved city.[94] Now they looked with dread upon the representations of many boats filled with armed soldiers, some of whom were entering a walled city. To forestall the prophecy they attempted to mutilate the offending reliefs.[95] Unfortunately for them, however, both columns depicted campaigns that were largely naval, making the complete destruction of all pictures of troops on boats impossible. Some of these reliefs from the column of Theodosius can still be seen, since fragments were used in building the Beyazid baths around 1504.[96] The images on the column of Arcadius were sketched by an anonymous artist in 1574.[97] Both columns are now lost.

Although he plainly hoped to seize the throne at some point, Mourtzouphlus made no attempt to put himself at the head of the popular uprisings. Perhaps he doubted the resolve of the mobs or perhaps they considered him, despite his show of valor against the Latins, to be too closely tied to Alexius IV's government. But he surely knew that matters could not continue as they were. A vicious cycle of political imperatives was tearing Alexius's administration into shreds. The angrier the populace became, the more the emperor wanted to preserve his ability to call on the Latins to defend his reign; the more he refused to attack the Latins, the angrier, in turn, the mobs became. The spiral was fatal. At last on 25 January an enormous throng descended on Hagia Sophia and compelled the senate and principal clergy to convene for the purpose of electing a new emperor. Nicetas, who as grand logothete still presided over the senate, played an important role in this meeting and provides a vivid picture of the events. The citizens asked the nobles to speak freely and nominate anyone they chose as the new emperor. They swore that, following a coronation, they would attack Alexius in Blachernae Palace and oust the hated youth. But Nicetas and his colleagues knew that it was not that simple. Despite their enthusiasm and numbers, the mass of citizens would have a difficult time removing Alexius IV from well-fortified and distant Blachernae, particularly while he still commanded the Varangian Guard. That was, after all, one of the reasons that emperors had begun to govern from Blachernae. Nicetas also knew, as he tells us in his history, that the moment Alexius heard of a rival emperor he would immediately appeal to the crusaders, who "would wrap their arms around Alexius and defend him." The man they would choose to lead this doomed insurrection "would be led out the very next day like a sheep led to slaughter." And so the senate and clergy remained silent. But the assembled were obstinate. They proclaimed that no one would leave Hagia Sophia until a new emperor was chosen. They would no longer be ruled by the hated Angeli. It was an emotional scene. Nicetas and his colleagues sympathized with the aims of the crowd, but they could not give them what they wished. Tears rolled down the cheeks of the senators as they beheld to what straits Alexius and his father had brought the Roman nation. Since the aristocracy would not choose, the crowd began to yell out names, many of whom were members of the mob. When none of these met with approval they began to ask individual senators to take the purple, hoping that one of them might accept. Each senator refused it as a deadly poison. Nicetas was reminded of the words of the prophet Isaiah who foretold a day when people would proclaim, "You have raiment, you be our leader, and rule this heap of ruins."[98]

The mob searched frantically for a leader for three days. Since the senate and clergy would not help and no one among the assembled would accept the dubious honor, the rebels began to propose nobles who were not there, thus forestalling their refusal. At first they settled on a noble named Radinos. When news reached the unlucky man, he immediately donned the garb of a monk and remained in this disguise until the whole thing blew over. Not finding him at home, the delegates of the revolution seized his wife and led her to Hagia Sophia. Despite intense questioning, she would not reveal her husband's whereabouts.[99] Frustrated in this choice, the mob turned to another: a young nobleman named Nicholas Canabus. Here they had more luck. On 27 January, he was seized, brought to Hagia Sophia, and informed of his new vocation. Although the people now had a warm body, they still lacked the support of the senate, the upper clergy, or even the imperial nominee. When Patriarch John Camaterus refused to crown Canabus, the common people did so themselves.[100] Poor emperor! His dominion never extended beyond the confines of Hagia Sophia. He ruled over his motley collection of devotees for only six days before meeting his death.

Alexius IV, of course, received intelligence of the meetings in the great church and the raising of Canabus, but he was powerless to disperse the crowd. Isaac, the older emperor, was on his deathbed. He no longer possessed power, in any case, having lost it to his son. Alexius saw that his throne and his life were in serious danger, but he did not guess the direction of the gravest threat. As Nicetas knew, Alexius had always planned to turn to the crusaders if his reign was seriously threatened. But the young man made that choice too quickly. Despite the racket, the uprising at Hagia Sophia remained very weak. It lacked support from the senate, clergy, or military. The rhetoric of destroying Alexius in Blachernae remained just that; the followers of Nicholas Canabus never left Hagia Sophia.[101] For his part, Alexius still probably controlled the army and he certainly commanded the Varangian Guard whose loyalty was only to the emperor. Alexius feared that unless he crushed this rebellion immediately it would escalate to more dangerous levels. He may also have believed that the imperial army would balk at orders to violate the sanctuary of Hagia Sophia to seize the pretender. The crusaders had shown themselves adept at breaking into Greek churches. And so Alexius ordered his protovestiarius, Mourtzouphlus, to cross over to the crusader camp and summon Boniface of Montferrat.[102] It was a foolish choice for an agent. As the leader of the anti-Latin party, Mourtzouphlus had been chiefly responsible for ousting Boniface from court affairs. The two had also squared off against each other in battle only three weeks earlier. If Boniface regained his position in court, Mourtzouphlus would be the first loser. Even worse for the scheming protovestiarius, Boniface's family ties to the Angeli through his two brothers (both Caesars) made his imperial pedigree more impressive than that of Mourtzouphlus.[103] For Alexius to have missed all of this suggests that he was politically tone-deaf, hopelessly preoccupied, or both.

In his last act of duty to his emperor, Mourtzouphlus crossed the Golden Horn and retrieved the marquis.[104] According to Nicetas, Boniface and Alexius conferred together over what should be done.[105] Their discussion obviously included many excuses and requests for forgiveness from the young emperor, as well as new assurances that he would meet every one of his commitments to the crusaders. At last, the two decided that Boniface should lead Latin forces into the city to expel Nicholas Canabus and his supporters from Hagia Sophia and any other part of the Great Palace complex they had occupied. Alexius probably offered the immensely wealthy Great Palace, or perhaps Blachernae Palace, as security on his outstanding debt. Boniface returned to the crusader camp to gather his troops.[106]

Mourtzouphlus was quicker. The protovestiarius could no longer bide his time, ruminating over his future coup. If he did not act immediately the Latin forces would again be in the city and he would be out of a job, or worse.

Boniface would see to that. The key to overthrowing Alexius was neutralizing the Varangian Guard; and the key to the Guard was Constantine Philoxenites, the eunuch of the Imperial Treasury. Constantine had already shown his effectiveness with the Guard back in July when he convinced them to accept blind Isaac as the emperor. Mourtzouphlus rounded up a number of his kinsmen and other members of his faction and paid a visit to Constantine.[107] The protovestiarius told the eunuch of the emperor's deliberations with the Latins and the impending invasion of crusader troops. More interesting to Constantine, however, were the promises of titles and money should the coup succeed. The eunuch accepted, and immediately assembled the Varangian Guard. As he had done in July, Constantine told the ax-bearers of the desperate straits to which the empire had been brought and the need, therefore, for desperate action. He related in full the details of Alexius's meeting with Boniface and the planned Latin occupation of the palace. These revelations must have struck the Varangians as odd and insulting. They had plenty of experience putting down insurrections in the city. Why did the emperor turn to the crusaders? They may also have wondered where they were to be quartered if Latin forces occupied the Great Palace or Blachernae. As he had done in July, Constantine assured the Guard of strong support for the imperial ouster. Indeed, he claimed that it would be supported by the entire population, which was largely true.[108] He probably also offered a sizable gratuity. The Guard's vow had been bruised by the reinstatement of Isaac II; it was now taking another battering. Whatever the specifics of their reasoning, the Varangians agreed not to stand in the way of Alexius's imprisonment.[109]

Late that night Mourtzouphlus burst into Alexius's bedchamber and shook him awake. In an excited tone (which was genuine, but for the wrong reasons) he told Alexius that just outside the palace stood an enormous crowd, which included not only rebellious citizens, but also Alexius's own blood relations and the Varangian Guard.[110] Having heard of his decision to bring the Latins back into the city, Mourtzouphlus said, they were bent on tearing him limb from limb. Frozen with fear, Alexius begged Mourtzouphlus to save him from certain death. The trusted protovestiarius threw a large cloak around the emperor and swiftly escorted him out of his chamber and to a pavilion in the palace complex. While the frightened youth was still whispering psalms, his legs were put into irons and he was cast into prison. Mourtzouphlus relieved Alexius of the purple and proclaimed himself emperor.[111]

Despite Mourtzouphlus's success in imprisoning the highly unpopular Alexius IV, Byzantines did not flock to accept him as their new emperor. For the masses, the true emperor was Nicholas Canabus, who had been crowned, albeit irregularly, the day before. In fact, Mourtzouphlus's coup against Alexius actually gave to Canabus what he previously lacked: support from the ruling classes. With no legally crowned emperor available, factions grew up around the two contenders. Nicetas implies that they were initially of equal strength and, given the tone of his rhetoric, it seems very likely that he backed Canabus. The senator remarks that Canabus was gentle, intelligent, and a skilled tactician, but that these attributes doomed him from the start. He goes on: "Inasmuch as the worst elements prevail among the Constantinopolitans (for truth is dearer to me than my compatriots), Doukas [Mourtzouphlus] grew stronger and increased in power, while Canabus' splendor grew dim like a waning moon."[112] Undoubtedly, Mourtzouphlus gained popular and aristocratic favor by reminding the citizens of his foray against the Latins and his continued determination to rid Constantinople of the barbarians, once and for all. Canabus probably made similar promises, but Mourtzouphlus had the benefit of controlling the imperial apparatus at Blachernae. According to the *Chronicle of Novgorod*, Mourtzouphlus offered Canabus a high position in his administration if he would relinquish his claim to the throne.[113] The emperor of Hagia Sophia may not have wanted the diadem in the first place, or not at the hands of an unreliable crowd, but, once he had been forced to accept it, he could not let it go. Psychologically, people do not like to have taken from them titles, honors, powers, or whatever, even if these were originally unwanted. Mourtzouphlus was not to be trusted, moreover. Whatever he promised, he would not actually allow such an obvious rival to survive. The lot of Canabus was tragic, for Mourtzouphlus lured away his fickle supporters with rewards and promises. On 2 February, the unfortunate emperor of six days was seized by armed men and put in prison. His party dispersed, none of those who had forced the crown upon him coming to his aid. The *Devastatio* tells us that he was decapitated.[114]

The problem of the still surviving emperor Isaac II resolved itself at some point between Alexius's imprisonment and Mourtzouphlus's formal accession to the throne. He had been for some time a sick man, withdrawn from the pains of the real world into his realm of fantasies. After hearing the news of his son's imprisonment, fear exacerbated his condition, and in a very short time he passed away.[115] There have been suspicions that Mourtzouphlus had Isaac murdered, but it appears that this was not necessary. The old emperor was no rival to fear. His death passed almost unnoticed. History has judged Isaac harshly. He was not richly endowed with talent or prepared for the responsibilities of the imperial role.[116] His judgment was not consistently good,[117] and he made grievous errors, but he also enjoyed some successes prior to his betrayal by his brother, Alexius III.[118] He loved luxury and splendor. He never wore the same garment twice, and he bathed, says Nicetas, every other day. His chefs set a magnificent table with mountains of good food and seas of rich wine, much enjoyed by the parasites he kept about him, who, in his last months, encouraged his foolishness.[119]

The crusaders on the other side of the Golden Horn were not unaware of events in Constantinople. It would have been impossible to conceal the power struggle between Hagia Sophia and Blachernae, which lasted almost a week.[120] Boniface would have noticed a change immediately on 29 January when the gates of the city were not opened for his troops. Reports of Alexius's imprisonment soon followed. From the French crusaders' feudal perspective, Mourtzouphlus was a felon, a disloyal vassal who had overthrown his lord. Even worse, the treacherous Greeks willingly accepted the usurper. Villehardouin exclaimed, "Now see if ever people were guilty of such horrible treachery!"[121] The two cultures were too different. What was an ordinary palace coup for Byzantines was an abhorrent act of disloyalty to the feudal knights.

The success of Mourtzouphlus did nothing to alter the crusaders' view of their legal, moral, or ethical position at Constantinople. In their eyes, Alexius IV remained the emperor of Byzantium—and he still owed them money, provisions, and service. They were still justified, therefore, in looting his lands for their rightful due; they were still obliged to "pay themselves."

In accordance with that policy, Henry, the brother of Baldwin of Flanders undertook an attack against Philia, a prosperous town northwest of Constantinople on the Black Sea. He took with him thirty knights and many mounted sergeants, according to Robert of Clari.[122] They left the camp around six o'clock in the evening, probably on 2 February, and rode all night, arriving at Philia late the following morning. The Latins seized the town without resistance, gaining great booty, including cattle and clothing, and many prisoners. Enough was captured to supply the army for fifteen days. Some of this they shipped down the straits to their camp. They remained in Philia for two days, enjoying the abundance of good food and amenities. Then, burdened with the remaining cattle and other booty, they set out on their return journey.[123]

On 5 February Mourtzouphlus was formally crowned Alexius V in Hagia Sophia.[124] Almost immediately, perhaps during the coronation ceremony itself, word reached the new emperor of Henry of Flanders' expedition to Philia.[125] Here was Mourtzouphlus's chance to make good on his anti-Latin rhetoric. With throne and people of one mind in hating the crusaders, Constantinople was now ready to fight back. Mourtzouphlus assembled a force of about four thousand men and immediately rode out to ambush Henry before he could return to the crusaders' camp.[126] He brought with him the miraculous icon of the Virgin, which the emperors often carried into battle in the belief that under its protection they could not be defeated.[127] At the edge of the woods, along the road from Philia to Constantinople, Mourtzouphlus laid an ambush for the returning crusaders. Henry and his followers unsuspectingly rode right into it. When the crusaders saw themselves surrounded they were filled with fear, and they began to call upon God and Our Lady to deliver them. Although fearful, they did not panic, saying to one another that if they fled they would be killed, so it would be better to die honorably fighting than to perish miserably in flight. The Greeks fell upon them furiously. When the crusaders saw the enemy coming at them from all sides, they discarded their lances, and struck about with swords, knives, and daggers. Despite tactical advantage, the Byzantine army again proved its lack of courage or skill. After fierce fighting that resulted in no Latin knights being unhorsed, the Greek soldiers considered the balance to be shifting against them. They took to flight. The Latins pursued them, killing some and capturing others. Mourtzouphlus and his bodyguard fled back toward the city, but a party of Latins remained in hot pursuit. Finally, to halt their progress, Mourtzouphlus discarded his imperial helmet, standard, and even the precious icon of the Virgin. Although costly, the ploy worked. The pursuing crusaders stopped to retrieve the gem-studded treasures and let Mourtzouphlus and his party return to the city. Robert of Clari, accepting the powers that the Greeks attributed to this image of the Virgin, believed that Mourtzouphlus was defeated because he had no right to bear it as emperor.[128]

When the crusaders in the camp heard that Henry had been ambushed, a rescue party spurred forth to aid him. They met him on the road, however, already victorious and proudly displaying the captured icon. As the returning crusaders drew near the camp, the Latin bishops and clergy came forth to meet them and received the precious image with rejoicing. They carried it in solemn procession to a church, where the clergy chanted a service of thanksgiving.[129] This icon, which is lost or unidentifiable today, is described as made of gold, adorned with precious stones, and provided with most sacred relics, such as a baby tooth of Christ and a part of the sacred lance.[130] The barons agreed that the holy prize should be given to Cîteaux, but there is no record of its having arrived there.[131]

Mourtzouphlus returned to the capital with the battered remains of his forces. Although his expedition was a disaster, the new emperor's defeat was militarily irrelevant. It does not even seem to have greatly affected his popularity, which remained quite high.[132] What Byzantines craved was someone who would fight the Latins; they had found that in Mourtzouphlus. As an emperor, Mourtzouphlus was the opposite of the vacillating young Alexius IV or the doddering Isaac II. He was resolute and active. Unlike his predecessors, Mourtzouphlus delegated almost nothing, refusing to hand out meaningless titles and taking full charge of all imperial affairs.[133] Those who had received titles and honors under the Angeli were stripped not only of their dignities, but also their wealth.[134] Nicetas Choniates managed to retain what little property he had after the great fire, but he soon learned that he was being replaced as grand logothete with Mourtzouphlus's father-in-law, Philokales.[135] The rest of Mourtzouphlus's relatives did not fare as well. Expecting plush jobs and stratospheric stipends, they flocked to their kinsman's court, only to be rebuked and sent packing. Mourtzouphlus further earned the respect of his countrymen by his continued willingness to engage the Latins face-to-face. In the coming months he would often respond to a report of a Latin raid by girding his sword and mace, mustering a detachment, and engaging the assailants. Victory was less elusive in some of these engagements than it had been on the road to Philia.[136]

The crusaders probably expected the loss of the miracle-working icon to have more of an impact on Mourtzouphlus's position than it did. A story began circulating, at least among the rank and file, that the usurper had claimed victory in the engagement against the Latins. When asked about the missing icon, Mourtzouphlus had replied that he had already stored it away for safekeeping. According to Robert of Clari, the crusaders disproved this lie by displaying the captured icon and imperial insignia on a galley, which rowed back and forth under the city walls.[137] If this happened, it did not make much of an impression on either side of the Golden Horn, since Clari is the only source for it. If anything, this display only inflamed the Greeks' rage against the Latins further, which in turn tightened Mourtzouphlus's grip on power all the more.

Mourtzouphlus had a mandate to stop the Latin raids and expel the barbarians from the region, and he meant to do just that. Alexius IV's strategy of waiting for March when the crusade leaders' covenant with the rank and file would take precedence over the Treaty of Zara was no longer viable. The fight with Henry of Flanders convinced Mourtzouphlus that expelling the large Latin force, now swollen with refugees from the city, by military means would be an extremely difficult operation, if it could be done at all. And so he turned to negotiations. On 7 February, only one or two days after Mourtzouphlus's loss of the icon, a meeting was arranged with Doge Enrico Dandolo.[138] Boniface of Montferrat, who had always served as the liaison between the crusaders and the emperor, was not even considered to represent the Latins this time. Mourtzouphlus and Boniface were hardly on the best of terms. Dandolo, on the other hand, was a pragmatist who had some knowledge of Constantinople. Unlike the other Western barons, the Venetian doge would not be impeded by a feudal outlook on an imperial matter.

The meeting took place in the open near the monastery of Saints Cosmas and Damian, the doge staying afloat in his galley, while Mourtzouphlus was mounted on shore. Only Nicetas and Baldwin record the details of this discussion. The two accounts are different, but not irreconcilable. According to Nicetas, Dandolo demanded that Mourtzouphlus pay five thousand gold pounds (or ninety thousand silver marks), which must have been Alexius's IV's outstanding debt to the crusaders. The doge then outlined "certain other conditions which were both galling and unacceptable to those who have tasted freedom and are accustomed to give, not take, commands." When Mourtzouphlus balked, Dandolo insisted that the demands were not burdensome. Suddenly, a Latin cavalry force appeared and swept down on Mourtzouphlus. Some of his bodyguard was captured, but the emperor escaped.[139] According to Baldwin of Flanders, Dandolo began the negotiations by declaring that the crusaders would not negotiate. Mourtzouphlus was a usurper. If he would agree to return Alexius IV to his rightful throne, then the crusaders would use their influence with the young man to reduce Mourtzouphlus's punishment for his crime. In the meantime, Mourtzouphlus should remind Alexius of his continued indebtedness to the crusaders. Alexius must immediately restore the Greek church to Roman obedience and prepare his troops to sail with the crusaders when they departed in March. According to Baldwin, Mourtzouphlus replied with empty words; he had nothing reasonable to say.[140]

Together the two accounts provide us with a good picture of the negotiations between emperor and doge. Nicetas, who saw the Latins as money-hungry savages, not surprisingly emphasizes the monetary demand of ninety thousand marks.[141] He then lumps the call for ecclesiastical union and aid in the Holy Land under "galling and unacceptable conditions." For his part, Baldwin, who was writing to the pope, omits the request for money, but plays up the insistence on Roman obedience and the crusade to the East. Baldwin, of course, omits the treacherous attempted ambush of the emperor, which, it seems likely, did occur. What emerges from this is striking. The three demands of the crusaders—money, union, and assistance—were the three components of their reward in the Treaty of Zara. Even now, the crusaders only wanted their contract to be honored.[142]

Mourtzouphlus clearly hoped that the Westerners would strike a new bargain with a new emperor. Perhaps he thought to tempt Dandolo by promising a restoration of Venice's favored commercial position in the empire after matters had cooled down.[143] Perhaps he offered to provide the Latins with provisions and a distant campsite if they would leave Constantinople. These would surely have been "empty words" in Baldwin of Flanders' estimation. What Mourtzouphlus certainly could not do, however, was come up with ninety thousand marks to buy off the crusaders. To do so would make him as unpopular as Alexius IV, and for the same reason. That was of no concern to the crusaders, since, according to Baldwin, they were only willing to accept payment from a restored Alexius. Neither the Franks nor the Venetians had any desire to deal with the usurper. For the feudal knights, Mourtzouphlus was simply a disloyal vassal. When he refused to relinquish power, they felt justified in attempting to capture him. For the Venetians, he was just one more in a line of treacherous imperial claimants. Mourtzouphlus could offer Dandolo and his countrymen nothing that they did not already have with Alexius. If, when March came, Mourtzouphlus was still on the throne, that would be the time for Venice to negotiate with the new emperor. Alexius V had sufficiently alienated all of the Italians, so Venice would have an equal chance at recouping its losses in the empire. Until then, it only made sense to insist on the reinstatement of the young man who owed them all so much.[144]

For the crusaders, the meeting between Dandolo and Mourtzouphlus changed nothing. They still felt justified in continuing their raids against Byzantine lands for provisions and wealth in payment on Alexius's outstanding debt. For Mourtzouphlus, the meeting told him all he needed to know about the crusaders' position. If Dandolo's words had not made it crystal clear, the attempted ambush did: the Latins would never accept Mourtzouphlus as emperor while Alexius IV lived. The young man was the sole moral and ethical underpinning for the crusaders' presence at Constantinople. If Alexius were dead, the Latins would no longer have reason before God or man to continue collection on the debt or further delay their crusader vows. It had been Alexius and then Isaac who had made covenants with the Latins, not Mourtzouphlus or the citizens of Byzantium.[145] And yet, if Mourtzouphlus simply executed Alexius, it might so enrage the Latins that they would become even more troublesome.

To rid himself of this liability, Mourtzouphlus tried twice to poison Alexius IV. Both times the young man was able to take antidotes.[146] Finally on the night of 8/9 February, Mourtzouphlus ordered him strangled.[147] Thus ended the life of the ambitious young man from whom so much tragedy had flowed, and would continue to flow. The next day it was announced throughout Constantinople that Alexius had died of natural causes. Mourtzouphlus gave him a full state burial and seemed genuinely to mourn him.[148] Although this show may have been of some benefit for any partisans of Alexius IV in the city (if any still existed), its primary intended audience was the Latin host.

Mourtzouphlus was in no danger of offending Byzantine sensibilities by proclaiming that he had ordered the murder of the previous emperor. He owed
his position to the citizens' loathing of the Angeli in general and Alexius IV
in particular. If the Latins, on the other hand, could be made to believe that
God had taken poor, young Alexius, they might be more willing to discuss
matters with his legitimate successor.[149]

The crusaders were not fooled. According to Clari, an arrow with a letter
attached was shot into the crusader camp, which divulged the secret that they
might otherwise have guessed: Mourtzouphlus had murdered Alexius. For
most crusaders, whether Alexius had died naturally or not was a distinction
without a difference. Clari reports that they greeted the news by exclaiming,
"a curse on anyone who cares whether Alexius is dead or not," because he had
not kept his word to them.[150] They were disgusted with the whole sordid affair and longed to shake the dust of Byzantium from their sandals. For the
crusade's highest leaders, however, the death of Alexius IV was momentous.
It brought the entire contractual house of cards that they had so painstakingly
built crashing to their feet. The Treaty of Zara was now void. The extension
of the Treaty of Venice, undertaken by Alexius IV to keep the crusaders at
Constantinople until March, was also defunct. Since the original Treaty of
Venice had already expired, the Venetian fleet no longer had an employer. It
was only the presence of the doge that kept the warships from returning to
the Adriatic and the transports from returning to trade. The only sworn commitments that still survived were the vows the leaders had made to the host
to bring them to Syria in March no matter the situation in Constantinople,
and the vow each crusader had made to God to deliver the land of his Son.[151]

The crusaders were in a horrible bind. The plans of the leaders, based
on the promises of Alexius, were in shambles. There would be no glorious
Latin/Byzantine fleet descending on the sultan of Egypt. More than one of the
dissidents at Corfu must now have proclaimed that they could have avoided
these straits if only their advice had been heeded. The cold and stormy Constantinopolitan winter was still upon them. Even if the weather had been
better, even if they had sufficient provisions, they would not have dared to
sail away, for in the midst of the disorder of embarkation the Greeks might
fall upon them.[152] They lacked the basic necessities of life, living from hand to
mouth by foraging, which required ever more distant and dangerous forays,
since the nearby areas had been plundered frequently. Many of their horses
had been eaten,[153] a thing that a feudal army would do only as a last resort,
for a knight without a horse felt impoverished and degraded. Before them
loomed the enormous fortified walls, whose strength they had already tested

once with disappointing results. If they could survive another month sustaining meager rations and continual harassment, the rank and file would demand to be taken to Syria. When the leaders claimed poverty, tidal forces would tear the crusade into pieces. After so much effort and heartache, the Fourth Crusade seemed to have reached a pitiful anticlimax.

The Second Conquest of Constantinople

Back in December 1203 when Villehardouin declared, "and so began the war," he also referred to its end: "and so the war lasted a long time until the heart of winter."[1] This passage is crucial to understanding the Latin view of events from December 1203 to April 1204. The "war" Villehardouin described, as we have seen, was directed against the property and wealth of Alexius IV and his lands. The crusaders saw it as a morally justified attempt to "pay themselves," since the emperor refused to pay them. The feudal knights, with their culture of chivalry steeped in honor, believed that their attacks on Byzantine lands were the natural result of Alexius IV's dishonorable refusal to live up to his sworn oaths. The Venetians, who saw things from a commercial perspective, agreed with their northern allies. Contracts had been made. If the required payment for services was not rendered, the Venetians believed they were justified in collecting the sum by force. French chivalric honor and Venetian bourgeois ethics bound the crusade from the start to scrupulously proceeding within the boundaries of their sworn commitments.[2] The Fourth Crusade lived and died by its contracts, oaths, and vows.

It is not surprising, then, that Villehardouin speaks of the "war" between the Latins and Greeks continuing only until the "heart of winter." In February 1204, Alexius IV's death had dissolved the rationalization for the crusaders' war against Byzantium. There were, of course, other reasons for a new war against the Greeks. They had cheated the crusaders, led attacks on Latins even when both sides were at peace, and supported the murderer of Alexius IV. As Raymond Schmandt has pointed out, all of the Fourth Crusade's engagements met the current standards for a just war.[3] But that was no longer good enough: the majority of the crusaders no longer cared for just wars. The Mediterranean was littered with just wars; it was not the crusade's duty to take part in them. On the contrary, it was their duty to avoid spilling Christian blood on their way to the land of Christ. No wonder so many crusaders greeted the

news of Alexius's death with a resounding "Who cares?"[4] His empty promises had kept them at Constantinople for too long. With Alexius's death, the
crusaders were transformed from hired hands into soldiers of Christ.[5]

The leaders did not see it quite that way. For them the collapse of their
web of treaties and oaths was cataclysmic.[6] It was clear, given the mood of
disgust in the camp and the always fervent desire of the majority to complete their vows, that the crusading host would demand from its leaders the
promised transportation to Syria in March. Fulfillment of this promise was
probably impossible. While the leaders still had permission from Innocent III
to forage in Greek lands if provisions were not forthcoming, they no longer
had any right to take money or other forms of wealth from the local population.[7] And great wealth it would take to bring the army to the Levant.
Large amounts of provisions would have to be gathered, far more than they
currently had or could easily find. The Venetian fleet would also require payment; it was not within Dandolo's power to provide so large an armada at
the republic's expense.

Faced with the utter collapse of the enterprise, the leaders in desperation turned to the crusading clergy. A parliament was called shortly after the
Latins learned of Alexius IV's death. Present were the leading barons, Doge
Dandolo, and the bishops and abbots of the crusade.[8] The secular leaders
were powerless, their collection of agreements of no value. March was only
weeks away. When the host demanded transport, and the leaders could not
deliver, the crusade would splinter and crumble. The leaders needed time. A
few of the barons probably also wanted something more: a mandate to attack
Constantinople itself. Boniface of Montferrat had yet again been outmaneuvered by Mourtzouphlus and he must naturally have wanted revenge. Like
his brothers, Boniface had now been very close to the glamour and allure of
imperial power. Psychologically, it would be difficult to leave all that behind
to lead an impoverished and strife torn crusade to Palestine.

As they had done at Zara when asked for uncanonical absolutions, the
clergy gave the leaders what they wanted. In their verdict, they proclaimed
that Mourtzouphlus was a murderer and therefore had no right to rule Byzantium. All those who supported him were, therefore, abettors of murder. Even
worse, they lamented, the Greek church was once again in open schism from
Rome. For all these reasons, they decreed, "this war is right and just, and if
you have a right intention of conquering this land and bringing it into Roman
obedience, all those who die after confession shall have part in the indulgence
granted by the pope."[9]

There are two parts to the clergy's decision. The first simply states that
Mourtzouphlus's crimes and the Byzantines' sanction of them made a new

war "right and just." The aim of this new war was no longer acquisition of their due, but rather outright conquest. Yet, this facet of the clerical response could not itself extract the leaders from their bind. Right and just the war might be, but it was not a crusade, and the rank and file would no longer accept anything less.[10] The second part of the decision then addresses this problem. As a result of the Greek church's return to schism, a new war against Constantinople was not only just, but also a de facto crusade. The "indulgence granted by the pope" can be none other than the crusading indulgence. What the high clergy was in fact asserting was that reclaiming Constantinople for Catholicism was the equivalent of reclaiming Jerusalem for Christendom, at least for those who died. There is a difference, of course, between granting a crusading indulgence for the fallen at Constantinople and declaring that the taking of the city would fulfill a crusader's vow.[11] The distinction is subtle, however, and was not made clear to the rank and file.[12] The crusaders now had neither reason nor right to demand transport to Syria in March, since the crusade's enemy was Constantinople itself. From the crusaders' point of view, Jerusalem was now on the Bosporus.[13]

As they had done at Zara, the leading clergy proved themselves willing to contradict the pope and canon law to provide the barons with the justification they desired. Their construction of an attack on Constantinople as the equivalent of a crusade, while eminently practical, was plainly wrong. In a letter sent at least eight months earlier, Innocent III had explicitly forbidden any attack on Greek territory. Anticipating a likely clerical justification, Innocent wrote, "Let no one among you rashly convince himself that he may seize or plunder the Greeks' lands on the pretext that they show little obedience to the Apostolic See." He then enjoined the host to redeem its sins by proceeding immediately to the Holy Land.[14] The clergy deserve our compassion and understanding for they were torn between religion and reality, between the laws of the church and the laws of necessity. Yet, while it is true that they were faced with a difficult situation that threatened to become disastrous, that cannot justify their endorsing in the pope's name what Innocent unambiguously forbade. It is no accident, we believe, that all clerical accounts of the crusade omit any mention of the crusading indulgence granted before the attack on Constantinople. Only secular sources record it: namely Villehardouin, Robert of Clari, and perhaps the *Chronicle of the Morea*.[15] When Baldwin of Flanders wrote to the pope, he omitted any mention of the indulgence from his otherwise detailed account of events. It is clear that the redefinition of the attack on Constantinople as a crusade against schismatics was a doctrinal sleight of hand that many hoped would later be forgotten.[16]

The decision of the clergy was immediately preached to the host, and it came as a great comfort to them all.[17] The question that had nagged each pilgrim, high or low, since he arrived at Constantinople was, "Why are you still here and not bound for Jerusalem?" Now each man had his answer: God's work is here. It is only now, in mid-February 1204, that work began on the Venetian fleet to prepare it for an assault on Constantinople itself.[18] The Greeks sensed the change as well. On or around 3 March, city officials expelled the last remnants of Latins from Constantinople to guard against possible espionage or sabotage attempts.[19]

In March 1204, the deadline that had shaped events for almost a year, the crusading leaders entered into a new contract, this one between Doge Dandolo on the one side and Boniface of Montferrat, Baldwin of Flanders, Louis of Blois, and Hugh of Saint Pol on the other.[20] Together these men controlled most of the crusading host, with Dandolo commanding the Venetian half and the four other barons the non-Venetian half of the pilgrims. The treaty begins by committing all parties to undertaking a vigorous attack on Constantinople. If, with God's help, they should gain entry into the city, all booty should be brought together into one place for an equitable division. But what was equitable? First and foremost, the crusaders wanted Alexius IV's debt to be paid off, not because they believed it was still binding after his death, but rather because his refusal to pay had hurt some crusaders worse than others.[21] When Alexius died he owed the crusaders as a whole approximately 100,000 silver marks on the Treaty of Zara. He also owed the Venetians an additional 100,000 or so silver marks for the extension of the Treaty of Venice, which he undertook. Therefore, the Venetians were robbed of 150,000 marks when Alexius was murdered and the Frankish crusaders lost 50,000 marks.[22] It was decided, therefore, that when booty was divided the Venetians would receive three portions for each single portion that went to non-Venetians. All foodstuffs should be divided equally right from the start. If they were able to lay hands on less than 200,000 marks, then both sides would have to live with their losses. If, on the other hand, the booty exceeded the total that Alexius IV had owed them, all further funds would be divided equally between the Franks and the Venetians in accord with the Treaty of Venice.[23] There was an expectation in these arrangements that the crusaders might gain entry into Constantinople, as the Venetians had done the previous year, but would only be able to seize a portion of the massive city. Nevertheless, they next turned in their treaty to the possibility that all of Constantinople might fall to them. It was decided that in that case six Franks and six Venetians should be chosen to elect as emperor the man they found best suited for the task.[24] The emperor they chose would receive a quarter of all the conquests, and he would also have both the Great Palace and Blachernae. The remaining three-quarters would be divided equally between the Franks and the Venetians, as had been agreed in the Treaty of Venice. If the emperor should be selected from among the Franks, the Venetians should have a right to Hagia Sophia and the patriarchate, and conversely. Twelve crusaders and twelve Venetians should also be elected from among the wisest men to allocate fiefs and offices among the leaders and to establish the services that the recipients should owe the emperor in return.[25] They agreed that all pilgrims should remain by the emperor's side until the end of March 1205, at which time everyone should be free to go where he pleased.[26] They also agreed that the emperor would not do business with any state while it was at war with Venice.[27] When this was completed each man was required to swear with his hands on holy relics that, with some minor exceptions, he would bring all booty to the common hoard and that he would not use force upon any woman or despoil her of any garment she was wearing. The penalty for violating this oath was death. Each man also had to swear that he would not break into monasteries or churches.[28]

During the weeks of February and March the crusaders and Venetians busied themselves with preparations for their assault upon the imperial city. Altogether they were a host of more than twenty thousand men: a very large force by medieval standards, although still a meager force in the history of Constantinople's assailants.[29] Their number was further reinforced by Latins who had fled the city. The leadership of the brave count Louis of Blois was lost to the crusaders, however, for all winter and spring he was ill of a quartan fever and took no active part in the final conquest.[30] The army's experience in attacking Constantinople in July of 1203 had revealed the very great difficulty of scaling the land walls, whereas the Venetians had been more successful in their assault across the harbor. So they now agreed to concentrate all their forces against the walls fronting the Golden Horn, as from the outset the Venetians had advised.[31] Venetians and Franks labored industriously to put their machines of war in working order. The northerners set up mangonels and petraries on the shore before the Blachernae Palace to harass and exhaust the defenders and to raise the threat of another attack from that quarter. The leaders regarded these machines as very damaging to the enemy. They also prepared rams, catapults, tortoise shells, and other devices for assaulting or mining the walls.[32] The Venetians once more set up missile throwing mechanisms on their ships to bombard the city. The assault bridges, which customarily were suspended from the superstructures were raised even higher than those used previously to compensate for the heightening of the walls by the emperor. The fleet was covered with timbers and vines to absorb the shock of projectiles and with hides to protect against fire. Dandolo not only directed much of the preparation, but also built up confidence in the capacity of the fleet and inspired the spirits of the weakhearted.[33]

Within the city Mourtzouphlus also made ready for the coming battle. Along the land curtain to the west he ordered many of the gates walled up with bricks.[34] He too recognized the advantage of the Venetians' assault bridges, which allowed the attackers to approach on a level with the defenders or even from above, over the scaling ladders with which the northern crusaders had attempted to mount the land walls the previous July. Along the harbor curtain, therefore, he had built of stout beams towers of several stories between the permanent stone towers and also had the latter raised by several stories of wood. These hoardings overhung the stone wall, and each story overhung the one below, so that stones, missiles, hot sand, and burning oil could be poured upon attackers at the wall's base. The temporary timbered fortifications were covered with hides against burning. Mangonels and petraries were mounted along the wall to fire upon the enemy ships. Mourtzouphlus ordered a double ditch dug between the curtain and the water, so that the attackers on foot would find it difficult to drag or push their wheeled machines to the foot of the fortifications.[35] Mourtzouphlus also further strengthened his already very large army with additional troops brought in from provinces still under Constantinople's control.[36]

Now came the tense time when the preparations were complete. The Venetian fleet was equipped and armed to the teeth, the machines of war were in place, and provisions had been put on board.[37] On Thursday, 8 April, the men boarded their assigned ships and the horses were once again loaded into the horse transports to be ready for sailing with the dawn.[38] Each division of the army had its own vessels, drawn up side by side, transports alternating with galleys and horse transports. Villehardouin notes the marvelous sight of this long line of ships awaiting the morrow.[39]

Before battle the men prepared themselves for possible death by confessing their sins with tears, receiving absolution, and partaking of the Body of Christ in the sacrament.[40] With the first light of day the ships moved forward in line of battle.[41] The galleys and horse transports were to discharge their troops ashore to attempt to undermine or scale the fortifications. The transports would try to effect a foothold on the walls with their flying bridges.[42] The ships moving forward along a front of a good mile, their colorful banners fluttering in the early light, made a spectacular sight. Soldiers crowded the decks. Some prepared to throw themselves ashore under the walls. Others stood by the machines for which they were responsible. Those on the transports made ready to clamber across the precarious bridges onto the heights of the fortifications.

From the decks the attackers could see plainly the vermilion tents of the emperor, which Mourtzouphlus had ordered pitched on the slope of the hill in front of the monastery of Christ Pantepoptos (the All-Seeing).[43] His silver trumpets were ringing and timbrels were shaking, creating a great din to arouse the spirits of the defenders.[44] The voices of the Greeks raised the emperor's battle-cry, "Jesus Christ conquers!"[45] Mourtzouphlus had chosen a good command post from which he could survey the movements of the enemy and evaluate what was done on the ships even as they came directly under the walls.[46] They were approaching the same part that the Venetians had assaulted in July 1203. In just this quarter Mourtzouphlus looked across the desolate ruins left by the fire that the Venetians had set on that occasion.[47]

As the ships neared the walls they attempted to establish a cover for the assault forces with volleys of stones, bolts, and arrows. The defenders showered the fleet with return fire, which smashed some of the equipment and made it dangerous for those exposed on the decks.[48] The galleys and horse transports drew as near to the shore as they could, some beaching and others of deeper draft running aground farther out, so that the assault troops had to splash ashore burdened with scaling ladders, pickaxes, and other gear. The protective wheeled shells were carefully unloaded. These troops attacked the walls from the narrow strip of land between the fortifications and the harbor. The defenders hurled great stones down from above upon the wooden equipment for breaching the wall, smashing their protective roofs and forcing the engineers to flee.[49] While some crusaders attacked from the shore, the transports with their flying bridges flung out and burdened with brave men assaulted the heights of the walls.[50] One vessel had been assigned to each tower, and each boldly pushed forward to attempt to anchor its bridge to the top of the fortifications so that its complement could achieve a foothold.[51] An unusual south wind hampered operations, driving the ships back from the walls. Only five of them succeeded in drawing close enough to their assigned towers so that the troops suspended high above the sea and the land exchanged strokes with the Greeks.[52] The defenders fought back with energy. None of the ships succeeded in affixing its assault bridge to the wall.[53] For a good part of the day the battle raged in more than a hundred different places.[54]

Those who had landed were driven back. Amid the shower of stones and arrows they were unable to hold the shore and took to their vessels.[55] The Byzantine garrison had also been able to fight off the flying bridges of the transports. The wooden superstructures that Mourtzouphlus had raised upon the towers had been a success.[56] Abandoning much of their equipment, the leaders of the crusade were constrained to give the order to retreat.[57] As the ships pulled away from the shore the Greeks on the walls hooted and jeered at the defeated attackers. Some of them let down their clouts and showed their bare buttocks in derision to the fleeing foe.[58] The attack was a complete failure. The disheartened pilgrims had clearly had the worst of it. They lost nearly a hundred dead.[59] We do not have a figure for the Greek losses, but they seem to have been very slight. Alexius V, who had supervised the defense from his hillside command post before the monastery, was pleased by the easy victory. Again his instruments sounded, this time in proud triumph.[60]

A wave of fear now swept through the crusading army, infecting both high and low alike. Enflamed by their rage against Mourtzouphlus and the perfidious Greeks, assured by the words of their clergy, and puffed up by the relative ease of their victory in July 1203, the crusaders' balloon of self-righteous confidence had been smashed on the mammoth walls of the ancient megalopolis. Their crushing defeat did not square with their divinely endorsed work. Particularly worrisome was the unusual south wind that had blown up so suddenly, keeping the Venetian vessels from ever seriously threatening the city walls. Surely this was a sign from God! Amid the jeers of the Greeks and the moans of their companions, the crusaders began to believe again that they did not belong at Constantinople.

These sentiments were not merely the grumblings of the formerly dissident leaders and the rank and file. Some of the chiefs who had steadfastly supported all of the crusade's previous engagements now began to fear that God was finally taking vengeance for the pilgrims' long delayed vows and the decision to attack this Christian city.[61] Even Villehardouin proclaimed that the crusaders' defeat was inflicted by God as punishment for their sins.[62] For the first time some of these leaders began to doubt their previous judgments concerning the Constantinopolitan venture. To deal with these problems, a parliament of the Latin magnates, the doge, and the clergy was called. They met that evening about six o'clock in a church. The meeting was contentious. Many of the assembled wanted to withdraw, to board the Venetian vessels and head east. They were no longer interested in the reassurances of the clergy. The smashing defeat that they had just experienced made clear how little God agreed with his representatives. Others argued that the tactics of the assault were deficient. Why attack the walls that Mourtzouphlus had so strongly reinforced? Why not bring the fleet out of the Golden Horn and attack the sea walls along the Bosporus or the Sea of Marmara? Doge Dandolo objected to this plan, pointing out that the strong current running down the strait would make a naval assault on the city impossible. The fleet would simply be swept away. Suspecting the motives of those who proposed the scheme, Villehardouin declares that the effects of the current were precisely what many wanted: "And you should know that there were those who wished that the current would bear them down the strait, or that the wind would do so. They cared only about leaving this land and going on their way, and that should not be surprising as they were all in great danger."[63] After much discussion the parliament decided to attack the city once more. They agreed to spend the next two days resting, refitting the ships, and repairing the equipment before assaulting the same walls on Monday, 12 April. They had discovered in the first engagement that the garrisons of the towers were large enough to beat off the attackers trying to gain a foothold from the flying bridge of a single transport. For the next assault they determined to bind the transports together two by two, so that a greater force could be brought to bear against each point of attack.[64]

While the fleet would again be ready for the attack, it increasingly seemed as if the host would not. The crusader rank and file remained angry and frightened, both because of their punishing defeat, and because of God's hand in it. They no longer accepted the assurances of their clergy and leaders. Promise after promise to them had been made and broken; they were tired of being lied to. March, the month they had anticipated for so long, had come and gone and they were no closer to completing their vows. Even worse, they were imperiling their souls by attacking the greatest Christian city in the world. From a purely strategic standpoint, another assault seemed foolhardy. Although the Venetians had successfully taken a portion of the wall in 1203, the Franks had met only defeat in all of their attacks on Constantinople. They were tired of it.

The crisis of faith that now afflicted the crusade threatened its very survival. The clergy moved quickly to stop the loss of will that the enterprise was actively hemorrhaging. On Sunday, 11 April, it was cried through the camp that everyone, including even the excommunicated Venetians, should come to divine services. The bishops of Soissons, Troyes, and Halberstadt and other prominent clergy, such as Baldwin's chancellor, the eloquent John Faicete, preached to large gatherings.[65] They sought to persuade the host, now in more vibrant terms, of the righteousness of their cause. Over and over again they stressed that the attack on Constantinople was not a sin, but rather a good deed.[66] The justifications they preached were not new: the murder of Alexius IV and the schism with Rome. But now the bishops embellished their speeches with explosive language that the common soldier could understand and respond to. When they railed at the treasonous nature of the Greeks who had murdered their lord, the bishops now added that the crime had made Byzantines "worse than Jews."[67] When they lashed out at the Greeks' refusal to accept the primacy of the pope, they supplemented, for the benefit of those less familiar with ecclesiological concerns, that the Greeks believed that those who followed the "law of Rome" were "dogs."[68] These sermons sought both to de-Christianize the Greeks and to personalize the struggle for the common soldier. In so doing, the bishops hoped to extinguish the growing belief that the attack on the Byzantines was sinful and to enflame the spirit of the soldiers by evoking base insults.[69] But they went even further. To underscore to the host that their war was in fact a crusade, they called all of the men to take communion. Even the Venetians appear to have been included; the fact that they were excommunicates was ignored. The clergy then heard confessions and imparted full absolution on "all those who should attack them [Byzantines], in the name of God, and by the authority of the Apostolic." Finally, the clergy ordered all camp prostitutes to be expelled.[70] These purifications were the usual preliminaries to crusader attacks on infidel lands; the clergy of the Fourth Crusade had never resorted to them before. Faced with the breakdown of the crusaders' will to fight, the clergy pulled out all the stops. The rank and file had no idea that the verdict of their bishops contradicted the commands of the pope. And so, the crusade crystallized once more around the episcopal invention. The soldiers were again convinced of the righteousness of their war.

At sunrise on Monday, 12 April, every available Latin soldier was in his place, ready to resume the assault. Forty of the large roundships had been tied together in pairs, so that each pair might attack a single tower, thus concentrating more men against its defenders. The fleet approached the same section of wall from the Blachernae to the monastery of Christ Evergetes, which they had unsuccessfully assailed on Friday.[71] Alexius V also occupied the same command post on the hill below Pantepoptos. Greek stone throwers hammered the fleet with boulders so large that a single man could not lift one, but the Venetians had protected their ships with timbers and grapevines, so that no serious damage was done. The roundships came as near the walls as they could, then cast anchors and rained arrows and stones upon the defenders. They were close enough also to disgorge Greek fire upon the wooden towers, but these were protected with hides, so they would not burn.[72] After their victory on Friday the Greeks had more confidence and less fear, and the walls and towers were now even more crowded with defenders. They fought well, according to witnesses on both sides, and amid the shouts of combat the conflict raged more furiously than before. Until about midday the defenders stood firm.[73]

Toward noon there arose a north wind that blew the ships toward the shore. Robert of Clari tells us that only four or five of the greatest vessels could reach with their assault bridges the tops of the wooden towers erected by Mourtzouphlus.[74] Two of these were the *Paradise* and the *Pilgrim*, which were bound together and assigned to the French bishops of Soissons and Troyes. A gust of wind and a surge of water drove them forward, so that for an instant the end of the flying bridge of the ship of the bishop of Soissons, the *Paradise*, banged against a tower near where Alexius V watched from his hill.[75] A courageous Venetian grabbed hold of the tower, clung to it with hands and feet, and somehow managed to pull himself upon it. He was quite alone. The Varangians and Greeks fell upon him with axes and swords, making of him a bloody corpse.[76] Tossed by wave and wind, the ship once more bumped the tower, and a French knight named André d'Ureboise of the household of Bishop Nivelon followed the example of the Venetian and clambered onto its summit on his hands and knees. The Varangians and Greeks also attacked him with their cruel weapons, but his armor protected him enough so that he was able to struggle to his feet and draw his own sword. With great force and valor he drove the defenders to a lower level of the tower, gaining time for his comrades to climb upon it after him. They secured the ship with stout ropes, and other pilgrims crossed the flying bridge to the tower. The surge of the sea, however, pulled at the ships so strongly that the whole tower trembled, so the ships had to cast off for fear of pulling down the superstructure with their own men upon it. Those who had crossed were enough. The crusaders' battle cry, "Holy Sepulcher!" resounded as the Varangians and the Greeks fled from the tower. The Latins who had taken it waved their hands over their heads in triumph and shouted encouragement to their comrades on the ships. Soon the banners of the two bishops were flying over the captured tower.[77] Emboldened by the success of the *Pilgrim* and the *Paradise*, Peter of Bracieux, who was not accustomed to being second to any in the fray, succeeded with his men in mounting upon another tower and taking it.[78] Other crusaders debarked on the shore and set up ladders to scale other towers.[79] Mourtzouphlus immediately sent reinforcements to the threatened sector. Seeing the multitude of soldiers which now swarmed onto the walls, neighboring towers, and the ground below, the Latins did not dare to venture beyond their captured towers.[80]

Robert of Clari was one of a party of about ten knights and sixty sergeants, led by Peter of Amiens, that landed on a narrow strip of ground between the walls and the shore. They discovered a postern gate that the defenders had walled up. The crusaders fell upon it zealously with picks, crowbars, axes, and even swords. It was hard going and dangerous, for from above the Greeks rained quarrels upon them, almost buried them under a torrent of immense stones, poured down pots of boiling pitch, and attempted to incinerate them with Greek fire. While some picked away at the postern, other crusaders covered them with their shields. Soon they succeeded in making a hole. Peering through it, they saw a huge crowd of Greeks inside; according to Robert it seemed that half of the world stood on the other side of that wall. They did not dare to enter. Robert's brother, Aleaumes, the same priest in hauberk who had distinguished himself in the taking of the tower of Galata, pushed forward to claim the honor of attempting entry. Robert, fearing for his brother's life, urged that he should not be so foolhardy, but Aleaumes got down on his hands and knees to crawl through the hole. Robert thereupon grabbed his foot to prevent him, but Aleaumes kicked loose from his clinging brother and dragged himself through.[81]

And then an amazing thing happened. With enormous confidence Aleaumes of Clari drew his sword, one man against a multitude, and ran toward the Greek troops. They fled like cattle. The story Robert tells seems so improbable that one is tempted to disbelieve it, but the prideful words of the lowly Picard knight are corroborated by the lamentations of Nicetas Choniates.[82] Now Constantinople reaped what the military reforms of Manuel Comnenus had sown. Poorly trained and martially inept, the largely provincial elements in the imperial army had shown themselves again and again willing to fight only when the danger to themselves was minuscule. Most had little stake in Constantinople and therefore refused to risk their lives for the sake of the capital. Instead they "took to their customary flight as the efficacious medicine of salvation."[83] How unlike the brave Greeks who would defend "the City" in 1422 or 1453 were these soldiers in 1204!

When the Greek troops near the hole turned tail, Aleaumes quickly called for his companions to follow him. Robert of Clari and Peter of Amiens entered the city, and the remainder of the ten knights and sixty sergeants slithered through the hole one by one. Fearing to progress any farther, the Latins remained with their backs to the walls. The precaution was unnecessary. When the Greek troops stationed at other points along the walls saw that the men had gained entry they fled their posts. Soon a domino effect occurred along the fortifications, as one tower was evacuated, the next followed suit. Seeing the impending collapse of his forces caused by such a tiny leak in his fortifications, Mourtzouphlus attempted to put his finger in the dike. At first he sounded his trumpets and beat his timbrels to frighten Peter and his men, but this had no effect. Finally, he spurred his horse and charged alone toward the Latins at a full gallop. Peter of Amiens ordered his men to stand fast; after routing the army they would not flee before the emperor. Indeed, they relished the opportunity to prove their mettle against "Mourtzouphlus the traitor." Sensing their resolve, the emperor halted, and turned back to his command post on the hill.[84]

Granted this respite, Peter dispatched some sergeants to break open the nearest gate, probably Petrion. In spite of the bolts and iron bars, the crusaders used axes and swords to tear it open. Seeing this, the Venetians brought the transports up to shore, and the remaining Latins and the crusaders' horses disembarked. The attackers swarmed into the city like killer bees. Additional gates swung wide, and a large force of Latins gathered at the foot of the hill where Mourtzouphlus had his headquarters. With their horses and a wide open space in which to fight, the Franks were now in their element. The heavily armed knights drew up to charge Mourtzouphlus and his imperial bodyguard. The emperor did not remain to give battle.[85] His situation was desperate. From his vantage point, Mourtzouphlus could see the large majority of the imperial army running helter-skelter for the land walls, leaving their posts and heading to their faraway homes.[86] At Pantepoptos he probably had no more than a token force of Varangians. If he had more he would hardly have ridden alone to face Peter of Amiens. His forces, therefore, were no match for the Frankish knights. Instead, he decided to use Constantinople's great size and density where her sea walls had failed. Retreating into the city, Mourtzouphlus entered the Great Palace where he could assess the damage.[87]

With no one to oppose them in far northern Constantinople, the crusaders and Latins fanned out with little order. They ran from place to place, looting, pillaging, and mercilessly slaughtering Greeks, regardless of age or sex.[88] We know of only one Latin killed during this carnage, a well known and noble knight who was killed when his horse fell into a pit while he was pursuing a Greek.[89] Peter of Amiens and his men seized the Pantepoptos hill.[90] Overall, however, the Latin army did not come away with much. Despite their position, they still did not control Blachernae Palace, which had its own fortifications and garrison. In fact, they currently held little more than the open field of desolation left behind by the Venetian fire nine months earlier. Constantinople was far too large and populous for the Latins to claim in the few remaining hours of daylight. Their victory that day was important, amazing, and unique, but it was not yet the conquest of New Rome.

As the sun sank the various groups of Latins assembled in the burned region for a general parliament.[91] The leaders spoke to the army of their dangerous situation. Constantinople, they believed, still had far more men under arms than did the Latins.[92] The crusaders must remain alert lest the Greeks catch them unaware. No one believed that Constantinople was taken, nor that it could be taken very soon. Villehardouin states bluntly that the leaders believed that even a month would be insufficient time to conquer so large a city.[93] The massive population, narrow streets, and dense buildings suggested brutal house to house fighting, which the Franks abhorred. They feared that should their troops venture into the city's snarl of backstreets and broad avenues they would easily be picked off by lone assassins, tumultuous mobs, or residents throwing down roof tiles.[94] They, therefore, forbade the army to seek quarters in the city. Most of the troops camped outside or just inside the sea walls near the Venetian vessels so that they could retreat in the event of a Greek attack.[95] Baldwin of Flanders occupied the emperor's colorful tent at Pantepoptos. His brother Henry spent the night just outside Blachernae Palace. Boniface of Montferrat with a small force, camped not far from the monastery of Christ Evergetes, close to the sea walls.[96] It was decided that on the morrow the Latins would draw up into battle ranks in the open burned region and meet Mourtzouphlus on that blackened field. If the Greeks refused battle, the Latins would again set fire to the city, burning out its defenders.[97]

But a few crusaders could not wait until morning. During the night, near the encampment of the marquis of Montferrat, a German count, identified by some historians as Berthold of Katzenellenbogen, fearing a surprise attack, set fire to the buildings between the Latins and the Greeks.[98] The fire spread into the city, raging from near Evergetes where it was set, through the lower elevations along the Golden Horn, until at Droungarios Gate it met the desolation left behind by the great fire of 19 August 1203.[99] This was the third fire the crusaders had inflicted upon Constantinople since their arrival in July 1203. Villehardouin estimated that more houses were destroyed in these three blazes than existed in the three largest cities in France.[100] He was close to the mark.[101] Altogether the Latins had turned one-sixth of Constantinople into smoldering ruins and eliminated perhaps one-third of her dwellings.[102] Looking out over the charred wastelands, Nicetas addressed his beloved city saying, "now your luxurious garments and elegant royal veils are rent and torn; your flashing eye has grown dark, and you are like an aged furnace woman all covered with soot. . . ."[103]

A very different drama was being played out in the other 90 percent of the city. To understand it, however, we must wrest ourselves from the Latin view of events and attempt to view the calamity of 12 April from the Byzantine perspective—a perspective shaped by the city's own unique history and culture. When Mourtzouphlus rode into the Great Palace he still hoped that he could turn things around. Most of the imperial army had fled or was in the process of doing so. There may have remained about ten thousand mounted troops, which probably constituted those permanently garrisoned in Constantinople.[104] Whether these soldiers would obey his commands any longer was another matter. Mourtzouphlus could, of course, count on the elite Varangian Guard, which stood at about six thousand men.[105] While formidable, the Varangians would hardly be sufficient to destroy twenty thousand Latins. Mourtzouphlus needed the remaining army, and particularly the population, which probably still numbered around four hundred thousand or more, to back an effort to expel the invaders. Like the crusade leaders, the emperor realized that the massive and destructive mobs could overwhelm the Latins if they so chose.

And yet, as strange as it may seem, the people of Constantinople wanted nothing to do with fighting the Latins. From hindsight, this seems to be a baffling response to the impending destruction of their city. With the hated enemy in the gates poised to destroy their homes, steal their goods, rape their women, and either expel or kill them, why did the frequently violent Byzantine population suddenly become so meek and mild? They had little difficulty expelling thousands of well-armed Pisans only a few months ago. Why did they now refuse to lift a finger to defend themselves? Even more amazing, the large majority of the citizenry did not even attempt to avoid the sack by leaving the city.[106] Instead, they simply waited. Why? Historians have offered various explanations for this extraordinary response. Some believe that Constantinople was simply weak from the start, a decrepit metropolis teetering on the edge of its inevitable demise.[107] Others accept that the city was still powerful, but that the people themselves either refused to defend it or were unable to do so.[108] None of these assertions, however, explains why the majority of the people did not flee immediately rather than waiting to endure the carnage of the sack—and then fleeing.

On the night of 12 April 1204, the majority of Constantinopolitans refused either to flee or to resist the Latins because they lacked the hindsight of medieval and modern historians. Instead, they viewed events from their own history and personal experiences, not from those of the Latins. There was no precedent for the final outcome of the events of 12 April in Constantinople: no foreign invader had ever gained entry into the city. But there was precedent for the specific events themselves. Armed conflicts were commonplace in Byzantium. Just in the twenty years before the crusaders' arrival on the Bosporus, there were at least nine separate armed rebellions whose aim was to carve autonomous states out of imperial territory, and nineteen other rebellions whose target was the imperial throne itself. Of the latter, thirteen involved the use of troops marshaled to depose forcibly the sitting emperor.[109] And those twenty years were not even considered, by Byzantine standards, all that tumultuous. Jean-Claude Cheynet has counted 223 revolts against imperial authority in the years between 963 and 1210. As he points out, civil war was for the Byzantine citizen an expected part of life.[110] This should not surprise us. Making war to claim supreme power was, after all, a venerable Roman tradition dating back to Sulla. The regularity of these armed coups made them expected events in a capital dweller's life. It would be astonishing, then, if the citizens of Constantinople did not view the actions of the crusaders in 1204 in that familiar light. After all, the installation of a rival imperial claimant was precisely the reason the Westerners had come to Byzantium in the first place. During their stay they had continued to support their claimant until he refused to pay them for their services. The crusaders' transformation into a conquering army attempting to take the city for themselves had only occurred in the crusaders' own minds two months earlier, when Alexius IV was killed. Most Byzantines seem to have been unaware of this shift. Indeed, even the crusaders had difficulty with it: witness the need for the fiery sermons on Sunday. In the Byzantine view, the crusaders were inextricably bound to the Angelan dynasty—they were that family's army. Even after the troops' falling out with Alexius IV in November, the army had never threatened Constantinople itself until Mourtzouphlus overthrew the Angeli in February.

When people are faced with new and terrifying situations they look to their cultural and personal experiences to guide them. We can get a better handle on the Byzantine view of events that night, therefore, if we examine other events that shaped that view. The situation on 12 April is strikingly similar to that of the Comnenian change of dynasty in 1081. After Alexius I had gained entry into Constantinople with his largely foreign mercenary army, the emperor Nicephorus still controlled the palace complex and, of course, the Varangian Guard. The imperial army largely evaporated. Rather than suffer a war within the walls, the citizens and clergy withdrew their support from Nicephorus, thus allowing Alexius to take the purple.[111] The people preferred a change in imperial dynasty over a destructive conflict in their city. Much more recently, in July 1203, the people favored accepting Alexius IV and his mercenary army of crusaders rather than suffering further damage to their city as occurred in the Venetian fire. Sensing this, Alexius III fled. Unlike Alexius I's foreign mercenaries in 1081,[112] however, Alexius IV's forces entered peacefully, respecting property and law. The night of 12 April 1204 the people of Constantinople remembered these events and made their customary decision. Rather than fight for the latest in a line of short-lived emperors, they chose once again to accept the crusading army's claimant to the throne. Although there was much bad blood between the crusaders and the Greeks, the latter undoubtedly hoped that the former would conduct themselves with the same restraint they showed nine months earlier. It was, after all, in no new emperor's interest to see his capital destroyed.

This view had one major flaw: the Latins had no imperial claimant. Yet that in itself was a very recent development: only a few days earlier the leaders had agreed to put off an imperial election until a later date. Even on 12 April most Latins believed Boniface of Montferrat would be elected. Most Byzantines, we know from subsequent events, believed that Boniface was waging war as an imperial rival to Mourtzouphlus.[113] As mentioned before, Boniface had a good imperial pedigree: his two brothers had married into the Angelus family and received the title of Caesar. The Montferrat clan was well known to the average Constantinopolitan, both for Renier's attempt to seize the throne for himself and his wife, and for Conrad's defense of the capital against the Branas revolt. From the Byzantine point of view, Boniface, a member of the Angelus family by marriage, was attempting to overthrow Mourtzouphlus, the destroyer of the Angelan dynasty. It seemed that Boniface would now reach the throne that had eluded his brothers. The fact that Boniface was a Latin Christian backed by a Latin army was sufficient reason for the populace to oppose him if it cost them little, but insufficient if it meant warfare within the city. The same citizens had, after all, joyously accepted Alexius IV, who was backed by the same army and had promised the submission of the Greek church to Rome.[114]

To save his throne, Mourtzouphlus had to rally the people to his side. He mounted his horse and rode through the streets, where there was more than the usual buzz of activity that fateful night. Some people, particularly those who had lost their homes in the great fire, were gathering their few belongings and leaving the city. Others, perhaps remembering the three days of looting that followed Alexius Comnenus's coup and not trusting the Latin soldiers in any event, were burying their wealth so that it could be retrieved later.[115] Still others were preparing the streets for the ritual procession of the new emperor to Hagia Sophia for his coronation.[116] Into all of this rode Mourtzouphlus. He did his best to convince the people to fight the Latins. The battle was not lost, he claimed. If they worked together they could crush the invaders between the irresistible populace and the immovable walls.[117] When they refused, he ridiculed the people for their fickleness. Had they forgotten their hatred for the Latins? Where was their Roman courage? From place to place Mourtzouphlus rode, but everywhere heard the same reply: silence or scorn. The commoners ignored his exhortations and the aristocrats fled from him, probably to avoid any association with the defeated emperor that could be used against them later.[118]

Nothing Mourtzouphlus said could convince the Greeks to defend their country, for, as they saw it, it was only his reign at stake. Neither he nor they envisioned the fall of Byzantium, only the imperial elevation of Boniface of Montferrat. The emperor's ride had a cultural subtext lost on moderns. Isaac II, who had died only a few months earlier and on whose account all of these calamities had occurred, saved his life and won the throne by riding through the city's streets rallying the people to his cause.[119] But where Isaac had succeeded, Mourtzouphlus failed. The populace had no moral obligation to support the current emperor with arms when another strove to take his place. These kinds of struggles were between two men, not two peoples. Issac II himself gave voice to this fact when he faced the army of Branas in

1187. He told those not committed to his reign, "I make of you a reasonable request: remain at home, offering assistance to neither side until the issue is resolved by battle and then submit with the others to the victor."[120] In the view of the citizens of Constantinople, the matter had been decided by battle, and Mourtzouphlus had lost. While many undoubtedly felt pity for the valiant man, the red glow of fire from the north told them of the fate of their city if they should continue to support him.[121]

Mourtzouphlus returned to the Great Palace with nothing to show for his efforts. The city had already forsaken him, preparing as it was to crown his successor. With the Varangian Guard he could hold the palace complex for a while, just as Andronicus I had done in 1187, but this would only prolong the inevitable. Mourtzouphlus knew what to expect from the hated Boniface and his army of self-righteous Westerners. As Nicetas put it, the emperor would be "put into the jaws of the Latins as their dinner or dessert."[122] It was time to leave the capital, he decided, and take his place as one of Byzantium's itinerant emperors. To further that career, he brought with him Euphrosyne, the wife of Alexius III, as well as her daughter, Eudocia, who was either now or shortly would be Mourtzouphlus's wife.[123] All three boarded a small fishing boat docked at the palace wharf and faded into the gloom of the Bosporus night.[124]

Mourtzouphlus made no secret of his decision to leave the city. As soon as he departed, the Varangian Guard drew up their ranks at their barracks in the Great Palace and just outside at the Milion.[125] This was usual for the Guard when the city lacked an emperor.[126] Inside Hagia Sophia, the remnants of Byzantine government attempted to grapple with an insoluble problem. Assembled in the shimmering light of gold lamps were Patriarch John Camaterus and a few aristocrats, probably including Nicetas Choniates. Overall, though, attendance was very sparse. With Alexius V gone, they turned their attention to choosing a new emperor. Given the difficulties they had encountered finding a willing candidate in January, they might have imagined more troubles now. In fact, however, they were faced with a surplus of candidates. Two young men vied for the imperial insignia: Constantine Ducas, probably a first cousin to Isaac II and Alexius III; and Constantine Lascaris, the brother of Theodore Lascaris whom Alexius III had left in control of Constantinople when he fled the city in 1203 and who later would be crowned the first emperor of Nicaea.[127] Both men, Nicetas reports, were sober and skilled in warfare, but they now fought only for the "captaincy of a tempest-tossed ship, for they viewed the great and celebrated Roman empire as Fortune's prize, depending upon the chance move of a chessman."[128] Both men were equal in accomplishments and experience (or lack thereof) making the choice difficult. So they cast lots, which fell to Constantine Lascaris. Yet when the patriarch moved to crown the victor, he refused the insignia. Lascaris knew what Mourtzouphlus knew: that the emperor, whoever he was, would suffer mightily if the Latins took the city. Lascaris would accept the supreme office only if he was assured of support by the people and the Varangian Guard. And so, accompanied by the patriarch, the emperor-elect walked out of Hagia Sophia and into the torchlit street near the Milion.

There, near the gilded arch of the milestone, stood the Varangian Guard, the only cohesive fighting force on which Constantinople could still rely. There also was a large number of citizens, some confused and frightened, others curious, others preparing for the next day's ceremonies. Like Mourtzouphlus, Lascaris attempted to rally the people to support him. He enjoined them to fight the Latins, to resist those who had already done them such injury. But the people remained obdurate; not a single person responded to his exhortations.[129] Lascaris then turned to the Varangians. The Guard was now accustomed to having its approval sought before a new emperor was installed. It is often assumed that the Varangians refused to fight for Lascaris, but that is not so.[130] Although Nicetas has nothing but scorn for the corps during Byzantium's darkest hour, he is forced to admit that they agreed to fight after Lascaris agreed to pay them more money.[131] Nicetas casts this as reprehensible extortion on the ax-wielders part, yet it was hardly that. The Varangians were, after all, mercenaries. If asked by an imperial claimant what their conditions were for approval, increased pay would naturally come up. Besides, the imperial bodyguards were being asked alone to defend the entire city: they deserved more money.

Having gained their assent, Lascaris sent the Varangian Guard off to engage the Latins on the morrow. To improve their resolve (which was granitic compared to the absent Greek soldiers), Lascaris reminded the Varangians that they fought not only as mercenaries but also for their own positions as well. If a Latin should seize the throne he would have no appreciation for the "far-famed gifts of honor of the imperial guard," nor would he pay the Varangians more than "a hair's worth." The speech ended, the Guard marched away from the Milion toward what could only be a hopeless battle.[132]

In the event, however, the Guard never had to fight that battle. Faced with the same calculus that had thwarted Mourtzouphlus, Constantine Lascaris realized that the Varangians could not single-handedly defeat the Latin host. He therefore followed his predecessor's example. Eschewing the imperial title, he entered the Great Palace and, probably with his brother Theodore, boarded a vessel in the palace harbor. They rowed across toward Asia and ultimately Nicaea.[133] There, Theodore Lascaris would found the Nicaean Empire, a prosperous state that would preserve the flame of the

Byzantine candle until it could return to Constantinople almost sixty years later. As for the Varangian Guard, when Lascaris deserted them they no longer had a reason to fight. Their vow was to the emperor, not the empire. They probably returned to their barracks in the Great Palace to await orders from the next emperor.[134] Those orders never came. Lascaris had been right about one thing: the Latins would have little money and less appreciation for the Varangian Guard. The corps' long history as a fighting force had come to an end.[135]

It is hard to imagine two peoples who understood each other less than the Greeks and Latins on the morning of 13 April 1204. As the sun rose above the hills of Scutari, the Latin soldiers awoke from their fearful sleep, donned their armor, and drew up their ranks. They expected this to be the first day in a very long and bloody struggle. How little they understood the Byzantines! Along the streets of the city, Greeks were already pouring out, well dressed, bearing icons and crosses, all jostling for position to acclaim the new emperor.[136] The rituals for welcoming a new leader whom the city had previously resisted were etched deeply in Byzantine culture. They were akin to the rituals for an imperial triumph, but had additional features and a different message: that despite its resistance, the city was now loyal to the victor.[137] The ritual always began in the early morning when a delegation of high clergy and an honor guard would greet the new emperor and deliver the city into his hands. This was sometimes symbolized by bestowing a golden crown. Then the delegation would point the way to the coronation and the procession would begin.[138]

The delegation to Boniface of Montferrat showed up promptly at sunrise that morning. As was traditional, it consisted of upper clergy (how high we do not know) bedecked in their splendid ecclesiastical vestments, as well as the Varangian Guard, probably also outfitted in their ceremonial dress.[139] Boniface, who may well have been familiar with the ceremony, came out to meet them. The delegation proclaimed that the city and all of its wealth belonged to Boniface and then did reverence to him as emperor by prostrating themselves at his feet.[140] The marquis drank in the scene, but he could not accept the honor. As much as he hoped to be elected emperor, he had no power to take the throne now. Whether Boniface understood the intent of the delegation or not, it was lost on the rest of the Latins. The author of the *Devastatio*, who may well have witnessed the ceremony, did not see this as the first step toward a coronation, but simply as the surrender of the city to the crusaders. His text implies that the later exodus of the Greeks was the natural result of their forfeiture of Constantinople.[141] When word reached the other crusaders they were flabbergasted. They could not believe that the vast city was surrendering itself to their mercy with so much flair and so little fight.[142] Immediately they fell out of ranks and fell upon the Queen of Cities.

Nicetas, who refuses to record the delegation to Boniface of Montferrat (one wonders if he was a member of it), now groans at the foolishness of his people. The narrow streets, broad avenues, and busy intersections that the crusaders had feared so much were cleared of all traffic to make way for the triumphal procession.[143] Unaware of what was coming, the citizens still stood by the side of the roads with their precious vestments and rich icons.[144] How little they understood the Latins! As the Westerners came in a torrent down these streets they found the Greeks had made the task of plunder, rape, and murder that much easier. The shouts of adulation were transformed into cries of terror. Nicetas laments that "their [Latins'] disposition was not at all affected by what they saw, nor did their lips break into the slightest smile, nor did the unexpected spectacle transform their grim and frenzied glance and fury into cheerfulness. Instead, they plundered with impunity and stripped their victims shamelessly, beginning with their carts."[145]

And so the sack began. Yet even the great violence the Latins would inflict on the city did not immediately shake the Greeks out of the cultural mindset that Constantinople could not be conquered; it could only change emperors.[146] Days later, Martin of Pairis still noticed that Greeks would greet a Latin by making the sign of the cross with their fingers and proclaiming, "Aiios Phasilieos marchio" (Holy Emperor the Marquis).[147] As wrong as the population of Constantinople was about the control Boniface had over the crusaders and the purpose of the Latins, they were right about Boniface's intentions. Subsequent events would prove that the marquis was willing to do anything, even make war against his fellow crusaders, to seize imperial power. But on 13 April, Boniface could not accept their honors. He was no Sulla; he was an Alaric. Previous lootings of Constantinople could not compare with 1204 because the army lacked an imperial claimant to restrain the destruction of his new city. The pact of March not only provided the means for the collection and division of the city's wealth, but also left the identity of the new emperor up in the air. Even the crusade's leaders, then, had incentive to pick the city clean, leaving only the bones for the dubious winner of the imperial election.

The Devastation of Constantinople

"What then should I recount first and what last of those things dared at that time by these murderous men?"[1] Nicetas's question still plagues anyone who would describe the Latin sack of Constantinople. For three days, the customary and accepted period of time for the sack of a conquered city, the victorious Latins feasted on the bloated corpse of New Rome. The crusading host and the Latin refugees were merged into a hideous mob driven by greed, lust, and hate. Oaths sworn on the Gospels to leave women and ecclesiastical buildings unmolested were forgotten in the frenzied anarchy. Many fanned out to the richest houses and palaces where they found the wealthy owners waiting— further evidence of the Greeks' drastic misunderstanding of the Latins' intentions.[2] Like those who had turned out for the procession, though, the Byzantine aristocrats learned immediately of their mistake. Soldiers stripped the homes of all wealth, took up quarters there, and, after forcing them to reveal their buried treasures, expelled the owners. With nowhere to live these bands of ragged lords streamed out of the city, leaving it to its Latin conquerors.[3]

Imperial palaces were occupied by the crusading leadership. After receiving the official submission of the city from the Byzantine delegation, Boniface of Montferrat avoided the main roads lined with acclaiming Greeks and took instead the most circuitous route possible, along the sea walls, to the Great Palace.[4] In so doing, the marquis avoided the appearance of accepting the crown from the Greeks, and remained close to his vessels if a retreat was necessary.[5] Although, according to the crusaders' pact, the Great Palace was reserved for the winner of the imperial election, the opportunity to grasp it was too great for Boniface to pass up.[6] The palace's inhabitants included the sister of Philip II of France, Agnes, who had been married to Alexius II, Andronicus I, and Theodore Branas. There also was the daughter of Bela III of Hungary, Margaret, the widow of Isaac II. On the condition that their lives be spared, the palace surrendered immediately to Boniface.[7] Control of both the Great Palace and Margaret, whom he would soon marry, gave Boniface the look of an emperor, if not yet the title. For his part, Baldwin of Flanders, through his brother Henry, took the palace of Blachernae at the opposite end of the city.[8] Blachernae, also, was supposed to be reserved for the new emperor.[9] It was hardly a coincidence that the two leading contenders for the imperial crown occupied the two most important imperial palaces. Enrico Dandolo, who lacked such aspirations, contented himself with another rich dwelling, probably the patriarchal palace.[10]

In the holy sanctuaries the Latins stripped the altars of all precious furnishings, smashed icons for the sake of their silver or gems, and defiled the consecrated Eucharist and Holy Blood. Patens were used as bread dishes and chalices as drinking cups.[11] Radiant Hagia Sophia was stripped of everything of value. The priceless altar fashioned from precious metals, gems, and marbles was smashed into pieces and divided among the looters. So much wealth was found in the great church that mules were brought in to carry it away. Unable to keep their footing on the slick marble floor, some of the beasts fell and were split open by sharp objects they carried, thus defiling the sanctuary with their excrement and blood. A prostitute was put on the throne of the patriarch, where she provided entertainment for the looters with her bawdy songs and high kicking dances.[12]

Equally sought after in the churches and monasteries were Constantinople's numerous relics. For most, this "pious thievery" was embarrassing enough that they later tried to conceal it. Bishop Nivelon of Soissons stole the crown of thorns, the Virgin's robe, the head of John the Baptist, and two large pieces of the True Cross from the Church of the Blessed Virgin at Pharos, yet the Anonymous of Soissons, who records the bishop's victory, says nothing of violating churches.[13] Bishop Conrad of Halberstadt seized a very large number of relics, including hair of the Virgin, pieces of the apostles Bartholomew, Simon, Thomas, and Paul, and the finger of Saint Nicholas, yet the *Gesta episcoporum Halberstadensium* passes over this procuration in silence. In later years Bishop Conrad even implied that he had acquired his sacred trove as a gift.[14] Enrico Dandolo also claimed relics, including a portion of a different head of John the Baptist, which he donated to the church of San Marco.[15] Robert of Clari records that the Shroud of Sydoine was missing from Saint Mary of Blachernae, but says nothing of the other hundreds of relics pilfered by the crusaders.[16] In fact, his account suggests that the crusaders honored their oaths to refrain from looting churches; an odd thing given that Robert himself seized church goods that he later donated to the abbey of Corbie.[17]

Among Latin sources only Gunther of Pairis records the crusaders' theft of relics, and he does so with gusto. Describing the activities of his abbot during the sack, he wrote, "Abbot Martin began to think also about his own booty and, lest he remain empty-handed while everyone else got rich, he resolved to use his own consecrated hands for pillage." Eschewing secular spoils, Martin piously limited his thievery to sacred relics. Like others, the abbot had heard that many Greeks had hidden their wealth and relics at the monastery of Christ Pantocrator. By the time he and a chaplain arrived there, however, Latins were already busy despoiling the rich buildings of their gold and silver. "Thinking it improper to commit sacrilege except in a holy cause," Martin began hunting for a secluded portion of the monastery where relics might be hidden. He soon came upon the cowering figure of an old priest, whom Martin threatened with death unless he told him the whereabouts of the monastery's relics. The priest quickly showed the abbot a large iron chest, which, when opened, revealed to the wide-eyed Martin a storehouse of sacred relics. "On seeing it, the abbot hurriedly and greedily thrust in both hands, and, as he was girded for action, both he and the chaplain filled the folds of their habits with sacred sacrilege." Unwilling to share with his fellow looters, Martin and his chaplain spirited the relics away to his boat where the abbot venerated his haul for three days.[18]

Aside from stealing ecclesiastical treasures, the crusaders also destroyed many priceless artifacts of antiquity. We have no way of knowing how many works of ancient authors were permanently lost as a result of the Fourth Crusade, but there were surely some.[19] We do know, however, that months later the Latin government of Constantinople ordered many hundreds, perhaps thousands, of ancient bronze statues melted down for coin.[20] These included monumental works like the Forum of Constantine's statue of Hera, whose head was so large that four oxen had difficulty carting it away, and a massive bronze mechanical device shaped like a pyramid, replete with warbling birds, piping shepherds, and swimming fish.[21] Lysippus's colossal bronze masterpiece depicting Hercules resting, tired and despondent after cleaning the Augean stables, was also tossed into the melting pots. The statue was so large, Nicetas tells us, "that it took a cord the size of a man's belt to go round the thumb, and the shin was the size of a man."[22] With only a few exceptions, the hundreds of bronze statues that adorned the Hippodrome's spina were also melted down.[23] The ancient Serpent Column of Delphi was spared, probably because it functioned as a fountain.[24] Enrico Dandolo was able to save four bronze horses that sauntered before a victorious charioteer over the Hippodrome's starting gates.[25] They were shipped to Venice and mounted over the entry to San Marco where these gilded steeds became a new symbol of Venetian prosperity and pride.[26] Virtually all of Constantinople's other bronze statues were destroyed, a cruel blow to later generations. The memory of a handful of these treasures was preserved by the meticulous and loving descriptions that Nicetas Choniates fashioned in his work *De Signis*.

During the sack and for some time after, Latins sated their sexual lusts on the women of Constantinople. And yet to attribute such shameful behavior to mere animal desire would too readily ignore the element of human perversity, stripped of inhibitions, committing sexual violence to satisfy twisted emotional needs. Women were raped publicly on streets and squares, even in churches.[27] Older women were also stripped and outraged. Byzantine men who tried to protect their wives or daughters were slaughtered mercilessly; others were killed for no reason at all. Women and children were also not spared the sword.[28] "There were lamentations and cries of woe and weeping in the narrow ways, wailing at the crossroads, moaning in the temples, outcries of men, screams of women, the taking of captives, and the dragging about, tearing in pieces, and raping of bodies heretofore sound and whole."[29]

Nicetas Choniates gives an excellent account of his own circumstances during the days of terror, an account that puts a human face on the abstract and distant tragedy. Unlike many of his friends, Nicetas no longer had a large palace in April 1204, since it had been destroyed in the great fire of August 1203. Instead, he lived in a more modest dwelling not far from Hagia Sophia. Less ostentatious and better hidden, Nicetas's home was not the first target of the looters.[30] It was not long, though, before the senator learned of the fate of his city from friends who had been expelled from their mansions.[31] Realizing that he would soon be forced to join them as refugees, Nicetas enlisted the aid of a Latin friend, a Venetian wine merchant named Domenico.[32] When most Latins had fled across the Golden Horn in August, Domenico and his family had fled to Nicetas Choniates, who had welcomed them into his home. Now it was Domenico's turn to repay the favor. When Latin victors descended on Nicetas's house, Domenico dressed in armor and, pretending to be one of them, told them that he had already claimed the dwelling. His cleverness and bravado worked well enough with other Venetians and Italians, but French marauders were much harder to discourage.[33] Finally, Domenico urged Nicetas and his family, as well as other Byzantine families that had come there for protection, to leave before the French seized the house. They took the advice, moving to another dwelling owned by Venetian friends of Nicetas. Yet when that part of the city was later claimed by the French, the Venetians despaired of further hiding the Greeks.[34] On 17 April, a cold and stormy day, Nicetas came to the bitter conclusion that he must leave Constantinople.[35] Because of their fear of the French, the senator, his family, and his friends had their hands bound and strung together. The good Domenico then pulled them along the streets as if they were his captives. At some point, when the danger no longer seemed extreme, Domenico released his friends and bade them farewell.[36]

Nicetas's ragtag group of nobles, which included such potentates as Patriarch John X Camaterus, was a pitiful sight.[37] The senator's pregnant wife was very close to term yet still had to walk the long Mese to the Golden Gate. Nicetas carried his young son who could not yet walk. As they made their way down the once beautiful avenue, friends and relatives joined them, expanding their group until it resembled a "throng of ants." Mese had become a gauntlet of armed Latins randomly stopping refugees to make certain they were not hiding precious fabrics or bags of money in their tattered clothing. Others were searching for attractive young women to violate. The women in Nicetas's party spread mud on their faces to make themselves less appealing and huddled in the center of the group "as though in a sheepfold."[38] This strategy worked during most of their trek, yet when they were almost to the Golden Gate, near the Church of Saint Mokios, an armed Latin burst into the group and plucked out the beautiful young daughter of a judge. The entire company shouted out in alarm as the soldier dragged the poor girl away. Her aged and sick father pursued the Latin, but he soon stumbled and fell into a mudhole, where he wallowed, helpless to get up. Racked with horror and grief, the old man turned to Nicetas, calling him by name, and begging him to stop the defilement of the young woman. At once, Nicetas went after the criminal and, on the way, convinced some Italian soldiers to help him in his cause.[39] Taking pity on the girl, many of them followed Nicetas to the house of the abductor. The criminal had locked the girl inside the dwelling and stood defiantly in the doorway, prepared to do battle with anyone who would deprive him of his prize. With angry tears and violent sobs, Nicetas denounced the man to the Latin troops, reminding them of the prohibitions of their leaders against rape and asking them to think of their own children and wives.[40] Moved by the senator's pleas, the soldiers demanded that the abductor release the young woman and threatened to hang him as a criminal if he did not. Seeing their resolve, the man released the girl, who was returned to her rejoicing father.[41]

After so harrowing a trip, at last Nicetas and his party passed through the Golden Gate and out of Constantinople. The senator now turned his gray head toward the mighty walls of Theodosius that stretched for miles to the north in monumental glory. Their proud strength and iron resolve to defend against any foe stood in stark contrast to the destruction of the city behind them. The absurdity of events was more than the senator could bear. He fell down on the ground weeping and cursing the fortifications. "If those things for whose protection you were erected no longer exist, being utterly de-

stroyed by fire and war, for what purpose do you still stand?"[42] The silence of
the stones mocked Nicetas as he and his company left Constantinople, torn
from their beloved city like "darling children from their adoring mother."[43]

After three days, on 15 April, the crusaders and other Latins were sub-
jected to some measure of control. As Nicetas Choniates's experience makes
plain, however, theft and rape continued after the official period of plundering. It is clear, even during the three days, that the crusaders did not abide by
their own rules. Despite their oaths and the threat of excommunication, they
ruthlessly and systematically violated Byzantium's holy sanctuaries, destroying, defiling, or stealing all they could lay hands on. Many also dishonored
their vows to leave the women of Byzantium unmolested. When Innocent III
heard of the conduct of his pilgrims he was filled with shame. He wrote to
his legate, "For they who are supposed to serve Christ rather than themselves, who should have used their swords against the infidel, have bathed
those swords in the blood of Christians. They have not spared religion, nor
age, nor sex, and have committed adultery and fornication in public, exposing
matrons and even nuns to the filthiness of their troops."[44] The crusaders too
felt shame: no Latin source even hints at the widespread sexual crimes, and
only Gunther of Pairis records the looting of churches.[45] Nicetas contrasted
the sack of Constantinople with the fall of Jerusalem to Saladin, judging that
Byzantium would have fared better had it been conquered by the infidel.[46]
He blamed the crusading leaders, who had boasted of their piety and moral
superiority over the "Greeks" (a slur the crusaders often used), yet presided
over rape, murder, and sacrilege.[47] He lashed out too at the common crusaders, who had sworn to deliver Jerusalem, promised to kill no Christians,
and even proclaimed that they would refrain from sex until they had arrived
in the Holy Land. "In truth, they were exposed as frauds. Seeking to avenge
the Holy Sepulcher, they raged openly against Christ and sinned by overturn-
ing the Cross with the cross they bore on their backs, not even shuddering to
trample on it for the sake of a little gold and silver."[48] The Byzantines' deep
sense of betrayal and bitter anger toward the Latins became the legacies of
1204 that would not die with the generation that experienced the events.[49]
They would animate centuries of tragic history and, for many, still live today.

The Western soldiers, who had struggled for so long with so little, were
now rich men, many living in luxurious surroundings.[50] Both Villehardouin
and Robert of Clari remarked on the enormous amounts of riches the host acquired, more than they had believed existed in the entire world. The marshal
of Champagne told of the "gold and silver, and vessels, and precious stones,
and satins, and silk clothing, and cloaks of vair, of grey, and of ermine, and
all the most precious things that could ever be found on earth."[51] The knight

of Picardy also celebrated the vast quantities of gold, silver, and jewels, claiming that not even Charlemagne or Alexander had ever found so much booty in one city. Indeed, Robert continued, more wealth was found in the walls of Constantinople than could be found in the world's forty next richest cities combined.[52] Since the Sunday following the capture of the city was Palm Sunday (18 April), the crusaders spent Holy Week and Easter praising God for the great victory he had bestowed on them.[53] For the Venetians it was particularly moving that Easter Sunday fell on the feast day of their patron, Saint Mark.

After the solemnities of the holy days, the crusaders turned their attention to the division of the vast booty. It was ordered throughout the host that all treasure was to be brought to three churches, each manned by equal numbers of Frankish and Venetian guards.[54] Streams of crusaders carried heavy loads of plunder to these common piles. The resulting mountains of riches were both truly enormous and bitterly disappointing. It was clear to all that the large majority of Constantinople's wealth was held back by individual looters. Villehardouin greatly blames those who brought forward only a portion of their spoils, greedily clinging to that which they had sworn to bring into the common pile. Indeed, the marshal blames the later misfortunes of the Latin Empire on the sins of these men, who selfishly brought down the wrath of God on the pious crusaders.[55]

The amount of booty has caused some scholarly controversy. According to Villehardouin, the collected sum was first divided between the Franks and the Venetians.[56] According to the pact of March, however, the Venetians were to receive three-quarters of the first 200,000 marks, or 150,000 marks, and the Franks one-quarter, or 50,000 marks.[57] Thus, Villehardouin states that after the initial equal division the Franks gave to the Venetians 50,000 marks. After making that payment, the Franks still had 100,000 marks to divide among themselves.[58] Therefore, the total amount brought together was 300,000 silver marks. The Franks had 50,000 marks as their share of Alexius's outstanding debt and 50,000 as their equal share of the excess booty. Likewise, the Venetians had 150,000 marks to pay off what Alexius owed to them, and their 50,000 equal share of the excess booty.

What has caused some confusion is Villehardouin's subsequent attempt to estimate the total amount of booty taken in Constantinople, but not necessarily brought into the common pool. He states that if all of the booty had been brought together and had the Franks not paid the Venetians, then the non-Venetian crusaders would have had 400,000 marks to divide, rather than just 100,000.[59] If the Franks had not paid the Venetians they would have had 150,000 marks. Thus, according to Villehardouin, the non-Venetians would have received 250,000 additional marks if so many had not stolen so much.

Since, according to the pact, the Venetians would receive equal share of all additional booty, this implies another 250,000 marks that would have gone to the Venetians. Villehardouin is stating, then (in a rather roundabout way) that 500,000 marks was held back. Adding this to the 300,000 marks that was assembled in the churches, Villehardouin's estimate of the crusaders' total take at Constantinople, both hidden and declared, was 800,000 silver marks.[60] While only an estimate, coming from the marshal of Champagne it was an educated one, and probably not too far from the mark.

While Villehardouin was troubled by the small amounts that were turned in for division, the poorer soldiers were horrified. They had expected that their shares would be very large: sums befitting a booty that outstripped those taken by Charlemagne or Alexander. Robert of Clari blames the guards of the treasure, who took what they wanted and let the rich knights do the same, leaving only the silver plate.[61] The author of the *Devastatio Constantinopolitana* was equally angered, characterizing the distributed amounts as "almost like certain downpayments." The same author also records that in the final division each knight received twenty marks, each sergeant or cleric ten marks, and each foot soldier five marks.[62] This is confirmed by Villehardouin's description of the treasure's distribution ratios, and fits with the marshal's report that the Franks had only 100,000 marks to distribute among themselves.[63] Elsewhere Villehardouin claims that the total number of Constantinople's assailants numbered 20,000.[64] A little less than half of these were probably Frankish, while the rest were Venetians and Pisans. Assuming that the 1:2:4 ratio of knights to sergeants to foot soldiers still prevailed, then the total paid out to 10,000 Frankish soldiers would have been 85,710 marks.[65] Since clergy were to receive a mounted sergeant's share, there would remain sufficient funds to pay out 1,429 clergy members, which suggests that there were as many churchmen as knights. Of the great many who held back treasure from the common pile, only a few were caught and hung. Most of these were commoners, but one was a knight who was hung with his crested shield around his neck.[66]

Aside from their share of the loot, the topic on everyone's mind was the identity of the new emperor. Boniface of Montferrat was the clear favorite. He was linked by marriage to the previous dynasty, well known to the Greeks (who had already hailed him as emperor and continued to see him as such), and had taken possession of the Great Palace. To further bolster his claim, Boniface was either married or engaged to marry Margaret, the widow of Isaac II.[67] The marquis's only serious rival for the throne was Count Baldwin of Flanders, who had occupied the Blachernae Palace.[68] Factions materialized around both claimants and tension rose. According to the March pact, the Franks and Venetians were each to choose six electors. Selecting the Frankish delegates was troublesome. In a series of parliaments, supporters of Baldwin and Boniface wrangled over choosing men favorable to their candidate. The stakes were high and neither side was willing to budge.[69] To grease the wheels and avoid a dangerous rift, some of the leaders suggested that the winner of the election should give to the loser all of the lands east of Constantinople. Baldwin and Boniface agreed to this, but came no closer on the electors.[70] Finally, both sides decided to select members of the high clergy, whom they hoped would be impartial.[71] The six they chose were Bishop Nivelon of Soissons, Bishop Garnier of Troyes, Bishop Conrad of Halberstadt, Bishop-elect Peter of Bethlehem, Bishop-elect John of Acre, and Abbot Peter of Locedio.[72] Some of these men, despite their clerical robes, were clearly partisan. John Faicete of Acre had been chancellor of Flanders; Conrad of Halberstadt was devoted to Philip of Swabia, and therefore favored his vassal, Boniface.[73]

The Venetians had much less trouble choosing their six electors. Venice, after all, was a republic with plenty of experience in assembling committees. Because of Venetians' distrust of concentrated power and their fear of faction, they generally selected committees by selecting other committees to name them. This put a buffer between an office and those who sought it. In this case, Dandolo chose four men who swore on relics that they would choose the best six men as electors. Each man they picked remained in a church until the time of the election and was forbidden to talk to anyone. In the same church, some time before the election, a mass of the Holy Spirit was sung, asking that God lead the six to make the right decisions.[74]

Sometime before the electors met on 9 May, Doge Dandolo suggested to the crusading leaders that Boniface of Montferrat and Baldwin of Flanders should evacuate their imperial residences. Both palaces were well fortified and the doge wanted to insure that the loser of the election was not tempted to disregard the results and force an armed siege.[75] After the imperial palaces were abandoned, the twelve electors met at Dandolo's palace, which was probably the patriarchal palace adjoining Hagia Sophia. The twelve were cloistered in a rich chapel in the same palace.[76] The barons waited anxiously in a nearby palace, perhaps another wing of the patriarchal complex or perhaps part of the senate building. Throngs of others stood outside, probably in the Augusteion. Time crawled by.[77]

We do not know how long the electors met or what was said during the process. In the end, however, the Venetian electors favored Baldwin of Flanders.[78] They had known him to be a scrupulously honest man who had respected his commitments to Venice.[79] He brought with him no baggage of past Byzantine governments. Boniface, on the other hand, was a partisan of Genoa, one of Venice's rivals in Constantinople. His close attachment to the

Angeli also worried the Venetians, who feared he might become as bad as Isaac II or Alexius III.[80] With six votes cast for Baldwin, the count of Flanders needed only one from the Frankish electors. The contentious disputes over delegates had been pointless. After the commission's decision was clear, electors who chose Boniface on the first ballot switched their votes to Baldwin for the sake of unanimity. Around midnight, Bishop Nivelon of Soissons announced the election of Baldwin of Flanders. The crusading host erupted with joy, although some of Boniface's supporters mumbled in disgust.[81]

Baldwin was carried to the Great Palace, where plans began for his coronation on 16 May. The event was splendid. The leading barons and Venetian nobles rode in procession to the palace to collect the emperor-elect and then proceeded to Hagia Sophia. There Baldwin was bedecked in the marvelously rich garments of a Roman emperor. Precious stones were so copious on his attire that it is a wonder he could carry them all. Even his shoes were studded with jewels. His mantle bore the imperial eagles in rubies, so brilliant that it seemed to Robert of Clari that it was on fire. Baldwin proceeded through the church to the high altar, accompanied by Louis of Blois bearing the imperial standard, Hugh of Saint Pol carrying the imperial sword, and Boniface of Montferrat holding the imperial crown that had just eluded him. Baldwin knelt before the altar where his garments were taken from him one by one until he wore nothing from the waist up. He was then anointed with oils and his robes and mantle were replaced. Next the crown was taken up by the crusader bishops and blessed. Then all of them, each holding the crown by one hand, placed it on Baldwin's head and proclaimed him emperor. Around the new Augustus's neck they hung a ruby the size of an apple that had formerly belonged to Manuel I.[82]

Emperor Baldwin I heard mass from his throne and then left the great church. Outside he mounted a white horse and rode back to the Great Palace where, in the massive throne room, he received the homage of the Western knights and the acclamation of the Greeks.[83] There in that room, so joyous and rich, the Fourth Crusade died and the Latin Empire was born. Although a few would push on to Syria, the vast majority would not. Their vows had been completed; at least that is what they had been led to believe by their clergy before the attack on Constantinople. They had sworn to remain until April 1205 to defend the new empire, and so they did. But when that year expired at least seven thousand, virtually the entire Frankish force, boarded Venetian vessels and went home.[84] For those who remained an additional year, the papal legate made it official, relieving them of their crusading vows.[85] But the legate could only give what many believed they already possessed. For them, the crusade was over, indeed, had ended when Constantinople fell.

Rather than crushing the sultan of Egypt, the crusaders had destroyed the emperor of Byzantium, and then usurped his throne. They never raised a sword against Islam. Difficult decisions, improbable events, and morally ambiguous situations had brought the Westerners to New Rome and mired them in its treacherous power struggles. The result no one could have foreseen, for it was the most improbable of all outcomes: a Flemish knight now reigned in the city of the Caesars.

Abbreviations

ASV	Archivio di Stato, Venice
CMH	*Cambridge Medieval History*
MGH, SS	*Monumenta Germaniae historica, Scriptores*, 32 vols. (Hannover, 1826–1934).
Migne, *PL*	*Patrologia Latina*, ed. J. P. Migne et al., 221 vols. (Paris, 1841–64).
Rec. hist. Gaules	*Recueil des historiens des Gaules et de la France*, ed. Martin Bouquet et al., 24 vols. (Paris, 1738–1904).
Register	*Die Register Innocenz' III.*, ed. Othmar Hageneder et al., 4 vols. (Vienna et al.: Österreichischen Akademie der Wissenschaften, 1964–95).
Rer. Brit. M. A. Script.	*Rerum Britannicarum Medii Aevi scriptores*, 99 vols. (London, 1858–96).
TTh	*Urkunden zur älteren Handels- und Staatsgeschichte der Republik Venedig*, ed. G. L. Fr. Tafel and G. M. Thomas, 3 vols. (Vienna: Kaiserlich-königlichen Hof- und Staatsdruckerei, 1856–57, repr., Amsterdam, 1967).

Notes

Chapter 1

1. Innocent III, *Die Register Innocenz' III*, ed. Othmar Hageneder and Anton Haidacher (Graz-Cologne: Hermann Böhlaus Nachf., 1964), 1:11, pp. 18–20 (Migne, *PL*, CCXIV: 9–10). Achille Luchaire, *Innocent III*, vol. 4, *La question d'Orient* (Paris: Librairie Hachette, 1907), pp. 6–7. This letter did not, however, constitute the proclamation of a crusade. Helmut Roscher, *Papst Innocenz III und die Kreuzzüge* (Göttingen: Vandenhoeck u. Ruprecht, 1969), pp. 51–52. In fact, the German crusade had not yet expired. Apprehensive that the last of the remaining German crusaders were about to return home, thereby weakening the defense of the Holy Land, Innocent offered crusading privileges to those who would support a crusader. Innocent III, *Register*, 1:302, pp. 430–33. The document is undated, but was probably issued about mid-year.

Unless otherwise stated, all English translations are by us.

2. Jonathan Riley-Smith, "An Approach to Crusading Ethics," *Reading Medieval Studies* 6 (1980): 3.

3. Since this study will be very much concerned with the motivations of Innocent III, Boniface of Montferrat, Enrico Dandolo, and others, let us emphasize at the outset an obvious point, which, it seems to us, many writers on the Fourth Crusade have overlooked. That Innocent stood to gain power and prestige for the papacy, Boniface lands for himself, and Dandolo wealth for Venice, does not require us to believe that they were insincere in their crusading sentiments. Quite often men's ideals and their profits are not in conflict. Scholars, for example, are not necessarily less dedicated scholars if they also gain professional stature or money from their writings.

4. Generally, Innocent did not favor royally directed expeditions in which his own role would be limited to issuing the summons. Hans Eberhard Mayer, *The Crusades* (rev. German ed., 1988), trans. John Gillingham (New York and Oxford: Oxford University Press, 1990), p. 196. See Franco Cardini, "La crociata nel Duecento. L''Avatara' di un ideale," *Archivio storico italiano* 135 (1977): 118–27; Michele Maccarrone, *Studi su Innocenzo III*, Italia sacra 17 (Padua: Editrice Antenore, 1972): 88–90.

5. Innocent III, *Register*, 1:336, pp. 498–505 (Migne, *PL*, CCXIV: 308–12). See also, ibid., 1:509, pp. 743–45, on the problem of collecting money for the Holy Land. Capuano went north, Soffredo south. The latter visited Venice to encourage sea support and transportation for the crusade. Werner Maleczek, *Petrus Capuanus: Kardinal, Legat am vierten Kreuzzug, Theologe (†1214)* (Vienna: Österreichischen Akademie der Wissenschaften, 1988), p. 98.

6. E.g., the cardinal-legate Peter Capuano was sent to France to gain a peace, or a truce. Innocent III, *Register*, 1:355, p. 531 (Migne, *PL*, CCXIV: 329); Maleczek, *Petrus Capuanus*, pp. 95–116. Also a papal legation was sent to try to make peace between Genoa and Pisa. *Gesta Innocentii*, Migne, *PL*, CCXIV: chap. 46, col. 91. In gen-

eral, see James Ross Sweeney, "Innocent III, Hungary and the Bulgarian Coronation: A Study in Medieval Papal Diplomacy," *Church History* 42 (1973): 320, and nn.

7. William E. Lunt, *Financial Relations of the Papacy with England to 1327* (Cambridge, Mass.: Medieval Academy of America, 1939), pp. 241–42; Giuseppe Martini, "Innocenzo III ed il finanziamento delle crociate," *Archivio della Deputazione Romana di Storia Patria*, n.s. 10 (1944): 318–19. Edgar H. McNeal and Robert Lee Wolff, "The Fourth Crusade," in *A History of the Crusades*, gen. ed. Kenneth M. Setton (Philadelphia: University of Pennsylvania Press, 1962), 2: 156–57; Roscher, *Papst Innocenz III*, p. 80, n. 128; Ronald P. Grossman, "The Financing of the Crusades" (Ph.D. diss., University of Chicago, 1965), pp. 91–95. Adolf Gottlob, *Die päpstlichen Kreuzzugssteuern des 13. Jahrhunderts* (Heiligenstadt: F. W. Cordier, 1892), pp. 22–23. This was probably not, however, the first tax of its kind: see Fred A. Cazel Jr., "The Financing of the Crusades," in *A History of the Crusades*, gen. ed. Kenneth M. Setton (Madison: University of Wisconsin Press, 1989), 6: 135–36.

See also Innocent III, "Rubrice Registri litterarum secretarum fel. rec. Domini Innocentii pape tertii de anno pontificatus sui III. IV. (XVIII. et XIX.)," in *Vetera monumenta slavorum meridionalium historiam illustrantia*, ed. Augustin Theiner (Rome: Academia Scientiarum, 1863), vol. 4, no. 123, p. 59. After much dispute the Cistercians agreed to a fixed sum of 2,000 marks, which they were still having difficulty in collecting in 1214. Ibid., no. 116, p. 59. Elizabeth A. R. Brown, "The Cistercians in the Latin Empire of Constantinople and Greece, 1204–1276," *Traditio* 14 (1958): 70–72.

8. Innocent III, *Die Register Innocenz' III*, vol. 2, ed. Othmar Hageneder, Werner Maleczek, and Alfred A. Strnad (Rome-Vienna: Osterreichischen Akademie der Wissenschaften, 1979), 2:257–60, pp. 488–503 (Migne, *PL*, CCXIV: 826–36). Cazal, "The Financing of the Crusades," p. 133; McNeal and Wolff, "The Fourth Crusade," p. 156. Luchaire, *Innocent III*, 4: 8. See also Joseph R. Strayer, "The Political Crusades of the Thirteenth Century," in Setton, *History of the Crusades*, 2: 347. As in other areas of papal activity, Innocent III enhanced the involvement of the papacy in the financing of the crusades. Grossman, "Financing of the Crusades," p. 87. Lay rulers had previously imposed crusading taxes, and Clement III in 1188 had ordered the clergy of Canterbury to give alms for the Holy Land. Lunt, *Financial Relations*, 1: 240 and 422; William E. Lunt, *Papal Revenues in the Middle Ages*, 2 vols. (New York: Columbia University Press, 1934), 1: 71–72. Gottlob argued that late Polish sources which recounted a papal tax by Clement III in 1188 and 1189 were unbelievable, but, in light of Lunt's evidence from England, one wonders whether there was not, at any rate, an order for the levy of compulsory alms. *Die päpstlichen Kreuzzugssteuern*, pp. 18–20. See, Cazal, "The Financing of the Crusades," p. 135, n. 69.

9. John M. O'Brien, "Fulk of Neuilly," *Proceedings of the Leeds Philosophical and Literary Society* 13 (1969): 114; Paul Alphandéry, *La chrétienté et l'idée de croisade*, completed from the authors notes by Alphonse Dupront, 2 vols. (Paris: Editions Albin Michel, 1954–59), 2: 47.

10. Quoted in O'Brien, "Fulk of Neuilly," p. 114.

11. Ibid., 118–20. Milton R. Gutsch, "A Twelfth-Century Preacher—Fulk of Neuilly," in *The Crusades and Other Historical Essays Presented to Dana C. Munro by His Former Students*, ed. Louis John Paetow (New York: F. S. Crofts, 1928), pp. 189–90.

12. John M. O'Brien, "Fulk of Neuilly" (Ph.D. diss., University of Southern California, Los Angeles, 1964), pp. 59–61; Gutsch, "Fulk of Neuilly," p. 191.

13. O'Brien, "Fulk of Neuilly," *Proceedings*, pp. 119–20.

14. Rigord, *Gesta Philippi Augusti Francorum Regis*, in *Rec. hist. Gaules*, 17: 48; Robert of Clari, *La conquête de Constantinople*, ed. Philippe Lauer (Paris: Edouard Champion, 1924), sec. 1, p. 1; O'Brien, "Fulk of Neuilly," *Proceedings*, pp. 122–23; Gutsch, "Fulk of Neuilly," pp. 193–98. Miracle seekers frequently tore pieces off his garments for medicinal purposes. On one occasion, molested by enthusiastic clothes snatchers, Fulk proclaimed that although his own clothes were not sacred, he would bless with the sign of the cross the garments of one of the members of the crowd. The clothing of this hapless person were promptly torn to shreds by the mob. Jacques of Vitry, *The Historia Occidentalis of Jacques of Vitry: A Critical Edition*, ed. John F. Hinnebusch (Fribourg: University Press, 1972), pp. 97–98.

15. Robert of Auxerre, *Chronicon*, ed. O. Holder-Egger, *MGH, SS*, 26: 258; Gutsch, "Fulk of Neuilly," p. 192; O'Brien, "Fulk of Neuilly," Ph.D. diss., pp. 61–62, 69–73.

16. Otto of Saint Blaise, continuation of Otto of Freising, *Chronicon*, ed. Roger Wilmans, *MGH, SS*, 20: 330.

17. Gutsch, "Fulk of Neuilly," p. 202.

18. Innocent III, *Register*, 1:398, p. 597 (Migne, *PL*, CCXIV: 375–76). Gutsch, "Fulk of Neuilly," pp. 202–3, gives a translation. The exact nature of this papal letter is debated; it is clearly not a crusade commission. See O'Brien, "Fulk of Neuilly," *Proceedings*, p. 128 and n. 116.

19. O'Brien, "Fulk of Neuilly," *Proceedings*, pp. 124–25. On the methods of crusade preachers' propaganda generally, see Colin Morris, "Propaganda for War: The Dissemination of the Crusading Ideal in the Twelfth Century," in *The Church and War*, ed. W. J. Sheils, (Oxford: Blackwell, 1983), pp. 79–101.

20. Alphandéry, *La chrétienté et l'idée de croisade*, 2: 64. O'Brien, "Fulk of Neuilly," *Proceedings*, p. 131, criticizes Norman Cohn's argument that Fulk preached a crusade exclusively for the poor. Alphandéry also comes close to Cohn's position. *La chrétienté et l'idée de croisade*, 1: 1. O'Brien is probably right, given Fulk's later preaching to the Cistercian assembly. The ideal of poverty, however, which was to culminate in Saint Francis, was already widespread. It is worth noting that Robert of Clari repeatedly refers to himself as a poor knight. Robert of Clari, *Conquête*, pp. ix–x. Also Mayer, *Crusades*, p. 198. Whether this is merely a means of identifying himself in contrast to the rich, whom he resented and envied, or whether it manifests a belief in the messianic character of the poor, we do not know. Perhaps both, for one's longings and one's ideals may be at odds, just as they might be mutually supportive.

21. Maleczek, *Petrus Capuanus*, pp. 98–103; Innocent III, *Register*, 1:336, p. 502; 1:345, p. 516; 1:346, p. 517 (Migne, *PL*, CCXIV: 309, 319–20). Innocent's letter confirming the truce: Innocent III, *Register*, 2:23–25, pp. 31–35 (Migne, *PL*, CCXIV: 552–54). Philip broke the truce, however, shortly after the death of Richard.

22. Innocent III, *Register*, 1:347–48, pp. 518–20 (Migne, *PL*, CCXIV: 320–22). Maleczek, *Petrus Capuanus*, p. 100.

23. Geoffrey of Villehardouin, *La conquête de Constantinople*, ed. Edmond Faral, 2 vols. (Paris: Société d'édition "les Belles lettres," 1938–39), sec. 3, 1: 4. (This form of

citation of Villehardouin, which will be used henceforth without comment, signifies that reference is found in sec. 3, vol. 1, p. 4 of the Faral ed.) In his ingenious article, E. John urges that the dating of the preliminaries of the crusade from the tournament at Ecry through the meeting at Compiègne should be set forward one year. "A Note on the Preliminaries of the Fourth Crusade," *Byzantion* 28 (1958): 95–103. It seems, though, that the lapse of time between the appointment of envoys at Compiègne and their departure would be incomprehensibly long. John does not claim convincing proof for his hypothesis.

24. Villehardouin, *Conquête de Constantinople*, sec. 3, 1: 4; Edgar H. McNeal, "Fulk of Neuilly and the Tournament of Ecry," *Speculum* 28 (1953): 374.

25. McNeal, "Fulk of Neuilly," pp. 371–75. O'Brien attempts to raise some questions about McNeal's conclusions, but not successfully. "Fulk of Neuilly," *Proceedings*, pp. 130–31, and n. 136. The Anonymous of Halberstadt, *Gesta Episcoporum Halberstadensium*, ed. L. Weiland, *MGH, SS*, 23: 117, does not unequivocally state that Fulk crossed Thibaut and Louis. Neither does Villehardouin "invariably" cite the name of the preacher involved when he tells of nobles taking the cross. *Conquête de Constantinople*, sec. 8, 1: 10–12.

26. James Brundage, *Medieval Canon Law and the Crusader* (Madison, Milwaukee and London: University of Wisconsin Press, 1969), pp. 32–33; Michel Villey, *La croisade: Essai sur la formation d'une théorie juridique* (Paris: J. Vrin, 1942), pp. 119–27.

27. Brundage, *Medieval Canon Law and the Crusader*, pp. 149–50. For legal support of this position, see Mayer, *Crusades*, pp. 30–37; Steven Runciman, *A History of the Crusades*, 3 vols. (Cambridge: Cambridge University Press, 1954), 1: 84; Frederick H. Russell, *The Just War in the Middle Ages* (Cambridge and New York: Cambridge University Press, 1975), p. 119: Raymond H. Schmandt, "The Fourth Crusade and the Just War Theory," *Catholic Historical Review* 61 (1975): 197–98 and n. 13; also C. R. Beazley, *The Dawn of Modern Geography* (New York: Peter Smith, 1901) 2: 117–18. See the martyrdom of Cacciaguida in Dante, *Paradiso*, Canto XV, 11.145–149. We strongly endorse Brundage's warning that we must beware of modern historians who "tend to devalue the spiritual motives" of their medieval ancestors, and who tend "to overemphasize correspondingly the force of economic, social (or antisocial), and other temporal factors in terms which for the Middle Ages may be more than a trifle anachronistic." As Brundage says: "it would be . . . foolish to write off the force of a genuine, if at times grotesque, spirituality." *Medieval Canon Law and the Crusader*, p. 144. The crusaders of the Fourth Crusade have been maligned more than any others.

28. C. J. Tyerman, "Were There Any Crusades in the Twelfth Century?" *English Historical Review* 105 (1995): 575–76.

29. Runciman, *Crusades*, I: 83–84.

30. Villey, *Croisade*, p. 22.

31. Runciman, *Crusades*, 1: 84. Pope Leo IV declared that those dying in battle in defense of the church would receive a heavenly reward; Pope John VIII declared them martyrs. See also Villey, *Croisade*, pp. 25–26.

32. Villey, *Croisade*, p. 88.

33. Russell, *Just War*, p. 35. Over the opposition of Peter Damian. Villey, *Croisade*, p. 33. See also Alphandéry, *La chrétienté et l'idée de croisade*, 1: 27.

34. Mayer, *Crusades*, p. 14.

35. Russell, *Just War*, pp. 38–39, 115–23; Jonathan Riley-Smith, *What Were the*

Crusades? (Totowa, N.J.: Rowman and Littlefield, 1977), pp. 18–24, 29–33; Tyerman, "Were There Any Crusades in the Twelfth Century?" pp. 559–62, 565–66.

36. Jules Tessier, *La quatrième croisade: La diversion sur Zara et Constantinople* (Paris: E. Laroux, 1884), p. 37; *L'esprit de croisade*, ed. Jean Richard (Paris: Les Editions du Cerf, 1969), p. 39, quoting Conon of Béthune.

37. Villehardouin, *Conquête de Constantinople*, sec. 3, 1: 6, and especially n. 5.

38. Villehardouin says that Thibaut was not more than twenty-two, Louis not more than twenty-seven. *Conquête de Constantinople*, sec. 3, 1: 4–6. Many scholars, however, follow Gislebert of Mons in dating the birth of Thibaut 13 May 1179. The best discussion of the sources is in John, "Preliminaries of the Fourth Crusade," pp. 98–99. See also Henri D'Arbois de Jubainville, *Histoire des ducs et des comtes de Champagne* (Paris: A. Durand et Pedone-Lauriel, 1865), 4: 73, 87–88, and 88, n. (a).

39. Arbois de Jubainville, *Histoire des ducs et des comtes de Champagne*, 4: 43–46, 63–65.

40. Jean Longnon, *Les compagnons de Villehardouin: Recherches sur les croisés de la quatrième croisade* (Geneva: Librarie Droz, 1978), pp. 79, 84; Villehardouin, *Conquête de Constantinople*, sec. 360, 2: 168–70; Robert of Clari, *Conquête*, sec. 112, p. 106; Robert Lee Wolff, "The Latin Empire of Constantinople," in Setton, *History of the Crusades*, 2: 203.

41. Villehardouin, *Conquête de Constantinople*, secs. 4–6, 1: 6–8.

42. Ibid., sec. 8, 1: 10–12.

43. Benjamin Hendrickx, "Boudewijn IX van Vlaanderen, de vrome keizer van Konstantinopel," *Ons Geestelijk Erf* 44 (1970): 227–29; Longnon, *Les compagnons de Villehardouin*, p. 137; Friedrich Hurter, *Storia di Papa Innocenzo III*, trans. from the third German ed. by T. Giuseppe Gliemone, 4 vols. (Milan: A. Arzione, 1857–58), 2: 324.

44. Because she was pregnant, Marie did not accompany Baldwin on the crusade. After the child was born, Marie managed affairs in Flanders until early 1204 when she left for the Holy Land. At Acre she heard of Baldwin's election to the imperial throne and made plans to join him in Constantinople. Tragically, for the two were very much in love, she never saw Baldwin again. Before leaving Acre, she fell sick and died on 9 August 1204. Baldwin would follow her to the grave within two years. Villehardouin, *Conquête de Constantinople*, secs. 317–18, 2: 124–26; Longnon, *Les compagnons de Villehardouin*, p. 140.

45. Villehardouin, *Conquête de Constantinople*, sec. 8, 1: 10–12.

46. Robert Lee Wolff, "The Latin Empire of Constantinople (1204–1261)" (Ph.D. diss., Harvard, 1947), p. 81. E.g., "cet homme doué d'une sagesse exquise." *Chronique de la conquête de Constantinople*, trans. J. A. Buchon (Paris: Verdiere, 1825), pp. 36–37.

47. Robert Lee Wolff, "Baldwin of Flanders and Hainaut, First Latin Emperor of Constantinople: His Life, Death and Resurrection, 1172–1225," *Speculum* 27 (1952): 283 and 304, n. 29; Wolff, "The Latin Empire," Ph.D., diss., p. 85. We are not in accord with those who believe that the great men among the French crusaders took the cross to escape the wrath of their sovereign Philip after the death of Richard Lion-Heart. It does, however, have some support in the sources: Ernoul and Bernard le Trésorier (hereafter cited as Ernoul-Bernard), *Chronique*, ed. Louis de Mas Latrie (Paris: Mme Ve J. Renouard, 1871), p. 337; Guillaume le Bréton, *Gesta Philippi Augusti*, in *Rec. hist.*

Gaules, 17: 76. See Leopoldo Usseglio, *I marchesi di Monferrato in Italia ed in Oriente durante i secoli XII e XIII* (Turin, 1926), 2: 173; Roberto Cessi, "Venezia e la quarta crociata," *Archivio Veneto*, ser. 5, 48–49 (1951): 9, n. 3; Roberto Cessi, "Politica, economia, religione," in *Storia di Venezia*, vol. 2, *Dalle origini del ducato alla IV crociata* (Venice: Centro internazionale delle arti e del costume, 1957), p. 449; Francesco Cognasso, *Storia delle crociate* (Milan: Dall'Oglio, 1967), p. 701. Cognasso's statement, which includes a denial of any religious motivation to the crusaders, is almost the antithesis to our thesis. On the narrower question of the reasons for taking the cross, we do not believe that the great vassals had much to fear from Philip Augustus at this stage in his career. Even if they did, they surely had no reason to believe that ecclesiastical sanctions protecting crusaders would deter him, if he were able to take vengeance upon them. Tessier, *Quatrième croisade*, p. 36; Sebastian Naslund, "The Crusading Policy of Innocent III in France, 1198–1202: An Evaluation from Secular and Ecclesiastical Sources" (seminar paper, University of Illinois, 1969), pp. 13–14.

48. Villehardouin, *Conquête de Constantinople*, sec. 10, 1: 12–14. For the relationship of Louis of Blois and Geoffrey of Perche, see p. 13, n. 7.

49. Ibid., sec. 9, 1: 12; Anna Maria Nada Patrone, in Robert of Clari, *La conquista di Costantinopli* (Genoa, 1972), p. 8, n. 28.

50. Villehardouin, *Conquête de Constantinople*, secs. 4–5, 1: 6–8.

51. Ibid., sec. 8, 1: 10–12.

52. Ibid., sec. 10, 1: 12–14.

53. Ibid., sec. 9, 1: 12.

54. McNeal and Wolff, "The Fourth Crusade," p. 160.

55. Villehardouin, *Conquête de Constantinople*, sec. 11, 1: 14.

56. Ibid., sec. 7, 1: 10.

57. Ibid., sec. 11, 1: 14.

58. The meeting cannot be dated with certainty. See Donald E. Queller, "L'évolution du rôle de l'ambassadeur: Les pleins pouvoirs et le traité de 1201 entre les Croisés et les Vénitiens," *Moyen Age* 19 (1961): 484 and n. 13. Also see this article for greater detail on the envoys and the negotiation of the treaty. H. Vriens asserted that a sort of "permanent central committee" met at Compiègne. "De kwestie van den vierden kruistocht," *Tijdschrift voor Geschiedenis* 37 (1922): 52. There is no documentation, and we do not follow him. Cf. Maleczek, *Petrus Capuanus*, p. 118, n. 13.

59. C. W. Previté-Orton, "The Italian Cities till c. 1200," *CMH*, 5: 293; E. J. Passant, "The Effects of the Crusades upon Western Europe," *CMH*, 5: 328; McNeal and Wolff, "The Fourth Crusade," p. 161.

60. Villehardouin, *Conquête de Constantinople*, sec. 11, 1: 14. One would like to know who participated in the agreement: the plenipotentiaries were sent in the names of Baldwin of Flanders, Louis of Blois, and Thibaut of Champagne. The failure of many crusaders to adhere to the treaty concluded by these plenipotentiaries becomes crucial for the fate of the crusade.

61. Robert of Clari, who was ill-informed concerning the preliminaries of the crusade, names only these two. *Conquête*, sec. 6: p. 6. Villehardouin, however, gives the full list, which is confirmed by official documents: he and Milo le Brébant representing Thibaut; John of Friaise and Walter of Gaudonville representing Louis; and Conon and Alard Maquereau representing Baldwin. *Conquête de Constantinople*, sec. 359, 2: 168. Tessier wrongly attributed preeminence to Conon, Geoffrey, and John, calling the others mere aides or assessors. *Quatrième croisade*, p. 256.

62. Villehardouin, *Conquête de Constantinople*, 1: 11, n. 10; McNeal and Wolff, "The Fourth Crusade," p. 160 and n. 21. He was criticized by another troubadour, Huon III d'Oisi, for returning home early with Philip Augustus. *Kreuzzugsdichtung*, ed. Ulrich Müller (Tübingen: M. Niemeyer, 1969), p. 35.

63. *Livre de la conqueste de la princée de l'Amorée: Chronique de Morée*, ed. Jean Longnon (Paris: Librarie Renouard, 1911), sec. 126, p. 43; *Chronique de la Conquête de Constantinople*, p. 31. Neither of these chronicles is a reliable source for the crusade, but they may serve to show the reputation of Villehardouin. See also Faral's introduction to Villehardouin, *Conquête de Constantinople*, 1: vii and x. Jean Longnon identifies him as the *marescallus comitis Henrici* on the Third Crusade. *Recherches sur la vie de Geoffroy de Villehardouin, suivies du catalogue des actes des Villehardouin* (Paris: E. Champion, 1939), pp. 59–63. He also finds him as arbiter of a dispute in 1198. Ibid., pp. 65–66.

64. Concerning organization and clarity see Faral's introduction to Villehardouin, *Conquête de Constantinople*, 1: xxxv. We should remember that he was a soldier writing his memoirs, not an analytical scholar. See Andrea's essay on primary sources below.

65. Faral's introduction to Villehardouin, *Conquête de Constantinople*, 1: vi.

66. For the list of his missions on behalf of the crusaders. see Queller, "L'évolution du rôle de l'ambassadeur," pp. 482–83, n. 11. The second in the list, however, was actually Geoffrey of Joinville.

67. Villehardouin, *Conquête de Constantinople*, sec. 13, 1: 16.

68. Emile Bouchet, in Geoffroy de Villehardouin, *La conquête de Constantinople*, ed. Emile Bouchet, 2 vols. (Paris, 1891), 2: 18–19.

69. Robert of Clari, *Conquête*, sec. 3, p. 7. Roberto Cessi accepts the prior attempts not only at Genoa and Pisa, but also at Marseilles. "Politica, economia, religione," p. 449.

70. Villehardouin, *Conquête de Constantinople*, sec. 32, 1: 32–34. Lacking compelling reason, one simply does not have the option of following the confused and ill-informed Robert instead of Villehardouin, who was a participant.

71. Wilhelm von Heyd, *Histoire du commerce du Levant au moyen âge* (1st German ed., 1879), trans. by Furcy Raynaud and revised and augmented by the author (1885; reprinted, 2 vols., Leipzig: O. Harrassowitz, 1936), 1: 204, 234–35, and 312.

72. H. Vriens, "De kwestie van den vierden kruistocht," p. 61.

73 Villehardouin, *Conquête de Constantinople*, sec. 14, 1: 18.

74. Luchaire, *Innocent III*, IV: 89; Tessier, *Quatrième Croisade, p.* 105; Francesco Cerone, "Il papa e i veneziani nella quarta crociata," *Archivio Veneto*, n.s. 36 (1888): 61.

75. *Gesta Innocentii*, chap. 46, col. 91.

76. Queller, "L'évolution du rôle de l'ambassadeur," p. 488, n. 22.

77. Innocent III, *Register*, 1:336, p. 502; 1:343, p. 513; and 1:536 (539), pp. 775–76 (Migne, *PL*, CCXIV: 311, 318, 493). See Cessi, "Venezia e la quarta crociata," p. 7, n. 3.

78. Queller, "L'évolution du rôle de l'ambassadeur," p. 488, n. 22.

79. For specific references to Carl Hopf, Paul Riant, Ludwig Streit, Edwin Pears, Walter Norden, F. C. Hodgson, H. Vriens, E. F. Jacob, and A. Frolow, see Donald E. Queller, "Innocent III and the Crusader-Venetian Treaty of 1201," *Medievalia et Humanistica* 15 (1963): 32, n. 8. Add Bouchet, in Villehardouin, *Conquête de Constantinople* (1891), 2: 20–21. Fliche believes not only that the pope had a peculiar mistrust of Venice, but that he favored Sicily as the point of concentration of troops

and fleets. Augustin Fliche, Christine Thouzelliers, and Yvonne Azais, "La chrétienté romaine," in Augustin Fliche and Victor Martin, *Histoire de l'eglise* (Paris, 1950), x: 60–61; see also John Godfrey, *1204: The Unholy Crusade* (Oxford: Oxford University Press, 1980), p. 51.

80. See Innocent's letter authorizing the Venetians to continue the trade in nonstrategic materials. Innocent III, *Register*, 1:536 (539), pp. 775–76 (Migne, *PL*, CCXIV: 493).

81. Benjamin of Tudela, *The Itinerary*, trans. Marcus Nathan Adler (London, 1903; repr. Malibu, Calif.: Joseph Simon Pangloss, 1987), p. 134.

82. Cerone, "Il papa e i veneziani nella quarta crociata," p. 59.

83. Schmandt, "Fourth Crusade and the Just War Theory," p. 221.

Chapter 2

1. Villehardouin does not give us their route to Venice, but he does provide an itinerary of the return. Villehardouin, *Conquête de Constantinople*, secs. 32–35, 1: 32–36. This return route conforms with the route of the journey to Venice given by the *Chronicle of Morea*, which is not in itself a reliable source for such details, and by the *Chronique de la conquête de Constantinople*. *Crusaders as Conquerors: The Chronicle of Morea*, trans. Harold E. Lurier (New York: Columbia University Press, 1964), pp. 76–77; *Chronique de la conquête de Constantinople*, p. 32. Faral's dates are slightly off, because he used 21 March, instead of 25 March, the correct date, for Easter 1201. For the date of arrival: Villehardouin, *Conquête de Constantinople*, sec. 14, 1: 18. The *Cronaca Bemba*, a fifteenth-century Venetian chronicle, gives the date as March, but the author is generally inaccurate on details concerning the Fourth Crusade. Such late Venetian sources have no value when contemporary documentation is available. One might be tempted to use them when contemporary documentation is lacking if they could be shown to conform closely and in detail to contemporary documents, and especially to official documents such as treaties, on other points, but this is not often the case. *Cronaca Bemba*, Biblioteca Marciana, cl. ital. 7, cod. 125 (7460), f. 33 (436) r.

2. Villehardouin, *Conquête de Constantinople*, sec. 15, 1: 18.

3. Villehardouin, *Conquête de Constantinople*, sec. 67, 1: 68; sec 351, 2: 160; sec. 364, 2: 172; Nicetas Choniates, *Historia*, ed. Jan-Louis Dieten in *Corpus Fontium Historiae Byzantinae*, XI/1 (Berlin and New York: De Gruyter, 1975), p. 538; *Venetiarum historia vulgo Petro Iustiniano Iustiniani filio adiudicata*, ed. Roberto Cessi and Fanny Bennato (Venice: Deputazione di Storia Patria per le Venezie, 1964), p. 131, (=*Historia ducum Veneticorum. Supplementum*, ed. H. Simonsfeld, *MGH, SS*, 14: 90); Andrea Dandolo, *Chronica per extensum descripta*, ed. Ester Pastorello, in *Rerum Italicarum Scriptores*, vol. 12, part. 1 (Bologna, 1938), p. 276.

4. Marino Sanudo, *Vitae ducum venetorum*, ed. Lodovico Antonio Muratori, in *Rerum Italicarum Scriptores* (Milan, 1733), vol. 22, col. 527.

5. Cf. Sara de Mundo Lo, *Cruzados en Bizancio: La quarta cruzada a la luz de las fuentes latinas y orientales* (Buenos Aires: Universidad de Buenos Aires, 1957), p. 78; Paul Rousset, *Histoire des croisades* (Paris: Payot, 1957), 2: 213; McNeal and Wolff, "The Fourth Crusade," p. 162; Donald M. Nicol, *Byzantium and Venice: A Study in Diplo-*

matic and Cultural Relations (Cambridge: Cambridge University Press, 1988), p. 119.

6. Thomas F. Madden, "Enrico Dandolo: His Life, His Family, and His Venice before the Fourth Crusade" (Ph.D diss., University of Illinois at Urbana-Champaign, 1993), pp. 63–65.

7. Villehardouin, *Conquête de Constantinople*, sec. 67, 1: 68; sec. 173, 1: 174; sec 351, 2: 160; sec. 364, 2: 172; Nicetas, *Historia*, p. 538.

8. Villehardouin, *Conquête de Constantinople*, sec. 67, 1: 68; see note 10 below.

9. Manuel was reportedly warned of Dandolo's future mischief by an imperial soothsayer. *The Chronicle of Novgorod, 1016–1471*, trans. Robert Michell and Nevill Forbes, Camden Third Series, 25 (London: Camden Society, 1914), p. 48.

10. Thomas F. Madden, "Venice and Constantinople in 1171 and 1172: Enrico Dandolo's Attitude Towards Byzantium," *Mediterranean Historical Review* 8 (1993): 181–82; cf. Giorgio Cracco, s.v. "Dandolo, Enrico," *Dizionario biografico degli Italiani*.

11. Runciman, *History of the Crusades*, 3: 114–15; McNeal and Wolff, "The Fourth Crusade," p. 169; Nicol, *Byzantium and Venice*, pp. 119–20, and passim; Robert Browning, *The Byzantine Empire*, rev. ed. (Washington, DC: Catholic University of America Press, 1992), p. 187. Runciman, cited above, in an apparent attempt to reconcile the rumor of Dandolo's blinding with the explanation Dandolo gave to Villehardouin, stated that the doge lost his sight in a street brawl in Constantinople. This is pure fabrication, but it is common to see it reported as fact: see, e.g., Godfrey, *1204: The Unholy Crusade*, p. 64, who even attributes the brawl to Villehardouin; Nicol, *Byzantium and Venice*, p. 84.

12. Villehardouin, *Conquête de Constantinople*, sec. 15, 1: 18; *Chronique de Morée*, sec. 15, p. 6; Edgar H. McNeal, introduction to Robert of Clari, *The Conquest of Constantinople* (New York: Columbia University Press, 1936; repr., 1966), p. 223. See also Donald E. Queller and Irene B. Katele, "Attitudes towards the Venetians in the Fourth Crusade: The Western Sources," *International History Review* 4 (1982): 1–36.

13. Madden, "Enrico Dandolo," passim.

14. E.g., Rousset, *Histoire des croisades*, p. 213; Mundo Lo, *Cruzados en Bizancio*, p. 78; Runciman, *History of the Crusades*, 3: 114–15; Nicol, *Byzantium and Venice*, pp. 119–20, 412, and passim.

15. While we must appreciate that medieval values were not the same as ours, it is astonishing that so many scholars accept as a virtuous motivation the feudal noble's desire to slay the infidel for his wrong faith (and to seize his land), while rejecting as unworthy the merchant's quest for profit. Neither, of course, seems especially saintly to us, but the merchant's values are as medieval as the knight's and surely appear, upon reflection, more acceptable to most of us. See Donald E. Queller and Gerald W. Day, "Some Arguments in Defense of the Venetians on the Fourth Crusade," *American Historical Review* 81 (1976): 717–37; Donald E. Queller and Thomas F. Madden, "Some Further Arguments in Defense of the Venetians on the Fourth Crusade," *Byzantion* 62 (1992): 433–73, esp. pp. 434–35, 445–46.

16. Villehardouin, *Conquête de Constantinople*, secs. 16–17, 1: 18–20. On the identification of Venetian constitutional bodies in Villehardouin's account see, Cessi, "Venezia e la quarta crociata," pp. 10–11, n. 4.

17. Madden, "Enrico Dandolo," pp. 199–200 and Appendix B.

18. Villehardouin, *Conquête de Constantinople*, sec. 18, 1: 20–22.

19. *TTh*, 1: 365. The treaty is also found in Longnon, *Recherches*, pp. 179–81,

and in Tessier, *Quatrième croisade*, pp. 252–54. For a discussion of whether the squires were noncombatant servants or sergeants on horseback, see Ferdinand Lot, *L'art militaire et les armées au moyen âge* (Paris: Payot, 1949), pp. 170 and 175 and n. 3. That horses were to be transported only for the knights argues that the squires were still servants. See also R. C. Smail, *Crusading Warfare (1097–1193)* (Cambridge: Cambridge University Press, 1956), pp. 108–9. Contra: Antonio Carile, "Alle origini dell'impero d'Oriente: Analisi quantitativa dell' esercito crociato e repartizione dei feudi," *Nuova rivista storica* 56 (1972): 291, n. 29. Anna Maria Nada Patrone wrote that the agreement was for the transportation of 100,000 men, which is probably a misreading of Robert of Clari's 104,000. *La quarta crociata e l'impero latino di Romania (1198–1261)* (Turin: G. Giappichelli, 1972), p. 76. Read accurately or not, Robert still should not be followed on matters of this sort, especially when there exists an official document. Fred A. Cazel, Jr. misreads "horses" for "knights," thus making the proposed crusader army "29,000 men and 4,500 horses." "Financing the Crusades," p. 141.

20. Villehardouin, *Conquête de Constantinople*, sec. 19, 1: 22. Godfrey sees evil intentions in the eight days Dandolo took to deliberate on the proposal. He "suspects that not only did Dandolo skillfully and patiently lead them [the envoys] to the admission that they would find the Venetian transports quite indispensable, but also that he adroitly flattered them to the point at which they convinced themselves that their Crusading army was going to be very large and imposing." *1204: The Unholy Crusade*, p. 49. There is no evidence for Godfrey's suspicions, which he goes on to treat as fact. Godfrey's certainty of Dandolo's clandestine designs is but one of the handicaps of his book.

21. Villehardouin, *Conquête de Constantinople*, sec. 21, 1: 22. Villehardouin says that the Venetians agreed to furnish provisions for nine months, but the treaty itself says a year. So does the *Chronicon gallicum ineditum*, in *TTh*, 1: 330 (improperly identified there). This is a rare example of conflict between Villehardouin's account and official documentation. *TTh*, 1: 365. Faral proposes two explanations: (1) Villehardouin subtracted from the year the three months of 1202 when the crusaders were at Venice and supplied by the Venetians; (2) three extra months of provisions were obtained by the envoys in subsequent negotiations. Villehardouin, *Conquête de Constantinople*, 1: 216. Queller now believes that he was wrong in preferring the former explanation. Queller, "L'évolution du rôle de l'ambassadeur," p. 490, n. 28. The sale of grain by the Venetians to the crusaders at inflated prices during their sojourn on the Lido is mentioned, so it would seem that the Venetians did not begin supplying them until the date of embarkation. *Devastatio Constantinopolitana*, ed. Alfred J. Andrea, in "The *Devastatio Constantinopolitana*, A Special Perspective on the Fourth Crusade: An Analysis, New Edition, and Translation," *Historical Reflections* 19 (1993): 132. Also in *Chroniques greco-romanes*, ed. Charles Hopf (Berlin, 1873; repr. Brussels: Culture et Civilisation, 1966), p. 87; *Annales Herbipolenses, MGH, SS*, 16: 9–12. Villehardouin also mentions that the Venetians held a market for all things needful for horses and men. *Conquête de Constantinople*, sec. 56, 1: 58.

22. The proposed division of booty makes clear the importance and expense of an armed fleet at this time. Had the Fourth Crusade sailed as planned, one quarter of the host (the Venetian sailors) would have received one half of the spoils. See Antonio Carile, *Per una storia dell'Impero Latino di Costantinopoli, 1204–1261*, rev. ed. (Bologna: Pàtron, 1978), p. 89.

23. Villehardouin, *Conquête de Constantinople*, secs. 20–30, 1: 22–30. This interpretation satisfactorily reconciles the figure of 94,000 marks given by Villehardouin in describing the offer of the doge and that of 85,000 marks, which appears in the treaty, especially since the difference represents a reduction of two marks per knight. See Queller, "L'évolution du rôle de l'ambassadeur," p. 490, n. 29. This explanation is not, however, without its skeptics: see Cazal, "Financing the Crusades," p. 141, n. 78. Another accurate description of the treaty is given by the fifteenth-century Venetian chronicler Lorenzo de Monacis, who seems to have had the document before him. *Chronicon de rebus venetis ab u. c. ad annum MCCCLIV*, ed. Fl. Cornelius (Venice, 1758), p. 134. Villehardouin's statement that the date of departure was to be Saint John's day (24 June) is one of his few errors of fact, not, of course, very significant. *Conquête de Constantinople*, sec. 30, 1: 30. On the mark of Cologne and the mark of Venice, see Louise Buenger Robbert, "The Venetian Money Market, 1150–1229," *Studi Veneziani* 13 (1971): 16.

24. The first to make the charge was Peter of Vaux-de-Cernay, *Petri Vallium Sarnaii monachi hystoria Albigensis*, ed. Pascal Guébin and Ernest Lyon, 3 vols. (Paris: Champion, 1926–30), 1: 107; on this passage, see Alfred J. Andrea, "Cistercian Accounts of the Fourth Crusade: Were They Anti-Venetian?" *Analecta Cisterciensia* 41 (1985), p. 14, n. 53. He was not the last: see, for example, John V. A. Fine, *The Late Medieval Balkans: A Critical Survey from the Late Twelfth Century to the Ottoman Conquest* (Ann Arbor: University of Michigan Press, 1987), p. 61; M. Hellweg, "Die ritterliche Welt in der franzosichen Geschichtsschreibung des vierten Kreuzzuges," *Romanische Forschungen* 52 (1938): 1–40. See also Georges Duby, *The Early Growth of the European Economy: Warriors and Peasants from the Seventh to the Twelfth Century*, trans. from the French 1st ed. of 1973 by Howard B. Clarke (Ithaca, N.Y.: Cornell University Press, 1974), p. 264, on the "simple minded debtors" from the north. On the negative myth of Venice, treating the Venetians as motivated solely by avarice, see Gina Fasoli, "Nascita di un mito," in *Studi storici in onore di Giacchino Volpe* (Florence: Sansoni, 1958), vol. 1, especially p. 449. Fasoli concedes that the chroniclers prior to Martin da Canal do not show any real Venetian interest in the conquest of the Holy Land for religious ends. Ibid., 162–63. The Venetians on the Fourth Crusade had religious motives as strong as most other crusaders. See Queller and Day, "Some Arguments in Defense of the Venetians on the Fourth Crusade," pp. 719–20.

25. The respect given to Villehardouin for his diplomatic skill can be inferred from the many missions assigned to him by the French nobility. For a list of these assignments, see Queller, "L'évolution du rôle de l'ambassadeur," p. 482, n. 11.

26. Grossman, "Financing of the Crusades," p. 17.

27. *Codice diplomatico della repubblica di Genova*, ed. Cesare di Imperiale, *Fonti per la storia d'Italia*, 79: 264–66, doc. 191. Grossman, "Financing of the Crusades," pp. 17–18.

28. Villehardouin, *Conquête de Constantinople*, sec. 76, 1: 76. Robert of Clari, *Conquête*, sec. 10, p. 9, and sec. 13, p. 13; see also Queller and Madden, "Some Further Arguments in Defense of the Venetians," pp. 435–36.

29. C. Manfroni, *Storia della marina italiana dalle invasioni barbariche alla caduta di Costantinopoli* (Livorno: R. Academia navale, 1899), 1: 313. The author emphatically accuses those who believe the contract extortionate of ignorance of such affairs. Where Manfroni gets 900 horses rather than 4,500 is unclear, but the correct figure would

strengthen his argument. Much better is the discussion by Maleczek, *Petrus Capuanus*, pp. 256–57. Maleczek also makes an attempt to assess the cost to Venice for the galleys, and arrives at the figure 28,500 marks. In an earlier study, Carile estimates the cost to have been more than 29,200 marks. *Per una storia dell'impero latino di Costantinopoli*, p. 90. Both figures assume, however, that specialists on the galleys required payment. They may have joined as crusaders, thus paying for the journey themselves, or simply for the promised share of booty.

30. Maleczek, *Petrus Capuanus*, pp. 122–23, 264–68.

31. "Et si Deo annuente per uim uel conuentione aliquid fuerimus aquisiti, comuniter uel diuisum, nos ex eo omni medietatem habere debemus, et uos aliam medietatem." *TTh*, 1: 367.

32. The Venetian constitution before the thirteenth century remains rather murky. We do, however, have Dandolo's oath of office, which makes clear how much authority was vested in the council. *Le Promissioni del doge di Venezia dalle origini alla fine del duecento*, ed. Gisella Graziato (Venice: Comitato per la pubblicazione delle fonti relative alla storia di Venezia, 1986), pp. 2–4; Madden, "Enrico Dandolo," pp. 150–52. On the nature of political power in this early period, see Enrico Besta, "Il diritto e le leggi civili di Venezia fina al dogado di Enrico Dandolo," *Ateneo Veneto* 22, no. 2 (1899): 232–37; Charles Diehl, *Une république patricienne: Venise* (Paris: E. Flammarion, 1915), pp. 85–88 and 107; Giuseppe Maranini, *La costituzione di Venezia dalle origini alla serrata del Maggior Consiglio* (Florence: La nuova Italia, 1927; repr. 1974), pp. 76–77, 113–31; Giovanni Cassandro, "Concetto e struttura dello stato veneziano," *Bergomum* 38 no. 2 (1964): 37–40; Roberto Cessi, "Venice to the Eve of the Fourth Crusade," *CMH* (Cambridge: Cambridge University Press, 1966), vol. 4, pt. 1, p. 272; Gerhard Rösch, *Der venezianische Adel bis zur Schließung des Großen Rats: Zur Genese einer Führungsschicht* (Sigmaringen: Jan Thorbecke, 1989), pp. 81–111.

33. A source of some disagreement: those who see Dandolo in the darkest terms attribute to him the ability to circumnavigate the constitutional restraints placed on him. E.g., William H. McNeill, *Venice: The Hinge of Europe, 1081-1797* (Chicago: University of Chicago Press, 1974), pp. 248–49; Nicol, *Byzantium and Venice*, p. 148. On the other side, Giorgio Cracco argues that old and blind Dandolo had virtually no power and, in fact, played little part in Venetian politics or the Fourth Crusade, s.v. "Dandolo." This is difficult to accept given the vast testimony of Dandolo's wisdom and vigorousness; e.g., Villehardouin, *Conquête de Constantinople*, sec. 173, 1: 174–76; sec. 364, 2: 172; Nicetas, *Historia*, p. 538. Frederic Lane was probably closest to the mark when he wrote that "the way in which he [Dandolo] dominated events showed that, although the doge of Venice could not go against the views of his councils, he could be as powerful a ruler as any king." *Venice: A Maritime Republic* (Baltimore: Johns Hopkins University Press, 1973), p. 93.

34. Villehardouin, *Conquête de Constantinople*, sec. 25, 1: 26. Cessi, "Venezia e la quarta crociata," pp. 10–11 and n. 4; Madden, "Enrico Dandolo," p. 201.

35. Villehardouin, *Conquête de Constantinople*, sec. 25, 1: 26. It is not possible, however, that ten thousand could have been crowded into San Marco.

36. It was diplomatic to say it, but it was not true. The envoys themselves had chosen Venice, as we have seen. Queller, "L'évolution du rôle de l'ambassadeur," p. 487 and n. 19.

37. Villehardouin, *Conquête de Constantinople*, secs. 26–29, 1: 26–30. Cazel

points out the corporate nature of the Venetian decision to accept, thus binding all citizens to the costs, profits, and merits of the enterprise. "Financing of the Crusades," p. 124.

38. There is a problem of dating that has not been satisfactorily resolved. Villehardouin says that the treaty was redacted on the day following the assembly at San Marco and that it was still Lent. *Conquête de Constantinople*, sec. 30, 1: 30. The treaty is actually dated in April. Easter was 25 March. For attempted reconciliations, see C. Klimke, *Die Quellen zur Geschichte des vierten Kreuzzuges* (Breslau: A. Neumann, 1875), p. 83, n. 2, and Faral in Villehardouin, *Conquête de Constantinople*, 1: 219. Contra, see Colin Morris, "Geoffrey of Villehardouin and the Conquest of Constantinople," *History* 53 (1968): 30–31.

39. Villehardouin, *Conquête de Constantinople*, sec. 31, 1: 32. *TTh*, nos. 89–91, 1: 358–62. For the use of blank parchments, see Donald E. Queller, "Diplomatic 'Blanks' in the Thirteenth Century," *English Historical Review* 80 (1965): 477–80.

40. Villehardouin, *Conquête de Constantinople*, sec. 30, 1: 30.

41. Gunther of Pairis, *Hystoria Constantinopolitana*, ed. Peter Orth (Hildesheim and Zurich: Weidmann, 1994), p. 121. Gunther anachronistically places Boniface of Montferrat among the barons who made this decision. The scholarly consensus seems to favor the view that the decision to sail to Egypt came from the barons rather than the envoys themselves. Carl Hopf believed that Egypt was selected by the barons at Compiègne. *Geschichte Griechenlands* in *Encylopädie*, ed. J. S. Ersch and J. G. Gruber, 85–86 (Leipzig: J. F. Gieditsch, 1867–68), p. 186. See also, Nicol, "The Fourth Crusade and the Greek and Latin Empires," *CMH*, vol. 4, pt. 1. (Cambridge: Cambridge University Press, 1966), pp. 276–77; Jonathan Riley-Smith, *The Crusades: A Short History* (New Haven, Conn.: Yale University Press, 1987), p. 123. Godfrey, *1204: The Unholy Crusade*, p. 48, holds that the envoys made the decision themselves. Gunther of Pairis does not really state that Innocent III selected Egypt as the goal of the crusade: Tessier, *Quatrième croisade*, pp. 51–56, has read the passage out of context. Also Adolf Schaube, *Handelsgeschichte der romanischen Völker des Mittelmeergebiets bis zum Ende der Kreuzzüge* (Munich and Berlin: R. Oldenbourg, 1906), p. 258. The *Gesta Innocentii*, chap. 83, col. 131, followed by a few modern authors, asserts that part of the force was to go to Syria and part to Egypt. Alberic of Trois-Fontaines's use of "Constantinopolim" must be a lapsus for Egypt or Cairo, because he only later tells how Alexius sent letters to the crusaders asking their aid. *Chronica*, ed. P. Scheffer-Boichorst, *MGH*, *SS*, 23: 880. Cessi's argument, "L'eredità di Enrico Dandolo," *Archivio Veneto*, ser. 5, 67 (1960): 2 and n. 2, that the intended place of debarkation was Palestine, that there was no agreement to go to Egypt, and that Villehardouin had merely voiced privately to the doge a personal opinion on the subject of Egypt is not supported by the evidence. For identification of "Babilloine" with Cairo, see Robert of Clari, *The Conquest of Constantinople*, p. 36, n. 15.

42. *Sigeberti continuato Praemonstratensis*, *MGH*, *SS*, 6: 456; Helene Wieruszowski, "The Norman Kingdom of Sicily and the Crusade," in Setton, *A History of the Crusades*, 2: 30.

43. William of Tyre, *Historia rerum in partibus transmarinis gestarum*, 19, 30, in *Corpus Christianorum, Continuatio medievalis*, ed. R. B. C. Huygens (Turnhout: Brepols, 1986), LXIIIA: 907–8; Gustave Schlumberger, *Campagnes du Roi Amaury Ier de Jérusalem en Egypte au XIIe siècle* (Paris: Plon-Nourrit, 1906), pp. 154–68; Mahmoud

Said Omran, "King Amalric and the Siege of Alexandria, 1167" in *Crusade and Settlement*, ed. Peter W. Edbury (Cardiff: University College Cardiff Press, 1985), pp. 191–96.

44. Schlumberger, *Campagnes du Roi Amaury Ier*, pp. 172–220.

45. Joshua Prawer, in Marino Sanudo (Torsello), *Liber secretorum fidelium crucis super Terrae Sanctae recuperatione et conservatione* (Hanover ed. of 1611; reprinted Toronto and Buffalo: University of Toronto Press, 1972), p. viii; William of Tyre, *Historia rerum in partibus transmarinis gestarum a tempore successorum Mahumeth usque ad annum Domini MCLXXXIV*, in *Recueil des historens des croisades: historiens occidentaux*, vol. 1, pt. 2, pp. 890–94, 902–13, 948–58, 962–69, 971–79; Runciman, *History of the Crusades*, 2: 436–37. Runciman dates Renaud's expedition in 1182, although other authorities give 1183. Hamilton A. R. Gibb, "The Rise of Saladin," *History of the Crusades*, ed. Setton, 1: 582; Joshua Prawer, *The Crusaders' Kingdom: European Colonialism in the Middle Ages* (New York, 1972), p. 28.

46. This argument is advanced by J. J. Saunders, *Aspects of the Crusades* (Christchurch, New Zealand: University of Canterbury, 1962), p. 28.

47. Gunther of Pairis, *Hystoria Constantinopolitana*, p. 121. Tessier, *Quatrième croisade*, p. 48, argues against Gunther that a country desolated by famine would offer scanty resources to invaders. For additional evidence of the famine see Shaul Shaked, *A Tentative Bibliography of Geniza Documents* (Paris: Mouton, 1964 [Mosseri Coll., no. 22]), p. 27. It was followed by a terrible plague. Eliahu Ashtor, *A Social and Economic History of the Near East in the Middle Ages* (Berkeley: University of California Press, 1976), p. 238. Roger de Hoveden, *Chronica*, ed. William Stubbs, 4 vols., *Rer. Brit. M. A. Script.*, 4: 186, quotes a letter describing the troubles in Egypt.

48. Queller and Madden, "Some Further Arguments in Defense of the Venetians," pp. 441–42.

49. Madden, "Enrico Dandolo," pp. 94–102.

50. Gunther of Pairis, *Hystoria Constantinopolitana*, p. 121.

51. Ernoul-Bernard, *Chronique*, pp. 340–41.

52. Tessier, *Quatrième croisade*, pp. 48–51. Otto of Saint Blaise, *Chronicon*, p. 327. In fairness to the Latins of the Levant, however, it should be borne in mind that the martial zeal of newly arrived Westerners often jeopardized the precarious kingdom.

53. Alphandéry, *La chrétienté et l'idée de croisade*, 1: 156–57.

54. Queller, "L'évolution du rôle de l'ambassadeur," p. 495, n. 47, for the bibliography on the secrecy concerning the Egyptian destination. Walter Norden offers the strange hypothesis that the Venetians intended to divert the crusade from Egypt to Syria. *Der vierte Kreuzzug in Rahmen der Beziehungen des Abendlandes zu Byzanz* (Berlin: E. Beck, 1898), pp. 86–87. See also Ludwig Streit, *Venedig und die Wendung des vierten Kreuzzugs gegen Konstantinopel* (Anklam: Richard Poettcke, 1877), p. 29.

55. Villehardouin, *Conquête de Constantinople*, sec. 32, 1: 32. See especially n. 5 for a brief discussion of the amount borrowed.

56. Queller, "Diplomatic 'Blanks,'" p. 479.

57. Tafel and Thomas, *Urkunden*, 1: p. 366; Villehardouin, *Conquête de Constantinople*, sec. 32, 1: 32. From whom the money was borrowed, Villehardouin does not say. Presumably from moneylenders at the Rialto markets.

58. Below, pp. 68–69.

59. Villehardouin, *Conquête de Constantinople*, sec. 56, 1: 58.

60. Robert of Clari, *Conquête*, sec. 7, p. 8, and sec. 11, pp. 9–10. The first citation is in that portion of the account prior to his own arrival in Venice, which is filled with errors. The second, though, occurs when the doge attempted to get the money owed the Venetians by the crusaders after Clari had arrived in the lagoon. Although Clari is the only source for this ducal order, it is borne out by documentary evidence and precedent. In Madden's examination of surviving overseas trade documents, he found that Venetian activity declined precipitously in 1201 and ground to a halt in 1202. "Enrico Dandolo," pp. 210–13. By happenstance, commercial records survive which document what must have been one of the last merchant voyages to the East before the crusade left. The great roundship called the *Paradise*, owned by Tomaso Viadro and captained by Deodato Blanco, left Venice for Syria in July 1201. After a lucrative voyage, the vessel made it back to Venice by July 1202 at the latest, but more probably sometime in June. The fleet was to be ready to sail on 29 June. The *Paradise* is one of the ships we know took part in the Fourth Crusade. *Documenti del commercio veneziano nei secoli XI–XIII*, ed. Raimondo Morozzo della Rocca and Antonino Lombardo, 2 vols. (Rome: R. Istituto storico italiano per il medio evo, 1940), vol. 1, no. 461, pp. 451–52; *Nuovi documenti del commercio veneto dei secoli XI–XIII*, ed. Antonino Lombardo and Raimondo Morozzo della Rocca (Venice: Deputazione di storia patria per le Venezie, 1953), nos. 53–54, pp. 59–61. The last two documents record payments to investors after the *Paradise*'s return. The first is dated July 1202. The second, dated November 1202, was paid rather late, perhaps because the investor, the future doge Pietro Ziani, was out of Venice or perhaps because of a disruption of business during the crusaders' stay in the lagoon. There are no other surviving documents recording Venetian overseas trade until 1205.

Such a cancellation of trade was not without precedent in Venice. Most recently, in 1188, Doge Orio Mastropiero ordered all Venetian vessels to return to the lagoon by Easter to take part in the Third Crusade. *TTh*, 1: 204–6; Andrea Dandolo, *Chronica per extensum descripta*, p. 270. In 1198 there was a similar, although less comprehensive, order in effect, probably in anticipation of further trouble from the Pisans with whom Venice had recently been at war. Lombardo and Morozzo della Rocca, *Nuovi Documenti*, no. 45, pp. 51–52.

61. Juergen Schulz, "Urbanism in Medieval Venice," in Anthony Molho, Kurt Raaflaub, and Julia Emlen, eds., *City States in Classical Antiquity and Medieval Italy* (Stuttgart: Franz Steiner, 1991), p. 428.

62. Louise Buenger Robbert, "Reorganization of the Venetian Coinage by Doge Enrico Dandolo," *Speculum* 49 (1974): 48–60, argued convincingly for a earlier minting of the *grosso*. With some refinements, this thesis met with general acceptance: Donald E. Queller, "A Note on the Reorganization of the Venetian Coinage by Doge Enrico Dandolo," *Rivista italiana di numismatica e scienze affini* 67 (1975): 167–72; Frederic C. Lane and Reinhold C. Mueller, *Money and Banking in Medieval and Renaissance Venice* (Baltimore: Johns Hopkins University Press, 1985), pp. 114–15, 501. Recently, scholars have begun to question the earlier dating: Peter Spufford, *Money and its Uses in Medieval Europe* (Cambridge: Cambridge University Press, 1988), p. 226; Alan Stahl, "Venetian Coinage: Variations in Production," in *Rythmes de la production monétaire de l'antiquité à nos jours*, ed. Georges Depeyvot, et al. (Louvain-la-Neuve: Séminaire de numismatique Marcel Hoc, 1989), p. 478; Madden "Enrico Dandolo," pp. 177–90. The debate has not ended. In a forthcoming article, Stahl returns to the

problem and concludes that the early date is probably correct. Alan Stahl, "The Coinage of Venice in the Age of Enrico Dandolo," in *Venice: Society and Crusade. Studies in Honor of Donald E. Queller*, ed. Thomas F. Madden and Ellen E. Kittell, forthcoming.

63. Robert of Auxerre, *Chronicon*, p. 261; Hurter, *Papa Innocenzo III*, 2: 149.

64. The galleys alone would require 6,000 men. Lane, *Venice*, p. 36. See Carile, *Per una storia dell'impero latino di Costantinopoli*, p. 90, who calculates the Venetian crusaders to have totaled 14,600 men. In an earlier study, he calculated the figure to be 17,264. "Alle origini dell'impero latino d'Oriente," pp. 287–88.

65. Clari, *Conquête de Constantinople*, sec. 11, pp. 9–10.

66. It is not uncommon to read that the force size was an impossibility in western Europe in 1201, and that the 85,000 mark price tag equaled almost twice the annual revenue of either the king of France or England. See, for example, Hans Jahn, *Die Heereszahlen in den Kreuzzügen* (Berlin: G. Nauck, 1907), p. 40; Lot, *L'art militaire*, 1: 174; Lane, *Venice*, p. 37. Maleczek, *Petrus Capuanus*, pp. 253–57, demonstrates that, in fact, 85,000 marks was roughly equal to one year's revenue at the end of Philip II's reign. There is some possible precedent for the troop size also. In 1174, William II of Sicily seems to have sent over 30,000 fighting men in his attack on Alexandria. See, Ferdinand Chalandon, *Histoire de la domination normande en Italie et en Sicile* (Paris: A. Picard et Fils, 1907), 2: 396; Wieruszowski, "Norman Kingdom of Sicily and the Crusades," p. 35. For refinement on this figure, see Queller and Madden, "Some Further Arguments in Defense of the Venetians on the Fourth Crusade," pp. 440–41, n. 21.

67. This view is especially expounded by Albert Pauphilet, "Robert of Clari et Villehardouin," in *Mélanges de linguistique et de litterature offerts à M. Alfred Jeanroy* (Paris: E. Droz, 1928), pp. 562, 564.

68. Faral, Introduction to Villehardouin, *Conquête de Constantinople*, 1: xiv–xvi. C. Klimke, *Quellen*, p. 4, believed that he used a diary from 1201 on.

69. Jean Dufournet, *Les écrivains de la quatrième croisade: Villehardouin et Clari*, 2 vols. (Paris: Société d'edition d'enseignement supérieur, 1973), 1: 202–3. This contains an extensive and judicious evaluation of Villehardouin. The author believes that he does conceal many things, but does not go to the extreme of labeling Villehardouin an "official" historian covering up a plot. See also Queller and Katele, "Attitudes towards the Venetians in the Fourth Crusade," p. 9; Vriens, "De kwestie van den vierden kruistocht," p. 82.

70. Queller, "Innocent III and the Crusader-Venetian Treaty of 1201," pp. 31–34.

71. Villehardouin, *Conquête de Constantinople*, sec. 31, 1: 32.

72. *Gesta Innocenti*, chap. 83, col. 131.

73. For the controversy, see Queller, "Innocent III and the Crusader-Venetian Treaty of 1201," p. 32, n. 8.

74. Innocent III, *Epistolae*, 7: 18, in Migne, *PL*, CCXV: 301–2.

75. This is the argument laid out more fully by Queller, "Innocent III and the Crusader-Venetian Treaty of 1201"; similar conclusions are drawn by John, "The Preliminaries of the Fourth Crusade," pp. 101–3. More recently, Maleczek has argued that Innocent refused to confirm the treaty on two grounds: because it was an unrealistic treaty that he and his advisers knew the crusaders could never meet, and because the pope would never accept the clause giving one-half of booty to the Venetians. *Petrus Capuanus*, pp. 121–23, 258–68. The first argument rests on the speculation that Inno-

cent III saw the infeasibility of a treaty that its participants did not. (Although, to be fair, Maleczek believes that the Venetians knew that the treaty was impossible to fulfill as well). The second argument has already been discussed above.

Chapter 3

1. Villehardouin, *Conquête de Constantinople*, sec. 32, 1: 32–34. Robert of Clari, *Conquête*, sec. 6, p. 8. Once more Robert, who has them accompanied by a Venetian patrician, cannot be relied upon for details before his own arrival in Venice. Ernoul-Bernard also has Venetian envoys accompanying the crusading envoys back to France. *Chronique*, pp. 338–40.

2. Villehardouin makes no mention of a visit to Boniface, but the *Chronique de Morée*, sec. 18, p. 7, states that such a meeting did take place. The visit is also related in the *Chronique de la conquête de Constantinople*, pp. 36–37. These sources are weak reeds upon which to rely, but the visit does seem probable.

3. Villehardouin, *Conquête de Constantinople*, sec. 41, 1: 42. Emile Bouchet, "Notices," in Villehardouin, *Conquête de Constantinople*, 2: 25; Carl Hopf, *Bonifaz von Montferrat, der Eroberer von Konstantinopel, und der Troubadour Rambaut von Vaqueiras*, ed. Ludwig Streit (Berlin: C. Habel, 1877), pp. 24–25; and Longnon, *Recherches*, p. 72, accept the visit as probable.

4. Ernoul-Bernard, *Chronique*, pp. 329–30. On the papal-Hohenstaufen struggle during Frederick II's minority, see Thomas C. Van Cleve, *The Emperor Frederick II of Hohenstaufen: Immutator Mundi* (Oxford: Clarendon, 1972), pp. 38–57; David Abulafia, *Frederick II: A Medieval Emperor* (Oxford: Oxford University Press, 1988), pp. 94–102.

5. Strayer, "The Political Crusades," p. 347; Elizabeth Kennan, "Innocent III and the First Political Crusade: A Comment on the Limitations on Papal Power," *Traditio* 27 (1971): 231–49; Norman Housley, "Crusades against Christians: their Origins and Early Development, c. 1000–1216," in *Crusade and Settlement*, Peter W. Edbury, ed. (Cardiff: University College Cardiff Press, 1985), pp. 27–28.

6. Villehardouin, *Conquête de Constantinople*, sec. 34, 1: 34.

7. Innocent also gave permission to King Emeric of Hungary to leave twelve crusaders at home to protect the kingdom. Innocent III, "Rubrice Registri," vol. 4, no. 109, p. 58; James Ross Sweeney, "Hungary in the Crusades, 1169–1218," *International History Review* 4 (1981): 475.

8. Villehardouin, *Conquête de Constantinople*, sec. 33, 1: 34.

9. Omer Englebert, *Saint Francis of Assisi*, trans. from the 2d French ed. by Eve-Marie Cooper, 2d Eng. ed. revised and augmented by Ignatius Brady and Raphael Brown (Chicago: Franciscan Herald Press, 1965), p. 64.

10. Ibid.

11. Van Cleve, *Frederick II*, pp. 50–51; Abulafia, *Frederick II*, p. 102.

12. Roscher underestimates the significance of the Apulian expedition for the Fourth Crusade. *Papst Innocenz III*, p. 91. It is the first manifestation of that fragmentation of the crusading host that made it impossible for the crusaders to fulfill their

contract with Venice. Villehardouin does not criticize Walter, as he does others who failed to join the army at Venice, perhaps because Walter was the chronicler's lord for the fief of Villehardouin. Jean Longnon, *L'empire latin de Constantinople* (Paris: Payot, 1949), p. 27; Dufournet, *Villehardouin et Clari*, 2: 316.

13. Thibaut's war chest had been filled in part by extortions from the Jews of his territory. Grossman, "Financing of the Crusades," p. 96.

14. Villehardouin, *Conquête de Constantinople*, secs. 32–37, 1: 32–38.

15. Damna redempturus Crucis et patriam Crucifixi
Struxerat expensis, milite, classe, viam
Terrenam quaerens, caelestam reperit urbem
Dum procul haec potitur, obviat ille domi.

Quoted by Hurter, *Papa Innocenzo III*, 2: 100, n. 224. A more complete version in Arbois de Jubainville, *Histoire des ducs et des comtes de Champagne*, 4: 96.

16. Robert of Clari, *Conquête*, sec. 2, p. 4.

17. Ernoul-Bernard, *Chronique*, pp. 339–40.

18. Paul Riant, "Innocent III, Philippe de Souabe et Boniface de Montferrat," *Revue des questions historiques* 17 (1875): 332–33; Fliche, Thouzellier, and Azais, "La chrétienté romaine," p. 63; Nicol, "The Fourth Crusade and the Greek and Latin Empires," p. 276; idem, *Byzantium and Venice*, p. 129; Godfrey, *1204: The Unholy Crusade*, p. 52.

19. As long ago as 1884 Jules Tessier doubted that Thibaut was the official leader. *Quatrième croisade*, pp. 76–77; McNeal and Wolff, "The Fourth Crusade," p. 164.

20. Benjamin Hendrickx, "Les chartes de Baudouin de Flandre comme source pour l'histoire de Byzance," *Byzantina (Thessalonica)* 1 (1969): 76.

21. Ellen E. Kittell, "Was Thibaut of Champagne the Leader of the Fourth Crusade?" *Byzantion* 51 (1981): 557–65.

22. *TTh*, 1: 362; Innocent III, *The Letters of Pope Innocent III (1198–1216) concerning England and Wales*, ed. C. R. Cheney and Mary G. Cheney (Oxford: Clarendon, 1967), p. 52, n. 318; Roger of Hoveden, *Chronica*, 4: 166; *Regesta pontificum romanorum*, ed. August Potthast, 2 vols., (Berlin: Rudolf de Decker, 1874–75; repr. Graz: Akademische Druck- u. Verlagsanstalt, 1957), vol. 1, no. 1346. In the Venetian *Liber Albus* and *Liber Pactorum* the oaths of the envoys are also given in that order. *TTh*, 1: 358–62.

23. Kittell, "Was Thibaut of Champagne the Leader of the Fourth Crusade?" pp. 557–65.

24. *TTh*, 1: 367.

25. Villehardouin, *Conquête de Constantinople*, sec. 39, 1: 40. The duke of Burgundy possibly refused because of the poor financial condition of the duchy, dating back to the administration of his predecessor, Hugh III. Grossman, "Financing of the Crusades," p. 11.

26. Villehardouin, *Conquête de Constantinople*, sec. 41, 1: 42.

27. McNeal and Wolff, "The Fourth Crusade," p. 164.

28. Villehardouin, *Conquête de Constantinople*, sec. 42, 1: 42.

29. According to the terms of the Treaty of Péronne, Baldwin received a strip of territory from Philip containing the thriving communes of Saint Omer and Aire and

Baldwin was also to receive the rest of Artois, the dowry of Philip's first wife, Baldwin's sister, in case the French king's son should die without heirs. F. M. Powicke, "Philip Augustus and Louis VIII," *CMH* (Cambridge: Cambridge University Press, 1936), 6: 315–16.

30. Mundo Lo, *Crusados en Bizancio*, p. 120.

31. Joseph Linskill, Introduction to Raimbaut de Vaqueiras, *The Poems of the Troubadour Raimbaut de Vaqueiras* (The Hague: Mouton, 1964), pp. 9–10, 14.

32. Usseglio, *I marchesi di Monferrato*, 2: 169–70.

33. Villehardouin, *Conquête de Constantinople*, sec. 498–499, 2: 312–14.

34. Raimbaut de Vaqueiras, *Poems*, p. 312, and Introduction, pp. 8–9 and 18.

35. David Brader, "Bonifaz von Montferrat bis zum Antritt der Kreuzfahrt," *Historischen Studien* 55 (1907): 171–72; Rousset, *Histoire des croisades*, p. 208.

36. *Gesta Innocentii*, chap. 83, col. 132.

37. Louis Bréhier believes that many crusaders who had sided with Richard against Philip took the cross out of fear of reprisals, so that they would scarcely consult him concerning the leadership. *L'Eglise et l'Orient au moyen âge* (1st ed., 1906; 6th ed., Paris: Lecoffre, J. Gabalda et fils, 1928), p. 151. Tessier, however, points out the appropriateness of seeking royal counsel. *Quatrième croisade*, pp. 79–80.

38. *TTh*, 1: 367.

39. Brader, "Bonifaz von Montferrat," p. 20.

40. Ibid., p. 89.

41. Ibid., pp. 97–102.

42. *Chronica regia Coloniensis (Annales maximi Colonienses)*, ed. Georgius Waitz, *MGH, Scriptores rerum Germanicarum*, vol. 18 (Hannover, 1880), pp. 168–69.

43. Usseglio, *I marchesi di Monferrato*, 1: 170; Brader, "Bonifaz von Montferrat," p. 157. It could also be argued that Innocent approved the election of Boniface to remove a powerful Ghibelline ally from Italy.

44. Usseglio, *I marchesi di Monferrato*, 1: 148; 2: 57–59.

45. Thomas Sherrer Ross Boase, *Kingdoms and Strongholds of the Crusaders* (London: Thames and Hudson, 1971), p. 123.

46. Ibid., p. 128.

47. Tessier, *Quatrième croisade*, pp. 81–82.

48. James A. Brundage, *Richard Lion Heart* (New York: Scribner, 1974), pp. 159–60. A new candidate, Count Henry of Champagne, Thibaut's brother, has been added to the list of those suspected of complicity in the murder. The list also includes Richard of England, Saladin, Guy of Lusignan, Humphrey of Toron, and, of course, Sinan, the Grand Master of the Assassins. Patrick A. Williams, "The Assassination of Conrad of Montferrat: Another Suspect," *Traditio* 26 (1970): 381–88.

49. Charles M. Brand, *Byzantium Confronts the West, 1180–1204* (Cambridge, Mass.: Harvard University Press, 1968), pp. 18–19.

50. Cf. Usseglio, *I marchesi di Monferrato*, 1: 161.

51. Robert Lee Wolff believes that this account is more plausible than has sometimes been supposed. "Greeks and Latins before and after 1204," *Ricerche di storia religiosa*, 1 (1957): 324. See also Paolo Lamma, *Comneni e Staufer: Ricerche sui rapporti fra Bisanzio e l'Occidente nel secolo XII*, 2 vols. (Rome: Istituto storico italiano per il Medio Evo, 1955–57), 1: 302.

52. Nicetas, *Historia*, pp. 170–71; 200–201; 260; Usseglio, *I marchesi di Monferrato*, 1: 151–57; 2: 59–63; Lamma, *Comneni e Staufer*, 1: 301–2; Brand, *Byzantium Confronts the West*, pp. 34–37, 45.

53. Brader, "Bonifaz von Montferrat," pp. 27, 182–84.

54. Nicetas, *Historia*, p. 382; English trans., *O City of Byzantium, Annales of Niketas Choniates*, by Harry J. Magoulias (Detroit: Wayne State University Press, p. 210).

55. Nicetas, *Historia*, p. 395; Usseglio, *I marchesi di Monferrato*, 2: 80–82; Brand, *Byzantium Confronts the West*, pp. 80–84; Francesco Cognasso, "Un imperatore bizantino della decadenza: Isaaco II Angelo," *Bessarione* 31 (1915): 48–50; Nada Patrone, *La quarta crociata*, p. 70.

56. Villehardouin, *Conquête de Constantinople*, sec. 42, 1: 42; Robert of Clari, *Conquête*, sec. 3, pp. 4–5. It is the *Chronicle of Morea*, pp. 74–75, that gives the place, "Lans" in the French version, "Lantza" or "Latza" in the Greek. Usseglio identified it as Castagnola delle Lanze. *I marchesi di Monferrato*, 2: 179–82.

57. Villehardouin, *Conquête de Constantinople*, sec. 43, 1: 42–44; Brader, "Bonifaz von Montferrat," p. 171; Cognasso, *Storia delle crociate*, p. 707; Robert of Clari, *Conquête*, secs. 3–4, pp. 5–6.

58. J. Folda, "The Fourth Crusade, 1201–1204: Some Reconsiderations," *Byzantinoslavica* 26 (1965): 277–78; Innocent III, *Regestum Innocentii III papae super negotio Romani imperii*, ed. Friedrich Kempf (Rome: Pontificia Universita gregoriana, 1947), no. 63, pp. 175–76; also in Migne, *PL*, CCXVI: 1068.

59. Villehardouin, *Conquête de Constantinople*, sec. 43, 1: 42–44; *Devastatio Constantinopolitana*, p. 131 (*MGH, SS*, 16: 10; Hopf ed., p. 86). Robert of Clari, *Conquête*, secs. 3–4, pp. 5–6; Brader, "Bonifaz von Montferrat," p. 171; Cognasso, *Storia delle crociate*, p. 707.

60. Treason theorists dwell upon the familial connections of the house of Montferrat in Byzantium. It should be remembered that they had equally strong connections and claims in Palestine. Boniface, the brother of William Longsword, was the uncle of the late boy-king Baldwin V. He was also brother to Conrad, who had married the heiress of the kingdom, Isabel. Their daughter, Baldwin's niece, conveyed the kingdom to her husband, John of Brienne, and the daughter of this marriage in turn brought it to Frederick II. For genealogies, see Runciman, *History of the Crusades*, vol. 2, Appendix 3, and vol. 3, Appendix 3.

61. Villehardouin, *Conquête de Constantinople*, sec. 43, 1: 44, and p. 45, n. 2.

62. Ibid., sec. 44, 1: 44. The *Gesta* of Innocent III seems to say that Boniface had earlier taken the cross, perhaps in 1200, but the chronology is not clear ("Misit ergo praefatum Sofridum, presbyterum cardinalem, ad ducum et populum Venetorum; ad cuius exhortationem ipse dux et multi de populo crucis characterem assumpserunt. Marchio quoque Montisferrati; episcopus Cremonensis, et abbas de Lucedio, multique alii nobiles de provincia Lombardiae." *Gesta Innocentii*, chap. 46, col. 90). Villehardouin's eyewitness and circumstantial account should be preferred. In both accounts Abbot Peter of Locedio receives the cross along with the marquis.

63. Villehardouin, *Conquête de Constantinople*, sec. 45, 1: 46; Brown, "The Cistercians in the Latin Empire," p. 65, n. 12a.

64. Brown, "The Cistercians in the Latin Empire," pp. 64, 70–72; Andrea, "Cistercian Accounts of the Fourth Crusade," p. 8. The Cistercians' crusading zeal was

probably dampened at first by Innocent's attempted imposition of a tax on the order for the crusade. However, by the time of the order's chapter general meeting in 1201, a compromise had been arranged between the monks and Pope Innocent. Above, Chapter 1, n. 7. For the problem of monks going on crusade, see James A. Brundage, "A Transformed Angel (x. 3.31.18): The Problem of the Crusading Monk," in *Studies in Medieval Cistercian History Presented to Jeremiah F. O'Sullivan* (Spencer, Mass: Cistercian Publications., 1971), pp. 55–62, and esp. pp. 57–59 on the liberalizing policy of Innocent III.

65. Ralph of Coggeshall, *Chronicon Anglicanum*, in *Rer. Brit. M.A. script.*, 66: 130; Alphandéry, *La chrétienté*, 2: 62.

66. Villehardouin, *Conquête de Constantinople*, sec. 45, 1: 46, listing some of those who took the cross.

67. Brown, "The Cistercians in the Latin Empire," p. 67; Alphandéry, *La chrétienté*, 2: 62.

68. Brown, "The Cistercians in the Latin Empire," p. 68; Usseglio, *I marchesi di Monferrato*, 2: 183; Brader, "Bonifaz von Montferrat," p. 172. For the tangled problem of the identification of Peter of Locedio, see John C. Moore, "Peter of Lucedio (Cistercian Patriarch of Antioch) and Innocent III," *Römische Historische Mitteilungen* 29 (1987): 221–49.

69. Robert of Clari, *Conquête*, sec. 17, p. 16; *Gesta Innocentii*, chap. 83, col. 132; Riant, "Innocent III," 17: 349; Usseglio, *I marchesi di Monferrato*, 2: 183. Villehardouin does not mention the visit to Hagenau, an important omission to those who doubt his veracity.

70. Robert of Clari, *Conquête*, sec. 17, p. 16; *Gesta Innocentii*, chap. 83, col. 132. There has been much scholarly debate about the date of young Alexius's arrival in the West. Defenders of Villehardouin and the theory of accidents have argued for the summer of 1202, while treason theorists have presented a date in 1201 to allow time for the hatching of a conspiracy. The controversy has been settled by Folda and Brand, who have firmly established Alexius's arrival in the fall of 1201. Folda, "The Fourth Crusade," pp. 279–86; Brand, *Byzantium Confronts the West*, pp. 275–76. Folda also succeeds, however, in preserving the integrity of Villehardouin. The arrival in 1201 does not necessarily support the theory of conspiracy. Folda, "The Fourth Crusade," pp. 289–90.

71. Folda, "The Fourth Crusade," p. 285. Later Venetian chroniclers agree that Alexius was twelve years old in 1195 when his uncle, Alexius III, deposed the boy's father, Isaac II, and imprisoned them both. Dandolo, *Chronica per extensum descripta*, p. 274; Marcantonio Sabellico, *Rerum venetarum ab urbe condita libri XXIII* (Venice, 1718), p. 172; Gian Giacopo Caroldo, *Historia de Venetia*, Biblioteca Marciana, cl. ital., vol. VII, cod. 127 (= 8034), 66r. (The chronicle attributed to Pietro Giustinian confuses the Venetian tradition, making Alexius twelve years old at the time of his flight to the West. *Venetiarum historia*, p. 136.) Nicephorus Chrysoberges declared in his oration honoring Alexius, 6 Jan. 1204: "manhood has not altogether altered the boy, nor, measured by very long years, has it marked pleasant down upon your cheeks." Charles M. Brand, "A Byzantine Plan for the Fourth Crusade," *Speculum* 43 (1968): 466. It is probably not helpful in our case, but it should be mentioned that Isidore of Seville *(Etymologiae*, bk. 11, chap. 2, sec. 5), defines *iuventus* as ages twenty-eight to fifty, *adolescens* as fourteen to twenty-eight. Cited by Josiah C. Russell, *Late Ancient*

and Medieval Population, Transactions of the American Philosophical Society, n.s., 48, part 3 (Philadelphia: American Philosophical Society, 1958), p. 33.

72. Nicetas, *Historia*, pp. 448–52.

73. Ibid., p. 536; Magoulias trans., p. 294.

74. Nicetas, *Historia*, pp. 536–37. There is another story in which young Alexius was hidden in a barrel with a false bottom. The officers of Alexius III drew the plugs out of the barrels, suspecting that he might be hidden in one, but when they saw water flow, they were deceived. *The Chronicle of Novgorod*, p. 44.

75. Nicetas, *Historia*, p. 537; Magoulias trans., p. 295.

76. Nicetas, *Historia*, p. 537.

77. *Chronicle of Novgorod*, p. 44.

78. Edgar N. Johnson, "The Crusades of Frederick Barbarossa and Henry VI," in Setton, *History of the Crusades*, 2: 91–109.

79. Ibid., pp. 118–19; Brand, *Byzantium Confronts the West*, pp. 176–82, 191, and 233.

80. Queller and Madden, "Some Further Arguments in Defense of the Venetians," pp. 460–63; M. Canard, "Les expéditions des Arabes contre Constantinople dans l'histoire et dans la légende," *Journal asiatique* 208 (1926): 61–121; Bryon C. P. Tsangadas, *The Fortifications and Defense of Constantinople* (Boulder: East European Monographs, 1980), pp. 80–106, 134–52.

81. Raymond Janin, *Constantinople byzantine: Développement urbain et répertoire topographique*, 2d ed. (Paris: L'institut français d'études byzantines, 1964), p. 266; Wolfgang Müller-Weiner, *Bildlexicon zur Topographie Istanbuls* (Tubingen: Ernst Wasmuth, 1977), pp. 286–319, esp. pp. 293, 303, 313–14.

82. On the phenomenon generally, see Sibyll Kindlimann, *Die Eroberung von Konstantinopel als politische Forderung des Westens im Hochmittelalter* (Zurich: Fretz & Wasmuth, 1969).

83. Queller and Madden, "Some Further Arguments in Defense of the Venetians," pp. 457–58.

84. George Ostrogorsky, *History of the Byzantine State*, trans. from the 2d German ed. of 1952 by Joan Hussey with revisions by the author. (New Brunswick: N.J.: Rutgers University Press, 1956), p. 350.

85. The bishop of Halberstadt was already excommunicated. Alfred J. Andrea, "Conrad of Krosigk, Bishop of Halberstadt, Crusader and Monk of Sittichenbach: His Ecclesiastical Career, 1184–1225," *Analecta Cisterciensia* 43 (1987): 17–23.

86. Riant, "Innocent III," 17: 339–40.

87. The evidence does not support Browning's assertion that Philip "felt himself obliged to overthrow the man who had deposed and blinded his father-in-law." *The Byzantine Empire*, p. 187.

88. Eduard Winkelmann, *Philipp von Schwaben und Otto IV von Braunschweig*, 2 vols. (Leipzig: Duncker and Humblot, 1873–78), 1: 52, the first of the German treason theorists.

89. *Gesta Innocentii*, chap. 83, col. 132.

90. Riant, "Innocent III," 17: 352–56; Winkelmann, *Philipp von Schwaben*, 1: 525.

91. Alphandéry, *La chrétienté*, 2: 76–77.

92. See, for example, the story of the Flemish knight who pursued his own ambitions. Below, Chapter 6.

93. Schmandt, "Fourth Crusade and the Just War Theory," p. 192.

94. Folda, "The Fourth Crusade," pp. 285–86.

95. This is the classic argument put forward by Henri Grégoire, "The Question of the Diversion of the Fourth Crusade, or, an Old Controversy Solved by a Latin Adverb," *Byzantion* 15 (1941): 165.

96. Innocent III, *Die Register Innocenz' III*, vol. 5, ed. Othmar Hageneder, Christoph Egger, Karl Rudolf, and Andrea Sommerlechner (Vienna: Osterreichischen Akademie der Wissenschaften, 1993), no. 121, pp. 239–42 (Migne, *PL*, CCXIV: 1123–24).

97. Kenneth M. Setton, *The Papacy and the Levant (1204-1571)* (Philadelphia: American Philosophical Society, 1976), 1: 4; Brand, *Byzantium Confronts the West*, pp. 225–30. Gerd Hagedorn, "Papst Innocenz III. und Byzanz am Vorabend des Vierten Kreuzzugs (1198–1203)." *Ostkirchliche Studien* 23 (1974): 11–12.

98. *Gesta Innocentii*, chap. 83, cols. 131–32; Winkelmann, *Philipp von Schwaben*, 1: 525; Brader, "Bonifaz von Montferrat," pp. 172–73; Folda, "The Fourth Crusade," p. 286.

99. Brader, "Bonifaz von Montferrat," pp. 172–73.

100. *Gesta Innocentii*, chap. 83, col. 132.

101. Usseglio, *I marchesi di Monferrato*, 2: 192.

Chapter 4

1. Gunther of Pairis, *Hystoria Constantinopolitana*, pp. 111–14.

2. These German enlistments support the argument that at least one of the reasons for the journey to Hagenau was to attempt to gain recruits.

3. Cessi, "Venezia e la quarta crociata," pp. 17–18.

4. Hurter, *Storia di Papa Innocenzo III*, 2: 44.

5. Even in the crusading songs the praise of knightly heroism is muted by the oppressive melancholy of facing the unknown. Cessi, "Venezia e la quarta crociata," pp. 17–18. For the many gifts made to monasteries, see Jean Longnon, *Les compagnons de Villehardouin*, passim.

6. Villehardouin, *Conquête de Constantinople*, sec. 46, 1: 46–48.

7. Ibid., sec. 47, 1: 50; Robert of Clari, *Conquête*, sec. 9, p. 8.

8. "Lai de la dame de Fayel," in *Recueil de chants historiques français*, ed. Antoine le Roux de Lincy, 1st ser. (Paris: C. Gosselin, 1841), pp. 105–8.

9. Conon de Béthune, in *Recueil de chants historiques français*, p. 113; Luchaire, *Innocent III*, 4: 78–79.

10. Usseglio, *I marchesi di Monferrato*, 2: 386–87. Raimbaut de Vaqueiras, *Poems*, pp. 31 and 304.

11. Jethro Bithell, *The Minnesingers* (London: Longmans, 1909), p. 31.

12. *Recueil de chants historiques français*, p. 114.

13. "Hisdem diebus innumera populorum milia, predicti Fulconis instantia iam annis aliquot per Gallias concitata, Iherololimitana iter arripiunt, tantaque fuit pere-grinantium numerositas, ut non solum precedentibus expeditionibus equari potuerit, sed preferri." Robert of Auxerre, *Chronicon*, p. 261.

14. Villehardouin, *Conquête de Constantinople*, sec. 47, 1: 50.

15. Theo Luykx, *De graven van Vlaanderen en de kruisvaarten* (Louvain, 1947), p. 171.

16. Usseglio, *I marchesi di Monferrato*, 2: 193.

17. *TTh*, 1: 366.

18. Villehardouin, *Conquête de Constantinople*, sec. 47, 1: 50.

19. *Devastatio Constantinopolitana*, p. 132 (*MGH, SS* 16: 10; Hopf ed., p. 87).

20. Christopher Tyerman, *England and the Crusades, 1095–1588* (Chicago: University of Chicago Press, 1988), pp. 95–96, 191.

21. Rousset, *Histoire des croisades*, p. 203; Vriens, "De kwestie van den vierten kruistocht," p. 52.

22. Villehardouin, *Conquête de Constantinople*, secs. 51–53, 1: 54–56; Longnon, *Recherches*, p. 75.

23. Robert of Clari, *Conquête*, sec. 10, p. 9. The Lido received its medieval name from the church of Saint Nicholas, which allegedly possessed that saint's relics. Robert of Clari, *Conquest of Constantinople*, trans. McNeal, p. 39, n. 21. For a wonderful account of the theft of the various bodies of Saint Nicholas from Myra, see Patrick J. Geary, *Furta Sacra: Thefts of Relics in the Central Middle Ages* (Princeton, N.J.: Princeton University Press, 1988), pp. 115–27. Nada Patrone incorrectly identifies Robert's island of Saint Nicholas as an isoletta near the Lido. Robert of Clari, *Conquista di Costantinopoli*, p. 134, n. 92.

24. *Devastatio Constantinopolitana*, p. 132 (*MGH, SS,* 16: 10; Hopf ed., p. 87).

25. Lane, *Venice*, pp. 18, 36. Freddy Thiriet estimates 50,000. *La Romanie vénitienne au moyen âge* (Paris: E. de Boccard, 1959), p. 66, n. 1.

26. McNeal, in Robert of Clari, *Conquest of Constantinople*, pp. 4–5; Villehardouin, *Conquête de Constantinople*, sec. 51–53, 1: 54–56. Robert and Peter did not leave before May, however, since Robert is a witness to his lord's act in Amiens during that month. Nada Patrone, *La quarta crociata*, p. 13.

27. For example, Robert of Clari places Boniface's election as commander of the crusade before the embassy of Villehardouin to Venice, and he states that the agreement between the crusaders and Venetians included transportation for one hundred thousand infantry rather than twenty thousand at a cost of eighty-seven thousand marks. *Conquête*, secs. 3–4, pp. 4–8. The eighty-seven thousand marks may be explicable, although one should not labor too hard to try to make sense of Robert's figures. He may have heard of the loan of two thousand marks made by the crusader envoys before they left Venice and added that to the eighty-five thousand, which was probably well known.

28. See the essay on primary sources in this volume by Alfred Andrea. See also Hopf, *Chroniques greco-romanes*, p. ix; Nada Patrone, in Robert of Clari, *Conquista di Costantinopoli*, pp. 26, 63–77. The introduction and the apparatus of this Italian translation should be used by any student of Robert of Clari.

29. Robert of Clari, *Conquête*, sec. 7, p. 8; sec. 10, p. 9; Villehardouin, *Conquête de Constantinople*, secs. 56–57, 59, 1: 58–60.

30. The Venetians prided themselves on their adherence to their promises. A century later Marino Sanudo (Torsello) gave as the first reason why his projected crusade should be entrusted to the Venetians: "quia Veneta gens ita bene attendit id quod

promittit, sicut aliqua gens de mundo." *Liber secretorum fidelium crucis*, bk. 2, pt. 1, chap. 2, p. 35. Such an attitude is fundamental to bourgeois ethics.

31. "Veneti tam magnificia navigia praeparaverant, ut a longis retro temporibus nedum visus, sed nec auditus fuerit tantus navalium apparatus." *Gesta Innocentii*, chap. 85, col. 138.

32. Above, Chapter 2 at nn. 59–60.

33. Madden, "Enrico Dandolo," pp. 207–8.

34. Ibid., pp. 210–13.

35. Manfroni, *Storia della marina italiana*, 1: 314.

36. Villehardouin, *Conquête de Constantinople*, secs. 48–55, 57, 1: 50–58; Robert of Clari, *Conquête*, sec. 11, pp. 9–10.

37. Villehardouin, *Conquête de Constantinople*, secs. 49–50, 54–55, 1: 52–56; Ernoul-Bernard, *Chronique*, p. 340; Robert of Auxerre, *Chronicon*, p. 261.

38. Villehardouin, *Conquête de Constantinople*, sec. 54, 1: 56.

39. Ibid., sec. 33, 1: 34; Manfroni, *Storia della marina italiana*, 1: 314.

40. Villehardouin says in sec. 103 that John of Nesle, "chevetaines" of the fleet, Thierry of Flanders, and Nicholas of Mailly sent to Baldwin for instructions. *Conquête de Constantinople*, 1: 102–4. In sec. 48, however, he gives all three as "chevetaines." Ibid., 1: 50–52.

41. Robert of Auxerre, *Chronicon*, p. 261.

42. Ernoul-Bernard, *Chronique*, p. 352.

43. Ibid., p. 352; Villehardouin, *Conquête de Constantinople*, sec. 50, 1: 52; Hurter, *Papa Innocenzo III*, 2: 147.

44. Cf. Jean Dufornet, "Villehardouin et les Champenois dans la quatriéme croisade," in *Les Champenois et la croisade*, ed. Yvonne Bellenger and Danielle Quéruel (Paris: Amateur de livres, 1989), pp. 55–69; Natalis de Wailly, "Eclaircissements," in Villehardouin, *Conquête de Constantinople* (3d ed., Paris, 1882), pp. 30, 458–59; Riant, "Innocent III," 17: 348–49. Contra: Tessier, *Quatrième croisade*, p. 65, n. 1.

45. Robert of Clari, *Conquête*, sec. 17, p. 16.

46. Schmandt, "Fourth Crusade and the Just War Theory," p. 192.

47. *TTh*, 1: 362.

48. Robert of Clari, our source for this assembly, says only that the crusading barons were summoned to a meeting at Corbie. *Conquête*, sec. 8, p. 8.

49. Villehardouin, *Conquête de Constantinople*, sec. 58, 1: 60.

50. Heinrich Kretschmayr, *Geschichte von Venedig*, vol. 1 (1st ed., 1905; repr. Gotha: Neudruck, 1964), pp. 282–83; Tessier, *Quatrième croisade*, p. 68.

51. Villehardouin, *Conquête de Constantinople*, secs. 51–55, 1: 54–56.

52. Ibid., secs. 52–53, 1: 54–56; sec. 56, 1: 58. Cognasso believes that Count Louis was opposed to an already concluded agreement to go to Constantinople. *Storia delle crociate*, p. 716. The hypothesis has little support in the evidence: there is no reason to believe that Louis of Blois ever opposed the idea of supporting the young Alexius after he had heard of the scheme. Nada Patrone is wrong in fixing Hugh's departure only in 1203. Robert of Clari, *Conquista di Costantinopoli*, p. 8, n. 28.

53. Villehardouin, *Conquête de Constantinople*, sec. 54, 1: 56.

54. Ibid. Alberic of Trois-Fontaines, on the contrary, records that Renaud left the army in the company of Simon de Montfort after the fall of Zara. *Chronica*, p. 880.

It is possible that Renaud spent the winter in Apulia and there joined the forces of Simon in the spring of 1203. It is also possible that Alberic was wrong, something not at all difficult to believe. Alfred Andrea brings an impressive array of materials to bear on this question, concluding that Renaud left Apulia in the spring of 1202. "Adam of Perseigne and the Fourth Crusade," *Cîteaux* 36 (1985): 30–31.

55. Ernoul-Bernard, *Chronique*, pp. 341–43; Andrea, "Adam of Perseigne," p. 30, n. 53; Hurter, *Papa Innocenzo III*, 2: 240; Jean Richard, *Le royaume Latin de Jérusalem* (Paris: Presses universitaires de France, 1953), pp. 167–68.

56. Villehardouin, *Conquête de Constantinople*, sec. 55, 1: 56; sec. 57, 1: 58–60; Donald E. Queller, Thomas K. Compton, and Donald A. Campbell, "The Fourth Crusade: The Neglected Majority," *Speculum* 49 (1974): 441. Faral points out that this is one of several examples of Villehardouin's judging of events in the light of subsequent experience. *Conquête de Constantinople*, pp. xiii–xiv.

57. Vriens, "De kwestie van den vierden kruistocht," pp. 81–82.

58. Ernoul-Bernard, *Chronique*, p. 340.

59. This proportion is close to the unit used in the treaty of 1201 itself, although the precise figures would be 1 knight, 2 squires, and 4.4 sergeants. *TTh*, 1: 365.

60. Villehardouin, *Conquête de Constantinople*, sec. 56, 1: 58. Benjamin Hendrickx has examined the question of the number of troops gathered in Venice. "A propos du nombre des troupes de la quatrième croisade et de l'empereur Baudouin I," *Byzantina (Thessalonica)* 3 (1971): 29–40. He gives a minimum figure of 11,167 (Villehardouin's "one third") and a maximum of 21,750 (p. 34). There is little reason to accept the assumption upon which the latter estimate is based: that one-half of the crusaders in Venice paid two marks each of the 83,000 or 85,000 marks owed. Moreover, 21,750 must be a mistake for 21,250 (p. 33). McNeal and Wolff estimate 10,000–12,000. "The Fourth Crusade," pp. 166–67. Robert of Clari says that there were not more than a thousand knights. *Conquête*, sec. 11, pp. 9–10. We know, however, how unreliable his numbers are. If he is correct, though, in stating that 50,000 marks remained to be paid (ibid., sec. 11, pp. 9–10), which seems reasonable and in line with Villehardouin's statement that less than half had been paid *(Conquête de Constantinople*, sec. 58, 1: 60), and if those present had paid at the contracted rate, this would indicate about 13,000 crusaders. This figure is in line with two Venetian chroniclers of the fourteenth century. The *Venetiarum historia*, p. 134, states that 5,000 horse and 8,000 foot arrived, thus 13,000 total troops. Similarly, Andrea Dandolo puts the number at 4,500 horse and 8,000 foot, or 12,500 troops (*Chronica per extensum descripta*, p. 276). Antonio Carile's elaborate attempts to quantify the crusading army are unconvincing. There are flaws in the reasoning, and too many soft figures are accepted as hard. Later iterations of the thesis make it no more clear or compelling. "Alle origini dell'impero latino d'Oriente," pp. 288–314; idem, *Per una storia dell'Impero Latino di Costantinopoli*, pp. 96–98, 369–72. Cf. Queller, Compton, and Campbell, "The Neglected Majority," pp. 446–47, n. 24.

61. *Devastatio Constantinopolitana*, p. 132 (*MGH, SS*, 16: 10; Hopf ed., p. 87). This is the episode misinterpreted as Innocent's selection of Venice as the port to which the crusaders' envoys should go to obtain transportation.

62. *Devastatio Constantinopolitana*, p. 132 (*MGH, SS*, 16: 10; Hopf ed., p. 87). In April the other legate, Soffredo, cardinal-priest of Saint Praxis, had been dispatched

to Palestine. Innocent III, *Register*, 5: 25, p. 48 (Migne, *PL*, CCXIV: 978); Maleczek, *Petrus Capuanus*, p. 135.

63. *Devastatio Constantinopolitana*, p. 132 (*MGH, SS*, 16: 10; Hopf ed., p. 87). In 1200 Innocent had decided that the indigent should not accompany a crusading army since they created additional problems for the success of the holy mission. Such people were allowed to remit their vows with a money contribution to the Holy Land equivalent to the expenses they would have incurred in the expedition and to any compensation they would have received for their labor. (This is ridiculous, of course: if they had that much money they would not have been a burden to the crusade.) Those who could afford to go on crusade and to contribute positive service to the undertaking, however, were still bound to fulfill their original vow. Maleczek, *Petrus Capuanus*, p. 136; Lunt, *Financial Relations*, p. 426. Lunt has republished the document, which was incorporated in the *Decretales*, in *Papal Revenues*, 2: 512–14 n. 556.

64. Although Roscher, *Papst Innocenz III*, p. 60, states that there had been no papal legate on the Third Crusade or that of Henry VI, Professor James Brundage informs us that there indeed were legates on both of these expeditions: Ubaldo Lanfranchi, archbishop of Pisa, for the Third Crusade, and an unnamed cleric for Henry VI's crusade. Still, as Professor Brundage points out, neither of these papal officials exercised much influence. Runciman, *Crusades*, 3: 31; Sidney Painter, "The Third Crusade: Richard the Lionhearted and Philip Augustus," in Setton, *History of the Crusades*, 2: 66, 69; Johnson, "Crusades of Frederick Barbarossa and Henry VI," p. 119.

65. Villehardouin, *Conquête de Constantinople*, sec. 107, 1: 108.

66. It is interesting that the only sources for the Venetian refusal to accept Peter Capuano are from the papal curia. The *Gesta Innocentii*, chap. 85, col. 138, states that the Venetians feared Peter would forbid the later attack on Zara. This seems unlikely, since the cardinal was still in Venice when the plan to go to Zara was adopted, and he refused to release crusaders from their vows who objected to the expedition. The refusal was an affront to the pope, which he mentioned often in later letters: Innocent III, *Register*, 6: 48, pp. 71–72 (Migne, *PL*, CCXV: 50); 7: 18, Migne, *PL*, CCXV: 302; 7: 200, Migne, *PL*, CCXV: 510; 9: 139, Migne, *PL*, CCXV: 957. No other contemporary sources, even those written by ecclesiastical authors, mention the Venetian rejection of the papal legate. This further underscores how unimportant Peter Capuano was to the host. The late-thirteenth-century chronicler Martin Da Canal rewrote history, saying that Doge Dandolo did great honor to Peter Capuano and even received the cross from his hands. Da Canal, *Les estoires de Venise: Cronaca veneziana in lingua francese dalle origini al 1275*, ed. Alberto Limentani (Florence: Leo S. Olschki, 1972), p. 46. See also, Queller and Katele, "Attitudes towards the Venetians in the Fourth Crusade," pp. 3–6, 21–22; Maleczek, *Petrus Capuanus*, p. 139.

67. Gunther of Pairis, *Hystoria Constantinopolitana*, pp. 117 and 120. There is some reason, however, to accept Gunther's figure of twelve hundred Germans with reservations, since he uses almost the identical phrase *numero quasi mille ducenti* in a completely different context, but also to end a hexameter line in the verse portion of his chronicle. It may derive more from metrical exigencies than numerical facts. Twelve hundred is not, however, an unreasonable figure. Francis R. Swietek, "Gunther of Pairis and the *Historia Constantinopolitana*," *Speculum* 53 (1978): 62, n. 105.

68. Alfred J. Andrea, trans., *The Capture of Constantinople: The "Hystoria Constantinopolitana" of Gunther of Pairis* (Philadelphia: University of Pennsylvania Press, 1997). We are grateful to Professor Andrea for making his manuscript available to us. See also, Alfred J. Andrea, "The *Historia Constantinopolitana*: An Early Thirteenth-Century Cistercian Looks at Byzantium," *Analecta Cisterciensia* 36 (1980): 276–77.

69. Gunther of Pairis, *Hystoria Constantinopolitana*, pp. 109–10.

70. Andrea, *The Capture of Constantinople: The "Hystoria Constantinopolitana."*

71. Gunther of Pairis, *Hystoria Constantinopolitana*, pp. 111–14. Martin's speech, as reported by Gunther, goes into surprising detail concerning the enormous possibilities for material wealth open to the crusader. This has led Penny J. Cole to remark on the extraordinary nature of this sermon. *The Preaching of the Crusades to the Holy Land, 1095–1270* (Cambridge, Mass.: Harvard University Press, 1991), pp. 92–96. Andrea argues, however, that the sermon was never delivered, but is rather the work of Gunther of Pairis. The imagined speech was set precisely into Gunther's history to act as a counterpoint to the later looting of Constantinople. Thus, Abbot Martin is made to unknowingly prophesy the wealth that the crusaders will enjoy. Andrea, *The Capture of Constantinople: The "Hystoria Constantinopolitana."*

72. Gunther of Pairis, *Hystoria Constantinopolitana*, pp. 115–20; see n. 67 above.

73. Gunther of Pairis, *Hystoria Constantinopolitana*, p. 120–21.

74. Complicating the date of the bishop's arrival is a charter he issued to the monastery of Hamersleben on 28 July 1202. The charter date, however, is probably defective. See Andrea, "Conrad of Krosigk," pp. 21–25.

75. Ibid., pp. 20–21.

76. Villehardouin, *Conquête de Constantinople*, sec. 74, 1: 74; *Gesta episcoporum Halberstadensium, MGH, SS*, 13: 116–17. Andrea, "Conrad of Krosigk," pp. 17–23; Tessier, *Quatrième croisade*, p. 151.

77. Anonymous of Halberstadt, in *Exuviae*, 1: 10–11, n. 1; Andrea, "Cistercian Accounts of the Fourth Crusade," pp. 32–33.

78. Villehardouin, *Conquête de Constantinople*, sec. 74, 1: 74. See also, Hans Wolfgang Kuhn, "Heinrich von Ulmen, der vierte Kreuzzug und die Limburger Staurothek," *Jahrbüch für westdeutsche Landesgeschichte* 10 (1984): 67–106; Longnon, *Les compagnons de Villehardouin*, pp. 242–49.

79. *Devastatio Constantinopolitana*, p. 132 (*MGH, SS*, 16: 10; Hopf ed., p. 87); Brader, "Bonifaz von Montferrat," pp. 177–78.

80. Tessier, *Quatrième croisade*, pp. 115–16.

81. Villehardouin, *Conquête de Constantinople*, sec. 73, 1: 74.

82. Gutsch, "Fulk of Neuilly," p. 205. Grossman believes that Baldwin of Flanders also received some of the money collected by Fulk. "Financing of the Crusades," pp. 95–96. The *Devastatio Constantinopolitana*, p. 131, reports that Odo Campaniensis and the castellanus de Colcith received custody of the money (*MGH, SS*, XVI: 10; Hopf ed., pp. 86–87). These are reasonably identified as Eudes of Champlitte and the castellan of Coucy by M. A. C. de Muschietti and B. S. Díaz-Pereyra, "Devastatio Constantinopolitana: Introduccion, traduccion y notas," *Anales de historia antigua y medieval*, 15 (1970): 171–200.

83. Villehardouin, *Conquête de Constantinople*, sec. 57, 1: 58–60; Robert of Clari, *Conquête*, sec. 11, pp. 9–10. Robert further reports that the crusaders agreed that each knight should pay four marks, as well as four marks for each horse, and each sergeant

two marks, while nobody should give less than one mark. The increase from the charge of two marks per knight specified in the treaty may represent an effort to make up for the deficit in numbers, but more likely is just another example of Robert's carelessness with figures. On the burden of Venice, see Manfroni, *Storia della marina italiana*, 1: 315, and Mundo Lo, *Cruzados en Bizancio*, p. 124.

84. Ernoul-Bernard, *Chronique*, pp. 343–46. Louis de Mas Latrie and others accepted it as fact. *Histoire de l'île de Chypre sous le règne des princes de la maison de Lusignan*, 3 vols. (Paris: Imprimerie imperiale, 1852–61), 1: 161–64. The false identification was by Carl Hopf, *Geschichte Griechenlands*, 1: 122. Hopf's identification was demolished by Gabriel Hanotaux, "Les Vénitiens ont-ils trahi la chrétienté en 1202?" *Revue historique* 4 (1877): 74–102. Runciman's reluctance to discard the false treaty (*History of the Crusades*, 3: 113) is surprising, as McNeal and Wolff have pointed out. "The Fourth Crusade," p. 170, n. 44. Speros Vryonis claims that the Venetians had negotiated with Egypt to keep the crusade from landing there. *Byzantium and Europe* (London: Thames and Hudson, 1967), p. 151. Like Hopf, Vryonis provides no evidence. Likewise, John Julius Norwich accepts fully that Venetians assured the sultan that they "had no intention of being party to any attack on Egyptian territory." For proof, Norwich is content to accept what he considers characteristic "double-dealing by Venetians at this time." *A History of Venice* (New York: Alfred A. Knopf, 1982), p. 128, and n. 1. Although Godfrey accepts that "there is no evidence of a formal treaty," nonetheless, he contends, an "understanding" of some kind was probably reached between Dandolo and the Egyptian sultan. Godfrey informs us that Dandolo probably had no intention of ever transporting the French to Egypt, no matter what they contracted. "If he [Dandolo] was going to land them anywhere on Muslim territory it would be Syria." *1204: The Unholy Crusade*, p. 72. Like much in this work, Dandolo's plans exist only in Godfrey's imagination.

85. Villehardouin, *Conquête de Constantinople*, sec. 59, 1: 60–62.

86. Ibid., sec. 60, 1: 62.

87. Ibid., sec. 61, 1: 64.

88. *Gesta Innocentii*, chap. 84, col. 132. This letter was written in 1200, as Potthast thought, not in 1201, as McNeal and Wolff have it. See Queller, "Innocent III and the Crusader-Venetian Treaty of 1201," p. 32, n. 7.

89. The financial cost of crusading was enormous for the ordinary pilgrim. The rise of the economy, favoring kings and powerful lords, and the limitation of the number of crusaders by the turn to the voyage by sea made it feasible for the wealthy, especially kings, to pay for their followers. This is one manifestation of the changing relationships between lords and vassals. Grossman, "Financing of the Crusades," p. 165.

90. Innocent III, *Register*, 2: 258 (270), p. 495 (Migne, *PL*, CCXIV: 830–31).

91. Some of the money raised by almsgiving was used by Innocent to purchase foodstuffs for the needy in the Holy Land, but in Sicily the cargo was converted back into money that was later distributed in Palestine. Connie Monk, "Papal Financing of the Fourth Crusade," seminar paper, University of Illinois, 1968–69, p. 13; Innocent III, *Register*, 2: 180 (189), pp. 345–46 (Migne, *PL*, CCXIV: 737–38); *Gesta Innocentii*, chap. 46, cols. 89–90.

92. Ernoul-Bernard, *Chronique*, pp. 337–38.

93. C. R. Cheney, "Master Philip the Notary and the Fortieth of 1199," *English Historical Review* 63 (1948): 346; Monk, "Papal Financing," p. 14.

94. Monk, "Papal Financing," p. 13. Martini failed to understand that the funds raised by the pope were not intended, for the greater part, to finance the crusading army. "Innocenzo III ed il finanziamento delle crociate," p. 319.

95. Robert of Auxerre, *Chronicon*, p. 261; *Devastatio Constantinopolitana*, p. 132 (*MGH, SS*, 16: 10; Hopf, ed., p. 87).

96. Robert of Clari, *Conquête*, sec. 11, p. 10. McNeal points out (in Robert of Clari, *The Conquest of Constantinople*, p. 40, n. 22) that a strict translation of *laissa* would give the opposite sense, i.e., that the doge did cut off their supplies. Confusion of *laissa* and *lassa* elsewhere in the text and Robert's favorable words about the doge at precisely this point, however, lead us to follow McNeal in assuming that *lassa* was intended. This has become the scholarly consensus. See, e.g., Setton, *Papacy and the Levant*, 1: 8; Nada Patrone, in Robert of Clari, *Conquista di Costantinopoli*, p. 136.

97. Robert of Auxerre, *Chronicon*, p. 261; *Devastatio Constantinopolitana*, p. 132 (*MGH, SS*, 16: 10; Hopf, ed., p. 87); Hurter, *Papa Innocenzo III*, 2: 149.

98. Ernoul-Bernard, *Chronique*, p. 349.

99. Robert of Auxerre, *Chronicon*, p. 261; Ernoul-Bernard, *Chronique*, p. 349; Robert of Clari, *Conquête*, sec. 12, pp. 10-11; Villehardouin, *Conquête de Constantinople*, sec. 61, 1: 62; *TTh*, 1: 385; Runciman, *History of the Crusades*, 3: 114.

100. Ernoul-Bernard, *Chronique*, p. 349; Robert of Auxerre, *Chronicon*, p. 261; Gunther of Pairis, *Hystoria Constantinopolitana*, pp. 122. According to the treaty, the crusaders were forbidden from obtaining food from the *terraferma*. It is not clear whether this was meant to refer only to acquisition of provisions for the crusade or was a more comprehensive prohibition. *TTh*, 1: 367, 371. The distinction surely made no difference to the poor crusaders. Cf. Maleczek, *Petrus Capuanus*, p. 120.

101. Villehardouin, *Conquête de Constantinople*, sec. 60, 1: 62; *Devastatio Constantinopolitana*, p. 132 (*MGH, SS*, 16: 10; Hopf ed, p. 87); Anonymous of Soissons, *De terra Iherosolimitana*, in Alfred J. Andrea and Paul I. Rachlin, "Holy War, Holy Relics, Holy Theft: The Anoymous of Soissons's *De terra Iherosolimitana*, An Analysis, Edition, and Translation," *Historical Reflections* 18 (1992): 159 (Riant, *Exuviae*, 1: 5–6). Rostang de Cluni wrote of Dalmase de Sercey and his companions: "a Veneticia venenatis dolose recepti sunt, qui transitum eis neque naulo neque alio pretio ex longo tempore concedere voluerant." *Exceptio capitis S. Clementis*, in Riant, *Exuviae*, 1: 133.

Chapter 5

1. Robert of Clari, *Conquête de Constantinople*, sec. 12, pp. 10-11.

2. For variations on this theme, see Godfrey, *1204: The Unholy Crusade*, p. 50; Nicol, *Byzantium and Venice*, p. 127.

3. On the basis of ducal instructions to Venetian envoys to Constantinople that anticipated possible Byzantine objections to a treaty, Charles Brand concludes that Enrico Dandolo was "foreseeing." He goes on: "It is reasonable to think that he applied the same skill to his relationship with the crusaders." "The Fourth Crusade: Some Recent Interpretations," *Medievalia et Humanistica* 12 (1984): 35.

4. One need only attend a few faculty, college, or departmental meetings to note how academics love to legislate, or at least debate, without ever having a motion on the floor, and without a thought to execution.

5. Villehardouin, *Conquête de Constantinople*, sec. 62, 1: 64.

6. Ibid., secs. 62–63, 1: 64–66. Robert of Clari's version reads: ". . . s'il nous veullent rendre ches .xxxvi. m. mars que il nous doivent des premeraines conquestes qu'il feront et qu'il aront a leur partie, que nous les messons outre mer." *Conquête*, sec. 12, p. 11. No mention of Zara.

7. Vitaliano Brunelli, *Storia della città di Zara* (Venice: Istituto Veneto di Arti Grafiche, 1913), p. 361.

8. Vriens, "De kwestie van den vierden kruistocht," p. 69; Alethea Wiel, *The Navy of Venice* (London: John Murray, 1910), p. 105.

9. Ludwig Steindorff, *Die dalmatinischen Städt im 12. Jahrhundert* (Vienna: Böhlau, 1984), pp. 124–25.

10. Giuseppe Praga, "Zaratini e veneziani nel 1190: La battaglia di Treni," *La rivista dalmatica* 8 (1925): 47–54.

11. Dandolo, *Chronica per extensum descripta*, p. 273; *Venetiarum historia*, p. 132 (=*Historia ducum Veneticorum, Supplementum*, p. 91); Praga, "Zaratini e veneziani," p. 54.

12. Pisa did attack Venice in the Adriatic, looting and briefly occupying nearby Pola. This was not, however, prompted by Venetian attacks on Zara, but rather open warfare between Venetians and Pisans in Constantinople after the accession of Alexius III. Dandolo, *Chronica per extensum descripta*, p. 273; *Annales Venetici breves*, p. 72; *Venetiarum Historia*, pp. 132–33, (=*Historia ducum Veneticorum, Supplementum*, p. 91); Madden, "Enrico Dandolo," pp. 161–63.

13. For more thorough treatments of Venetian-Zaran relations in this period, see Steindorff, *Die dalmatinischen Städt*, pp. 74–91, 121–26; Brunelli, *Storia della città di Zara*, pp. 359–63; Roberto Cessi, *La Repubblica di Venezia e il problema adriatico* (Naples: Edizioni scientifiche italiane, 1953), pp. 50–51; Thomas of Spalato, *Historia Spalatina*, ed. L. de Heinemann, *MGH, SS*, 29: 576.

14. See pp. 22–23 above.

15. Queller and Madden, "Some Further Arguments in Defense of the Venetians," pp. 446–47.

16. Robert of Clari, *Conquête*, secs. 12–14, pp. 11–12. According to the version of Ernoul-Bernard, *Chronique*, pp. 349–50, the crusaders would be quit of the sum owed. Martin da Canal, a Venetian chronicler of the late thirteenth century, states that Dandolo did not reveal to the crusaders his plan to attack Zara until the fleet was there, and he rejected the aid that the crusaders offered. *Les estoires de Venise*, sec. 11, 1: 48. See also Giorgio Cracco, "Il pensiero storico di fronte ai problemi del commune veneziano," in *La storiografia veneziana fino al secolo VI: Aspetti e problemi*, ed. Agostino Pertusi (Florence: Leo S. Olschki, 1970), pp. 54–55.

17. Robert of Clari, *Conquête*, secs. 11–12, pp. 11–12; Villehardouin, *Conquête de Constantinople*, sec. 63, 1: 66.

18. Robert of Clari, *Conquête*, secs. 12–13, pp. 11–12.

19. Cessi, on the other hand, attempts to use the same evidence to argue that the crusaders were not to participate in the attack upon Zara, which was strictly a Venetian undertaking. "Venezia e la quarta crociata," p. 24, n. 1, and p. 27; "L'eredità di Enrico Dandolo," p. 6, n. 1; "Politica, economia, religione," p. 453. This interpretation is problematic. It assumes that Venice required their allies' assent to stop at Zara. Yet Venice required no such assent to stop at all of the other Dalmatian cities to enforce their loyalty. This was clearly an accepted right. Further, the interpretation is belied

by the subsequent events. The Zarans offered to surrender and the Franks were compelled to fight because the latter were committed to a siege if it were required. Cessi's interpretation has attracted no adherents.

20. Villehardouin, *Conquête de Constantinople*, sec. 63, 1: 66.

21. Robert of Clari, *Conquête*, sec. 12, pp. 11–12.

22. Villehardouin rather ambiguously dates this event, placing it on a Sunday, which was also a high feast day. He also implies that it followed the decision of the barons to accept Dandolo's terms for deferment of their debt, and states that following the event "September approached" (*li setembre aprocha*). Villehardouin, *Conquête de Constantinople*, sec. 69, 1: 70. Some old manuscripts state that this was the feast of Saint Mark, 25 April, which is logistically impossible and contradicts Villehardouin. Ibid., 1: 70, n. 1. In 1202, April 25 fell on a Thursday. Roberto Cessi argued that the proper date was the Assumption of the Virgin on 15 July. Cessi, "Venezia e la quarta crociata," p. 25, n. 1. There are two primary problems with this date: the feast of the Assumption is celebrated on 15 August, and neither 15 July nor 15 August fell on a Sunday in 1202. Although the Nativity of the Virgin does meet the criteria of being both a high feast and one that fell on a Sunday in 1202, it does seem to contradict somewhat Villehardouin's statement that "September approached." Yet there does not seem to be an earlier alternative. In August 1202 no major feasts fell on Sunday. Faral pointed out in his gloss that the presence of an article before the word September suggests that a word is missing, perhaps *fins* or *chief*. The latter makes little sense, but the former fits nicely. Thus, after the event "the end of September approached." This makes September 8 very likely. The only other possibility would be Michaelmas, 29 September, which is a high feast day falling on a Sunday, but seems too late. Villehardouin, *Conquête de Constantinople*, 1: 71, n. 1.

23. Villehardouin, *Conquête de Constantinople*, sec. 65, 1: 66–68.

24. On this crusade see Donald E. Queller and Irene B. Katele, "Venice and the Conquest of the Latin Kingdom of Jerusalem," *Studi Veneziani* n.s. 12 (1986): 29–39; Jonathan Riley-Smith, "The Venetian Crusade of 1122–1124," in *I comuni italiani nel regno crociato di Gerusalemme*, ed. B. Z. Kedar and G. Airaldi (Genoa: Università di Genova, 1986), pp. 337–50.

25. Madden, "Enrico Dandolo," pp. 14–20.

26. Agostino Pertusi considers the crimson headgear in the form of a truncated cone depicted in the mosaic of the south transept of San Marco to be the type worn by the doge in the late twelfth century. "Quedam regalia insignia: Ricerche sulle insegne del potere ducale a Venezia durante il medioevo," *Studi Veneziani* 7 (1965): 83–84.

27. Villehardouin, *Conquête de Constantinople*, sec. 66, 1: 68. The *Gesta Innocentii*, chap. 46, col. 90, reports that the doge and many Venetians had already taken the cross in mid-August 1198. Robert of Clari reports a conscription of Venetians to go with the fleet before the doge's demand for payment, the proposal to go to Zara, and the crossing of Dandolo. Pairs of waxed balls were prepared, one of each two containing a summons to service. These were blessed by a priest and drawn by him, giving one ball to each eligible male. Faral believed that this occurred after the taking of the cross, and so he doubts the Venetian zeal to take up the crusaders' burden. Villehardouin, *Conquête de Constantinople*, 1: 69, n. 3. Without evidence to the contrary, there is no reason to rewrite the primary source. Carile estimates that a fleet of this size required a complement of 17,264 men. "Alle origini dell' impero latino d'Oriente," pp. 287–88. Probably somewhat overestimated.

28. Villehardouin, *Conquête de Constantinople*, sec. 68, 1: 68–70.

29. See, for example, Runciman, *History of the Crusades*, 3: 115; Norwich, *History of Venice*, p. 129. Nicol does not go so far as to claim that Dandolo's emotional state was contrived, but does conclude that Dandolo could now "lead them where he wished." *Byzantium and Venice*, p. 132. Ostrogorsky, however, has no qualms about declaring that Dandolo was "entirely unmoved by the genuine crusading spirit." *History of the Byzantine State*, p. 413.

30. Godfrey, *1204: The Unholy Crusade*, p. 77.

31. Maranini, *La costituzione di Venezia*, pp. 180–81. Interestingly, on 27 June 1203, Ranier Dandolo selected a kinsman to act as vice-doge for him while he was away. ASV, S. Zaccaria, B. 12, perg.

32. Cracco, "Dandolo, Enrico," pp. 454–55.

33. For Dandolo's oath of office, see Graziato, *Le Promissioni del doge di Venezia*, pp. 2–4.

34. Madden, "Enrico Dandolo," pp. 153–55, 215, n. 80.

35. Gunther of Pairis, *Hystoria Constantinopolitana*, p. 122. On the other hand, if this were so, why did those who defected at Zara not do so at this point? Perhaps the discontent arose simply from their long delay and their poverty. Perhaps a certain amount of disaffection is to be expected in armies.

36. Gunther of Pairis, *Hystoria Constantinopolitana*, p. 122; Tessier, *Quatrième croisade*, pp. 129–30; Riant, "Innocent III" 17: 363–64, 18: 40. Riant, however seems to be confused chronologically, placing these happenings before the arrival of Peter Capuano on 22 July.

37. William M. Daly, "Christian Fraternity, the Crusaders, and the Security of Constantinople, 1097–1204: The Precarious Survival of an Ideal," *Medieval Studies* 23 (1960): 84.

38. Robert of Clari, *Conquête*, sec. 13, p. 12.

39. Innocent III, *Register*, 5: 161 (162), pp. 318–19 (Migne, *PL*, CCXIV: 1180).

40. Ibid., 5: 160 (161), pp. 315–17 (Migne, *PL*, CCXIV: 1178–1179). See also, Queller, "Innocent III and the Crusader-Venetian Treaty of 1201," pp. 33–34.

41. Villehardouin, *Conquête de Constantinople*, sec. 50, 1: 52–54. The statement is, of course, self-serving and partisan, but nonetheless correct.

42. Gunther of Pairis, *Hystoria Constantinopolitana*, pp. 122–23. Gunther says that the cardinal additionally imposed upon Martin responsibility for all the Germans, but this is simply more Guntherian puffery. It is likely, however, that Martin was one of the four Cistercian abbots whom Peter ordered to remain with the host to provide spiritual leadership. *Gesta episcoporum Halberstadensium*, p. 117. Martin was probably given that charge for the German crusaders, a duty later inflated by Gunther to encompass complete command. See Andrea, *The Capture of Constantinople: The "Hystoria Constantinopolitana."* For a summary of views on what the individual should do when confronted with participation in an unjust war, see Schmandt, "Fourth Crusade and the Just War Theory," pp. 201–2, 204–8.

43. *Gesta episcoporum Halberstadensium*, p. 117; Andrea, "Cistercian Accounts of the Fourth Crusade," p. 39.

44. In a subsequent letter reproaching the crusaders for the conquest of Zara, Innocent states that Peter had taken care to expose to some of them the papal prohibition against attacking Christians. *Register*, 5: 160 (161), p. 317 (Migne, *PL*, CCXIV: 1179). There is no indication of the date of the warning. This may refer to the later

prohibition sent by the hands of the abbot of Locedio after Peter and Boniface had been to Rome. Cf. Maleczek, *Petrus Capuanus*, p. 139.

45. Villehardouin, *Conquête de Constantinople*, secs. 71–72, 1: 72. It is difficult to be precise on the date for this first sounding of the crusading leaders on the trip to Constantinople. It certainly occurred after 15 August, when Boniface of Montferrat arrived in Venice. Thus the envoys may have arrived at any time in the six weeks between August 15 and the departure of the fleet in the first week of October. It seems unlikely that this episode would have happened before the decision to land at Zara, since before then the crusaders were doubtful that the crusade would sail at all, let alone sail to Constantinople. It therefore probably occurred in September. See Queller and Madden, "Some Further Arguments in Defense of the Venetians," p. 455–56.

46. Villehardouin, *Conquête de Constantinople*, secs. 70–72, 1: 70–74.

47. Robert of Auxerre, *Chronicon*, pp. 265–66; *Chronicle of Novgorod*, p. 44.

48. Folda, "The Fourth Crusade," pp. 289–90. Folda's interpretation concerning the arrival of Alexius in the West and Villehardouin's ignorance of his presence there prior to this time has solved a very troublesome problem.

49. That seems to be the implication. Villehardouin speaks of the envoys telling the story to "al marchis Boniface de Monferrat, qui sires ere de l'ost, et as autres barons." The astonished reaction comes simply from "li baron." Boniface is here included in the plural "the barons," since in the previous sentence the group is referred to as "Boniface . . . and the other barons." Villehardouin, *Conquête de Constantinople*, sec. 72, 1: 72.

50. Ibid., sec. 72, 1: 72.

51. Innocent III, *Register*, 5: 121 (122), pp. 241–42 (Migne, *PL*, CCXIV: 1124).

52. Maleczek, *Petrus Capuanus*, pp. 139–40; Cerone, "Il papa e i veneziani," p. 292. Sara de Mundo Lo is good on this point. *Cruzados en Bizancio*, p. 128.

53. Riant, "Innocent III," 17: 369–70; Hurter, *Papa Innocenzo III*, 2: 157. Boniface's presence in Rome is not certain; it is based on the *Gesta Innocentii*, chap. 85, col. 139: "et hanc inhibitionem et excommunicationem [Innocentius] fecit eis per abbatem Locedio certius intimari Marchio vero Montisferrati, qui fuerat super hoc a domino papa viva voce prohibitus, se prudenter absentans, non processit cum illis ad Jaderam expugnandam." It certainly is not explicit regarding a journey by Boniface to Rome, but it can sustain that interpretation. We also know from Villehardouin that Boniface left Venice at this time to take care of personal business. *Conquête de Constantinople*, sec. 79, 1: 80. The argument is not compelling, but represents sound speculation. For an opposing view, see Maleczek, *Petrus Capuanus*, p. 140, n. 125.

54. *Gesta Innocentii*, chap. 85, col. 139.

55. Innocent III, *Epistolae*, 3: 3, Migne, *PL*, CCXIV: 871–73; Milan Loos, *Dualist Heresy in the Middle Ages*, trans. Iris Lewitova, (Prague: Academia, 1974), pp. 162–66.

56. Sweeney, "Hungary in the Crusades," pp. 475–76.

57. Innocent III, *Register*, 5: 102 (103), p. 205 (Migne, *PL*, CCXIV: 1100); James Ross Sweeney, "Papal-Hungarian Relations During the Pontificate of Innocent III, 1198–1216," (Ph.D. diss., Cornell University, 1971), pp. 99, 118–19.

58. Monique Zerner-Chardavoine and Hélène Piéchan-Palloc, "La croisade albigeoise, un revanche: Des rapports entre la quatrième et la croisade albigeoise," *Revue historique* 267 (1982): 9–10.

59. Steven Runciman, *Byzantine Civilisation* (London: E. Arnold and Co., 1933), p. 70; Charles Diehl, "The Government and Administration of the Byzantine Empire," *CMH*, o.s. (Cambridge: Cambridge University Press, 1923), 4: 728; W. Ensslin, "The Government and Administration of the Byzantine Empire," *CMH*, n.s. 4: 5.

60. The patriarch wrote a very cordial but firm letter, pointing out ecclesiological differences, and extolling Alexius III in February 1199. Innocent III, *Epistolae*, 3: 208, Migne, *PL*, CCXIV: 756–58. Innocent responded with his famous letter of 12 November 1199, which laid out the Western church's views on Roman primacy. *Epistolae*, 3: 209; Migne, *PL*, CCXIV: 758–65. Camaterus responded with a long and erudite discussion of Rome's claims, refuting the idea of Roman primacy. There are two editions of this letter: Aristeides Papadakis and Alice Mary Talbot, "John X Camateros Confronts Innocent 3: An Unpublished Correspondence," *Byzantinoslavica* 31 (1972): 33–41; and Jannis Spiteris, *La critica bizantina del primato Romano nel secolo XII* (Rome: Pontificium institutum orientalium studiorum, 1979), pp. 324–31. The Papadakis and Talbot edition has received some criticism (Spiteris, p. 254, n. 161). Spiteris provides an excellent discussion of the correspondence and its implications, as well as an Italian translation (pp. 248–99). See also Alfred J. Andrea, "Latin Evidence for the Accession Date of John X Camaterus, Patriarch of Constantinople," *Byzantinische Zeitschrift*, fasc. 2 (1973): 354–58.

61. Although the text of Alexius III's communication with the pope is no longer extant, we can surmise its contents from Innocent's reply of 16 November 1202. Innocent III, *Register*, 5: 121, pp. 239–43 (Migne, *PL*, CCXIV: 1123–25).

62. Nicetas, *Historia*, pp. 540–41; Magoulias trans., p. 296.

63. Villehardouin, *Conquête de Constantinople*, sec. 76, 1: 76.

64. *TTh*, 1: 385–86; Morozzo della Rocca and Lombardo, *Documenti del commercio veneziano*, 1: 452, no. 462.

65. ASV, S. Lorenzo, B. 21. See Madden, "Enrico Dandolo," pp. 209–10, and Appendix C.

66. On the state of the Piazza San Marco at this time, see Juergen Schulz, "La piazza medievale di San Marco," *Annali di architettura* 4/5 (1992/1993): 134–36.

67. Patriotic Venetian historians of the seventeenth and eighteenth centuries provided additional names, but they cannot be accepted without earlier confirmation. See, for example, Paolo Ramusio, *De bello Costantinopolitano et imperatoribus Comnenis per Gallos, et Veneto restitutis . . .* (Venice, 1634). Alvise Loredan uses Ramusio uncritically, giving him as much weight as Villehardouin or Nicetas Choniates. *I Dandolo* (Varese: Dall'Oglio, 1981), pp. 100–141, 426. Because of Loredan's willingness to mix primary sources with much later works, often without alerting the reader, his book should be used with great caution. See also the criticisms by Juergen Schulz, "The Houses of the Dandolo: A Family Compound in Medieval Venice," *Journal of the Society of Architectural Historians* 52 (1993): 392, n. 2.

68. Villehardouin, *Conquête de Constantinople*, sec. 76, 1: 76; *Devastatio Constantinopolitana*, p. 132 (*MGH*, *SS*, 16: 10; Hopf ed., p. 87); *Gesta episcoporum Halberstadensium*, p. 117.

69. Edwin Pears, *The Fall of Constantinople* (New York: Harper and Bros., 1886), p. 254 (New York ed.) This interpretation squares with the possibility that the fleet was divided. Below, p. 72.

70. Lot, *L'art militaire*, 1: 174.

71. Hugh of Saint Pol. *Epistola*, in *TTh*, no. 306; *Devastatio Constantinopolitana*, p. 132 (*MGH, SS*, 16: 10; Hopf ed., p. 87); Nicetas, *Historia*, p. 539. Antonio Carile's statement that among the thirteenth-century sources only the *Devastatio* gives a figure for the size of the fleet is incorrect. "Alle origini dell'impero d'Oriente," pp. 287–88; idem, *Per una storia dell'Impero Latino*, p. 89.

72. The transition to the trireme does not occur until about the end of the thirteenth century. Frederic C. Lane, *Venice and History* (Baltimore: Johns Hopkins University Press, 1966), p. 192, and *Venetian Ships and Shipbuilders of the Renaissance* (Baltimore: Johns Hopkins University Press, 1934), p. 9, n. 14.

73. Lane, *Venetian Ships*, pp. 7–9; Manfroni, *Storia della marina italiana*, 1: 452–55; McNeal, in Robert of Clari, *Conquest of Constantinople*, pp. 132–33; Richard W. Unger, *The Ship in the Medieval Economy* (London and Montreal: Croom Helm, 1980), pp. 121–22; John H. Pryor, *Geography, Technology, and War* (Cambridge: Cambridge University Press, 1988), pp. 57–86. For a larger estimate of oarsmen and others, see Carile, "Alle origini dell'impero d'Oriente," p. 287, n. 3; idem, *Per una storia dell'Impero Latino*, p. 90.

74. The most detailed and exhaustive examination of transport vessels is John H. Pryor, "The Naval Architecture of Transport Ships: A Reconstruction of some Archetypes for Round-Hulled Sailing Ships," *Mariner's Mirror* 70 (1984): 171–219, 275–92, 363–83. See also Lane, *Venetian Ships*, pp. 7–9; Manfroni, *Storia della marina italiana*, 1: 458; Unger, *The Ship in the Medieval Economy*, pp. 123–27; Michel Mollat, "Problèmes navals de l'histoire des croisades," *Cahiers de civilisation medievale* 10 (1967): 352.

75. Robert of Clari, *Conquête*, sec. 74, p. 73.

76. John H. Pryor, "Transportation of Horses by Sea during the Era of the Crusades: Eighth Century to 1285 A.D.," *Mariners' Mirror* 68 (1982): 9–21; Mollat, "Problèmes navals," pp. 352–53.

77. Villehardouin, *Conquête de Constantinople*, sec. 156, 1: 154; Pryor, "Transportation of Horses," pp. 21–22.

78. Our thanks to Professor John Pryor for bringing these considerations to our attention.

79. On the banner and the silver trumpets, see Pertusi, "Quedam regalia insignia," pp. 89–91.

80. Villehardouin, *Conquête de Constantinople*, secs. 75–76, 1: 76–78; Robert of Clari, *Conquête*, sec. 13, pp. 12–13. Robert was a romantic, of course, but such romanticism played as important a role as calculation in the crusade.

81. *Devastatio Constantinopolitana*, p. 132 (*MGH, SS*, 16: 10; Hopf ed., p. 87); Villehardouin, *Conquête de Constantinople*, sec. 79, 1: 80; secs. 315–16, 2: 122–24.

82. Villehardouin, *Conquête de Constantinople*, secs. 315–16, 2: 122–24.

83. Ibid., sec. 79, 1: 80.

84. Brunelli, *Storia della città di Zara*, p. 368; Cessi, "Venezia e la quarta crociata," p. 26; Wiel, *Navy of Venice*, p. 133; Robert of Clari, *Conquête*, sec. 13, p. 13. On the obligation to provide men, see Manfroni, *Storia della marina italiana*, 317–18.

85. This is on the assumption that Dandolo sailed on 8 October. If he sailed on 1 October, this would be 2 October. *TTh*, 1: 387.

86. Kretschmayr, *Geschichte von Venedig*, pp. 288–89; Dandolo, *Chronica per extensum descripta*, pp. 276–77; *TTh*, 1: 387–88. This treaty is commonly misdated

5 October, even in the headnote in *TTh*, 1: 386. This would necessitate a 1 October departure for part of the fleet and would raise disturbing questions about the elapsed time between this treaty and the arrival at Zara. The text reads: ". . . die quinto exeunte, mense Octubri." (The comma is an error.) This means 27 October. Historians of the period should know the meaning of *exeunte*. They also ought not follow headnotes while ignoring the texts. Marino Sanudo, *I Diarii*, 58 vols., ed. Rinaldo Fulin et al. (Venice: Deputazione R. Veneta di Storia Patria, 1897–1903), 7: 447, summarizes and has the correct date

87. *TTh*, 1: 386–403. Lorenzo de Monacis, *Chronicon*, pp. 134–35, accurately describes the pacts, which he probably had before him. Also see *Venetiarum historia*, pp. 134–35 (=*Historia ducum Veneticorum. Supplementum*, p. 92); *Devastatio Constantinopolitana*, p. 132 (*MGH, SS*, 16: 10; Hopf ed., p. 87).

88. Robert of Clari, *Conquête*, sec. 13, p. 13.

89. Manfroni, *Storia della marina italiana*, 1: 317–18, and 318 n. 1.

90. Robert of Clari, *Conquête*, sec. 13, p. 13.

91. Riant, "Innocent III," 17: 369.

92. Robert of Clari, *Conquête*, sec. 13, p. 12.

93. ". . . ad dedicionem compulerunt." *Devastatio Constantinopolitana*, p. 132 (*MGH, SS*, 16: 10; Hopf ed., p. 87).

94. John H. Pryor, "Winds, Waves, and Rocks: The Routes and the Perils Along Them," in *Maritime Aspects of Migration*, ed. Klaus Fiedland (Cologne-Vienna: Böhlau, 1989), p. 78.

95. Manfroni, *Storia della marina italiana*, 1: 317–18.

96. For a colorful description of the site of Zara, see Brunelli, *Storia della città di Zara*, pp. 36–37.

97. Robert of Clari, *Conquête*, sec. 14, p. 13; Villehardouin, *Conquête de Constantinople*, scc. 77, 1: 78. Faral, in a note to his text of Villehardouin (1: 79, n. 4), says that the *Devastatio* mentions the sinking of a ship named the *Workhorse*. Indeed, Pertz's edition of the *Devastatio* (*MGH, SS*, 16: 10) reads: "Iaderam navigaverunt, in qua iumentum periit." "Iumentum" does mean "workhorse," but comparing this passage to one closely preceding, "Viola navis periit," we note that in our questionable passage there is no juxtaposed word, "navis." Again, Pertz undoubtedly did not consider "iumentum" to be the name of a ship, for he left the word uncapitalized. The loss of a horse would have been too insignificant an event for the author of the *Devastatio* to mention. Probably with this objection in mind, Hopf emended Pertz's text to read: "Iaderam navigaverunt, in qua iuramentum periit" (Hopf ed., p. 87). The passage is then translated not as, "They sailed to Zara, where the *Workhorse* sank," but rather as, "They sailed to Zara, where their (crusading) oath went for naught." The manuscript itself does, in fact, use the word "iumentum" not "iuramentum." Alfred Andrea, in his edition and translation of the *Devastatio*, follows Hopf by substituting the word "iuramentum" (p. 132). Emending a manuscript ought to be done only for a compelling reason, which we think is lacking here. The loss of a vessel in these treacherous waters would hardly be unusual. While it is true that oaths and contracts are a central theme in the *Devastatio*, it is hard to see how the attack on Zara could destroy the crusading vow. Not even the pope believed that.

98. Villehardouin, *Conquête de Constantinople*, sec. 78, 1: 78.

99. Ibid., sec. 80, 1: 80. Zaran narrative sources name the heads of the delegation, Damiano de Varicassi and Berto de Matafarri. Brunelli, *Storia della città di Zara*, p. 375, n. 56.

100. In November 1187, Enrico Dandolo made a sizable voluntary contribution of 150 lire to the Venetian state to prosecute a new war against Zara. Gino Luzzatto, *I prestiti della repubblica di Venezia (Sec. XIII–XV)* (Padua: A. Draghi, 1929), pp. 12–16, no. 3.

101. Villehardouin, *Conquête de Constantinople*, sec. 80, 1: 80.

102. Zerner-Chardavoine and Piéchon-Palloc, "La croisade albigeoise," pp. 16–17.

103. Guy of Vaux-de-Cernay was also a promoter of the Albigensian Crusade. His nephew, Peter, who accompanied him on the Fourth Crusade, inserts in his history of the Albigensian Crusade an account of the expedition from the viewpoint of those who interpreted their vows strictly. Peter of Vaux-de-Cernay, *Hystoria Albigensis*, 1: 106–11. See also, Zerner-Chardavoine and Piéchon-Palloc, "La croisade albigeoise," pp. 12–15.

104. Zerner-Chardavoine and Piéchon-Palloc, "La croisade albigeoise," pp. 15–16.

105. Peter of Vaux-de-Cernay, *Hystoria Albigensis*, 1: 108–9; *Gesta episcoporum Halberstadensium*, p. 117; *Gesta Innocentii*, chap. 85, cols. 138–39. Robert of Clari says that Zara had secured a letter from Innocent saying that anyone who should attack them would be excommunicated, and they sent this letter to the doge and the pilgrims. *Conquête*, sec. 14, p. 14. This is probably the story, somewhat garbled, that circulated among the rank and file. Alfred J. Andrea and Ilona Motsiff argued that Peter of Locedio arrived in Venice with the papal letter before the fleet set sail, but that he lacked the courage to make it public. "Pope Innocent III and the Diversion of the Fourth Crusade Army to Venice," *Byzantinoslavica* 33 (1972): 17–18. But Moore points out the great trust Innocent continued to put in the abbot of Locedio during and after the crusade. He would not have felt that way had Peter withheld the papal letter. "Peter of Lucedio," p. 243. Andrea later followed Brown, stating that Peter of Locedio did not return to the host until after the siege of Zara, although both scholars accept the arrival of the papal letter before the siege. Andrea, "The *Historia Constantinopolitana*," p. 273, n. 14; idem, "Adam of Perseigne and the Fourth Crusade," p. 24, n. 19; Brown, "The Cistercians in the Latin Empire," p. 74. Professor Andrea has recently suggested to us another, very plausible, possibility: Peter carried the letter to Venice, but handed it over to Guy of Vaux-de-Cernay, who departed with the fleet. Peter then remained with Boniface in Italy until after the fall of Zara. This elegant solution reconciles all of the evidence.

106. Villehardouin, *Conquête de Constantinople*, sec. 81, 1: 82.

107. Ibid., sec. 82, 1: 82.

108. Ibid., sec. 83, 1: 82–84.

109. Peter of Vaux-de-Cernay, *Hystoria Albigensis*, 1: 109.

110. Villehardouin, *Conquête de Constantinople*, sec. 83, 1: 82–84.

111. Villey, *La croisade*, p. 142.

112. Villehardouin, *Conquête de Constantinople*, sec. 84, 1: 84.

113. Ibid.; Robert of Clari, *Conquête*, sec. 14, p. 14.

114. Robert of Clari, *Conquête*, sec. 14, p. 14; Peter of Vaux-de-Cernay, *Hystoria Albigensis*, 1: 108

115. Brunelli, *Storia della città di Zara*, p. 368.

116. Innocent III, *Register*, 5: 160 (161), p. 316 (Migne, *PL*, CCXIV: 1178).

117. Villehardouin, *Conquête de Constantinople*, sec. 85, 1: 84–86; Brunelli, *Storia della città di Zara*, p. 368.

118. Gunther of Pairis, *Hystoria Constantinopolitana*, pp. 124–25. Gunther, it is true, exercised artistic liberties with Martin's words, but his testimony here makes sense in general and in view of the abbot's own reluctant participation.

119. Thomas of Spalato, *Historia*, p. 576; *Gesta episcoporum Halberstadensium*, p. 117. According to the *Devastatio Constantinopolitana*, p. 132 (*MGH, SS*, 16: 10; Hopf ed., p. 88), the siege lasted fifteen days. If we count from the first day of the siege on 11 November, this means the siege ended on 25 November.

120. Villehardouin, *Conquête de Constantinople*, secs. 85–87, 1: 84–88; Thomas of Spalato, *Historia*, p. 576; Robert of Clari, *Conquête*, sec. 14, pp. 14–15; *Gesta episcoporum Halberstadensium*, p. 117; *Devastatio Constantinopolitana*, pp. 132–33 (*MGH, SS*, 16: 10; Hopf ed., p. 88).

121. Gunther of Pairis, *Hystoria Constantinopolitana*, p. 125.

122. Innocent III, *Register*, 5: 160 (161), p. 316 (Migne, *PL*, CCXIV: 1178).

123. Thomas of Spalato, *Historia*, p. 576.

124. Hurter, *Papa Innocenzo III*, 2: 160–61; Brunelli, *Storia della città di Zara*, p. 369.

125. Innocent III, *Epistolae*, 7: 203, Migne, *PL*, CCXV: 511–12.

126. Queller and Madden, "Some Further Argument in Defense of the Venetians," pp. 449–50.

127. Runciman, *History of the Crusades*, 3: 114; A. A. Vasiliev, *History of the Byzantine Empire, 324–1453*, 2d Eng. ed. rev., (Madison: University of Wisconsin Press, 1952), p. 454.

Chapter 6

1. Pryor, *Geography, Technology, and War*, pp. 87–89; Vriens, "De kwestie van den vierden kruistocht," p. 71.

2. Villehardouin, *Conquête de Constantinople*, sec. 86, 1: 86–88. According to Robert of Clari, Dandolo told the crusaders that they would winter in Zara when he first proposed his plan to the host before leaving Venice. *Conquête*, sec. 13, p. 12.

3. Brunelli, *Storia della città di Zara*, pp. 36–37.

4. *Devastatio Constantinopolitana*, p. 133 (*MGH, SS*, 16: 10; Hopf ed., p. 87).

5. Gary Blumenshine, "Cardinal Peter Capuano, the Letters of Pope Innocent III, and the Diversion of the Fourth Crusade to Zara" (Seminar paper, University of Illinois, 1968–69), n. 29; Wiel, *Navy of Venice*, p. 136. No source says this explicitly, but it seems a probable cause of the fight between Venetians and Franks.

6. Villehardouin, *Conquête de Constantinople*, secs. 88–90, 1: 88–90; Robert of Clari, *Conquête*, sec. 15, p. 15; *Devastatio Constantinopolitana*, p. 133 (*MGH, SS*, 16: 10; Hopf ed., p. 87).

7. Letter of Enrico Dandolo, in Innocent III, *Epistolae*, 7: 202, Migne, *PL*, CCXV: 511; Queller and Madden, "Some Further Arguments in Defense of the Venetians," pp. 448–49.

8. Ernoul-Bernard, *Chronique*, p. 350.

9. Innocent III, *Register*, 5: 160 (161), pp. 315–17 (Migne, *PL*, CCXIV: 1178–79). As for the date of the letter, since it occasioned Bishop Nivelon of Soissons' supplicatory embassy, which probably arrived in Rome no later than mid-February, 1203, it must have been written around the New Year. Maleczek, *Petrus Capuanus*, pp. 144–45, 271–72; Tessier, *Quatrième croisade*, pp. 276–81. Contra Roscher, *Papst Innocenz III*, p. 107.

10. McNeal and Wolff, "Fourth Crusade," p. 175; Andrea, "Conrad of Krosigk," p. 27, n. 74; idem, "Cistercian Accounts of the Fourth Crusade," p. 15, n. 57; Maleczek, *Petrus Capuanus*, p. 143. There are a few who doubt the ban altogether: see e.g., Helene Tillmann, *Papst Innocenz III* (Bonn: L. Rohrscheid, 1954), p. 285, n. 30; Roscher, *Papst Innocenz III*, p. 107; Gill, "Franks, Venetians, and Pope Innocent III, 1201–1203," *Studi Veneziani* 12 (1970): 93, n. 39. For a fuller examination of this question, see the forthcoming study by Alfred J. Andrea, "Innocent III and the Greeks of Constantinople: A Re-assessment of the Pope's Role in the Fourth Crusade," in *Venice: Society and Crusade. Studies in Honor of Donald E. Queller*, ed. Thomas F. Madden and Ellen E. Kittell, forthcoming.

11. On 7 February 1204, Innocent wrote a letter to the crusaders after discovering that they had again disobeyed him by sailing to Constantinople. As a result of this decision, he stated that he was afraid that they were once again excommunicated ("vos iterato excommunicationis esse"). Innocent III, *Register*, 6: 229 (230), p. 388 (Migne, *PL*, CCXV: 260). See also *Gesta episcoporum Halberstadensium*, pp. 117–18; Gunther of Pairis, *Hystoria Constantinopolitana*, p. 125.

12. Villehardouin, *Conquête de Constantinople*, secs. 105–7, 1: 104–8.

13. ". . . apud Jaderam incurrimus excommunicationem apostolicam, vel incurrisse nos timemus." Innocent III, *Register*, 6: 99, p. 160 (Migne, *PL*, CCXV: 104).

14. Peter of Vaux-de-Cernay, *Hystoria Albigensis*, pp. 109–10.

15. Andrea, "Cistercian Accounts of the Fourth Crusade," p. 15, n. 57.

16. Zerner-Chardavoine and Piéchon-Palloc, "La croisade albigeoise," p. 10. The authors go on to contend, rightly we think, that Peter of Vaux-de-Cernay's description of the Fourth Crusade is greatly affected by Simon de Montfort's subsequent adventures in Syria and in the Albigensian Crusade. It was a bitter disappointment to Simon's party that they went on to the Holy Land and accomplished nothing, while the Fourth Crusade went on to conquer Constantinople, gaining great fame and wealth. Despite their repeated disobedience to the pope, the crusaders were absolved of all, released from their vows, and hailed as heroes. Peter wants to make clear, therefore, that Simon de Montfort removed himself from men who were sinners and betrayers of the Holy Land, no matter what everyone else thought of them.

17. Innocent III, *Epistolae*, 5: 161 (162), pp. 318–20 (Migne, *PL*, CCXIV: 1180).

18. Villehardouin, *Conquête de Constantinople*, sec. 105, 1: 104–6. Other sources confirm Villehardouin's testimony by mentioning one or two of the four men: Innocent III, *Register*, 6: 231 (232), p. 391 (Migne, *PL*, CCXV: 262); Robert of Clari, *Conquête*, sec. 15, p. 15; *Gesta Innocentii*, chap. 87, col. 139; Ernoul-Bernard, *Chronique*, p. 351.

19. Villehardouin, *Conquête de Constantinople*, sec. 106, 1: 106; Robert of Clari, *Conquête*, sec. 15, p. 15.

20. Gunther of Pairis, *Hystoria Constantinopolitana*, pp. 125–26.

21. Riant, *Exuviae*, 1: lxxxii, n. 2; Brown, "The Cistercians in the Latin Empire," pp. 75–76; Usseglio, *I marchesi di Monferrato*, 2: 213, n. 1.

22. Andrea, "Cistercian Accounts of the Fourth Crusade," p. 19, n. 69.

23. Innocent III, *Register*, 6: 102, pp. 166–67 (Migne, *PL*, CCXV: 107–8). Robert of Clari, *Conquête*, sec. 15, p. 15, is not credible in making the Venetians participate in the mission and in the absolution.

24. Villehardouin, *Conquête de Constantinople*, sec. 91, 1: 90.

25. *Devastatio Constantinopolitana*, p. 133 (*MGH, SS*, 16: 10; Hopf ed., p. 88); Villehardouin, *Conquête de Constantinople*, sec. 91, 1: 90; *Gesta episcoporum Halberstadensium*, p. 118. Robert of Clari, unaware of the previous negotiations but well aware of Boniface of Montferrat's ties to Philip of Swabia, reconstructed the events differently. He stated that Doge Dandolo pointed out the wealth of Greece, and how useful that would be to the crusade if they only had some reason to go there. On cue, Boniface arose, saying that he knew of the plight of the young Alexius, and suggested sending envoys to Philip of Swabia. Helping the boy would give them the perfect excuse to go to Greece. *Conquête*, sec. 17, p. 16. As he frequently does, Robert reports imagined dialogues between high men to explain the events that occurred around him. His literary technique should not be given more credence than the testimony of Villehardouin, who was there and participated in the discussions. Maleczek accepts Clari's version, buttressing it with Boniface's characterization of Dandolo and the Venetians as his friends in a later letter. *Petrus Capuanus*, p. 150–51.

26. Charles Brand suggests that Dandolo may have himself negotiated with Alexius earlier, s.v. "Dandolo, Enrico," *Oxford Dictionary of Byzantium* (Oxford: Oxford University Press, 1991). There is no evidence for this.

27. *Gesta episcoporum Halberstadensium*, p. 118; Villehardouin, *Conquête de Constantinople*, sec. 91, 1: 90–92. Tessier, *Quatrième croisade*, p. 155, makes a persuasive argument that this was the Hohenstaufen's first attempt to influence the course of the crusade. The German treason theorists, such as Riant, concede that it was the first *open* effort. "Innocent III," 18: 5-6.

28. Villehardouin, *Conquête de Constantinople*, sec. 91, 1: 92.

29. Jonathan Riley-Smith, "Crusading as an Act of Love," *History* 65 (1980): 177–85, 190–92.

30. Villehardouin, *Conquête de Constantinople*, secs. 91–94, 1: 90–94; *Devastatio Constantinopolitana*, p. 133 (*MGH, SS*, 16: 10; Hopf ed., p. 88).

31. Nicetas, *Historia*, pp. 539, 550–51.

32. Hugh of Saint Pol, *Epistola*, in *Annales Coloniensis maximi, MGH, SS*, 17: 812; *Chronicle of Novgorod*, p. 44.

33. Villehardouin, *Conquête de Constantinople*, sec. 72, 1: 72–74.

34. Gunther of Pairis, *Hystoria Constantinopolitana*, p. 128.

35. Riant, "Innocent III," 18: 17.

36. In one extreme example, Fine states that Dandolo "jumped at the chance" to accept Alexius's proposal and then single-handedly negotiated for the union of the churches and help in the Holy Land "to placate the pope." *The Late Medieval Balkans*, p. 61. See also Alexander Kazhdan, s.v. "Venice," *Oxford Dictionary of Byzantium*

(Oxford: Oxford University Press, 1991); Browning, *The Byzantine Empire*, p. 187; Ostrogorsky, *Byzantine State*, p. 415.

37. This was Nicetas Choniates's view. *Historia*, p. 538. Some modern followers include: Steven Runciman, "Byzantium and the Crusades," in *The Meeting of Two Worlds: Cultural Exchange between East and West during the Period of the Crusades*, ed. Vladimir P. Gozz and Christine Verzar Bornstein (Kalamazoo, Mich.: Medieval Institute Publications, 1986), p. 22; Fine, *Late Medieval Balkans*, p. 61; Ostrogorsky, *History of the Byzantine State*, pp. 413–14; Vasiliev, *History of the Byzantine Empire*, p. 453.

38. For example, Pears, *The Fall of Constantinople*, pp. 239–40; McNeal and Wolff, "The Fourth Crusade," p. 169; Brand, *Byzantium Confronts the West*, p. 203, Godfrey, *1204: The Unholy Crusade*, p. 64; Fine, *Late Medieval Balkans*, p. 61; Nicol, *Byzantium and Venice*, pp. 119–20.

39. Madden, "Venice and Constantinople in 1171 and 1172," 178–79.

40. The dating of the reconciliation is complex. See, Thomas F. Madden, "Venice's Hostage Crisis: Diplomatic Efforts to Secure Peace with Byzantium between 1171 and 1184," in *Venice: Society and Crusade*, forthcoming; cf. Ralph-Johannes Lilie, *Handel und Politik zwischen dem byzantinischen Reich und den italienischen Kommunen Venedig, Pisa und Genua in der Epoche der Komnenen und der Angeloi (1081–1204)* (Amsterdam: Adolph M. Hakkert, 1984), pp. 549–50; M. E. Martin, "The Venetians in the Byzantine Empire before 1204," *Byzantinische Forschungen* 13 (1988): 213; Brand, *Byzantium Confronts the West*, pp. 196–97.

41. Madden, "Venice's Hostage Crisis"; on the duties of the legate, see Silvano Borsari, *Venezia e bisanzio nel XII secolo: I rapporti economici* (Venice: Deputazione di storia patria per le Venezie, 1988), pp. 57–58.

42. *TTh*, 1: 179–203, 206–11; Louise Buenger Robbert, "Venice and the Crusades," in Setton, *History of the Crusades*, 5: 409–10; Lilie, *Handel und Politik*, pp. 29, 34; Chryssa A. Maltezou, "Il quartière veneziano di Costantinopoli (Sacali marittimi)," *Thesaurismata* 15 (1978): 33; Nicol, *Byzantium and Venice*, p. 116.

43. Brand, *Byzantium Confronts the West*, p. 200; Robbert, "Venice and the Crusades," p. 410; Nicol, *Byzantium and Venice*, pp. 118–19.

44. *TTh*, 1: 246–80; Lilie, *Handel und Politik*, pp. 41, 581; Nicol, *Byzantium and Venice*, pp. 121–23.

45. Queller and Madden, "Some Further Arguments in Defense of the Venetians," pp. 454–55.

46. It is incomprehensible why some scholars argue that Venice wished to divert the crusade from Egypt because she probably had commerical treaties with the sultan. We know that Venice had vitally important commerical treaties with Byzantium; why then does not the same logic apply?

47. Gunther of Pairis, *Hystoria Constantinopolitana*, p. 147.

48. Schmandt, "The Fourth Crusade and the Just War Theory," p. 195; Thomas F. Madden, "Vows and Contracts in the Fourth Crusade: The Treaty of Zara and the Attack on Constantinople in 1204," *International History Review* 15 (1993): 443.

49. Only the *Devastatio Constantinopolitana* links Simon with this disaccord, p. 133 (*MGH, SS*, 16: 11; Hopf ed., p. 87). Villehardouin does not mention his presence in the discussions over Alexius's proposals. Peter of Vaux-de-Cernay, *Historia Albigensis*, 1: 110, and Robert of Clari, *Conquête*, sec. 14, p. 14, report that Simon departed in defiance of the army's decision to attack Zara, that is, before the discussions

about Constantinople. Since Peter of Vaux-de-Cernay and the *Devastatio* link Simon and Guy of Vaux-de-Cernay together and we know from Villehardouin that the abbot took part in the Constantinopolitan argument, it is quite likely that Peter and Robert have confused the crusader quarrel over Alexius with the earlier one about Zara. Ville-hardouin, *Conquête de Constantinople*, sec. 95, 1: 96, and sec. 97, 1: 98. In any event, it is a certainty that, despite what Robert says and Peter implies, Simon de Montfort was still in Zara until at least February or March 1203. See the thoroughly researched examination by Andrea, "Cistercian Accounts of the Fourth Crusade," p. 17, n. 61. Since he was there, it is impossible to believe that Simon did not support the position of Guy of Vaux-de-Cernay.

50. The group was led by Renaud of Montmirail, Villehardouin, *Conquête de Constantinople*, sec. 101, 1: 102; Riant, "Innocent III," 18: 16.

51. Villehardouin, *Conquête de Constantinople*, sec. 97, 1: 97–98; Longnon, *Les compagnons de Villehardouin*, p. 165.

52. Longnon, *Les compagnons de Villehardouin*, p. 235; on Innocent's great trust in the abbot, see Moore, "Peter of Lucedio," pp. 230–39.

53. Riant, "Innocent III," 18: 14–15. Faral, in support of Villehardouin's denunciation of those who went their own way, pointed out that the abbot of Vaux-de-Cernay, as well as Simon de Montfort, later took part in the Albigensian Crusade against Christians. In Villehardouin, *Conquête de Constantinople*, p. xxii. B. Ebels Hoving, however, distinguishes between the two cases. *Byzantium in Westerse Ogen, 1096–1204* (Assen: Van Gorcum, 1971), p. 223, n. 540.

54. Brown, "The Cistercians in the Latin Empire," p. 75. The abbot of Perseigne was not present at Zara. Andrea, "Adam of Perseigne," p. 24.

55. Andrea, "Conrad of Krosigk, pp. 28–39.

56. See the excellent analysis of Conrad's decision and motives by Andrea, "Conrad of Krosigk," pp. 35–41. Like Andrea, we suspect that Martin and Conrad also genuinely recoiled at the idea of attacking Christians.

57. Longnon, *Les compagnons de Villehardouin*, pp. 13–14.

58. Riant, "Innocent III," 18: 13–14.

59. Villehardouin, *Conquête de Constantinople*, sec. 95, 1: 95–96. Monique Zerner-Chardavoine has argued that Guy of Vaux-de-Cernay suffered isolation and blame from his brother monks after the Fourth Crusade became so materially successful. He had stood against the plan, and this did not sit well with those Cistercians who had supported and profited greatly from it. "L'abbé Gui des Vaux-de-Cernay: Prédicateur de croisade," *Cahiers de fanjeaux* 21 (1986): 188–94.

60. The church had made definite pronouncements on the subject of inter-Christian warfare. The Council of Narbonne in 1054 announced "Primo ergo ominum institutionum nostrarum, quae in hoc tomo scribenda sunt, monemus Dei, et nostrum, ut nullus Christianorum alium quemlibet Christianum occidit: quia qui christianum occidit, sine dubio Christi sanquinem fundit." *Sacrorum conciliorum nova et amplissima collectio*, edited by Giovanni Mansi, 53 vols. (Paris: H. Welter, 1901–27), 19: 827. Peter Damian expresses a similar sentiment: "Quomodo ergo pro rerum vilium detrimento fidelis fidelem gladiis impetrat, quem secum utique redemptum Christi sanquine non ignorat?" *Epistolae*, 4: 9, Migne, *PL*, CXLIV: 316. Cited by Villey, *La croisade*, pp. 36–37.

61. Innocent had already pledged his support to Alexius III and had assured

the emperor that the papacy considered the young Alexius's claims to the throne to be without foundation. *Register*, 5: 121 (122), pp. 239–41 (Migne, *PL*, CCXIV: 1123).

62. Charles Brand, "The Byzantines and Saladin, 1185–1192: Opponents of the Third Crusade," *Speculum* 37 (1962): 169–79. *Regesten der Kaiserurkunden des Oströmischen Reichs von 565–1453*, ed. Franz Dölger, 5 vols. (Munich and Berlin: Oldenbourg, 1924–65), vol. 2, doc. 1591, p. 95.

63. Villehardouin, *Conquête de Constantinople*, sec. 97, 1: 96–98.

64. Villehardouin, *Conquête de Constantinople*, sec. 96, 1: 96. This argument from necessity is the only one put into the mouths of the proponents of the Hohenstaufen proposal by Hugh of Saint Pol and Robert of Clari. *Epistola*, in *MGH, SS*, 17: 812–14; *Conquête*, sec. 33, p. 32. It is probably legitimate to conclude that this was the primary consideration but that the proponents of the argument grasped at whatever straws they could to buttress their position.

65. Longnon, *L'empire latin de Constantinople*, p. 31; Lodovico Sauli, *Della colonia dei genovese in Galata* (Turin: G. Bocca, 1831), pp. 31–32.

66. Innocent III, *Register*, 6: 210 (211), p. 359 (Migne, *PL*, CCXV: 238). The letter is from the crusaders to the pope.

67. Riant, "Innocent III," 18: 19–20; Alphandéry, *La chrétienté*, pp. 81–82; Nicol, "Fourth Crusade," pp. 279–80. Robert of Clari, *Conquête*, sec. 39, p. 40.

68. Bede, *De locis sanctis*, chap. 20, in *Itineraria Hierosolymitana et descriptiones terrae sanctae bellis sacris anteriora*, ed. Titus Tobler and Augustus Molinier (Geneva, 1879), pp. 232–33.

69. Paul Riant, "Les dépouilles religieuses enlevées a Constantinople au XIIIe siècle," *Memoires de la Société Nationale des Antiquaires de France*, series 4, 6 (1875): 11–12; Nicol, "Fourth Crusade," pp. 279–80. The difficulty with the emphasis put upon relics by Alphandéry and especially Frolow, and by Riant before them, is that it is impossible to prove that the desire for relics was a motive for the taking of Constantinople. There is ample evidence after the fact for the importance of the relics, but the desire to liberate relics does not appear to have been used as an argument in the debates over the Constantinopolitan venture.

70. Gunther of Pairis, *Hystoria Constantinopolitana*, p. 129; Hurter, *Papa Innocenzo III*, 2: 216, n. 365; Alphandéry, *La chrétienté*, pp. 88–89; Hagedorn, "Papst Innocenz III," p. 134; Schmandt, "Fourth Crusade and the Just War Theory," p. 212.

71. Villehardouin, *Conquête de Constantinople*, sec. 98, 1: 98.

72. Hugh of Saint Pol, *Epistola*, in *MGH, SS*, 17: 812; Innocent III, *Epistolae*, 8: 133, Migne, *PL*, CCXV: 710–11.

73. Innocent III, *Epistolae*, 8: 133, Migne, *PL*, CCXV: 710–11. Since Capuano was not at Zara, if this occurred, it must have been at Venice when envoys of Alexius first contacted the leaders of the crusade.

74. Villehardouin, *Conquête de Constantinople*, sec. 99, 1: 99–101; Hendrickx, "Les chartes de Baudouin de Flandre," p. 70.

75. For example, when introducing the abbot of Vaux-de-Cernay and his party's argument against going to Constantinople, Villehardouin says of the faction, "Et parla l'abes de Vals, de l'ordre de Cystiaus, et cele partie qui voloit l'ost deprecier," *Conquête de Constantinople*, sec. 95, 1: 94–96.

76. Ibid., sec. 99, 1: 98–100. There is no evidence supporting Brand's statement that the crusaders sent a deputation to gain the pope's approval of the project.

Byzantium Confronts the West, p. 228. He appears to be relying upon Innocent's letter of 16 November 1202, which refers to the earlier contact between envoys of Alexius and the crusaders at Venice. Innocent III, *Register*, 5: 121, pp. 241–42 (Migne, *PL*, CCXIV: 1124).

77. Roger of Hoveden, *Chronica*, 4: 111. It is simply not true, as Fine states, that the crusaders were "easily persuaded by the huge pay-off" to go to Constantinople. *Late Medieval Balkans*, p. 61.

78. *Devastatio Constantinopolitana*, p. 133 (*MGH, SS*, 16: 10; Hopf ed., p. 88).

79. Gunther of Pairis, *Hystoria Constantinopolitana*, p. 125.

80. Villehardouin, *Conquête de Constantinople*, sec. 106, 1: 106.

81. Innocent III, *Register*, 6: 99, pp. 159–61 (Migne, *PL*, CCXV: 104).

82. Villehardouin, *Conquête de Constantinople*, sec. 106, 1: 106.

83. Innocent III, *Register*, 6: 231 (232), p. 391 (Migne, *PL*, CCXV: 262).

84. The papal reaction is made plain in the letters to the crusaders dicussed below.

85. Andrea has argued convincingly for the two letters and instructions that the envoys bore. "Conrad of Krosigk," pp. 28–33; Andrea and Motsiff, "Pope Innocent III and the Diversion of the Fourth Crusade Army to Zara," pp. 23–24.

86. Innocent III, *Register*, 5: 161 (162), pp. 318–20 (Migne, *PL*, CCXIV: 1179–82). See Innocent's later account of his action, *Register*, 6: 231 (232), pp. 391–92 (Migne, *PL*, CCXV: 262). For contrary views on the relationship of letters V: 162, and V: 161, see Gill, "Franks, Venetians, and Pope Innocent III," pp. 93, n. 39, and Tessier, *Quatrième croisade*, p. 284; see also Maleczek, *Petrus Capuanus*, pp. 269–73. On the question of who was to absolve the crusaders, see Faral in Villehardouin, *Conquête de Constantinople*, 1: 109, n. 1.

87. On the dating and purpose of this letter, Andrea and Motsiff, "Pope Innocent III and the Diversion of the Fourth Crusade Army to Zara," p. 20, n. 69; p. 23, n. 77; cf. Maleczek, *Petrus Capuanus*, p. 155, n. 214; Gill, "Franks, Venetians, and Pope Innocent III," pp. 97–99; Joseph Gill, *Byzantium and the Papacy, 1198–1400*, (New Brunswick, NJ: Rutgers University Press, 1979), pp. 18–19; and Roscher, *Papst Innocenz III*, p. 109, n. 52, who favor the letter's position in the register, thus dating it to late June 1203.

88. Alfred J. Andrea, "The Relationship of Sea Travellers and Excommunicated Captains under Thirteenth Century Canon Law," *Mariners' Mirror* 68 (1982): 205; Brundage, *Medieval Canon Law and the Crusader*, p. 155.

89. Innocent III, *Register*, 6: 102, p. 168 (Migne, *PL*, CCXV: 107–10).

90. Andrea, "The Relationship of Sea Travellers and Excommunicated Captains," pp. 205–6.

91. Gunther of Pairis, *Hystoria Constantinopolitana*, p. 130; Andrea and Motsiff, "Pope Innocent III and the Diversion of the Fourth Crusade Army to Zara," p. 22, n. 72.

92. There is no extant letter from Innocent III to Alexius III asking the emperor to prepare provisions, nor is there any letter from the emperor promising them. This leads Andrea to conclude that Innocent told a small lie to the crusaders, allowing them to alleviate their poverty without going to Constantinople where, the pope believed, they would certainly be destroyed. "Conrad of Krosigk," pp. 32–33. John C. Moore has suggested to us that Innocent may have sent such a letter but that it does not survive.

93. Innocent III, *Register*, 6: 102, p. 168 (Migne, *PL*, CCXV: 109). The pope cited Gideon's punishment of the cities that would not give his army food (Judges 8:4–17) and Jesus' reference to the Pharisees of David's example in feeding his men with sacred bread (Luke 6:1–5). See also Gunther of Pairis, *Hystoria Constantinopolitana*, p. 130.

94. Andrea, "Conrad of Krosigk," pp. 30–41. Andrea shows that the leaders and bishops knew of the prohibitions but did not inform the crusaders.

95. Robert of Clari, *Conquête*, sec. 15, p. 15.

96. Villehardouin, *Conquête de Constantinople*, sec. 107, 1: 108.

97. Andrea, "Conrad of Krosigk," pp. 38–39.

98. Robert of Clari, *Conquête*, sec. 39, pp. 39–40; Gunther of Pairis, *Hystoria Constantinopolitana*, p. 129. Andrea points out the possibility that this may have come straight from the pope's mouth in Rome. This was an oversimplification of Innocent's concerns, but useful for the crusaders nonetheless. "Conrad of Krosigk," p. 34, n. 101.

99. *Devastatio Constantinopolitana*, p. 133 (*MGH, SS*, 16: 10; Hopf ed., p. 88). The *Devastatio* places this before the arrival of the embassy from King Philip. It probably belongs with the defections placed by Villehardouin after the debate over the Constantinopolitan proposal, although it might refer to the same events as the Anonymous of Halberstadt. *Gesta episcoporum Halberstadensium*, p. 117.

100. The *Devastatio Constantinopolitana*, p. 133 (*MGH, SS*, 16: 10; Hopf ed., p. 88), reports that two of the ships were lost. The drowning of the five hundred aboard one ship comes from Villehardouin, *Conquête de Constantinople*, sec. 101, 1: 100.

101. Villehardouin, *Conquête de Constantinople*, sec. 101, 1: 100–102. Clearly these defectors are not to be equated with those of the Anonymous of Halberstadt, because they did not reach their goal.

102. Ibid., sec. 102, 1: 102, and sec. 315, 2: 122–24; Tessier, *Quatrième croisade*, p. 69.

103. Villehardouin, *Conquête de Constantinople*, sec. 109, 1: 110–11; Robert of Clari, *Conquête*, sec. 14, p. 14. Robert, not to be much trusted on chronology, places Simon's defection before the debate on Alexius.

104. Peter of Vaux-de-Cernay, *Hystoria Albigensis*, 1: 104–5.

105. See above, note 49.

106. Villehardouin, *Conquête de Constantinople*, sec. 109, 1: 112; Ernoul-Bernard, *Chronique*, p. 351. The Anonymous of Halberstadt tells us of "Quedam autem abbatum qui aderant, recedendum esse a Venetis propter hoc factum [the conquest of Zara] publice proclamabant, et quamplures peregrinorum versus Hungariam discesserunt." *Gesta episcoporum Halberstadensium*, p. 117. He must be dealing with the departure of Simon, because of his reference to the abbots. No abbots could be assigned to an earlier defection.

107. Peter of Vaux-de-Cernay, *Hystoria Albigensis*, 1: 110.

108. Villehardouin, *Conquête de Constantinople*, secs. 48–49, 1: 50–52, and sec. 103, 1: 102–4. Some authors confuse the issue of the failure of the Flemish fleet to rendezvous with the main body by assuming that Countess Marie of Flanders was aboard. For example, Hurter, *Papa Innocenzo III*, 2: 238, n. 491, and Riant, "Innocent III," 18: 40. This is based upon a misinterpretation of Villehardouin, *Conquête de Constantinople*, sec. 317, 1: 126. Villehardouin actually says that Marie sailed some time after

the birth of Margaret, from Marseilles, but he does not say that she joined the fleet under John of Nesle. That fleet, in fact, arrived in Palestine in the late spring or, at the latest, the early summer of 1203. Marie, Villehardouin tells us, arrived a year later, for she had just landed when messengers brought news of Baldwin's election as emperor. See also Benjamin Hendrickx, "Het Regentschaap van Vlaanderen en Henegouwen na het vertrek van Boudewijn IX (VI) op kruisvaart (1202–1211)," *Revue belge de philologie et d'histoire* 48 (1970): 386, n. 1. Incidentally, if Baldwin had been involved in a conspiracy to conquer Constantinople *instead of* Jerusalem, he would scarcely have allowed his wife to sail for Acre.

109. Villehardouin, *Conquête de Constantinople*, sec. 229, 2: 28–30.

110. See Queller, Compton, and Campbell, "The Neglected Majority," pp. 441–42.

111. Ernoul-Bernard, *Chronique*, pp. 352–53. See Mas Latrie, *Histoire de l'île de Chypre*, 1: 156–59.

112. Ernoul-Bernard, *Chronique*, p. 353.

113. Peter of Vaux-de-Cernay, *Hystoria Albigensis*, 1: 110; Ernoul-Bernard, *Chronique*, p. 360. On the defectors in general, see Queller, Compton, and Campbell, "The Neglected Majority," pp. 441–65.

114. Gunther of Pairis, *Hystoria Constantinopolitana*, p. 131. See also, Brown, "Cistercians in the Latin Empire," p. 77, n. 70; Gill, "Franks, Venetians, and Pope Innocent III," p. 93, n. 38. Andrea has most convincingly untangled the knotty problem of the whereabouts of Peter Capuano and Martin of Pairis during the winter of 1202–1203. *The Capture of Constantinople: "The Hystoria Constantinopolitana,"* chap. 9, n. 117.

115. *Gesta Innocentii*, chap. 88, col. 160.

116. Innocent III, *Register*, 6: 48, pp. 71–72 (Migne, *PL*, CCXV: 50). There is an error in the Migne edition. In the sentence: "Cum Francis autem, si sequi voluerint perfidiam Venetorum, secure procedas, et super absolutione baronum" the word "voluerint" should be "noluerint," which makes much more sense. We are very grateful to John C. Moore, who is one of the scholars producing the new editions of Innocent's letters, for pointing out this error in the old edition.

117. Innocent III, *Register*, 6: 99, pp. 159–61 (Migne, *PL*, CCXV: 103–4).

118. Innocent III, *Register*, 6: 100, pp. 161–62 (Migne, *PL*, CCXV: 105); *Epistolae*, 7: 202, Migne, *PL*, CCXV: 511. *Gesta Innocentii*, chaps. 87–88, cols. 139–40; Gunther of Pairis, *Hystoria Constantinopolitana*, p. 131. Gunther gives the date of embarkation as 4 April, which is very unlikely. The pope wrote to Capuano in Italy on 21 April (6: 102). Andrea has argued that Capuano and Martin left for Syria in late April or early May, perhaps on 25 April. *The Capture of Constantinople: The "Hystoria Constantinopolitana,"* chap. 9, nn. 117 and 118; see also, Maleczek, *Petrus Capuanus*, pp. 154–55.

119. Robert of Clari, *Conquête*, sec. 15, p. 15.

120. Above, p. 68. Events such as these are ignored by those anxious to cast the Venetians as ruthless opportunists willing to sell their souls for material profit. See, for example, the very poor book by Basile G. Spiridonakis, *Grecs, Occidentaux et Turcs de 1054 à 1453: Quatre siècles d'histoire de relations internationales* (Thessalonica: Institute for Balkan Studies, 1990), pp. 105–6.

121. Innocent III, *Register*, 6: 100, pp. 161–62 (Migne, *PL*, CCXV: 105). Riant reads *abbati Laudensi* as the abbot of Loos. "Innocent III,"18: 15. Usseglio argues that

it was the abbot of Locedio on the grounds of his close connection with Boniface. *I marchesi di Monferrato*, 2: 213. It is difficult to see the derivation of Locedio from a name with the dative form "Laudensi." In this same letter Boniface tells the pope that Dandolo and some Venetians had said that they were sending their own envoys to Rome. It is not clear whether Boniface or Dandolo invented this story. In any event, it is clear that no delegation was ever sent.

122. Innocent III, *Register*, 6: 102, p. 168 (Migne, *PL*, CCXV: 110).

123. Villehardouin, *Conquête de Constantinople*, sec. 108, 1: 110; *Gesta episcoporum Halberstadensium*, p. 118; *Venetiarum historia*, p. 135 (=*Historia ducum Veneticoru, Supplementum*, p. 92); Thomas of Spalato, *Historia*, p. 576. Andrea Dandolo and Gunther of Pairis imply that the walls were destroyed before winter. *Chronica per extensum descripta*, p. 277; *Hystoria Constantinopolitana*, p. 125.

124. *Venetiarum historia*, p. 137 (=*Historia ducum Veneticorum, Supplementum*, p. 93); Dandolo, *Chronica per extensum descripta*, pp. 277–78.

125. Villehardouin, *Conquête de Constantinople*, sec. 99, 1: 100.

126. Ibid., sec. 111, 1: 112–14; *Devastatio Constantinopolitana*, p. 133 (*MGH, SS*, 16: 10; Hopf ed., p. 88); Robert of Clari, *Conquête*, sec. 31, p. 31.

127. *Gesta episcoporum Halberstadensium*, p. 118. We have less confidence in the veracity of the report of the prophesying hermit than does Andrea. "Conrad of Krosigk," p. 42.

128. Villehardouin, *Conquête de Constantinople*, sec. 112, 1: 114; Alberic of Trois-Fontaines, *Chronica*, p. 880.

129. Villehardouin, *Conquête de Constantinople*, sec. 111, 1: 112–14; *Gesta episcoporum Halberstadensium*, p. 118.

130. Villehardouin, *Conquête de Constantinople*, sec. 111, 1: 114.

131. Ibid., sec. 112, 1: 115; *Gesta episcoporum Halberstadensium*, p. 118. Robert of Clari can be interpreted as saying that Alexius was led to Boniface's tent, which would emphasize the domination of the marquis over the young prince. *Conquête*, sec. 31, p. 31. Villehardouin is absolutely clear, however, that the marquis had his own tent pitched close by that of Alexius. The question is not trivial, for it involves the relative status of Alexius and Boniface.

132. *Gesta episcoporum Halberstadensium*, p. 118.

133. Ibid. It is difficult to believe that the crusaders destroyed the entire island, as the *Gesta episcoporum Halberstadensium* asserts. Corfu is very large and mountainous. The crusaders undoubtedly caused damage, but they were too few to utterly devastate it. Andrea also doubts that the fleet was forced to leave the harbor. "Conrad of Krosigk," p. 43, n. 133.

134. Riant argues that in this crisis Alexius was compelled to bribe the leaders to keep them to their agreement. "Innocent III," 18: 36–37.

135. Hugh of Saint Pol, *Epistola*, in *MGH, SS*, 17: 812.

136. *Conquête*, sec. 33, p. 32 (translation by Edgar H. McNeal); Hugh of Saint Pol, *Epistola*, in *MGH, SS*, 17: 812; Villehardouin, *Conquête de Constantinople*, secs. 113–14, 1: 116–18.

137. Villehardouin, *Conquête de Constantinople*, sec. 113, 1: 116.

138. Ibid., sec. 114, 1: 118.

139. Hugh of Saint Pol, *Epistola*, in *MGH, SS*, 17: 812.

140. Robert of Clari, *Conquête*, sec. 39, p. 40; Usseglio, *I marchesi di Monferrato*, 2: 216.

141. Hugh of Saint Pol says that there were only a few more than twenty who advocated the Constantinopolitan expedition. *Epistola*, in *MGH, SS*, 17: 812. One manuscript of this letter, the one published by Martene, lists the following names: Boniface of Montferrat, Louis of Blois, Matthew of Montmorency, Geoffrey of Ville-hardouin, Conon of Béthune, Miles the Brabantine, John Foisnon, John of Friaise, Peter of Bracheux, Anseau of Cayeux, Renier of Trith, Macaire of Ste. Menehould, Miles of Lille, the bishops of Troyes and Halberstadt, and John Faicete. There are two surprising omissions, undoubtedly erroneous: Baldwin of Flanders and Hugh himself. See Hendrickx, "Les chartes de Baudouin de Flandre," p. 70. Riant, "Innocent III," 18: 22, mistakenly places this at Zara. See Queller, Compton, and Campbell, "The Neglected Majority," p. 460, n. 102.

142. Villehardouin, *Conquête de Constantinople*, sec. 115–17, 1: 118–20; Hugh of Saint Pol, *Epistola*, in *MGH, SS*, 17: 812; Elizabeth Siberry, *Criticism of Crusading, 1095–1274* (Oxford: Clarendon, 1985), p. 172.

143. Robert of Clari, *Conquête*, sec. 39, p. 40.

Chapter 7

1. Villehardouin, *Conquête de Constantinople*, sec. 119, 1: 122. The *Devastatio Constantinopolitana* (p. 133) places the crusaders' departure one day later, on Whitsunday itself (*MGH, SS*, XVI: 10; Hopf ed., p. 88).

2. Raimbaut de Vaqueiras, *Poems*, p. 218. The body of Saint Nicholas had only been relocated to Bari in 1100, when merchants there stole it from Myra before Venetians could lay hands on it. As a result, the church of Saint Nicholas on the Lido had to content itself with the body of its patron's uncle, as well as a few reputed pieces of the saint himself. The issue remained a sore point between Venice and Bari. See Queller and Katele, "Venice and the Conquest of the Latin Kingdom," p. 22.

3. Villehardouin, *Conquête de Constantinople*, secs. 119–20, 1: 122.

4. Innocent III, *Register*, 6: 48, pp. 71–72 (Migne, *PL*, CCXV: 50).

5. Andrea, "Conrad of Krosigk," pp. 37–38, n. 115.

6. Luchaire, *Innocent III*, 4: 116.

7. Innocent III, *Register*, 6: 101, pp. 163–65 (Migne, *PL*, CCXV: 106–7).

8. *Regesta*, vol. 1, no. 1948. Tessier, *Quatrième croisade*, pp. 281–83. Others who argue for the earlier date include Andrea, "Conrad of Krosigk," p. 37, n. 115; Maleczek, *Petrus Capuanus*, p. 155, n. 214. Schmandt speculates on the grounds of the silence of Villehardouin and Robert of Clari that the letter miscarried or was suppressed, but does not take into consideration the tardiness of its dispatch. "Fourth Crusade and the Just War Theory," p. 213.

9. E.g., Nicol, "Fourth Crusade," p. 280; M. A. Zaborov, "Papstvo i zachvat Konstantinopolya krestonostsami v nacale XIII v," *Vizantiiskii Vremennik*, n.s. 5 (1952): 152–77; idem, "K Voprosu o predistorii cetvertogo krestovogo pochoda," *Vizantiiskii Vremennik*, n.s. 6 (1953): 223–35.

10. E.g. McNeal and Wolff, "Fourth Crusade," p. 176; Colin Morris, *The Papal Monarchy: The Western Church from 1050 to 1250* (Oxford: Oxford University Press, 1989), p. 440.

11. Gill, "Franks, Venetians, and Innocent III," pp. 97–99, 105; Andrea, "Conrad of Krosigk," pp. 37–38, n. 115.

12. If these were some of those who had sailed under John of Nesle, they had had a very rapid voyage and return, allowing time for a pro forma appearance in the Holy Land at most. The Flemish fleet probably left Marseilles late in March 1203. Villehardouin, *Conquête de Constantinople*, sec. 103, 1: 102–4. The journey to the Holy Land probably required close to two months. Roscher, *Papst Innocent III*, p. 57, n. 33. Thus the Flemings probably arrived in Syria in May, and the encounter between the fleet's remnants and the main crusading force took place in the first week of June. This seems a rather tight chronology.

13. Villehardouin, *Conquête de Constantinople*, secs. 121–22, 1: 124. The quotation is from the translation by M. R. B. Shaw, Villehardouin, *The Conquest of Constantinople* (1963; repr. Baltimore: Penguin Books, 1967), p. 57.

14. Pryor, "Winds, Waves, and Rocks," pp. 82–83. For a discussion on life aboard these transport vessels, see Jean Richard, "Le transport outremer des croisés et des pélerins (XIIe–XVe siècles)," in *Maritime Aspects of Migration*, ed. Klaus Fiedland (Cologne-Vienna: Böhlau, 1989), pp. 37–44.

15. Villehardouin, *Conquête de Constantinople*, secs. 123–24, 1: 124–26; Runciman, *History of the Crusades*, 3: 117.

16. Pryor, "Winds, Waves, and Rocks," pp. 83, 85.

17. Villehardouin, *Conquête de Constantinople*, secs. 125–26, 1: 126–28. Recall that the pope had taken the position that if the emperor did not supply them, they might help themselves. Innocent III, *Register*, 6: 102, pp. 167–68 (Migne, *PL*, CCXV: 109–10).

18. Anonymous of Halberstadt gives a somewhat confused version of the journey omitting Negroponte. *Gesta episcoporum Halberstadensium*, p. 118. Alberic of Trois-Fontaines is utterly confused on the geography. *Chronica*, pp. 880–81.

19. Some have argued against the prevailing belief that twelfth-century Byzantium was in the throes of economic decay. See Michael F. Hendy, "Byzantium, 1081–1204: An Economic Reappraisal," *Transactions of the Royal Historical Society* 20 (1970): 31–52; Lilie, *Handel und Politik*, p. 470. Hard evidence, however, is lacking on both sides of the question, as Hendy points out.

20. Alan Harvey, *Economic Expansion in the Byzantine Empire, 900–1200* (Cambridge: Cambridge University Press, 1989), pp. 466–68, and passim.

21. Freddy Thiriet, *Histoire de Venise*, 4th ed. (Paris: Presses universitaires de France, 1969), p. 40; Robert Lee Wolff, "Greeks and Latins," pp. 324–25; Anthony Bryer, "The First Encounter with the West—AD, 1050–1204," in *Byzantium: An Introduction*, ed. Philip Whitting (Oxford: Blackwell, 1971).

22. Nicetas, *Historia*, pp. 547–48.

23. Ibid., pp. 458–59; Brand, *Byzantium Confronts the West*, p. 118.

24. Nicetas, *Historia*, p. 484.

25. E.g., Ibid., pp. 477–78; Brand, *Byzantium Confronts the West*, p. 117.

26. Nicetas, *Historia*, pp. 530, 548.

27. Ibid., pp. 496–97; Brand, *Byzantium Confronts the West*, p. 117.

28. Nicetas, *Historia*, p. 460; Louis Halphen, "Le rôle des 'Latins' dans l'histoire intérieure de Constantinople à la fin du XIIe siècle," *Mélanges Charles Diehl* (Paris: E. Laroux, 1930), 1: 145. Halphen believed that Euphrosyne was a member of a nationalistic faction and that she actually ruled in place of her weak husband.

29. Nicetas, *Historia*, p. 541.

30. Hélène Ahrweiler, *Byzance et la mer: La marine de guerre, la politique et les institutions maritimes de Byzance aux VIIe–XVe siècles* (Paris: Presses universitaires de France, 1966), p. 244; M. Sesan, "La flotte byzantine à l'époque des Comnènes et des Anges (1081–1204)," *Byzantinoslavica* 21 (1960): 52–53.

31. Sesan, "La flotte byzantine," pp. 52–53.

32. Ibid., Ahrweiler, *Byzance et la mer*, p. 288. Sometimes the Byzantines unwillingly received such pirates into their services. Wolff reports an incident in which the Calabrian pirate Stinone forced the Greeks to pay him an indemnity and to make him an admiral in the Byzantine navy. "Greeks and Latins," p. 325.

33. Nicetas, *Historia*, p. 482; Brand, *Byzantium Confronts the West*, pp. 147, 213–14.

34. Usseglio, *I marchesi di Monferrato*, 2: 218.

35. Nicetas, *Historia*, pp. 540–41.

36. Ibid., p. 541; Brand, *Byzantium Confronts the West*, p. 147.

37. Paul Magdalino, *The Empire of Manuel I Komnenos, 1143–1180* (Cambridge: Cambridge University Press, 1993), pp. 176–77, 231–33; George Ostrogorsky, *History of the Byzantine State*, pp. 329–31; idem, *Pour l'histoire de la féodalité byzantine* (Brussels: Editions de l'Institut de philologie et d'histoire orientales et slaves, 1954), pp. 9–61. The timing of the effect of the *pronoia* is still debated. For a contrary view, see David Jacoby, "The Encounter of Two Societies: Western Conquerors and Byzantines in the Peloponnesus after the Fourth Crusade," *American Historical Review* 78 (1973): 876–77.

38. Nicetas, *Historia*, pp. 208–9. Magdalino doubts that the foreign element in the army was as large or destructive as is often maintained. *The Empire of Manuel I Komnenos*, pp. 176, 231–32.

39. Byzantine sources provide no estimation of troop levels in the city. Western estimates vary widely. According to Robert of Clari, in April 1204, the Byzantines had one hundred times as many men under arms as did the crusaders: in other words, a little less than two million men—a preposterous figure. *Conquête*, sec. 78, pp. 78–79. According to Villehardouin, who is much better with numbers, there were four hundred thousand men in Constantinople, although he does not say if these were armed. *Conquête de Constantinople*, sec. 251, 2: 57. In a subsequent letter to the pope, the crusading leaders put the entire opposing force at sixty thousand men. Innocent III, *Register*, 6: 210 (211), p. 360 (Migne, *PL*, CCXV: 238). This seems to be confirmed by the descriptions of the army that Alexius III brought outside of the walls in July 1203, which probably numbered over thirty thousand men. See Chap. 8, note 42 below. These would not constitute all of the Byzantine regular forces, many of whom remained behind for the city's defense. Subtracting foreign mercenaries (see below) from the leaders' estimate of sixty thousand yields the figure fifty thousand, which seems a realistic figure for the Byzantine army in the city.

40. After the fire of August 1203, Villehardouin recorded that fifteen thousand Latins fled Constantinople. *Conquête de Constantinople*, sec. 205, 1: 210. According to

Nicetas, a large portion of these were Pisans. *Historia*, p. 552. We can conservatively estimate, therefore, that at least eight thousand of the refugees were Pisans. Thus, the figure of two thousand fighting men seems reasonable.

41. Benjamin of Tudela, *Itinerary*, p. 71.

42. Sigfús Blöndal, *The Varangians of Byzantium*, rev. and trans., Benedikt S. Benedikz (Cambridge: Cambridge University Press, 1978), p. 120.

43. Anna Comnena, *The Alexiad*, trans. Elizabeth A. S. Dawes (London: Routledge and K. Paul, 1967), pp. 63–64.

44. Blöndal, *The Varangians of Byzantium*, pp. 161–62; Richard M. Dawkins, "The Later History of the Varangian Guard: Some Notes," *Journal of Roman Studies* 37 (1947): 39–40.

45. Nicetas, *Historia*, pp. 525–26.

46. Blöndal, *The Varangians of Byzantium*, pp. 162–63.

47. Nicetas, *Historia*, p. 541.

48. Villehardouin, *Conquête de Constantinople*, sec. 127, 1: 128. Robert of Clari, *Conquête*, sec. 40, p. 40; Hugh of Saint Pol, *Epistola*, in *MGH, SS*, 17: 812.

49. Magdalino gives an excellent account of what the crusaders could see as they sailed through Marmara and the Bosporus. *The Empire of Manuel I Komnenos*, pp. 119–20.

50. Villehardouin, *Conquête de Constantinople*, sec. 128, 1: 130; Robert of Clari, *Conquête*, sec. 40, p. 40; Hugh of Saint Pol, *Epistola*, in *MGH, SS*, 17: 812.

51. Robert of Clari, *Conquête*, sec. 92, p. 90; McNeal, trans., p. 112.

52. For an excellent compilation of modern estimates, see David Jacoby, "La population de Constantinople à l'époque byzantine: Un problème de demographie urbaine," *Byzantion* 31 (1961): 82–83 and accompanying notes. See also Queller and Madden, "Some Further Arguments in Defense of the Venetians," pp. 461–62, n. 110, which lays out the relevant arguments, but concludes with a figure we now believe is too high.

53. Villehardouin, *Conquête de Constantinople*, secs. 129–31, 1: 130–32. For the tactical considerations influencing the doge's proposal, see Manfroni, *Storia della marina italiana*, 1: 321.

54. Villehardouin, *Conquête de Constantinople*, sec. 132, 1: 132–34.

55. Pears, *Fall of Constantinople*, p. 304. Pears was not a very good historian, but he did know Constantinople and its surroundings.

56. Villehardouin, *Conquête de Constantinople*, sec. 133, 1: 134; Robert of Clari, *Conquête*, sec. 40, p. 40; Nicetas, *Historia*, p. 542.

57. Janin, *Constantinople byzantine*, p. 1.

58. Villehardouin, *Conquête de Constantinople*, secs. 134–35, 1: 134–36.

59. Ibid., sec. 136, 1: 136–38; F. C. Hodgson, *Early History of Venice* (London: George Allen, 1901), p. 371.

60. Villehardouin, *Conquête de Constantinople*, sec. 137, 1: 138.

61. Hugh of Saint Pol, *Epistola*, in *MGH, SS*, 17: 812.

62. Innocent III, *Register*, 6: 210 (211), p. 359 (Migne, *PL*, CCXV: 238).

63. Villehardouin, *Conquête de Constantinople*, sec. 137, 1: 138.

64. Innocent III, *Register*, 6: 210 (211), p. 359 (Migne, *PL*, CCXV: 238). Since this never became a rallying point of contention against accepting the young Alexius or later opposing his rule it seems unlikely that it was a foremost consideration in

most people's minds. Perhaps the rumor was not widely spread or the populace gave it little credence.

65. Virtually all armed coups were undertaken with the help of some Latin troops. Alexius Comnenus had made his bid for the throne with a predominantly Latin force. Ostrogorsky, *History of the Byzantine State*, p. 350.

66. Nicetas, *Historia*, p. 385; Magoulias trans., p. 211.

67. This is according to Villehardouin. Nicetas places the scene at Damatrys on the Sea of Marmara southwest of Scutari. See Brand, *Byzantium Confronts the West*, p. 235.

68. Nicetas, *Historia*, p. 542. On the identity of the Greek commander, see Faral, in Villehardouin, *Conquête de Constantinople*, 1: 141, n. 2.

69. Villehardouin, *Conquête de Constantinople*, secs. 138–40, 1: 138–42.

70. Axel Wallensköld, in Conon of Béthune, *Les chansons de Conon de Béthune* (Paris: H. Champion, 1921), pp. iii–v; Longnon, *Les compagnons de Villehardouin*, p. 146; Rousset, *Histoire des croisades*, p. 205.

71. Queller, "L'évolution du rôle de l'ambassadeur," pp. 482–83, n. 11.

72. Villehardouin, *The Conquest of Constantinople*, trans. M. R. B. Shaw, p. 63.

73. Villehardouin, *Conquête de Constantinople*, secs. 141–44, 1: 142–46. Robert of Clari, *Conquête*, sec. 41, pp. 40–41; Hugh of Saint Pol, *Epistola*, pp. 812–13.

74. Villehardouin, *Conquête de Constantinople*, sec. 145, 1: 146. On the possibility of approaching within ten feet of the walls, see Pears, *Fall of Constantinople*, pp. 305–6.

75. Nicol disagrees. In his view, Dandolo came to Constantinople with the firm intention of fighting. The unwise exhibition of young Alexius was "little more than a charade, stage-managed by the Doge, to prove the point that now the crusade would have to fight to achieve what it had come to do." *Byzantium and Venice*, p. 136. This view is not only contradicted by the evidence, but suggests that the doge was an utter fool. Why would he prefer fighting over a peaceful and profitable settlement? In his zeal to apportion blame for 1204 on Dandolo, Nicol is often forced to explain away events like this by imagining what was in the old doge's soul.

76. On Byzantium's general antipathy for Italians in general and Venice in particular, see Herbert Hunger, *Graeculus Perfidus — Ἰταλός ἰταμός· Il senso dell'alterità nei rapporti greco-romani ed italo-bizantini* (Rome: Unione internazionale degli istituti di Archeologia, storia e storia dell'arte in Roma, 1987), pp. 33–43; Catherine Asdracha, "L'image de l'homme occidental à Byzance: Le témoignage de Kinnamos et de Choniatès," *Byzantinoslavica* 44 (1983): 33–37.

77. Villehardouin, *Conquête de Constantinople*, secs. 145–46, 1: 146–48; Robert of Clari, *Conquête*, sec. 41, p. 41; Innocent III, *Register*, 6: 210 (211), pp. 359–60 (Migne, *PL*, CCXV: 238).

78. Villehardouin, *Conquête de Constantinople*, sec. 147, 1: 148.

79. Usseglio, I *marchesi di Monferrato*, 2: 221.

80. Villehardouin, *Conquête de Constantinople*, sec. 147, 1: 148.

81. For the armor worn by foot soldiers, see Christopher Marshall, *Warfare in the Latin East, 1192–1291* (Cambridge: Cambridge University Press, 1992), p. 89; Smail, *Crusading Warfare*, pp. 115–16.

82. Faral, in Villehardouin, *Conquête de Constantinople*, p. ix.

83. Villehardouin, *Conquête de Constantinople*, sec. 379, 2: 188.

84. Faral, in Villehardouin, *Conquête de Constantinople*, pp. xxxii–xxxv.

85. Villehardouin, *Conquête de Constantinople*, secs. 148–53, 1: 148–52.

86. Innocent III, *Register*, 6: 210 (211), pp. 360 (Migne, *PL*, CCXV: 238).

87. Villehardouin, *Conquête de Constantinople*, sec. 154, 1: 152; Robert of Clari, *Conquête*, sec. 41, pp. 41–42.

88. Robert of Clari, *Conquête*, sec. 41, p. 42; Villehardouin, *Conquête de Constantinople*, secs. 155–56, 1: 154–56.

89. Robert of Clari, *Conquête*, sec. 42, p. 42.

90. Ibid., secs. 42–43, p. 42; Villehardouin, *Conquête de Constantinople*, sec. 156, 1: 156; Hugh of Saint Pol, *Epistola*, in *MGH, SS*, 17: 813. Clari makes it clear that the knights issued mounted from the transports. Probably lesser men led the horses down the ramps into the water. See Pryor, "Transportation of Horses by Sea," p. 22.

91. Robert of Clari, *Conquête*, sec. 43, pp. 42–43; Villehardouin, *Conquête de Constantinople*, secs. 157–58, 1: 156–58; Hugh of Saint Pol, *Epistola*, in *MGH, SS*, 17: 813. This Tower of Galata, located on the seashore, must not be confused with the fourteenth-century tower, which still stands on the hillside at a considerable distance from the shore.

92. Villehardouin, *Conquête de Constantinople*, sec. 158, 1: 158; Ernoul-Bernard, *Chronique*, p. 363.

93. Pears, *Fall of Constantinople*, p. 308.

94. Robert of Clari, *Conquête*, sec. 43, p. 43; Villehardouin, *Conquête de Constantinople*, sec. 159, 1: 158.

95. Robert of Clari, *Conquête*, sec. 43, p. 43; Villehardouin, *Conquête de Constantinople*, sec. 159, 1: 158; Hugh of Saint Pol, *Epistola*, in *MGH, SS*, 17: 813; Manfroni, *Storia della marina italiana*, 1: 323, n. 2. Hugh names as defenders of the tower "Anglici, Pysani, Leventiani, Dachi."

96. Robert of Clari, *Conquête*, sec. 44, p. 43; Villehardouin, *Conquête de Constantinople*, sec. 160–61, 1: 158–60; Hugh of Saint Pol, *Epistola*, in *MGH, SS*, 17: 813; Nicetas, *Historia*, pp. 542–43.

97. Robert of Clari, *Conquête*, sec. 75, p. 75, sec. 106, p. 102 (on the height of Peter). On the cloudy question of the right of a cleric to bear arms against the infidel, see Russell, *Just War*, pp. 105–12.

98. Villehardouin, *Conquête de Constantinople*, sec. 160, 1: 160.

99. Ernoul-Bernard, *Chronique*, p. 362.

100. Dandolo, *Chronica per extensum descripta*, p. 322. The *Historia ducum Veneticorum*, p. 93, mentions a bridge over the chain by means of which men passed back and forth between Constantinople and Galata. It was supposedly struck and broken by the *Eagle*.

101. Robert of Clari, *Conquête*, sec. 44, p. 43; Nicetas, *Historia*, p. 543.

102. Alberic of Trois-Fontaines, *Chronica*, p. 881.

Chapter 8

1. Villehardouin, *Conquête de Constantinople*, sec. 162, 1: 160–62; Robert of Clari, *Conquête*, sec. 44, pp. 43–44. Martin da Canale puts into the mouth of Dandolo in 1204 a remark concerning the French lack of experience in fighting from the flying

bridges mounted on ships. *Les estoires de Venise*, pt. 1, sec. 51, p. 57 (in the older ed., p. 332).

2. This was the strategy used by Constantinople's attackers in 626, 717, 1422, and 1453, as well as other times.

3. Tsangadas, *Fortifications and Defense of Constantinople*, p. 19; Janin, *Constantinople byzantine*, pp. 262–63; Müller-Wiener, *Bildlexicon zur Topographie Istanbuls*, pp. 287, 290.

4. Tsangadas, *Fortifications and Defense of Constantinople*, p. 40; Janin, *Constantinople byzantine*, pp. 407–8.

5. Villehardouin, *Conquête de Constantinople*, sec. 163, 1: 162.

6. Villehardouin, *Conquête de Constantinople*, sec. 163, 1: 162–64; Robert of Clari, *Conquête*, sec. 44, p. 44; Hugh of Saint Pol, *Epistola*, in *MGH, SS*, 17: 813. Brand ignores the demolition of the bridge by the Greeks. *Byzantium Confronts the West*, p. 238.

7. Nicetas, *Historia*, p. 543; Villehardouin, *Conquête de Constantinople*, sec. 164, 1: 164–66; Ernoul-Bernard, *Chronique*, p. 364. Villehardouin says they could besiege one gate, which Faral identifies as the Blachernae Gate. Nicetas's identification of the gate as Gyrolimne Gate, however, makes sense and should not be discounted. Gyrolimne no longer exists. The Blachernae section of the wall was rebuilt and repaired by the Palaeologi who did away with the gate. Tsangadas, *Fortifications and Defense of Constantinople*, p. 164; Janin, *Constantinople byzantine*, pp. 283–84.

8. Hugh of Saint Pol, *Epistola*, in *MGH, SS*, 17: 813; Robert of Clari, *Conquête*, sec. 44, p. 45; Nicetas, *Historia*, p. 544.

9. Tsangadas, *Fortifications and Defense of Constantinople*, p. 164; Clive Foss and David Winfield, *Byzantine Fortifications: An Introduction* (Pretoria: University of South Africa, 1986), pp. 56–58.

10. Janin, *Constantinople byzantine*, p. 284.

11. Tsangadas, *Fortifications and Defense of Constantinople*, pp. 22–27, 163–65; Alexander Van Millingen, *Byzantine Constantinople: The Walls of the City and Adjoining Historical Sites* (London: J. Murray, 1899), pp. 131 53.

12. Van Millingen, *Byzantine Constantinople*, p. 109; Magdalino, *The Empire of Manuel I Komnenos*, pp. 115–16. Pears, *Fall of Constantinople*, p. 310.

13. Tsangadas, *Fortifications and Defense of Constantinople*, pp. 22–32.

14. To a certain extent, this was the strategy the crusaders employed after their entry into the city on 12 April 1204.

15. The crusading leaders believed that it would be madness to invade the city directly, since the crusaders were heavily outnumbered and easily subject to guerrilla tactics and assassins. See Villehardouin, *Conquête de Constantinople*, sec. 244, 2: 46; Robert of Clari, *Conquête*, sec. 78, pp. 78–79.

16. Villehardouin, *Conquête de Constantinople*, sec. 166, 1: 168; Hugh of Saint Pol, *Epistola*, in *MGH, SS*, 17: 813; Nicetas, *Historia*, pp. 511–15.

17. Probably these bridges were operated by a pulley system similar to that used on a land-based siege tower in the Fifth Crusade at Damietta. James M. Powell, *Anatomy of a Crusade, 1213–1221* (Philadelphia: University of Pennsylvania Press, 1986), pp. 142–44.

18. At least one scholar has equated the terror inspired in medieval man by Greek fire to the modern psychological effects of atomic weaponry. While the com-

parison may be overdone, it does emphasize the very real "superstitious awe" with which this device was regarded. H. R. Ellis Davidson, "The Secret Weapon of Byzantium," *Byzantinische Zeitschrift* 66 (1973): 61.

19. Robert of Clari, *Conquête*, sec. 44, p. 44; Wiel, *Navy of Venice*, p. 142.

20. Villehardouin, *Conquête de Constantinople*, sec. 165, 1: 166.

21. Nicetas, *Historia*, p. 544.

22. Villehardouin, *Conquête de Constantinople*, secs. 165–66, 168, 1: 166–70.

23. Ibid., sec. 169, 1: 170. The sallies must have emanated from the southern gates, since those closer to the crusaders had no drawbridges.

24. Ibid.

25. Ibid., sec. 165, 1: 166. Villehardouin, *The Conquest of Constantinople*, trans. by Shaw, p. 69. The marshal estimates that they could maintain the siege for three weeks. In the letter of the crusading leaders to Innocent III, they estimate only fifteen days. Innocent III, *Register*, 6: 210 (211), p. 360 (Migne, *PL*, CCXV: 238).

26. Villehardouin, *Conquête de Constantinople*, sec. 170, 1: 170–72; Hugh of Saint Pol, *Epistola*, in *MGH, SS*, 17: 814.

27. Nicetas, *Historia*, p. 545.

28. Villehardouin, *Conquête de Constantinople*, sec. 170, 1: 170–72.

29. The conjecture is Van Millingen's. *Byzantine Constantinople*, p. 172.

30. Villehardouin, *Conquête de Constantinople*, sec. 171, 1: 172–74.

31. Brand says, "Three casts of a stone-thrower," but he is following Villehardouin incorrectly. *Byzantium Confronts the West*, p. 240. Villehardouin, *Conquête de Constantinople*, sec. 172, 1: 174.

32. Nicholas Mesarites, *Epitaphios*, in *Neue Quellen zur Geschichte des lateinischen Kaisertums und der Kirchenunion, 1: Der Epitaphios des Nikolaos Mesarites auf seinen Bruder Johannes*, ed. A. Heisenberg, in *Sitzungsberichte der bayerischen Akademie der Wissenshaften. Philosophisch-philologische und historische Klasse*, Abh. 5 (Munich, 1923), p. 41.

33. Villehardouin, *Conquête de Constantinople*, sec. 172, 1: 174.

34. Ibid., secs. 173–74, 1: 174–76.

35. Nicetas, *Historia*, pp. 544–45. Western chroniclers make no mention of the ram, and Raimbaut says specifically "the wall breached in many places without the battering ram." Linskill, in Raimbaut de Vaqueiras, *Poems*, pp. 305, 310, and 332, n. to line 42.

36. Villehardouin, *Conquête de Constantinople*, sec. 175, 1: 176, lists twenty-five towers, but Hugh of Saint Pol, *Epistola*, in *MGH, SS*, 17: 814, says thirty.

37. Michael Maclagen, *The City of Constantinople* (London: Thames and Hudson, 1968), pp. 35–36.

38. Nicetas, *Historia*, pp. 544–45; Villehardouin, *Conquête de Constantinople*, secs. 175–76, 1: 178. It is not clear how far the Venetians advanced into the city. Villehardouin only implies an advance by describing the retreat. Alberic of Trois-Fontaines claims that the Venetians advanced one-half league into the city: an absurdity. *Chronica, MGH, SS*, 23: 881. No other source mentions a Venetian advance into the city.

39. Thomas F. Madden, "The Fires of the Fourth Crusade in Constantinople, 1203–1204: A Damage Assessment," *Byzantinische Zeitschrift* 84/85 (1992): 73–74, 88.

40. Villehardouin, *Conquête de Constantinople*, sec. 179, 1: 180–82.

41. Ernoul-Bernard, *Chronique*, pp. 364–65.

42. Villehardouin estimated that the emperor's force numbered 100,000 mounted warriors, but also described it as 40 very large battalions. *Conquête de Constantinople*, sec. 179, 2: 39. According to Robert of Clari there were only 17 Byzantine battalions, but he agrees that the mounted soldiers numbered 100,000. Clari also describes the French force as numbering 7 battalions of 700 knights. *Conquête*, sec. 44, p. 45. In this case, Clari's numbers may be superior to those of Villehardouin. The odd number of 17 batallions is more convincing than the round number of 40. Since all sources agree that the Byzantines covered the entire plain outside of the city in this engagement, the Byzantine battalions must either have been much larger than their Frankish counterparts, as Robert of Clari in fact states, or there must have been more of them, as Villehardouin contends. Accepting the first premise, if we postulate that the Byzantine batallions were thrice as large as the mounted warriors outside the walls they would have numbered 5,100 (300 knights times 17 batallions)—far fewer than Villehardouin's and Clari's 100,000. Assuming that Byzantine forces followed the 1:2:4 ratio of knights to squires to infantry, then total Byzantine troops outside the walls in July 1203 would number around 35,700.

43. Villehardouin, *Conquête de Constantinople*, sec. 179, 1: 180–82.

44. Ibid.

45. Ibid., secs. 177–79, n. 178–80.

46. Ibid., sec. 178, 1: 180; Robert of Clari, *Conquête*, secs. 45–46, pp. 45–47. Brand, *Byzantium Confronts the West*, pp. 239–40, reverses the numbers of the attacking and guarding battalions.

47. Robert of Clari, *Conquête*, sec. 44, p. 45; Hugh of Saint Pol, *Epistola*, in *MGH, SS*, 17: 814.

48. Robert of Clari, *Conquête*, sec. 45, p. 46.

49. Villehardouin, *Conquête de Constantinople*, sec. 180, 1: 182.

50. Robert of Clari, *Conquête*, sec. 47, pp. 47–49.

51. Ibid., sec. 48, pp. 50–51.

52. Anna Comnena, *The Alexiad*, p. 342; Smail, *Crusading Warfare*, p. 115, n. 1. In fact, a mounted knight was useless against fortifications.

53. Villehardouin has the emperor retreat to the Philopatrion, which was a palace outside the walls. *Conquête de Constantinople*, sec. 180, 1: 182. Other sources, however, have him withdrawing into the city. Robert of Clari, *Conquête*, sec. 48, p. 51; Nicetas, *Historia*, p. 546; Innocent III, *Register*, 6. 210 (211), p. 360 (Migne, *PL*, CCXV: 238).

54. Raimbaut de Vaqueiras, *Poems*, pp. 305 and 310.

55. Robert of Clari, *Conquête*, sec. 48, p. 51.

56. Brand, on the other hand, arranges the chronology differently. He believes that it might have been the news of the Venetian success against the harbor wall that caused Alexius III to return to the city. *Byzantium Confronts the West*, p. 240. This seems unlikely since the crusaders summoned the Venetians to rescue them, presumably when they learned that the emperor had come out of the city in force. The Venetian success had been achieved already at that time.

57. Villehardouin, *Conquête de Constantinople*, sec. 181, 1: 182–84.

58. Robert of Clari, *Conquête*, sec. 50, p. 52.

59. The author of the *Chronicle of Novgorod* (p. 44) gives the fire's devastation as the primary reason for Alexius III's flight.

60. Nicetas, *Historia*, p. 546.

61. Robert of Clari, *Conquête*, sec. 51, p. 52; Hugh of Saint Pol, *Epistola*, in *MGH, SS*, 17: 814.

62. Nicol, *Byzantium and Venice*, p. 110. For the entire gruesome story see Nicetas, *Historia*, pp. 348–51.

63. George Acropolita, *Annales*, in *Corpus scriptorum historiae Byzantinae*, vol. 27 (Bonn, 1836): 7.

64. Nicetas, *Historia*, pp. 485–89.

65. Anonymous of Gaeta, *Qualiter caput beati Theodori martyris de Constantino-politana urbe ad Caietam translatum est*, in *Exuviae*, 1: 152.

66. Linskill, in Raimbaut de Vaqueiras, *Poems*, p. 335, n. to line 58.

67. Nicetas, *Historia*, pp. 546–47.

68. Jean-Claude Cheynet, *Pouvoir et contestations à Byzance (963–1210)* (Paris: Publications de la Sorbonne, 1990), p. 460.

69. Ibid.

70. Nicetas Choniates, *Orationes et Epistulae*, ed. Jan Louis Van Dieten, *Corpus Fontium Historiae Byzantinae*, Series Berolinensis, III (Berlin and New York: De Gruyter, 1972), p. 126; Nicolas Oikonomides, "La décomposition de l'empire byzantin à la veille de 1204 et les origines de l'empire de Nicée: A propos de la *Partitio Romaniae*," in *XVe Congrès international d'études byzantine: Rapports et co-rapports* vol. 1/1 (Athens: Association internationale des études byzantines, 1976), pp. 23–24; Cheynet, *Pouvoir et contestations*, p. 460.

71. Cheynet, *Pouvoir et contestations*, pp. 171–73.

72. Nicetas, *Historia*, pp. 549–50.

73. Ibid., p. 347.

74. Ibid., p. 550.

75. Ibid.; Villehardouin, *Conquête de Constantinople*, sec. 182, 1: 184.

76. Nicetas, *Historia*, pp. 550–51; Villehardouin, *Conquête de Constantinople*, secs. 182–83, 1: 184–86.

77. Villehardouin, *Conquête de Constantinople*, sec. 184, 1: 186–88; Robert of Clari, *Conquête*, sec. 52, p. 52.

78. A letter written by Isaac to Saladin and quoted by Raymond H. Schmandt gives some indication of the Byzantine emperor's duplicity: "[Barbarossa] has experienced every type of deception on the way; the sufferings he has endured and the shortage of his supplies have weakened and troubled him. He will not reach your country in any shape useful to himself or his army." "Orthodoxy and Catholicism: Public Opinion, the Schism, and the Fourth Crusade," *Diakonia* 3 (1968): 295.

79. Villehardouin, *Conquête de Constantinople*, secs. 184–85, 1: 186–88. Van Millingen identifies their entry point as probably Gyrolimne. *Byzantine Constantinople*, p. 127.

80. Janin, *Constantinople byzantine*, pp. 126–27.

81. Nicetas, *Historia*, p. 452.

82. Villehardouin, *Conquête de Constantinople*, sec. 185, 1: 188.

83. Ibid., secs. 186–89, 1: 188–92.

84. Some Western sources obfuscate the restoration of Isaac, probably deliberately. The letter of the crusaders to the pope had Alexius elected during the night and Isaac raised from prison by his son. Innocent III, *Register*, 6: 210 (211), p. 360

(Migne, *PL*, CCXV: 239). Robert of Clari also has Isaac rescued from prison by Alexius, although he does concede the imperial seat to his father. *Conquête*, sec. 52, pp. 52–53. Perhaps Robert tells the story as he honestly viewed it. See also *Devastatio Constantinopolitana*, p. 134 (*MGH, SS*, 16: 11; Hopf ed., p. 89), and Dandolo, *Chronica per extensum descripta*, pp. 278–79.

85. Villehardouin, *Conquête de Constantinople*, sec. 190, 1: 192; Robert of Clari, *Conquête*, sec. 52, pp. 52–53; Nicetas, *Historia*, p. 551; Innocent III, *Register*, 6: 210 (211), p. 360 (Migne, *PL*, CCXV: 239).

86. Rudolf Pokorny, "Zwei unedierte Briefe aus der Frühzeit des lateinischen Kaiserreichs von Konstantinopel," *Byzantion* 55 (1985): 209.

Chapter 9

1. Anna Comnena, *The Alexiad*, pp. 65–66.

2. Nicetas, *Historia*, pp. 243–50; William of Tyre, *Historia*, pp. 1022–24; Cheynet, *Pouvoir et contestations*, pp. 111–12.

3. Villehardouin, *Conquête de Constantinople*, sec. 191, 1: 194; Gunther of Pairis, *Hystoria Constantinopolitana*, p. 142; Innocent III, *Epistolae*, 7: 152, Migne, *PL*, CCXV: 447.

4. Robert of Clari, *Conquête*, sec. 55, pp. 55–56.

5. Ibid.; Villehardouin, *Conquête de Constantinople*, sec. 191, 1: 194. Clari adds that the French and Venetians agreed between themselves to have about a hundred yards of the city wall dismantled to discourage the Greeks from betraying their new allies. Getting the Byzantines to agree to this was another matter, and there is no evidence that any of Constantinople's defensive works were demolished in 1203. That neither Villehardouin nor Nicetas Choniates, who were both in a much better position to know, mention Robert's broken wall makes it very unlikely.

6. Faral in Villehardouin, *Conquête de Constantinople*, 1: 228–29.

7. Brand, *Byzantium Confronts the West*, p. 241.

8. Such is also Riant's opinion. "Innocent III," 18: 43–44; also in *Exuviae*, 1: lxxxiii.

9. See nn. and , above.

10. One wonders whether the date was chosen because of the association of Saint Peter with the Roman See. Professor Andrea has suggested to us that some may have compared the crusaders with the angel of the Lord that broke Peter's chains, just as the Latins had destroyed those of Isaac and Alexius.

11. Innocent III, *Register*, 6: 210 (211), p. 360 (Migne, *PL*, CCXV: 239); Villehardouin, *Conquête de Constantinople*, sec. 193, 1: 196.

12. See Faral, in Villehardouin, *Conquête de Constantinople*, 1: 229, and sources cited there.

13. Nicetas, *Historia*, p. 551.

14. According to the sixteenth-century chronicle of Galeotto del Carretto, young Alexius promised Crete to Boniface at Corfu. *Chronica di Monferrato*, ed. Gustavo Avrogado, in *Monumenta historiae patriae*, 5: 1141. McNeal and Wolff, "Fourth Crusade," p. 177, accept this as probable. If true, he would likely have re-

ceived the island after Alexius's installation. Boniface's transfer of it to the Venetians on 12 August 1204 is well known. *TTh*, 1: 512–15.

15. Villehardouin, *Conquête de Constantinople*, sec. 193, 1: 196.

16. Robert of Clari, *Conquête*, sec. 56, p. 56. Clari's total payment figure is borne out by the Treaty of Partition of March 1204. See Chap. 12, below. The thirty-six thousand marks paid to the Venetians should probably read thirty-four thousand, since that was the outstanding debt. Setton, *Papacy and the Levant*, 1: 11.

17. Faral misinterprets a passage in a letter of the crusaders to the pope to say that at this point they also received provisions for a year and two hundred thousand marks. Villehardouin, *Conquête de Constantinople*, 1: 197, n. 2. As we read the passage the emperor began to pay the sum of money promised under the Treaty of Zara and made new promises in addition. "Hiis peractis, ad solutionem promissorum prosilit Imperator, et promissa rebus accumulat, victualia servitio Domini profutura nobis omnibus praebet in annum; ducenta marcarum millia nobis solvere pergit, et Venetis sumptibus suis stolium prolongat in annum, seque juramento astringit, quod engere nobiscum debeat regale vexillum, et in passagio Martii nobiscum ad servitium Domini proficisci, cum quantis potent millibus armatorum." *TTh*, 1: 431 (Innocent III, *Register*, 6: 210 (211), pp. 360–61 [Migne, *PL*, CCXV: 239]). We translate the crucial passage as follows: "he offers supplies for us all for a year in the future for the service of God; he is proceeding to pay two hundred thousand marks to us." Both verbs are in the present tense. Robert of Auxerre, also using the present, does seem to say that Alexius had performed these things: "restituit precia navium, liberat nostros a debitis Venetorum, victualia omnibus copiose administratet sumptibus suis stolum prologat in annum, ducenta milia marchas argenti nostris et Venetis de imperiali munificentia dilargitur." *Chronicon*, pp. 265–66. Benjamin Hendrickx, "Baudouin IX de Flandre et les empereurs byzantins Isaac II l'Ange et Alexis IV," *Revue belge de philologie et d'histoire* 49 (1971): 486, n. 6, also reads the crusaders' letter as reporting that two hundred thousand marks had been paid. Dandolo refers to an earlier Venetian chronicle that states that the "Franks" were paid, but the Venetians were not. *Chronica per extensum descripta*, pp. 278–79.

18. Villehardouin, *Conquête de Constantinople*, sec. 192, 1: 194.

19. This is from the description given by the twelfth-century traveler Benjamin of Tudela. *Itinerary*, p. 54.

20. Cessi, "Venezia e la quarta crociata," pp. 2–3.

21. Hurter, *Papa Innocenzo III*, 2: 219; quotation from W. B. Yeats, "Sailing to Byzantium."

22. Janin, *Constantinople byzantine*, pp. 59–62; Müller-Weiner, *Bildlexicon zur Topographie Istanbuls*, pp. 248–49; Glanville Downey, "Justinian as Achilles," *Transactions of the American Philological Association* 71 (1940): 70–73.

23. Cyril Mango, *The Brazen House: A Study of Vestibule of the Imperial Palace* (Copenhagen: I kommission hos Munksgaard, 1959), pp. 56–60; Gilbert Dagron, *Naissance d'une capitale: Constantinople et ses institutions de 330 à 451* (Paris: Presses universitaires de France, 1974), pp. 138–39.

24. Müller-Weiner, *Bildlexicon zur Topographie Istanbuls*, pp. 216–18.

25. The literature on the Great Palace is vast. See the bibliography in Müller-Weiner, *Bildlexicon zur Topographie Istanbuls*, p. 237.

26. Van Millingen, *Byzantine Constantinople*, p. 269.

27. Janin, *Constantinople byzantine*, p. 115.

28. Rodolphe Guilland, "Etudes sur l'Hippodrome de Byzance," *Byzantino-slavica* 26 (1965): 12–39; 27 (1966): 26–40; Cyril Mango, Alexander Kazhdan, and Anthony Cutler, s.v. "Hippodromes," *Oxford Dictionary of Byzantium* (Oxford: Oxford University Press, 1991). Cyril Mango has convincingly argued that chariot races in medieval Constantinople were no longer really games of sport, but civic rituals acted out with complex ceremony. "Daily Life in Byzantium," *Jährbuch der Österreichischen Byzantinistik* 31 (1981): 344–49.

29. Rodolphe Guilland, "Etudes sur l'Hippodrome de Byzance," *Byzantino-slavica* 27 (1966): 289–307; 28 (1967): 262–77; 29 (1968): 24–33; J. Théodorides, "Les animaux des jeux de l'Hippodrome et des ménageries impériales à Constantinople," *Byzantinoslavica* 19 (1958): 73–84.

30. Cyril Mango, "L'Euripe de l'hippodrome de Constantinople: Essai d'identi-fication," *Revue des études byzantine* 7 (1949–50): 180–93.

31. Thomas F. Madden, "The Serpent Column of Delphi in Constantinople: Placement, Purposes, and Mutilations," *Byzantine and Modern Greek Studies* 16 (1992): 111–22; Werner Gauer, "Weihgeschenke aus den Perserkriegen," in *Istanbuler Mitteilungen*, Beiheft 2 (1968): 74–96.

32. Erik Iversen, *Obelisks in Exile* (Copenhagen: G. E. C. Gad, 1972), 2: 9–11.

33. Müller-Weiner, *Bildlexicon zur Topographie Istanbuls*, p. 65.

34. Ibid., pp. 255–57; Janin, *Constantinople byzantine*, pp. 77–80.

35. Müller-Weiner, *Bildlexicon zur Topographie Istanbuls*, pp. 258–64; Janin, *Constantinople byzantine*, pp. 81–82.

36. Müller-Weiner, *Bildlexicon zur Topographie Istanbuls*, pp. 250–53.

37. See Chap. 10, note 94 below.

38. Nicholas Mesarites tells how palpably the presence of Christ was felt in Constantinople, thanks to the innumerable relics, and especially the relics of the Nativity and the Passion. A. Frolow, *Recherches sur la déviation de la IVe Croisade vers Constantinople* (Paris, 1955), pp. 63–64. Constantinople did possess the greater part of the surviving remants of the Cross. Ibid., p. 50.

39. For a full interpretation of the importance of the True Cross to the crusaders' motivation, see ibid., pp. 59–71.

40. Robert places his description of the marvels of the city after the account of the second conquest, but he does tell us that after the first conquest the crusaders went to the city whenever they wished. Some of the things he describes, like the Hippodrome statuary, were destroyed after the second conquest. His description, then, probably comes from sight-seeing in 1203. *Conquête*, secs. 82–92, pp. 81–90. The translated portions are from McNeal. See also Regine Colliot, "Fascination de l'or à Byzance d'après le chroniqueur Robert of Clari," *Senefiance* 12 (1983): 89–110.

41. This monastery was founded by John II Comnenus (1118–1143) and had become one of the wealthiest and most important monasteries in the city. Raymond Janin, *La géographie ecclésiastique de l'empire byzantin*, part 1, *Le Siège de Constantinople et le patriarcat oecuménique*, vol. 3, *Les églises et les monastères*, 2d ed. (Paris: L'institut français d'études byzantines, 1969), pp. 515–23. Unlike Holy Apostles, the church is still extant, now a mosque called Zeyrek Kilise Camii. Müller-Weiner, *Bildlexicon zur Topographie Istanbuls*, pp. 209–15.

42. McNeal in Robert of Clari, *Conquest of Constantinople*, p. 17.

43. On Heraclius as a "crusader," see Frolow, *Recherches*, p. 75.

44. According to Procopius, with the outstretched right hand of the statue, the emperor "commands the barbarians in that quarter to remain at home and to advance no farther." *Buildings*, trans. H. B. Dewings (Cambridge, Mass.: Harvard University Press, 1954), p. 35. Actually, the statue did have an inscription on it, but it would have only confused Robert more. On the horse was the inscription: "FON GLORIAE PERENNIS THEODOSI." It seems that Justinian appropriated a colossal bronze horse that had formerly been in an equestrian statue of Theodosius (or at least planned to be) and put his own statue on its back. See P. W. Lehmann, "Theodosius or Justinian? A Renaissance Drawing of a Byzantine Rider," *Art Bulletin* 41 (1959): 39–57.

45. Hopf, *Chroniques gréco-romanes*, p. 68, n. 2; see citations by Philippe Lauer in Robert of Clari, *Conquête*, p. 116.

46. Robert states that the statues used to "play" by enchantment, suggesting they took part in the games. This is similar to the story which appears in the *Saga of Sigurd*, written less than a century earlier. According to the Norse writer, the bronze statues "appear to be living things; and to the people it appears as if they were really present in the games." Snorre Sturlason, *Heimskringla: The Norse King Sagas*, trans. Samuel Laing (New York: Dutton, 1930), p. 286.

47. Benjamin Hendrickx suggests that he could have been the king of Al-Magurra, 'Alwa, or perhaps Ethiopia. "Un roi Africain à Constantinople en 1203," *Byzantina (Thessalonica)* 13 (1985): 895–98.

48. Robert of Clari, *Conquête*, sec. 54, pp. 54–55.

49. Villehardouin, *Conquête de Constantinople*, sec. 192, 1: 194.

50. Nicetas, *Historia*, p. 557. The Greek historian calls Alexius a "foolish, inexperienced child." Ibid., p. 551.

51. Ibid., p. 539. Runciman's observation that "Alexius IV soon found that an emperor cannot be as irresponsible as a pretender" is trenchant. *History of the Crusades*, 3: 19.

52. Nicetas, *Historia*, pp. 551–52.

53. Ibid; cf. George Acropolita, *Annales*, p. 8.

54. Brand, *Byzantium Confronts the West*, p. 140. Alexius III had, however, stripped the imperial tombs in the Church of the Holy Apostles of their precious ornaments to pay the so-called German tax to Henry VI. J. M. Hussey, "The Later Macedonians, the Comneni and the Angeli, 1025–1204," *CMH*, vol. 4, pt. 1 (Cambridge: Cambridge University Press, 1966), pp. 247–48.

55. Innocent III, *Register*, 6: 209 (210), p. 357 (Migne, *PL*, CCXV: 236–37). Brand, *Byzantium Confronts the West*, p. 243, rightly observes that it would have been foolhardy to do so. Setton suggests that Alexius's letter was written by a Western cleric who understood the proper ecclesiological terminology that the pope wanted to hear. *Papacy and the Levant*, 1: 11.

56. See above, Chap. 5, note 60. See also the Nicephorus Chrysoberges's address of 1202 to the patriarch, which extols Camaterus's epistolary victory over the pope, and derides the pontiff as a sniveling barbarian. Robert Browning, "An Unpublished Address of Nicephorus Chrysoberges to Patriarch John X Kamateros of 1202," *Byzantine Studies* 5 (1978): 59–62.

57. Innocent III, *Register*, 6: 229 (230), pp. 388–89 (Migne, *PL*, CCXV: 260–61).

58. Gunther of Pairis, *Hystoria Constantinopolitana*, p. 142.

59. According to Gunther, Alexius's subjects had no qualms about denouncing the emperor's association with the crusaders to his face. Ibid. It was probably done with the flourish and flattery of the oration written for Alexius IV by Nicephorus Chyrsoberges. Brand, "A Byzantine Plan for the Fourth Crusade," pp. 462–75.

60. Villehardouin, *The Conquest of Constantinople*, trans. Shaw, p. 77.

61. Villehardouin, *Conquête de Constantinople*, secs. 194–99, 1: 196–202. The treaty Alexius signed with the Venetians has not survived. The emperor probably agreed to pay around ninety thousand marks for the contract. Madden, "Vows and Contracts in the Fourth Crusade," p. 466.

62. Nicolas Oikonomides, "La décomposition de l'empire byzantin," pp. 16–17; Cheynet, *Pouvoir et contestations*, p. 461.

63. Villehardouin, *Conquête de Constantinople*, sec. 201, 1: 205.

64. Nicetas, *Historia*, p. 556.

65. Villehardouin, *Conquête de Constantinople*, sec. 201, 1: 204–6. Robert of Clari, on the other hand, says that a good half of the host went with Alexius. *Conquête*, sec. 57, p. 57. Villehardouin, sec. 203, 1: 206–8, and Robert of Clari in the passage just cited indicate that Alexius was out of the city with the expeditionary force before the time of the great fire, which broke out on 19 August. The letter from Alexius IV to Innocent III offering submission to Rome is somewhat troublesome, since it is dated in *Urbe Regia VIII Kal. Septembris*, which would seem to place Alexius in Constantinople at the time of the fire. Innocent III, *Registor*, 6: 209 (210), p. 358 (Migne, *PL*, CCXV: 237). Could the document have been prepared before his departure, but issued with the date a few days later?

66. Villehardouin, *Conquête de Constantinople*, sec. 200, 1: 204.

67. Nicetas, *Historia*, p. 556.

68. Ibid.; Villehardouin, *Conquête de Constantinople*, sec. 203, 1: 206; Robert of Clari, *Conquête*, sec. 57, p. 57.

69. Nicetas describes the expedition after his account of the riot and the fire (Historia, pp. 552–56) but this is not the correct chronological sequence. Nicetas frequently groups events thematically rather than chronologically. The *Devastatio Constantinopolitana* also relates the riot and fire before the expedition, but it begins its description of the latter with *interea*, thus implying that the emperor was absent when the conflagration erupted (p. 135 [*MGH, SS*, 16: 11; Hopf ed., pp. 89–90]).

70. Nicetas, *Historia*, p. 553; *Devastatio Constantinopolitana*, p. 135 (*MGH, SS*, 16: 11; Hopf ed., p. 89). For the dating of the riot and fire, see Madden, "Fires of the Fourth Crusade," p. 74, n. 12.

71. Horatio Brown, "The Venetians and the Venetian Quarter in Constantinople to the Close of the Twelfth Century," *Journal of Hellenic Studies* 40 (1920): 75–76.

72. Nicetas, *Historia*, p. 552.

73. Hubaldus of Pisa, *Das Imbreviaturbuch des Erzbischöflichen Gerichtsnotars Hubaldus aus Pisa*, ed. Gero Dolezalek (Cologne-Vienna: Böhlau, 1969), p. 32.

74. Nicetas, *Historia*, p. 552.

75. Madden, "Fires of the Fourth Crusade," pp. 76–77.

76. Ibid., p. 553.

77. For the identification and location of the mosque, see Madden, "Fires of the Fourth Crusade," pp. 75–76.

78. According to the *Devastatio Constantinopolitana*, p. 134 (Hopf ed., p. 89), the

expedition's goal was to aid Latins in the city who were under attack. This is unlikely since the riot had abated, probably the previous day, and most of the Latins had already fled. The author of the *Devastatio* seems to be collapsing the events of 18 and 19 August together. See the fuller discussion in Madden, "Fires of the Fourth Crusade," p. 77.

79. Nicetas, *Historia*, p. 553.

80. Madden, "Fires of the Fourth Crusade," pp. 76–77.

81. Nicetas, *Historia*, p. 553–54; Magoulias trans., p. 303.

82. Villehardouin, *Conquête de Constantinople*, sec. 203, 1: 208.

83. Nicetas, *Historia*, p. 587.

84. Madden, "Fires of the Fourth Crusade," pp. 77–83.

85. Ibid., p. 74.

86. Ibid., pp. 83–84, 86–87.

87. Nicetas, *Historia*, p. 587.

88. Madden, "Fires of the Fourth Crusade," p. 88.

89. Villehardouin, *Conquête de Constantinople*, sec. 205, 1: 210.

90. Madden, "Fires of the Fourth Crusade," p. 77.

91. Villehardouin, *Conquête de Constantinople*, sec. 205, 1: 210.

Chapter 10

1. Robert of Clari, *Conquête*, sec. 57, p. 57. They returned on Saint Martin's Day, 11 November. Villehardouin, *Conquête de Constantinople*, sec. 207, 2: 6.

2. *Devastatio Constantinopolitana*, p. 135 *(MGH, SS*, 16: 11; Hopf ed., p. 90). The author adds that Boniface remained with the army with "a few Christians."

3. A few well-connected Latins still remained. A Venetian wine merchant named Domenico was able to remain in the city, protected by Nicetas Choniates. Domenico later returned the favor after the fall of the city. Nicetas, *Historia*, p. 588; Magoulias trans., p. 407, n. 1598.

4. Robert of Clari, *Conquête*, sec. 57, p. 57.

5. This is Robert's conclusion. Ibid., sec. 57, pp. 57–58.

6. Villehardouin, *Conquête de Constantinople*, sec. 207, 2: 6.

7. Ibid.; Nicetas, *Historia*, p. 556. On the Byzantine triumphal rituals, see Michael McCormick, *Eternal Victory: Triumphal Rulership in Late Antiquity, Byzantium, and the Early Medieval West* (Cambridge: Cambridge University Press, 1986), pp. 189–230.

8. Nicetas, *Historia*, p. 556–57.

9. Robert of Clari, *Conquête*, sec. 57, p. 58; Villehardouin, *Conquête de Constantinople*, sec. 207, 2: 6–8.

10. Villehardouin, *Conquête de Constantinople*, sec. 208, 2: 8.

11. Usseglio, *I marchesi di Monferrato*, 2: 229.

12. Cheynet, *Pouvoir et contestations*, pp. 459–65.

13. The patriarch of Constantinople, John Camaterus, was likely also a member of this faction. Letter of Baldwin of Flanders, in Innocent III, *Epistolae*, 7: 152, Migne, *PL*, CCXV: 447–48. See Brand, *Byzantium Confronts the West*, pp. 242–43, and

"A Byzantine Plan for the Fourth Crusade," p. 463. Brand asserts that Isaac II and his faction controlled the state before Alexius's progress through Thrace. Alexius IV then joined forces with the members of the faction of Alexius III who had been responsible for blinding Isaac. With their help, Alexius IV was able to take over the court. This scenario, however, contradicts Nicetas, who records that upon his return to the palace Alexius IV ordered all those involved with Isaac's blinding and deposition to be hung. Nicetas, *Historia*, p. 556.

14. Madden, "Vows and Contracts in the Fourth Crusade," p. 447.

15. Nicetas, *Historia*, p. 561.

16. See his words of caution to the mob against electing a new emperor in January 1204. Nicetas, *Historia*, p. 562.

17. Villehardouin, *Conquête de Constantinople*, sec. 208, 2: 8.

18. Nicephorus Chrysoberges, *Ad Angelos orationes tres*, ed. Maximilian Treu (Breslau, 1892), p. 28; trans. Brand, "A Byzantine Plan for the Fourth Crusade," p. 467.

19. Baldwin says that he was influenced by his father, the patriarch, and the mass of the nobles. In Innocent III, *Epistolae*, 7: 152, Migne, *PL*, CCXV: 447–48.

20. Villehardouin, *Conquête de Constantinople*, sec. 208, 2: 8.

21. Nicetas, *Historia*, p. 561 is the source for the meaning of Alexius Ducas's nickname. K. P. Symeonides has suggested that it may also have meant sullen or melancholy. "Τὸ βυζαντινὸ παρωνύμιο 'Μούρτζουφλος,'" *Byzantina* 13 (1985): 1621–28.

22. Alberic of Trois-Fontaines, *Chronica*, p. 870, Gunther of Pairis, *Hystoria Constantinopolitana*, p. 143; Cheynet, *Pouvoir et contestations*, p. 129; Benjamin Hendrickx and Corinna Matzukis, "Alexios V Doukas Mourtzouphlos: His Life, Reign, and Death (?–1204)," *Hellenika* 31 (1979): 111; Brand, *Byzantium Confronts the West*, pp. 248–49.

23. Nicholas Mesarites, *Die Palastrevolution des Johannes Komnenos*, ed. A. Heisenberg (Würzburg: Konigl. Universitatsdruckerei von H. Sturtz, 1907); Cheynet, *Pouvoir et contestations*, pp. 136–37.

24. Nicetas, *Historia*, p. 528; Robert of Clari, *Conquête*, sec. 52, p. 53; sec. 58, p. 58; sec. 61, p. 61; Hendrickx and Matzukis, "Alexios V Doukas Mourtzouphlos," pp. 112–13.

25. Brand, *Byzantium Confronts the West*, p. 248. Hendrickx and Matzukis dispute Brand's assertion, arguing that there is no evidence that anti-Latinism led Mourtzouphlus to support John Comnenus in 1201 as Brand suggests. They therefore doubt that Mourtzouphlus led an anti-Latin faction in 1203; in fact, they doubt the very existence of such a faction in the aristocracy. "Alexios V Doukas Mourtzouphlos," pp. 117–18. Yet even Hendrickx and Matzukis are forced to accept that Mourtzouphlus became fiercely anti-Latin after Alexius IV's return from his campaign in Thrace. That is the extent of our concern here.

26. Hendrickx and Matzukis, "Alexios V Doukas Mourtzouphlos," p. 111.

27. Baldwin of Flanders, in Innocent III, *Epistolae*, 7: 152, Migne, *PL* CCXV: 448; Nicetas, *Historia*, p. 563; Villehardouin, *Conquête de Constantinople*, sec. 221, 2: 20.

28. Nicetas, *Historia*, p. 566.

29. For a brief sketch of Mourtzouphlus, see Usseglio, *I marchesi di Monferrato*, 2: 230.

30. Nicetas, *Historia*, p. 566.

31. Ibid.

32. *Chronicle of Novgorod*, p. 45. The context does not inspire confidence in the accuracy of details, although the author does have the gist of what happened.

33. Brand, "A Byzantine Plan for the Fourth Crusade," p. 473.

34. Nicetas, *Historia*, p. 565

35. Ibid., pp. 556–57.

36. Ibid., pp. 557–58.

37. Cognasso, "Un imperatore bizantino della decadenza: Isaaco II Angelo," p. 40.

38. Nicetas, *Historia*, pp. 557–58.

39. Robert of Clari, *Conquête*, sec. 58, p. 58.

40. Villehardouin, *Conquête de Constantinople*, sec. 209, 1: 8. The same sentiment occurs in the letter written by Baldwin of Flanders to the pope in 1204 after he had become the Latin emperor: ". . . et ex insperato seu innata malitia, seu graecorum seductus perfidia animo recedit a nobis, qui tanta beneficia contulimus, imperator, et in omnibus cum patre, patriarcho, et mole nobilium, nobis promissis periuris et mendax tot incurrit periuria, quot nobis praestitit iuramenta." Innocent III, *Epistolae*, V2: 152, Migne, *PL*, CCXV: 447–48.

41. Villehardouin, *Conquête de Constantinople*, sec. 208, 2: 8.

42. Runciman, *History of the Crusades*, 3: 119.

43. Robert of Clari, *Conquête de Constantinople*, sec. 58, p. 58.

44. Gunther of Pairis, *Hystoria Constantinopolitana*, p. 142; Andrea, "The *Historia Constantinopolitana*," p. 297.

45. Brand identifies the Latins as "tourists," but given the great hatred most Greeks felt for Latins in the wake of the great fire, it would seem that the time for touring had passed. *Byzantium Confronts the West*, p. 248. Runciman states that Mourtzouphlus "organized" the riot, for which there is no evidence. *History of the Crusades*, 3: 120.

46. ". . . qui tam temere contra Grecos arma moverant." *Devastatio Constantinopolitana*, p. 135 *(MGH, SS,* 16: 11; Hopf ed., p. 90).

47. Ibid.

48. Madden, "Vows and Contracts in the Fourth Crusade," pp. 448–49.

49. *Devastatio Constantinopolitana*, p. 135 (*MGH, SS,* 16: 11; Hopf, p. 90).

50. Villehardouin, *Conquête de Constantinople*, sec. 210, 2: 8–10; Madden, "Vows and Contracts in the Fourth Crusade," p. 448, n. 1.

51. Villehardouin, *Conquête de Constantinople*, secs. 211–14, 2: 10–12.

52. See p. 143 above.

53. Madden, "Vows and Contracts in the Fourth Crusade," p. 449.

54. Alexius's response to the envoys is frequently misunderstood by historians. The confusion arises from Robert of Clari's multiple accounts of Alexius's attitude toward his indebtedness to the crusaders. In his typical style, Robert attempts to explain events that affected him by inventing the conversations of high men. He relates that in a private conversation between Alexius and Mourtzouplus, the latter advised the emperor that he had already paid the crusaders too much and should not pay them more; *Conquête*, sec. 58, p. 58. Robert then describes all of the counts and barons of the host visiting Alexius and demanding payment. Here Alexius responds that he can pay

them no more—still not an outright refusal to pay. In response the knights issue a defiance and depart. Ibid. Finally, according to Robert, two knights were sent as envoys to Alexius to again request payment. At this meeting Robert has Alexius say the words that he imagines Mourtzouphlus gave to him: "he would not pay them anything and he had already paid them too much." Ibid., sec. 59, pp. 58–59. As a lowly knight, not privy to the doings of the mighty, Robert is doing his best to explain the situation, but his relations of diplomatic meetings should not be accepted over those of Villehardouin, who was there and took part in the discussion. Brand uses Villehardouin's account of the meeting, but injects Robert's version of Alexius's reply. *Byzantium Confronts the West*, p. 249. In the first edition of this book, Queller repeated this error. *The Fourth Crusade*, pp. 126–27. Godfrey states that Alexius protested to the crusaders that he had already paid them a great deal and implored them to leave his lands. Godfrey cites Villehardouin who says nothing of the kind. *1204: The Unholy Crusade*, p. 116. Also citing Villehardouin, Nicol states that "the emperor was stung to reply that he would not pay a penny more to such insolent persons." *Byzantium and Venice*, p. 140. Fine does not appear to rely on any sources when he writes, "the crusaders issued an ultimatum that Alexius deliver on his promises immediately or else they would re-take the city." *Late Medieval Balkans*, p. 62.

55. Villehardouin, *Conquête de Constantinople*, secs. 215–16, 2: 14.

56. Ibid., sec. 216, 2: 14.

57. In his confused way, Robert appends to his story another meeting between the emperor and a prominent crusader, this time Doge Dandolo. As Faral has argued, in Villehardouin, *Conquête de Constantinople*, 2: 15, n. 1, this is surely a confused and misplaced account of the later meeting between Dandolo and Mourtzouphlus. Still, it is worth quoting for its revelation of the feelings of the men in the ranks. Dandolo said: "Alexius, what do you think you are doing? Just think how we rescued you from great wretchedness, and made you lord, and crowned you emperor. Will you not keep your agreements with us?" To which Alexius replied that he would do no more for them. "No?" said Dandolo. "Evil boy! We pulled you out of shit, and into shit we will throw you back! I defy you, and let you know for certain that I will do you all the harm in my power." *Conquête*, sec. 59, p. 59. In this we have rejected the customary euphemisms to better express the feelings of the Latin troops.

58. "Ensi comença la guerre . . ." Villehardouin, *Conquête de Constantinople*, sec. 216, 2: 14.

59. Robert of Clari, *Conquête*, sec. 60, pp. 59–60.

60. Cf. Nicetas, *Historia*, p. 560; Villehardouin, *Conquête de Constantinople*, sec. 216, 2: 14; sec. 226, 2: 25; *Devastatio Constantinopolitana*, pp. 135–36 (*MGH, SS*, 16: 11; Hopf ed., p. 91).

61. *TTh*, 1: 505.

62. Robert's confusion may arise from his defective understanding of the meeting between Dandolo and Mourtzouphlus, which actually occurred in February 1204. Robert puts it in December 1203 and substitutes Alexius for Mourtzouphlus. His assertion about the delay in preparing the vessels for an attack on Constantinople immediately follows this episode. *Conquête de Constantinople*, secs. 59–60, pp. 59–60.

63. "Forfist qui forfaire pot." Villehardouin, *Conquête de Constantinople*, sec. 216, 2: 14.

64. Robert of Clari, *Conquête*, sec. 58, p. 58.

65. Nicetas, *Historia*, p. 560; *Devastatio Constantinopolitana*, p. 136 (*MGH, SS*, 16: 11; Hopf ed., p. 91).

66. Villehardouin, *Conquête de Constantinople*, sec. 216, 2: 14; Nicetas, *Historia*, p. 560.

67. On the justness of this course of action, see Schmandt, "Fourth Crusade and the Just War Theory," p. 217, n. 72.

68. Madden, "Vows and Contracts in the Fourth Crusade," p. 451.

69. Ibid.

70. See Nicetas's assessment of Alexius's strategy; *Historia*, p. 562.

71. Gunther of Pairis, *Hystoria Constantinopolitana*, p. 142; Madden, "Vows and Contracts in the Fourth Crusade," p. 452; Andrea, "Conrad of Krosigk," p. 46.

72. Nicetas, *Historia*, pp. 560–61; Magoulias trans., p. 307.

73. Nicetas, *Historia*, p. 561.

74. This is the implication of his assessment of the eventualities should the populace elect a rival emperor. Ibid., p. 562.

75. Hendrickx and Matzukis suggest that Mourtzouphlus instigated the fire ship attacks. "Alexios V Doukas Mourtzouphlos," p. 116. While possible, there is no evidence for it. In any event, it would not have been against Alexius IV's wishes.

76. Robert of Clari, *Conquête*, sec. 60, pp. 59–60; Baldwin of Flanders, in Innocent III, *Epistolae*, 7: 152, Migne, *PL*, CCXV: 448.

77. *Devastatio Constantinopolitana*, p. 135 (*MGH, SS*, 16: 11; Hopf ed., p. 91).

78. Villehardouin, *Conquête de Constantinople*, secs. 217–20, 2: 16–18; Robert of Clari, *Conquête*, sec. 60, p. 60; *Devastatio Constantinopolitana*, p. 135 (*MGH, SS*, 16: 11; Hopf ed., p. 91). Baldwin of Flanders in his letter to Innocent III and others (Innocent III, *Epistolae*, 7: 152, Migne, *PL*, CCXV: 449) places this second attack after the ascension to the throne of Alexius Ducas, probably erroneously. See Faral, in Villehardouin, *Conquête de Constantinople*, 2: 17, n. 1. Hendrickx and Matzukis accept Baldwin, arguing that there were at least three fire ship attacks. "Alexios V Doukas Mourtzouphlos," pp. 122–23, n. 5. This conclusion would be strengthened if Baldwin, or any other source, mentioned three attacks.

79. Robert of Clari, *Conquête*, sec. 60, p. 60.

80. Alberic of Trois-Fontaines, *Chronica*, p. 882.

81. Robert of Clari, *Conquête*, sec. 60, p. 60.

82. Alberic of Trois-Fontaines, *Chronica*, pp. 882–83.

83. The two sources for this sortie are Nicetas Choniates and the *Devastatio Constantinopolitana*. Both see it from different points of view. Nicetas gives no exact date for the sortie, but does supply information about the Greek commander, Mourtzouphlus. The *Devastatio* gives the precise date and the name of the Latin commander, Boniface of Montferrat. Given the extreme paucity of Greek sorties against the Latins at this time, it seems certain that the two sources are referring to the same event. See Faral in Villehardouin, *Conquête de Constantinople*, 2: 15, n. 2.

84. Ibid., p. 561.

85. Janin, *Constantinople byzantine*, p. 467; Heyd, *Commerce du Levant*, 1: 210, n. 1, and "Nuova serie di documenti sulle relazioni di Genova coll' impero bizantino," ed. Angelo Sanguineti and Gerolamo Bertolotto, *Atti della Società Ligure di Storia Patria* 28 (1896–98): 346.

86. Nicetas, *Historia*, p. 561.

87. *Devastatio Constantinopolitana*, pp. 135–36 (*MGH, SS*, 16: 11; Hopf ed., p. 91).

88. Nicetas, *Historia*, p. 561.

89. *Devastatio Constantinopolitana*, pp. 135–36 (*MGH, SS*, 16: 11; Hopf ed., p. 91). Baldwin of Flanders also tells of another skirmish, which probably occurred around this time. He gives no date, but it appears after a discussion of the second fire ship attack. Unfortunately, Baldwin misplaces the second fire ship attack, putting it after Mourtzouphlus took the throne. According to the story, the crusaders were crossing the bridge at the head of the Golden Horn and took up a position before one of the gates near the Blachernae Palace. They drew up in wedge-shaped formations with the cross borne before them. A single Byzantine noble foolishly, if valorously, sought to prove his mettle by an unsupported charge upon the army. He met the hero's death he apparently sought. In Innocent III, *Epistolae*, 7: 152, Migne, *PL*, CCXV: 449.

90. Nicetas, *Historia*, p. 561.

91. Ibid., pp. 558–59.

92. See R. J. Jenkins, "The Bronze Athena at Byzantium," *Journal of Hellenic Studies* 67 (1947): 31–33; idem, "Further Evidence Regarding the Bronze Athena at Byzantium," *Annual of the British School at Athens* 46 (1951): 72–74. The latter argues, based on miniatures in Byzantine texts, for the theory of the missing shaft.

93. Nicetas, *Historia*, pp. 558–59.

94. Both columns were believed to bear prophecies in their reliefs, but the Arcadius column seems to have had a longer tradition of such properties. See *Scriptores originum constantinopolitanarum*, ed. Theodor Preger (Leipzig: B. G. Teubneri, 1901–7), 2: 176–80; Gilbert Dagron, *Constantinople imaginaire: Etudes sur le recueil des "Patria"* (Paris: Presses universitaires de France, 1984), p. 149.

95. Robert of Clari, *Conquête*, sec. 92, p. 89; Gunther of Pairis, *Hystoria Constantinopolitana*, p. 166.

96. Stanley Casson and David Talbot Rice, *Second Report upon the Excavations Carried Out In or Near the Hippodrome of Constantinople in 1928* (London: Oxford University Press, 1929), pp. 57–60; Janin, *Constantinople byzantine*, pp. 81–82; Müller-Wiener, *Bildlexicon zur Topographie Istanbuls*, p. 264.

97. E. H. Freshfield, "Notes on a Vellum Album Containing Some Original Sketches of Public Buildings and Monuments, Drawn by a German Artist Who Visited Constantinople in 1574," *Archaeologia* 72 (1921–22): plates 15–23.

98. Nicetas, *Historia*, pp. 561–62; Magoulias trans., pp. 307–8. The biblical reference is Isaiah 3:6. Nicetas quotes only the first part of the sentence ("You have raiment, you be our leader . . ."), but the second half, which he knew, is equally appropriate.

99. *Chronicle of Novgorod*, p. 45. The *Chronicle* errs, however, when it places Isaac II's death before this insurrection.

100. Ibid.; Nicetas, *Historia*, p. 562. Alberic of Trois-Fontaines wrongly dates this after the skirmish in which Mourtzouphlus lost the icon. *Chronica, MGH, SS*, 23: 883. The *Devastatio Constantinopolitana* mentions the event, but gives Nicholas's surname as "Macellarius," p. 136 (Hopf ed., p. 91).

101. *Chronicle of Novgorod*, p. 45.

102. Nicetas, *Historia*, p. 563; *Chronicle of Novgorod*, p. 45; Baldwin of Flanders, in Innocent III, *Epistolae*, 7: 152, Migne, *PL*, CCXV: 448. Brand casts Mourtzouphlus

as the crafty adviser who treacherously gave Alexius IV the idea of reintroducing the Latins. Mourtzouphlus's purpose, according to this theory, was to create an anti-Latin revolution that would put him on the throne in place of the tainted young emperor. *Byzantium Confronts the West*, p. 250. While an interesting theory, it lacks supporting evidence. One indication that it is not true is the failure of Nicetas to mention it, thus passing up a good opportunity to vilify further his enemy, Mourtzouphlus. The question is not whether Mourtzouphlus was treacherous, but whether he initiated the embassy to Boniface. The scenario also seems far too risky from Mourtzouphlus's standpoint. To grasp the throne he would have to invite his enemy, Boniface, back into the imperial court. The protovestiarius could not know that Boniface would wait until the following day to bring troops into the city.

103. Hendrickx and Matzukis reject that Mourtzouphlus was the messenger sent to the crusader camp because Baldwin of Flanders is the source and Nicetas Choniates does not mention it. They also contend that had Mourtzouphlus acted as messenger he would not have had sufficient time to effect his coup. "Alexios V Doukas Mourtzouphlos," pp. 118–19. On the merits of both sources, see note 104 below. We do not accept, furthermore, that the retrieval of Boniface required all that much time. It was obviously concluded in sufficient time for Boniface and Alexius to confer extensively in the palace. This was more than enough time for Mourtzouphlus to perform the few necessaries for his clever imprisonment of Alexius.

104. Baldwin of Flanders, in Innocent III, *Epistolae*, 7: 152, Migne, *PL*, CCXV: 448. There are two sources for the meeting of Alexius IV and Boniface of Montferrat: Baldwin of Flanders' letter to Innocent III after he became emperor and Nicetas Choniates's history. Both are secondhand and they differ enormously. Generally Baldwin is the better source for events in the crusader camp, while Nicetas is superior for events in Byzantium. In this case, the identification of the envoy who escorted Boniface to the palace comes from Baldwin, who may have been present when the surprise visitor arrived. Baldwin goes on to say, however, that when Boniface arrived at court, Alexius greeted the marquis with scorn and derision. This is very unlikely. Baldwin's account to the pope was meant to excuse the conquest of Constantinople. It is not surprising, then, that it greatly exaggerates Greek sins and avoids any discussion of Latin transgressions. It seems that Baldwin is simply casting Alexius as a typically deceptive Greek. It has been suggested that Baldwin's account may be correct, and that Alexius's abrupt change of heart occurred because Greek nobles got wind of the secret deliberations. Alexius was, therefore, attempting to forestall a coup by deriding the chief Latin. This theory rests on shaky ground, however, for it relies on the gossipy and ill-informed *Chronicle of Novgorod* (p. 45) for its disaffected aristocracy. It also makes little sense. The coup against Alexius was caused by his acceptance of Latin aid, not his rejection of it. Nicetas, on the other hand, had excellent information and was familiar with court activities. Furthermore, he lacked a motive to fabricate a story since he hated all the participants equally—Alexius, Boniface, and Mourtzouphlus. We have, therefore, favored Nicetas's account for events in Alexius's court when it contradicts Baldwin's.

105. According to Baldwin of Flanders, the agreement was worked out in the crusader camp between Boniface and Mourtzouphlus. In Innocent III, *Epistolae*, 7: 152, Migne, *PL*, CCXV: 448

106. Nicetas, *Historia*, pp. 562–63; Baldwin of Flanders, in Innocent III, *Epistolae*, 7: 152, Migne, *PL*, CCXV: 448. According to Baldwin, Mourtzouphlus offered

Blachernae Palace to the crusaders as security on the outstanding debt when he crossed over to meet with Boniface. Nicetas, on the other hand, states clearly that Boniface was "to bring Latin forces into the palace to expel the new emperor and the populace who had elected him assembly." Magoulias trans., p. 308. Since Hagia Sophia was considered part of the Great Palace complex, this suggests that the crusaders were to occupy that palace and then hold it as security.

107. Nicetas, *Historia*, p. 563; *Chronicle of the Morea*, p. 88.

108. Nicetas, *Historia*, p. 563.

109. Ibid.

110. This was a lie. Neither Alexius's relations nor the Varangians were outside the palace. Blöndal asserts that the Varangian actually staged a riot of sorts to bolster Mourtzouphlus's claims. *The Varangians of Byzantium*, p. 165. As bodyguard, the Varangians were stationed inside the palace, indeed right outside the emperor's bedroom. If they had wished to take an active role in the coup they would not have moved outside the palace simply to make noise.

111. Nicetas, *Historia*, pp. 563–64; Villehardouin, *Conquête de Constantinople*, sec. 222, 2: 20–22; Baldwin of Flanders, in Innocent III, *Epistolae*, 7: 152, Migne, *PL*, CCXV: 148.

112. Nicetas, *Historia*, p. 564; Magoulias trans., pp. 308–9.

113. *Chronicle of Novgorod*, p. 45.

114. *Devastatio Constantinopolitana*, p. 136 (*MGH, SS*, XVI: 12; Hopf ed., p. 91); Nicetas, *Historia*, p. 564; Baldwin of Flanders, in Innocent III, *Epistolae*, 7: 152, Migne, *PL*, CCXV: 448; Alberic of Trois-Fontaines, *Chronica*, p. 883.

115. Nicetas, *Historia*, p. 562; Villehardouin, *Conquête de Constantinople*, sec. 223, 2: 22.

116. Brand, *Byzantium Confronts the West*, pp. 76, 114, and 115.

117. Hussey, "The Later Macedonians, the Comneni, and the Angeli, 1025–1204," p. 247. Hussey's judgment is harsher and lacks the nuances of Brand's.

118. Brand, *Byzantium Confronts the West*, pp. 113–14.

119. Nicetas, *Historia*, p. 448.

120. According to Gunther of Pairis, Mourtzouphlus concealed his coup against Alexius and then sent messengers to the crusaders in the young man's name, hoping to lure the Latin leaders into a trap. His scheme was foiled by the ever-cautious Dandolo, who suspected the ploy. *Hystoria Constantinopolitana*, pp. 144–45. Aside from the logistics of keeping secret from the Latins what the population of Constantinople knew for days, Gunther's story has other serious flaws. He ignores the imprisonment of Alexius, putting this subterfuge after Alexius's death, when we know Mourtzouphlus was openly proclaiming that the young man had died naturally (a deception of a different sort). Andrea has pointed out that no other source mentions this scheme, suggesting that Gunther fabricated it for embellishment. He further notes that given both Villehardouin's and Clari's insistence on the sagacity of Enrico Dandolo, it is odd that neither mentions this excellent example of it. Andrea, ed., *The Capture of Constantinople: The "Hystoria Constantinopolitana,"* chap. 14, nn. 166 and 170. Most scholars accept Gunther's account; e.g., Brand, *Byzantium Confronts the West*, p. 252; Hendrickx and Matzukis, "Alexios V Doukas Mourtzouphlos," pp. 121, 124; Godfrey, *1204: The Unholy Crusade*, p. 117.

121. Villehardouin, *Conquête de Constantinople*, sec. 222, 2: 20.

122. Robert of Clari, *Conquête*, sec. 66, p. 65. Alberic of Trois-Fontaines says a thousand men. *Chronica, MGH, SS*, 23: 883. So does Baldwin. In Innocent III, *Epistolae*, 7: 152, Migne, *PL*, CCXV: 449. Villehardouin says that he took a great part of the best men. *Conquête de Constantinople*, sec. 226, 2: 24. The *Devastatio Constantinopolitana*, p. 136 (*MGH, SS*, 16: 12; Hopf, ed. p. 91), describes them only as "a large number of knights and footsoldiers."

123. Villehardouin, *Conquête de Constantinople*, sec. 226, 2: 24; Robert of Clari, *Conquête*, sec. 66, p. 65; Baldwin of Flanders, in Innocent III, *Epistolae*, 7: 152, Migne, *PL*, CCXV: 449; Alberic of Trois-Fontaines, *Chronica, MGH, SS*, 23: 883; *Devastatio Constantinopolitana*, p. 136 (*MGH, SS*, 16: 12; Hopf, ed. p. 91); Nicetas, *Historia*, p. 567. Nicetas incorrectly attributes the raid to Baldwin of Flanders.

124. *Chronicle of Novgorod*, p. 46; Villehardouin, *Conquête de Constantinople*, sec. 222, 2: 20–22. Clari mistakenly places the coronation after the death of Alexius IV. *Conquête*, sec. 62, p. 61. Nicetas omits any mention of Mourtzouphlus's coronation. Given his rapid fall from grace under the new emperor, this is not surprising. Nicetas does, however, provide a date for the crowning by means of the reign duration of two months and sixteen days, which refers to the night of 28 January when Mourtzouphlus imprisoned Alexius IV. *Historia*, p. 571. This was when the usurper donned the imperial insignia and was proclaimed by his faction as emperor, but his formal crowning in Hagia Sophia was not until 5 February.

125. According to Villehardouin, Henry of Flanders' raid occurred around 2 February. It took one day to reach Philia, and the knights remained there for two days before returning. *Conquête de Constantinople*, secs 226–28, 2: 24–28. If they left on 2 February, then, they would have arrived on 3 February, remained there on 4 February, and returned on 5 or 6 February. All sources put the ambush after Mourtzouphlus's coronation.

126. Clari's figures for Mourtzouphlus's troop strength seem the most reasonable. He fixes it at four thousand men. *Conquête*, sec. 66, pp. 65. Alberic of Trois-Fontaines says ten thousand. *Chronica, MGH, SS*, 23: 883. The *Devastatio Constantinopolitana*, p. 136 (*MGH, SS*, XVI: 12; Hopf ed., p. 91) says fifteen thousand. Alberic says that he took so many because of fear that those remaining might try to prevent his reentry.

127. On the role of the Virgin, her icons, and relics in protecting Constantinople and its environs, see Norman Baynes, "The Supernatural Defenders of Constantinople," *Analecta Bollandiana* 67 (1949): 171–76.

128. Villehardouin, *Conquête de Constantinople*, secs. 226–28, 2: 24–28; Robert of Clari, *Conquête*, sec. 66, pp. 65–67; Nicetas, *Historia*, pp. 567; *Devastatio Constantinopolitana*, p. 136 (*MGH, SS*, 16: 12; Hopf ed., p. 91); Baldwin of Flanders, in Innocent III, *Epistolae*, 7: 152, Migne, *PL*, CCXV: 449. Alberic of Trois-Fontaines gives a very colorful account of this ambush, most of which is pure invention. According to Alberic, Mourtzouphlus's vanguard was commanded by a certain Peter of Navarre, who proudly rode into battle unhelmed, his head encircled by a band of gold. Henry of Flanders is supposed to have dealt Peter so hard a blow on the head that his sword broke the gold band and split his skull to the depth of two fingers. Alberic also reports that the patriarch of Constantinople, Samson, took part in the battle and carried the icon. Peter of Bracieux, he continues, killed the patriarch, who then dropped the icon. Courageously, Peter dismounted in the swirl of battle to pick up the precious object.

Chronica, MGH, SS, 23: 882–83. The greatest problem with Alberic's testimony is that it is seldom reliable on other events, and it contradicts Clari, who may well have been an eyewitness to the ambush. It was also not written until 1241. More damning for this story is the fact that no other source mentions the patriarch taking part in the battle. The patriarch's name was also not Samson, but John X Camaterus. John Camaterus, in fact, did not die in 1204, but rather in exile in Bulgaria on 26 June 1206. Nicetas, *Historia,* p. 633; P. Wirth, "Zur Frage eines politischen Engagements Patriarch Johannes' X. Kamateros nach dem vierten Kreuzzug," *Byzantinische Forschungen* 6 (1972): 248–51; Papadakis and Talbot, "John X Camateros," p. 27; Spiteris, *La critica bizantina del primato Romano,* pp. 253–54. Professor Queller humbly confesses to having followed the colorful account of Alberic in the first edition of this book.

129. Robert of Clari, *Conquête,* sec. 66, p. 67.

130. Alberic of Trois-Fontaines, *Chronica, MGH, SS,* 23: 883. Alberic again may be stretching the truth, but Clari confirms that the icon was very richly adorned. *Conquête,* sec. 66, p. 67.

131. Robert of Clari, *Conquête,* sec. 66, p. 67; Alberic of Trois-Fontaines, *Chronica, MGH, SS,* 23: 883; Baldwin of Flanders, in Innocent III, *Epistolae,* 7: 152, Migne, *PL,* CCXV: 449. Andrea, "The *Historia Constantinopolitana,*" p. 274, n. 18.

132. Nicetas, *Historia,* p. 566.

133. Ibid., p. 565.

134. Ibid., p. 566.

135. Ibid., p. 565.

136. Ibid., p. 566; Hendrickx and Matzukis, "Alexios V Doukas Mourtzouphlos," p. 126.

137. Robert of Clari, *Conquête,* secs. 66–67, pp. 67–68.

138. The date is given by Baldwin, who places the meeting the day before the murder of Alexius, which occurred on 8 February. In Innocent III, *Epistolae,* 7: 152, Migne, *PL,* CCXV: 450; and note below.

139. Nicetas, *Historia,* pp. 567–68; Magoulias trans., p. 312.

140. In Innocent III, *Epistolae,* 7: 152, Migne, *PL,* CCXV: 449–50. Brand interprets the incident described by Nicetas as a personal meeting distinct from what he believes was a written correspondence described by Baldwin. That is, however, not what the texts say. *Byzantium Confronts the West,* p. 252. Godfrey puts this meeting after the death of Alexius IV, which makes the crusader demands incomprehensible. *1204: The Unholy Crusade,* p. 118.

141. E.g., Nicetas, *Historia,* p. 551.

142. Madden, "Vows and Contracts in the Fourth Crusade," pp. 457–58.

143. Carile, *Per una storia dell'impero latino,* p. 146.

144. Madden, "Vows and Contracts in the Fourth Crusade," pp. 458–59.

145. The Treaty of Zara was a private contract between Alexius and the crusaders. The young man had no power to bind the Byzantine state to a treaty before his coronation and there is no hint in any sources that he did so afterward. He also did not bind his heirs or successors, a clause that was common in Venetian contracts of the time but is absent in all agreements concerning the Fourth Crusade. In every case the crusaders demanded their payment from Alexius alone, even after his imprisonment. Furthermore, no source, Latin or Greek, suggests that Byzantium still owed the crusaders money after the death of Alexius IV.

146. Villehardouin, *Conquête de Constantinople*, sec. 223, 2: 22; Nicetas, *Historia*, p. 564.

147. The date is given by Nicetas as the sixth month, the eighth day of the reign of Alexius, which began officially on 1 August 1203. *Historia*, p. 564. According to Nicetas, Mourtzouphlus ordered the strangulation, which was usual. The word spread in the crusader camp, however, that the usurper had done the deed himself. Villehardouin, *Conquête de Constantinople*, sec. 223, 2: 22; Robert of Clari, *Conquête*, sec. 62, p. 61; *Devastatio Constantinopolitana*, p. 136 (*MGH, SS*, 16: 12; Hopf, ed. pp. 91–92); Alberic of Trois-Fontaines, *Chronica, MGH, SS*, 23: 883. Baldwin of Flanders added further gruesome details to underscore the treacherous and vile nature of his predecessor on the throne. He contended that Mourtzouphlus crushed Alexius's sides and ribs and beat him with an iron implement. In Innocent III, *Epistolae*, 7: 152, Migne, *PL*, CCXV: 450. A story reached Syria that Alexius had had a dream of being strangled by a wild boar of brass that was in the great palace. When he awoke, he had the statue destroyed, but could not avert his fate. Ernoul-Bernard, *Chronique*, pp. 369–70.

148. Villehardouin, *Conquête de Constantinople*, sec. 223, 2: 22.

149. Madden, "Vows and Contracts in the Fourth Crusade," p. 460.

150. *Conquête*, sec. 62, p. 62; trans. McNeal in Robert of Clari, *Conquest of Constantinople*, p. 86.

151. Madden, "Vows and Contracts in the Fourth Crusade," pp. 460–61.

152. Gunther of Pairis, *Hystoria Constantinopolitana*, p. 145.

153. Alberic of Trois-Fontaines, *Chronica, MGH, SS*, 23: 883.

Chapter 11

1. Villehardouin, *Conquête de Constantinople*, sec. 216, 2: 14.

2. This is evident in all Latin sources, but especially in the *Devastatio Constantinopolitana*. See Andrea's commentary, in "The *Devastatio Constantinopolitana*," pp. 121–22.

3. Schmandt, "Fourth Crusade and the Just War Theory," pp. 191–221.

4. Robert of Clari, *Conquête*, sec. 62, p. 62.

5. Madden, "Vows and Contracts in the Fourth Crusade," p. 462.

6. Godfrey, *1204: The Unholy Crusade*, p. 118.

7. See p. 156 above.

8. Villehardouin, *Conquête de Constantinople*, secs. 224–25, 2: 22–24.

9. Ibid., sec. 224, 2: 22–24.

10. Schmandt, "Orthodoxy and Catholicism," p. 297.

11. Norman Daniel, "The Legal and Political Theory of the Crusade," in Setton, *A History of the Crusades*, 6: 8–16; Russell, *The Just War in the Middle Ages*, pp. 197–200, 294–96.

12. So many considered their vow to be fulfilled after the fall of Constantinople that the papal legate later relieved the host of their vow. Innocent III, *Epistolae*, 8: 126, Migne, *PL*, CCXV: 701.

13. Paul Rousset, *Histoire d'une idéologie: La croisade* (Lausaune: L'age d'homme, 1983), p. 84; Madden, "Vows and Contracts in the Fourth Crusade," p. 463. The monk

of San Giorgio in Venice asserted that God wished to punish the pride and disrespect of the Greeks even more than to avenge the wrongs committed by the Saracens. *Translatio corporis beatissimi Pauli martyris de Constantinopoli Venetias*, in Riant, *Exuviae*, 1: 141.

14. Innocent III, *Register*, 6: 101, p. 164 (Migne, *PL*, CCXV: 106–7).

15. Villehardouin, *Conquête de Constantinople*, secs. 225, 2: 24; Robert of Clari, *Conquête*, sec. 72, p. 71; *Chronicle of the Morea*, pp. 89–91. The jumbled *Chronicle of the Morea* may have confused the clerical verdict given before the attack on Constantinople with the attack on Zara. It states that before the crusaders attacked Zara the clergy proclaimed, "all those who died on this expedition would receive forgiveness and remission of their sins as if they had died at the tomb of Christ." Ibid., p. 82. No such proclamation was made at Zara.

16. Madden, "Vows and Contracts in the Fourth Crusade," p. 464.

17. Villehardouin, *Conquête de Constantinople*, sec. 225, 2: 24.

18. Baldwin of Flanders, *TTh*, 1: 506.

19. Acropolita, *Annales*, p. 9; Hendrickx and Matzukis, "Alexios V Mourtzouphlos," p. 124.

20. There are two texts of the treaty, one in the name of Dandolo, the other in the names of the other crusading leaders. There are insignificant differences and one major discrepancy. Text B, the one in the names of the crusaders, says that three-quarters of the booty should go "nobis et hominibus Venetie," which is obviously a misreading of "vobis." Text A also has "nobis," in this case correctly. *TTh*, 1: 444–52. Christopher G. Ferrard became confused by trying to follow text B. "The Amount of Constantinopolitan Booty in 1204," *Studi Veneziani* 13 (1971): 102–3, n. 17.

21. The treaty names only Alexius IV as their debtor, not the Byzantine state or people, and speaks of the debt in the past tense: "soluere tenebatur." It is not true, as it is common to read, that the first division was considered to be monies owed only to Venice. The treaty explicitly defines it as a sum owed to both the Franks and the Venetians. *TTh*, 1: 446; Antonio Carile, "Partitio terrarum imperii romanie," *Studi Veneziani* 7 (1965): 126. For examples of this common error see: George Finlay, *A History of Greece from its Conquest by the Romans to the Present Time*, B.D. 146 to A.D. 1864 (Oxford: Clarendon Press, 1877), 3: 265–66; Nicol, "Fourth Crusade," p. 285; idem, *Byzantium and Venice*, p. 141; McNeal and Wolff, "Fourth Crusade," p. 182; Brand, *Byzantium Confronts the West*, p. 254; Setton, *Papacy and the Levant*, 1: 12; Godfrey, *1204: The Unholy Crusade*, p. 120.

22. Alexius had paid half of the promised 200,000 marks shortly after he came to the throne. Robert of Clari, *Conquête*, sec. 56, p. 56. Additional payments trickled in, but these were very small. When Dandolo met with Mourtzouphlus, he demanded 90,000 silver marks, which must have taken into account the token payments. In working out the pact of March, however, these token payments were apparently factored back out. This is the only way to account for the fact that when the treasure division was later made the Franks gave the Venetians 50,000 marks out of their share to reflect the initial 3-to-1 division. Villehardouin, *Conquête de Constantinople*, sec. 254, 2: 59. The cost of the extension of the Venetian fleet's service for one year is not recorded, but it too can be deduced from the later treasure division and this pact. The Venetians had initially asked for 94,000 marks from the crusaders, which was later bargained down to 85,000. Dandolo would not likely have given so generous a discount to the emperor.

One hundred thousand marks seems the probable figure, and the only one which, again, justifies the Franks' giving 50,000 marks to the Venetians during the treasure division. Thus, in the event, the first 200,000 marks of loot was initally divided equally, with 100,000 to each side, and the transfer of 50,000 from the Franks to the Venetians represented the proper payment of all of Alexius's debts. See Chap. 12 below.

23. Nicol is incorrect when he states that Venice had first pick of all booty. *Byzantium and Venice*, p. 141; idem, "Fourth Crusade," p. 285.

24. Boniface of Montferrat, as commander in chief, remained the obvious candidate. The treaty itself seems to single him out, for it provides for its own amendment by the doge and his six councillors and Montferrat and his six. *TTh*, 1: 448 and 452.

25. Wolff has pointed out that the division of territories undercut, from the beginning, the foundations of the new state. *The Latin Empire*, p. 70. Nicol indicts the Venetians in the partition agreement for listing "numerous towns, ports, islands and provinces which were nothing but names to the crusaders." *Byzantium and Venice*, p. 142. The treaty of March mentioned no place names, only the amount each party would receive. The document Nicol is referring to is the later Treaty of Partition, which was not drawn up until after the conquest.

26. In addition to the treaty, see Villehardouin, *Conquête de Constantinople*, sec. 235, 2: 36.

27. It is not true, as some scholars have maintained, that Venice excluded her rivals—only her enemies. Cf. Joseph Gill, "Venice, Genoa, and Byzantium," *Byzantinische Forschungen* 10 (1985): 62; J. M. Hussey, *The Orthodox Church in the Byzantine Empire* (Oxford: Clarendon, 1986), p. 184.

28. Robert of Clari, *Conquête*, sec. 68, pp. 68–69.

29. Villehardouin, *Conquête de Constantinople*, sec. 251, 2: 55. Hendrickx formulates an equation to determine the number of non-Venetian crusaders, which he finds insoluble. We are told by Villehardouin that among them they divided 100,000 marks (sec. 254, 2: 58). He also tells us that the 100,000 marks were divided as follows: "II. serjanz a pié contre un a cheval, et .II. serjanz a cheval contre un chevalier," or a ratio of 1:2:4. The *Devastatio Constantinopolitana* and Ernoul-Bernard support this. According to the latter, Dandolo proposed to give each knight 400 marks, each mounted sergeant 200, and each sergeant on foot 100, but the actual distribution was 20 marks per knight, 10 per mounted sergeant, and 5 per sergeant on foot. (*Chronique*, pp. 375–76.) Hendrickx thus sets up the formula: $100,000 = 400x + 200y + 100z$, but he finds no way to arrive at numbers for x, y, and z. "A propos du nombres des troupes de la quatrième croisade," pp. 34–35. It should be $100,000 = 20x + 10y + 5z$, and there seems to be a means of solving the equation. If we assume that the proportions were in accord with the treaty of 1201, we can say that $y = 2x$ and $z = 4.44x$, or

$$100,000 = 20x + 20x + 22.2x$$
$$100,000 = 62.2x$$
and therefore:
$$1,608 = x$$
$$3,216 = y$$
$$7,140 = z$$
for a total of 11,964 non-Venetian crusaders.

Or, we might obtain a slightly different result by using the ratio 1:2:4, which is considered common for an army at this time. (This may be the right key since it would mean that the 100,000 marks were divided into three equal shares for knights, mounted sergeants, and foot sergeants.) We would then have the equation:

$$100,000 = 20x + 20x + 20x$$
$$100,000 = 60x$$
and therefore:
$$1,667 = x$$
$$3,334 = y$$
$$6,668 = z$$
for a total of 11,669 non-Venetian crusaders.

Neither of these is an unreasonable figure, if we interpret Villehardouin's one-third of the anticipated number of crusaders actually arriving at Venice as a rather rough figure. McNeal calculates 9,900. Robert of Clari, *Conquête*, p. 131.

30. Villehardouin, *Conquête de Constantinople*, sec. 245, 2: 48.

31. Ibid., sec. 162, 1: 162.

32. For description of some of these machines, see Nada Patrone's trans. of Robert of Clari, *Conquista di Costantinopoli*, p. 202, nn. 74, 76, and McNeal, in Robert of Clari, *Conquest of Constantinople*, p. 92, n. 91.

33. Robert of Clari, *Conquête*, sec. 69, p. 69; Manfroni, *Storia della marina italiana*, 1: 335.

34. Nicetas, *Historia*, p. 567.

35. Ibid.; Villehardouin, *Conquête de Constantinople*, sec. 233, 2: 32–34; Baldwin of Flanders, in Innocent III, *Epistolae*, 7: 152, Migne, *PL*, CCXV: 448–49; Robert of Clari, *Conquête*, secs. 61, pp. 60–61, and sec. 69, p. 69.

36. Gunther of Pairis, *Hystoria Constantinopolitana*, p. 145. According to the usually unreliable Alberic of Trois-Fontaines, in order to strike terror into the hearts of the attackers, Mourtzouphlus ordered three Venetian prisoners drawn with iron hooks and burned to death in full view of their friends and allies. *Chronica, MGH, SS*, 23: 883.

37. Villehardouin, *Conquête de Constantinople*, sec. 236, 2: 36.

38. Carile has confused the dating: "Il 9 aprile, *joesdi aprés mi quaresme*, i crociati lanciarono l'attacco alle mura della città e dopo parecchie ore di lotta dovettero riparare al campo." "Partitio," p. 131. They *boarded* their vessels on Thursday, 8 April, and attacked at break of day on Friday, 9 April. Villehardouin, *Conquête de Constantinople*, secs. 236–37, 2: 36–38. Inexplicably, Runciman fixes the attack on 6 April. *History of the Crusades*, 3: 122.

39. Villehardouin, *Conquête de Constantinople*, sec. 236, 2: 36–38; Robert of Clari, *Conquête*, sec. 70, pp. 69–70.

40. Anonymous of Soissons, *De terra Iherosolimitana*, p. 160 (Riant, p. 6).

41. Villehardouin, *Conquête de Constantinople*, secs. 236–37, 2: 36–38. Pears conjectured that the galleys and horse transports formed a first line and the transports a second. *Fall of Constantinople*, p. 347. Some MSS support this interpretation, but Faral rejects it. In Villehardouin, *Conquête de Constantinople*, 2: 39, n. 1.

42. Villehardouin, *Conquête de Constantinople*, sec. 237, 2: 38.

43. Robert of Clari, *Conquête*, sec. 70, p. 70; Nicetas, *Historia*, p. 568.

44. Robert of Clari, *Conquête*, sec. 70, p. 70.

45. Van Millingen, *Byzantine Constantinople*, p. 183.

46. Robert of Clari, *Conquête*, sec. 70, p. 70; Nicetas, *Historia*, p. 568.

47. Nicetas, *Historia*, p. 568. From Blachernae Palace to the monastery of Christ Evergetes.

48. Ibid., pp. 568–69.

49. Robert of Clari, *Conquête*, sec. 71, p. 70.

50. Villehardouin, *Conquête de Constantinople*, sec. 237, 2: 38.

51. Ibid., sec. 240, 2: 42.

52. *Devastatio Constantinopolitana*, p. 137 (*MGH, SS*, 16: 12; Hopf ed., p. 92).

53. Robert of Clari, *Conquête*, sec. 71, p. 70.

54. Villehardouin, *Conquête de Constantinople*, sec. 237, 2: 38.

55. Ibid., sec. 238, 2: 38.

56. Robert of Clari, *Conquête*, sec. 71, p. 70.

57. Baldwin of Flanders, in Innocent III, *Epistolae*, 7: 152, Migne, *PL*, CCXV: 450

58. Robert of Clari, *Conquête*, sec. 71, pp. 70–71.

59. *Chronicle of Novgorod*, p. 46. The *Devastatio Constantinopolitana*, p. 137 (*MGH, SS*, 16: 12; Hopf ed., p. 92), says that the losses were heavy on both sides. Baldwin of Flanders seems to say that the defeat occurred without much loss of Latin blood. In Innocent III, *Epistolae*, 7: 152, Migne, *PL*, ccxv: 450. Tafel and Thomas tentatively supply "non." *TTh*, 1: 506. So does the version addressed to the archbishop of Cologne, but none of the others has it. Prevenier, *De Oorkonden der graven van Vlaanderen (1191–aanvang 1206)*, ed. W. Prevenier, 3 vols. (Brussels: Paleis der Academien, 1964), 2: 570, 581 (Cologne version), 588, and 598. Villehardouin confesses that the Latins lost more men than did the Greeks. *Conquête de Constantinople*, sec. 238, 2: 38–40.

60. Robert of Clari, *Conquête*, sec. 71, p. 71. Clari also imagines the emperor proclaiming to his people, "Never did you have so good an emperor! Have I not done well? We need fear them no longer. I will have them all hanged and dishonored." McNeal trans., p. 93.

61. Robert of Clari, *Conquête*, sec. 72, p. 71.

62. Villehardouin, *Conquête de Constantinople*, sec. 238, 2: 38. This may or may not refer specifically to their vows or their attack upon Christian Constantinople. Villehardouin's simple faith leads him to believe that the righteousness of any action is manifested in God-given victory or defeat.

63. Ibid., sec. 239, 2: 40. Janin, *Constantinople byzantine*, p. 2, reports that the current, due to the overflow of the Black Sea, runs at 3–5 km/hr.

64. Villehardouin, *Conquête de Constantinople*, sec. 240, 2: 40–42.

65. Robert of Clari names Abbot Simon of Loos among the preachers. *Conquête*, sec. 73, p. 71. Villehardouin has him dead in late autumn 1203. *Conquête de Constantinople*, sec. 206, 2: 7. See Brown, "The Cistercians in the Latin Empire," p. 76, and Schmandt, "Fourth Crusade and the Just War Theory," p. 216, n. 67. The latter points out that Simon generally agreed with Villehardouin, for that reason received special attention, and would therefore have been mentioned by the chronicler were he living. On the eloquence of John Faicete, see Villehardouin, *Conquête de Constantinople*, sec. 290, 2: 98.

66. Robert of Clari, *Conquête*, secs. 72–73, pp. 71–72.

67. Ibid., sec. 73, p. 71.

68. Ibid., sec. 72, p. 71.

69. Unfortunately for Frolow's argument concerning the attractive force of the relics of Constantinople, there is no evidence that the preachers exhorted their hearers to liberate the holy remains from the Greeks. There is plenty of evidence, assembled by Riant in the *Exuviae*, of the great importance of the relics after the conquest, but no indication that the existence of the relics in Constantinople was used as an argument for attacking the city. Frolow, *Recherches*, p. 71. If Frolow's thesis is sound, it is difficult to understand why such an obvious appeal would not have been made. Mayer still accepts Frolow's basic thesis. *The Crusades*, p. 200.

70. Robert of Clari, *Conquête*, secs. 73–74, p. 72.

71. *Chronicle of Novgorod*, p. 46.

72. Robert of Clari, *Conquête*, sec. 74, p. 73. Greek fire, it seems, was no longer a secret weapon of the Greeks.

73. Villehardouin, *Conquête de Constantinople*, sec. 241, 2: 42; Nicetas, *Historia*, p. 569.

74. Robert of Clari, *Conquête*, sec. 74, p. 73.

75. There is some disagreement in the sources concerning which of the two ships approached the tower. Villehardouin, *Conquête de Constantinople*, sec. 242, 2: 245, states that it was the *Pilgrim*. Robert of Clari, *Conquête*, sec. 74, p. 73, says that it was the ship of the bishop of Soisson, which was the *Paradise*. Baldwin of Flanders, *TTh*, 1: 506 names the *Paradise*.

76. Venetian tradition named him Pietro Alberti. See Zorzi Dolfin, *Chronica*, Biblioteca Marciana, cl. ital. vii, cod. 794 (= 8503). Dolfin and the Venetian tradition generally, however, are not very reliable on the Fourth Crusade. Dolfin also has him bearing the standard of Saint Mark.

77. Robert of Clari, *Conquête*, sec. 74, pp. 73–74; Villehardouin, *Conquête de Constantinople*, sec. 242, 2: 42–44; Baldwin of Flanders, in Innocent III, *Epistolae*, 7: 152, Migne, *PL*, CCXV: 450; Nicetas, *Historia*, pp. 568–69; Ernoul-Bernard, *Chronique*, p. 372; Anonymous of Soissons, *De terra Iherosolimitana*, p. 160 (Riant, pp. 6–7). On the identity of André, see Riant, *Exuviae*, 1, iv.

78. Robert of Clari, *Conquête*, sec. 74, p. 74; Ernoul-Bernard, *Chronique*, p. 372.

79. It is not clear whether the crusaders managed to seize more than two towers. According to Villehardouin, they took altogether either four or five towers, depending on whether one counts the first tower taken as one of the four he claims or not. *Conquête de Constantinople*, sec. 243, 2: 44. Yet Robert of Clari, who was in the thick of battle, states that the crusaders took only two towers, from which they did not dare move. *Conquête*, sec. 74, pp. 74–75.

80. Robert of Clari, *Conquête*, sec. 75, p. 75.

81. Ibid., secs. 75–76, pp. 75–76.

82. Ibid., sec. 76, p. 76; Nicetas, *Historia*, pp. 569–70. Nicetas knows only the commander's name, Peter, whom he credits with routing the imperial army. He also refers to him as "nearly nine fathoms [54 ft.] tall." A phrase from the *Odyssey* obviously not meant to be taken literally. Magoulias trans., p. 406, n. 1510.

83. Nicetas, *Historia*, p. 570; Magoulias trans., p. 313.

84. Robert of Clari, *Conquête*, secs. 76–78, pp. 76–77. In another position be-

neath the walls the poet-companion of Boniface of Montferrat, Raimbaut de Vaqueiras, was wounded. Linskill, in Raimbaut de Vaqueiras, *Poems*, pp. 305 and 310, and
notes. This gives a slight indication of the place of Boniface and his followers in the
battle.

85. Robert of Clari, *Conquête*, sec. 78, p. 77; Villehardouin, *Conquête de Constantinople*, sec. 243, 2: 44–46.

86. According to Villehardouin, many soldiers fled to Blachernae Gate when
the crusaders entered the city. *Conquête de Constantinople*, sec. 244, 2: 46. Nicetas states
that they fled to the other extreme of the land walls, the Golden Gate. *Historia*, p. 570.
Villehardouin is probably referring only to those troops he witnessed flee. Blachernae
gates were all that were visible to the crusaders at that time. Nicetas is probably high-
lighting those who fled through the Golden Gate to contrast the cowardly defeat of
the imperial troops with the victorious symbolism of the ceremonial portal. Fleeing
troops certainly made use of not just these two gates, but all those in between as well.

87. Villehardouin, *Conquête de Constantinople*, sec. 243, 2: 46; Robert of Clari,
Conquête, sec. 78, p. 77.

88. Nicetas, *Historia*, p. 570; Anonymous of Soissons, *De terra Iherosolimitana*,
p. 160 (Riant, pp. 6–7); Villehardouin, *Conquête de Constantinople*, sec. 244, 2: 46.
Gunther of Pairis blames the slaughter on the former Latin residents of Constantinople. This seems very reasonable, although no other source suggests this exculpation
of the crusading army. *Hystoria Constantinopolitana*, p. 156.

89. Gunther of Pairis, *Hystoria Constantinopolitana*, p. 156.

90. Robert of Clari, *Conquête*, sec. 78, p. 78.

91. Villehardouin, *Conquête de Constantinople*, sec. 244, 2: 46; Nicetas, *Historia*,
p. 568.

92. Robert of Clari heard that the Greeks still had one hundred times more fighting men than the crusaders. *Conquête*, sec. 78, p. 78. Villehardouin claimed that there
were four hundred thousand men in the city. *Conquête de Constantinople*, sec. 251, 2: 54.

93. Villehardouin, *Conquête de Constantinople*, sec. 244, 2: 46.

94. Robert of Clari, *Conquête*, sec. 78, p. 78.

95. Ibid., p. 79; Villehardouin, *Conquête de Constantinople*, sec. 244, 2: 46.

96. Villehardouin, *Conquête de Constantinople*, sec. 245, 2: 46–48; Nicetas, *Historia*, p. 570.

97. Robert of Clari, *Conquête*, sec. 78, p. 78.

98. Villehardouin says only that the incendiaries were certain unknown persons.
Conquête de Constantinople, sec. 247, 2: 48. Gunther of Pairis identified the leader as
"quidam comes Theotonicus." *Hystoria Constantinopolitana*, p. 154. Riant conjectures
Berthold. *Exuviae*, 1: xxxiv, and "Innocent III," 18: 52–53. In the latter he speculates
that the fire was set by command of Boniface. Usseglio, *I marchesi di Monferrato*,
2: 237–38, and Brand, *Byzantium Confronts the West*, p. 257, follow Riant. See also
Andrea, *The Capture of Constantinople: The "Hystoria Constantinopolitana,"* chap. 18.

99. Nicetas, *Historia*, p. 570; Madden, "Fires of the Fourth Crusade," pp. 84–85.

100. Villehardouin, *Conquête de Constantinople*, sec. 247, 2: 50.

101. Madden, "Fires of the Fourth Crusade," pp. 87–88.

102. Ibid., pp. 88–89.

103. Nicetas, *Historia*, p. 577; Magoulias trans., p. 317.

104. This is a difficult figure to get at, and essentially irrelevant for future events.

In the booty taken by the crusaders, Villehardouin speaks of "ten thousand mounts." *Conquête de Constantinople*, sec. 255, 2: 60. Presumably, these belonged to someone. The word, *chevaucheüres*, which Villehardouin uses, means mounts. Pears, following Natalis De Wailly's 1870 edition, read this as suits of armor. Faral glosses no variants on this word in any copy, and translates it as mounts, not armor. *Conquête de Constantinople*, sec. 255, 2: 61. Both English translators follow Faral. Sir Frank Marzials, trans. (New York: E. P. Dutton, 1908), p. 66; Shaw, trans., p. 95. The 10,000 suits of armor still pop up, however, in literature. E.g., McNeal and Wolff, "The Fourth Crusade," p. 185. According to Godfrey, the booty included 10,000 horses *and* 10,000 suits of armor! *1204: The Unholy Crusade*, p. 130.

105. See p. 107 above.

106. It is not true, as it is often asserted, that most of the population of Constantinople fled the city the night of 12/13 April. E.g., Wolff, "The Latin Empire," p. 189; Dawkins, "Later History of the Varangian Guard," p. 43. The great exodus was still to come. The only sources for a massive migration that night are foreign, unreliable, and not in a position to know. Robert of Clari, describing the surrender ceremony of the following day, which he did not witness, states that the clergy reported that "all the Greeks had fled and no one was left in the city but the poor people." *Conquête*, sec. 80, p. 79. Gunther of Pairis states that on the morning of 13 April only women, children, and the elderly remained, which suggests that every able-bodied male Greek abandoned his family to the crusaders' mercy. *Hystoria Constantinopolitana*, p. 157. Villehardouin states simply that all those who could flee did so. *Conquête de Constantinople*, sec. 246, 2: 56. Putting these three Westerners' testimonies together we would have to conclude that the only residents left in Constantinople the morning of 13 April were poor, non-Greek, women, children, or elderly who were unable to make it to the city gates. According to Nicetas only "some chose to leave the city" that night. *Historia*, p. 571. The *Chronicle of Novgorod*, p. 47, speaks only of Mourtzouphlus, the patriarch, and the "nobles" fleeing. The author is incorrect about the patriarch, who remained, and as for "nobles" this must refer only to those members of Mourtzouphlus's faction, since Nicetas and many others remained. The *Devastatio* speaks of "all the Greeks" surrendering the following day, and then fleeing after that. *Devastatio Constantinopolitana*, p. 137 (Hopf ed., p. 92). In short, those who either were Greek or had dealings with Greeks before the sack state that only a few decided to abandon the city that night.

107. E.g. Maleczek, *Petrus Capuanus*, pp. 131–32; Hans Delbrück, *History of the Art of War*, vol. 3, *Medieval Warfare*, trans. Walter J. Renfroe Jr. (Lincoln and London: University of Nebraska Press, 1982), p. 196.

108. According to Godfrey, the Byzantines refused to take up arms because they believed that "by paying taxes for the maintenance of an army citizens were absolved from the duty of serving in it." *1204: The Unholy Crusade*, p. 119. There is no evidence that Greeks saw things that way, and the violent nature of the Byzantine mob throughout its history contradicts the assertion. Godfrey goes on to blame also "the Venetian spies, who were working like moles and using their money to weaken the will of the people to defend their city." Ibid. As usual, Godfrey provides no source, but he is probably relying on Runciman, who wrote "there were traitors in Venetian pay inside the city." *A History of the Crusades*, 3: 122. Runciman, and Godfrey's elaboration, rely on nothing but imagination. E. Frances saw the refusal of the citizens to

defend themselves as a revolt of the masses who refused to protect the wealth of the bourgeois elite. "Sur la conquête de Constantinople par les Latins," *Byzantinoslavica* 15 (1954): 25. See also Carile, *Per una storia dell'impero latino*, pp. 177–78, who agrees with this view. This line of reasoning assumes, however, that to further their social-ist agenda, the people of Constantinople were willing to endure the ravages of theft, rape, and murder as long as the same was also meted out to the aristocracy.

109. Cheynet, *Pouvoir et contestations*, pp. 114–39; cf. Nicetas, *Historia*, p. 420.

110. Cheynet, *Pouvoir et contestations*, passim.

111. Anna Comnena, *The Alexiad*, pp. 64–69; Cheynet, *Pouvoir et contestations*, pp. 356–57.

112. Anna Comnena, *The Alexiad*, pp. 65–66.

113. See Gunther of Pairis, *Hystoria Constantinopolitana*, p. 157.

114. "Latin" as used by historians refers both to religion and usually ethnicity. Ethnicity, however, was not as important to medieval Byzantines as it is to modern scholars. A diverse group of ethnic stocks had held the imperial throne during its his-tory: western Europeans had long been a large share of that mix.

115. Nicetas, *Historia*, p. 571.

116. It is difficult to know how many people were busy with the preparations for Boniface's procession, but a great many showed up in their finery the next day, bearing icons and offerings. Nicetas, *Historia*, pp. 572–73. According to Nicetas, the people were simply "wandering aimlessly about." *Historia*, p. 570. Throughout his narrative of the night of 12/13 April, Nicetas views events through the prism of the subsequent sack. The expectation of a gala procession and coronation the following day seemed absurd later, and so the senator only mentions it briefly, and only as a tool to further castigate the Latins. See *Historia*, p. 572. The fact that Nicetas himself remained in the city until 17 April suggests that he too believed that something besides what happened would happen. Given his previous position as grand logothete under the Angeli, he probably hoped to be restored to that office from which Mourtzouphlus had removed him. Cf. Pears, *Fall of Constantinople*, p. 345.

117. Baldwin of Flanders, in Innocent III, *Epistolae*, 7: 152, Migne, *PL*, CCXV: 451.

118. Nicetas, *Historia*, p. 570; *Chronicle of Novgorod*, p. 47.

119. Nicetas, *Historia*, p. 342.

120. Ibid., p. 385; Magoulias trans., p. 211.

121. Ivan Dujčev argues that the extreme loss of prestige and "humanization" of the emperors over the last three decades led the Byzantines to no longer see their em-peror as divinely appointed, thus robbing the rulers of the people's respect and awe. Dujcev blames much of the catastrophe of 1204 on this loss of imperial prestige. *La crise idéologique de 1203–1204 et ses répercussions sur la civilization byzantine* (Paris: Mai-sonneuve, 1976), passim. Without disagreeing with his fundamental thesis, it is hardly true that all Byzantine emperors before Andronicus I were revered with awe by the common people. The Nika Riot against Justinian is only the most famous example. In any event, the citizens of Constantinople would never support an emperor if it meant open warfare in their city.

122. Nicetas, *Historia*, p. 571; Magoulias trans, p. 314.

123. On the question of Mourtzouphlus's marriage to Eudocia, see Hendrickx and Matzukis, "Alexios V Doukas Mourtzouphlos," pp. 127–28.

124. Nicetas, *Historia*, p. 571. According to Villehardouin, Mourtzouphlus fled through the Golden Gate. *Conquête de Constantinople*, sec. 246, 2: 56. When a Latin source is at variance with Nicetas on topographic matters, it is always better to favor the native. Villehardouin probably chose the Golden Gate because it supported his prior statement that Mourtzouphlus "rode through other streets as far as he could from those of the host." Ibid. Surely a great many people did leave Constantinople that night through the Golden Gate, so it is not surprising that Villehardouin would assume Mourtzouphlus to be one of them. Cf. Robert of Clari, *Conquête*, sec. 79, p. 79.

125. Nicetas, *Historia*, p. 572.

126. In 1081, before Nicephorus surrendered to Alexius Comnenus, the Varangians returned to the Milion, where they were drawn up in ranks, either to defend against Alexius or attack his mercenaries, who had already begun to plunder the town. Anna Comnena, *The Alexiad*, p. 69; Blöndal, *Varangians of Byzantium*, p. 120. In 1118, the Varangians stationed at the Great Palace refused to allow the clandestinely crowned John II to enter until they had received word of his father's death. Nicetas, *Historia*, p. 7.

127. Nicetas, *Historia*, p. 571. On Constantine Ducas, see Demetrios J. Polemis, *The Doukai: A Contribution to Byzantine Prosopography* (London: Athlone, 1968), p. 195; Brand, *Byzantium Confronts the West*, p. 258. There is some disagreement concerning Constantine Lascaris. A fourteenth-century manuscript of Nicetas's *Historia* names both candidates as Theodore. B. Sinogowitz follows Bekker and Van Dieten, in arguing that both were named Constantine. "Über das byzantinische Kaisertum nach dem vierten Kreuzzuge (1204–1205)," *Byzantinische Zeitschrift* 155 (1952): 345–51. Wolff argues for Theodore, since Theodore Lascaris did go on to become emperor of Nicaea. "The Latin Empire of Constantinople," p. 201, n. 11. Runciman also names Theodore Lascaris, yet this may be an error: his treatment of the fall of Constantinople in 1204 is extremely confused. *History of the Crusades*, 3: 122. Brand accepts Nicetas at his word, but wonders why Theodore was not chosen. *Byzantium Confronts the West*, p. 258. In light of subsequent events, logic lies on Wolff's side, but Nicetas's words do not. More recent studies have accepted Constantine Lascaris as the chosen man. E.g., Nicol, *Byzantium and Venice*, p. 143; Godfrey, *1204: The Unholy Crusade*, p. 124.

128. Nicetas, *Historia*, p. 571; Magoulias, trans., p. 314.

129. Nicetas, *Historia*, p. 572.

130. E.g., Brand, *Byzantium Confronts the West*, p. 258; Nicol, *Byzantium and Venice*, p. 143.

131. Nicetas, *Historia*, p. 572.

132. Ibid., Magoulias trans., p. 314.

133. Robert of Clari, *Conquête*, sec. 79, p. 79. Interestingly, Nicetas omits Lascaris's departure from his account, perhaps to further discredit the Varangian Guard for failing to fight the next day. See note 134 below.

134. According to Nicetas, the Varangian Guard "took flight to save themselves" when the Latins arrayed their forces the next day. *Historia*, p. 572. It may have seemed that way to Nicetas, or he may be simply blaming the English and Danes for the Greeks' refusal to fight. The fact is that the Varangian Guard *never* fought except at the command of the emperor: no emperor, no fighting. Since Nicetas omits Constantine Lascaris's flight the night before, he may have believed that the young man was still present in the morning and was therefore betrayed by the Varangians. More

likely, since he omits any mention at all of the departure of Lascaris, Nicetas is simply removing the rationale for the Varangians' refusal to fight, so that he can substitute cowardice. If Latin forces had stood against six thousand Varangians and put them to flight, as Nicetas contends, at least one of the Latin sources would mention it. None do.

135. Almost completely made up of English, the Varangian Guard continued to exist after 1204 only as an honor guard, house guard, or prison guard for Byzantine emperors. Their numbers were severely reduced. The Latins may have retained some as honor guards, but not for very long. Mark C. Bartusis, *The Late Byzantine Army: Arms and Society, 1204–1453* (Philadelphia: University of Pennsylvania Press, 1992), pp. 272–76; Blöndal, *Varangians of Byzantium*, pp. 167–76.

136. Nicetas, *Historia*, p. 572.

137. McCormick, *Eternal Victory*, pp. 82–83.

138. Ibid., pp. 198–99; cf. also pp. 210–12.

139. *Devastatio Constantinopolitana*, p. 137, (Hopf ed., p. 92); Robert of Clari, *Conquête*, sec. 80, p. 79. The author of the *Devastatio* gives a brief description, perhaps as an eyewitness. That the ceremony was for Boniface of Montferrat also jibes with Gunther of Pairis's observation. *Hystoria Constantinopolitana*, p. 157. Clari provides a richer description, but has the delegation come to the Franks rather than Boniface. This may be garbled (a common affliction for Clari) or it may represent another delegation. Robert goes on to say that the clergy and the Varangians announced that all the Greeks had left, which is incomprehensible. The high clergy, not to mention the populace, were certainly Greek.

140. *Devastatio Constantinopolitana*, p. 137 (Hopf ed., p. 92).

141. After describing the prostration and submission of the city, the author's next sentence is: "Then we took possession of places for lodging, and the Greeks fled the city." Ibid. Andrea trans., p. 148.

142. Robert of Clari, *Conquête*, sec. 80, p. 79; Villehardouin, *Conquête de Constantinople*, sec. 248, 2: 50.

143. Nicetas, *Historia*, p. 572.

144. Ibid. Nicetas describes the procession the people had prepared for as *paneguris* (solemn festival) and *pompeia* (solemn or religious procession). These are also the words he uses elsewhere in his history to describe other imperial triumphs, particularly those of Manuel Comnenus in 1161 and 1168. Ibid., pp. 118–19, 157.

145. Ibid., pp. 572–73; Magoulias trans., p. 314.

146. First noticed by Pears, *Fall of Constantinople*, pp. 343–45.

147. Gunther of Pairis, *Hystoria Constantinopolitana*, p. 157.

Chapter 12

1. Nicetas, *Historia*, p. 573; Magoulias trans., p. 314.

2. Nicetas, *Historia*, p. 586.

3. Ibid., pp. 586–87.

4. Villehardouin, *Conquête de Constantinople*, sec. 249, 2: 50–52.

5. Boniface had spent the previous night close to his boats for that same reason.

6. *TTh*, 1: 447, 450.

7. Villehardouin, *Conquête de Constantinople*, sec. 249, 2: 50–52; Usseglio, *I marchesi di Monferrato*, 2: 241.

8. Villehardouin, *Conquête de Constantinople*, sec. 250, 2: 52.

9. *TTh*, 1: 447, 450.

10. Villehardouin, *Conquête de Constantinople*, sec. 259, 2: 64. According to later Venetian tradition, Dandolo's palace was on the Augusteion. Paolo Ramusio, *De bello Constantinopolitano*, p. 136. Longnon postulates that this refers to part of the Great Palace. *L'empire latin de Constantinople*, p. 50, n. 2. While this is consistent with the tradition (which may after all be false), it supposes that Boniface of Montferrat would be willing to share his accommodations with the doge. It seems much more likely that the palace in question was the patriarchal complex, which was also on the Augusteion.

11. Nicetas, *Historia*, p. 573; J. Darrouzès, "Le mémoire de Constantin Stilbès contre les Latins," *Revue des études byzantines* 21 (1963): 82–83.

12. Nicetas, *Historia*, pp. 573–74; Darrouzès, "Le mémoire de Constantin Stilbès," 81–82.

13. Anonymous of Soissons, *De terra Iherosolimitana*, pp. 161–62; Andrea and Rachlin, "Holy War, Holy Relics, Holy Theft," pp. 153–53.

14. Andrea, "Conrad of Krosigk," pp. 65–67.

15. Agostino Pertusi, "*Exuviae sacrae Constantinopolitanae*: A proposito degli oggetti bizantini esistenti oggi nel tesoro di San Marco," *Studi Veneziani*, n.s. 2 (1978): 251–55; reprinted in idem, "Venezia e Bisanzio: 1000–1204," *Dumbarton Oaks Papers* 33 (1979): 13–16.

16. Robert of Clari, *Conquête*, sec. 92, p. 90.

17. The donated items were a crystal cross reliquary taken from a church near Blachernae and another processional cross. Riant, *Exuviae*, 2: 175–76, 197–99; Carile, *Per una storia dell'impero latino*, pp. 281–82; Andrea, "Conrad of Krosigk," pp. 68–69.

18. Gunther, *Hystoria Constantinopolitana*, pp. 158–60; Andrea, trans., *The Capture of Constantinople: The "Hystoria Constantinopolitana,"* chap. 19.

19. We know of no source that mentions lost manuscripts, but it is true that Constantinople harbored a great many ancient texts found nowhere else in the world. See, Alexander P. Kazhdan and Ann Wharton Epstein, *Change in Byzantine Culture in the Eleventh and Twelfth Centuries* (Berkeley: University of California Press, 1985), pp. 133–41. Presumably some of these would have been lost either in the three fires or in the looting of palaces and monasteries. Nicetas does record that the largely illiterate crusaders often mocked Byzantines by taking a quill and pretending to write in books. *Historia*, p. 594. This disdain for Greek learning and literacy probably took more tangible forms on occasion. We can find no evidence, however, to support David Nicholas's statement that "the crusaders burned the entire city, including the imperial library and its irreplaceable manuscripts." *The Evolution of the Medieval World: Society, Government and Thought in Europe, 312–1500* (London and New York: Longmans, 1992), p. 270. They, in fact, burned only one-sixth of the city and, to the best of our knowledge, there was no formal imperial library in Constantinople.

20. Nicetas dates this to some time after the arrival of Thomas Morosini at the end of July 1204. Nicetas Choniates, *De Signis*, ed. Jan Louis van Dieten, in *Corpus Fontium Historiae Byzantinae*, XI/1 (Berlin and New York: de Gruyter, 1975), pp. 647–48. On the question of the identity of the coins, see Michael F. Hendy, *Coinage and*

Money in the Byzantine Empire, 1081–1261 (Washington, D.C.: Dumbarton Oaks, 1969), 191ff; Anthony Cutler, "The *De Signis* of Nicetas Choniates: A Reappraisal," *American Journal of Archaeology* 72 (1968): 116.

21. Nicetas, *De Signis*, p. 648. See also, Cutler, "The *De Signis*," p. 113, and n. 7.

22. Nicetas, *De Signis*, pp. 649–50; Magoulias trans., p. 359. Both Strabo and the elder Pliny describe this statue. It was transported from the acropolis at Tarentum to Rome in 209 B.C. and then moved to Constantinople in A.D. 325. See Cutler, "The *De Signis*," pp. 116–17 and sources cited there.

23. Nicetas, *De Signis*, pp. 651–54. A useful introduction to the spina's treasures can be found in Sarah Guberti Bassett, "The Antiquities in the Hippodrome of Constantinople," *Dumbarton Oaks Papers* 45 (1991): 87–96. Bassett's conclusions, however, rest on a Byzantine popular cognizance of antiquity and artistic expression that we doubt.

24. Madden, "Serpent Column of Delphi," pp. 120–21.

25. A great deal of literature has been and continues to be produced on the San Marco horses. A truly excellent introduction is given by L. Borelli Vlad and A. Guidi Toniato, "The Origins and Documentary Sources of the Horses of San Marco," in *The Horses of San Marco*, ed. Guido Perocco, trans. Valerie Wilton-Ely and John Wilton-Ely (London: Thames and Hudson, 1979), pp. 127–36. Although the San Marco group probably came from the famous quadriga on the carceres, Vlad and Toniato point out that there was another charioteer group on the Hippodrome spina. Ibid., pp. 127–28.

26. Michael Jacoff has recently argued that the statues were placed before an image of Christ and the evangelists, thus the four horses represented the four evangelists drawing the Word behind them. *The Horses of San Marco and the Quadriga of the Lord* (Princeton: Princeton University Press, 1993). We leave the assessment of this theory to those better qualified than ourselves, yet it is noteworthy that the Venetians misplaced the horses if they were to represent a quadriga.

27. Innocent III, *Epistolae*, 8: 126, Migne, *PL*, CCXV: 701.

28. Nicetas, *Historia*, pp. 574–75, 586–87, 594; Darrouzès, "Le mémoire de Constantin Stilbès," p. 85.

29. Nicetas, *Historia*, p. 574; Magoulias trans., p. 315.

30. Nicetas describes the dwelling as "my house whose entranceway, dark and difficult to approach, was covered by a low portico." *Historia*, p. 587; Magoulias trans., p. 323.

31. Nicetas, *Historia*, p. 587.

32. Ibid., p. 588; Magoulias trans., p. 407, n. 1598.

33. Since Nicetas states that Domenico could converse "in their own barbaric tongue" with the first looters who appeared at his door, this suggests they were Venetian or, at least, Italian. The senator does, however, clearly distinguish the French "who were not like the others in temperament or physique and boasted that the only thing they feared was heaven." Nicetas, *Historia*, p. 588; Magoulias trans., p. 323.

34. Nicetas, *Historia*, p. 588.

35. Ibid., p. 589.

36. Ibid., p. 588.

37. Ibid., p. 593.

38. Ibid., p. 589.

39. Nicetas does not distinguish between the various races of Latins at this

point in his narrative, but he does state that the soldiers he appealed to knew Greek. *Historia*, p. 590. This suggests strongly that they were Venetian or Pisan. See Pertusi, "Venezia e Bisanzio," pp. 16–17. Very few French or Germans could understand Greek.

40. Nicetas, *Historia*, pp. 590–91.

41. Ibid., p. 590.

42. Ibid., p. 591; Magoulias trans., p. 325.

43. Nicetas, *Historia*, pp. 591–92; Magoulias trans., p. 325.

44. Innocent III, *Epistolae*, 8: 126, Migne, *PL*, CCXV: 701. Although Innocent's first letters to the crusaders after he heard of their conquest of Constantinople were very cordial, calling the event the miraculous work of God, his subsequent letters included bitter rebukes. Cf. *Epistolae*, 7: 153, 154, 164, Migne, *PL*, CCXV: 454–61, 471–72; 8: 126, Migne, *PL*, CCXV: 699–702; 9: 139, Migne, *PL*, CCXV: 957–59. Joseph Gill has argued, rightly we think, that the first letters were dispatched before the pope learned the details of the sack of the city. *Byzantium and the Papacy*, p. 27.

45. Godfrey defends ecclesiastical plundering based on the fact that the emperors had done the same thing previously. *1204: The Unholy Crusade*, p. 129. The difference, of course, is one of degree. In any event, despoiling churches was prohibited under all circumstances in the West. Innocent clearly considered it to be among the crusaders' gravest sins. Innocent III, *Epistolae*, 8: 126, Migne, *PL*, CCXV: 701.

46. Nicetas, *Historia*, p. 576.

47. Ibid., p. 575.

48. Ibid., pp. 575–76; Magoulias trans., p. 316.

49. Dujcev, *La crise idéologique de 1203-1204*, p. 39; Hélène Ahrweiler, "Constantinople Seconde Rome: Le tournant de 1204," in *Roma, Costantinopoli, Mosca: Da Roma alla Terza Roma, documenti e studi (seminario 1981)* (Naples: Edizioni Scientifiche Italiane, 1983), pp. 312–15; cf. Asdracha, "L'image de l'homme occidental à Byzance," pp. 34–37.

50. Villehardouin, *Conquête de Constantinople*, sec. 251, 2: 54.

51. Ibid., sec. 250, 2: 52.

52. Robert of Clari, *Conquête*, sec. 81, pp. 80–81.

53. Villehardouin, *Conquête de Constantinople*, sec. 250, 2: 52.

54. Ibid., sec. 252, 2: 56; Robert of Clari, *Conquête*, sec. 81, pp. 80–81. According to the *Devastatio*, three large towers were filled with silver. *Devastatio Constantinopolitana*, p. 137.

55. Villehardouin, *Conquête de Constantinople*, sec. 253, 2: 56–58. Ernoul-Bernard accuses the Venetians of secretly putting much of the booty on their ships under cover of darkness, thus again cheating the French. *Chronique*, p. 375. While Venetians were surely just as guilty of concealing booty as other members of the crusade, there is no hint from any of the eyewitness sources, or any other sources save Ernoul-Bernard, that they systematically depleted the pool by spiriting treasure away. Both Robert of Clari and the author of the *Devastatio* blame the rich knights, not the Venetians. See below. Modern writers who view Venice in the worst light, not surprisingly, find Ernoul-Bernard reliable on this point. E.g., Brand, *Byzantium Confronts the West*, p. 263; Godfrey, *1204: The Unholy Crusade*, p. 130.

56. "Ce qui aus moustiers fu aportez assemblez fu et departiz des Franz et des Venisiens par moitié, si cum la compaignie ere juree." Villehardouin, *Conquête de Constantinople*, sec. 254, 2: 58.

57. See Chap. 11, above.

58. "Et sachiez que, quant il orent parti, que il paierent de la lor partie .L. mil mars d'argent as Venitiens; et bien en departirent .CM. entr'als ensemble par lor gent." Villehardouin, *Conquête de Constantinople*, sec., 254, 2: 58.

59. "Bien poez savoir que granz fu li avoirs: que, sanz celui qui fu emblez, et sanz la partie des Venitiens, en vint bien avant .CCCC. .M. mars d'argent. . . ." Ibid., sec. 255, 2: 60.

60. In tabular form, Villehardouin's estimate is thus:

	Venetians	Franks	Total
Common pile (first 200,000 marks)	150,000	50,000	200,000
Common pile (excess amount)	50,000	50,000	100,000
Amount held back	250,000	250,000	500,000
Total	450,000	350,000	800,000

The largest pitfall for scholars trying to estimate the total booty is to ignore Villehardouin's statement that after the 50,000 marks were paid to the Venetians, the Franks had only 100,000 marks to divide among themselves. The second largest pitfall is to treat Villehardouin's estimate of all booty, both surrendered and held back, as the total that was actually brought together. See, for example, McNeal and Wolff, "The Fourth Crusade," p. 185; Godfrey, *1204: The Unholy Crusade*, p. 130. Brand confuses matters more when he describes the surrendered booty as equaling 400,000 marks, plus 50,000 paid to the Venetians, out of which only 100,000 were divided among the soldiers. *Byzantium Confronts the West*, p. 263. Nicol characterizes the 50,000 marks as a payment made to Enrico Dandolo before the division for everyone else. *Byzantium and Venice*, p. 144. Ferrard made an attempt to clear up the subject, but with disappointing results. According to Ferrard, Villehardouin described the Frankish share of the surrendered booty as equaling 400,000 marks *after the Venetians had taken their share* (emphasis his). This is not correct, although the wording can be confusing. Villehardouin states that "without that which was stolen and without the Venetians' part there would have been 400,000 marks. . . ." See note 59 above. In other words, there were 400,000 marks minus (*sanz*) the payment to the Venetians and minus the stolen loot. The total of this equation is given in Villehardouin's preceding paragraph as 100,000 marks. Ferrard compounds the error by figuring that the Frankish share was 450,000 marks before they paid the Venetians 50,000 marks, and thus the total surrendered to the common pool was 900,000 silver marks! He concludes that the real booty taken was many times larger. "The Amount of Constantinopolitan Booty," pp. 98, 104. This figure ignores the actual sum that Villehardouin records the Franks dividing in the preceding paragraph, and it also makes no accounting for the division plan agreed to in the March pact. It is further contradicted by the final distribution amounts as recorded by the *Devastatio Constantinopolitana*. See below. Although he does not cite him, Mayer accepts Ferrard's figure. *The Crusades*, p. 204. Runciman incorrectly extends the land division ratios to the booty division, thus claiming that Venice received three-eighths of the total loot. *A History of the Crusades*, 3: 124. Louise Buenger Robbert follows Runciman on this, and further adds that Venice's three-eighths totalled

400,000 marks. "Monetary Flows—Venice, 1150–1400," in *Precious Metals in the Later Medieval and Early Modern Worlds*, ed. J. F. Richards (Durham, N.C.: Carolina Academic Press, 1983), p. 65. We, too, have been guilty of this error. Queller and Madden, "Some Further Arguments in Defense of the Venetians," pp. 467–68.

61. Robert of Clari, *Conquête*, secs. 81, 98, pp. 79–81, 95–96. While this might have happened to some limited extent, the time for thievery was not while so many were watching the hoard, but rather before it was brought together. The disappearance of gems and other precious items that did not lend themselves to division, however, is not that surprising. Many of these goods were sold to Greek and Latin merchants to acquire liquid assets that could more easily be distributed. See, e.g., Nicetas, *Historia*, p. 594.

62. *Devastatio Constantinopolitana*, pp. 137, 149 (Hopf ed., p. 92)

63. Villehardouin, *Conquête de Constantinople*, sec. 254, 2: 58.

64. Ibid., sec. 251, 2: 54.

65. The computations are:

1428 knights receiving 20 marks each	=	28,560 marks
2858 sergeants receiving 10 marks each	=	28,580 marks
5714 foot receiving 5 marks each	=	28,570 marks
Total dispersed to soldiers	=	85,710 marks

66. Villehardouin, *Conquête de Constantinople*, sec. 255, 2: 60.

67. Ibid., sec. 262, 2: 68.

68. Ibid., sec. 256, 2: 62.

69. Ibid.; Robert of Clari, *Conquête*, sec. 94, p. 92. Robert states that the parliaments met daily for fifteen days before coming to a decision.

70. Villehardouin, *Conquête de Constantinople*, secs. 257–58, 2: 62–64; Carile, *Per una storia dell'impero latino*, p. 180.

71. Robert of Clari, *Conquête*, sec. 94, p. 92.

72. Letter of Baldwin of Flanders, in Innocent III, *Epistolae*, 8: 152, Migne, *PL*, CCXV: 451.

73. Longnon, *Les compagnons de Villehardouin*, pp. 165–67; Andrea, "Conrad of Krosigk," p. 46.

74. Robert of Clari, *Conquête*, sec. 94, p. 92. Robert errs when he says that the Franks and Venetians chose ten electors each, rather than six. He may be wrong on other details as well, but the method of Venice's elector selection he describes is typically Venetian. Doges were chosen at this time by a four-man commission, which selected a forty-man body of ducal electors. Beginning in the sixteenth century, Venetian chroniclers started giving a list of the six electors: Doge Enrico Dandolo, Vitale Dandolo (allegedly admiral of the fleet), Ottavio (or Ottone) Querini, Bertuccio Contarini, Nicolò Navigaioso, and Pantaleone Barbo. Antonio Carile, *La cronachistica veneziana (secoli XII–XVI) di fronte alla spartizione della Romania nel 1204* (Florence: Leo S. Olschki, 1969), pp. 497, 501, 506, 519, 524, 528. It is hard to take this list seriously when it is always followed by what we know to be a completely erroneous list of the Frankish electors. There is also no contemporary or near-contemporary evidence that the doge himself served as an elector. Indeed, Villehardouin makes it clear that Dandolo was with the rest of the nobles when the committee's decision was an-

nounced. *Conquête de Constantinople*, sec. 260, 2: 66. Paolo Ramusio in the seventeenth century dropped Enrico Dandolo from the list, saying that the sixth elector was variously named in his sources as either Giovanni Baseggio or Giovanni Michiel. *De bello Constantinopolitano*, p. 136.

75. Robert of Clari, *Conquête*, sec. 93, p. 91. Robert says that all imperial palaces were to be evacuated, but mentions only the departure of Boniface from the Great Palace. There were a number of imperial palaces in the city. Boniface and Baldwin were only the two most consipicuous inhabitants.

76. According to Nicetas, the electors met in the Church of the Holy Apostles. *Historia*, p. 596. The senator left Constantinople almost one month before the election. As a result, his description of the event is extremely flawed.

77. Robert of Clari, *Conquête*, sec. 95, pp. 92–93; Villehardouin, *Conquête de Constantinople*, sec. 259, 2: 64–66.

78. There is a long tradition among Venetian chroniclers, dating as far back as Martin da Canal in the thirteenth century, that Enrico Dandolo was the initial choice to be emperor. Da Canal, *Les estoires de Venise*, p. 60; Dandolo, *Chronica per extensum descripta*, p. 279. Later chronicles asserted that on the Frankish side were chosen four French and two Lombards. When the election was held the four French voted for Baldwin of Flanders, the two Lombards for Boniface of Montferrat, five of the six Venetians for Enrico Dandolo, and one Venetian, Pantaleone Barbo, remained silent. Since the French favored Dandolo over Boniface, and the Lombards favored the doge over Baldwin it seemed that Dandolo would be elected. Just then, however, Barbo arose and said that if they elected the doge the French soldiers would leave and the empire would be defenseless. This convinced the Venetians to change their votes to Baldwin, and the others followed suit. Carile, *La cronachistica veneziana*, pp. 343, 363, 401, 411, 431, 466, 479. Another Venetian chronicle, attributed to Nicolò Trevisan, reports that all of the Venetian electors voted for Dandolo on the first ballot, while all of the Franks chose Baldwin. Then Ottavio Querini stood up and gave the same speech usually attributed to Pantaleone Barbo. As a result the Venetians switched their votes to Baldwin, thus unanimously electing him. Ibid., p. 510; Freddy Thiriet, "Les chroniques vénétiennes de la Marcienne et leur importance pour l'histoire de la Romanie gréco-vénitienne," *Mélanges d'archéologie et d'histoire: Ecole Française de Rome* 66 (1954): 265. These are late sources, puffed up with Venetian patriotism and family pride, but they may contain a nugget or two of truth. The breakdown of votes in most chronicles giving five for Dandolo, four for Baldwin, two for Boniface, and one abstention, is not unlikely given the leanings of the Frankish electors. A Pantaleone Barbo was alive in May 1187, but there is no evidence that he traveled to Constantinople with the crusade. Luzatto, *I Prestiti*, pp. 8–11, no. 2. Ottavio Querini, on the other hand, was a man with good familiarity with Constantinople. We find him there in a commerical document of May 1189. ASV, Canc. Inf. B. 178, 5. notai Superancio. (Codice diplomatico Lanfranchi, 3939). Enrico Dandolo chose him in 1198 as one of his ambassadors to Constantinople charged with negotiating the chrysobull with Alexius III. *TTh*, 1: 249. Three years after the imperial election Querini was appointed podesta of Constantinople. Nicol, *Byzantium and Venice*, p. 154. Nicetas Choniates states that Enrico Dandolo was excluded from consideration because of his blindness. *Historia*, p. 596. That seems unlikely, since that principle of exclusion had been eroded when Isaac II

was reinstated. Robert of Clari, in any event, saw Dandolo as a possible candidate. *Conquête*, sec. 93, p. 91.

79. Even Nicetas has great praise for Baldwin's moral character: "He was, furthermore, devout in his duties to God, and was reported to be temperate in his personal conduct; for as long as he was separated from his dear wife, he never so much as cast a glance at another woman. In singing the praises of God and in the face of every distress, he was unwavering. Most important, twice a week in the evening he had a herald proclaim that no one who slept within the palace was to have sexual intercourse with any woman who was not his legal wife." *Historia*, p. 597; Magoulias trans., p. 328.

80. Nicetas charged that the entire election process was manipulated by Dandolo through "fraud and deceit." This is easily chalked up to the senator's extraordinary hatred for the old doge. Such manipulations were unnecessary with the Venetian electors, who naturally opposed Boniface, and with the Frankish delegates, at least one of whom would surely favor Baldwin. Nicetas explains the Venetian reasoning by claiming that they wished to avoid having the emperor's lands so close to home, lest by running afoul of Byzantium they invited invasion of Venice. This may have been a minor consideration, although one wonders how seriously the marquis of Montferrat could threaten the lagoon city even in the best of times. Nicetas also points out that Boniface was an experienced statesman, while Baldwin was young, pliable, and deferred to Dandolo as a son does to a father. *Historia*, pp. 596–97. Here, the senator is at least partially right. A few months later, Dandolo was able to convince Emperor Baldwin to cease his war against Boniface of Montferrat by simply sending some messengers. The emperor "did not want to alienate the doge of Venice." Villehardouin, *Conquête de Constantinople*, sec. 295, 2: 102. Nonetheless, it was not in Dandolo's interest to have a weak emperor and therefore unstable empire. See the excellent arguments layed out by J. K. Fotheringham, *Marco Sanudo* (Oxford: Clarendon, 1915), pp. 22–24.

81. Villehardouin, *Conquête de Constantinople*, sec. 260, 2: 66; Robert of Clari, *Conquête*, sec. 95, p. 93.

82. Robert of Clari, *Conquête*, sec. 96, pp. 93–95; Villehardouin, *Conquête de Constantinople*, sec. 263, 2: 68–70; Letter of Baldwin of Flanders, in Innocent III, *Epistolae*, 7: 152, Migne, *PL*, CCXV: 451–52.

83. Robert of Clari, *Conquête*, sec. 97, p. 95; Villehardouin, *Conquête de Constantinople*, sec. 263, 2: 68–70.

84. Villehardouin, *Conquête de Constantinople*, sec. 376, 2: 184.

85. Innocent III, *Epistolae*, 8: 126, Migne, *PL*, CCXV: 701; Maleczek, *Petrus Capuanus*, pp. 193–94.

Bibliography

Essay on Primary Sources

Alfred J. Andrea

The most comprehensive eyewitness account of the Fourth Crusade is Geoffrey of Villehardouin's *La conquête de Constantinople*, and consequently any discussion of that crusade's sources must begin with Villehardouin's chronicle. Without his memoirs, which trace the course of the crusade from Fulk of Neuilly's preaching in 1198 to the death of Boniface of Montferrat in 1207, our knowledge of the events that made up the Fourth Crusade would be severely diminished. Geoffrey, who was about fifty years of age when he took the crusade vow in late 1199, had been the marshal of Champagne since 1185. As the count of Champagne's chief logistical officer and first deputy in all administrative and military matters, Villehardouin was widely respected for his good sense and organizational skills. Despite the fact that he was not a major feudal lord, Villehardouin's experience, maturity, and deserved reputation for sober judgment assured him a place in the second rank of the Fourth Crusade's leadership and full participation in the councils of the barons where all of the major strategic and tactical decisions were made. In fact, it was Geoffrey who had suggested to the French barons that they offer leadership of the army to Boniface of Montferrat. Villehardouin's crusade colleagues so trusted Geoffrey that they chose him to serve on a number of critical missions. He was one of the six plenipotentiaries who negotiated the army's treaty with Venice in 1201. Along with Hugh of Saint Pol, Villehardouin was sent in the early summer of 1202 to Pavia to convince Count Louis of Blois and large numbers of other French crusaders not to renege on their commitment to embark from Venice. On 18 July 1203 Villehardouin functioned as spokesman for the four-man crusader delegation that forced Emperor Isaac II to ratify the Treaty of Zara, and in November of that same year he was one of six crusader envoys chosen for the difficult and dangerous task of entering Blachernae Palace to demand full imperial compliance with the Treaty of Zara and, failing Alexius IV's acknowledgment of his obligation, to defy the emperor formally, thereby initiating a state of war. In brief, as a member of the crusade's inner circle of decision-makers and as one of its major actors, Geoffrey of Villehardouin possessed a knowledge of events unequaled by any other chronicler of the Fourth Crusade.

Several other characteristics also set Villehardouin's chronicle apart from most others. In an age whose writers generally exhibited little regard for quantitative precision, Villehardouin stood almost alone as a reporter whose numbers had the ring of authenticity. As we might well expect from a man whose office in Champagne had placed him in charge of all military preparations, Geoffrey of Villehardouin had a deep respect for correct facts and figures. When he informs us that, following the fire of 19–20 August 1203, some 15,000 resident Latins fled Constantinople to take refuge in the crusader camp, we can be reasonably sure that Villehardouin had not arbitrarily chosen some high figure as an artistic means of indicating that a large but indeterminate number of refugees had sought shelter in the crusader encampment. A man who was responsible for mustering armies naturally counted heads and possessed a good eye for estimating the size of crowds.

A good memory is also a desirable attribute for any successful staff officer, but even more important is that person's ability to keep and use records. When Villehardouin, then marshal of the entire Latin Empire of Constantinople, began to narrate his memoirs sometime prior to his death in 1212/1213, he possibly had access to copies of various official crusade documents, such as its treaties. Some historians have maintained that a number of passages in the *Conquest of Constantinople* appear to have been composed with such documents before the author's eyes. I remain unconvinced of this, but I do believe that the chronicle's rich details, which are unmatched by any other account of this crusade, suggest that Villehardouin used a personal journal or some form of notes as an aid to memory.

Given his position, talents, and access to information, Geoffrey of Villehardouin could and did proudly claim that he never knowingly uttered a false word in this account. A number of scholars, most notably Edmond Faral, who has produced the best modern edition of the *Conquête de Constantinople*, essentially accept Villehardouin's self-judgment as true. Other modern historians, however, are less sanguine when it comes to judging Villehardouin's reliability and even his veracity. The reason for their skepticism is simple. Villehardouin's position within the crusade leadership strongly suggests to them that his account is biased to the point of distortion and even contains deliberate falsehoods or, at least, suppressions of the whole truth. These skeptics often refer to Villehardouin as the crusade's "official historian." By that many of them mean he twisted or concealed facts that could damage the reputations of his colleagues and himself—all of whom, in some manner or other, had diverted the crusade to Constantinople for their own ends. Other, perhaps more charitable, skeptics simply see him as a dupe. Although he was not personally involved in a plot to divert the crusade, he was too ingenuous to probe deeply into the factors that drove the army to Constantinople. Therefore, he naively believed that the apparent happenstances that led the army to Constantinople constituted a series of totally random "accidents," when actually darker forces were at work.

As is often the case in such matters, the truth concerning Villehardouin's reliability as a witness seems to lie somewhere between the extremes. It would be foolish to believe that what we have in this chronicle is pure, unvarnished truth reported by an objective, uninvolved narrator. Such sources do not exist. At the same time, it is not inconceivable that Villehardouin honestly attempted to render a truthful and fairly complete account of the Fourth Crusade and its aftermath, and did a reasonably good job of it, despite blindspots, prejudices, and values that inevitably colored his narrative, as well as sharing the natural tendency of all memoir-writers to conveniently forget or underplay embarrassing details.

The thesis of Queller and Madden's study of the Fourth Crusade is that there was no conspiracy to divert the crusade in order to capture Constantinople. If one accepts that conclusion, then Villehardouin is exonerated of all charges of complicity in some putative plot to cover up the guilt of the crusade leadership. He also can no longer be viewed as a simple-minded dupe who was blind to the machinations of his feudal superiors. All of this in no way, however, belies what is to me the obvious reality that Villehardouin reported and interpreted events from the perspectives of his class, his culture, and the crusade leadership and that he also, at times, failed to report certain disquieting facts that could place the crusades, and especially the leaders, in a bad light. These unreported events include Boniface of Montferrat's meeting with Alexius the Younger at Christmas in 1201 and the sacking of Constantinople's churches in April of 1204.

As one of the architects of the 1201 Treaty of Venice, a treaty that Queller and Madden point to as the fatal flaw that ultimately led to the crusade's diversions to Zara and Constantinople, Villehardouin had a natural affinity with the party of the leadership that sought to keep the army together, whatever the price, and that resisted the party of conscientious recusants that, from Geoffrey's simplistic point of view, was continually working to break up the army. Needless to say, his history reflects his "spin" on the events that drove the crusade. From his perspective, the crusade leaders, of which he was one, acted reasonably and prudently in the face of a series of unforeseen crises. What is more, they acted honorably. Villehardouin was a *chevalier*, that particular type of professional warrior who cherished the ideals of chivalry, particularly the virtues of courage, honor, and loyalty. A blunt military man who tended to see life in black and white terms and who was not given to self-doubt or deep introspection, Villehardouin clearly identified the heroes and villains of his prose *chanson de geste*. The heroes were those who scrupulously kept their word and faith by remaining with the army, no matter the peril or vicissitudes of fortune; the villains were those, crusaders and Greeks alike, who proved false by abandoning or selling out the army, no matter their motives.

When we accept his account for what it is, the memoirs of a deeply involved and partisan crusade leader, who desired to tell *most* of the truth as he saw it and who was well-informed and unusually keen on details, then we must admit that, for all its shortcomings, Geoffrey's *Conquête de Constantinople* is one of the great historical sources to survive from medieval Europe. Persons who wish to read it in the original should consult the Faral edition, which is accompanied by a modern French translation. M. R. B. Shaw's 1963 English translation is available in an inexpensive Penguin paperback edition; Sir Frank Marzials's superior 1908 translation was reprinted in 1963. Patrick Tull narrates translated excerpts from the chronicle in a four-and-a-half-hour program on three audio cassettes from Recorded Books.

A second source, also titled *La conquête de Constantinople*, serves as a counterbalance to Villehardouin's view from the top. Narrated by Robert of Clari, a poor Picard knight, this account, which traces the fortunes of the crusade down to early 1205, allows us to view the crusade from the ranks and to see, close up, the face of battle. Clari, as is true of every rank-and-file soldier throughout history, was not privy to the plans of his leaders. Whereas Villehardouin gives us close-up views of the formulation of grand strategy, Clari gives us camp rumors and the grim realities of hand-to-hand combat. For those who seek the certainties of chronology and similar incontestable facts, Clari is most disappointing. In fact, he is scandalously unreliable on dates and all quantifiable data.

Notwithstanding this exaggeration of perspective, he tells an honest story, and regarding events that he actually witnessed or in which he participated, Clari contributes many interesting details to help fill in our picture of this crusade. He also serves as a healthy corrective to some of Villehardouin's oversights or selective lapses of memory. For example, he mentions the fact that Boniface and Alexius met in Germany in 1201. More important than these details is what Robert's story tells us of rank and file attitudes and beliefs. Some of the pieces of misinformation that he relates allow us to infer that at times the leaders, including Villehardouin, deliberately misled the army, probably out of a sense that certain information was dangerous in the wrong hands. For example, Robert incorrectly tells us that Pope Innocent III absolved the Venetians for their transgression at Zara—a convenient lie from the leaders' perspective. Even more telling are the attitudes that Robert reflects. In his view, Greeks are treacherous and cowardly, and he seems to accept without reservation the judgment by the army's ranking clerics that the Byzantines were "enemies of God." Although he presents a favorable view of the Venetians and their doge, and certainly does not implicate Dandolo or any other crusade leader in any plot to capture Constantinople for themselves, Robert does articulate what appears to have been a widespread dissatisfaction among the lower ranks toward the way in which their leaders had cheated them in the distribution of Constantinople's spoils. Although artlessly narrated, Clari's account is a compelling story that brings alive, in ways a more polished piece of prose could never capture, the experiences and perspectives of a common soldier in the field.

Philippe Lauer has edited Clari's work, and Edgar H. McNeal provides an English translation with good notes and introduction. On the other hand, the notes accompanying Anna Maria Nada Patrone's Italian translation of Clari's account should be used with some caution.

Because most Fourth Crusade sources were composed by either clerics or high-ranking secular leaders, Clari is rare in providing us a view from the crusade's rank and file. The only other source that can claim a similar perspective is the *Devastatio Constantinopolitana*. This short, anonymous history was probably the work of a low-ranking cleric from the German Rhineland who participated in the crusade and, following the capture of Constantinople in 1204, was left with the feeling that the crusade's leaders had sold out the crusader poor—the *Pauperes Christi*—for their own profit. According to the *Devastatio*, at each crucial juncture of the crusade—Venice, Zara, and Constantinople—the poorer elements were exploited by their superiors, first the Venetians, then the barons, and finally the Venetians and barons in concert. In the process, the crusade foundered on the rock of greed as the not-so-noble nobles betrayed their crusade vow and the commoners who had kept faith with that vow and their leaders.

In addition to providing this special viewpoint, the *Devastatio* abounds in factual data. Very much like Villehardouin, this clerical author was a record keeper and delighted in providing generally reliable numbers, dates, prices, payments, and losses. In fact, the *Devastatio*'s dates are more numerous and precise than those provided by Villehardouin. All of this suggests that the author held some low-level administrative post, possibly in a cathedral, and composed his history from notes or a personal journal after he had returned to the Rhineland.

Because of its concentration on the progress of the crusade pilgrimage undertaken by those who were "poor in the eyes of the world" and its author's concomitant fixation with providing accurate facts and figures, the *Devastatio Constantinopolitana* nicely complements both Villehardouin and Clari. Those who wish to read the *Devastatio* should consult my recent new edition of the text and its accompanying English translation with notes and analytical introduction in *Historical Reflections*, 19 (1993). Older editions are in *Chroniques gréco-romanes* by Charles Hopf and volume 16 of the *Monumenta Germaniae historica, Scriptores*. M. A. C. de Muschietti and B. S. Díaz-Pereyra have published a Spanish translation with notes and introduction, but one must be careful in using the notes because they contain a number of factual errors.

Despite its underlying religious message, the *Devastatio* is devoid of overt expressions of conventional piety, and miracles play no role whatsoever in this rather sober and somber history. Such was not the case for three other histories, each of which celebrated the triumphs of their respective ecclesiastical heroes, who carried home from Constantinople sacred relic spoils as signs of divine favor and crusade success. However, although they share a common genre by virtue of their celebrating and cataloging these translations of relics, the three histories are dissimilar in many essential respects.

The lengthiest, most complex, and most important of the three is the *Hystoria Constantinopolitana* by Gunther, a Cistercian monk of the Alsatian abbey of Pairis. Gunther was not a crusade participant but based his history on the reminiscences of his abbot Martin, who apparently commissioned the work in which he plays a major role. The abbot of Pairis preached the crusade in his native Basel in 1201 and then joined the army in Venice during the high summer of 1202. Leaving the main body of crusaders at Zara, Abbot Martin sailed by way of Italy to the Holy Land, which he reached in midspring of 1203. Later he rejoined the army, arriving at Constantinople on 1 January 1204, just in time to witness the last stages of the crusader-Byzantine conflict and to participate in the April sack of the city. During this pillage Martin robbed the abbey church of the Pantocrator of numerous sacred relics, which he brought back with high ceremony to his monastery in March of 1205. Before the year was over Gunther had essentially completed the *Hystoria*.

Gunther, who had entered the Cistercian order in midlife, was already a celebrated man of letters in southwestern Germany. When Abbot Martin commissioned Gunther to write what became the *Hystoria Constantinopolitana*, he probably envisioned a simple work that would celebrate his exploits and justify his pious thievery. What he received was something quite extraordinary. Gunther's apologetical history did defend Abbot Martin from all possible charges of impropriety, but it also went well beyond that objective by justifying the crusader capture of Christian Constantinople as the handiwork of Divine Providence. Using all of his considerable literary skills and intellectual powers, Gunther crafted a tightly constructed masterpiece of interspersed prose and poetry in which every element is subordinated to the work's overarching theme: all the deeds mentioned in this history, even those that are apparently impious, were done under the direction of God in order to effect a historically significant change in the course of human events and to offer his servants an opportunity to cooperate in the salvation of their souls.

Gunther's grand view of human history resulted in his twisting certain historical phenomena to fit his metahistorical mold. His apologetical purposes also compromised the *Hystoria*'s worth as a factual source. Errors abound in the work and, were we to use it uncritically, we would be misled on many points. Certainly the *Hystoria Constantinopolitana* has limited value for anyone concentrating on the political and military aspects of the Fourth Crusade, but we should not be surprised by that fact. Both Gunther and Martin were clerics and, more specifically, monks. Each had, at best, only a meager understanding of and interest in military grand strategy and battlefield tactics. Abbot Martin had not been involved in the high councils of the crusade leaders nor had he directly participated in the assaults on Zara and Constantinople. His memories of these battles could not have been more than hazy impressions. When Martin's imperfect recollections combined with Gunther's artistic, apologetical, and theological purposes, the result was an account heavy with factual errors. However, it would be foolish to dismiss all of the *Hystoria*'s statements as fabrication. It provides some reliable details that are verifiable from other sources and that do fill out our story of the Fourth Crusade. Supported as it is on a number of significant points, the *Hystoria* definitely is not a totally worthless source for even the strictly political-military events of the crusade. However, its value far exceeds its being simply an adjunct to the accounts of Villehardouin and Clari.

As a clerical history, the *Hystoria Constantinopolitana* provides important insights for historians specializing in medieval religious culture and the psychosocial environment of the crusades. One example must suffice in this brief overview. In chapter 3 Gunther "records" the crusade sermon delivered by Abbot Martin in Basel. Although surely the sermon as written was crafted by Gunther, in all likelihood it contains the basic elements of Martin's sermon. As such, it reveals the major motives of the rank and file crusader: a conviction that he was called to this duty by Christ who needed his help; a belief that the

Holy Land possessed a special sanctity—the sanctity of a relic—which had to
be defended against the defilement of the unbeliever; and the hope that God
would reward him for this holy work with both salvation and earthly prosperity. We must understand this expectation of a sure reward at the expense of
those whom God judges unworthy, if we wish to understand Abbot Martin's
later pious pilferage of relics, which was born, Gunther tells us, out of a desire,
not to "remain empty-handed while everyone else got rich." To refuse these
heaven-endowed rewards would be tantamount to denying the will of God.

Presently the best available edition of Gunther's work is now that of
Peter Orth, which appeared in 1994. The older edition can be found in Paul
Riant's *Exuviae*. My English translation, with analytical introduction and
notes, appears under the title *The Capture of Constantinople*. The bibliography
that accompanies the book lists several articles by Francis Swietek and me
that analyze the *Hystoria* as a historical source and piece of literature.

One of the more important insights that the *Hystoria* offers is to show
how Abbot Martin wrestled with the conflicting claims of private conscience
and group loyalty at Zara, thereby shedding light on the meaning of the crusade vow to the average pilgrim. A second German source, the account written by the so-called Anonymous of Halberstadt, deals with the same issue,
and there are a number of other striking similarities between these two Fourth
Crusade sources, even though they differ greatly so far as scope of vision and
artistic merit are concerned. As already noted, each serves, in part, to catalog and authenticate sacred relics brought to Germany from Constantinople.
Each was composed by a stay-at-home ecclesiastical subordinate from the testimony of a high-ranking clerical crusader, and both attempt to vindicate the
individuals whose memories they record. In the case of the Anonymous of
Halberstadt, that crusader was Conrad of Krosigk, bishop of Halberstadt in
Saxony.

Written by an unknown clerk of the cathedral of Halberstadt around
1208–1209, the Anonymous of Halberstadt's account of Bishop Conrad's adventures is incorporated into the final pages of the *Gesta*, or *The Deeds of the
Bishops of Halberstadt*. Insofar as the last segment of the *Gesta episcoporum Halberstadensium* is a defense of the often troubled pontificate of Conrad, who
served as Halberstadt's bishop from 1201 to 1208, this crusade account must
be read in the context of the larger story to which it is subordinated. Like the
pages that precede and follow, the Anonymous of Halberstadt's story of the
Fourth Crusade helps to develop the theme that Bishop Conrad was a righteous man, despite the fact that he lay under a papal ban of excommunication
while on crusade. In order not to weaken that argument, the Halberstadt
chronicler fails to mention or passes briefly over a fair amount of potentially
embarrassing material. Indeed, he devotes only a single lengthy sentence to

the entire fourteen-month period in which Conrad was in and around Constantinople. We read nothing about the slaughter of fellow Christians at Constantinople or the sack of its churches. The value of the Anonymous of Halberstadt's account lies in what he tells us of the events preceding the army's arrival at Constantinople, especially in regard to its stopovers at Zara and Corfu, and Conrad's adventures in the Holy Land and Rome after the capture of Constantinople. Like the *Hystoria Constantinopolitana*, this chronicle is especially valuable for those who study the psychology of the crusading movement.

Paul Riant has excerpted the Latin text of the crusade portions of the *Gesta episcoporum Halberstadensium* in his *Exuviae*, where he argues that this account should be detached from the chronicle in which it appears. For reasons articulated above, I disagree. The full text appears in the *Monumenta Germaniae historica, Scriptores*, volume 23. My articles on Fourth Crusade Cistercian sources and Conrad of Krosigk contain fuller treatments of the Anonymous of Halberstadt, and my translation and analysis of the portions of the *Gesta episcoporum Halberstadensium* relating to the Fourth Crusade appears in *Historical Reflections*.

The third major clerical source to authenticate and catalog relics taken in the sack of Constantinople is the little work with the big title: *De terre Iherosolimitana et quomodo ab urbe Constantinopolitana ad hanc ecclesiam allate sunt reliquie (Concerning the Land of Jerusalem and the Means by Which Relics Were Carried to This Church from the City of Constantinople)*, by an author known simply as the Anonymous of Soissons. This unnamed person was probably a canon of Soissons cathedral, who received his information from Nevelon de Chérisy, bishop of Soissons (r. 1176–1207) and chief prelate of the Fourth Crusade army. The account tells us very little about the political and military aspects of the crusade, but it is a rich religious document. Like Gunther of Pairis, the Anonymous of Soissons not only wrote a *translatio*, in which he dealt with the translation of relics, but he also composed a theodicy, in which he attempted to demonstrate the workings of Divine Justice in the face of evil and human suffering. In brief, this work places the events of 1202–1204 into the context of over one hundred years of crusade history, and its thesis is that the conquest of Constantinople and the subsequent transfer of sacred relics to the West was an acceptable, albeit incomplete, realization of the crusade quest. As a justification of the Fourth Crusade, this work must be studied by anyone interested in "crusader mentalities."

A study, critical edition, and English translation of this Latin text appears in the article Paul Rachlin and I co-authored for *Historical Reflections*. An earlier edition appears in Riant's *Exuviae*.

Other ecclesiastical documents that merit careful attention are the registers, or recorded letters, of Pope Innocent III (r. 1198–1216) and the *Gesta Innocentii III* (*The Deeds of Innocent III*), an adulatory biography of the pope written around 1208 by an unknown curial official, probably a functionary in the papal chancery, or secretariat. The *Gesta* gives us the official curial position on the crusade and also provides numerous details that would otherwise be lost. For example, it is the only source that mentions Boniface of Montferrat's meeting with the pope in March of 1202. Perhaps the greatest value of this biography is that its author interspersed in his text large numbers of papal letters, some of which are not preserved in the extant registers of Pope Innocent III.

Innocent's correspondence, however preserved, is likewise an important body of evidence for anyone who wishes to understand the Fourth Crusade in all of its complexity. As official, carefully crafted documents, the papal letters offer interesting testimony to the policies and public postures of the pope. Innocent, who was one of the most capable individuals ever to hold the papal throne, was, in some respects, exceedingly ill-informed about a crusade that he was incapable of controlling, no matter how hard he tried. His lack of adequate information and frustration over his inability to control events come through clearly in many of his letters regarding the crusade. On some issues, to the contrary, he possessed unique firsthand knowledge, and often in these cases his letters provide eloquent evidence of his attempts to turn his knowledge to the advantage of the Church and the crusade whose success was so close to his heart. When studying Innocent's role in regard to the Fourth Crusade, we must begin with letters that he sent out as early as 1198 and must carry our investigation down through at least 1205. One area that needs particular attention, but which is often overlooked by historians of the Fourth Crusade, is the pope's convoluted relations with Emperor Alexius III from 1198 through 1202.

The *Gesta Innocentii III*, which is sorely in need of a new edition, is presently available for most researchers only in Migne's *Patrologia Latina*, volume 214. However, David Gress-Wright's 1981 Ph.D. dissertation at Bryn Mawr, "The *Gesta Innocentii III*: Text, Introduction and Commentary," gives promise of a forthcoming published edition, and Professor John C. Moore of Hofstra is also presently working on a new edition of this valuable text. I am working on a translation, with commentary, of those portions of the *Gesta* that relate to the Fourth Crusade, as well as Innocent's relations with the Greeks of Constantinople. Theodosius Haluščynskyj has edited many of Innocent's letters that relate to Eastern Christian matters, including the crusade, in *Acta Innocentii III*, the second volume of a series of papal materials relating to all Eastern churches produced by the Papal Commission for the

Codification of Oriental Canon Law (1944). In 1964 Othmar Hageneder and others inaugurated a totally new edition of all of Innocent's extant correspondence. To date they have produced four volumes that cover the pontifical years 1198–1199, 1199–1200, 1202–1203, and 1203–1204. Until this massive project is completed, the best available collection remains Migne's *Patrologia Latina*, volumes 214–217. For those who read Greek, two letters by Patriarch John X Camaterus to Innocent III sent in 1199 and 1200 have been edited by A. Papadakis and Alice Mary Talbot in *Byzantinoslavica*, 31 (1972). The second letter, which apparently Innocent never saw, is especially important for the light it sheds on the depth of the ecclesiastical differences between Rome and Constantinople on the eve of the Fourth Crusade. As noted by Queller and Madden, however, the Papadakis and Talbot edition has its critics. In 1979 Jannis Spiteris reedited the crucial second letter and provided an Italian translation of it. A thirteenth-century Latin translation of the patriarch's first letter exists in the registers for Pope Innocent's second pontifical year.

G. L. F. Tafel and G. M. Thomas have also published a number of Pope Innocent's more important letters relating to the Fourth Crusade in volumes 1 and 2 of *Urkunden zur älteren Handels- und Staatsgeschichte der Republik Venedig*, along with numerous other documents concerning Venice's involvement in the Levant. These include the Treaty of Venice of 1201 and the pre-conquest compact of 1204 between the Venetians and their fellow crusaders concerning partition of the empire. Antonio Carile has provided a better edition of this latter treaty, known as the *Partitio Terrarum Imperii Romanie*, in volume 7 (1965) of *Studi veneziani*. Tafel and Thomas also provide copies of two important crusader letters composed shortly after each capture of Constantinople: the letter of Hugh of Saint Pol to Duke Henry of Louvain written toward the end of 1203 and the encyclical letter of Emperor Baldwin I sent out in the summer of 1204. Emperor Baldwin's letter, as well as the general letter sent to the West during the summer of 1203 in the names of Baldwin of Flanders, Hugh of Saint Pol, and Louis of Blois, is located in a number of other collections, most notably and recently in volume 2 of *De Oorkonden der graven van Vlaanderen (1191–aanvang 1206)*, edited by W. Prevenier.

The value of these three baronial letters, two from 1203 and one from 1204, is that, unlike the memoirs of Villehardouin and Clari, they were written quite soon after the events they describe. One historian has gone so far as to claim that, because of their immediacy, they collectively constitute the best source for the Fourth Crusade. I do not go that far, but I agree that historians have tended to grossly undervalue them. Of the three, I especially favor Count Hugh's letter to his friend Henry of Louvain. Unlike the other two baronial letters, it was not a partisan brief intended for a general audience and written in defense of questionable actions. It was a letter from one warrior to another describing how the crusade army managed to find itself at Constantinople and providing a vivid description of the combat that ensued prior to the city's first capitulation in 1203. More than that, it clearly shows Count Hugh's belief that, following a winter respite in Constantinople, the army would set sail to fight its "tournament against the sultan of Babylon in the city of Alexandria." Anyone who believes that Hugh of Saint Pol, one of the five chief leaders of the crusade, was part of a conspiracy to divert the army permanently to Constantinople and to capture the city for some Western lord must necessarily explain away the evidence provided by this letter.

Another major crusade source that has a value no less great than that of Villehardouin's memoirs is Nicetas Choniates's *History*. Nicetas, whose history spans the years 1118 to 1207, is the principal Byzantine historian for the period 1180–1205, an era in which he played a major role in governmental affairs. Having lived through the events of 1203–1204, he wrote about them in detail and with passion. Choniates had no doubt that Constantinople's capture and the subsequent miseries that he and his family endured were the consequence of a plot laid by Enrico Dandolo, in order to pay the empire back for injuries suffered by the Venetians in 1171. He further believed that Innocent III, as well as Philip of Swabia, openly supported the diversion to Constantinople. At the same time, Nicetas believed that the Byzantines shared in the blame for the disasters of 1203 and 1204 and pointed to years of imperial shortsightedness and gross malfeasance that combined to weaken the empire to a critical point. We might question Nicetas's theory of a Western plot to capture Constantinople, but there is no reason to dismiss the rich details he provides as he presents the story of the Fourth Crusade as seen from within the walls of the imperial capital by a high-ranking senator. Whereas the Western sources are almost universally silent concerning the three-day sack of the city, which began on 13 April 1204, Nicetas provides a vivid and emotionally moving account of the pillage. To underscore the brutality of the Latin capture of the city, he appended to his history a description of some of the more notable works of art destroyed by the crusader captors of Constantinople. To be sure, Choniates, as is true of every other source, had his prejudices and blindspots. He certainly had nothing but contempt for both the Latin crusaders and the four Byzantine emperors who held the throne during the fateful year in which the city was twice captured. When, however, those perspectives are taken into account, one must acknowledge that Nicetas Choniates's *History* is one of our most important sources for the Fourth Crusade, and without it we would know considerably less about this crusade and its major actors.

Jan-Louis van Dieten published the definitive edition of the *History* in 1975, and Harry J. Magoulias has translated the work into English under the title *O City of Byzantium, Annals of Niketas Choniates* (1984). Magoulias's accompanying notes and introduction are as solid as his fine translation.

A second Eastern Christian source comes to us from the pages of the Russian *Chronicle of Novgorod*. The account is confused and fanciful in places, but it does have its value. If we can believe it, this source clearly states that Alexius IV deposed his father Isaac II, who then entered a monastery and predeceased his son. It also provides a short description of the crusader ransacking of Hagia Sophia and other churches and monasteries. Also, for what it is worth, the chronicler denies that Pope Innocent and King Philip of Swabia sought the capture and sacking of Constantinople and the establishment of a Latin empire there.

This exculpation of the pope and the Hohenstaufen king of Germany, as well as a few word choices that vaguely suggest a Low German connection, have led two scholars to conclude that the chronicler had a connection with the German crusader camp and specifically with Bishop Conrad von Krosigk, the eventual eyewitness source for the Anonymous of Halberstadt. I am totally unconvinced by this thesis. What I think we can say with some assurance is that the Novgorod chronicler was drawing from the memory of someone who was in Constantinople in April of 1204 and who had equal sympathy for "the God-preserved city of Constantine" and the Roman pope and German king.

The best English translation of this account, with commentary, is Jared Gordon, "The Novgorod Account of the Fourth Crusade," *Byzantion*, 43 (1973): 297–311. The most recent edition of the text, with a French translation, is Sylvain Patri, "La relation russe de la quatrième croisade," *Byzantion*, 58 (1988): 461–501. D. Freydank argues for a connection with the Bishop of Halberstadt in his 1968 article in *Byzantinoslavica*.

One eyewitness source that only takes us as far as Zara, but is quite important for shedding light on that pivotal episode, is Peter of Vaux-de-Cernay's *Hystoria Albigensis*. This history of the later Albigensian Crusade, in which Simon of Montfort and Abbot Guy of Vaux-de-Cernay played such prominent roles, was composed by Abbot Guy's nephew, the Cistercian monk Peter, who had accompanied his uncle and Simon of Montfort to Zara and with them departed from Zara for the Holy Land by way of Apulia. Except for possibly the *Gesta Innocentii III*, Peter's account of the affair at Zara is the most anti-Venetian of all the Western sources for the Fourth Crusade, and that is largely due the view shared by the party of Simon of Montfort that one's first loyalty must lie totally with the crusade vow and not with any army or treaty. Needless to say, this opinion differed radically from that held by Villehardouin.

Pascal Guébin and Ernest Lyon have edited Peter's *History* in three volumes. My article on Cistercian sources deals with this account, as well as all other Fourth Crusade sources composed by or for Cistercian monks, including two minor sources not mentioned in this essay—the later, secondhand accounts of Alberic of Trois-Fontaines and Abbot Ralph of Coggeshall.

One secondhand account that looks at the crusade from a considerable distance of time and space that should be listed here is the *Chronique* of Ernoul-Bernard. This multi-authored work is a continuation of the crusading history of William of Tyre and reflects the perspective, knowledge, and opinions of Latins residing in the crusader states of the Holy Land. Ernoul-Bernard should not be taken seriously regarding the plans and motives of the leaders of the Fourth Crusade who sailed from Venice, but the chronicle does provide important information on those crusaders, what Queller terms "the neglected majority," who proceeded by other means to Palestine.

Louis de Mas Latrie prepared the standard edition of this chronicle in the nineteenth century. M. R. Morgan, *The Chronicle of Ernoul and the Continuations of William of Tyre* (1973), sheds light on the complex history of this chronicle.

Finally, thanks to Donald Queller's first edition of *The Fourth Crusade*, historians of the crusades are now aware that the poems of Raimbaut de Vaqueiras, friend and companion of Boniface of Montferrat, who probably died with Boniface on the field of battle in 1207, offer us some interesting insights into the emotions of those who swore the cross. We also learn much about the character of Boniface from Raimbaut's poetic testimony, and his *Epic Letter* provides a few minor, but nonetheless solid details concerning the conquest of Constantinople. Joseph Linskill has edited, translated, and analyzed Raimbaut's work.

There are numerous minor sources, many of them of marginal value due to their distance from the events, which could also be mentioned here, but to do so would serve no practical purpose due to their lack of substantive worth and their general unavailability. Many of the above-mentioned major sources are presently available in English translation, and more will be translated before the turn of the millennium. When assembled by the enterprising student, even one who has no Latin and less Greek, they collectively make it possible for the historian-as-detective to delve into the fascinating mystery of the Fourth Crusade with reasonable hope of drawing intellectually defensible conclusions. The Fourth Crusade is too important and interesting to be left exclusively to professional historians.

Primary Sources

Acropolita, Georgius. *Annales*. Ed. Immanuel Bekker. In *Corpus scriptorum historiae Byzantinae*, vol. 27. Bonn, 1836.

Alberic of Trois-Fontaines. *Chronica*. Ed. P. Scheffer-Boichorst. *MGH, SS*, 23: 631–950.

Annales Venetici breves. Ed. H. Simonsfeld. *MGH, SS*, 14: 69–72.

Anonymous of Gaeta. *Qualiter caput beati Theodori martyris de Constantinopolitana urbe ad Caietam translatum est*. In *Exuviae sacrae Constantinopolitanae*, ed. Paul Riant, 1: 150–55. Paris: E. Leroux, 1877–1904.

Anonymous of Halberstadt. *De peregrinatione in Greciam et adventu reliquiarum de Grecia libellus*. In *Exuviae sacrae Constantinopolitanae*, ed. Paul Riant, 1: 10–21. Paris: E. Leroux, 1877–1904. (Riant urges that the *De perigrinatione in Greciam* should be detached, as it is here, from the Chronicle of Halberstadt.) Also in the *Gesta episcoporum Halberstadensium*. Ed. Ludewicus Weiland, in *MGH, SS*, 23: 73–123. (We have used both versions, but have cited the *MGH, SS* for the convenience of the reader.) Eng. translation by Alfred J. Andrea, in "The Anonymous Chronicler of Halberstadt's Account of the Fourth Crusade: Popular Religiosity in the Early Thirteenth Century." *Historical Reflections* 27 (1996): 457–77.

Anonymous of Langres. *Historia translationum reliquiarum s. Mamantis*. In *Exuviae sacrae Constantinopolitanae*, ed. Paul Riant, 1: 22–34. Paris: E. Leroux, 1877–1904.

Anonymous of Soissons. *De terra Iherosolimitana et quomodo ab urbe Constantinopolitana ad hanc ecclesiam allate sunt reliquie*. Ed. Alfred J. Andrea. In Alfred J. Andrea and Paul I. Rachlin, "Holy War, Holy Relics, Holy Theft: The Anonymous of Soissons's *De terra Ihersolomitana*, An Analysis, Edition, and Translation." *Historical Reflections* 18 (1992): 157–75. Also in *Exuviae sacrae Constantinopolitanae*, ed. Paul Riant, 1: 1–9. Paris: E. Leroux, 1877–1904.

Arnold of Lübeck. *Chronica Slavorum libri VII*. Ed. J. M. Lappenberg. *MGH, SS*, 21: 115–20.

Baldwin of Flanders. *Epistola* (addressed to Innocent III). In *De Oorkonden der graven van Vlaanderen (1191–aanvang 1206)*, ed. W. Prevenier, 2: 564–77, no. 271. Brussels: Paleis der Academien, 1964. Also in Migne, *PL*, CCXV: 447–54; TTh., I: 502–11. The same letter, addressed to Adolph, Archbishop of Cologne, is in Prevenier, *Oorkonden*, 2: 577–83, no. 272. Also in *Annales Coloniensis*, MGH, SS, 17: 815–18. The same letter, addressed to the abbot of Cîteaux and other abbots of the order, is in Prevenier, *Oorkonden*, 2: 583–91, no. 273. The same letter, addressed to all Christians, is in Prevenier, *Oorkonden*, 2: 591–603, no. 274. Also in Arnold of Lübeck, *Chronica Slavorum*, *MGH, SS*, 21: 226–30. We have cited the version addressed to the pope, assuming it to be the original, and the edition in Migne, *PL*, since it is widely available. Prevenier, however, is much to be preferred.

Baldwin of Flanders, Louis of Blois, Hugh of Saint Pol, and other barons and knights. *Epistola*. In *De Oorkonden der graven van Vlaanderen (1191–aanvang 1206)*, ed. W. Prevenier, 2: 542–45, no. 260. Brussels: Paleis der Academien, 1964; in *Rec. hist. Gaules*, 18: 515–16; (with a different address) in Arnold of Lübeck, *Chronica Slavorum, MGH, SS*, 21: 224–26.

Bede, *De locis sanctis*. Chap. 20 in *Itineraria Hierosolymitana et descriptiones terrae sanctae bellis sacris anteriora*, ed. Titus Tobler and Augustus Molinier. 3 vols., Geneva, 1879.

Benjamin of Tudela. *The Itinerary*. Trans. Marcus Nathan Adler. London, 1903; repr. Malibu, Calif.: Joseph Simon Pangloss, 1987.

Caroldo, Gian Giacopo. *Historia de Venetia*. Biblioteca Marciana, cl. ital. VII, cod. 127 (=8034).

Chronica regia Coloniensis (Annales maximi Colonienses). Ed. George Waitz. *MGH, Scriptores rerum Germanicarum*, 18 (Hannover, 1880).

The Chronicle of Novgorod (1016–1471). Trans. Robert Michell and Nevill Forbes in Camden Third Series. Vol. 25. London: Camden Society, 1914. A more recent translation is by Jared Gordon, "The Novgorod Account of the Fourth Crusade." *Byzantion* 58 (1973): 297–311. The most recent edition, accompanied by a French translation, is by Sylvain Patri. "La relation russe de la quatrième croisade." *Byzantion* 58 (1988): 461–501.

Chronicon Hanoniense quod dicitur Balduini Avennensis. Ed. Joh. Heller. *MGH, SS*, 25: 419–67.

Chronique de la conquête de Constantinople. Trans. J. A. Buchon. Paris: Verdiere, 1825.

Codice diplomatico della repubblica di Genova. Ed. Cesare di Imperiale. In *Fonti per la storia d'Italia*, vol. 79. Rome, 1936–42.

Comnena, Anna. *The Alexiad*. Trans. Elizabeth A. S. Dawes. London: Routledge and K. Paul, 1967.

Conon of Béthune. *Les chansons de Conon de Béthune*. Ed. Axel Wallensköld. Paris: H. Champion, 1921. Also in *Recueil de chants historiques français*. Ed. Antoine le Roux de Lincy. 1st ser. Paris: C. Gosselin, 1841.

Cronaca Bemba. Biblioteca Marciana, cl. ital. VII, cod. 125 (=7460).

Crusaders as Conquerors: The Chronicle of Morea. Trans. Harold E. Lurier. New York and London: Columbia University Press, 1964. (See *Livre de la conqueste de la princée de l'Amorée*.)

Da Canal, Martin. *Les estoires de Venise: Cronaca veneziana in lingua francese dalle origini al 1275*. Ed. Alberto Limentani. Florence: Leo S. Olschki, 1972. An older edition is *La cronique des Veniciens*, ed. Filippo-Luigi Polidori, Ital. trans. Giovanni Galvani, *Archivio Storico Italiano*, ser. 1, 8 (1845): 229–776.

Dandolo, Andrea. *Chronica per extensum descripta*. Ed. Ester Pastorello. *Rerum Italicarum Scriptores*, vol. 12, part. 1: 1–327. Bologna, 1938.

———. *Chronica brevis*. Ed. E. Pastorello. *Rerum Italicarum Scriptores*, vol. 12, part. 1: 329–73. Bologna, 1938.

Del Carretto, Galeotto. *Cronica di Monferratto*. Ed. Gustave Avrogado. In *Monumenta historiae patriae*. Vol. 5: 1081–1300.

Devastatio Constantinopolitana. Ed. and trans. Alfred J. Andrea, in "The *Devastatio Constantinopolitana*, a Special Perspective on the Fourth Crusade: An Analysis, New Edition, and Translation." *Historical Reflections* 19 (1993): 131–49. Also in

Chroniques gréco-romanes, ed. Charles Hopf Berlin, 1873; repr. Brussels: Culture et Civilisation, 1966 pp. 86–92. Also in the *Annales Herbipolensis*, ed. Karl Pertz. *MGH, SS*, 16: 9–12. "*Devastatio Constantinopolitana*: Introduccion, traduccion y notas," ed. M. A. C. de Muschietti and B. S. Díaz-Pereyra. In *Anales de historia antiqua y medieval* 15 (1970): 171–200.

Documenti del commercio veneziano nei secoli XI–XIII. Ed. Raimondo Morozzo della Rocca and Antonino Lombardo. 2 vols. Rome: R. Istituto storico italiano per il medio evo, 1940.

Documents relatifs au comté de Champagne et de Brie (1172–1361). Ed. Auguste Longnon. 2 vols. Paris: Imprimerie nationale, 1901–14.

Dolfin, Zorzi. *Chronica*. Biblioteca Marciana, cl. ital. VII, cod. 794 (=8503).

Ernoul and Bernard le Trésorier. *Chronique*. Ed. Louis de Mas Latrie. Paris: Mme Ve J. Renouard, 1871. (Consult M. R. Morgan, *The Chronicle of Ernoul and the Continuations of William of Tyre* [Oxford: Oxford University Press, 1973]. We do not have the original chronicle of Ernoul, which, in any case, ends in 1197. For the Fourth Crusade all the texts are almost the same, and all should be used with some caution.)

Exuviae sacrae Constantinopolitanae. Ed. Paul Riant. 3 vols. Paris: E. Leroux, 1877–1904.

Gesta Innocentii PP. III. Ed. in Migne, *PL*, CCXIV: 18–228.

Guillaume le Bréton. *Gesta Philippi Augusti*. In *Rec. hist. Gaules*, 17: 62–116.

Gunther of Pairis. *Hystoria Constantinopolitana*. Ed. Peter Orth. Hildesheim and Zurich: Weidmann, 1994. The older edition is *Historia Constantinopolitana* in *Exuviae sacrae Constantinopolitanae*, ed. Paul Riant, 1: 57–126. Paris: E. Leroux, 1877–1904. Trans. into German by Erwin Assman, Cologne-Graz, 1956. Alfred J. Andrea has kindly let us use his translation and notes in manuscript form (published by the University of Pennsylvania Press as *The Capture of Constantinople: The "Hystoria Constantinopolitana" of Gunther of Pairis* [1997]).

Historia ducum Veneticorum. Supplementum. Ed. H. Simonsfeld. *MGH, SS*, 14: 89–94.

Hubaldus of Pisa. *Das Imbreviaturbuch des Erzbischöflichen Gerichtsnotars Hubaldus aus Pisa*. Ed. Gero Dolezalek. Cologne-Vienna: Böhlau, 1969.

Hugh of Saint Pol. *Epistola*. Ed. in *Annales Coloniensis maximi, MGH, SS*, 17: 812–14. Also in *TTh.*, 1: 304–11, and in *Rec. his. Gaules*, 18: 517–19. Another version of this letter, addressed differently, with some minor variations and, most importantly, an additional paragraph, is found in Rudolf Pokorny, ed., "Zwei unedierte Briefe aus der Frühzeit des lateinischen Kaiserreichs von Konstantinopel." *Byzantion* 55 (1985): 203–9.

Innocent III. *Epistolae*. In Migne, *PL*, CCXIV–CCXVII.

———. *The Letters of Pope Innocent III (1198–1216) concerning England and Wales*. Ed. and trans. C. R. Cheney and Mary G. Cheney. Oxford: Clarendon, 1967.

———. "Lettres inédites d'Innocent III." Ed. Léopold Delisle. *Bibliothèque de l'Ecole des Chartres*, 34 (1873): 397–419.

———. *Regestum Innocentii III papae super negotio Romani imperii*. Ed. Friedrich Kempf. Rome: Pontificia Universita gregoriana, 1947.

———. *Die Register Innocenz' III*. Vol. I. Ed. Othmar Hageneder and Anton Haidacher. Graz-Cologne: Hermann Böhlaus Nachf., 1964. Vol. II. Ed. Othmar Hageneder, Werner Maleczek, and Alfred A. Strnad. Rome-Vienna: Österreichischen Akademie der Wissenschaften, 1979. Vol. V. Ed. Othmar Hageneder, Christoph Egger, Karl Rudolf, and Andrea Sommerlechner. Vienna: Österreichischen Akademie der Wissenschaften, 1993. Vol. VI: Ed. Othmar Hageneder, John C. Moore, and Andrea Sommerlechner. Vienna: Österreichischen Akademie der Wissenschaften, 1995.

———. *Registrum de negotio Romani Imperii*. In Migne, *PL*, CCXVI.

———. "Rubrice Registri litterarum secretarum fel. rec. Domini Innocentii pape tertii de anno pontificatus sui III. IV. (XVIII. et XIX.)." In *Vetera monumenta slavorum meridionalium historiam illustrantia*, ed. Augustin Theiner, pp. 47–70. Rome: Academia Scientiarum, 1863.

Jacques of Vitry. *The Historia Occidentalis of Jacques de Vitry: A Critical Edition*. Ed. John F. Hinnebusch. Fribourg: University Press, 1972.

Kreuzzugsdichtung. Ed. Ulrich Müller. Tübingen: M. Niemeyer, 1969.

"Lai da le dame de Fayel." In *Recueil de chants historiques français*, ed. Antoine le Roux de Lincy. 1st ser. Paris: C. Gosselin, 1841. pp. 105–8.

Lectiones Longipratenses. In *Exuviae sacrae Constantinopolitanae*, ed. Paul Riant, 2: 10–22. Paris: E. Leroux, 1877–1904.

Livre de la conqueste de la princée de l'Amorée: Chronique de Morée (1204–1305). Ed. Jean Longnon. Paris: Librairie Renouard, 1911. (There are Greek and other versions.) Trans. Harold E. Lurier as *Crusaders as Conquerors: The Chronicle of Morea*. New York: Columbia University Press, 1964.

Lorenzo de Monacis. *Chronicon de rebus venetis ab u. c. ad annum MCCCLIV*. Ed. Fl. Cornelius. Venice, 1758.

Matteo d'Amalfi. *Translatio sancti Andreae*. In *Exuviae sacrae Constantinopolitanae*, ed. Paul Riant, 1: 165–78. Paris: E. Leroux, 1877–1904.

Mesarites, Nicholas. *Epitaphios*. In *Neue Quellen zur Geschichte des lateinischen Kaisertums und der Kirchenunion, I: Der Epitaphios des Nikolaos Mesarites auf seinen Bruder Johanne*, ed. A. Heisenberg. In *Sitzungsberichte der bayerischen Akademie der Wissenshaften. Philosophisch-philologische und historische Klasse*, Abh. 5. Munich, 1923.

———. *Die Palastrevolution des Johannes Komnenos*. Ed. A. Heisenberg. Würzburg: Konigl. Universitatsdruckerei von H. Sturtz, 1907.

Monk of San Giorgio. *Translatio corporis beatissimi Pauli martyris de Constantinopoli Venetias*. In *Exuviae sacrae Constantinopolitanae*, ed. Paul Riant, 1: 141–492. Paris: E. Leroux, 1877–1904.

Nicephorus Chrysoberges. *Ad Angelos orationes tres*. Ed. Maximilian Treu. Programm des Konigl. Friedrichs Gymnasiums zu Breslau. Vol. 127. Breslau, 1892.

Nicetas Choniates. *Historia*. Ed. Jan-Louis van Dieten. 2 vols. (*Corpus Fontium Historiae Byzantinae*, XI/1.) Berlin and New York: De Gruyter, 1975. Older edition, with Latin translation, by Immanuel Bekker, *CSHB*, vol. 33. Bonn: Weber, 1835. English trans. by Harry J. Magoulias as *O City of Byzantium, Annales of Niketas Choniates*. Detroit: Wayne State University Press, 1984. There is also a German translation by Franz Grabler, Graz-Vienna-Cologne: Verlag Styria, 1958.

———. *Orationes et Epistulae*, Ed. Jan-Louis Van Dieten. (*Corpus Fontium Historiae Byzantinae*, III.) Berlin and New York: De Gruyter, 1972.

———. *De Signis*. Ed. Jan-Louis van Dieten. 2 vols. (*Corpus Fontium Historiae Byzantinae*, XI/1) Berlin and New York: De Gruyter, 1975. English trans. by Harry J.

Magoulias as *O City of Byzantium, Annales of Niketas Choniates*. Detroit: Wayne State University Press, 1984.

"Nuova serie di documenti sulle relazioni di Genova coll'impero bizantino." Ed. Angelo Sanguineti and Gerolamo Bertolotto. *Atti della Società Ligure di Storia Patria* 28 (1896–98).

Nuovi documenti del commercio veneto dei secoli XI–XIII. Ed. Antonino Lombardo and Raimondo Morozzo della Rocca, in Monumenti Storici della Deputazione di Storia Patria per le Venezie, n.s., vol. 7. Venice: Deputazione di storia patria per le Venezie, 1953.

Ogerius Panis. *Annales Ianuensis*. Ed. Luigi Tommaso Belgrano and Cesare Imperiale. *Fonti per la storia d'Italia*. 12: 67–154. Rome, 1901.

De Oorkonden der graven van Vlaanderen (1191–aanvang 1206). Ed. W. Prevenier. 3 vols. Brussels: Paleis der Academien, 1964.

Otto of Saint Blaise. Continuation of Otto of Freising. *Chronicon*. Ed. Roger Wilmans. *MGH, SS*, 20: 302–37.

Peter of Vaux-de-Cernay. *Petri Vallium Sarnaii monachi hystoria Albigensis*. Ed. Pascal Guébin and Ernest Lyon. 3 vols. Paris: Champion, 1926–39.

Procopius. *Buildings*. Trans. H. B. Dewings. Cambridge, Mass.: Harvard University Press, 1954.

Le Promissioni del doge di Venezia dalle origini alla fine del duecent,. Ed. Gisella Graziato. Venice: Comitato per la pubblicazione delle fonti relative alla storia di Venezia, 1986.

Raimbaut de Vaqueiras. *The Poems of the Troubadour Raimbaut de Vaqueiras*. Ed. Joseph Linskill. The Hague: Mouton, 1964.

Ralph of Coggeshall. *Chronicon Anglicanum*. In *Rer. Brit. M. A. script.*, 66: 1–208.

Ramusio, Paolo. *De bello Costantinopolitano et imperatoribus Comnenis per Gallos, et Veneto restitutis* . . . Venice: Marc. Ant. Brogiolum, 1634.

Recueil de chants historiques français. Ed. Antoine le Roux de Lincy. 1st ser. Paris: C. Gosselin, 1841.

Regesta Pontificum romanorum. Ed. August Potthast. 2 vols. Berlin: Rudolf de Decker, 1874–75; repr., Graz: Akademische Druck- U. Verlagsanstalt, 1957.

Regesten der Kaiserurkunden des Oströmischen Reichs von 565–1454. Ed. Franz Dölger. 5 vols. Munich and Berlin: Oldenbourg, 1924–1965.

Rigord. *Gesta Philippi Augusti Francorum Regis*. In *Rec. hist. Gaules*, 17: 1–62.

Robert of Auxerre. *Chronicon*. Ed. O. Holder-Egger. *MGH, SS*, 26: 219–76.

Robert of Clari. *La conquête de Constantinople*. Ed. Philippe Lauer. Paris: Edouard Champion, 1924. *The Conquest of Constantinople*. English trans. by Edgar H. McNeal. New York: Columbia University Press, 1936; repr. 1966. *La conquista di Costantinopoli*. Italian trans. with introduction and apparatus by Anna Maria Nada Patrone. Genoa: n.p., 1972.

Roger of Hoveden. *Chronica*. Ed. William Stubbs. 4 vols. *Rer. Brit. M. A. script.*, 51. London, 1868–71.

Rostaing de Cluni. *Exceptio capitis S. Clementis*. In *Exuviae sacrae Constantinopolitanae*, ed. Paul Riant, 1: 127–40. Paris: E. Leroux, 1877–1904.

Sabellico, Marcantonio. *Rerum venetarum ab urbe condita libri XXIII*. Venice, 1718.

Sacrorum conciliorum nova et amplissima collectio. Ed. Giovanni Mansi. 53 vols. Paris: H. Welter, 1901–27.

Sanudo, Marino. *I Diarii*. Ed. Rinaldo Fulin et al. 58 vols. Venice: Deputazione R. Veneta di Storia Patria, 1897–1903.

———. *Vitae ducum venetorum*. Ed. Lodovico Antonio Muratori, in *Rerum Italicarum Scriptores*, vol. 22. Milan, 1733.

Sanudo, Marino (Torsello). *Istoria del regno di Romania*. In *Chroniques gréco-romanes*, ed. Charles Hopf, pp. 99–170. Berlin, 1873; repr. Brussels: Culture et civilisation, 1966.

———. *Liber secretorum fidelium crucis super Terrae Sanctae recuperatione et conservatione*. Hanover ed. of 1611. Toronto and Buffalo: University of Toronto Press, 1972.

Scriptores originum constantinopolitanarum. Ed. Theodor Preger. Leipzig: B. G. Teubneri, 1901–7.

Sigeberti continuato Praemonstratensis, MGH, SS, 6: 447–56.

Snorre Sturlason. *Heimskringla: The Norse King Sagas*. Trans. Samuel Laing. New York: Dutton, 1930.

Thomas of Spalato. *Historia Spalatina*. Ed. L. de Heinemann. *MGH, SS*, 29; 570–98.

Urkunden zur älteren Handels- und Staatsgeschichte der Republik Venedig. Ed. G. L. Fr. Tafel and G. M. Thomas. 3 vols. Vienna: Kaiserlich-königlichen Hof- und Staatsdruckerei, 1856–57, repr., Amsterdam, 1967.

Venetiarum historia vulgo Petro Iustiniano Iustiniani filio adiuidicata. Ed. Roberto Cessi and Fanny Bennato. Venice: Deputazione di storia patria per le Venezie, 1964.

Vetera monumenta Slavorum meridionalium historiam illustrantia. Ed. Augustin Theiner. Vol. 1. Rome: Academia Scientiarum, 1863.

Villehardouin, Geoffrey of. *La conquête de Constantinople*. Ed. Edmond Faral. 2 vols. Paris: Société d'édition "les belles lettres," 1938–39. Also several editions beginning in 1870 by Natalis de Wailly and the 1891 ed. by Emile Bouchet. *The Conquest of Constantinople*. Trans. M. R. B. Shaw, 1963; repr. Baltimore: Penguin Books, 1967. Also by Sir Frank Marzials, New York: E. P. Dutton, 1908, and later reprints.

William of Tyre. *Historia rerum in partibus transmarinis gestarum*. In *Corpus Christianorum, Continuatio medievalis*. Ed. R.B.C. Huygens. Turnhout: Brepols, 1986. Older edition: *Recueil des historens des croisades: historiens occidentaux*. Paris, 1844.

Essay on Literature

For an extended discussion of the literature on the Fourth Crusade see Donald E. Queller and Susan J. Stratton, "A Century of Controversy on the Fourth Crusade," *Studies in Medieval and Renaissance History* 6 (1969): 235–77. The reader can sample the literature and the sources in *The Latin Conquest of Constantinople*, ed. Donald E. Queller. For views on more recent scholarship see Charles M. Brand, "The Fourth Crusade: Some Recent Interpretations," *Medievalia et Humanistica* 12 (1984): 33–45; and Thomas F. Madden, "Outside and Inside the Fourth Crusade," *International History Review* 17 (1995): 726–43.

For centuries historians of the Fourth Crusade simply followed Villehardouin, but in the second half of the nineteenth century, under the influence of nationalism, economic determinism, and the rise of a more critical historical method, they began to debate the straightforward narrative of the marshal. The first of the so-called treason theorists was Count Louis de Mas Latrie in his *Histoire de l'île de Chypre sous le règne des princes de la maison de Lusignan*. The editor of Ernoul, Mas Latrie chose to follow the Palestinian source, discovering a supposed Venetian plot in collusion with the sultan to divert the crusade from Egypt. Villehardouin is dismissed as a dupe of Venetian duplicity.

In his *Geschichte Griechenlands* the distinguished Byzantine historian Carl Hopf appeared to have discovered the treacherous treaty that the Venetians signed with the sultan. There was no documentation, but Hopf's great scholarly reputation carried the day for a time. Gabriel Hanotaux shortly proved, however, that Hopf's evidence consisted only of certain conventions of a later date already published in the *Urkunden*, and that the supposed negotiations between the sultan and the Venetians could not have taken place. This should have laid the false treaty to rest, but it still pops up here and there.

A rival Swabian or German conspiracy theory took the field with Eduard Winkelmann's *Philipp von Schwaben und Otto IV. von Braunschweig*. According to Winkelmann, the hard-pressed Philip diverted the crusade with the help of Boniface of Montferrat in order to embarrass Innocent III, who supported his rival for the German throne. He had not much power, but achieved his aim through skillful diplomacy—and the opportune appearance in the West of his refugee brother-in-law, Prince Alexius.

The Swabian treason was developed by Count Paul Riant in two articles in the *Revue des questions historiques* of 1875 and 1878. With great erudition and a massive command of minor sources, Riant wove a plot among Philip, Boniface, and young Alexius, who met at the German court at Christmas 1201. The Venetians, whose supposed treaty with Egypt Riant accepted on Hopf's word, accepted the plan willingly. Despite his great learning, Riant's work is flawed by excessive speculation and his too facile acceptance of the false treaty.

Ludwig Streit returned to the Venetians as the culprits in his *Venedig und die Wendung des vierten Kreuzzugs*, but he introduced a new element into Fourth Crusade historiography, an insistence upon setting the crusade in historical perspective by tracing the deterioration of relations between Venice and Byzantium in the twelfth century.

Edwin Pears's *The Fall of Constantinople* is not very good history. Unaware of Hanotaux's criticism of Hopf, Pears perpetuates the false treaty between the Venetians and the sultan. He regards Villehardouin as a suppressor of unpleasant facts, choosing to follow instead Robert of Clari, Ernoul-Bernard, and Nicetas Choniates. Because it remained the only book-length account of the Fourth Crusade in English for many years, *The Fall of Constantinople* has been unfortunately influential in the English-speaking world. A more recent popularization, *The Sundered Cross* (also titled *The Great Betrayal*), by Ernle Bradford, follows Pears with lavish praise for a work that was inadequate when it was written over a century ago. Bradford has a lively style and a knowledge of ships and sailing lacking to armchair historians, but his history is atrocious.

Despite the treason theorists, Villehardouin's theory of accidents retained supporters, among them the learned French scholar Jules Tessier. In his *La quatrième croisade: La diversion sur Zara et Constantinople* late nineteenth-century French patriotism took a peculiar turn. He resented the idea that the German king or the Venetian doge had been able to manipulate the barons of France like stupid dupes. Tessier follows Villehardouin, whom he affectionately calls "our old chronicler from Champagne." Tessier was too good a scholar, however, merely to retell the narrative of Villehardouin. He did take account of the critical work of the previous generation of scholarship, even though he rejected much of it.

A milestone in Fourth Crusade historiography was reached at the end of the nineteenth century with Walter Norden's *Der vierte Kreuzzug in Rahmen der Beziehungen des Abendlandes zu Byzanz*. The genuine political and economic insights of those who saw a conspiracy to divert the crusade and the sophisticated defense of Villehardouin by Tessier find fruition in what can be called the modified theory of accidents. Like Streit, but more broadly, Norden places the Fourth Crusade in the framework of Western-Byzantine relations, not just those of Venice, but of Normans, Germans, Venetians, and crusaders of all Latin lands. No one could have possessed sufficient foreknowledge to conspire to divert the crusade, but there were underlying reasons and deep-seated causes that predisposed the crusaders and Venetians to grasp at the opportunity offered by young Alexius. Villehardouin was essentially truthful, in the eyes of Norden, but superficial. Norden's thesis has become extremely influential.

Achille Luchaire's *Innocent III: La question d'Orient* interprets the Fourth Crusade as the triumph of increasing secularism over the moral concerns of the church. Innocent did not wish the diversion, but was himself enough of a secularist to draw advantage from events he was powerless to prevent. Among writers on the Fourth Crusade, Luchaire is best known for his dictum that "historical science has something better to do than to discuss indefinitely an insoluble problem," the question of the diversion. It is, of course, impossible even for Luchaire to write of the Fourth Crusade without discussing it. The debate over the diversion, moreover, is not a mere jumble of conflicting views, but an orderly process in which later scholars, although still unable to agree, profited from the debates of their predecessors to write more and more sophisticated history.

Leopoldo Usseglio's commonsense approach to the Fourth Crusade in *I marchesi di Monferrato in Italia ed in Oriente durante i secoli XII e XIII* is much too little known. Solidly in the tradition of Norden, this is an admirable scholarly work.

The most ardent defender of Villehardouin since Tessier is Edmond Faral, the marshal's most recent editor. His article on Villehardouin's sincerity in the *Revue historique* of 1936 scores off all Geoffrey's rival chroniclers and detractors. Faral follows Villehardouin's theory of accidents with the barest nod in the direction of Norden and his disciples.

Henri Grégoire, on the other hand, continued to see a conspiracy behind the attack on Constantinople. He sought to lay the groundwork for a new attempt to prove a Swabian plot by showing that young Alexius arrived in the West in 1201, not 1202 as Villehardouin seems to say, thus allowing time for the meeting at Hagenau and the development of a conspiracy. His article in *Byzantion* in 1941, which was not entirely convincing to some of us, has been decisively confirmed by J. Folda in *Byzantinoslavica* in 1965. The question of the date of the arrival of Alexius is now closed: it was 1201. Folda does not, however, incline very much toward the treason theory and he explains the discrepancy in Villehardouin as an error made in good faith.

Another famous Byzantinist, Charles Diehl, represented over his long career a gradual softening of the theory of Venetian responsibility. In his rather romantic *Une république patricienne* (1915) he clearly pointed the finger at Dandolo, a man "capable of every self-sacrifice, careless also of every scruple when the greatness of the Republic was at stake." In more recent works, however, Diehl showed appreciation for the various underlying factors that made the diversion attractive to northern crusaders, as well as Venetians, and he did not attempt to prove that the Venetians planned the diversion as early as April 1201, when the Treaty of Venice was signed. He did still hold a moderate belief in Venetian responsibility.

As far as the Fourth Crusade is concerned the popularity and influence of Sir Steven Runciman's *A History of the Crusades* is somewhat unfortunate, for the author failed to integrate into his account the several generations of scholarship on the diversion question. There are a number of errors on details. He is also inexplicably reluctant to give up the false Venetian-Egyptian treaty. Much better are the treatments by Hans Eberhard Mayer in his revised edition of *The Crusades*, as well as Jonathan Riley-Smith's in *The Crusades: A Short History*.

Donald M. Nicol has turned his considerable talents toward the Fourth Crusade on a number of occasions. His chapter in the new *Cambridge Medieval History* contained a number of factual errors, but these have largely been corrected in his book, *Byzantium and Venice*. Nicol remains convinced, however, that Venice in general and Dandolo in particular were responsible for the diversion to Constantinople. The old doge, Nicol contends, held a "personal grudge" and an "obsessive" hatred toward Byzantium. In Nicol's view, the Treaty of Venice was merely the means by which Dandolo entrapped the northerners. The doge, he contends, "hid his purpose under a cloak of piety. But Constantinople was in his mind from the outset."

Further underscoring that treason theories are not dead is John Godfrey's book, *1204: The Unholy Crusade*. Godfrey is not a specialist and his book is not meant for a scholarly audience. Nevertheless, he has read the major sources for the crusade as well as some secondary literature, including the first edition of this volume. As an outsider Godfrey could have brought a fresh perspective, but instead he simply trots out the shopworn treason theories for yet another airing. The tiny number of footnotes in the book means that most of Godfrey's assertions must remain unsupported. In many cases no support exists, as the book is marred by many serious errors. Although a popularization, *1204: The Unholy Crusade* has found its way into the footnotes of works by solid scholars, who favor Godfrey's condemnation of Venice. Brand's rather forced apologetic for Godfrey in his historiographical article is not convincing.

At the opposite pole of opinion stood the eminent Venetian historian Roberto Cessi, whose various articles on the subject (notably in *Archivio Veneto* of 1951 and 1960) attempt to justify his beloved Venice. There was, for example, no plan to go to Egypt, and for another, no request that the northern crusaders join in the Venetian undertaking at Zara. Cessi's great knowledge of Venetian history commands attention and respect, but his startling interpretations are hard to accept.

The most satisfactory short synthesis of Fourth Crusade scholarship is found in the chapter by Edgar McNeal and Robert Lee Wolff in the multiauthored *A History of the Crusades*, edited by Kenneth M. Setton. McNeal and Wolff possess a notable command of the sources and literature and they weigh motives and causes judiciously.

Sibyll Kindlimann's *Die Eroberung von Konstantinopel als politische Forderung des Westens im Hochmittelalter* has contributed to the placing of the Fourth Crusade within a framework of long-range causes and motivations. She traces the rise of the feeling in the West that Byzantium was an obstacle to the crusading movement unworthy to survive. Although notably weak on the Venetian relations with the Greeks, she successfully confirms and extends the tradition of Walter Norden.

Setting the stage from the Byzantine point of view is Charles M. Brand's excellent book, *Byzantium Confronts the West, 1180–1204*. Brand's characterization of the Fourth Crusade as "the failure of Byzantine foreign policy" sets the Latin expedition into the landscape of Byzantine political events. Others have followed Brand's lead. Nicolas Oikonomides, in his article "La décomposition de l'empire byzantin," demonstrated the already heavily fragmented nature of imperial power that existed in Byzantium when the crusaders arrived, thus leaving Constantinople with control over only a fraction of the empire. Jean-Claude Cheynet, in his fascinating work, *Pouvoir et contestations à Byzance*, examines the role of rebellion in the empire. In so doing, Cheynet puts the activities of the crusaders at Constantinople into the larger framework of similar and frequent imperial coups.

A number of scholars have illuminated specific aspects of the Fourth Crusade while dealing primarily with Byzantine concerns. Sigfús Blöndal's *The Varangians of Byzantium* is a first attempt to understand the role of the elite bodyguard in Byzantine history. The treatment of the Fourth Crusade, however, leaves something to be desired. Benjamin Hendrickx and Corinna Matzukis shed some light on the dark figure of Alexius V Mourtzouphlus in their article in *Hellenika* of 1979. Thomas Madden, in a *Byzantinische Zeitschrift* article of 1992, has examined the devastation of Constantinople by the three crusader fires and suggested the effects they had on the outcome of the Fourth Crusade.

In the first volume of his magisterial *The Papacy and the Levant*, Kenneth M. Setton examines the crusade from Innocent III's perspective, but provides a very competent narration of the event from other angles as well. Joseph Gill also looks at Innocent's side in his book *Byzantium and the Papacy*, pointing out the pope's overriding concerns of rescue of the Holy Land and union of the Greek and Latin churches under the Roman pontiff.

A number of scholars have attempted to capture an interior history of the expedition from the perspective of the Western crusaders. A. Frolow has examined the influence of the cult of relics upon the minds of the crusaders in his *Recherches sur la déviation de la quatrième croisade vers Constantinople*. Riant had suggested this long ago, but historians preoccupied with modern nationalism and economic causation failed to grasp this key to medieval mentality. Paul Alphandéry went further in *La chrétienté et l'idée de croisade*. He attempted to plumb other religious and psychological factors that moved the crusaders. These factors, such as the twelfth-century emphasis upon the humanity of Christ and expectations of the Last Judgment, were peculiarly medieval, and

Alphandéry scorned the imposition of modern stereotypes upon medieval men. He is especially concerned with the thoughts and feelings of the anonymous mass of crusaders inspired by Fulk of Neuilly. Jonathan Riley-Smith has also taken up this issue in a number of articles and books, particularly his 1980 article in *History* and his little book *What Were the Crusades?* Riley-Smith explodes the idea of crusaders as self-serving second sons out for plunder and land and stresses the importance of piety and self-sacrifice inherent in the crusading vow. He points out that crusading was, in fact, an act of Christian charity and love.

John Pryor has produced an impressive body of work on the maritime history of the crusades, an important aspect of the Fourth Crusade. His two-part article on horse transports in the 1982 issue of *Mariner's Mirror* and his three-part essay on crusader transport ships in the 1984 issue of the same journal are both impressive and exhaustive. In his book *Geography, Technology, and War*, Pryor presents the various routes to the East and the concerns of a maritime expedition. Also of importance is Richard W. Unger's *The Ship in the Medieval Economy*.

The largest growing aspect of Fourth Crusade historiography seems to be studies of individual crusaders. Aside from his prolific work on the minor sources of the crusade, Alfred J. Andrea has studied Adam of Perseigne and, more importantly, Bishop Conrad of Krosigk. The latter work, which appeared in *Analecta Cisterciensia* in 1987, is a truly comprehensive study of one of the crusade's highest clerics. Hans W. Kuhn has done a similarly exhaustive examination of Henry of Ulmen. In two very good articles, Monique Zerner-Chardavoine has looked at the roles of Guy of Vaux-de-Cernay and Simon de Montfort, placing them into the context of their subsequent activities in the Albigensian Crusade. In his book *Petrus Capuanus*, Werner Maleczek examines the role of the papal legate in the Fourth Crusade. He concludes that Capuano's influence on the course of the expedition was slight, but blames the pope's inaction and the Venetian's willfulness for the situation.

Jean Longnon also looked at individual crusaders, but he did not stop at one or two. In his *Les compagnons de Villehardouin*, Longnon catalogs hundreds of mostly French soldiers who took up the cross. Although he relies only on published sources, Longnon's work will remain an essential resource for historians of the Fourth Crusade for a long time and will provide a good jumping off point for scholars delving deeper into the archival records for individual crusaders.

LITERATURE

Abulafia, David. *Frederick II: A Medieval Emperor*. Oxford: Oxford University Press, 1988.

Ahrweiler, Hélène. *Byzance et la mer: La marine de guerre, la politique et les institutions maritimes de Byzance aux VIIe–XVe siècles*. Paris: Presses universitaires de France, 1966.

———. "Constantinople Seconde Rome: Le tournant de 1204." In *Roma, Costantinopoli, Mosca: Da Roma alla Terza Roma, documenti e studi (seminario 1981)*. Naples: Edizioni Scientifiche Italiane, 1983.

Alphandéry, Paul. *La chrétienté et l'idée de croisade*. Completed from the author's notes by Alphonse Dupront. 2 vols. Paris: Editions Albin Michel, 1954–59.

Andrea, Alfred J. "Adam of Perseigne and the Fourth Crusade." *Cîteaux* 36 (1985): 21–37.

———. "Cistercian Accounts of the Fourth Crusade: Were They Anti-Venetian?" *Analecta Cisterciensia* 41 (1985): 3–41.

———. "Conrad of Krosigk, Bishop of Halberstadt, Crusader and Monk of Sittichenbach: His Ecclesiastical Career, 1184–1225." *Analecta Cisterciensia* 43 (1987): 11–91.

———. "The *Historia Constantinopolitana*: An Early Thirteenth-Century Cistercian Looks at Byzantium." *Analecta Cisterciensia* 36 (1980): 269–302.

———. "Innocent III and the Greeks of Constantinople: A Re-assessment of the Pope's Role in the Fourth Crusade." In *Venice: Society and Crusade, Studies in Honor of Donald E. Queller*, ed. Thomas F. Madden and Ellen E. Kittell. Forthcoming.

———. "Latin Evidence for the Accession Date of John X Camaterus, Patriarch of Constantinople." *Byzantinische Zeitschrift*, fasc. 2 (1973): 354–58.

———. "The Relationship of Sea Travellers and Excommunicated Captains under Thirteenth Century Canon Law." *Mariners' Mirror* 68 (1982): 203–9.

Andrea, Alfred J., and Ilona Motsiff. "Pope Innocent III and the Diversion of the Fourth Crusade Army to Venice." *Byzantinoslavica* 33 (1972): 6–25.

Andrea, Alfred J., and Paul I. Rachlin. "Holy War, Holy Relics, Holy Theft: The Anonymous of Soissons's *De terra Iherosolimitana*: An Analysis, Edition, and Translation. *Historical Reflections* 18 (1992): 146–56.

Arbois de Jubainville, Henri d'. *Histoire des ducs et des comtes de Champagne*. Paris: A. Durand et Pedone-Lauriel, 1869.

Asdracha, Catherine. "L'image de l'homme occidental à Byzance: Le témoignage de Kinnamos et de Choniatès." *Byzantinoslavica* 44 (1983): 31–40.

Ashtor, Eliahu. *A Social and Economic History of the Near East in the Middle Ages*. Berkeley: University of California Press, 1976.

Atiya, Aziz S. *Crusade, Commerce, and Culture*. Bloomington: Indiana University Press, 1962.

———. *The Crusade: Historiography and Bibliography*. Bloomington: Indiana University Press, 1962.

Bagley, C. P. "Robert of Clari's *La Conquête de Contantinople*." *Medium Aevum* 40 (1971): 109–15.

Balard, Michel. "Les transports des occidentaux vers les colonies du Levant au Moyen

Age." In *Maritime Aspects of Migration*, ed. Klaus Fiedland. Cologne-Vienna: Böhlau, 1989.

Bartusis, Mark C. *The Late Byzantine Army: Arms and Society, 1204–1453*. Philadelphia: University of Pennsylvania Press, 1992.

Bassett, Sarah Guberti. "The Antiquities in the Hippodrome of Constantinople." *Dumbarton Oaks Papers* 45 (1991): 87–96.

Baynes, Norman. "The Supernatural Defenders of Constantinople." *Analecta Bollandiana* 67 (1949): 165–77.

Beazley, C. R. *The Dawn of Modern Geography*. New York: Peter Smith, 1901.

Beck, Hans Georg. "Byzanz und der Westen im 12. Jahrhundert." *Probleme des 12. Jahrhunderts*. Vortrage und Forschungen vom Konstanzer Arbeitskreis für mittelalterliche Geschichte, 12. Constance-Stuttgart: J. Thorbecke, 1968.

Berry, Virginia G. "The Second Crusade." In *A History of the Crusades*, ed. Kenneth M. Setton. 1: 463–512. Philadelphia: University of Pennsylvania Press, 1958.

Besta, Enrico. "La cattura dei Veneziani in oriente per ordine dell'imperatore Emanuele Comneno e le sue consequenze nella politica interna ed esterna del commune di Venezia." *Antologia veneta* I (1900): 35–46, 111–23.

———. "Il diritto e le leggi civili di Venezia fina al dogado di Enrico Dandolo." *Ateneo Veneto* 22, no. 2 (1899): 61–93, 202–48.

Bithell, Jethro. *The Minnesingers*. London: Longmans, 1909.

Blake, E. O. "The Formation of the 'Crusade Idea.'" *Journal of Ecclesiastical History* 21 (1970): 11–31.

Bloch, Marc. *The Historian's Craft*. Trans. Peter Putnam. New York: Vintage Books, 1964.

Blöndal, Sigfús. *The Varangians of Byzantium*. Rev. and trans. Benedikt S. Benedikz. Cambridge: Cambridge University Press, 1978.

Blumenshine, Gary. "Cardinal Peter Capuano, the Letters of Pope Innocent III, and the Diversion of the Fourth Crusade to Zara." Seminar paper, University of Illinois, 1968–69.

Boase, Thomas Sherrer Ross. *Kingdoms and Strongholds of the Crusaders*. London: Thames and Hudson, 1971.

Bormans, S., and J. Halkin, eds. Vol. 11, pt. 1, of *Table chronologique des chartes et diplomes imprimés concernant l'histoire de la Belgique*. Brussels, 1907.

Borsari, Silvano. "Per la storia del commercia veneziano col mondo bizantino nel XII secolo." *Rivista storica italiana* 88 (1976): 104–26.

———. *Venezia e bisanzio nel XII secolo: I rapporti economici*. Venice: Deputazione di storia patria per le Venezie, 1988.

Brader, David. "Bonifaz von Montferrat bis zum Antritt der Kreuzfahrt." *Historische Studien* 55 (1907).

Bradford, Ernle. *The Sundered Cross: The Story of the Fourth Crusade*. Englewood Cliffs, N.J.: Prentice-Hall, 1967.

Brand, Charles M. "A Byzantine Plan for the Fourth Crusade." *Speculum* 43 (1968): 462–75.

———. "The Byzantines and Saladin, 1185–1192: Opponents of the Third Crusade." *Speculum* 37 (1962): 167–81.

———. *Byzantium Confronts the West, 1180–1204*. Cambridge, Mass.: Harvard University Press, 1968.

————. s.v. "Dandolo, Enrico." *Oxford Dictionary of Byzantium*. Oxford: Oxford University Press, 1991.

————. "The Fourth Crusade: Some Recent Interpretations." *Medievalia et Humanistica* 12 (1984): 33–45.

Bréhier, Louis. *L'Eglise et l'Orient au moyen âge*. 1st ed., 1906; 5th ed., Paris: Lecoffre, J. Gabalda et fils, 1928.

————. *Vie et mort de Byzance*. Paris: Albin Michel, 1948.

Brown, Elizabeth A. R. "The Cistercians in the Latin Empire of Constantinople and Greece, 1204–1276." *Traditio* 14 (1958): 63–120.

Brown, Horatio. "The Venetians and the Venetian Quarter in Constantinople to the Close of the Twelfth Century." *Journal of Hellenic Studies* 40 (1920): 68–88.

Browning, Robert. *The Byzantine Empire*. Rev. ed. Washington, D.C.: Catholic University of America Press, 1992.

————. "An Unpublished Address of Nicephorus Chrysoberges to Patriarch John X Kamateros of 1202." *Byzantine Studies* 5 (1978): 37–68.

Brundage, James. *Medieval Canon Law and the Crusader*. Madison, Milwaukee, and London: University of Wisconsin Press, 1969.

————. *Richard Lion Heart*. New York: Scribner, 1974.

————. "A Transformed Angel (X. 3.31.18): The Problem of the Crusading Monk." In *Studies in Medieval Cistercian History Presented to Jeremiah F. O'Sullivan*. Spencer, Mass.: Cistercian Publications, 1971.

————. "The Votive Obligations of Crusaders: The Development of a Canonistic Doctrine." *Traditio* 24 (1968): 77–118.

Brunelli, Vitaliano. *Storia della città di Zara*. Venice: Istituto Veneto di Arti Grafiche, 1913.

Bryer, Anthony. "The First Encounter with the West—AD, 1050–1204." In *Byzantium: An Introduction*, ed. Philip Whitting. Oxford: Blackwell, 1971.

Burdach, Konrad. "Walter von der Vogelweide und der vierte Kreuzzug." *Historische Zeitschrift* 145 (1931): 19–45.

Canard, M. "Les expéditions des Arabes contre Constantinople dans l'histoire et dans la légende." *Journal asiatique* 208 (1926): 61–121.

Cardini, Franco. "La crociata nel Duecento. L'Avatara' di un ideale." *Archivio storico italiano* 135 (1977): 101–39.

Carile, Antonio. "Alle origini dell'impero d'Oriente: Analisi quantitativa dell' esercito crociato e repartizione dei feudi." *Nuova rivista storica* 56 (1972): 285–314.

————. *La cronachistica veneziana (secoli XII–XVI) di fronte alla spartizione della Romania nel 1204*. Florence: Leo S. Olschki, 1969.

————. "Episodi della IV crociata nel mosaico pavimentale de S. Giovanni Evangelista di Ravenna." In *Corsi di cultura*, ed. P. Angiolini Martinelli, G. Brizzi, et al., vol. 23, pp. 109–30. Ravenna: Longo, 1976.

————. "Partitio terrarum imperii romanie." *Studi Veneziani* 7 (1965): 125–305.

————. *Per una storia dell'impero latino di Costantinopoli, 1204–1261*. Rev. ed. Bologna: Pàtron, 1978.

Cassandro, Giovanni. "Concetto e struttura dello stato veneziano." *Bergomum* 38, no. 2 (1964): 33–55.

Casson, Stanley, and Rice, David Talbot. *Second Report upon the Excavations Carried*

Out In or Near the Hippodrome of Constantinople in 1928. London: Oxford University Press, 1929.

Cazel, Fred A., Jr. "The Financing of the Crusades." In *A History of the Crusades*, ed. Kenneth M. Setton. 6: 116–49. Madison: University of Wisconsin Press, 1989.

Cerone, Francesco. "Il papa e i veneziani nella quarta crociata." *Archivio Veneto*, n.s. 36 (1888): 57–70, 287–98.

Cessi, Roberto. *Le colonie medioevali italiane in Oriente.* Bologna: "La Grafolito," 1942.

———. "L'eredità di Enrico Dandolo." *Archivio Veneto*, ser. 5, 67 (1960): 1–25.

———. "Politica, economia, religione." In *Storia di Venezia*, vol. 2, *Dalle origini del ducato alla IV crociata.* Venice: Centro internazionale delle arti e del costume, 1957.

———. *La Repubblica di Venezia e il problema adriatico.* Naples: Edizioni scientifiche italiane, 1953.

———. *Storia della Repubblica di Venezia.* 2 vols. Milan and Messina, 1944–46; repr., Milan: Giuseppe Principato, 1968.

———. "Venezia e la quarta crociata." *Archivio Veneto*, ser. 5, 48/49 (1951): 1–52.

———. "Venice to the Eve of the Fourth Crusade." *Cambridge Medieval History*, vol. 4, pt. 1. Cambridge: Cambridge University Press, 1966.

Chalandon, Ferdinand. *Histoire de la domination normande en Italie et en Sicile.* Vol. 2. Paris: A. Picard et Fils, 1907.

Charanis, Peter. "Aims of the Medieval Crusades and How They Were Viewed by Byzantium." *Church History* 21 (1952): 123–34.

Cheney, C. R. "Master Philip the Notary and the Fortieth of 1199." *English Historical Review* 63 (1948): 342–50.

Cheynet, Jean-Claude. *Pouvoir et contestations à Byzance (963–1210).* Paris: Publications de la Sorbonne, 1990.

Cognasso, Francesco. "Un imperatore bizantino della decadenza: Isaaco II Angelo." *Bessarione* 31 (1915): 29–60.

———. *Storia delle crociate.* Milan: Dall'Oglio, 1967.

Cole, Penny J. *The Preaching of the Crusades to the Holy Land, 1095–1270.* Cambridge, Mass.: Harvard University Press, 1991.

Colliot, Regine. "Fascination de l'or à Byzance d'après le chroniqueur Robert of Clari." *Senefiance* 12 (1983): 89–110.

Cracco, Giorgio. S.v. "Dandolo, Enrico." *Dizionario biografico degli Italiani.*

———. "Il pensiero storico di fronte ai problemi del commune veneziano." In *Le storiografia veneziana fino al secolo VI: Aspetti e problemi.* Ed. Agostino Pertusi. Florence: Leo S. Olschki, 1970.

———. *Società e stato nel medioevo veneziano (secoli XII–XIV).* Florence: Leo S. Olschki, 1967.

Cutler, Anthony. "The *De Signis* of Nicetas Choniates: A Reappraisal." *American Journal of Archaeology* 72 (1968): 113–18.

Dagron, Gilbert. *Constantinople imaginaire: Etudes sur le recueil des "Patria."* Paris: Presses universitaires de France, 1984.

———. *Naissance d'une capitale: Constantinople et ses institutions de 330 à 451.* Paris: Presses universitaires de France, 1974.

Daly, William M. "Christian Fraternity, the Crusaders, and the Security of Constantinople, 1097–1204: The Precarious Survival of an Ideal." *Medieval Studies* 23 (1960): 43–91.

Da Mosto, Andrea. *I dogi di Venezia nella vita pubblica e privata*. Milan: Aldo Martello, 1960.

Daniel, Norman. "The Legal and Political Theory of the Crusade." In *A History of the Crusades*, ed. Kenneth M. Setton. 6: 3–38. Madison: University of Wisconsin Press, 1989.

Darrouzès, J. "Le mémoire de Constantin Stilbès contre les Latins." *Revue des études byzantines* 21 (1963): 50–100.

Davidson, H. R. Ellis. "The Secret Weapon of Byzantium." *Byzantinische Zeitschrift* 66 (1973): 61–74.

Dawkins, Richard M. "The Later History of the Varangian Guard: Some Notes." *Journal of Roman Studies* 37 (1947): 39–46.

Delbrück, Hans. *History of the Art of War*. Vol 3, *Medieval Warfare*. Trans. Walter J. Renfroe Jr. Lincoln and London: University of Nebraska Press, 1982.

Diehl, Charles. *Byzance: Grandeur et décadence*. Paris: E. Flammarion, 1919.

———. "The Fourth Crusade and the Latin Empire." In *Cambridge Medieval History*. Vol. 4. Cambridge: Cambridge University Press, 1923.

———. "The Government and Administration of the Byzantine Empire." In *Cambridge Medieval History*. Vol. 4. Cambridge: Cambridge University Press, 1923.

———. *Histoire de l'Empire Byzantin*. Paris: A. Picard, 1919.

———. *Une république patricienne: Venise*. Paris: E. Flammarion, 1915.

Downey, Glanville. "Justinian as Achilles." *Transactions of the American Philological Association* 71 (1940): 68–77.

Duby, Georges. *The Early Growth of the European Economy: Warriors and Peasants from the Seventh to the Twelfth Century*. Trans. from the French 1st ed. of 1973 by Howard B. Clarke. Ithaca, N.Y.: Cornell University Press, 1974.

Dufournet, Jean. *Les écrivains de la quatrième croisade: Villehardouin et Clari*. 2 vols. Paris: Société d'edition d'enseignement supérieur, 1973.

———. "Villehardouin et les Champenois dans la quatriéme croisade." In *Les Champenois et la croisade*, ed. Yvonne Bellenger and Danielle Quéruel. Paris: Amateurs de livres, 1989.

———. "Villehardouin et les Vénitiens." *L'information littéraires*. 21 (1969): 7–19.

Dujčev, Ivan. *La crise idéologique de 1203–1204 et ses répercussions sur la civilisation byzantine*. Paris: Maisonneuve, 1976.

Ebels-Hoving, B. *Byzantium in Westerse Ogen, 1096–1204*. Assen: Van Gorcum, 1971.

Englebert, Omer. *Saint Francis of Assisi*. Trans. from the 2d French ed. by Eve-Marie Cooper. 2d Eng. ed. revised and augmented by Ignatius Brady and Raphael Brown. Chicago: Franciscan Herald Press, 1965.

Ensslin, W. "The Government and Administration of the Byzantine Empire." In *Cambridge Medieval History*. Vol. 4, pt. 2. Cambridge: Cambridge University Press, 1966.

Erdmann, Carl. *Die Entstehung des Kreuzzugsgedankens*. Stuttgart: W. Kohlhammer, 1935.

Faral, Edmond. "Geoffroy de Villehardouin: La question de sa sincérité." *Revue historique* 176 (1936): 530–82.

Fasoli, Gina. "Nascita di un mito." In *Studi storici in onore di Giacchino Volpe*, vol. 1. Florence: Sansoni, 1958.

Ferrard, Christopher G. "The Amount of Constantinopolitan Booty in 1204." *Studi Veneziani* 13 (1971): 95–104.

Fine, John V. A. *The Late Medieval Balkans: A Critical Survey from the Late Twelfth Century to the Ottoman Conquest*. Ann Arbor: University of Michigan Press, 1987.

Finlay, George. *A History of Greece from Its Conquest by the Romans to the Present Time, B.C. 146 to A.D. 1864*. Oxford: Clarendon, 1877.

Fliche, Augustin, Christine Thouzelliers, and Yvonne Azais. "La Chrétienté romaine." In *Histoire de l'eglise*, vol. 10, ed. Augustin Fliche and Victor Martin. Paris, 1950.

Folda, J. "The Fourth Crusade, 1201–1204: Some Reconsiderations." *Byzantinoslavica* 26 (1965): 277–90.

Fotheringham, J. K. "Genoa and the Fourth Crusade." *English Historical Review* 25 (1910): 26–57.

———. *Marco Sanudo*. Oxford: Clarendon, 1915.

Foss, Clive, and David Winfield. *Byzantine Fortifications: An Introduction*. Pretoria: University of South Africa, 1986.

Frances, E. "Alexis Comnène et les privilèges octroyés à Venise." *Byzantinoslavica* 29 (1968): 17–23.

———. "Sur la conquête de Constantinople par les Latins." *Byzantinoslavica* 15 (1954): 21–26.

Freshfield, E. H. "Notes on a Vellum Album Containing Some Original Sketches of Public Buildings and Monuments, Drawn by a German Artist Who Visited Constantinople in 1574." *Archaeologia* 72 (1921–22): 87–104.

Freydank, D. "Die altrussische Erzählung über die Eroberung Konstantinopels, 1204." *Byzantinoslavica* 29 (1968): 334–59.

Frolow, A. *Recherches sur la déviation de la quatrième croisade vers Constantinople*. Paris: Presses universitaires de France, 1955.

Gardner, Alice. *The Lascarids of Nicaea*. London: Methuen, 1912.

Gauer, Werner. "Weihgeschenke aus den Perserkriegen." In *Istanbuler Mitteilungen*. Beiheft 2 (1968).

Geary, Patrick J. *Furta Sacra: Thefts of Relics in the Central Middle Ages*. Princeton: Princeton University Press, 1988.

Gerland, Ernst. "Der vierte Kreuzzug und seine Probleme." *Neue Jahrbücher für das klassische Altertun und für Pädagogik* 13 (1904): 505–14.

Gibb, Hamilton A. R. "The Rise of Saladin." In *A History of the Crusades*, ed. Kenneth M. Setton, 1: 563–89. Philadelphia: University of Pennsylvania Press, 1958.

Gilchrist, John. "The Erdmann Thesis and the Canon Law, 1083–1141." In *Crusade and Settlement*, ed. Peter W. Edbury. Cardiff: University College Cardiff Press, 1985.

———. "The Papacy and the War against the 'Saracens.'" *International History Review* 10 (1988): 174–97.

Gill, Joseph. *Byzantium and the Papacy, 1198–1400*. New Brunswick: Rutgers University Press, 1979.

———. "Franks, Venetians, and Pope Innocent III, 1201–1203." *Studi Veneziani* 12 (1970): 85–106.

———. "Innocent III and the Greeks: Aggressor or Apostle?" In *Relations between East and West in the Middle Ages*, ed. Derek Baker. Edinburgh: Edinburgh University Press, 1973.

———. "Venice, Genoa, and Byzantium." *Byzantinische Forschungen* 10 (1985): 57–73.

Godfrey, John. *1204: The Unholy Crusade*. Oxford: Oxford University Press, 1980.

Gordon, Jared. "The Novgorod Account of the Fourth Crusade." *Byzantion* 43 (1973): 297–311.

Gottlob, Adolf. *Die päpstlichen Kreuzzugssteuern des 13. Jahrhunderts*. Heiligenstadt: F. W. Cordier, 1892.

Grégoire, Henri. "The Question of the Diversion of the Fourth Crusade, or, an Old Controversy Solved by a Latin Adverb." *Byzantion* 15 (1941): 158–66.

Grossman, Ronald P. "The Financing of the Crusades." Ph.D. diss., University of Chicago, 1965.

Grousset, René. *L'empire du Levant*. Paris: Payot, 1949.

———. *Histoire des croisades et du Royaume Franc de Jérusalem*. 3 vols. Paris: Plon, 1934–36.

Guilland, Rodolphe. "Etudes sur l'Hippodrome de Byzance." *Byzantinoslavica* 26 (1965): 12–39; 27 (1966): 26–40, 289–307; 28 (1967): 262–77; 29 (1968): 24–33.

Gutsch, Milton R. "A Twelfth-Century Preacher—Fulk of Neuilly." In *The Crusades and Other Historical Essays Presented to Dana C. Munro by his Former Students*, ed. Louis John Paetow. New York: F. S. Crofts, 1928.

Hagedorn, Gerd. "Papst Innocenz III. und Byzanz am Vorabend des Vierten Kreuzzugs (1198–1203)." *Ostkirchliche Studien* 23 (1974): 3–20, 105–26.

Halphen, Louis. "Le rôle des 'Latins' dans l'histoire intérieure de Constantinople à la fin du XIIe siècle." In *Mélanges Charles Diehl*. Vol. 1. Paris: E. Leroux, 1930.

Hanotaux, Gabriel. "Les Vénitiens ont-ils trahi la chrétienté en 1202?" *Revue historique* 4 (1877): 74–102.

Harvey, Alan. *Economic Expansion in the Byzantine Empire, 900–1200*. Cambridge: Cambridge University Press, 1989.

Hazlitt, W. C. *The History of the Origin and Rise of the Venetian Republic*. 4th ed. London: Adam and Charles Black, 1915. Reprinted, 2 vols., New York, 1966.

Hellweg, M. "Die ritterliche Welt in der franzosichen Geschichtsschreibung des vierten Kreuzzuges." *Romanische Forschungen* 52 (1938): 1–40.

Hendrickx, Benjamin. "A propos du nombre des troupes de la quatrième croisade et de l'empereur Baudouin I." *Byzantina (Thessalonica)* 3 (1971): 29–40.

———. "Baudouin IX de Flandre et les empereurs byzantins Isaac II l'Ange et Alexis IV." *Revue belge de philologie et d'histoire* 49 (1971): 482–89.

———. "Boudewijn IX van Vlaanderen, de vrome keizer van Konstantinopel." *Ons Geestelijk Erf* 44 (1970): 227–32.

———. "Les chartes de Baudouin de Flandre comme source pour l'histoire de Byzance." *Byzantina (Thessalonica)* 1 (1969): 59–80.

———. "Het Regentschaap van Vlaanderen en Henegouwen na het vertrek van Boudewijn IX (VI) op kruisvaart (1202–1211)." *Revue belge de philologie et d'histoire* 48 (1970): 337–93.

———. "Recherches sur les documents diplomatiques non conservés concernant la Quatrième Croisade et l'Empire Latin de Constantinople pendant les premières années de son existence (1200–1206)." *Byzantina (Thessalonica)* 2 (1970): 107–84.

———. "Un roi Africain à Constantinople en 1203." *Byzantina (Thessalonica)* 13 (1985): 895–98.

———. "Wat vonden de kruisvaarders in 1203/4 in Constantinopel en wat dachten zij over de Griekse schatten en het Griekse verleden?" *Hermeneus* 41 (1970): 72–79.

Hendrickx, Benjamin, and Corinna Matzukis. "Alexios V Doukas Mourtzouphlos: His Life, Reign, and Death (?–1204)." *Hellenika* 31 (1979): 108–32.

Hendy, Michael F. "Byzantium, 1081–1204: An Economic Reappraisal." *Transactions of the Royal Historical Society* 20 (1970): 31–52.

———. *Coinage and Money in the Byzantine Empire, 1081–1261.* Washington, D.C.: Dumbarton Oaks, 1969.

Heyd, Wilhelm von. *Histoire du commerce du Levant au moyen âge.* 1st German ed., 1879. Trans. by Furcy Raynaud and revised and augmented by the author, 1885. Reprinted, 2 vols., Leipzig: O. Harrassowitz, 1923.

Hodgson, F. C. *Early History of Venice.* London: George Allen, 1901.

Hopf, Carl. *Bonifaz von Montferrat, der Eroberer von Konstantinopel, und der Troubadour Rambaut von Vaqueiras.* Ed. Ludwig Streit. Berlin: C. Habel, 1877.

———. *Geschichte Griechenlands.* In *Encylopädie*, ed. J. S. Ersch and J. G. Gruber. Vols. 85–86. Leipzig: J. F. Gieditsch, 1867–68.

Housley, Norman. "Crusades against Christians: Their Origins and Early Development, c. 1000–1216." In *Crusade and Settlement*, ed. Peter W. Edbury. Cardiff: University College Cardiff Press, 1985.

Hunger, Herbert. *Graeculus Perfidus—'Ιταλός ἰταμός: Il senso dell'alterità nei rapporti greco-romani ed italo-bizantini.* Rome: Unione internazionale degli istituti di Archeologia, storia e storia dell'arte in Roma, 1987.

Hurter, Friedrich. *Storia di Papa Innocenzo III.* Trans. from the third German ed. by T. Giuseppe Gliemone. 4 vols. Milan: A. Arzione, 1857–58.

Hussey, J. M. "The Later Macedonians, the Comneni and the Angeli, 1025–1204." *Cambridge Medieval History.* Vol. 4, pt. 1. Cambridge: Cambridge University Press, 1966.

———. *The Orthodox Church in the Byzantine Empire.* Oxford: Clarendon, 1986.

Ivanov, A. "Zakhvat Konstantinopolia Latinianami v 1204 godu." *Zhurnal Moskovskoi Patriarchii* (1954): 64–73.

Iversen, Erik. *Obelisks in Exile.* 2 vols. Copenhagen: G. E. C. Gad, 1972.

Jacoby, David. "The Encounter of Two Societies: Western Conquerors and Byzantines in the Peloponnesus after the Fourth Crusade." *American Historical Review* 78 (1973): 873–906.

———. "Pélerinage médiéval et sanctuaires de Terre Sancte: La perspective vénitienne." *Ateneo Veneto* 24 (1987): 27–58.

———. "La population de Constantinople à l'époque byzantine: Un problème de demographie urbaine." *Byzantion* 31 (1961): 81–109.

Jacoff, Michael. *The Horses of San Marco and the Quadriga of the Lord.* Princeton: Princeton University Press, 1993.

Jahn, Hans. *Die Heereszahlen in den Kreuzzügen.* Berlin: G. Nauck, 1907.

Janin, Raymond. *Constantinople byzantine: Développement urbain et répertoire topographique.* 2d ed. Paris: L'institut français d'études byzantines, 1964.

———. *La Gèographie ecclèsiastique de l'empire byzantin.* Part 1. *Le Siège de Constantinople et le patriarcat oecumènique.* Vol. 3. *Les èglises et les monastères*, 2d ed. Paris: L'institut français d'études byzantines, 1969.

Jenkins, R. J. "The Bronze Athena at Byzantium." *Journal of Hellenic Studies* 67 (1947): 31–33.

————. "Further Evidence Regarding the Bronze Athena at Byzantium." *Annual of the British School at Athens* 46 (1951): 72–74.

John, E. "A Note on the Preliminaries of the Fourth Crusade." *Byzantion* 28 (1958): 95–103.

Johnson, Edgar N. "The Crusades of Frederick Barbarossa and Henry VI." In *A History of the Crusades*, ed. Kenneth M. Setton. 2: 87–122. Philadelphia: University of Pennsylvania Press, 1962.

Kandel, M. "Quelques observations sur la Devastatio Constantinopolitana." *Byzantion* 4 (1927–28): 79–88.

Kazhdan, Alexander. s.v. "Venice." *Oxford Dictionary of Byzantium*. Oxford: Oxford University Press, 1991.

Kazhdan, Alexander, and Ann Wharton Epstein. *Change in Byzantine Culture in the Eleventh and Twelfth Centuries*. Berkeley: University of California Press, 1985.

Kennan, Elizabeth. "Innocent III and the First Political Crusade: A Comment on the Limitations of Papal Power." *Traditio* 27 (1971): 231–49.

Kindlimann, Sibyll. *Die Eroberung von Konstantinopel als politische Forderung des Westens im Hochmittelalter*. Zurich: Fretz and Wasmuth, 1969.

King, Archdale A. *Citeaux and Her Elder Daughters*. London: Burns and Oates, 1954.

Kirfel, Hans Joachim. *Weltherrschaftsidee und Bündnispolitik: Untersuchungen zur auswärtigen Politik der Staufer*. Bonn: L. Rohrscheid, 1959.

Kittell, Ellen E. "Was Thibaut of Champagne the Leader of the Fourth Crusade?" *Byzantion* 51 (1981): 557–65.

Klimke, Carl. *Die Quellen zur Geschichte des vierten Kreuzzuges*. Breslau: A. Neumann, 1875.

Kretschmayr, Heinrich. *Geschichte von Venedig*. Vol. 1. Gotha: Neudruck, 1905; repr. 1964.

Kuhn, Hans Wolfgang. "Heinrich von Ulmen, der vierte Kreuzzug und die Limburger Staurothek." *Jahrbüch für westdeutsche Landesgeschichte* 10 (1984): 67–106.

Lamma, Paolo. *Comneni e Staufer: Ricerche sui rapporti fra Bisanzio e l'Occidente nel secolo XII*. 2 vols. Rome: Istituto storico italiano per il Medio Evo, 1955–57.

————. "Venezia nel giudizio delle fonti bizantine dal X al XII secolo." *Rivista storica italiana* 74 (1962): 457–79.

Lane, Frederic Chapin. "From Biremes to Triremes." In *Venice and History: The Collected Papers of Frederic C. Lane*. Baltimore: Johns Hopkins University Press, 1966.

————. *Venetian Ships and Shipbuilders of the Renaissance*. Baltimore: Johns Hopkins University Press, 1934.

————. *Venice: A Maritime Republic*. Baltimore: Johns Hopkins University Press, 1973.

Lane, Frederic Chapin, and Reinhold C. Mueller. *Money and Banking in Medieval and Renaissance Venice*. Baltimore: Johns Hopkins University Press, 1985.

Lehmann, P. W. "Theodosius or Justinian? A Renaissance Drawing of a Byzantine Rider." *Art Bulletin* 41 (1959): 39–57.

Lemerle, Paul. "Byzance et la croisade." In *Relazioni del X Congresso Internazionale di Scienze Storiche*. Vol. 3. Florence: Sansoni, 1955.

Lewis, Archibald R. "The Danube Route and Byzantium, 802–1195." In *Actes du XIVe congrès international des études byzantines*. Bucharest: Editura Academiei Republicii socialiste Romania, 1974.

———. "The Economic and Social Development of the Balkan Peninsula during Comneni Times, A.D. 1081–1185." In *Actes du IIe congrès international de études du Sud-Est Européen*. Athens: s.n., 1972.

———. *Nomads and Crusaders, A.D. 1000–1368*. Bloomington: Indiana University Press, 1988.

Lilie, Ralph-Johannes. *Byzanz und die Kreuzfahrerstaaten: Studien zur Politik des byzantinischen Reiches gegenuber den Staaten der Kreuzfahrer in Syrien und Palastrina bis zum vierten Kreuzzug (1096–1204)*. Munich: Adolph M. Hakkert, 1981.

———. *Handel und Politik zwischen dem byzantinischen Reich und den italienischen Kommunen Venedig, Pisa und Genua in der Epoche der Komnenen und der Angeloi (1081–1204)*. Amsterdam: Adolph M. Hakkert, 1984.

Longnon, Jean. *Les compagnons de Villehardouin: Recherches sur les croisés de la quatrième croisade*. Geneva: Librarie Droz, 1978.

———. "Domination franque et civilisation grecque." In *Mélanges d'archéologie et d'histoire offerts à Charles Picard*. Vol. 2. Paris: Presses universitaires de France, 1949.

———. *L'empire latin de Constantinople*. Paris: Payot, 1949.

———. *Les français d'outre-mer au moyen age*. Paris: Perrin, 1929.

———. *Recherches sur la vie de Geoffroy de Villehardouin, suivies du catalogue des actes des Villehardouin*. Paris: E. Champion, 1939.

———. "Sur les croisés de la quatrième croisade." *Journal des savants* (1977): 119–27.

Loos, Milan. *Dualist Heresy in the Middle Ages*. Trans. Iris Lewitova. Prague: Academia, 1974.

Lopez, Robert S. "Foreigners in Byzantium." *Miscellanea Charles Verlinden*. In *Bulletin de l'institut historique belge de Rome* 44 (1974): 341–52.

———. "Fulfillment and Diversion in the Eight Crusades." In *Outremer: Studies in the History of the Crusading Kingdom of Jerusalem Presented to Joshua Prawer*, ed. Benjamin Z. Kedar, Hans Eberhard Mayer, and R. C. Smail. Jerusalem: Yad Izhak Ben-zvi Institute, 1982.

Loredan, Alvise. *I Dandolo*. Varese: Dall'Oglio, 1981.

Lot, Ferdinand. *L'art militaire et les armées au moyen âge*. Paris: Payot, 1949.

Luchaire, Achille. *Innocent III: La question d'Orient*. Paris: Librairie Hachette, 1907.

Lunt, William E. *Financial Relations of the Papacy with England to 1327*. Cambridge, Mass.: Medieval Academy of America, 1939.

———. *Papal Revenues in the Middle Ages*. 2 vols. New York: Columbia University Press, 1934.

Luykx, Theo. *De graven van Vlaanderen en de kruisvaarten*. Louvain, 1947.

Luzzatto, Gino. *I prestiti della repubblica di Venezia (Sec. XIII—XV)*. Padua: A. Draghi, 1929.

———. *Storia economica di Venezia dall'XI al XVI secolo*. Venice: Centro internazionale delle arti e del costume, 1961.

Maccarrone, Michele. *Studi su Innocenzo III*. Italia sacra 17. Padua: Editrice Antenore, 1972.

Maclagen, Michael. *The City of Constantinople*. London: Thames and Hudson, 1968.

Madden, Thomas F. "Enrico Dandolo: His Life, His Family, and His Venice before the Fourth Crusade." Ph.D diss., University of Illinois at Urbana-Champaign, 1993.

———. "The Fires of the Fourth Crusade in Constantinople, 1203–1204: A Damage Assessment." *Byzantinische Zeitschrift* 84/85 (1992): 72–93.

———. "Outside and Inside the Fourth Crusade." *International History Review* 17 (1995): 726–43.

———. "The Serpent Column of Delphi in Constantinople: Placement, Purposes, and Mutilations." *Byzantine and Modern Greek Studies* 16 (1992): 111–45.

———. "Venice and Constantinople in 1171 and 1172: Enrico Dandolo's Attitude Towards Byzantium." *Mediterranean Historical Review* 8 (1993): 166–85.

———. "Venice's Hostage Crisis: Diplomatic Efforts to Secure Peace with Byzantium between 1171 and 1184." In *Venice: Society and Crusade. Studies in Honor of Donald E. Queller*, ed. Thomas F. Madden and Ellen E. Kittell. Forthcoming.

———. "Vows and Contracts in the Fourth Crusade: The Treaty of Zara and the Attack on Constantinople in 1204." *International History Review* 15 (1993): 441–68.

Magdalino, Paul. *The Empire of Manuel I Komnenos, 1143–1180.* Cambridge: Cambridge University Press, 1993.

Maleczek, Werner. *Petrus Capuanus: Kardinal, Legat am vierten Kreuzzug, Theologe (†1214).* Vienna: Österreichischen Akademie der Wissenschaften, 1988.

Maltezou, Chryssa A. "Il quartière veneziano di Costantinopoli (Sacali marittimi)." *Thesaurismata* 15 (1978): 30–61.

Manfroni, C. *Storia della marina italiana dalle invasioni barbariche alla caduta di Costantinopoli.* Vol. 1. Livorno: R. Accademia navale, 1897.

Mango, Cyril A. *The Brazen House: A Study of Vestibule of the Imperial Palace.* Copenhagen: I kommission hos Munksgaard, 1959.

———. "Daily Life in Byzantium." *Jährbuch der Österreichischen Byzantinistik* 31 (1981): 337–53.

———. "L'Euripe de l'hippodrome de Constantinople: Essai d'identification." *Revue des études byzantine* 7 (1949–50): 180–93.

Mango, Cyril A., Alexander Kazhdan, and Anthony Cutler. s.v. "Hippodromes." *Oxford Dictionary of Byzantium.* Oxford: Oxford University Press, 1991.

Maranini, Giuseppe. *La costituzione di Venezia dalle origini alla serrata del Maggior Consiglio.* Florence: La nuova Italia, 1927; repr. Florence, 1974.

Marshall, Christopher. *Warfare in the Latin East, 1192–1291.* Cambridge: Cambridge University Press, 1992.

Martin, M. E. "The Venetians in the Byzantine Empire before 1204." *Byzantinische Forschungen* 13 (1988): 201–14.

Martini, Giuseppe. "Innocenzo III ed il finanziamento delle crociate." *Archivio della Deputazione Romana di Storia Patria*, n.s. 10 (1944): 309–35.

Mas Latrie, Louis de. *Histoire de l'île de Chypre sous le règne des princes de la maison de Lusignan.* 3 vols. Paris: Imprimerie imperiale, 1852–61.

Mayer, Hans Eberhard. *The Crusades.* Rev. German ed., 1988; trans. John Gillingham, New York and Oxford: Oxford University Press, 1990.

Mayer, Hans Eberhard, and Joyce McLellan. "Select Bibliography of the Crusades." Ed. Harry W. Hazard. In *A History of the Crusades*, ed. Kenneth M. Setton. 6: 511–664. Madison: University of Wisconsin Press, 1989.

McCormick, Michael. *Eternal Victory: Triumphal Rulership in Late Antiquity, Byzantium, and the Early Medieval West.* Cambridge: Cambridge University Press, 1986.

McNeal, Edgar H. "Fulk of Neuilly and the Tournament of Ecry." *Speculum* 28 (1953): 371–75.

McNeal, Edgar H., and Robert Lee Wolff. "The Fourth Crusade." In *A History of the Crusades*, ed. Kenneth M. Setton. II: 153–85. Philadelphia: University of Pennsylvania Press, 1962.

McNeill, William H. *Venice: The Hinge of Europe, 1081–1797*. Chicago: University of Chicago Press, 1974.

Mollat, Michel. "Problèmes navals de l'histoire des croisades." *Cahiers de civilisation medievale* 10 (1967): 345–59.

Monk, Connie. "Papal Financing of the Fourth Crusade." Seminar paper, University of Illinois, 1968–69.

Moore, John C. "Count Baldwin of Flanders, Philip Augustus and the Papal Power." *Speculum* 37 (1962): 79–89.

———. "Peter of Lucedio (Cistercian Patriarch of Antioch) and Innocent III." *Römische Historische Mitteilungen* 29 (1987): 221–49.

Morris, Colin. "Geoffrey of Villehardouin and the Conquest of Constantinople." *History* 53 (1968): 24–34.

———. *The Papal Monarchy: The Western Church from 1050 to 1250*. Oxford: Oxford University Press, 1989.

———. "Propaganda for War: The Dissemination of the Crusading Ideal in the Twelfth Century." In *The Church and War*, ed. W. J. Sheils. Oxford: Blackwell, 1983.

Müller-Weiner, Wolfgang. *Bildlexicon zur Topographie Istanbuls*. Tubingen: Ernst Wasmuth, 1977.

Mundo Lo, Sara de. *Cruzados en Bizancio: La quarta cruzada a la luz de las fuentes latinas y orientales*. Buenos Aires: Universidad de Buenos Aires, 1957.

Nada Patrone, Anna Maria. *La quarta crociata e l'impero latino di Romania (1198–1261)*. Turin: G. Giappichelli, 1972.

Naslund, Sebastian. "The Crusading Policy of Innocent III in France, 1198–1202: An Evaluation from Secular and Ecclesiastical Sources." Seminar paper, University of Illinois, 1969.

Nicholas, David. *The Evolution of the Medieval World: Society, Government and Thought in Europe, 312–1500*. London and New York: Longman, 1992.

Nicol, Donald M. *Byzantium and Venice: A Study in Diplomatic and Cultural Relations*. Cambridge: Cambridge University Press, 1988.

———. "The Crusades and the Unity of Two Worlds." In *The Meeting of Two Worlds: Cultural Exchange between East and West during the Period of the Crusades*, ed. Vladimir P. Goss and Christine Verzár Bornstein. Kalamazoo: Medieval Institute Publications, 1986.

———. "The Fourth Crusade and the Greek and Latin Empires, 1204–1261." *Cambridge Medieval History*, vol. 4, pt. 1. Cambridge: Cambridge University Press, 1966.

———. *The Last Centuries of Byzantium, 1261–1453*. 2d ed. Cambridge: Cambridge University Press, 1993.

Norden, Walter. *Der Papstum und Byzanz*. Berlin: B. Behr, 1903; reprinted, New York: B. Franklin, 1958.

————. *Der vierte Kreuzzug in Rahmen der Beziehungen des Abendlandes zu Byzanz.* Berlin: E. Beck, 1898.

Norwich, John Julius. *A History of Venice.* New York: Alfred A. Knopf, 1982.

O'Brien, John M. "Fulk of Neuilly." Ph.D. diss., University of Southern California, Los Angeles, 1964.

————. "Fulk of Neuilly." *Proceedings of the Leeds Philosophical and Literary Society* 13 (1969): 109–48.

Ohnsorge, Werner. *Abendland und Byzanz.* Darmstadt: H. Gentner, 1958.

Oikonomides, Nicolas. "La décomposition de l'empire byzantin à la veille de 1204 et les origines de l'empire de Nicée: A propos de la *Partitio Romaniae.*" In *XVe Congrès international d'études byzantines: Rapports et co-rapports.* Vol. 1/1. Athens: Association internationale des études byzantines, 1976.

Oman, Charles. *The Art of War in the Middle Ages.* 1885; rev. and ed. John H. Beeler. Ithaca, N.Y.: Cornell University Press, 1953.

Omran, Mahmoud Said. "King Amalric and the Siege of Alexandria, 1167." In *Crusade and Settlement,* ed. Peter W. Edbury. Cardiff: University College Cardiff Press, 1985.

Ostrogorsky, George. *History of the Byzantine State.* Trans. from the 2d German ed. of 1952 by Joan Hussey with revisions by the author. New Brunswick, N.J.: Rutgers University Press, 1956.

————. *Pour l'histoire de la féodalité byzantine.* Brussels: Editions de l'Institut de philologie et d'histoire orientales et slaves, 1954.

Packard, Sidney R. *Europe and the Church under Innocent III.* New York: H. Holt and Co., 1927.

Painter, Sidney. "The Third Crusade: Richard the Lionhearted and Philip Augustus." In *A History of the Crusades,* ed. Kenneth M. Setton. 2: 45–85. Philadelphia: University of Pennsylvania Press, 1962.

Papadakis, Aristeides, and Alice Mary Talbot. "John X Camateros Confronts Innocent III: An Unpublished Correspondence." *Byzantinoslavica* 31 (1972): 26–41.

Passant, E. J. "The Effects of the Crusades upon Western Europe." *Cambridge Medieval History.* Vol. 5. Cambridge: Cambridge University Press, 1948.

Pauphilet, Albert. "Robert de Clari et Villehardouin." In *Mélanges de linguistique et de littérature offerts à M. Alfred Jeanroy.* Paris: E. Droz, 1928.

————. "Sur Robert de Clari." *Romania* 57 (1932): 289–311.

Pears, Edwin. *The Fall of Constantinople.* London: Longmans, 1885; and New York: Harper and Bros., 1886 (same, but with differing pagination).

Pertusi, Agostino. "*Exuviae sacrae Constantinopolitanae*: A proposito degli oggetti bizantini esistenti oggi nel tesoro di San Marco." *Studi Veneziani,* n.s. 2 (1978): 251–55. Reprinted in "Venezia e Bisanzio, 1000–1204," pp. 13–16.

————. "Quedam regalia insignia: Ricerche sulle insegne del potere ducale a Venezia durante il medioevo." *Studi Veneziani* 7 (1965): 3–123.

————. "Venezia e Bisanzio: 1000–1204." *Dumbarton Oaks Papers* 33 (1979): 1–22.

Petre, Dan A. "Le proche et le lointan: Lieux et images de l'altérité chez les historiens de la IVe croisade." *Revue roumaine d'histoire* 19 (1990): 137–40.

Pokorny, Rudolf. "Zwei unedierte Briefe aus der Frühzeit des lateinischen Kaiserreichs von Konstantinopel." *Byzantion* 55 (1985): 180–209.

Polemis, Demetrios. *The Doukai: A Contribution to Byzantine Prosopography*. London: Athlone, 1968.

Powell, James M. *Anatomy of a Crusade, 1213–1221*. Philadelphia: University of Pennsylvania Press, 1986.

Powicke, F. M. "Philip Augustus and Louis VIII." *Cambridge Medieval History*. Vol. 6. Cambridge: Cambridge University Press, 1936.

Praga, Giuseppe. "Zaratini e veneziani nel 1190: La battaglia di Treni." *La rivista dalmatica* 8 (1925): 47–54.

Prawer, Joshua. *The Crusaders' Kingdom: European Colonialism in the Middle Ages*. New York: Praeger, 1972.

Previté-Orton, C. W. "The Italian Cities till c. 1200." *Cambridge Medieval History*. Vol. 5. Cambridge: Cambridge University Press, 1948.

Primov, Borislav. "The Papacy, the Fourth Crusade and Bulgaria." *Byzantinobulgarica* 1 (1962): 183–211.

Pryor, John H. *Geography, Technology, and War*. Cambridge: Cambridge University Press, 1988.

———. "The Naval Architecture of Transport Ships: A Reconstruction of Some Archetypes for Round-Hulled Sailing Ships." *Mariners' Mirror* 70 (1984): 171–219, 275–92, 363–83.

———. "Transportation of Horses by Sea during the Era of the Crusades: Eighth Century to 1285 A.D." *Mariners' Mirror* 68 (1982): 9–30, 103–26.

———. "Winds, Waves, and Rocks: The Routes and the Perils Along Them." In *Maritime Aspects of Migration*, ed. Klaus Fiedland. Cologne-Vienna: Böhlau, 1989.

Purcell, Maureen. "Changing Views of Crusade in the Thirteenth Century." *Journal of Religious History* 7 (1972): 3–19.

Queller, Donald E. "Diplomatic 'Blanks' in the Thirteenth Century." *English Historical Review* 80 (1965): 476–91.

———. "L'évolution du role de l'ambassadeur: les pleins pouvoirs et le traité de 1201 entre les Croisés et les Vénitiens." *Moyen Age* 19 (1961): 479–501.

———. *The Fourth Crusade: The Conquest of Constantinople, 1201–1204*. Philadelphia: University of Pennsylvania Press, 1977.

———. "Innocent III and the Crusader-Venetian Treaty of 1201." *Medievalia et Humanistica* 15 (1963): 31–34.

———. "A Note on the Reorganization of the Venetian Coinage by Doge Enrico Dandolo." *Rivista italiana di numismatica e scienze affini* 67 (1975): 167–72.

Queller, Donald E., ed. *The Latin Conquest of Constantinople*. New York: John Wiley and Sons, 1971.

Queller, Donald E., Thomas K. Compton, and Donald A. Campbell. "The Fourth Crusade: The Neglected Majority." *Speculum* 49 (1974): 441–65.

Queller, Donald E., and Gerald W. Day. "Some Arguments in Defense of the Venetians on the Fourth Crusade." *American Historical Review* 81 (1976): 717–37.

Queller, Donald E., and Irene B. Katele. "Attitudes towards the Venetians in the Fourth Crusade: The Western Sources." *The International History Review* 4 (1982): 1–36.

———. "Venice and the Conquest of the Latin Kingdom of Jerusalem." *Studi Veneziani* n.s. 12 (1986): 15–43.

Queller, Donald E., and Thomas F. Madden. "Some Further Arguments in Defense of the Venetians on the Fourth Crusade." *Byzantion* 62 (1992): 433–73.

Queller, Donald E., and Susan J. Stratton. "A Century of Controversy on the Fourth Crusade." *Studies in Medieval and Renaissance History* 6 (1969): 235–77.

Renouard, Yves. *Les hommes d'affaires italiens du moyen âge.* Rev. according to the author's notes by Bernard Guillemain. Paris: A. Colin, 1968.

Riant, Paul. "Le changement de direction de la quatrième croisade." *Revue des questions historiques* 23 (1878): 71–114.

———. "Les dépouilles religieuses enlevées a Constantinople au XIIIe siècle." *Mémoires de la Société Nationale des Antiquaires de France*, ser. 4, 6 (1875): 1–214.

———. "Innocent III, Philippe de Souabe et Boniface de Montferrat." *Revue des questions historiques* 17 (1875): 321–75; 18 (1875): 5–75.

Richard, Jean. *Le royaume Latin de Jérusalem.* Paris: Presses universitaires de France, 1953.

———. "Le transport outremer des croisés et des pélerins (XIIe–XVe siècles)." In *Maritime Aspects of Migration*, ed. Klaus Fiedland. Cologne-Vienna: Böhlau, 1989.

Richard, Jean, ed. *L'Esprit de croisade.* Paris: Les Editions du Cerf, 1969.

Riley-Smith, Jonathan. "An Approach to Crusading Ethics." *Reading Medieval Studies* 6 (1980): 3–19.

———. *The Crusades: A Short History.* New Haven, Conn.: Yale University Press, 1987.

———. "Crusading as an Act of Love." *History* 65 (1980): 177–92.

———. "The Venetian Crusade of 1122–1124." In *I comuni italiani nel regno crociato di Gerusalemme*, ed. B. Z. Kedar and G. Airaldi. Genoa: Università di Genova, 1986.

———. *What Were the Crusades?* Totowa, N.J.: Rowman and Littlefield, 1977.

Robbert, Louise Buenger. "Monetary Flows—Venice, 1150–1400." In *Precious Metals in the Later Medieval and Early Modern Worlds*, ed. J. F. Richards. Durham, N.C.: Carolina Academic Press, 1983.

———. "Reorganization of the Venetian Coinage by Doge Enrico Dandolo." *Speculum* 49 (1974): 48–60.

———. "The Venetian Money Market, 1150–1229." *Studi Veneziani* 13 (1971): 3–94.

———. "Venice and the Crusades." In *A History of the Crusades*, ed. Kenneth M. Setton, 5: 379–451. Pennsylvania: University of Pennsylvania Press, 1985.

Rösch, Gerhard. *Der venezianische Adel bis zur Schließung des Großen Rats: Zur Genese einer Führungsschicht.* Sigmaringen: Jan Thorbecke, 1989.

Roscher, Helmut. *Papst Innocenz III und die Kreuzzüge.* Göttingen: Vandenhoeck u. Ruprecht, 1969.

Rousset, Paul. *Histoire des croisades.* Paris: Payot, 1957.

———. *Histoire d'une idéologie: La croisade.* Lausaune: L'âge d'homme, 1983.

Runciman, Steven. *Byzantine Civilisation.* London: E. Arnold and Co., 1933.

———. "Byzantium and the Crusades." In *The Meeting of Two Worlds: Cultural Exchange between East and West during the Period of the Crusades*, ed. Vladimir P. Gozz and Christine Verzar Bornstein. Kalamazoo, Mich.: Medieval Institute Publications, 1986.

———. *The Eastern Schism.* Oxford: Clarendon, 1955.

———. *A History of the Crusades.* 3 vols. Cambridge: Cambridge University Press, 1954.

Russell, Frederick H. *The Just War in the Middle Ages*. Cambridge and New York: Cambridge University Press, 1975.

Russell, Josiah C. *Late Ancient and Medieval Population*. Transactions of the American Philosophical Society. Vol. 48, pt. 3. Philadelphia: American Philosophical Society, 1958.

Sauli, Lodovico. *Della colonia dei genovese in Galata*. Turin: G. Bocca, 1831.

Saunders, J. J. *Aspects of the Crusades*. Christchurch, New Zealand: University of Canterbury, 1962.

Sayers, Jane. *Innocent III: Leader of Europe, 1198–1216*. London and New York: Longman, 1994.

Schaube, Adolf. *Handelsgeschichte der romanischen Völker des Mittelmeergebiets bis zum Ende der Kreuzzüge*. Munich and Berlin: R. Oldenbourg, 1906.

Schlumberger, Gustave. *Campagnes du Roi Amaury Ier de Jérusalem en Egypte au XIIe siècle*. Paris: Plon-Nourrit, 1906.

Schmandt, Raymond H. "The Fourth Crusade and the Just War Theory." *Catholic Historical Review* 61 (1975): 191–221.

———. "Orthodoxy and Catholicism: Public Opinion, the Schism, and the Fourth Crusade." *Diakonia* 3 (1968): 284–99.

Schreiner, Peter. "Genua, Byzanz und der 4. Kreuzzug: Ein neues Dokument in Staatsarchiv Genua." *Quellen und Forschungen aus Italienischen Archiven und Bibliotheken* 63 (1983): 292–97.

Schulz, Juergen. "The Houses of the Dandolo: A Family Compound in Medieval Venice." *Journal of the Society of Architectural Historians* 52 (1993): 391–415.

———. "La piazza medievale di San Marco." *Annali di architettura* 4/5 (1992/1993): 134–56.

———. "Urbanism in Medieval Venice." In *City States in Classical Antiquity and Medieval Italy*, ed. Anthony Molho, Kurt Raaflaub, and Julia Emlen. Stuttgart: Franz Steiner, 1991.

Sesan, M. "La flotte byzantine à l'époque des Comnènes et des Anges (1081–1204)." *Byzantinoslavica* 21 (1960): 48–53.

Setton, Kenneth M. "The Fourth Crusade." In *The Year 1200: A Symposium*. New York, 1975.

———. *The Papacy and the Levant (1204–1571)*. Vol. 1. Philadelphia: American Philosophical Society, 1976.

Setton, Kenneth M., gen. ed. *A History of the Crusades*. Vols 1 and 2. Philadelphia: University of Pennsylvania Press, 1958 and 1962. Vols 5 and 6. Madison: University of Wisconsin Press, 1985 and 1989.

Shaked, Shaul. *A Tentative Bibliography of Geniza Documents*. Paris: Mouton, 1964.

Siberry, J. Elizabeth. *Criticism of Crusading, 1095–1274*. Oxford: Clarendon, 1985.

Sinogowitz, B. "Über das byzantinische Kaiertum nach dem vierten Kreuzzuge (1204–1205)." *Byzantinische Zeitschrift* 155 (1952): 345–56.

Smail, R. C. *Crusading Warfare (1097–1193)*. Cambridge: Cambridge University Press, 1956.

Spiridonakis, Basile G. *Grecs, Occidentaux et Turcs de 1054 à 1453: Quatre siècles d'histoire de relations internationales*. Thessalonica: Institute for Balkan Studies, 1990.

Spiteris, Jannis. *La critica bizantina del primato Romano nel secolo XII*. Rome: Pontificium institutum orientalium studiorum, 1979.

Spufford, Peter. *Money and Its Uses in Medieval Europe*. Cambridge: Cambridge University Press, 1988.

Stahl, Alan. "The Coinage of Venice in the Age of Enrico Dandolo." In *Venice: Society and Crusade. Studies in Honor of Donald E. Queller*, ed. Thomas F. Madden and Ellen E. Kittell. Forthcoming.

———. "Venetian Coinage: Variations in Production." In *Rythmes de la production monétaire de l'antiquité à nos jours*, ed. Georges Depeyvot, et al. Louvain-la-Neuve: Séminaire de numismatique Marcel Hoc, 1989.

Steindorff, Ludwig. *Die dalmatinischen Städte im 12. Jahrhundert: Studien zu ihrer politischen Stellung und gesellschaftlichen Entwicklung*. Vienna: Böhlau, 1984.

Strayer, Joseph R. "The Political Crusades of the Thirteenth Century." In *A History of the Crusades*, ed. Kenneth M. Setton, 2: 377–428. Philadelphia: University of Pennsylvania Press, 1962.

Streit, Ludwig. *Venedig und die Wendung des vierten Kreuzzugs gegen Konstantinopel*. Anklam: Richard Poettcke, 1877.

Sweeney, James Ross. "Hungary in the Crusades, 1169–1218." *International History Review* 4 (1981): 467–81.

———. "Innocent III, Hungary and the Bulgarian Coronation: A Study in Medieval Papal Diplomacy." *Church History* 42 (1973): 320–44.

———. "Papal-Hungarian Relations During the Pontificate of Innocent III, 1198–1216." Ph.D. diss., Cornell University, 1971.

Swietek, Francis R. "Gunther of Pairis and the *Historia Constantinopolitana*." *Speculum* 53 (1978): 49–79.

Symeonides K. P. "Τὸ βυζαντινὸ παρωνύμιο 'Μούρτζουφλος?'" *Byzantina* 13 (1985): 1621–28.

Tessier, Jules. *La quatrième croisade: La diversion sur Zara et Constantinople*. Paris: E. Leroux, 1884.

Thayer, William R. *A Short History of Venice*. New York: Macmillan, 1905.

Théodorides, J. "Les animaux des jeux de l'Hippodrome et des ménageries impériales à Constantinople." *Byzantinoslavica* 19 (1958): 73–84.

Thiriet, Freddy. "Les chroniques vénitiennes de la Marcienne et leur importance pour l'histoire de la Romanie gréco-vénitienne." *Mélanges d'archéologie et d'histoire: École Française de Rome* 66 (1954): 241–92.

———. *Histoire de Venise*, 4th ed. Paris: Presses universitaires de France, 1969.

———. *La Romanie vénitienne au moyen âge*. Paris: E. de Boccard, 1959.

Tillmann, Helene. *Papst Innocenz III*. Bonn: L. Rohrscheid, 1954.

Tsangadas, Bryon C. P. *The Fortifications and Defense of Constantinople*. Boulder: East European Monographs, 1980.

Tyerman, Christopher J. *England and the Crusades, 1095–1588*. Chicago: University of Chicago Press, 1988.

———. "Were There Any Crusades in the Twelfth Century?" *English Historical Review* 110 (1995): 553–77.

Unger, Richard W. *The Ship in the Medieval Economy*. London and Montreal: Croom Helm, 1980.

Uspenskii, F. I. *Istoriia Vizantiiskoi Imperii*. Vol. 3. Moscow and Leningrad: Izd-vo Akademii nauk SSSR, 1948.

Usseglio, Leopoldo. *I marchesi di Monferrato in Italia ed in Oriente durante i secoli XII e XIII.* Vol. 2. Turin: s.n., 1926.

Van Cleve, Thomas C. *The Emperor Frederick II of Hohenstaufen: Immutator Mundi.* Oxford: Clarendon, 1972.

Van Millingen, Alexander. *Byzantine Constantinople: The Walls of the City and Adjoining Historical Sites.* London: J. Murray, 1899.

Vasiliev, A. A. *History of the Byzantine Empire, 324–1453.* 2d Eng. ed. rev. Madison: University of Wisconsin Press, 1952. Repr. in two volumes, 1958, 1962.

Vasilievskii, V. G. Review of Fedor Uspenskii, *Obrazovanie votorogo Bolgarskogo tsarstva.* In *Zhurnal Ministerstva Narodnogo Proshveshcheniia* 204 (1879): 337–48.

Verbruggen, J. F. *Het leger en de vloot van de graven van Vlaanderen vanaf het ontstaan tot in 1305.* Brussels: Paleis der Academien, 1960.

Villey, Michel. *La croisade: Essai sur la formation d'une théorie juridique.* Paris: J. Vrin, 1942.

———. "L'idée de la croisade chez les juristes du moyen âge." *Relazioni del X Congresso Internazionale di Scienze Storiche.* Vol. 3. Rome, 1955.

Vlad, L. Borelli, and A. Guidi Toniato. "The Origins and Documentary Sources of the Horses of San Marco." In *The Horses of San Marco.* Ed. Guido Perocco. Trans. Valerie Wilton-Ely and John Wilton-Ely. London: Thames and Hudson, 1979.

Vriens, H. "De kwestie van den vierden kruistocht." *Tijdschrift voor Geschiedenis* 37 (1922): 50–82.

Vryonis, Speros. *Byzantium und Europe.* London: Thames and Hudson, 1967.

Waas, Adolf. *Geschichte der Kreuzzüge.* 2 vols. Freiburg: Herder, 1956.

Wiel, Alethea. *The Navy of Venice.* London: John Murray, 1910.

Wieruszowski, Helene. "The Norman Kingdom of Sicily and the Crusade." In *A History of the Crusades,* ed. Kenneth M. Setton. 2: 3–42. Philadelphia: University of Pennsylvania Press, 1962.

Williams, Patrick A. "The Assassination of Conrad of Montferrat: Another Suspect." *Traditio* 26 (1970): 381–88.

Winkelmann, Eduard. *Philipp von Schwaben und Otto IV von Braunschweig.* 2 vols. Leipzig: Duncker and Humblot, 1873–78.

Wirth, P. "Zur Frage eines politischen Engagements Patriarch Johannes' X. Kamateros nach dem vierten Kreuzzug." *Byzantinische Forschungen* 6 (1972): 248–51.

Wolff, Robert Lee. "Baldwin of Flanders and Hainaut, First Latin Emperor of Constantinople: His Life, Death and Resurrection, 1172–1225." *Speculum* 27 (1952): 281–322.

———. "Greeks and Latins before and after 1204." *Ricerche di storia religiosa* 1 (1957): 320–34.

———. "The Latin Empire of Constantinople (1204–1261)." Ph.D. diss., Harvard University, 1947.

———. "The Latin Empire of Constantinople." In *A History of the Crusades,* ed. Kenneth M. Setton. 2: 187–233. Philadelphia: University of Pennsylvania Press, 1962.

Zaborov, M. A. "Papstvo i zachvat Konstantinopolya krestonostsami v nacale XIII v." *Vizantiiskii Vremennik,* n.s. 5 (1952): 152–77.

———. "K Voprosu o predistorii cetvertogo krestovogo pochoda." *Vizantiiskii Vremennik,* n.s. 6 (1953): 223–35.

Zakythinos, Denis A. "La conquête de Constantinople en 1204, Venise et le partage de l'Empire Byzantin." In *Venezia dalla prima crociata alla conquista di Costantinopoli del 1204*, ed. Vittore Branca. Florence: Sansoni, 1965.

Zerner-Chardavoine, Monique. "L'abbé Gui des Vaux-de-Cernay: Prédicateur de croisade." *Cahiers de fanjeaux* 21 (1986): 183–204.

Zerner-Chardavoine, Monique, and Piéchan-Palloc, Hélène. "La croisade albigeoise, un revanche: Des rapports entre la quatrième et la croisade albigeoise." *Revue historique* 267 (1982): 3–18.

Index